A PROPHET IN HIS OWN COUNTRY

A Prophet
in
His Own Country

THE TRIUMPHS AND DEFEATS OF

ADLAI E. STEVENSON

BY KENNETH S. DAVIS

> For the main point in biography is to present the
> man in all his relations to his time, and to show to
> what extent it may have opposed or prospered his
> development. What view of mankind and the
> world he has shaped from it, and how far he may
> himself be an external reflection of its spirit.
> —GOETHE *Dichtung und Wahrheit*

1957

DOUBLEDAY & COMPANY, INC.

GARDEN CITY, NEW YORK

TO FLO

. . . *When the tumult and the shouting die, when the bands are gone and the lights are dimmed, there is the stark reality of responsibility in an hour of history haunted with those gaunt, grim spectres of strife, dissension and materialism at home, and ruthless, inscrutable and hostile power abroad.*

The ordeal of the Twentieth Century—the bloodiest, most turbulent era of the Christian age—is far from over. Sacrifice, patience, understanding and implacable purpose may be our lot for years to come. Let's face it! Let's talk sense to the American people!

—ADLAI E. STEVENSON

Contents

viii   *Contents*

Preface

1. CONCERNING THE WRITING OF PARALLEL LIVES

Plutarch, as everyone knows, created his masterpiece as a series of *Parallel Lives*. In each he wrote of one Greek and one Roman whose careers seemed to him in some sense "parallel," concluding with an essay comparing and contrasting the two men. It has occurred to me that, within the severe limits of my talent, I have been emulating Plutarch in this "parallelism." Late in 1945 I published a biography of Dwight D. Eisenhower,[1] in late 1956 I completed this biography of Adlai E. Stevenson, and in the concluding sections of the latter work it has been necessary to compare and contrast the two men.

There is even a sense, I suppose, in which the two "lives" might be said to deal with a Greek and a Roman. Certainly Dwight Eisenhower—the pragmatic administrator, the general who applies the military-staff concept to government, the politician who has become a prime focus and symbol of "human engineering" in our time—seems to fit fairly well our stereotyped view of the Roman man of affairs. Adlai Stevenson seems to fit equally well our stereotyped view of the Greek in his aversion to all forms of excess, his espousal of a temperate and individualistic reasonableness in an age of conformist passions, his personal example of growth-in-balance toward an integrity of spirit and body. Moreover, to some readers of this book the latter's political fate might seem to be such as a Periclean Athenian might have suffered who was born in Rome during the first century B.C.

In any case, the difference between the two men renders far different the problems a writer faces who would present full-length portraits of them while they are yet living, influential, and hence controversial public figures.

Vividly do I remember the initial struggle I had to make to come to grips with Eisenhower as "problem" during the last year of World War II. I spoke of it in the closing pages of my book about him, quoting there some notes written in Normandy in July and August,

[1] Kenneth S. Davis, *Soldier of Democracy: A Biography of Dwight Eisenhower* (New York: Doubleday & Co., Inc., 1945. Revised Edition, 1952).

1944.[2] "It is almost impossible to write a biography of any depth, any significant density, when its subject is a man who has no interior life," said one of these notes. "Eisenhower . . . is a man whose whole mental life is involved in *external* strategy. If he cares about *meanings*, even historical ones, I am not aware of it. . . . Yet he is caught up in historic circumstances. In writing about him, one is impelled to carry meanings to him. . . ." Said another note: "Meaning, significance, is not rooted in him; it only *adheres* to him. His significance is all external, imposed. He drifts with a destiny he probably does not understand, and he does nothing (practically) to determine it." Still another note said: "Eisenhower is a mirror of democracy. Use Sidney Hook's neat distinction between 'eventful' and 'event-making' men. Ike mirrors events, colors them with his personality, but never (in the deep sense) *causes* them." It was in the midst of the latter note that my mind, apparently, worked its way from a negative to a positive attitude toward my subject, for I went on: "But to color such mighty events as these is in itself a creative act. . . . History may yet write Eisenhower's special qualities down as determining forces in the world stream."

The book I then wrote was imbued with a warm liking for the man personally and with a profound admiration of his career up till then. If sharply critical of the handling of political arrangements in North Africa, it absolved Eisenhower of blame for these, since his political role there was "passive." The book's major focus, however, was not upon the individual man as mind or spirit, clearly distinguishable from his historic context; rather was it upon that context whereby the man was molded and through which he grew into a potent, active symbol of democracy in arms.

Far different was the struggle attending my introduction to Stevenson as biographical "problem." At no point did I feel that I was "impelled to carry meanings to him" or that he drifted "with a destiny . . . he does not understand." On the contrary, Stevenson's sense of history and of the role he was playing in it was as profound as it was objective, and one of the writer's tasks was to sharpen his own sense of these against that of his subject when he and his subject held somewhat different views. When beginning the Eisenhower project I wrote to myself: "Don't try so hard to understand him. . . . Be passive. . . . Let him work on you. Stick to *facts*, as he does."[3] No

[2] Ibid., pp. 541–42.
[3] Ibid., p. 542.

such notes were written at the beginning of the "research" on Stevenson. From the first I realized that a full knowledge of the external facts could never lead very far toward an understanding of this extremely complicated personality, this far from simple mind, this "infinite wit and variety." The bare facts, indeed, might be misleading, hiding from a biographer the complex motives from which these facts often sprang.

Nor was it possible to arrive at understanding merely by accepting the man in his complexity and then letting him "work" on one's mind. One might feel confident that he "knew" Eisenhower well almost from the moment of meeting him, provided one knew his past history, since his appearance was, with relatively slight modification, his reality. One could be reasonably sure that he would remain essentially as he then appeared to be and that whatever changes were later made in one's assessment of him would be due, not to changes in the essential man, but to shifts of context whereby aspects of him that had theretofore been "played down" were "played up," and vice versa. No such confidence attended one's initial knowledge of Stevenson. The understanding of him was a very active and even arduous labor, albeit a fascinating one, since he was full of surprises. It depended rather more upon intuition than upon factual survey or logical analyses, though the latter were necessary. And the conclusions at which one at last arrived were tentative and general, being a knowledge of process rather than event, of tendency rather than static entity.

Even more tentative and general must be one's conclusions as to Stevenson's future historical importance. Assuming that his political career ended on November 6, 1956 (though the assumption may conceivably prove unwarranted), what will his significance prove to have been?

The whole economic tendency of our age, spurred by every technological advance, seems to be toward an ever more inclusive collectivism. The great political question of our age, I am persuaded, is whether this collectivism is to be responsible or irresponsible in democratic terms—whether it is to enhance or deny the essential individual freedoms of speech, inquiry, and conscience. If it is to do the former, if the ends of liberty are to be served, then surely there is required increasingly a politics that is truly educative, one that sharpens instead of blurring real issues as it "talks sense" to the people.

In terms of this fundamental question, then, has Stevenson been an anachronism in American politics, engaged in a forlorn attempt to restore eighteenth-century rationalism to the public life of an age which is far "beyond" it? Will his implicit insistence upon the individual life as the proper aim and source of all public activity seem absurdly reactionary, at so late a date, to a people absorbed in huge and tightly organized economic endeavors, their leisure increasingly devoted to the pleasures of the senses? Or will he prove a harbinger of the future, anticipating a whole "new school" of politicians who, in the years ahead, will help us create on a world-wide scale such organizations as will maintain individual liberty against the mass pressures of atomic energy, electronic automation, and a standardized communications system?

2. CONCERNING OBLIGATIONS AND SOURCES

To such knowledge of Stevenson as I have been able to obtain, and to such success as I have had in presenting it here interestingly, a great many extremely busy people have made contributions. This book was not conceived as a promoter in any way of Mr. Stevenson's personal ambitions; it was to be a full-length portrait, honestly drawn, of an interesting and important man who just *might* (as it then appeared) become President of the United States. No urgently interested motives, therefore, prompted the co-operation I received from Adlai Stevenson, his family and friends, and his working associates during a year of intense pressures upon all of them. I am more grateful to them than I can say and fervently hope that they will not be too greatly disappointed by the uses to which their contributions have been put. This co-operation, I should add, was given me freely; no strings were attached to it. Several of the people most intimately involved, including Mr. Stevenson, have read all or most of the work in manuscript and have made corrections of factual errors as well as suggested changes in interpretations. None has imposed censorship. Sometimes the suggestions have been followed, sometimes they have not been, and for whatever mistakes the book contains I am wholly responsible.

My greatest obligation, of course, is to Mr. Stevenson himself, who has given generously of his precious time, out of personal kindness and a sense of public obligation rather more, I'm afraid, than out of a desire to have me write his story. Without his support, of course, I could not have received the co-operation I did from his family and intimate friends. Of these, the most helpful single person was Mr. Stevenson's sister, Mrs. Ernest L. Ives of Bloomington, Illinois, who gave me through interviews great masses of otherwise unobtainable information, facilitated my interviews with other people, and read most of the book as it progressed. She also gave me access to books and family papers I could not otherwise have seen. I have depended greatly upon her co-operation and upon her book, *My Brother Adlai,* for information concerning my subject's early life. I am grateful also to her and her husband for their review of the manuscript as the work progressed.

Mr. Stevenson's aunts, Miss Letitia Stevenson and Mrs. Martin D. (Julia) Hardin of St. Louis, were invaluable sources of information about the family background and about the Adlai Stevenson they have known at various stages of his development. They turned over to me family papers without which it would have been impossible for me to portray, even as well as I have done, their nephew's paternal ancestry, and they checked in manuscript those portions of the book dealing with family history. I am also indebted to the Stevenson sons—Adlai, Borden, and John Fell—for insights they have given me, inadvertently perhaps, and to Mrs. Ellen Borden Stevenson.

Many of my other debts, and their nature, are indicated in the book itself. Suffice it here to say that I have profited hugely from interviews with, among others: Dr. E. M. Stevenson, Mr. and Mrs. Carl Vrooman, Mr. Joe Bohrer, Mr. Loring Merwin, Mr. Lawrence Rust, and Miss Alverta Duff, all of Bloomington; the Reverend Dr. Richard Graebel and the late Mr. Harry Edward Pratt of Springfield, Illinois; Mr. and Mrs. Quincy Wright, Mr. and Mrs. Clifton Utley, Mr. Edward D. McDougal, Jr., Mr. and Mrs. Hermon Dunlap Smith, Mrs. Edison Dick, Mrs. John P. Welling, Mr. Walter T. Fisher, Mr. Walter Johnson, Mr. Fred K. Hoehler, and Mr. and Mrs. Stanley Pargellis, all of greater Chicago; Mr. Kenneth Anderson and Mr. Milo Sutton, Emporia, Kansas; Mr. John Young, Salina, Kansas; Mr. Richard Stengel, Rock Island, Illinois; Mr. Arthur Schlesinger, Jr., Cambridge, Massachusetts; and Mr. Wilson Wyatt, Louisville, Kentucky.

Of particular value to me have been my interviews with those who have been members of Stevenson's immediate staff during all or part of the time since 1948. These include Mr. Carl McGowan, who was Governor Stevenson's closest working associate in Springfield and is now a Chicago lawyer; Mr. William McC. Blair, Jr., Mr. W. Willard Wirtz, and Mr. Newton Minow, all of whom are now law partners of Mr. Stevenson; Miss Carol Evans, personal secretary to Mr. Stevenson since 1948; Miss Phyllis Gustafson and Mrs. Juanda Higgens, both of whom have worked closely with Mr. Stevenson since the days of the governorship; and Mr. J. Edward Day, a personal aide of Governor Stevenson in Springfield who was formerly associated with him in a Chicago law firm.

For documentary materials I leaned heavily upon personal letters of Adlai Stevenson, as boy and young man, to his mother, father, and sister, and upon letters they wrote to him. I also found invaluable in the portrayal of the early years albums of pictures kept in the Ives home in Bloomington and microfilms of the Bloomington (Illinois) *Pantagraph* kept in the library of the McLean County (Illinois) Historical Society. Voluminous scrapbooks of clippings kept by and for Mr. Stevenson from his first years in Chicago through his two presidential campaigns were constantly consulted. The war years were illuminated for me by a personal diary kept sporadically by Mr. Stevenson through the early 1940s. The Stevenson papers for the years of the governorship and for the 1952 campaign are temporarily housed, in intimidating volume, in the Newberry Library of Chicago, and were of course a principal documentary source of material for this period. I also consulted continuously bound or microfilm copies of the Chicago *Daily News*, the Chicago *Tribune*, and the New York *Times* in the Newberry Library, and of course counted heavily upon these and other current periodicals for information of the period during which the book was being written, checking this information when necessary against that I could obtain simply by reaching for a telephone and calling people directly involved. At several of the events described in latter portions of the book, I was personally present. Copies of all of Mr. Stevenson's speeches and writings in recent years were made available to me by his office.

There is no need to present here, I think, a complete bibliography, but a partial listing of books found useful might conceivably be of help to such future historians as may consult this work. For the history of Mr. Stevenson's ancestry, I found particularly valuable *Historic Families of Kentucky*, First Series, by Thomas Marshall Green

(Cincinnati: Robert Clarke and Co., 1889); *Quaker Pioneers*, by Harriet Fyffe Richardson (privately printed on the Press of Gillett and Co., J. Louis Wolff, Milwaukee 2, Wisconsin, 1940); *A History and Genealogical Record of the Stevenson Family, From 1748 to 1926*, by the Reverend Samuel Harris Stevenson, the Reverend J. A. Harris, and the Honorable W. F. Stevenson (privately printed, apparently in 1926); and *The Life of Jesse W. Fell*, by Francis Milton I. Morehouse (University of Illinois Studies in the Social Sciences, Vol. V, No. 2, June, 1916). The first Adlai Ewing Stevenson's *Something of Men I Have Known* (Chicago: A. C. McClurg and Co., 1909), though telling little of Vice-President Stevenson directly, was revealing of his temperament and associates. Robert Dale Richardson's *Abraham Lincoln's Autobiography* (Boston: The Beacon Press, 1947) gives valuable information concerning the close association of Mr. Stevenson's maternal great-grandfather, Jesse Fell, with Lincoln. The *Dictionary of American Biography* was consulted often when material for early portions of the book was being gathered.

Extensive use was of course made of the two earlier books about Mr. Stevenson: John Bartlow Martin's *Adlai Stevenson* (New York: Harper & Brothers, 1952) and Noel F. Busch's *Adlai E. Stevenson of Illinois* (New York: Farrar, Straus & Young, 1952); and of *My Brother Adlai*, by Elizabeth Stevenson Ives and Hildegarde Dolson (New York: William Morrow & Co., 1956). Heavily used were Mr. Stevenson's own books: *Major Campaign Speeches of Adlai E. Stevenson, 1952* (New York: Random House, 1953); *Call to Greatness* (New York: Harper & Brothers, 1954); and *What I Think* (New York: Harper & Brothers, 1956). For factual information concerning the general historical context of Mr. Stevenson's life I consulted such standard works as *Contemporary America, The National Scene Since 1900*, by Harvey Wish (New York: Harper & Brothers. Revised Edition, 1955); *The United States, American Democracy in World Perspective*, by Ray A. Billington, Bert J. Loewenberg, S. H. Brockunier (New York: Rinehart & Co., 1947); *Our Times*, Volumes IV and V, by Mark Sullivan (New York: Charles Scribner's Sons, 1932); *Only Yesterday*, by Frederick Lewis Allen (New York: Harper & Brothers, 1931); *Since Yesterday*, by Frederick Lewis Allen (New York: Harper & Brothers, 1940); *The Great Crash, 1929*, by John Kenneth Galbraith (Boston: Houghton Mifflin Company, 1955); and *Depression Decade*, by Broadus Mitchell (New York: Rinehart & Co., 1947).

While writing of Mr. Stevenson's Princeton years I referred to *Woodrow Wilson, Life and Letters, Princeton 1890–1910*, by Ray Stannard Baker (Garden City: Doubleday, Page & Co., 1927); *Wilson, The Road to the White House*, by Arthur S. Link (Princeton University Press, 1947); *Princeton*, by Varnum L. Collins (New York: Oxford University Press, American Branch, 1914); *Historic Princeton* (Princeton: The Princeton Municipal Improvement, Inc., 1940); and *The Far Side of Paradise, A Biography of F. Scott Fitzgerald*, by Arthur Mizener (Boston: Houghton Mifflin Company, 1951). Arthur Meeker's *Chicago, with Love* (New York: Alfred A. Knopf, 1955) gives some of the flavor of the society in which Mr. Stevenson lived when he first came to Chicago and contains accounts of several of the people with whom he associated.

The writing of Mr. Stevenson's life through the early 1940s and the years after the United States' entry into World War II was aided by references to *William Allen White's America*, by Walter Johnson (New York: Henry Holt & Company, 1947); and *Roosevelt and Hopkins*, by Robert Sherwood (New York: Harper & Brothers. Revised and Enlarged Edition, 1950). Walter Johnson's *How We Drafted Adlai Stevenson* (New York: Alfred A. Knopf, 1955) was of help to the writing of the 1952 Democratic National Convention, and while writing of the years since 1952 I had occasion to refer to Clinton Rossiter's *The American Presidency* (New York: Harcourt, Brace & Co., 1956); *Eisenhower, The Inside Story*, by Robert J. Donovan (New York: Harper & Brothers, 1956); *The Eisenhower Years, Affairs of State*, by Richard Rovere (New York: Farrar, Straus & Cudahy, 1956); *The Future of American Politics*, Revised Second Edition, by Samuel Lubell (New York: Doubleday Anchor Books, Doubleday & Co., 1956); *Politics in America*, by D. W. Brogan (New York: Harper & Brothers, 1954); and *Through These Men*, by John Mason Brown (New York: Harper & Brothers, 1956).

My wife, Florence Olenhouse Davis, was of invaluable assistance throughout this labor. She did all of the first, basic research among the Stevenson papers stored in the Newberry Library, made constant and valuable criticisms and suggestions as the writing of the book progressed, and typed all of the manuscript twice and major portions of it a third time as the work proceeded from its rough to its finally revised form.

K.S.D.

Book One

BACKGROUND AND BEGINNINGS

CHAPTER ONE

Introducing the Stevensons
of Bloomington

In the late afternoon of March 4, 1909, a man riding southward from Chicago across the flat Illinois prairie might look out from his train window upon a scene fairly typical of both the body and spirit of America. It was, predominantly, a country scene. Wilderness-bordered streams wound through a wide, rather lonely landscape, across which spread farms and villages and far-spaced towns in a mixture not far different from that prevailing over the nation as a whole.

True, the urbanization of American culture had been proceeding at an accelerating rate since the Civil War; already less than 35 per cent of the population lived on farms. True, the automobile had already established itself as a fact of increasing importance; a combine called General Motors had just been organized and Henry Ford was preparing to announce a new cheap automobile he called the Model T. But agrarian social, economic, and cultural views yet persisted throughout the country, and in Washington that day a new President rode to his inauguration, not in an automobile, but in a black victoria drawn by four black horses. Census takers were finding that the center of the country's population now lay in Bloomington, Indiana, and a sociologist might conclude that the center of gravity of American life lay also in a town of that size and general complexion—some such town, perhaps, as Bloomington's namesake in Illinois.

II

It was toward Bloomington, Illinois, his home town and the home town of his family for two generations back, that a man named Lewis

Green Stevenson was riding that day. In his fortieth year he was slender, of medium height, rather intense-looking, almost perfectly bald (his only hair was a close-cropped fringe across his temples and around the back of his skull), with large clear wide-spaced eyes, a straight, rather fleshy nose, and finely modeled lips. A cleft in his chin was matched by an even deeper cleft in his forehead, just above his nose, as though his eyebrows had been often drawn together in a frown of physical pain. And, indeed, they had been. In recent months he had begun to suffer periodically from migraine headaches so intense they totally incapacitated him for days at a time; this disability was added to a severe injury of his right shoulder, which occurred when he was fourteen and from which he would never fully recover. Its pain, though he'd never confess it, had for years been a virtually constant dull ache. Small wonder that he, notably intelligent, was known in Bloomington as a man of rather intimidating wit; and that, despite his remarkable self-control, he was sometimes irritable, occasionally too sharp and quick in his responses to challenges that were only mildly hostile if hostile at all. The wonder is that he was, on the whole, so jolly and capable a man.

The injury and his response to it were significant both of the quality of the man and of the family attitudes in which he'd been raised. With other boys he'd gone hunting on a Sunday, though his Presbyterian father, whose family tree was studded with Presbyterian divines, frowned upon such desecrations of the Lord's Day. Lifting his gun for a quick shot, he'd failed to pull the stock tightly against his shoulder. The recoil had sent him staggering backward, blind with pain, and by the time he reached home his shoulder, blackly bruised, was hot and swollen. But he said nothing to his parents about it—not that day, nor the next, nor the next. Not until weeks of pain had passed was the injury revealed, and even then it may have been discovered by the parents rather than confessed by the boy. He was, of course, taken at once to the doctors: an operation was performed, the bone was scraped: but too much time had passed and a chronic infection had developed which the doctors could not truly cure, nor even accurately diagnose in that year of 1882. Probably the ailment was tuberculosis of the bone. One result was a permanent slight crippling of his right arm, seldom noticed by others save when he shook hands. Shaking hands, he shoved his right shoulder forward and braced his elbow slightly against his side —and smiled.

Much of his life had been a quest for health. It had sent him West
in his manhood. He'd been educated at Phillips Exeter Academy in
Exeter, New Hampshire, and then at Illinois State Normal Univer-
sity. The latter was in the town of Normal, a community so close to
Bloomington as to be virtually one with it. A distinguished former
member of State Normal's faculty (from 1866 to 1872) was Major
John Wesley Powell, principal architect and present chief of the U. S.
Geological Survey, who had also taught at Illinois Wesleyan in
Bloomington itself. Major Powell had for forty years been a friend
of Lewis Stevenson's father and the friendship extended to the
Stevenson son. What then was more natural than that the son should
ask Powell for a place on a Geological Survey party into the Southwest, or that Powell should grant the request? Young Stevenson had
had grand adventure along the Colorado; he loved the desert and
believed that its climate had improved his health.

He'd adventured, too, for several months in Japan and China during the 1890s and had written some newspaper reports from the
theater of war when the Sino-Japanese conflict broke out. This was
enough to cause him to be labeled a "former war correspondent" in
news stories about him. If the label was inaccurate, in that he'd never
actually been a member of the working press, it did point to one
important fact about him: one way and another his life had been, and
remained, intimately concerned with newspapers.

He held a Chicago newspaper in his hands as the train rolled
southward through the gathering dusk. Its first page featured portrait
photographs of President William Howard Taft and Vice-President
James Schoolcraft Sherman, and was wholly devoted to two detailed
reports, one of the inaugural and the other of Chicago's reaction to
it. Reading the latter, Stevenson may have smiled a bit wryly. Surely
a lifelong Democrat might be excused for doing so! Especially a
Democrat whose father had entered politics with Greenback-party
support in the '70s, had been a champion of the "free silverites" in
the '80s and '90s, and had in 1900 been a running mate of the same
William Jennings Bryan whom Taft had defeated (it was Bryan's
third and last presidential defeat) in the preceding autumn. . . .
The festivities in Washington had been marred, the paper said, by
the "worst blizzard to strike the capital city in ten years"; not since
1893, the paper said, had snow fallen in Washington on an inaugural
day. Reading this, Lewis Stevenson folded up his paper and sat for a
time gazing out into the almost-fallen night, musing.

On March 4, 1893, Stevenson himself, then a young man of twenty-four, had been in Washington, playing a personal role in the great national ceremony. On that day his own father, Adlai Ewing Stevenson, had been installed as Vice-President of the United States. He remembered vividly the two inches of snow that had blanketed the city, the dirty slush through which they had all tramped across the Capitol plaza, and the dull gray light that had fallen upon the great platform on the Capitol steps as Grover Cleveland, after an interval of four years, became again the nation's President.

He remembered, too, with equal vividness, the bright June day in Chicago when his father was nominated as Cleveland's running mate. Two of his sisters had been there that day, the dark-haired eighteen-year-old Julia and the light-haired nineteen-year-old Mary. (Just three years later, in 1895, Mary, who'd been so gentle, so quietly lovely, had died of tuberculosis; the loss was yet deeply felt by Lewis, as it was by all who had known her well.) His youngest sister, reddish-haired sixteen-year-old Letitia, remained in Bloomington with their mother, in the big family home on McLean Street, facing Franklin Park, a house now pointed out to Bloomington visitors as a historic show place. What excitement there'd been in that house when its occupants were informed by telephone (the Adlai Stevensons had been among the first people in Bloomington to have one) of the great triumph in Chicago!

Grandmother Stevenson was staying that day in the house of Lewis's uncle William, a younger brother of Adlai. A reporter for the Bloomington *Pantagraph* told of how the eyes of the "venerable mother" (she then approached her seventy-third birthday) glowed with a quiet pride when she was told of the great honor that had come to her son. "He has always been a good son," she'd said, "and a good man."

She was proud of all her children, worthy descendants, she felt, of ancestors of whom she was also very proud. She'd been born Eliza Ann Ewing in Iredell County, North Carolina. The man she married in 1832, Major John Turner Stevenson of sturdy Scotch Presbyterian stock, had been born there, too, just a year before she was and, like her, had moved as a child to Christian County, Kentucky, and been raised there in the Bluewater country. Here her seven children, a girl and six boys, were born. Then, on July 7, 1852, the John Turner Stevensons had arrived in Bloomington. In the spring of 1857, at the age of forty-nine, the husband died, and ever since that tragic day

Eliza Ewing Stevenson had felt herself to be living in and through her children.

Of them, none had been more loving and dutiful than Adlai. He was her second-born, the eldest son, whose lot it was to take his father's place as head of the family. He'd become a vibrant, jovial, dominant personality, immensely liked and respected even by those (and they were the majority in Republican Illinois) who strongly opposed his political views. A sparkling conversationalist and a generous outgoing personality, he'd become one of the great raconteurs of the day. The latter talent, combined as it was with a mastery of public speaking, had served him well in politics. His had been an intensely active life, but no matter how busy he was he'd sent his mother, every single day, some token of his affection and esteem for her: a letter, a few scrawled lines on a postal card, or some little gift.

This was typical of his thoughtfulness of others; it was consistent with his essential attitude toward the world. He was a man who focused so much of his attention outside himself, a man so intensely interested in other people, that he had little left of interest or attention to spend upon himself. There was no malice in him. His observations and judgments of those about him, uncomplicated by self-consciousness, were on the whole remarkably kindly; when they were not he seldom expressed them.

This generous quality was evident in the book Adlai Stevenson was completing that spring, for publication in October by A. C. McClurg and Co. of Chicago. As one of McClurg's editors had mildly complained to Lewis Stevenson in a recent conversation, the publishers had believed they were buying the autobiography of an interesting man who had had an interesting life; but what they were getting was a book of sketches of other men, drawn from Adlai Stevenson's memory. The author was calling it, accurately, *Something of Men I Have Known*.

Certainly all the men of whom he wrote had been well worth knowing, and many had been of major importance to history. In his teens he had known John Todd Stuart, Stephen A. Douglas, Abraham Lincoln. Several times he had heard Lawyer Lincoln at the bar of the old courthouse at Metamora, a village some thirty miles northwest of Bloomington, where he himself opened a law office in 1859 and where, in 1864, he'd been elected state's attorney for the circuit.

In September 1854, when he was yet a student at Bloomington's

Wesleyan University, he was among a group who called upon the visiting Stephen A. Douglas in the latter's room in Bloomington's National Hotel. Barely four months before, the Little Giant had pushed his Kansas-Nebraska Bill through the most turbulent session of Congress ever seen up till then—and the storm provoked by the act's repeal of the Missouri Compromise was yet rising across the land. Chief among the callers that day was the Honorable Jesse W. Fell, who was also by general consent the chief citizen of Bloomington and Normal, and the youthful Adlai had listened with rapt attention as Fell, a close friend of Lincoln, proposed to Douglas that the senator engage with Lincoln in a "joint discussion" of the issues raised by Kansas-Nebraska. Young Adlai would never forget the emphatic way in which Douglas had declined the suggestion. But when Lincoln himself entered the hotel room a few minutes later, he and Douglas greeted one another with great affection. . . .

Four years later Fell's suggestion had borne historic fruit. The elderly Adlai Stevenson recalled with "pleasure," in his book, how he'd watched Abraham Lincoln and Stephen Douglas shake hands on the crude platform at Ottawa, evincing great mutual respect, before launching the first of the seven great debates which made Lincoln a national figure. No man now held Abraham Lincoln in greater esteem than this same Adlai Stevenson who, only two weeks before, on Lincoln's one-hundredth birthday, had eulogized the Great Emancipator in florid oratory before a large audience in Bloomington.

But Lewis Green Stevenson knew that his father, on the record, had not been among Lincoln's political supporters during the Civil War. In the year of the Lincoln-Douglas debates, Adlai Stevenson, having read law in Bloomington after returning from Centre College in Danville, Kentucky, was admitted to the Illinois bar. He actively supported Stephen Douglas for the Senate that year. In April of the following year he'd met and become a good friend of Robert G. Ingersoll, in Metamora—the Ingersoll who'd later become so famous an orator and so notorious a religious agnostic. In 1860 he'd joined Ingersoll, who was himself a Democratic candidate for Congress, in strong support of Douglas for the presidency—and four years later he'd been elected elector-at-large on the Democratic ticket and had canvassed Illinois for McClellan.

Thereafter he'd been continually active in Democratic politics. When in 1869 he moved from Metamora to Bloomington, forming a law partnership with his double first cousin, James S. Ewing, his desk was at once a focal point of the Illinois Democracy and his will a potent force in the party counsels. Twice, in 1874 and '78, he'd won election to the Congress in one of the most solidly Republican districts in the state, having become a leading spokesman for bimetallism, "fiscal reform," and drastic tariff reductions in order to help farmers and others of the debtor class in the West and South.

His fiscal views had been opposed by Grover Cleveland. So had been his views as to the proper exercise of patronage in the building up of political party organization. But, significantly, these facts were not mentioned in the sketch of "Cleveland as I Knew Him," which was now in the editor's hands. Appointed first assistant postmaster-general in 1885, Stevenson, like most Democratic politicians, had disagreed with the President's efforts wholly to abolish the "spoils system." When Pulitzer's New York *World* editorially chided the President for forgetting "the obligations which an administration elected by a great historical party owes to that party," Adlai Stevenson had boldly issued a statement of agreement: "Although it is daily asserted that hundreds of postmasters are being appointed, yet the six months which have elapsed since Cleveland's accession finds only between ten and twelve percent of the offices occupied by Democrats." In the end, of course, Cleveland had been forced to yield. Adlai Stevenson himself had gained fame in his party, and notoriety among his opponents, by removing some forty thousand Republican postmasters and replacing them with deserving Democrats. He'd been dubbed "The Headsman," and for this exercise in practical politics his party had been glad to reward him with the vice-presidential nomination in 1892—particularly so, since there was need to mollify the "silverites," Cleveland being so strong a gold-standard man.

This last, the nomination of Stevenson as a "sop to the silverites," was a piece of "politicking" that very nearly backfired on the gold-standard men. The country at large still did not know it,[1] but in the summer of 1893 Adlai Stevenson came very close to becoming President of the United States. In June of that year a malignant growth as large as a quarter dollar had been found in the roof of Cleveland's mouth, necessitating an immediate operation in which the entire upper left jaw was removed. The President made a strong recovery, and every hint of his illness, published months later in the press, was

[1] The full facts were not revealed until 1918. See Allan Nevins's *Grover Cleveland* (New York: Dodd, Mead & Company, 1933), pp. 528–33.

flatly denied by men close to him. But the doctors knew, and Adlai Stevenson and his son also knew, that Cleveland's life had been gravely threatened. . . .

It would be a fine thing, Lewis Stevenson thought, if this present book of his father's could have a sequel in which he wrote more of his personal experience and expressed more of his personal opinion. His father, for instance, in a genuinely autobiographical work, must inevitably tell something about his marriage, for there was no doubt that his wife, Letitia, Lewis's mother, was a remarkable woman— quite as remarkable in her way as he was in his. Her presence beside him had been a major factor in his success.

How she'd enjoyed the social life which was hers as the wife of the Vice-President of the United States! With what grace and charm had she presided as Second Lady over the society of Washington! Nor did this official life absorb all her vital energies. She had an abundance left over for other concerns. She had, for instance, taken an active part in the activities of the New York Avenue Presbyterian Church. (John Watson Foster, Secretary of State in 1892–93, was a leading elder of this church; Foster's grandson, named John Foster Dulles, would be not unknown to future history.) One of her fellow members was Mrs. Phoebe Apperson Hearst of California, wealthy widow of Senator George R. Hearst of California, who'd made his millions out of copper and gold mines in the West. Mrs. Hearst's power-hungry son, William Randolph, having made a great commercial success of the San Francisco *Examiner*, launched the New York *Journal* in the third year of Cleveland's administration, and with it a "yellow journalism" of which the elder Stevensons could not but disapprove—but Mrs. Hearst herself was a "great and pious lady," as the Stevensons always said, whose energy and fortune were devoted to good works. As one of Mrs. Stevenson's closest friends, she joined with Mrs. Stevenson in the founding of the Mothers' Congress, forerunner of the Parent-Teachers' Association. Mrs. Stevenson had also taken the lead in founding the Daughters of the American Revolution and had been a pioneer member of the Colonial Dames and of the Women's Clubs of America. . . .

Those had been crowded years for Lewis Stevenson, too—years through which he'd swiftly grown to be the man who now gazed out the train window across a darkling plain, seeing the light of lonely stars reflected on earth, as it seemed, by the lamps of lonely farmsteads.

In November of 1893 he married his childhood sweetheart, Helen Davis, daughter of W. O. Davis, the proprietor of the Bloomington *Pantagraph*. Helen's mother had been born Eliza Fell, daughter of Jesse Fell, and the *Pantagraph* had been one of the many enterprises which Fell had launched. In the 1830s and '40s, when it was called, first, the *Observer* and, later, the *Intelligencer,* the newspaper had been a Whig organ; in the 1850s, soon after being named the *Pantagraph,* it had become an organ of the new Republican party and the earliest editorial supporter of Abraham Lincoln for the presidency. Staunchly Republican the *Pantagraph* remained, reflecting the conservative views of Davis, under whose management it had grown into one of the most influential and prosperous papers in Illinois. Thus Davis had never been a political friend of Adlai Stevenson. Quite the contrary. But he was a kindly, pacific Quaker gentleman who would not permit political differences to blind him to another's human qualities, and he'd made no objection to the romance between his daughter and Stevenson's son. . . . The wedding had been the most brilliant social event of the year in central Illinois.

Lewis had taken his bride to Washington, where he served as private secretary to his father. Two years later he'd made his journey alone to the warring Far East where he'd been introduced to the Empress of China. And in Washington, of course, the newly married couple became good friends of Mrs. Phoebe Hearst. The friendship had proved rewarding when, after the vice-presidential term ended, Lewis again went West in quest of health. Mrs. Hearst employed him to help with the management of her mining properties in Arizona and New Mexico, particularly of the Santa Rita copper mine in the latter state. In 1899 he'd moved from Fort Bayard, New Mexico, to Los Angeles, continuing to help with management of Hearst estates. Nor had all the profit from this arrangement accrued to him. Looking back from this March day, 1909, he could say with perfect confidence that he had been a successful steward: enterprising, an effective organizer, an astute manager both of finances and of men. Mrs. Hearst had not hesitated to recommend him highly to her son when William Randolph in 1904, having added the Los Angeles *Examiner* to his swiftly growing newspaper empire, was in search of an assistant general manager of that property. The post had been offered Lewis, and he'd accepted it.

He had become, by that time, widely known in southern California, particularly in Democratic political circles. Just a few months after his arrival in Los Angeles in 1900, he'd been the subject of an extended feature story in the city's leading paper. The occasion was his father's nomination as Vice-President on the ticket headed by William Jennings Bryan. Mounted now in a family scrapbook at home, the article recorded that the Democratic national convention at which his father was nominated that year was the first Lewis Stevenson had missed "since he was a boy of six or eight." He was, the writer added, "exceptionally bright, a thorough specimen of a twentieth century unassuming American." Other later publicity, telling of his effective role at some party meeting or other, recorded with apparent surprise that he looked "not the type of political henchman." He looked, instead, "scholarly," but had proved himself a hardheaded politician just the same.

All this had done him no harm in the eyes of William Randolph Hearst, himself a Democratic member of Congress from New York, with high political ambitions, when the Los Angeles *Examiner* became a Hearst property. The Hearst newspaper connection had, of course, made young Stevenson yet better known to the southern California public. He'd received a great deal of personal publicity, for instance, as a result of the great earthquake of April 18, 1906, which devastated San Francisco. By that time he'd moved from Los Angeles to Berkeley, into a house near the famous "Hacienda," the home of Mrs. Phoebe Hearst, and then, after a brief time, had moved back to the southern city. When news of the San Francisco disaster came, the Los Angeles *Examiner* recruited doctors and nurses, gathered together quantities of medical and other supplies, and dispatched these northward on a much-publicized special train. Of that train—the first relief train to reach the stricken city—Lewis Stevenson was in charge, and he'd done yeoman service in helping to organize relief work in the flame-swept city where hundreds had died, thousands had been injured, and scores of thousands made homeless. A number of babies, born in relief tents, were named after him by grateful parents.

It appeared to many that he might look forward to a successful public career on the West Coast.

Yet in that very year of the earthquake he had abandoned all his western projects and returned to Bloomington, Illinois. There were several reasons. For one thing, neither Lewis nor Helen had ever felt really at home in the West; their roots ran deep into the Illinois earth and their vital interests had continued to center in Bloomington, where they visited for extended periods every year. For another thing, their parents wanted and perhaps even needed their return. Helen's father was by then a widower; he approached his seventieth year. Lewis's father was now seventy-one, and he'd more than hinted that, in his declining years, he wished that his son were beside him. But the final determinant had been the expanding enterprises of Mrs. Matthew Scott, Lewis's aunt Julia, who had been left a widow in 1901. Adding more and more land to the extensive holdings left to her, she had soon some forty-nine farms comprising more than twelve thousand acres. She asked Lewis to become her farm manager. She offered a good salary. Without much hesitation, he accepted.

Thus it was primarily as a farmer that he thought of himself, this evening of March 4, 1909, as his train came close to Bloomington. He found time to engage in other activities, politics for example: just last fall he'd managed his father's unsuccessful campaign for the governorship of Illinois—a campaign Lewis had strongly opposed and the enfeebled elderly ex-Vice-President had reluctantly undertaken at his party's insistence. (Adlai Stevenson had run far ahead of the national ticket, losing by a mere 22,000 whereas the Democratic presidential candidate lost Illinois by 179,000.) But his major energies, physical and mental, were devoted to the problems of scientific land management.

Of these concerns was his mind filled up, who now felt the train brake and slow and saw the lights of houses coming closer together through the window. A trainman came through the coach calling, "Bloomington." Lewis Green arose and donned his coat. A few minutes later he handed his traveling bag to a hack driver beside the Bloomington station and, mounting, gave the driver his home address.

III

Bloomington and her sister community, Normal, contained in that year approximately thirty thousand people—something over twenty thousand in the former place, something less than ten thousand in the latter. In general plan, Bloomington was a fairly typical midwestern county-seat town. Its center, from which all else spread out, was the courthouse square, around which were built the leading stores, banks, and hotels, plus a "Grand Opera House" in which operas were very seldom if ever performed, and a theater, the Castle, in which a five-thousand-dollar organ was being installed that year. As the business center of the second richest agricultural county in the United States (only Lancaster County, Pennsylvania, surpassed McLean County, Illinois, in this respect), the town's economic life very largely depended on agriculture, but there was a healthy admixture of other economic elements: a candy factory, an insurance company destined to grow into a very large enterprise, the Alton Railroad shops, several small manufacturing concerns, and two colleges—Illinois Wesleyan in Bloomington itself, and the State Normal College in the town next door.

Many retired farmers lived along the quiet streets through which Lewis Stevenson rode that night, and everywhere in the town the farmer's attitudes and way of life were evident. Nevertheless Bloomington was not at all a "hick" community, viewed from an urban standpoint. It had a degree of sophistication far from typical of towns of its size and general composition, for it had drawn to itself a remarkable number of exceptional people. Among these, of course, were the grandparents and parents of Lewis Stevenson and his wife. Others were famous figures of the Lincoln era: Ward H. Lamon, David Davis, Leonard Swett, William F. Arny. Two "inspirational" writers, Frank Crane and Elbert Hubbard, had been Bloomingtonians; Rachel Crothers, soon to become a famous playwright, was a Bloomingtonian. So were James G. Harbord, the soldier; Margaret Illington, the actress; Clark Griffith, the baseball pitcher; and several others of equal note.

Any town so productive of celebrities must feel itself to be in the main stream of national life, and Bloomington's sophistication was increased by the presence of many wealthy, widely traveled, and well-educated people—a "Society" more brilliant than that of most towns two or three times its size. Of it, Lewis Stevenson himself, of course, was a leading member, and the house toward which he now rode was one of its focal points.

This house, at 1316 East Washington Street, was a two-story ten-room structure set far back from the street on the north side, with high-pitched gables bounding an attic almost large enough to be considered another story. The long lot on which the house was set had, when the Stevensons bought the place three years before, a small grove of box elders at the back, a great sycamore tree rising above the northwest corner of the house, an ash tree, and no landscaping or shrubbery at all. Now, thanks to Helen Stevenson, there were a good many young trees and shrubs. Clingstone peach trees replaced the box elders; from them would come many quarts of white peaches for the Stevenson fruit cellar. Ginkgo trees were planted. The house was walled with gray clapboard in 1909, but three years later it would be "pebble-dashed"—that is, stuccoed—and would no longer merge so easily into the darkness as it did on this night of Lewis Stevenson's arrival.

The front door of the house opened into an entrance hall from which a stairway climbed to the second floor. Its walls held many mementos of Lewis Stevenson's travels to the Orient, including Japanese and Korean ceremonial swords, a carved elephant tusk, and Egyptian embroideries. From it opened three doors into downstairs rooms: the drawing room across the whole south front of the house, the dining room on the east side behind the hall, and the library.

The drawing room, with its floor-to-ceiling windows, had an astonishingly various though pleasing *décor*. Its walls were covered with gray grass cloth; its highly polished oak floors were almost covered with dark red oriental rugs and runners. A tiger-skin rug, brought from China, sprawled before the white-tiled fireplace and hearth, and a fire screen with a cut-velvet peacock design upon it stood at the tiger's head. On the fireplace mantel stood a Sèvres clock and a leopard modeled in white marble. There were tall wing-backed chairs in this room and tall-backed pull-up chairs, and at one end a Baldwin piano, over which was draped a brightly colored ancient Chinese mandarin coat. There was a tall richly carved cabinet, seventeenth-century Italian, on which stood a Chinese goddess, while nearby stood a plain walnut table made by some Quaker forebear in Pennsylvania, probably during the Colonial period.

But the drawing room was strictly a special-occasion room, rarely entered by the children of the house save when they were brought in by their parents to bow or curtsy before guests. The library was the true "living room" of the house. A west room, it was approximately ten feet wide by fifteen feet long, though it seemed longer because at its west end were three large bay windows.

On this March evening, as on most chill evenings when the Stevensons were in Bloomington, a coal fire blazed cheerfully in a quite elaborate though not overly large fireplace whose scroll-topped columns sustained a marble mantel. The fireplace was in the southeast corner of the room. On the wall at its left, lighted by the flickering orange-red flames, hung a cross-stitched sampler containing the alphabet in various colors and a stitched-in name and date: Eliza Brown, 1825. On the wall to the right of the fireplace hung a framed facsimile of the autobiography of Abraham Lincoln, in Lincoln's handwriting, with below it the printed statement that this had been presented to the public by Jesse W. Fell of Normal, Illinois, on March 20, 1872, and was published by James R. Osgood and Company, Boston. Across the room from it, on a homely but comfortable brown leather sofa, sat the great-granddaughter of Eliza Brown, the granddaughter of Jesse W. Fell, Mrs. Helen Davis Stevenson.

In her fortieth year she was a tall, slender woman with a long, narrow face, pale of complexion, topped by a mass of dark hair brushed back from her high forehead to a soft bun. Her eyes were gray and heavy-lidded, her nose straight and cleanly chiseled. She did not appear physically strong; three years before, in Berkeley, she'd come near dying of pneumonia and her former strength (she'd never been really robust) had not returned to her. But there was in her appearance another kind of strength—the strength of a forceful personality—and this appearance did not belie reality. Even in the present moment of utter informality, she sat upon the sofa like a queen. With the light of a green-shaded lamp shining down upon her she would have dominated the room even had she been silent.

But she was not silent. A book was opened in her hands and from it she read aloud to her two children, an eleven-year-old girl and a nine-year-old boy. The little boy—a very chubby little boy—leaned against his mother as she read, and gazed round-eyed upon the fire, and was very still. His sister, who sat at the mother's right, was different from him both in appearance and manner. She was tall for her age, and slender and regal, almost a perfect childish replica of her mother, and she was less quiet than her brother. She stirred restlessly from time to time, and her eyes glanced continually about the room. She may even have been conscious of a desire to read aloud herself, for she was already becoming interested in "readings" and play-acting, already dreaming of someday going on the stage. Almost certainly she was conscious, as her absorbed little brother was not, of the *way* her mother read, of the dramatic inflections of her mother's richly resonant voice.

It was a voice not only naturally lovely, a contralto, but highly trained. As a girl, Helen Stevenson had studied singing in Germany and in Paris, and she often sat at the Baldwin and played accompaniments to the songs she sang: German *lieder,* French art songs, Civil

War ballads, folk songs, sentimental songs of the day. The children loved to hear her. "You can't holler down my rain barrel," "Can she bake a cherry pie, Billy boy, Billy boy?" "The Bicycle Built for Two" —these they loved, and also the sad songs from the great American war about boats coming down the river, and the prisoner who dreamed of Mother dear as he sat within the stockade.

But tonight she read—and what was she reading? It is impossible precisely to say, but quite likely it was a selection from *The Family Album of Poetry and Song,* a collection from "the Best Poets, English, Scottish, Irish and American," edited by William Cullen Bryant. This was a favorite book of hers, and of her children. Marked in it were certain special favorites, whose list would grow longer as the children grew older. Already marked were Byron's *The Prisoner of Chillon* and selections from his *Childe Harold;* Thomas Buchanan Read's *Sheridan's Ride;* Oliver Wendell Holmes's *Old Ironsides* and *The Wonderful One-Hoss Shay;* Sir Walter Scott's *Marmion;* and Tennyson's *Charge of the Light Brigade.* Most favored of all, on certain wintry evenings (and this might well have been one of them), was Whittier's *Snow-Bound.*

When the mother read from Whittier she sometimes reminded her children that Whittier was a Quaker poet and that he might be said to speak more directly to them than to most people because Quaker blood flowed in their veins too. She herself came from Quaker stock. Her grandfather Fell had been raised a Quaker and so had her grandmother Hester Brown Fell. (It was Hester's mother who had cross-stitched that sampler by the fireplace.) Quaker, too, in heritage, was her father W. O. Davis, whose forebears had settled in Pennsylvania as early as 1670. Of course all these Quakers had become Unitarians in Bloomington, but if they'd broken the confines of a rigid Quaker piety, accepting a more "liberal" faith, they'd retained many of the Quaker ways and much of the Quaker spirit— a love of peace, an inward serenity which increased rather than reduced effective activity in the world. Often, then, the mother would be led by her children's questions to tell stories about her ancestors, who were, by that same token, *their* ancestors as well—and when she did this they sensed and perhaps even pondered the mystery by which "blood" was said to flow out of the distant past through their own veins toward the future. The past was alive in them.

The past was certainly present in that room. Ancestors were too. It was a room of relics and heirlooms. Upon shelves which lined all but the fireplace wall were books that ancestors had bought and bequeathed to them: Hume's *History of England* in six volumes; the works of Tennyson in eight volumes; Prescott's *Conquest of Mexico* in three volumes; Boswell's *Life of Samuel Johnson* in four volumes; a set of Shakespeare in tall, slender volumes, beautifully bound in white calf. Many of these books, the children knew, came from their grandfather Davis who was an omnivorous reader and whose library was full to overflowing. The sewing rocker, with its cane back and seat, was an heirloom. The antique clock upon the fireplace mantel was an heirloom. So were the needle-point and crochet-covered cushions in the chairs. The dark-oak writing table beside the bay window was not, but it looked as though it were and it had been built, obviously, for the ages. Equally solid was the heavy carved oak straight-back chair beside the table where, in later years, the children would study their school lessons and write their "compositions" and letters, using the silver inkstand and penholder on which, now, the firelight dully glittered.

Thus the little boy and girl, as their mother spoke of ancestors and of the many historic things they'd done, saw history solidified in objects wherever they looked in that room, and saw the colors of time in the dark brown of the stained pine woodwork, in the wine-red of the thick carpet, in the leaping flames of the fire, even in the narrow glare cast down by bronze green-shaded lamps. Many years later, when the little girl was a grown woman living in far countries, she'd remember not just the firelit lamplit evenings in the library but the sunsets too; she'd recall and write about the quiet warmth which pervaded this room whenever a setting sun shone through the gay English linen chintz of curtains hung across the great bay windows. And the little boy, when a grown man caught up in what often seemed to him a devastating tornado of history, would also remember with pleasure this room where time seemed not an immediate pressure but a gentle though vivid dream; sometimes he'd even return to this place, finding his bearings again and renewing himself here at what seemed to him a still center of the whirling world.

Generally the mother read to her children for a stated period and sent them upstairs to bed at a scheduled hour. On this early March night, however, the reading ended when the front door opened to admit Lewis Green Stevenson and with him a sense of the present as vibrant colorful energy. He was full of the news of the day ("'Tis a sad day for Democrats," said he, seeming not sad at all) and of his own activities as, gaily, he greeted wife and children. The latter flew to his embrace. The little girl he called "Sheep," perhaps because she was the very opposite of "sheepish" in her quality—though she was, she confessed in later years, a little inclined to "stray" from strictly conventional pastures, like the sheep of the nursery rhyme. The little boy was called "The Brute," because he was such a gentle and conscientious and well-behaved little boy, even a "saintly" little boy, as his mother and aunts, and his sister, too, in later years, often said. Then the father asked questions about his wife's day and about the children's. Eagerly the latter spoke of events at the red-brick East Washington public school, where their attendance was still a somewhat novel experience for them. Not until this year had either of them gone to a regular school for any length of time; they'd moved around the country so much, and had been taught rather erratically by their mother. . . . A great event on this particular day, they told their father, was a little talk each of their teachers had given about the ceremony in Washington, where President Taft was inaugurated.

"And my teacher spoke about Grandfather," the little girl said proudly, "and how he was inaugurated too, once."

"Yes," said their father, smiling, "*that* was a great day for Democrats. Today, as I've said, is a sad one. Right, Brute?"

The two children climbed the gloomy stairs to bed, past the ancient spinning wheel on the landing, up into the second-floor hallway where a gas jet burned with a blue flame in a ceiling fixture: the mother retained it when electricity was installed, because it was "so cheerful." From this hallway five doors opened, each with a transom above it. One opened into the guest room in the northeast corner of that floor. Another opened into the little girl's room in the southeast corner. A third opened into the relatively large master bedroom, directly over the drawing room. A fourth opened into the bathroom with the mother's dressing room attached, where there was a gas burner beside which the children huddled into their clothes on cold mornings.

Soon the little boy ran on bare feet across the floor of his room and jumped, shivering a little, between the chilly sheets of his bed. The window beside his bed was wide open: fresh air was "good" for one. He pulled sheets and blankets up over his chin and huddled deep into the bed—but his eyes looked out, seeing the naked twigs and branches of the giant sycamore swaying in patterns across the star-strewn sky. A wintry breeze softly sighed through the barren sycamore, and through the young naked ginkgo trees, and the cling-stone peaches.

How warm and cozy was his bed after he'd lain in it a little while! How warm and cozy was his world! He was perfectly secure in it and looked toward all his tomorrows with a happy anticipation. He'd go to school next day. On the next day after, Saturday, he'd play, with his cousin Dave Merwin perhaps, by the frozen stream meandering through the cow pasture which spread beyond all the back yards in that block. On Sunday he'd go to Sunday school in the plain yet graceful Unitarian church, and afterward they'd have Sunday dinner at his grandfather Stevenson's. In the afternoon he'd play, no doubt, with Joe Bohrer, who was just his age and a neighbor of the elderly Adlai Stevenson. Joe Bohrer's mother would be the first woman to be elected to the state Senate of Illinois, and his maternal grandfather, "Private Joe" Fifer, had once been governor of Illinois and was a close friend of the little boy's own grandfather Davis.

A cozy world. A warm cozy world.

But as he lay in his bed he heard, far across the prairie night, the haunting cry of a train whistle. It was a cry which always evoked in him strange and powerful emotions. With it, there seemed to enter his consciousness a lyric sense of distances in space and time so vast that even this world of his was lost in them. His world was an island, after all—a tiny island compared to the cold emptiness by which it was surrounded. Tragedy was therefore possible. But far from frightening him or in any way dismaying him, this sense of tragic possibilities seemed to enhance his joy in the present moment, his pleasure in looking forward and looking back along the stream of history. He loved the sad wail of a distant train whistle in the night. He would always love it. In the 1950s, as a mature man, one of his regrets about "Progress" would be that it banished steam locomotives from the nation's railways, and with them the long aching evocative calls of steam whistles across lonely miles of the prairie he loved so well.

CHAPTER TWO

Of History
as a Family Matter

The family of this little boy was one which carefully preserved both its records and its legends. A future historian would be overwhelmed by the bulk of books and manuscripts it had accumulated about itself. Nor could he ignore this material who would understand the man into whom the little boy would grow. To the boy, American history was largely a family matter; to the man, it was of his essence. . . .

During the period from 1906 through 1911, family custom decreed that the Lewis Green Stevensons take Sunday dinner with the elderly Adlai Stevensons, where the little boy listened, fascinated, to stories of the early Stevensons and of all the collateral lines which had fused to make *him*, through his own father. The Ewings, for instance. And the Osbornes. It was after the little boy's great-great-great-grandfather, Adlai Osborne, that Grandfather Stevenson had been named, the word originally coming from the twenty-ninth verse of the twenty-seventh chapter of the Book of Chronicles, where it is recorded that one "Shapat, the son of Adlai" was placed "over the herds in the valleys" in the time of David. Probably it was at Sunday dinner that the little boy first heard the story of the founder of the American Stevensons, William, a Scotch-Irishman who'd come to Pennsylvania in 1748 and moved in 1763 to what was later Iredell County, North Carolina, where he, a farmer and notably pious Presbyterian convert, became a ruling elder of the Fourth Creek Church in what is now Statesville.

This pious William Stevenson had been dubbed "Little Gabriel" because, though small in size, he was great in voice and could pray with a fervor, a fluency, and a volume amazing to all who heard him. Famous was the occasion on which he "prayed the devil out of Doctor Hall." The latter, pastor of the Fourth Creek Church, was subject to fits of melancholia during which he was so convinced of his own sinfulness that he could not preach. One such spell lasted for a year and a half and might never have ended had not Little Gabriel mounted the pulpit to intercede with the Almighty on his pastor's behalf. At the close of this prayer, as long as it was fervent, delivered with stentorian volume, the Reverend Dr. Hall went slowly to the pulpit and preached again; it is reported that "he was not troubled by these melancholy spells for many years after Little Gabriel's prayer and never so seriously as before."

Little Gabriel, the boy learned, was a great-great-great-grandfather of his sister and himself, and was as prolific of children as he was fervent in prayer. Of his twelve children, the eldest was killed as a soldier in the Revolutionary War. From the fifth child, James, the little boy could trace his own descent. James Stevenson had married Nancy Brevard, a daughter of Colonel Hugh Brevard who was a leader at the Battle of Ramseur's Mills during the Revolution and was a brother of the Ephraim Brevard who authored the Mecklenburg Declaration of Independence. Hence the boy may well have learned before he could read a fact most Americans never learn, namely that Mecklenburg County, North Carolina, had declared her independence from England and established a government of her own by May 20, 1775, nearly fourteen months before the great Declaration which Thomas Jefferson penned in Philadelphia. The event had for him a personal meaning: his own great-great-uncle had been a leader of the enterprise.

He must have learned, too, how James Stevenson with his wife Nancy, his brother-in-law, his younger brother Moses, and a large party of emigrants crossed the mountains and settled in Christian County, Kentucky, where they established a Presbyterian church almost before they'd established their homes. James, too, was prolific of children: he had nine of them, the sixth of whom was little Adlai's great-grandfather John Turner Stevenson. He it was who married Eliza Ewing, daughter of Adlai Osborne Ewing, and fathered Adlai Ewing Stevenson I, Vice-President of the United States. They were sturdy yeoman stock, these people, farmers and Presbyterian preachers, strong of physique and equally strong in their Protestant faith. The boy was rightly taught to take pride in them.

But yeoman's blood did not flow unmixed through his father's veins, and hence through his own. With it was mingled the blood of aristocrats. As Grandfather Stevenson looked down the table at Grandmother Stevenson he sometimes spoke, and she did too, of how this mingling had come about.

In the late 1850s Adlai I had gone with Cousin James Ewing from Bloomington, where they'd attended Illinois Normal in the sister town of Normal, to Danville, Kentucky, where they enrolled as students in Centre College, a Presbyterian institution. The president of Centre College at that time was the Reverend Lewis Warner Green, D.D., whose daughter Adlai I was destined to marry and who became, thereby, the grandmother of the little boy. Yes, she was the tiny but vibrant old lady who smiled so kindly upon him as he eagerly listened. . . .

This Reverend Dr. Green, the boy heard, came from a very distinguished family indeed. He had been born in 1806 on a large and lovely estate near Danville called "Waveland," established by his father, Willis Green, in 1795. Willis Green was the son of Duff Green of the Shenandoah Valley in Virginia—scion of one of the greatest colonial families—and of Anne Willis Green, whose father, Harry Willis, was also among the greatest of Virginians. And for his second wife (his first had died at Waveland of "galloping consumption" shortly after her wedding), the Reverend Dr. Green had taken one Mary Peachy Fry, whose ancestry was quite as distinguished as his own.

She, as the little boy early learned, was directly descended from Colonel Joshua Fry, a graduate of Oxford who, in 1732, became professor of mathematics in Virginia's William and Mary College. Professor Fry had collaborated with Thomas Jefferson's father, Peter, in preparing a map by order of the King, the first accurate one of the "Inhabited Parts of Virginia," and had been commissioned a colonel by King George III, commanding Virginia militia during the French and Indian War. On the march to Fort Duquesne he was thrown from his horse, died of his injuries, and was buried on May 31, 1754, under an oak tree near Mills Creek, Maryland. (His command devolved upon his twenty-two-year-old lieutenant colonel, George Washington, who cut into the oak: "Under this tree lies the body of the good, the just and noble Fry.") He left a son, John, who had a son, Joshua Fry II, and this second Joshua, after returning from Oxford where he'd been sent for his education, served as a soldier in the Revolution. He then emigrated to Mercer County, Kentucky, where, having inherited a large landed estate, he was enabled to devote his energies to a school which he opened for the education of his own children and his neighbors. Many who later became prominent Kentuckians owed their education to him.

Joshua Fry II took as wife one Peachy Walker, daughter of Dr. Thomas Walker, physician, surveyor, explorer (he named the Cumberland Gap), and scientific engineer, who had become the commissar-general of Braddock's army. (His house, Castle Hill, still stood outside Charlottesville, Virginia, in the 1950s and would be visited then by the boy become a man.) One of his sons, also named Thomas, was the father of the Mary Peachy Fry, who, as a young widow (she'd married a Colonel Lawrence and had a son by him), married Lewis Warner Green.

By the time the little boy first heard of her, this Mary Peachy Fry Green, his great-grandmother, was a legendary figure in the family. She was a formidable aristocrat in the southern tradition, who in all her life—at least until she came to live with her daughters in Bloomington—had never so much as buttoned her own shoes or made a cup of coffee. She was an arrogant, haughty, black-haired beauty at the time of her second marriage, and she remained arrogant and haughty—and black-haired too—until, in her eighties, she died. But she had charm and vital force; an aura of excitement surrounded her; and if she was excessively patrician and proud and too much devoted to worldly matters, she perhaps provided a needed counterbalance to the Reverend Dr. Green's tendency toward excessive otherworldliness.

For the Reverend Lewis Green had been raised in the strict Calvinist faith, convinced of the doctrine of original sin and of the necessity of God's grace to absolve each man of his innate wickedness. Good works were needed too. Dr. Green saw man's wickedness institutionalized in Negro slavery—not an easy view to take in his time, and place, and circumstances. He himself inherited some twenty-two slaves. But he joined his fiery kinsman, editor James Birney of Danville's leading newspaper, in sponsorship of the "Liberia Project," and as soon as he obtained his inheritance he not only freed his slaves but also financed the emigration of several of them to West Africa's new Negro Republic. Thus did he keep the faith.

And at the time of his second marriage this faith had been, or seemed, as solid as a rock, as bright as a beacon. Alas, he took his bride to Germany. There he studied in universities swept by that tide of skepticism which was later called the "Higher Criticism." Before long his faith was dissolved, the shining light went out. He walked in utter darkness through the streets of Alleghany City, where he was president of the Presbyterian Theological Seminary; he yet walked in gloom when, after a period as president at Hampden-Sydney College in Virginia and of Transylvania (now the state university) in Kentucky, he returned to Danville as president of Centre College. And who knows but what his very life might have failed for lack of purpose had he not had beside him a proud, aristocratic girl whose zest for life was wholly undisturbed by metaphysical doubts?

Long years afterward his granddaughter Julia Stevenson—the little boy's aunt Julia Hardin—met an elderly lady who had been one of the Reverend Green's parishioners in the Danville Presbyterian church. This lady told Julia how, one evening, she met her minister as he walked slowly up the path to the president's house. His head was bowed, his face drawn with weariness, and she stopped him to ask, rather anxiously, how he was.

"Faint, yet pursuing," he'd replied, lifting his hat and bowing in his usual courtly way. "Faint, yet pursuing."

And indeed, as Aunt Julia told her young nephew, Dr. Green, though faint with doubt and confusion, did pursue the truth until at last he found it in a more serene and mature faith than any he had known before.

He must have been just emerging from his period of "darkness" when young Adlai Stevenson I, with his cousin James Ewing, first met him at Centre College, but there was nothing faint about the impression he made upon the two students. That impression was strong and glowing—nor did it ever weaken or fade. The boy never heard Grandfather Stevenson speak of Dr. Green save with reverence and gratitude; the same was true of Cousin James, who became Minister to Belgium and whom the boy knew as a most distinguished old gentleman with walrus mustaches, a soft pleated shirt front, and a long black frock coat.

There was always a twinkle in Grandfather Stevenson's eye, however, when in the presence of Grandmother he spoke of his first meeting with the great teacher, for it was at that meeting that he also first saw Letitia Green, the reverend doctor's daughter. It was on a Sunday. The two shy cousins, just arrived in Danville, were invited to dinner at the president's house. They were years older than most entering students, and to Letitia, then in her early teens and not uninfluenced by her mother's aristocratic ways, the two looked old indeed. And very dull. That evening her father told her that she must include the two cousins among her guests at a party she was planning. Bitterly, she rebelled. She'd rather give up the party altogether, she said, than have it spoiled by "old" Stevenson and "old" Ewing. Her father, however, prevailed, as in such matters he always did. The party was held. The two cousins came.

"And so I met your grandmother," Grandfather Stevenson would say to his grandson and namesake. "And so we were married."

The latter event did not occur, however, until some nine years later, after a great war had been fought and Dr. Green had died. It was said that "his tired heart was broken by fratricidal strife," and well it might have been, for though he himself was an ardent Union man he had beloved kinsmen and close friends in both the Union and Confederate armies. All that he stood for, all that he had worked for—all kindness and love—seemed to be consumed in the conflagration. Grandmother Stevenson spoke movingly of his spiritual agony. . . .

But the little boy, listening round-eyed at Sunday table, was more impressed by certain adventures Grandmother Stevenson herself had had as a young girl in those violent bloody years. After the battle of Perryville, fought some miles from Danville, the Confederates retreated through the latter town; the girl Letitia Green watched them stream past the president's house, worn and bedraggled. That night, as she lay abed in her room on the house's first floor, she was awakened by the sound of snipers shooting in the streets. She started up. She rushed for the door. And just as she reached it a bullet struck the pillow where her head had lain.

"Now where would *you* be," she asked the little boy, gently smiling, "if I had not reached that door? But never mind. I did reach it—and here you are!"

She'd been at Miss Haynes's Fashionable Finishing School for Young Ladies, at No. 10 Gramercy Park in New York, when news of her father's last illness reached her. To get home she'd traveled by train to Lexington and thence through the battle lines to Danville in a stagecoach repeatedly halted by soldiers who demanded her passport. A terrible journey. The most terrible journey of all her long life. The boy saw and heard and felt it all as she told of it:

the wild wind tossing tree branches against the sky, the sound of firing in the distance, the yellow lanterns at night glinting on bayonets and shining on the grim young faces of soldiers as they peered in upon the girl (though it was strange to think of grandmother as a young girl) who sat, grief-stricken, in the coach. When she reached home at last she was barely in time to see her father die.

Then it was, or shortly thereafter, that young Letitia with her widowed mother had come to live with the elder daughter, Julia, who had married Mr. Matthew Scott, formerly of Lexington, Kentucky, and now a resident of central Illinois. So flat and, in those days, yet relatively treeless, central Illinois seemed a dreary landscape after the lush rolling beauty of Kentucky, but Matthew Scott was a wealthy, canny man who had the means to re-create, in the raw prairie state, much of the grace and ease of the old plantation South and, so far as Dr. Green's widow was concerned, to maintain the aristocratic attitudes too. It was inevitable, therefore, that the Widow Green (how she'd have bridled at the name!) should regard with small favor the suit for her daughter's hand which was at once pressed by Adlai Stevenson I. He was then thirty-one years old, was prosecuting attorney at Metamora and well known in political circles, but he seemed far "beneath" the Scotts and Greens. Letitia, however, knew her own mind and heart, and her mother at last gave a reluctant consent to that which she was powerless to prevent.

The wedding took place on December 20, 1866, in the Matthew Scott home. Chicago was deemed too crude a town to supply the wedding feast, or the waiters for it; everything—ices, salads, cakes, and waiters—came from that much older and more sophisticated city, St. Louis. And it came frozen by a sudden bitter cold wave. Everything had to be thawed out before the feast could proceed. But it did proceed, in high style. Afterward, Adlai Stevenson I drove his bride to Metamora, whose muddy streets had been frozen to the consistency of iron, and as his buggy jarred over snow-covered ruts it passed an old farmer in a sleigh.

"Hi, Stevenson," the old man called out. "I hear you got hitched. Bring your old woman around to see us."

Grandfather Stevenson always chuckled as he told this part of the story: how he'd looked down at his elegant little bride, fearful of the effect the old farmer might have made upon her.

"Your grandmother has always been a fine figure of a woman," he slyly said to his grandson, "but she was more slender then than now.

She had a wasplike waist. She looked too fine and frail, if I may say so, for pioneer life. For it was still a pioneer life, pretty much, at Metamora. We were ten muddy miles from the nearest railroad. Do you know what her wardrobe consisted of, as we began that pioneer life? Silks and satins and fine muslins! Can you wonder at my worry over her response to that 'old woman'? But she didn't mind at all."

And why should she have? asked Grandmother Stevenson, smiling. She knew that she was no "old woman" in that far-off year. She'd be more likely to be offended if someone called her "old woman" now.

The wedding anniversary, ever since, had been celebrated as a family festival, with joy and solemnity. That it should be seemed right and proper to the boy in his early childhood; later the justification seemed even greater, for he came to realize that this marriage had been a singularly happy one. The tiny Letitia Green Stevenson looked up at her six-foot-tall husband with loving pride and respect. He looked down upon her in adoration, and with an equivalent respect. And in their relationship with one another, in the household they established, they maintained from first to last a formality which, somehow, gave a richer meaning to all their words and all their gestures. Always he addressed her as "Mrs. Stevenson," and she addressed him as "Mr."

She appeared far from strong—and indeed, in terms of muscular power, she was far from strong. Yet she had borne many burdens without flagging. Two of her children—Lewis, and Mary, who'd died so young—had been frail and required frequent nursing, though the other two, little Adlai's aunt Julia and aunt Letitia, had been robust enough, and boisterous. They grew up to be beautiful girls, belles of Washington society where Letitia of the reddish-golden hair was called "The Lily," while dark-haired Julia became "The Rose."

II

Often on fine afternoons in the spring and autumn a phaeton from the livery stable drew up beside the porch at 1316 East Washington. The little girl and her younger brother rushed out to get into it, while their mother came more sedately. Then they all went for a drive, with the mother expertly driving, through the streets of the town and out into the open country. On such drives the two children heard a great deal from their mother's lips about "when I was a little girl," and heard, too, about ancestors very different, in temperament and tradition, from the Stevensons and Ewings, the Greens and Frys and Walkers.

Of these maternal ancestors, the greatest according to popular belief—certainly the greatest in influence upon the little boy—was Great-grandfather Jesse Weldon Fell. The Fell influence was pervasive; it was, indeed, inescapable in that community, being everywhere visible as well as talked about.

Driving, the mother and two children passed an impressive mansion at the edge of Bloomington, with a park of several landscaped acres around it. There, said the mother, is the site of the first house Jesse Fell lived in after his marriage, way back in 1838, to Hester Vernon Brown. Jesse was thirty, then—and as lawyer, newspaperman, road builder, town builder, political leader, he was already a major power in central Illinois. His bride was nineteen. . . . Best man at that wedding, the mother went on, was David Davis, Jesse's friend and law associate to whom these acres were later sold. Davis, like Fell, was later a close friend of Abraham Lincoln; he was Lincoln's floor manager during the 1860 Republican convention and became an associate justice of the Supreme Court of the United States and executor of Lincoln's will. Judge Davis it was who built the mansion they now saw, on the site of Jesse Fell's relatively modest cottage.

"The judge had lots of money, and he needed lots of room," Helen Stevenson explained, "for he was a very *big* man in every respect. He must have weighed three hundred pounds."

Then she reminded her children that she'd once taken them to visit Hester Brown Fell, their great-grandmother, an old, old lady whose hair was drawn tightly back against her skull in the old Quaker style, whose smile was tired and a little sad, but whose gray eyes had a rare serenity as, looking back into a full and happy life, she awaited death. It seemed impossible to the boy that she had ever been young, and just a few months later (this was in 1907) she was dead at the age of eighty-eight, having survived her husband by twenty years. Her father, William Brown, as the boy heard, had been the great man of Delavan, Illinois, where she was raised. A *good* man, too. All through central Illinois he was known as "Joseph" because in a year of general crop-failure he had sold his own good corn crop to his distressed neighbors for the normal price of one dollar a bushel instead of at the inflated prices others were charging.

He was a man of means. From the Quaker community of Chester County, Pennsylvania—the same county that Fell came from—he'd come West with his family in a carriage! His very first cabin had had glass panes in its windows! He could afford tutors for his children! It was as tutor to the Brown children that Jesse Fell in 1832, having just come to Illinois, first saw his future bride.

When the phaeton rolled past the plain red-brick structure on the corner of East and Jefferson streets, the mother might remind her children that this church where they worshiped on Sunday mornings had been founded in 1859 by Jesse Fell with his brother Kersey (who first proposed Lincoln as Republican candidate for President) and some twenty other "religious liberals." Of course Fell by then had fallen entirely away from the Quaker piety in which he had been raised (his house, incidentally, was one of the few in that community in which dancing was permitted), but this piety, as the mother explained, had never been rigidly orthodox. His father, a hatter, had forsaken the Friends for Methodism in middle years, while his mother had been a preacher of the Hicksites, who constituted the "liberal branch" of the Society of Friends and were opposed to set creeds and doctrinal statements. Thus when the slim blue-eyed young Fell started West in the fall of 1828, his mind, unhampered by religious dogma, could swiftly learn from books and practical experience. He became salesman for a book firm in Pittsburgh; he set type in a Wheeling newspaper office; he "paused for two years" (the phrase delighted the boy grown up, who always quoted it with relish) in Steubenville to study law; he passed his Bar examinations in Steubenville in October, 1832; and he arrived in eastern Illinois a month later, ready to begin one of the most useful careers in midwestern history.

"His was such a *free* mind," Helen Stevenson said.

At first the religious group he helped to organize in Bloomington was called the Free Congregational Society, she went on. It met in historic Phoenix Hall upon the square. A decade later, when the present church was built (with a spire now, alas, destroyed), it became Unitarian. But from its very beginning its faith was a rational one. Human reason is man's only sure guide to truth, the members believed, and to use one's mind honestly and well in quest of truth is therefore an act of devotion to the Supreme Intelligence. This implied a commitment to free inquiry and free speech.

The faith, the commitment, had not gone untested during the Civil

War. Indeed, of all the stories the little boy heard about his great-grandfather Fell, none produced on him an effect more profound and educative than the story of the little church's greatest trial.

This was in April 1865, after Lincoln's assassination. The news of that tragedy had been especially dismaying to Bloomington, where so many of the President's personal friends resided, and of these friends none had been more grief-stricken than Jesse Fell. He presided over a great mass meeting of sorrowing citizens, in the square, on the day after Lincoln's death and spoke there "with singular eloquence of his old friend." Even the boy, therefore, could understand the emotions aroused among members of the Free Congregational Church when its pastor, the Reverend Charles Ellis, a New Englander of fervent abolitionist views, chose in his sermon for April 23, 1865, to hold Abraham Lincoln morally responsible for his own assassination.

Before God, the minister argued, John Wilkes Booth was less to blame for Lincoln's murder than were the Founding Fathers, for these had permitted slavery to be woven as a fatal flaw into the fabric of the Republic at the time of the Constitutional Convention. As for Abraham Lincoln, he had supported this slave constitution until forced by events to issue the Emancipation Proclamation. "He had not the moral courage to step forth like a strong man in his might and do what his better nature told him was his highest duty," cried Mr. Ellis.

The effect of this, and of much more in similar vein, was an angry disturbance in the church. Mr. Ellis was barely permitted to complete his sermon. And a few days later a full meeting of church members was held for the avowed purpose of demanding the pastor's resignation.

The boy become a man could imagine with some vividness his great-grandfather's emotions on this occasion. Jesse Fell could hardly fail to deplore, personally, the assessment Mr. Ellis had made of Lincoln's character. He might well have questioned the judgment and sensitivity of a man who could so deliberately salt an open wound. Yet Jesse Fell stood firmly against the proposed action. As substitute for the proposed action he submitted resolutions which (a) refused to censure the sermon, asserting the right of any man to express his ideas untrammeled in this church; and (b) reproved the "mob" which had caused the disturbance last Sunday. It is evidence of Fell's persuasive power that these resolutions were almost unanimously adopted, for this meant that several members of the reproved "mob" must have voted for them.

Instructive, too, for one who would make a career in politics, was the effect of all this on Mr. Ellis himself. Though he had been publicly vindicated, he voluntarily resigned his pulpit a few days later, convinced that his usefulness in Bloomington was at an end. . . .

Fell, himself, though if anyone could be called the founder of the Republican party in Illinois, it was he, and though he was always active in politics, had never (the boy learned) permitted himself to be a candidate for elective office. He preferred that others, notably Abraham Lincoln, give official expression of his political views. Famous in history was the story of how Jesse Fell, having toured the Old Northwest and the New England states while Lincoln and Douglas engaged in those great debates Fell had suggested, returned to join his brother Kersey in urging Lincoln to become Republican candidate for President in 1860. Lincoln had become a national figure; Fell urged his friend to write out an autobiographical sketch which might be used for campaign purposes. Lincoln at first refused, saying the idea was a "foolish" one, but Fell continued to press him until finally, on December 20, 1859, Lincoln handed Fell the brief sketch whose facsimile was now framed on the wall of the library at 1316 East Washington. At once Fell sent it to his friend, Joseph L. Lewis, in West Chester, Pennsylvania, and Lewis's use of it played no small part in swinging the Pennsylvania Republicans, a key delegation, behind Lincoln's candidacy.

If Helen Stevenson drove east or west or south, she must cross railroad tracks and be reminded (and remind her children) that these rail lines ran through Bloomington largely because Jesse Fell had fought so hard in the 1830s and '40s to put them there. If she crossed the tracks northward she drove along a three-mile dirt road leading to Normal. The road was named Fell Avenue, and well it might be (the mother said), since Normal was even more completely Fell's town than Bloomington was. He was a great founder of towns, was Jesse Fell: Pontiac, Lexington, Towanda, Clinton, Leroy, El Paso—all had been largely initiated by him. And one of the towns he had started was Normal, laid out in 1854. It was called North Bloomington at first; the name was changed when the State Normal School, the first teachers' college west of the Alleghanies, was established there. For this, too, Fell (explained the mother) was largely responsible. He it was who donated the land for the campus and who led the subscription drive which raised one hundred and forty-one thousand dollars, thus outbidding Peoria for the college; he it was who directed the inspection trip which presented the proposed site to officials in the best possible light, despite heavy rains which had transformed the bare prairie into a sea of mud; he it was who led eighty prominent Bloomingtonians in the underwriting of the pledged funds, after lawyer Abraham Lincoln had drawn up the bond.

"And one of the things which made the inspectors favor this site for the college was—this," the mother said, gesturing toward the great elms and maples arching over the streets of Normal where the phaeton now rolled. "They were very young trees then. Jesse Fell had planted them. He planted some ten thousand trees here in Normal alone. He always planted trees on land he owned. After Pennsylvania, this treeless prairie country looked so bleak to him, you see, and he became the greatest tree planter in the Middle West, I guess, supplying scores of thousands of them from his own nursery."

In Normal the phaeton often rolled past the site of Fell Park, Jesse's home, where the little boy's grandfather Davis had been married to Eliza Brown Fell, and where Helen Stevenson herself often played as a little girl. The house, though removed from its original site, still stood—a large square structure, not beautiful at all but very comfortable-looking, with a cupola at the peak of its roof and verandas around three sides. Great-grandfather Fell, Helen Stevenson said, had had two horses, Pet and Dolly, who'd played a large role in her childhood fun. A sawdust ring had been made in the barn at Fell Park and those two patient, gentle horses (they apparently had "Quaker manners") had circled the ring endlessly while Helen and her sister and friends "played circus." Sometimes—and this made a great impression on the little boy—they'd hung from the horses' tails as they did their "stunts."

"I always loved animals," the mother said, as they drove past the house, "but not as my mother did. She was really very sentimental about them. It used to amuse your grandfather."

And then she might talk of the other blood stream, the Davis ancestral line, which blended with the Fell's in her veins and with the Stevenson's and Green's in the little girl and boy.

The Davis traditions were not really very different from the Fells'. This family, too, was Quaker, and came from Chester County, Pennsylvania, where the first of the line, John, died in 1719. William Osborne Davis was of the sixth generation. He was born in a house the family had lived in, father and son, for well over one hundred years, his own father, Hibbard, being one of the wealthiest and most respected farmers in this community. But William Osborne Davis had early evinced a dislike for farming, coupled with a yearning toward intellectual pursuits. While yet in his teens, Helen Stevenson told her children, he accumulated a considerable library of serious literature: Shakespeare, Burns, Byron, Plutarch: and at the boarding school he attended—the Greenwood Dell School on the historic Brandywine—he impressed the master, a venerable Quaker named Jonathan Gauss, with his "warm heart and sensitive temperament" as well as with his scholarship. Later he himself taught in that school.

Then, at the behest of one of the Fell family, he came West, arriving in Bloomington shortly after his twentieth birthday, in the fall of 1859. He taught school that winter in Normal, became a friend of Jesse Fell's, and in 1860 went into the wilderness of the Nebraska Territory in vain search for gold. (That his frail, scholarly grandfather should ever have engaged in such Wild West adventuring seemed to the little boy very strange.) Returning to Illinois, he did guard duty in Springfield in the first year of the Civil War. In 1862, when Jesse Fell was appointed army paymaster with the rank of major by Abraham Lincoln, W. O. Davis became Fell's clerk. And in 1868 he became Fell's son-in-law, later taking over active management of the *Pantagraph*, of which he became sole editor and proprietor in 1871. . . .

Had Helen Stevenson not given her children these details of their grandfather Davis's life during the afternoon buggy rides and at other times, the boy might never have learned them—and this despite the fact that he and his grandfather were very close to one another during those years. Grandfather Davis would never talk about himself, even when urged to do so: this was one of his distinguishing characteristics. He talked wittily on many subjects, including (with some vehemence) politics, but of himself as a person, and of purely personal experience, he said not a word. He listened. He had a knack for "drawing out" other people, thus gaining an acute sense of the public temper in his community, which served him and the *Pantagraph* well.

His effects on the boy were very great, and would be manifest in the man. It might be said that through Grandfather Davis the influence of Jesse Fell upon the boy was deepened and widened. For though Grandfather Davis refused to talk of himself, he talked a great deal about his father-in-law, whom he strove in many ways to emulate. There were similarities between the two. Both were shrewd, unassuming, conscientious, devoted to the public weal, peace-loving, tidy in their personal habits, and in general immensely capable.

But there were differences, too, and the differences, as personified in Grandfather Davis, were perhaps as influential on the boy as the similarities were.

Prudence and acquisitiveness were more important in Davis's character than they were in Jesse Fell's. There was in Fell a largeness of vision, a creative imagination, a generosity of spirit which Grandfather Davis had in far smaller degree, perhaps because he was far less robust physically. Consistent with this was the fact that neatness and orderliness, notable in Fell, were almost a passion in his son-in-law. It was as if his vital energies were so meager that he was compelled carefully to ration them. The little girl would write in a later year of this dominant trait in Grandfather Davis—how his bureau drawers "were so neat that even the collar buttons had their place!" Once he sent her to fetch a little black booklet; it was, said he, in the left-hand corner of the back end of the upper right-hand drawer, second from the top, in his bureau. She opened that drawer. The book was precisely there! "His spectacles had a special spot on top of his bureau," she wrote. "His high black laced boots stood in an even, neat row in the closet; the pencils on the night table had freshly-made points; his bow tie seemed always in its place on his spotless collar. His beautiful gray hair showed it certainly must have been brushed with clean brushes!"

It can hardly be said that the boy "took after" his grandfather in this respect: his room, as his sister often complained, was almost too cluttered to get into, being jammed with collections of coins, baggage checks, luggage tags, wood for carving, tadpoles in Mason jars, and the tiny pictures of boxers and baseball players and actresses that came in the cigarette packages of those days. He was untidy, too, with his clothes; often they lay strewn around the room.

But in another respect he and Grandfather Davis were very similar, the old man's example encouraging what seems to have been a natural tendency in the boy. The grandfather, of course, kept close track of his money: he was even said to be "close" with money. (It is recorded that his standard advice to young men was "never spend more than half your income and keep accounts" but that the wage scale on the *Pantagraph* was not high enough to make his advice practical for most of the "young men" he employed there. His hostility toward organized labor, particularly when it "invaded" his paper, was implacable and moralistic.) He carried a pocket notebook in which he jotted down all expenditures, and he deplored every form of waste and extravagance, though he and his family lived very well indeed in a material way. Even in his purchases of books—and his love and need for books was immense—his expenditures, as his granddaughter later said, were "modest." The grandson, of course, would differ from his grandfather in views on labor relations, but his personal thriftiness would become famous. With amusement, reporters would record how the man went around turning off lights in empty rooms, was likely to grow absent-minded when checks for meals were presented, tipped waitresses a standard 15 per cent instead of the customary politician's dollar, and was reputed to be "always worrying about money—his own, the State's, anybody's."

It was Jesse Fell, however—and not his maternal or paternal grandfather—who became the boy's "favorite ancestor" and even, as he'd say, his "favorite historical character." Fell was the kind of man he himself would most like to be, the "best sort of citizen," a rare combination of visionary and shrewd practical man, eminently "useful."

"He looked ahead," the man would say. "He saw possibilities where others did not. In land. In towns. In Abraham Lincoln. And he always did something about them, something effective."

Then, with a wry smile, he'd mildly regret that Great-grandfather Fell had not been just a bit more concerned to profit in a material way from his enterprise and foresight.

"Life would be simpler for me now if he had. He once owned a lot of land here in Chicago, you know—just outside the Loop. If only he'd held onto it—but he let it go for the mortgage. Oh, he did well enough financially, I suppose, but he seemed to lose interest in an enterprise at about the point at which it was about to yield really big money. He went on to something else. Judge David Davis, for instance, who started as a clerk in his office, I think, died a very wealthy man."

For Jesse Fell's character and personality the man's admiration was unbounded. Though moderate and pacific, he'd say, Jesse Fell was a great natural leader of men, who'd persist patiently and stubbornly when principle was at stake. Fell was utterly fearless. He had, too, a kind of instinctive grasp of the proper balance between force and persuasion in the achievement of human goals. One of the great-grandson's favorite stories about him was of the occasion when Fell, as schoolteacher, was forced to whip a bully larger than himself. He did a thorough job of it. But afterward the youthful teacher gave the bully a lecture which mingled kindness and flattery so effectively that the bully reformed himself and became a Methodist Episcopal minister "of fine character and widespread influence."

Another favorite story revealed that Fell, for all his Quaker background, reacted in the way his great-grandson would also, as boy and as man, when pushed too far. Fell and another lawyer, in a courtroom where Abraham Lincoln was present, became engaged in an argument so heated that Fell was flatly accused of lying. "I told him that would have to be settled outside the courtroom," Fell himself wrote years later, "so when court adjourned, we promptly went out to settle it in the time-honored way. Neither of us gained much advantage over the other, as while he was the stronger, I was quicker, and we were parted before we could finish. We had fought hard enough however to be willing to shake hands. In the morning we were indicted for fighting 'to the disturbance and alarm of the people.' My defense was that nobody was at all alarmed, much to Lincoln's amusement, and the indictment was quashed."

III

Of all the boy's ancestral influences, then, Jesse Fell's was most important. Fell's influence might even be said to have become a central strand of meaning, around which was woven the fabric of the boy's education. But to say this is not to say that the other ancestral strands were unimportant. Each added to the others, each to some extent neutralized the others, so that he was literally forced to make vital choices among them (while retaining the rejected ones as elements of himself) and thus, through his choices, to make of himself a unique individual.

There was in him such a mingling of opposite traditions! He could trace out, as components of himself, the great aristocrat and the petty bourgeois, the poor artisan and the wealthy businessman, the small farmer and the powerful planter, the soldier and the pacifist, the abolitionist and the slave-owner, the free thinker and the rigid Calvinist, the settled Easterner and the westering pioneer, the Unionist and the Confederate, the rabid Republican and the equally rabid

Democrat. No one, in terms of heritage, could come closer to being an "All-American Boy." And no man, molded by such a heritage, and conscious of it, could easily yield to partial views, or become a dogmatist, or commit that "pure" act so beloved of men like Teddy Roosevelt and so devoid, often, of responsible intelligence. The man's "weaknesses" would be of a nature far different from these—so different indeed as to constitute actual strengths, perhaps, in an age all too prone to despair of reason and indulge in totalitarian passions. The man would have a sense of alternative values, an awareness of historic relevancies and implications, so acute as to render difficult the "making-up" of his mind on vital questions immediately. He'd ponder long before deciding. But once his mind was made up, it might be better made than most men's are, with a larger view of objective truth than most men obtain. One of his own favorite quotations came from Bacon's essays, which was a favorite book of his mother's and from which she read often to her children: "If a man will begin with certainties, he shall end in doubts; but if he will be content to begin with doubts, he shall end in certainties."

Certainly his consciousness of history as a family matter made history for him a vividly human drama written by the daily thought and passion and action of individual men and women, yet written, too, in terms of a design more vast and meaningful than any individual could comprehend. There was a pattern. Hence there must be purpose. And the purpose seemed to be moral. He developed a sense of historical process, and of the need for tradition, which was rare in his America. Tradition was that strand of continuity on which historic events are strung like beads; only in terms of a living tradition could current events be understood in such a way as to make intelligent action possible; and this tradition was clearly within as well as beyond himself. Being alive, it was not fixed and rigid. Rather was it that permanence which is the very essence of change, and he himself would re-create it at the same time as he was judged by it when, through present action, he helped to shape the future.

Even the little boy who heard train whistles crying across the night as he lay abed in the first decade of the twentieth century may well have sensed the profound mystery of time and identity: how he was not only himself, isolate, but also others; and how others, though isolate, were also *him*. His ancestors were alive in him. He would be alive in his sons and his sons' sons. And all their lives had meaning, through their every moment, because all were involved in history.

CHAPTER THREE

The Son
of Lewis Stevenson

The boy's own individual story, in the telling of it, often began some ten or eleven months before he was born. . . .

In the spring of 1899 Eliza Brown Fell Davis came to Fort Bayard, New Mexico, for an extended visit with her daughter, Helen Louise Stevenson. With her she brought the two small children of her only son, Hibbard, whose wife had died tragically some five years before. In her fifty-sixth year this eldest daughter of Jesse W. Fell was a slight, frail-appearing figure, but her health had been good in recent years. She had all her old quiet sparkle as she greeted her daughter and son-in-law and bestowed a special greeting upon her infant granddaughter, Elizabeth Stevenson, who'd been born in the Davis home in Bloomington on July 16, 1897. Moreover she had come, as her son-in-law informed her, to a remarkably healthful climate: the brilliant sunshine, the dry desert air, seemed designed to draw from aging bones whatever aches might be.

But, alas, she had enjoyed this climate for only a few happy weeks when a strangely persistent physical pain, deep and gnawing, drove her back with her two grandsons to her home in Bloomington. An operation in Chicago confirmed her suspicions: she was dying of cancer. In November her husband took her to San Antonio, Texas, there to await what both knew to be a swiftly approaching end.

There was, however, a balance, a continuity: as Eliza Brown Fell Davis was dying out of the family, another new life was growing into it. The tall, slender, bearded William Osborne Davis had gray heavy-lidded eyes which appeared always to be gazing across great distances and had always in them, even in his frequent moments of laughter, a quality of quiet sadness. His was a sensitive, brooding intelligence, quickened rather than dulled by long bouts with ill-health, and he must have felt acutely that a race between death and life was being run through that bitter autumn and early winter. Soon he would be a widower—but soon also he would be again a grandfather: Helen Stevenson was again with child. The first news had come from Fort Bayard; later news came from Los Angeles, whence the Stevensons removed that summer; and it must have brought some slight cheer into his life, and into the waning life of his wife. She must have hoped, they both must have hoped, that she might hold this new life in her arms before she died.

If so, they hoped in vain. Eliza Brown Fell Davis died at one o'clock in the morning on January 21, 1900.

By that time Helen Stevenson was very big with child. It was a hard pregnancy. Often she was too ill to rise in the mornings from her bed. Often she sat in the great dormer window of the large white house they'd rented on Los Angeles' Monmouth Avenue, sat and stared in dull sickness out into gray winter rains. Her husband grew increasingly worried about her as January gave way to February and the time for her taking seemed overdue. He communicated his anxiety to his parents, and to the widowed father-in-law, now returned to Bloomington. The anxiety seemed more than justified on the morning of February 5; the birth, too, was hard. . . . But when the Stevenson nurse, Cora Galbraith, returned from a nearby park to which she'd taken the two-and-a-half-year-old Elizabeth (there were orange trees in that park; the little girl had picked up bright oranges from the ground), she was informed that Elizabeth now had a baby brother. A perfectly *enormous* baby brother: he weighed eleven pounds and eight ounces!

It had been long decided what name Lewis Stevenson's son should bear. The telegrams which went out that day to Bloomington announced the birth of a second Adlai Ewing Stevenson. And on the next morning, in wintry Bloomington, Lewis's mother wrote to her daughter-in-law:

February 6, 1900

My dear Helen:
This proud day's sun must not set until I have sent you a line of most heart-felt congratulations to both you and the triumphant father, and a glad welcome to the dear grandson, Adlai.

That he may fill all your most ardent expectations is my earnest prayer. If the new Adlai only comes up to the splendid standard established by his two grandfathers, you will have nothing to regret in the pain and suffering of yesterday. With all good wishes and prayer for your speedy recovery, I remain

Always yours,
Letitia Green Stevenson

A week later she wrote to her son:

February 13, 1900

My dear Lewis:

You know now what it is and all it means to say "my dear boy". May he grow dearer to you each hour of his life and may he be to you and to his mother all you have been to us all these years.

Father is as happy as a king over his first grandson and real name-sake. He often says if Adlai Jr. only turns out such a boy as Elizabeth is a girl his highest ambition will have been attained. How I wish it were possible to peep in upon your little household—not so very little either—this splendid, cold, clear morning!

I am so glad Elizabeth loves the boy. A child is apt to carry through life the feelings it had when its first rival arrives in the world.

Heaven bless you and yours and make the boy in all things to be like you, his proud father and mother.

Devotedly,
Mother

But it was Helen's father who wrote the letter which, in later years, would be most quoted. On the first Sunday following his new grandson's birth, W. O. Davis wrote to his daughter from Bloomington:

Dear Helen:

Tell Lewis that I rec'd his second letter, written since the advent of little Adlai, this morning and I want to thank him for writing so promptly, and while I should reply to him now I want to wait until I have written to you.

We are all highly gratified to hear of the successful launching of this little Presidential craft and to know that you are safely through it. We have been anxious, and were filled with dread until relieved by your telegram—but now that you are believed to be out of danger, the joy the little cherub is to all of us, will compensate a good

deal for your tribulations. Little Elizabeth will enjoy a little brother.
She will be so wise in protecting him, and utterly spoil him, as I
was spoiled by my older sisters. Then I suppose Lewis's ecstatic con-
dition is such that it is hardly safe to permit him to be left alone.
Bert and Lewis B. both insist that he had his thumbs on the scales,
determined that the little fellow should outweigh little Jessie Davis
Merwin. I know Lewis's delight is unbounded, and I scarcely know
anyone who enjoys their children better than he. And it is such a
fine thing to have children in the household, and enjoy them. I do
not know what I would do now without these little boys of ours—
they are developing so well—

Yours lovingly,
W. O. Davis

II

From all accounts, Adlai Ewing Stevenson II was a placid baby, sweet-tempered, passive, and very fat. Nevertheless he squalled sometimes, and loudly. It was said in later years that he once lay in the dormer window of the Monmouth Avenue house squalling with such vehemence and for so long that the nurse, Cora, finally lifted him from his crib and gently dropped him through the open window onto the grassy yard. What happened then is unreported. The story, he himself later believed, was apocryphal: no doubt it seemed consistent with his later career that the first clear glimpse of him should show him with his mouth wide open, bawling for the world's attention; and there were many, he supposed, who wished they might dispose of him by just dropping him out a window.

It is a historic truth that he was in the national political news within six months after his birth. In the summer of 1900 he and his sister were taken by their mother, with Cora to help her, to the Davis summer cottage at Charlevoix, Michigan. On the way they stopped in Bloomington where Grandfather Stevenson was photographed holding his namesake in his arms. The resulting picture showed Adlai E. Stevenson I, Democratic candidate for the vice-presidency, looking with stern directness at the world, his lips clamped tightly shut beneath a thick white mustache, his brow puckered in a slight frown, his bald pate fringed by a fuzz of white hair. Adlai E. Stevenson II, who was certainly very large for his age, leaned passively against his grandfather's left side and looked away to his left, neither smiling nor frowning, his fat little hands resting loosely on the hand which held him. The picture was published on July 20 as a four-column cut in Hearst's brand-new Chicago *American,* with the caption: "The next Vice-President and his Grandson." Below was the legend: "Governor (Theodore) Roosevelt says that this citizen of Illinois . . . in common with all other Democrats, 'stands for dishonesty and dishonor, for license and disaster at home and cowardly shrinking from duty abroad.' There are some citizens of Illinois who probably do not agree with Mr. Roosevelt's view, and who will probably tell him so next November."

When this infant Adlai had grown into a man he would never be sure that he actually remembered the Monmouth Avenue house where he'd been born. He did remember vividly—it was one of his earliest memories—a lagoon with water birds upon it, probably in West Lake Park in Los Angeles. There were ducks and plumed birds. They excited him and perhaps frightened him a little by coming right up to him as he threw handfuls of food toward them. He thought it was miraculous that these creatures, who had always seemed so free and wild and far away, should come close enough actually to eat out of his hand. . . .

Of extended memories from his California years, his earliest perhaps were of the life in Berkeley. There was a little girl next door with the improbable name of Arida Loeshner (this was the spelling he later gave it) whose parents came from Germany. Her father was an astronomer on the faculty of the University of California. She was a rosy-cheeked little girl who was just the age of Adlai's sister, and she joined that sister in "knocking me about."

By that time he had conferred upon his sister the nickname she would bear for the rest of her life. When he first began to talk, "Elizabeth" was more than his tongue could manage; he called her "Buff," which soon became "Buffie," and it was as Buffie that she was thereafter chiefly known to her family and intimate acquaintances. She called him "Brod" (his mother called him "Laddie") and she was indeed a very "managing" little girl where he was concerned.

She seems never to have regarded him as a rival for her parents' affection, and seldom to have resented his presence as a hindrance to her play, perhaps because his responses to the world were so different from hers. "What different children we were!" she'd say in a later year. "I impulsive, emotional, and flying from one thing to another; he concentrated, even-tempered, never angry." Of course it wasn't true that he was *never* angry. She delighted in her "responsibility" for him, assuming toward him, from the outset, a maternal attitude—and sometimes he rebelled against her dominance: when they quarreled, which was seldom, it was generally because of this. But for the most part he was a quite passive recipient of her "management" and her adoration. She did adore him. She always would. When she compared herself with him, she saw his dominant traits as "virtues" and hers as "vices," and she'd say to herself and to others that he was so "good," so "sweet," so "gentle." Others who knew him well agreed with her in this latter judgment. He was, as a little boy, not at all aggressive. He seemed not to care at all for that limelight which to her spirit was as food and drink.

There was psychological significance, perhaps, in a charade they once played together in Charlevoix. He lay curled up on the floor, his eyes closed; she danced into the room, her arms high over her head, her hands clasped. What did it mean? Adlai explained that he was a "sunbeam on the rug" while she was "soaring like a soul."

All his earliest memories seem to have been, not of things he himself did, but of things heard and seen and felt: the gentle lapping of waves upon the shore of Pine Lake at Charlevoix; the sound of wind through the Michigan pines; trains roaring along the rails of the Père Marquette near the Davis summer cottage; a white wall of fog creeping silently across the San Francisco Bay, as seen from the hills of Berkeley; the great high-ceilinged hall—a truly baronial hall with a vast fireplace at the end of it—in the "Hacienda," where Mrs. Phoebe Hearst lived in the hills back of Oakland. Mrs. Hearst he remembered as a "very old lady" (she was then in her mid-sixties) who was "very kind" to him. Once she took him to the fireplace, where a great log fire was blazing, and picked up from the hearthstone a box of finely ground colored powders. "Now you watch!" she said. "These are magic powders. When I throw some of them on the fire, the fire will have beautiful colors." She did, and it did, and little Adlai was enraptured.

He remembered, too, from very early in his life, the fireplace at Charlevoix, with its chimney and hearth of large stones from the Lake Michigan shore. His tall gray-bearded grandfather Davis knelt upon the hearth, carefully building a fire, showing Buffie the proper way to do it. First, old newspapers must be loosely rolled and laid between the andirons, then kindling must be laid, crisscrossed above the paper, then the three white-barked birch logs must be carefully placed where the draft would suck the flames around them and up the chimney, with no smoke entering the room. It was a ritual. With ceremony, the match was struck. The flames leaped up, driving back the evening gloom and the evening chill, for always in early June and late August the nights were chilly in that north country.

Then Grandfather Davis took a book from the shelf. Often it was a collection of Bobby Burns' poetry—a large volume bound in red leather, bought in Philadelphia in 1857, not long before W. O. Davis set out for the West. It had cost two dollars. In that far-off year the warm blood of youth had flowed in his veins, but now he was old: his blood ran thin and cold, his brittle bones ached in the chill. As he settled into his easy chair he wrapped a plaid blanket closely around his legs, even though he sat near the blazing fire, and he took little Adlai up into his lap while Buffie pulled a chair close to him. The little boy, become a man, would yet hear his grandfather's simulated but effective Scottish brogue reading *To a Louse* to him (he saw that louse so clearly upon the prideful bonnet!), and *To a Mouse* and *The Cottar's Saturday Night*. His grandfather, he'd remember, had loved Bret Harte's verse, too; the little boy listened round-eyed as his grandfather spoke *Plain Language from Truthful James*. A few years later he'd listen to the legend of Ichabod Crane and Mark Antony's funeral oration over the body of Caesar, in Grandfather's stirring rendition, and both he and Buffie would *see* the headless horseman and the gesturing Mark Antony in firelight and flickering shadow upon the cottage wall.

Charlevoix was more his home than the California cities ever were, even in his first years. Every summer he and Buffie were taken there by their mother, with Cora (the children called her "Codie"), and lived there for three or four months in a colony of well-to-do people, many of them from Bloomington, centered in and about the Belvedere Hotel.

It is at Charlevoix that we catch our first glimpse of him at play, a play which seems at first to have been quite passive and often solitary. For hours he sat alone in the sand, a "sensitive imaginative little boy" (as Buffie would remember him) pushing a piece of wood through silica waves and making a noise "like a motorboat"—a "put-

putting" sound, for there were no speedboats roaring up the lake in those days. Later he developed a passion for making things. He spent hours with his Meccano set, building bridges and skyscrapers. He and Buffie had leather-burning sets with which they, and especially Adlai, traced designs: Indians, boats, all manner of things burned into the leather with a red-hot needle. In Charlevoix, too, he and Buffie were taken for rather formal "observation" walks, during which a guide would point out flowers and rocks and animals and birds, and give little talks about them. They were required to make drawings of these things: the notebooks of the walks could still be seen in the Bloomington house four decades later. No doubt they stimulated what, in any case, would have become a major trait in Adlai's character—a deep, lyric, and knowledgeable love of nature and landscape beauty. He loved to wander along the lake shore, through the woods and fields, and as he did so he was always acutely *aware* of sights and sounds and smells.

He lived much in and upon the water at Charlevoix—boating, swimming, watching the pleasure boats, the lumber schooners, and the ore boats come and go. A boat horn blew hoarsely as a boat approached the channel bridge, the bridge tender replied with three little toots of his whistle, and little Adlai rushed down to the shore to watch the bridge open and the boat come through. Many of the boats, he felt, were personal friends: he knew them from afar by their color and their silhouette against the sky. At least once each summer Adlai and Buffie were taken by their mother on a boat which went far up the lake to Irontown, there to visit cousins. When he was a little older Adlai joined other boys in the strictly forbidden pleasure of diving from a high trestle into the channel through which the freight boats came. Sometimes he and the family returned to Chicago by boat, the great *Manitou*, an overnight trip, instead of by train. . . .

Trains fascinated him from the beginning of his conscious life. Almost every morning he was at the little station when the Chicago train came in. His chubby figure and eager face became familiar to engineers and firemen and stationmaster, all of whom grew fond of him. From the stationmaster he collected baggage tags stamped with the names of different railway lines and of far places, hanging them from nails driven into the white pine walls of his bedroom. The railroad lore thus acquired was translated into his play with a wind-up model train, whose tracks he laid out in many shapes and whose switches he expertly manipulated. Often he went far down the tracks to watch ecstatically as the roaring wheels of a freight train flattened into spears and other strange designs the pins and nails and pennies he'd placed upon the rails. This last was also a forbidden pleasure; his indulgence in it was among his few acts of deliberate disobedience while he was yet small, requiring that he sneak down the embankment, out of his parents' sight.

And trains, certainly, were as important in his real as in his fantasy life. He spent a great deal of time upon them—and part of his individual story, preserved in family legends, was of the manner in which he took to train travel.

One trip was in January of 1907, just a few months after the family had moved from California to Bloomington. Grandfather Davis, whose health was far from good in his declining years, went to Florida, taking with him his daughter Helen and the two Stevenson grandchildren. Lewis was then in Europe. Grandfather Davis insisted that people should not read on trains but should instead observe the world flowing by the windows and learn from it. As far as little Adlai was concerned, the advice was needless. Eagerly he followed his grandfather's pointing finger and listened to his grandfather's explanations of the things they saw. Eagerly he counted freight cars and observed the fields (he was very early conscious of "good" and "bad" farming country, because there was so much talk of farming in the family), and studied the towns they went through—so eagerly indeed as to interfere with his eating when the little table was set before them in the sleeping car and the wondrous contents of the lunch basket were spread before them. This despite the fact that he was a hearty eater always. When conductors and trainmen came through the car he was likely to wander after them. Porters might delight in his interest in them or be irritated by it, but they could never ignore it: his interest was so intense.

Their destination, that trip, was Winter Park, Florida, where they lived for many weeks in a rented house beside a golf course. There little Adlai made friends with colored boys who caddied for the golfers, tried to play golf with them, and often brought them home, asking the servant to "give my brother some dinner." It was from Winter Park that he wrote, on March 1, 1907, his earliest extant composition—a letter to his father in Europe:

Dear father

I hope you will come home soon?

I will make you a pictire of a cow.

It was also in Winter Park that he had his first brief taste of formal schooling. Grandfather Davis told of it in a letter, dated January 15, 1907, to Lewis.

"Adlai began attendance at the public school a week ago," he wrote. "Elizabeth conducted him the first morning and ushered him into the presence of the teacher, who assigned him a seat, and some work. He was a pretty raw scholar, had no ideas of the rules, talked out loud, and moved about with a good deal of freedom. He was dressed in the fringed suit Miss Woodbury gave him, so the scholars nicknamed him Indian. On his return home at noon, he felt quite a little chesty and told of his experience chiefly in the rough-house at the recess at 10 o'clock. He said, 'There is one boy I must get rid of so I swatted him some good ones on the slats and soaked him a warm one in the face, and was oftener on top than I was under.' Meanwhile some of the boys hollered, 'Give it to him, Indian.' It was all intended to be playful but [was] altogether different from anything in his previous career."

The incident was so amusing to Grandfather Davis and the others precisely because it was so incongruous with the little boy's temperament and usual demeanor. Once in Bloomington, a year or so later, he was "jumped" by some older, larger boys and had his nose broken in the resulting melee (later, at Charlevoix, he tripped over a garden wire in the dark and broke his nose again, permanently bending it to the left). He himself would remember that he had "many fights at school." But others remarked in him a most peaceable disposition and a distaste for fighting, if no apparent fear of being hurt himself.

From the very first he was a sensitive and almost excessively conscientious little boy. Virtually every piece of wrongdoing, in his case, was an inadvertence for which he suffered great remorse. Apparently this stern conscience was an innate part of him: certainly it was not the product of punishment, for he was not sternly raised and never suffered a corporal "correction" more severe than a mild slap on his hands.

Once, in Charlevoix, his grandfather Davis gave him a red-handled jackknife of which he was very proud. But somehow he mislaid it. His grandfather found it and had it in his pocket when at lunch he asked the boy, intending a gentle reproof, if the gift had pleased him. "I lost it!" cried Adlai, and burst into a storm of remorseful tears before Grandfather Davis could place the knife before him.

On another occasion, in Denver, where his father experimented with investment banking briefly, little Adlai pulled some glasses and silver from a table set for a dinner party. For this he suffered a maximum punishment: his hands were slapped and he was put outdoors. Later, when the family searched for him, he could not be found. His parents were almost frantic when at last they discovered him, curled up asleep beside the dog in the dog kennel, his dirty face streaked with tears. He never outgrew this initial conscientiousness. Deliberately to hurt another through an act of aggression was, for him, a moral impossibility.

He was certainly mischievous enough as a boy. He engaged in all the standard Halloween tricks involving the overturning of outhouses and the hoisting of wheeled vehicles onto roofs; he was not above robbing another's tomato patch (his love for tomatoes would become legendary) and trespassing over various kinds of forbidden ground. But when he at last entered the Washington School in

Bloomington, in January of 1908, his teacher, Miss Catherine (Kitty) Cowles, found him remarkable as others had for obedience and sweetness of temper. She graded him "excellent" in deportment.

She could not, however, grade him high in other respects. He enrolled at the very end of the semester in grade 2B: the record shows that he attended only ten days, having been absent eighty days that semester: and he was not promoted to grade 2A until the second examination in the fall of 1908, though he was permitted to enter the class on trial in early September. His erratic tutelage had left him less well prepared for regular classwork than most of his contemporaries were. His grades for 2B were "low" for reading and spelling and "fair" in writing. In the first semester of the 1908–9 school year he attended sixty-five days and was absent twenty-two, his grades being "fair" in reading, spelling, and writing, and "excellent" in deportment. In the second half of that school year he attended sixty days and was absent twenty-eight (as usual the family went South that winter, this time to New Orleans); his grades were somewhat improved. He was "fair" in reading and "good" in spelling, arithmetic, and writing. His deportment, as always, was "excellent."

Going to school in Bloomington was a joyous neighborhood ritual, of a morning, on upper East Washington Street, where so many of the town's "better people" lived. For Buffie and Adlai the ritual seemed to begin, often, in the darkness of early morning, with the sound of the furnace man shaking down the fire he or Adlai had carefully banked the night before. Next came the rush for the gas heater in their mother's dressing room, and a thorough scrubbing of face and hands, a thorough brushing of teeth and hair in the bathroom. Then a breakfast whose main dish was invariably gray lumpy oatmeal that had sat on the back of the coal stove in the kitchen overnight; it was eaten dutifully but without relish. Finally came the bundling up and the rush out the side door—seldom were the children permitted the use of the front door—and down a walk which, if snow had fallen, had been cleared by Adlai, to earn pin money. On the Washington Street sidewalk the two joined a parade which, beginning at the far end of the street, grew as it proceeded westward toward the school. Really there were two parades, one of girls, the other of boys, the latter rollicking and showing off before the former.

By the time the family moved to Bloomington, when Adlai was six, his initial physical passivity had been sloughed off. He'd devel-

oped a passion for all sports. He was interested in everything; he
seemed to want to do something about every interest. It was almost
as though he feared in himself the tendency he'd seemed at first to
have toward brooding withdrawals, toward a solitary passive dream-
iness, and was reacting against this tendency with an almost feverish
busyness. At any rate he was now "always on the go" and he would
remain so, driven (as it seemed) by an inexhaustible electric energy,
all his life long.

At supper he had always a prodigious appetite, he used up so
much energy every day. Buffie would never forget one occasion on
which their mother, dismayed by a huge second helping her son had
taken at supper, protested against it. They had as servant at that
time a stocky cheerful colored boy named Sam White, who was very
fond of Adlai and of whom Adlai was very fond ("He helped raise
me from the time I was eight or nine till I was fourteen or fifteen,"
Adlai later said). Sam leaned forward from his position behind the
mother's chair.

"Now, Mrs. Stevenson," he gently said, "Adlai's just a growin' boy.
Let him eat."

It was Sam who tried without much success to teach Adlai how
to handle a pump in the basement, whereby rain water from the
cistern in the back yard was forced up into a large storage tank in
the attic. Pumping, like snow shoveling in the winter and dandelion
digging in the spring, was among the chores by which Adlai earned
his dimes and quarters. According to Sam, there was an easy trick
to it: with a slight bowing movement from the waist he'd pump
easily, rapidly. But Adlai had to use his whole body, grunting and
groaning. "What a big satisfaction, to pump and earn!" wrote Buffie
long afterward in an unpublished manuscript describing her brother's
childhood. Her brother himself had a different, grimmer memory. In
the margin of his sister's manuscript he penciled: "Chained like a
galley slave—what he thought."

His play world at Bloomington contained many of those who
populated it in Charlevoix. Joe Bohrer, for instance, was a companion
in both places; so was his cousin, Davis Merwin (Helen Stevenson's
sister Jessie had married L. B. Merwin), who lived just two doors
up the street from him and was almost exactly his age. And one
of the centers of his play world was the shop Walter Williams had
set up in the back yard of his father's home—the C. U. Williams home
across the street from the Lewis Stevensons. Walter, who was nine

years older than Adlai, was a precocious mechanical genius. He'd motorized his sled with a motor removed from his mother's washing machine when he was only ten. In his mid-teens, having earlier skipped school with great regularity, he went into business for himself; he'd become a master of all the mysteries of internal-combustion engines and electric motors. He was also an inventor. As a young man he would invent the Oil-O-Matic, among other things, and make himself a fortune. He was, of course, a fascinating figure to the youngsters of Bloomington, none of whom was more fascinated than little Adlai.

Another center of his play world was the yard of the Coolidges, who lived two doors to the west of the Stevensons. Mrs. Coolidge was a sister of Sidney Smith, a Bloomington boy who had become famous as the creator of "Andy Gump" in the funny papers. Her two children, Hesketh and Betty, were among Adlai's favorite companions. Especially Betty was, when he was eleven and twelve; she was a very pretty girl with reddish golden hair, and Buffie noticed that when Betty was to take part in one of the plays Buffie was continuously producing in yard or attic her brother did not need to be urged to take part too. . . .

Still other play places were his grandfather Stevenson's yard, Grandfather Davis's where he and Dave Merwin played mumbletypeg with their jackknives for hours at a time, Joe Bohrer's yard, and Franklin Park where he and his companions played ball, and rode bicycles. (Tennis, in Charlevoix in the summers, early became his favorite game, and one at which, by his mid-teens, he was expert.) In Davis's pasture just beyond the fence bounding his back yard, where cows wandered, he hunted crayfish along the meandering stream and played "cowboys and Indians" and "Civil War" upon a grassy sward that would become the golf course of the country club a few years later.

Most important of all, of course, was the yard of his own home, and the basement where he took the stray kittens he collected one year, to his family's frequent annoyance. The latter enterprise had as one effect a lifelong abhorrence of cats on Buffie's part. Once one of the strays had a fit in the kitchen, causing Buffie to clamber, terrified, onto the kitchen table. Her reaction seems wickedly to have amused her brother, who a little later placed a black cat upon her bed. He was dismayed, though, by her hysterical screams on that occasion, and the mad rush with which she fled her room. . . .

He was a "normal" boy. He did the things that most boys of his time and place and social class were doing. None of his playmates of those years (when he was eight, and ten, and eleven) would later remember that there was anything remarkable about him. They would recall no particular anecdotes concerning him which might reveal any marked capacity or forecast a distinguished future. He did not star in sports; he had no outstanding mechanical ability; he manifested no artistic or literary genius; he was no brilliant scholar. Far from being intellectually precocious, he seemed to lag behind most of his contemporaries at school in his mental development, though not so greatly as to make even this a distinguishing characteristic. Most people found him very likable. Older people especially were impressed by his "good manners," sensing that these proceeded not merely from training but from a genuine concern for other people and for the principles of right conduct.

III

Of all the influences which played upon him, the most potent by far was family. This included not only his immediate family but also, as has been indicated, his grandparents and aunts and cousins and all those ancestors whose stories went back two centuries and more into the national history. Some outside observers claimed it was fortunate for little Adlai that he had this larger family to sustain his vital growth, since the immediate family situation at 1316 East Washington was, in their view, a not wholly happy one.

Lewis and Helen Stevenson were brilliant, witty, willful people who were scintillating company on social occasions. But they were irritable in the literal meaning of that word—sensitive, high-strung —perhaps because their general physical health was none too good. Their nerve ends seemed to be more nakedly exposed to the world than most people's are. They were therefore aware of environmental pressures too slight to enter the average consciousness; they were chafed to the point of pain by things most people can ignore. Often, it was said, they chafed one another, and because each of them could use words like knives, stabbing and slashing with precision, it was said that they wounded one another deeply.

One of the exacerbating differences between them had to do with their attitudes toward money. Helen was thrifty, Lewis extravagant, in money matters. To count costs was, for Helen, almost an expression of piety; not to count them was, for Lewis, an expression of human warmth. She had been horrified when she learned that before their marriage he had bought a diamond ring to be buried with his sister Mary, just because "Mary always wanted a diamond." She was more resentful than grateful when he showered upon her such gifts as an elaborate silver toilet set (her old one was "perfectly good") and a gold bracelet shaped as a coiled snake with diamonds for eyes (her taste would never have chosen it). Perhaps she sensed in his extravagant giving an element of aggression. Sometimes it was as if he felt a need to "buy back" affections forfeited during spells of pain-provoked irritability, an effort which might seem insulting to the person he strove thus to manipulate. At other times it was as if he enjoyed flouting Helen's cautious thrift, defying her and so "getting even."

Lewis had other characteristics which, while often amusing, were certainly not conducive of peace and quiet in the home. He was often dramatic, even theatrical, in his reactions to stimuli. He kept a loaded revolver in his bedroom as a protection against burglars, and he heard far more burglars in the night than could possibly have entered 1316 East Washington. One night Buffie had Jessie Clark of California as house guest (this was the first time Buffie had had a guest overnight); after midnight both girls were awakened by a great and terrifying commotion in the upstairs hall. Lewis had rushed from his room, clad in his nightshirt, revolver in hand, and was leaning over the stair railing shouting: "I hear you! I hear you! If you take another step I'll shoot!" Then he crept down the stairs into the now lighted lower hall. No one was there.

Some outsiders believed that the relationship between Lewis and Helen Stevenson was such as to encourage the latter to become very much a mother, lavishing upon her children a loving care which even some insiders (cousins, aunts) felt to be excessive. It was a common thing in that prosperous neighborhood for children to be "over-mothered," according to the lights of less privileged people. But Helen Stevenson was believed to go beyond the neighborhood average in this respect.

Her concern for her children's health amounted to an almost constant anxiety. (Lewis, too, was a health-worrier. "You'll never know what happiness is unless you are healthy," he said.) This was explainable by her own and her husband's frequent ill-health; nevertheless it somewhat limited the range of her children's activity and might have encouraged in them a species of hypochondria. They themselves would remember with a wry amusement, in later years, various dietary fads which both mother and father adopted and foisted upon their offspring: Battle Creek foods ("Hay!" snorted Grandmother Stevenson; she'd not have such hay at her table), "Fletcherizing" (chewing each mouthful of food an incredible number of times), the consumption of gallons of milk and orange juice, the use of onion soup as a "specific" against headaches. When exercise with dumbbells and Indian clubs was decreed, Lewis Stevenson was among the first to obey. When regulated deep breathing before open windows was the fad no family breathed more deeply than the Stevensons. When sleeping porches were recommended Helen Stevenson promptly built one over the back porch (this was in the fall of 1912), to the anguish of Buffie and Adlai, who were forced to sleep there even on bitterly cold nights. Similarly with cold baths. Once when Lewis Stevenson was on a farm-inspection trip in Indiana he wrote his son asking if the latter were taking his daily cold baths. "I hope so," he said. "In a lecture the other day I heard a doctor say a man would gain thirty per cent resistance power (to prevent catching disease) if he had taken daily cold baths from childhood." No family was more conscious of hostile "germs."

And the mother's concern was by no means limited to matters of physical health. She was equally concerned to form in her children habits of work and play which would be conducive of moral probity and worldly success. The letters she wrote to Adlai when she was separated from him were full of the most detailed advice as to his general attitudes, his social conduct, his schoolwork. When they were together she watched over him with a closeness sometimes embarrassing to him. If she were in the vicinity of the school at closing time, for example, she often picked him up in her electric car, a procedure he did nothing to encourage. Once he hid from her under a bearskin robe on the floor of another student's car, so that he might ride home with his companions. . . .

"Quarrelsomeness" and "love" are not necessarily antithetical, however, in such temperaments as Lewis's and Helen's. The former may manifest the latter—and that it did so in this case is the testimony of the most intimate observers. The Democratic Vice-President's son and the Republican publisher's daughter had known one another well from earliest childhood. They could scarcely remember a time when they had not loved one another and taken it for granted that they'd marry. Thus there had never been between them that quality of courtship whereby each strives to impress the other with his or her most lovable qualities while avoiding all that might anger or annoy. They were utterly frank with one another; it was hardly possible for them to be anything else. What to outsiders appeared bitter, wounding quarrels seem therefore to have had, as essential reality, a very different quality: they were a "blowing off of excess steam," a release of tensions which might otherwise have strangled love. And this seems to have been recognized by their children. "Those were lovers's quarrels," Buffie would say long afterward, adding that her father "got a kick out of a fight." ("Your father is a brilliant fighter," Helen Stevenson told her children. "He has the courage of a lion.")

Thus the net effect on the children seems to have been the opposite of pernicious. It was the removal from them, too, through a free expression, of what might otherwise have become dangerously repressed anxieties. Adlai's reaction (different from Buffie's) was, in part, a determination to avoid quarrelsomeness and malice in his own conduct. In later years, when his sister and his wife engaged in critical gossip about their friends, he invariably protested; if the gossip continued, he arose and left the room. . . .

"Oh, but there was so much *love* in our family!" Buffie said, in the 1950s, when she reviewed her girlhood. "Our parents were both strong-minded people who both could and did fully express themselves. As one of our friends once told me, we were a very explosive family. But underneath and all the time there was so much love!"

Adlai, she added, was always the peacemaker in moments of strife, not so much by what he did as by what he was. He had such sweetness of temper, a kind of inward radiance felt by all who were around him. In this, perhaps, he took after the Quakers—the Fells, the Browns, the Davises—in his maternal line.

Buffie and her brother always remembered the laughter and bubbling wit which, as a normal thing, made the dinner table a stimulating experience. The two children, Buffie recalled, "never opened our mouths except to eat," but their ears were wide open, and the "steady stream of banter" between the parents was delightful to hear. One of the parents would start a story, the other would embroider it, and as they handed the story back and forth it grew in hilarity. They'd revise it as they went along; sometimes they'd go back and begin again. Finally, satisfied, they'd agree, *"There!* That's good."

Whereupon they'd tell it all over again, smoothly this time, and climax it with infectious laughter. Lewis, particularly, was an expert mimic, and both of them loved to puncture flatulent pomposities and all other forms of pretentious behavior.

Adlai would remember his father as a "funny man—I believe the funniest man I've ever known." He'd recall many stories his father told, including one of a visit to Egypt, sometime in the 1890s, before there was much protection of relics in that ancient land. His father had returned with a mummy, "just a little one," Adlai would explain, spreading his hands to indicate the size of a small child. Adlai was sure his father had bought it in some market, but his father was always mischievously mysterious about it, hinting that he had robbed an Egyptian tomb in defiance of the fatal curse placed upon those who do so. The story of the difficulties he'd encountered as he transported the mummy back to the States past suspicious and outraged customs officials built toward a climax which always left the family in tears of laughter.

As for the mother's "oversolicitude," there was no evidence later that it had hindered her son's development of strength and courage and independent judgment. On the contrary, it seemed to have increased his inner security, enabling him to focus upon the world an unusually candid gaze and face it with a rare lack of fear. Certainly his gay gallantry in times of mortal danger was astonishing to later associates, and so was his endurance of fatigue and sustained mental and emotional pressures. Even as a little boy, seemingly so plastic, he had a steely core of integrity; he could only be pushed so far. Once a schoolmate of his got into a scrape which Helen Stevenson thought disgraceful. Impetuously she ordered her children to have nothing more to do with the disgraced one. Buffie reportedly agreed readily enough, but Adlai didn't. "Don't ask me to do that!" he protested. "He's my friend." And the mother, shamed, yielded to him.

On his development as a mind, her efforts were lasting and beneficent. They were achieved in large part through her reading to him and to Buffie of an evening, her tastes in reading matter fortunately supplementing those of Grandfather Davis. She loved Greek mythology, and Adlai's imagination absorbed that wild, wonderful, yet beautifully ordered world of heroes and heroines, gods and goddesses, dominated by towering Olympus. He *saw* Perseus slaying the Gorgon Medusa as his mother read in her richly musical voice. He went with Jason in quest of the Golden Fleece and fought for fair Helen before the gates of Troy and roamed the wide world with far-wandering Ulysses. He was sure, he later said, that he suffered every horror of the Labyrinth, and confessed to a peculiar fascination with the story of that "mighty artificer" Daedalus, who, having fashioned the Labyrinth, was himself imprisoned there and escaped with his son Icarus on wings fashioned from feathers. Even more meaningful to him, judging from the repeated references he later made to it, was Prometheus' defiance of the gods and the agony he suffered for it: the theft of fire from heaven, the terrible wrath of Zeus, the long torment on the mountain. But Greek myths were by no means all that his mother read to him. She read Roman fables (which didn't much interest him), Norse myths (which did), and all the legends of King Arthur's Round Table, both in prose and in Tennyson's *Idylls of the King*. She read Hawthorne's *Wonder Book*, and Scott's Waverly Novels, and a great deal of Dickens, whose *A Child's History of England* made a special impression on him. She read *The Last of the Mohicans, Treasure Island,* an abridged version of *Les Miserables*. The list is endless, and it was largely through her and his grandfather Davis that the whole wonderful world of literature was opened up to him.

But his grandfather Stevenson was also a great reader-aloud, as well as a grand storyteller. His choice of reading matter was not always perfectly suited to the age of his listeners. Adlai's maiden aunt Letitia, Lewis's sister, was fond of recounting how Adlai E. Stevenson, the elder, sometimes called in from play Adlai E. Stevenson, the younger, particularly when the Hardin cousins were also present. (Aunt Julia had married a Presbyterian minister, the Reverend Martin Hardin of Kentucky, and had three sons and a daughter who came to Bloomington for holidays.) "They, thinking they were going to be fed ice cream and chocolate cake, settled themselves in enormous leather chairs in the library," Aunt Letitia wrote years later, "where they slid around alert with expectancy of a treat. Then Father [Grandfather Stevenson] would take down from the library shelves ponderous tomes, for he believed that great literature, delightful to people of sixty, must be equally enjoyable to men of six. In a deep-voiced impressive manner he'd read the funeral oration Robert Ingersoll delivered over the body of his brother, an oration Father himself had heard, or excerpts from *Hamlet*, dark and bloody. The boys, paralyzed with horror as they listened, stared at their adoring grandfather with glazed eyes, until rescued by their grandmother who thawed them out with hot chocolate blanketed with whipped cream and sent them out into the bright sunshine to resume their play."

Yet it was his grandfather Stevenson, Adlai later believed, who did most to arouse in him an interest in national history so intense that he read all thirteen volumes of Markham's *The Real America in Romance* before he reached high school. . . .

CHAPTER FOUR

An Era Ends

In 1910 the Lewis Stevensons had as cook and maid a blond Scandinavian girl named Susie Anderson, who was so pretty that Bloomington's grocery clerks and delivery boys paid her very special attention. So did the motormen and conductors of streetcars. Returning from downtown on the streetcar, she was let off, not at the corner as ordinary mortals were, but directly in front of 1316 East Washington, the motorman clanging the bell loudly in tribute to her. The family was very fond of her. When W. O. Davis, with Buffie and Adlai, boarded a train for the South on January 27, Susie went along. Helen Stevenson remained behind to close up the house; she would join her father and children a few days later.

For Susie the trip was a memorable one. She was amused, though sympathetic, when she observed how "cold-blooded" Grandfather Davis was—how, despite the long underwear and the several pairs of socks he wore, he kept a blanket wrapped around his legs and took a teaspoonful of whiskey now and then, for warmth's sake, carefully pouring it from a small silver flask with his monogram upon it. She was also amused by the dramatic suspense and sly winks with which he invested the approach of a ticket-collecting conductor; he ordered Buffie to "scrouge down now, scrouge down!" so that she might ride for half fare, though she was six months beyond her twelfth birthday and was tall for her age. But Susie was not amused at all—she had a will of her own—when she was ordered to lay aside the magazine she was reading and look instead out the window, thus "improving" her mind. But she obeyed. W. O. Davis was accustomed to being obeyed.

When a little later, he ordered Adlai to cease his window-gazing for the time being in order to write a letter to his mother, the boy obeyed, too, and promptly—though this was less surprising than Susie's meek acquiescence, since dutiful obedience ("often very painful," he would note years later) was one of the boy's characteristics. He wrote:

Dear mother:

We are on our way south. We are almost 200 miles from Chicago. We will reach New-orleans in the morning at ten fifteen.

The train is a very nice one and my sister and myselfe are having a fine time altho I did not want to go at first.

There is very much to see. The land is very good for farming. . . . I hope you are well and I would not be surprised if father has a sick headache. But I am well you beat. I must say good by now.

Yours truery

Ad Stevenson

At the bottom of the sheet the boy drew, in a shaky hand, a crude picture of a locomotive.

This visit to New Orleans, and the following summer in Charlevoix, became increasingly memorable for Buffie and Adlai, as time passed. Never again would they go South in the winter or North in the summer with their grandfather Davis. In June of 1911, after forty years as proprietor of the *Pantagraph*, W. O. Davis died at the age of seventy-three and was buried in the Bloomington cemetery.

With him ended an era in the life of the Stevenson children.

Always afterward they recalled with nostalgic pleasure, and with regret for their ending, those rich full summers in Michigan: the mahogany rowboat with Grandfather Davis in visored cap sitting nervously in its stern; the feel of oars in hands and pulling muscles as Grandfather set the rhythm of their rowing and cautioned, "You're pulling too hard on your right oar, Buffie"; the whine of the sawmill growing louder as they approached the far shore of Round Lake, and the smell of fish upon that shore; the farmers' wagons rolling along the road into the village, loaded with fruits and vegetables; the huge dray horses straining up the slope from the docks, with the freight wagons behind them piled high; the sound of wind at night through the pines, and the sight of deciduous trees—the maples, and beeches, and white birches—as their leaves turned to a brilliant red and gold and yellow in the early autumn; the dancing classes at the

Casino and tennis playing on the Belvedere courts; the shock of cold water (it was always cold) as they dove into the lake, and the glow of warmth returning as they swam; the whole graceful leisurely summer life among a secure and happy and prosperous people.

This Charlevoix life, as they lived it, was "pure" nineteenth century and, even had Grandfather Davis lived, it must have drawn soon to a close. Already, in the last summer, the lake was noisier with motorboats than it had ever been before, and the quiet of country roads was increasingly interrupted by the roar of "machines." The change was not at all resisted by the boy Adlai, psychologically or in any other way. He grew enamored of motors. "Pet cocks," "spark plugs," and "feed lines" were already part of his vocabulary, and a grease-stained tinkering with automobile engines would soon become one of his major pleasures. Yet he could be sorry for the price of "progress" as paid in the loss of the old slow rhythms of organic life and their replacement, increasingly, by the harsher, swifter rhythms of the inorganic: metal and oil and gasoline. He loved country living too. He always would. Machines fascinated him; he was stirred by the pride of cities; but the feel of a natural earth beneath his feet, the long views across open fields under open skies, the wind singing quiet away from crowds of men, these were for him actual vital needs.

A century seldom dies all at once, however, for those who have lived in it. Nor is a new century likely to be abruptly born. The old dies element by element into the new, each element fading into and merging with its successor so gradually that only in retrospect can one say that *this* was an ending, *this* a beginning. Charlevoix, in the summer of 1911, was replaced by a visit to the eastern seaboard— but surely the nineteenth century continued for Helen Stevenson and her children as they stayed in the Holland House and "did the sights" in leisurely fashion, and were entertained by family friends, especially Edward Clark, manager of the Hearst estate, who was a very special friend of Lewis Stevenson. One evening the Stevensons went to the theater where Bert Williams was starring, and for weeks afterward the mother and Buffie imitated him; in the fourteen-year-old girl the desire for a stage career, already strong, was further strengthened. From New York they went by boat to Boston, where they stayed in the old nineteenth-century Thorndike and also soaked up eighteenth-century atmosphere along with the New England Renaissance on Beacon Hill, in Louisburg Square, and in Cambridge.

Of the nineteenth century, too, in flavor and quality, was the trip abroad which the Stevensons took a few months later. They sailed from New York in December 1911 on the *Lusitania*. Edward Clark saw them off, his son presenting to Buffie her first bouquet. "Violets!" Buffie's diary records. She also wrote ecstatically about the luxury of "mahogany and white and gold" saloons, and of many of the state-rooms—but the Stevensons themselves occupied inside cabins "down in the depths of the ship." They traveled first class, as Grandfather Davis would have done, but with a concern to achieve the greatest possible value for every dollar spent, as he also would have done.

Adlai spent much time roaming over the ship, clambering through lifeboats and visiting with crew members, but he did not wholly enjoy the voyage. He suffered, apparently, from homesickness—a fact worth recording because it was, for him, so unusual an experience: he had traveled so much from early infancy, and been made "at home" in so many widely scattered places, that he very seldom suffered that sense of being uprooted and cast among strangers in a coldly indifferent world which most people suffer when they break home ties. He suffered, certainly, from seasickness—a fact also worth recording as an unusual if not unique experience for him: in later years he was never seasick or airsick, not even in the roughest weather when fellow passengers grew very sick indeed. He himself pictured the voyage, as he experienced it, in a brief "essay" submitted in his school composition class the following autumn. Under the heading, "A Lonely Day at Sea," he wrote:

The sea is a leaden grey and as far as the eye can reach, there is not a ship in sight, the sky is overcast and sullin; a storm is expected and the air is heavy and damp. All on board are depressed and irritabli; the sailors are grumbling in groups together.

Visions of home pass before the mind; of familiar faces of parents and friends and cheerful fires. Then the eye wanders around the deck and the mind comes slowly back to the dismal present.

The "Admiral Benhow" with all its horros of the Old Sea Dog would be a welcome sight, and he longs to be at home among green trees, blooming flours and singing birds. To him nothing could be more dreadful than a life at sea.

Once he arrived in England, however, his homesickness for a time departed. The Stevensons stayed in the Hotel Cecil in London, from which the two children were taken on determinedly "educational" sight-seeing tours by Miss Lucy Youngman, a Bloomington school-teacher whom Helen Stevenson had brought along in order to keep them from falling too far behind in their schoolwork. "Poor, patient, sweet Miss Lucy," as Buffie later described her, cannot have had a perfectly enjoyable time. Her charges were all too frankly bored by her guidebook lectures, and Adlai took a disproportionate interest, from her point of view, in medieval armor in Windsor Castle and the torture chambers as well as the armor in the Tower of London.

In Paris he developed a sudden but lasting passion for collecting stamps and was continually darting away to buy stamps in kiosks "with what, for him, was spendthrift abandon," as Buffie wrote in a later year. In Florence he was so much taken by a basket of puppies for sale at the entrance to the Pitti Palace that Miss Youngman had difficulty enticing him inside; when she did, the old masters quickly bored him.

In Rome she tried a shift in tactics. She took her two charges to the graves of Keats and Shelley, where they read aloud from the works of these poets. This seemed to work very well. But next day, when she took her charges to the Colosseum and there attempted to give them a Latin lesson (they were supposed to "keep up" with their classes in Latin), she failed miserably. Adlai—and Buffie, too —were far too much interested in the manner in which lions were loosed upon hapless Christians. "Poor Miss Lucy" soon thereafter returned to Bloomington, whence Lewis Stevenson had already gone to prepare his farms for the coming season.

Miss Youngman was mistaken, however, if she concluded (as she might be excused for doing) that the European tour was a failure as education for the twelve-year-old boy and the fourteen-year-old girl. The boy soaked up impressions of a Europe soon to be torn to bloody bits; a Europe dominated by humanistic values to a degree that would seem almost incredible a generation hence; a Europe through which one might travel with a freedom never again possible, perhaps, in his lifetime. The impressions would grow steadily more meaningful as the years passed. Nor was the tour a failure in terms of immediate education. If the boy learned little that was of value to him from Miss Youngman's earnest lectures, he learned a great deal from his sight-seeing and stamp collecting and the European friends he made. The brightly colored bits of paper, carefully mounted, gave him an immense aesthetic pleasure, one which grew in proportion to the size of his collection, and they stimulated his curiosity. A particularly beautiful stamp with the head of the Czar Nicholas upon it aroused his interest in imperial Russia. A stamp from British East Africa opened Africa to his inquiring mind. He pored for hours over maps, read books of geography and travel and national history, and drew into himself more completely than he'd otherwise have done the scenes of every land he visited.

The European visit also stimulated in him a fascinated interest in the Middle Ages. In England the romances of Scott, the legends of Arthur, the tales of Robin Hood came vividly alive to him. And in France and Italy the monuments of the Age of Faith and Chivalry inspired an awe he never entirely lost. The cathedrals! The castles! "It seemed wonderful to me that men, so long ago, could build such vast structures on hills," he said long afterward. "It still does. All through my early teens I reveled in historical novels about the Crusades, and the Hundred Years' War, and in histories of Joan of Arc and the whole medieval period. The 1912 trip had a lot to do with that."

For Buffie, too, education proceeded—a valuable education, if along lines Miss Youngman could not have laid out. One evening when Buffie, having returned from a long and tiresome tramp through the Louvre, ate with her family in the little hotel dining room in Paris, her mother indicated a beautiful young lady at a table nearby. Her mother urged Buffie to note the lady's "lovely deportment" and "perfect enunciation." The young lady, it turned out, was the actress Elsie Ferguson, and Buffie needed no urging to study her every gesture or to listen to her every word. A few evenings later, Buffie saw the great Sarah Bernhardt in *L'Aiglon*. "I have decided to become an actress—I'll die if I am not," she wrote in her diary. "I 'Sarah Bernhart' around the room all day. I dream about Sarah every night. It is really getting serious." She did spend hours reading *L'Aiglon* aloud in French, and acting the leading role. Later, in Rome, her mother took her to hear Yvette Guilbert, whose stage gestures, too, became a part of Buffie's repertoire.

Further education—its end might be called "sophistication"—derived from a very stylish and wealthy cousin named Mrs. Charles (Letty) Bromwell, with whom the Stevensons stayed at the Hotel Savoy in Lausanne. Letty Bromwell had a huge Packard, a chauffeur to drive it, a Pomeranian named Ko-Ko, and a pretty daughter named Mildred: she took all these, and the Stevensons too, down the valley of the Rhône to Nice (the trip took three days) at carnival time. Surely, to motor through France in 1912 was an experience rare enough to produce "sophistication," even though at journey's end Helen Stevenson insisted that the Packard be parked a block away from the hotel she had chosen so that the manager would not see it as she bargained, successfully, for lower rates. Almost equally rare, for Illinoisians, was a sun-bathed three-week stay on the Riviera in midwinter.

There was even education of a formal sort, in Lausanne. With a tutor, Buffie improved her French, while Adlai attended a day school for boys at Ouchy.

When summer came they went up into the Alps and climbed a little, though by no means as often or as high as Adlai wanted to do. From Switzerland he wrote to his friend Sam White, the houseboy at 1316 East Washington:

We are at Val d'illiez Switzerland. Val d'illiez is a verry little village at the foot of the Dent du Midi.

The Dent du Midi is one of the highest Swisse Mountains it is all covered with snow. The chalet that we live in is all of wood, everything is of wood. We hear French spoken all the time. We are the only people in the Village that speak English. Everybody that comes [here] comes for Mountain climbing. They carry a large sack for food and things. Also an alpine stick which is a pole with a pick and hatchet at one end, and a point at the other.

He illustrated this letter as was then his custom. At the top was a drawing of "Sam Driving the Auto" and being chased by a "Motorcycle Cop" who cried out, "Halt in the Name of the Law." At the bottom was a careful drawing of an alpine stick.

Meanwhile, the stylish Letty Bromwell was having, apparently, a subversive effect on Helen Stevenson. The two went to Paris on a shopping expedition and, for once in her life, Lewis's wife was as extravagant as Lewis habitually was. When the *Oceanic* docked in New York at the end of July, and the traveling Stevensons were met at customs by Lewis Stevenson, the duties on Helen's Paris clothes amounted to $257—an amount so staggering, under the circumstances, that it was precisely listed in Buffie's diary.

II

In Illinois that summer, Lewis Stevenson said, they were having good corn-growing weather—hot and humid—but for that very reason Bloomington would be unbearable to people accustomed to the summer temperatures of northern Michigan. He proposed, therefore, that they all go to a hotel in Spring Lake, New Jersey, for a few weeks.

No doubt his wife looked at him closely, with a little knowing smile on her face, as he made this proposal, though she accepted it quickly enough. Spring Lake, she knew, was near Sea Girt; at Sea Girt, she knew, the governor of New Jersey had his summer mansion; and the governor of New Jersey, as everybody knew, was Woodrow Wilson, former president of Princeton and now the Democratic candidate for President of the United States. Wilson had received the nomination at the Baltimore convention despite the bitter opposition of Lewis's former employer, William Randolph Hearst, and despite the publication of a private letter of some years before in which the then president of Princeton expressed the hope that William Jennings Bryan, whose fiscal policies Wilson opposed, might be "knocked into a cocked hat." The latter fact might have given some slight pause to the elderly Adlai Ewing Stevenson back in Bloomington, but apparently it did not do so. As for the former Vice-President's son, his admiration for the "Princeton Schoolmaster" was unbounded.

A day or so after their arrival in Spring Lake, Lewis took his son with him to Sea Girt, to the white two-story green-shuttered colonial house where Wilson was ensconced. There, on a wide Grecian-columned porch facing the sea, the boy Adlai Stevenson was introduced to a man destined to become one of his heroes and a potent influence upon his own political thought. He looked up into a long, narrow face, ascetic, intellectual, the very opposite of mobile—and into gray eyes which, behind rimless pince-nez spectacles, seemed rather stern, even though Wilson was smiling. Then he sat on the porch steps and looked out across the lawn and the campground sloping gently toward the Atlantic, listening to the sea's steady moan mingled with the voice of his father and Woodrow Wilson through most of what seemed to him a long afternoon.

The conversation, so Woodrow Wilson wrote to the elderly Adlai Stevenson in Bloomington on August 22, was "instructive and illuminating to me." Certainly the "situation" they discussed was well calculated to lift Democratic hearts. Teddy Roosevelt, "strong as a Bull Moose," was forming his own party, the Progressive. The resulting split in Republican ranks made Democratic chances look bright indeed. When Lewis Stevenson returned to Bloomington in

September his somewhat dubious personal strategy would be to "talk up" Teddy Roosevelt among the Republicans he met on his travels through Republican Illinois, on the grounds that votes for Teddy by such men were tantamount to votes for Woodrow Wilson.

Thus the boy Adlai that autumn lived a more consciously "political" life than he'd ever done before, having for the first time some awareness of issues as well as of personalities in a campaign. When his own grandfather Stevenson had run for governor four years before, he'd been excited because the grownups were, and he could see that politics was, for them, a matter of vital import. The parades and shouting crowds, the suspense as election day drew near—these had impressed him. But far more interesting to him personally was the fact that an extra telephone was installed in his grandfather's house to receive the returns on election night, and that this extra phone, instead of being mounted on the wall, sat on a table and had no crank. In the fall of 1912, however, hearing politics talked day in and day out, with Roosevelt damned and Taft deplored and Wilson extolled at every meal, he learned that there was something called the "Payne-Aldrich Tariff," and it was very bad because it aided "special privilege"; that Taft was a poor President because he was a "tool of the interests"; that there was something called "conservation," and it meant that you must keep selfish men from stealing the trees and minerals that belonged to all the people. He learned from his mother that Governor Wilson had not only a "great mind" but also a "deep concern for humanity." He learned from his father that Republicans in general believed that businessmen should run the government as they did their own businesses, to make money for themselves; whereas Democrats believed that *all* people should be represented by government and *all* should be served by it, with equal justice. Of course Republicans often talked like Democrats in election years, but that was just to fool the voters.

Easy would it have been for the boy Adlai to conclude that the struggle between Democrats and Republicans was one between "good" people and "bad." But he was constantly reminded that Grandfather Davis—a good, kind man—had been a very rigid Republican. The Merwins were Republicans. Most of their Bloomington friends, fine people all, were Republicans. To be a Republican, then, was not to be wicked, but only sadly mistaken. . . .

That fall William Jennings Bryan came to town. He stayed in Grandfather Stevenson's house, and the Lewis Stevensons were all invited to dine with the great man. The meal was bountiful; the boy Adlai tried to match Bryan's famous intake of fried chicken. Then they all went out to the coliseum, where thousands of people had gathered for the giant rally. Buffie in her best dress and Adlai in dark suit and stiff wide Eton collar (he hated it, but his mother always insisted) sat with their parents on the platform, listening to preliminary speeches which, as always at such occasions, were too many and too long. Finally the Great Commoner, gracefully introduced by Grandfather Stevenson, arose and swayed the multitude with that tongue of silver which had made of the Cross of Gold a great symbol of political iniquity. Buffie, as she later recorded, "caught the excitement" and gloried in it—but when she turned to see how her brother was taking it, she "almost died" of embarrassment. Adlai was sound asleep!

He stayed awake, however, on election night, until the decisive returns were in. The Stevensons were all in Grandfather Stevenson's house when, shortly before ten o'clock on November 5, the *Pantagraph* office phoned to tell the former Vice-President of Wilson's triumph. Take it all in all, it was an impressive victory. When the complete returns were in, it would be found that Wilson polled 6,286,214 votes, Roosevelt 4,126,020, and Taft 3,483,922. Thus Wilson lacked a popular majority, but he'd carried forty-one of the forty-eight states and obtained 435 of the 531 votes in the electoral college, and his party, for the first time in many years, controlled both houses of Congress. The Stevensons were elated; within an hour after Taft and Roosevelt had conceded, Grandfather Stevenson wired the President-elect. Next day Wilson telegraphed his thanks.

"Your congratulations," said he, "came to me like a benediction. . . ."

Nor was the national victory all that the Stevensons celebrated that night. Edward Fitzsimons Dunne, former mayor of Chicago and a long-time political friend of both Lewis and the former Vice-President, had won the governorship of Illinois, the first Democrat to do so since John Peter Altgeld's victory in 1892. This meant that Lewis would probably be offered an appointive office of some kind, and that his personal political prospects—for he was developing political ambitions at that time—would be greatly enhanced.

A few weeks later this expectation was fulfilled. The governor-elect asked Lewis to serve as chairman of the Illinois State Board of Pardons, and Lewis accepted. It would be the first public office he had ever held, and he prepared for it with thoroughness and enthusiasm.

They were a particularly happy, busy family that fall and early winter, with the lives of the parents as well as of the children opening out into new and rich experiences. Never had the world seemed more amiable to them; never had the political climate of Illinois and of the nation seemed more favorable to such ambitions as this highly political family might hold. Buffie, in University High School in Normal, was happily taking part in school dramatics and falling in and out of love every week. Adlai was happily exploring, and mastering, the mysteries of the family Locomobile (Lewis always called it, with a certain reverence, "The Machine"), bought in 1911, paying at least as much attention to these as he paid to his schoolwork.

Christmas came and passed with a round of parties and family feasts.

For Buffie the following days were enlivened by the presence of Margery McClelland, one of her old Charlevoix playmates, who had come for a holiday visit. She asked and received permission to entertain a group of her contemporaries, with Margery as guest of honor, including among her guests a girl named Ruth Merwin, a cousin of the Merwin children who, in turn, were Buffie's cousins. With Ruth, Buffie had formed a special friendship at University High.

The party evening came.

With it—swiftly, starkly, incredibly—came tragedy. . . .

Since it was to be a supper party and Adlai was deemed "too young" for it, he had his supper early that evening of December 30, 1912, going up afterward to his room. Lewis and Helen Stevenson went out to pay a neighborhood call while Buffie took her guests into the drawing room. One of the boys, Bob Whitmer, proudly offered to demonstrate the manual of arms which he had learned at military school—if only he had a gun. Whereupon Buffie went out into the hallway and called up to Adlai, asking him to go into the attic and fetch down the old .22 rifle which was kept there. Eagerly Adlai did so.

First Bob Whitmer carefully examined the gun to make sure there were no bullets in the barrel or magazine, explaining professionally that this was always required at school. Then, with professional smartness, he executed the manual and was warmly applauded. The gun was given back to Adlai to be returned to the attic. As he left with it he excitedly imitated Whitmer's movements. The gun went off. Ruth Merwin dropped limply to the floor.

She was dead.

Later examination revealed that the ejecting mechanism had a rusty spring that had probably prevented the emergence of the single bullet. But no one was concerned with this at the moment. Everyone stared helplessly, unbelievingly, at the girl who an instant before had been gaily laughing and talking and who now lay so still upon the hallway carpet. The front door opened. Lewis and Helen Stevenson entered.

"I did it!" said Adlai, in response to a sharp exclamation from his father.

He turned and went up the stairs. He went to his mother's room. He closed the door and flung himself face down upon his mother's bed.

Buffie would never forget, though she could never describe, how she herself felt when she came up the stairs and saw her dead friend's coat lying across the bed in her room.

"Why, Ruth will never wear this again!" she thought in grief-stricken amazement. Then, through the closed door to her mother's room, she heard Adlai moaning. "Oh, he moaned and moaned!"

The dead girl's mother, Mrs. Clarence Merwin, proved herself to be "a very great woman," as the family gratefully acknowledged ever after. On that very night, in the midst of her own terrible grief, she comforted Adlai's mother, and talked to Adlai, too, telling the boy that he must not blame himself. He *must* not! She realized that this tragedy could be devastating to anyone as sensitive and imaginative and excessively conscientious as this boy was. He seemed, that night, utterly lost. . . .

The day of the funeral Helen Stevenson took Adlai, Dave Merwin, Margery McClelland, and Claire, the French maid whom Helen had hired in Paris during the summer, to Chicago on an early train. There they stayed at Aunt Julia Hardin's home; Uncle Martin Hardin had by then become pastor of the city's Third Presbyterian Church. Lewis and Buffie went to Ruth Merwin's funeral. "Adlai Stevenson, prostrated by grief, was unable to be present," the *Pantagraph* reported. When Helen and the others returned to Bloomington the tragic event was not referred to, nor was it ever mentioned again in the family, or by Adlai himself, until a reporter questioned Adlai about it forty years later.

"We just went on home and started back to school," said Buffie in 1955. "We just went on, and so it has always been with us after every tragedy—we go on!"

What effect did the tragedy have upon the development of Adlai Stevenson the man?

Precisely to answer this question is of course impossible. The man himself probably could not have done so if he would—and certainly he would not. When William Glasgow of *Time* magazine, with some hesitation, brought the subject up in 1952 Stevenson "looked away for a moment" and then "told me the whole story, in a quiet matter of fact way." Later interviewers would find him similarly matter-of-fact on this subject as on all others which, though they concerned his intimate life, were necessarily exposed to the public gaze as he became an increasingly important public figure. To the facts as he recounted them, no evident emotion would adhere. Yet one need not be particularly perceptive to see that this apparent frankness was, in reality, the agency of a profound reticence. He seemed to tell all; he revealed nothing that was of the essence.

There is no doubt, however, that the tragedy did have an effect, a deep and lasting one, giving rise to some of the subtler complexities of an exceedingly complex man. Objective reason could convince him that he need feel no guilt for Ruth Merwin's death. Nevertheless, had he acted differently, she would have continued to live. Such knowledge, whether or not he admitted it to full consciousness, must increase his sense of being in the world on sufferance, required to earn his way by being especially dutiful, especially "good," especially politic. It must decrease the force of whatever tendencies he had toward egoistic self-assertiveness. It might partially account for certain distinctive traits of the mature man: a diffidence of manner, a tendency toward self-deprecation. Recurrent in his public speech, forty years later, would be the phrase: "If you please . . ."

Even his far-famed wit might be shaped in part by his awareness—born of this tragic experience—that blind chance can frustrate the strongest will, that it may assume at any moment the shape of a black malevolence, that death in any case awaits us all. He who holds his head too high while striding pridefully into a country of bogs is likely to end up in the muck; better to look down humbly, accepting

the absurdity of trembling knees and slippery footing. In this spirit
Adlai Stevenson would make himself the butt of his own best jokes,
using as a shield that which his political opponents feared as a
sword.

III

But no one could have predicted the Adlai Stevenson of the 1950s
from even the most intimate knowledge of the boy who, in his sister's
phrase, "went on" from the tragic close of 1912 through the winter
and into the spring of 1913. His schoolwork continued, neither more
nor less distinguished than before; his play continued as before. If
there was a shadow upon his inner life, it was hidden by those who
saw him day by day. A letter to his father, who was away on a farm-
inspection trip, records that there was "consibrel snow" in Bloomington on January 20, that he played in Dave Merwin's house
that afternoon with Betty Coolidge and others ("We made popcorn
balls, and had lots of fun in the attick"), that he had made "a big
Wind Mill with my American Model builder," and was going to at-
tach his motor to it "and see how fast the fan will go round." He
would go to school next day, and next day after that "they have a
Geography test and I don't have to go because I don't have to take
it." In the lower right-hand corner he drew a little picture of a man
in an overcoat facing a cow, with an arrow labeled "you" pointing to
the man.

That spring Lewis and Helen Stevenson took their children South
to a winter hotel, the Pine Forest Inn (here, too, the nineteenth
century lingered) in Summerville, South Carolina. When they returned to Bloomington both children began making weekly trips to a
Dr. Noyes in Chicago, to have their teeth straightened. In Chicago
they visited with their aunt Julia and uncle Martin and the four
Hardin cousins, and attended matinees at which they saw Sothern
and Marlowe in *Romeo and Juliet,* William Faversham in *Julius
Caesar,* and Cyril Maude in *Grumpy.* Buffie's theatrical ambitions
fed on these, and on Chatterton Opera House performances, in
Bloomington, of *Everybody's Doing It* ("Direct from The Winter
Garden, New York City") and *Uncle Tom's Cabin* ("With Ten
Cuban and Russian Bloodhounds").

In September, Buffie was enrolled in University High School on
Normal's college campus—a special tuition school to which many

children of Bloomington's "better families" were sent in preference to city high schools. Both Buffie and Adlai went there partly out of family tradition, Normal having been Fell's school, and that autumn Adlai was enrolled in the Metcalf Training School on Normal's campus. There he began for the first time to rebel a little, quietly but stubbornly, against maternal domination. On September 22 he addressed a letter to his mother, who was visiting in the East:

I am writing this letter on the couch with my new fountain pen. Dave [Merwin] and I bought 2 dozen bottels of pop for 60 cents a few days ago. We made what we paid for it the first day. Father bought 3 bottels, and Mr. Linn 4, Uncle 2.

I started this letter last night and am finishing it this morning. Buffie got your letter this morning in which you said you would not let me play football for another year. That is what you and father have been telling me for so long and anyway you promised me . . . that you would let me play this fall.

If I wait another year I will not be able to play. All doctors say its a bad game but all doctors haven't played it, and more than that they do not play like we play at Normal. Everybody these days have such terrable conceptions of football when they now nothing about it, just because they have read of accidents in for instances, a Harvard and Yale game. this is the third Normal team.

Everything is all right at school. I think Normal is easy.

!!!Lots of love!!!

Adlai

P.S. All the games you mencioned in your letter are out of season.
A.E.S.

In the end his mother yielded, but apparently she failed to communicate her decision to her husband, for a few days later Adlai wrote her asking her to "telegraph Father," as she'd promised to do. "I have been deprived of that pleasur for so long," he said. At last, permission granted, he became a member of the third team and played gamely and happily, though apparently with no starring ability.

During this year and the following ones he and his father grew closer together. They began to share common interests. They went hunting together and occasionally played golf together. Lewis drove his Locomobile on his farm-inspection trips and often he took his son with him. In the hot Illinois summers father and son would load the back seat of the Locomobile with a huge tin box of provisions, a tent, folding beds, and a spirit stove. Father and son would tramp together through the fields, with the tenant farmers showing them the results of new farming practices Lewis was always introducing: new rotations, new fertilizer treatments, new methods of cultivation: and at night they'd camp in a farmyard or pasture, which Lewis Stevenson always preferred to the farmhouse. They'd bathe in the morning, sometimes, in creek or river, as proud as they were happy to be "roughing it." Often they were stuck in mud, for there were no surfaced roads. Memories of these trips would be among the pleasantest of Adlai's boyhood: the purple shadows of night rising out of the hollows in the earth as sunset colors faded down the western sky, the prosaic meadows and cornfields turning lyric under silver moons, the woods along the Sangamon and Mackinaw and other streams looking just as they had when young Abe Lincoln of New Salem knew them.

Yet there remained between father and son a certain tension. They were so very different in mind and temperament: Adlai even-tempered, quiet, notably cool in judgment; Lewis volatile, gay, and quick-tempered, and inclined toward swift judgments made sometimes in the heat of anger—judgments often as quickly changed. Letters from this period seem to show that the mother and two children regarded themselves, now and then, to be in a secret alliance against the father's frequent storms. Father had to be humored. He had to be handled. One must not take his flat orders too seriously, for he was likely to remorsefully reverse himself without notice. But these same letters also reveal Lewis Stevenson's great capacity for love: one had again the sense of a warm, generous, extroverted personality battling gallantly against recurrent severe bodily pain, and losing the battle, sometimes, in an angry constrictive exasperation.

That Lewis Stevenson would have gone far in politics had his health permitted was one of the convictions of Adlai Stevenson the man—and there is considerable evidence in support of this conviction. However erratic he might sometimes be in his role of *pater-familias*, he was in his professional life notably practical, ingenious, and imaginative. By the time his son reached high school Lewis had earned a national reputation as a leader of scientific agriculture, and a few years later he would be among the first men to be listed in Who's Who in America under the classification of "farmer." (He pioneered, for instance, in the use of soybeans as a major crop, making the planting of soybeans both as a cash crop and for soil-building purposes a condition of the lease among his tenants.) As chairman of the Board of Pardons, he introduced many improvements in the administration of the parole laws; the governor was proud of him and could be counted on to support whatever ambitions he might have for further public service.

Politics, certainly, was "in his blood," and he wanted to carry on the family's political tradition. He may even have felt an obligation to do so, as his mother and father, their lives declining through the first months of Woodrow Wilson's administration, finally "passed the torch" to him and departed. . . .

On Sunday, December 28, 1913, the Lewis Stevenson family, in solemn black, attended the funeral of Letitia Green Stevenson, wife of the former Vice-President of the United States. Services were held in Bloomington's Presbyterian church, which was filled to overflowing. Prominent among the mourners were members of the Bloomington chapter—the Letitia Green Stevenson chapter—of the Daughters of the American Revolution.

Her husband survived her by only five months. On June 13, 1914, Adlai Ewing Stevenson I was dead. His funeral, three days later, was the largest and most widely publicized in Bloomington's history —so much so that both Buffie and Adlai "had a sudden queer feeling of mourning for a stranger." There was such a mob of people! Dignitaries from all over the country were there, reporters scribbled notes in pads during the services as if reporting a political rally, and Pathé newsreel men had their cameras set up on tripods by the church entrance, cranking away industriously. Next day, newspapers all over the country carried a picture of the Vice-President's namesake, clad in knickerbockers, holding with his sister a crepe-draped American flag at the church door.

It was the end of an era in the Stevenson family history, and it coincided with the end of an era in world history—for barely ten days after Grandfather Stevenson's funeral, in a far country of which few Bloomingtonians had heard and of which Grandfather Stevenson's namesake had heard only because he had Serbian stamps in his stamp collection, the Archduke Franz Ferdinand, heir to the Austro-Hungarian throne, was shot to death in the streets of Sarajevo, capital of Bosnia. Six weeks later war flamed on the Russian border, and in the tiny Belgian village of Visé dazed civilians were being led before German firing squads for having dared to fire upon invading German troops. Soon all western Europe was ablaze in a conflagration that would not end until the last effective vestiges of the nineteenth century were consumed, not only in Europe but in America.

Among the casualties of the war would be the fame of Adlai Ewing Stevenson I. His career would seem to have no vital connection with the America that emerged from the war; his speeches and writings would be largely forgotten because they said little that seemed relevant to the generations of men among whom his namesake must make a life. There would remain of him, in the minds of his family and friends, the memory of an extraordinarily rich and lovable personality.

CHAPTER FIVE

An Era Begins,
and Family Ties Are Loosened

In August of 1914, Carl Vrooman of Bloomington was appointed Assistant Secretary of Agriculture in the Wilson administration, under Secretary David Houston. The event heightened the interest at 1316 East Washington in Wilson's farm politics, for Vrooman had married Julia Green Scott, daughter of Mrs. Matthew T. Scott, in 1896, and had thus become "Cousin Carl" to the Lewis Stevensons. He was, in some respects, a strange husband for an aristocratic heiress. Raised in Kansas through years of farm depression, he had become a Populist, the author of a book called *Taming the Trusts* and of another, *American Railway Problems*, which argued from European examples that U.S. railroads should be nationalized. In Washington he and his wife became the center of a brilliant social life in which the Lewis Stevensons, from time to time, would share.

A few weeks after the Vrooman appointment there was a new beginning for Lewis Stevenson himself. The Democratic landslide two years before had swept into the office of secretary of state for Illinois a plump-faced bespectacled young man named Harry Woods who soon proved to be mentally unbalanced. He feuded with everyone, flew into frequent shouting rages, wrapped the most commonplace subjects in mystery. He aspired to be United States Senator, filing for that office in 1914 with every confidence that he would be nominated, and spending a great deal of money on his campaign. He ran a poor third in the primary—fourth in his home Chicago ward. The blow crushed him. On the morning of October 11 his wife found him dead in his garage at the rear of his Springfield home, a bullet wound in his forehead, a revolver in his hand. Two days later, on October 13, the governor announced that Lewis G. Stevenson of Bloomington had been appointed to fill out Woods's term, which would expire in January 1917. The appointment, a complete surprise to politicians and reporters, was made because of "my personal observation of Mr. Stevenson's conduct of the Board of Pardons," the governor said.

Lewis Stevenson moved at once to Springfield, and for Adlai, who remained in Bloomington with his mother to complete the school term, was soon transformed into the story in the newspapers, side by side with the stories of Governor Dunne, of President Wilson, of the bloody stalemate in France following the Battle of the Marne, and of the struggle to preserve American neutrality. The 1915 session of Illinois's General Assembly was made memorable by a bitter battle over the speakership of the House. For five stormy weeks, during which angry passions flamed high and no less than sixty-seven ballots were cast without decisive result, Lewis Stevenson was the House's presiding officer. His mastery of parliamentary procedure, his adroitness in handling men, his sense of justice, his self-control under fire—all were severely tested. His greatest personal fear during this ordeal was that he might be struck down by one of those terrible migraines and incapacitated for a day or two, but, miraculously, this did not happen. When at last the speaker was chosen, the House gave the secretary of state a unanimous vote of thanks for the impartiality and efficiency with which he discharged his duties.

By that time Adlai and his mother had moved to Springfield, where he was enrolled in the Springfield high school. Buffie had been enrolled, the preceding autumn, in the University School for Girls, on Lake Shore Drive in Chicago, but had so rebelled against the enforced separation from her family that she was permitted to return to the family circle in Springfield that spring. They lived in a house rented from former Governor Richard Yates. Next door lived the Medill McCormicks, while the General Assembly was in session, for McCormick, publisher of the Chicago *Tribune*, was a state senator —Republican, of course—and, strange as it might seem in a later year, the two families were close friends.

II

On the evening of May 7 thick black headlines proclaimed that the Cunard liner *Lusitania*—the ship on which the Stevensons had crossed to Europe three years before—had been sunk without warn-

ing off the Irish coast, with the loss of 1198 persons, including 114
Americans. Among the Americans was an ex-Bloomingtonian, Elbert
Hubbard of *Message to Garcia* fame; another casualty, a glamorous
figure to Buffie, was Charles Frohman, the theatrical producer. To
both Buffie and Adlai it seemed incredible that the huge floating palace they had known now lay in the ooze of the ocean floor, fathoms
deep in sea-green water. Fishes swam through its white and gold
saloons, its mahogany staterooms, among dead men trapped there—
and dead women, too! And children!

There arose in Adlai a martial patriotism such as he had never
known before, but it had dimensions deeper and wider than were
common to the moods of his contemporaries or, indeed, to those of
Americans in general. Mingled with his martial ardor was a lyric
sense of the American past, whose values must be preserved. Springfield encouraged it. Springfield, to an Illinoisian, was a central focus
of national history.

For through Springfield's streets at midnight walked Abraham Lincoln, that "quaint great figure . . . the prairie-lawyer, master of us
all," as Vachel Lindsay sang in a poem all the town was quoting that
spring. Lindsay, the Springfield poet, was among those who came to
dine with the Stevensons. A strange, intense man of passionate
political convictions, he was very talkative. Buffie found him boring
after an hour or so. Adlai did not. The boy sat with his head bent
slightly forward and a little to one side, silent and absorbed, as Lindsay talked and talked and then declaimed in a throbbing chant:

> *It is portentious and a thing of state*
> *That here at midnight, in our little town*
> *A mourning figure walks, and will not rest,*
> *Near the old court-house pacing up and down. . . .*
>
> .   .   .   .
>
> *And we who toss and lie awake for long*
> *Breathe deep, and start, to see him pass the door.*

Adlai saw that figure—saw and knew that the Lincoln of whom
Lindsay sang was no Republican of the twentieth century. (Could
two leaders be more different than William Howard Taft and the
Great Emancipator?) Rather was Lindsay's Lincoln a prophet of
"the league of sober folk, the Workers' Earth," belonging, he felt, in
the same liberal tradition as the "Bryan, Bryan, Bryan, Bryan" of

whom Lindsay also sang—the tradition of Woodrow Wilson, and of the Stevensons of Bloomington.

Nor was it just at midnight that Abraham Lincoln walked the streets which fifteen-year-old Adlai came to know that spring. Lincoln, it seemed, was everywhere and all the time in Springfield— especially for a great-grandson of Jesse Fell.

Adlai began to be interested in girls. He had "dates" and indulged what he called the "manly art of dancing." And his favorite "date" in Springfield was a pretty, vivacious girl named Mary Douglas Hay, daughter of Mr. and Mrs. Logan Hay, good social friends of the Lewis Stevensons. Logan Hay was one of Illinois's most prominent attorneys; he was also one of the nation's foremost Lincoln scholars. He was a cousin of John Hay, Lincoln's secretary and biographer, and a son of Milton Hay who had been one of Lincoln's close friends, having a law office on the same floor with Lincoln and Herndon. His mother, born Mary Logan, was the daughter of Judge Stephen T. Logan, who had been senior partner of the law firm of Logan and Lincoln in the early 1840s. Thus when Adlai visited the Hay home he listened with eager attention to much talk about Old Abe.

A few weeks after school was out Buffie was sent to a girls' camp and Adlai to a boys' camp near Oxford, Maine. He wrote full reports to his mother on his activities: he distinguished himself at bat and at third base in a baseball game with Lake Pleasant Camp; he was his camp's singles champion in tennis, representing his fellows in a match with Camp Kohut which he lost, but "only after three sets." Meanwhile his father was insisting, in letters from Springfield, that Adlai write to him twice a week: the boy must learn to express himself in writing and "to observe people carefully . . . to analyze them, and if you get into the practice of doing this early in life, it will be of immense value to you in later years."

With regard to his son's indulgence in athletics "Pop" was typically self-contradictory. "I am so glad you are going in for athletics, and that you take the licking you got in such a manly way," he wrote in an early letter. In his next letter he was "delighted to know you are doing so well in your athletics." But just a few days later he wrote, "I must urge you not to go in for so much athletics. . . . The purpose of your being there and my spending so much money to keep you there, is not for you to take long hikes and overdo yourself in athletics, but to get in good physical condition so you can have your tonsils removed without any harm." The boy changed his reports to his father rather more than he changed his ways (a few days later he climbed Mount Washington, which is sixty-three hundred feet high) but he returned to Bloomington in the fall glowing with health, and had his tonsils removed "without any harm." . . . ("He was so strong," says Buffie's diary, "that they had to give him lots of ether.")

This minor operation, as a matter of fact, was a major turning point in Adlai's life. Theretofore he had been plagued with bronchitis in the winters, one reason (his mother's tendency toward colds was another) for going South during the coldest months. Thereafter, he had, as he himself said, "remarkable health." ("Never missed a day's work from Feb., 1933, to June, 1952," he once boasted. "That's nineteen years *plus!*")

Family ties were loosened that autumn. Lewis Stevenson remained in Springfield as his wife and children returned to 1316 East Washington in Bloomington. Adlai was enrolled in University High. Buffie, a tall, slender, vivid girl with an actress's temperament, had become eighteen in July; high time she was "finished"; so she was entered in Miss Wright's School for Young Ladies, in Bryn Mawr. She was reluctant to go, if not actually rebellious. "How ghastly to break up the home," she wrote in her diary before she left. "I suppose we will never all live together again." Helen Stevenson went East with her daughter, planning to stay there for some weeks.

Before the mother left she hired as housekeeper a nineteen-year-old colored girl named Alverta Duff whose life, from that point on, would be intimately involved with Stevenson lives. She was the daughter of one Peter Duff, the son of a Mississippi slave who had come as a boy of fourteen to the house of Jesse Fell in Normal, where he was taken in and given odd jobs to do "on condition that he go to school." He went to school, and by the 1900s the Duff family was highly respected in the community. Fannie Duff, Alverta's mother, feared that the big house at 1316 East Washington might be "too much" for her daughter, who had never worked before for anyone save her mother, and was not particularly strong, but Helen Stevenson was insistent: Adlai was being left alone for the first time and they must have a housekeeper whom she could absolutely trust to look after him.

As it turned out, Alverta's mother need not have worried. The girl was more than a superb housekeeper; she was also, from the first, a close friend of Adlai's. He was "a wonderful boy—so kind and considerate, and sweet-tempered always." If he wanted to bring some boys home for dinner he always called her well ahead of time to ask if it would be all right. He had, always, a kind of serene gaiety and zest for life; he seemed to lack completely those sharp edges of personality, the slashing knife of brilliance, which made both Lewis and Helen—and particularly Lewis—such formidable and even wounding (though exciting) characters. Adlai, though intensely active and quick, was endlessly patient. "He was always so *happy*, too," Alverta said, long afterward; it made her feel good just to be around him. "And conscientious," she added. "So conscientious." She would remember how he studied at the library table at night, with the green-shaded lamp shining down over his bent, absorbed head. Her belief was that he studied hard and long.

Perhaps he did. Having entered school so late—and having attended so erratically, with frequent long interruptions ever since—he had handicaps to overcome. But his teachers believed he limited his formal studies to a barely acceptable minimum. They repeatedly told him and his parents that he had the mental ability to make excellent marks if only he would "concentrate more." He was too actively interested in too many things, they said. As it was, his grades in the fall of 1914 had averaged 77 (out of a possible 100) in algebra, 77 in English, and 76 in zoology. He was absent from Normal during the spring term, at Springfield, where his grades were if anything a little lower than his University High ones. Next year, when Alverta first knew him, his record was somewhat improved. In the fall of the 1915–16 year he averaged 86 in English, 77 in geometry, and 83 in history; in the winter he scored 91 in geometry, 93 in history, and 81 in Latin. In the spring he averaged 86 in English, 83 in geometry, and 83 in Latin.

He seems to have thought he was "working extremely hard in school," in the fall of 1915. He said so in an October letter to his sister (who wrote him rather acid reports of her life at "Miss Wright's Fashionable Finishing School"), drawing at the bottom of the page a sketch of an emaciated, bespectacled professor, all head and no body, labeled "Me, 20 years hence, Professor of Latin and Greek." He also, in a note at the top of the page, undertook to correct Buffie's erratic spelling: "Condescend *not* condesend. Ablution *not* abolution —Use the Dic!" But his letters reveal that he engaged in a great many activities that had nothing to do with his studies. "I am going over to Decatur tomorrow with the football team. . . . I was at the basketball game this afternoon, and we were beaten, sad to relate, by the little town of Lexington. . . . Tonight I am going out to Normal to the Jesters play called *The Admirable Crighton*. I am going to dancing school every week and am becoming some artist in the manly sport. I got a bid to the Iota B dance the other day which comes off New Years Eve. . . . My frat does not give a dance this winter as we are going to have the convention in Springfield next spring and have to save our money. But the dance next spring during the convention will be a peach. . . . I just wrote the 'old man' asking for fifty seeds (dollars). I am expecting a hot reply."

Of his greatest personal "triumph" and most vivid experience that year, his letters—at least those that have been preserved—said not a word. . . .

By far the most glamorous creature in University High in 1915–16 was a beautiful blond girl with a lovely figure, a ravishing dimpled smile, and a sparkling personality. Her name was Josephine Sanders; a few years later, under the stage name of Irene Delroy, she would become famous as a musical-comedy star. Virtually every boy in the school was smitten by her charms, so much so that, after forty years had passed, graying men in Bloomington would speak of her in dreamy tones, regretting a romantic beauty departed from their lives; yes, and the fact that they had been forced, so long ago, to worship that beauty from afar. Among the smitten ones was Adlai Stevenson. Largely for her, he became proficient on the mandolin; for her he improved his dancing, learning all the new steps; to her he sang in a far-from-musical voice, strumming an accompaniment, George M. Cohan's "I'm Awfully Strong for You." And of all the school, she chose him! They exchanged notes in class signed "ETA" for *ego te amo*—as both he and Buffie would remember, greatly amused by the Latin, forty years later. They exchanged letters, too. Josephine's missives, appearing in the mailbox at 1316 East Washington, were reportedly purloined, sometimes, by Helen Stevenson, who looked upon the budding romance with a coldly disapproving eye and was thankful that Josephine, ambitious for a stage career, was not likely to become "*too* serious" about a Bloomington boy. . . . When the senior prom was held in the spring Adlai was Josephine's escort, and to the pleasure of being with her was added the prideful pleasure that must come, even to such a nature as his, from the knowledge that one is envied.

But apparently this was the climax of the romance. Josephine Sanders, with a Broadway star's career ahead of her, was, after that one brief season, only a memory. . . .

Meanwhile Buffie was having triumphs of her own. During the spring vacation, her father came East and took her to Washington, where they stayed with glamorous Cousin Letty Bromwell, sister of Julia Vrooman, in her house on Q Street. The main purpose of the trip was a ceremony unveiling a portrait of Grandmother Stevenson in the D.A.R.'s Continental Hall. Buffie it was who pulled the cord, and had pictures of herself doing it in all the papers next day. Cousin Letty, who had had such a subversive effect on Helen Stevenson during the Paris shopping expedition in 1912, had a somewhat similar effect on Buffie during that holiday. The girl's hair was pulled back severely and tied in a knot; this, said Cousin Letty, was atrocious, and she proceeded to redo the hair. The girl's lips were without rouge; this, said Cousin Letty, would never do, and she proceeded to paint the lips. The girl's hats were without chic; Cousin Letty insisted on loaning Buffie one of hers—"a white feather toque with an egret sticking up like an antenna," as Buffie would always remember. The girl sat and walked awkwardly; Cousin Letty gave lecture-demonstrations, both to Buffie and her own daughter Millie, on the proper way to sit, and stand, and move. Buffie was an eager pupil, so much so that her father found her terribly affected and began to mimic her talk and movements with that deadly accuracy for which he was both famed and feared in Bloomington. Nevertheless, he took her to the White House to call upon President Wilson, who, she promptly reported in her diary, "is a dear!!!!"

But when she returned to Bloomington, in early June, she was not so toplofty as to be uninfluenced by certain changes in her brother. He met her at the train, and she sensed at once that their relationship from now on would be different from what it had been before. No longer was he "little brother," meekly acquiescent to her "bossing." He was almost a young man and, in his unassertive way, an impressive one. She found herself suddenly concerned as to what he thought of things she said and did; she began to ask him for his opinions of people and events. She even asked him, in an unprecedented tone of humility, if he would teach her to drive the new Hudson Super-six, for he drove so expertly (if rather too fast) himself.

And this sense of his growth toward an independent maturity, in which he would be a poised individual with great capacities, was strengthened in her as she sat at the University High School's senior banquet, where he gave his first public speech of any importance. (In the autumn of 1914, according to Buffie's diary, he'd made his very first speech, "for the Boys' Anti-Cigarette League"—at his mother's behest. His speech that night was entitled "To the Senior Celebrities," and neither he nor Buffie would have any remembrance of what he said, after a few years had passed. But Buffie would never forget how proud she was of him.

In his sixteenth year he had reached his full height of five feet nine inches. Because he was so slender he seemed taller than that, however, as he stood before the crowd, apparently perfectly at ease. He looked handsome, too, in his dark suit, with his thick brown hair neatly parted at the left. Dr. Noyes had done a good job with the boy's teeth: they were now very even and flashed white when he smiled. His deeply cleft chin, rather thin cheeks, and overhanging upper lip gave him an "aesthetic" look, confirmed by a certain moodiness in his large blue eyes, but those eyes had sparkle as well as depth and they looked out upon the world candidly, interestedly, with an expression that was both unassuming and unafraid.

III

It was well that he did not assume too much that early June. Had he done so, his would have been the pride that goeth before a fall.

Lewis and Helen Stevenson had decided that Adlai should go East to college, preferably to Princeton. There were family reasons for favoring Princeton: Adlai Osborne had graduated from that institution in 1764 and Great-grandfather Lewis Warner Green had also gone there, to the Theological Seminary. Moreover Woodrow Wilson, the family's great political hero, had not only graduated from Princeton but had made his academic career there, gaining national fame as its president during the first decade of the century.

Alas, University High School had failed to prepare Adlai for the Eastern college-entrance board examinations required by Princeton. Adlai took three of these early that summer. He failed all three. "I don't think the scores I made added up to passing in one," he confessed to one of his biographers, John Bartlow Martin, long afterward.

One can imagine the effect this produced on short-tempered Lewis

Stevenson. Lewis himself was no scholar and had no particular desire that his son become one, but he *did* want Adlai to be a "well-rounded man"—and how could the boy become that if he couldn't even get into a first-rate college? It was disgraceful! He would never admit that a son of his could be as stupid as these examinations seemed to indicate! But then he was quickly reminded that perhaps the preparation had something to do with it. So he immediately set about securing his son's entrance into Choate School in Connecticut where Davis Merwin had already gone, only to discover that, even for this, Adlai was inadequately prepared. The boy was deficient in French!

"Well, you'll just have to make it up this summer," Lewis said to him in threatful tones. "I'll arrange for a tutor, and *you* will study! You'll study hard!"

But, characteristically, Lewis was almost equally insistent that his son take an active interest in the political developments of that intensely political summer. It was high time, he said, that Adlai "learn about such things first hand." So in early June he wired both Adlai and Buffie, ordering them to meet him in Chicago to observe the Republican National Convention. . . .

What Adlai learned during those hot and hectic days in Chicago could hardly have furthered his preparation for Choate, but it was useful to his later career. This was his first national political convention—strange that this "first" should be Republican!—and the boy was fascinated by the color, the excitement. He gained, too, a clear insight into the basic issues and essential strategy of the huge, noisy gathering.

Harold Ickes helped him to understand. Ickes took Adlai and Buffie over to the Bull Moose convention, which was meeting in Chicago simultaneously with the Republican "regulars." As Buffie reported, the Bull Moose was "much more fun than the Republicans!" It was also more sad, for those who really cared (as Ickes did) about Progressivism. Adlai felt the tenseness, the bitterness of the crowd, as it listened to a message from Teddy Roosevelt in which the author of the Bull Moose virtually destroyed his handiwork by indicating that he would not accept the Progressive nomination; at the same time he urged Progressives to return to the Republican fold. Ickes, in pungent bitter phrase, explained what this meant. Once the breach the Progressives had made was closed, the Republican party would be more monolithically conservative than it had been at any time since McKinley's death, for the Old Guard was now vindicated, the party's liberal wing was discredited, and one could be sure that the former would punish the latter by denying it any real power.

For Ickes as for most insurgents, and most Democrats, too, the basic issues of the coming campaign did not lie in the realm of foreign policy, where Woodrow Wilson seemed inclined to place them. True, the lengthening shadows of war lay heavier upon the land, day by day; the threats looming across the Atlantic would make the slogan "He Kept Us Out of War" an appealing one, so long as it was balanced by the words and deeds of "Preparedness." But how could there be much difference between the foreign policy of Republicans and Democrats in a situation where there were virtually no free choices? No, the real issues lay between an extension of the New Freedom and a resurgence of McKinley Republicanism—and the Republican strategy, particularly the choice of Charles Evans Hughes as standard-bearer, was deliberately designed to blur this issue as much as possible in the general public's mind while sharpening it as much as possible in the mind of the business community.

Thus did the Chicago adventure—interpreted for him by Ickes, and Lewis Stevenson, and a dozen other sophisticated men—impress upon young Adlai the basic pattern in terms of which the events of the campaign might be understood. He was not permitted to go with his father to the Democratic convention, which opened in St. Louis two days after the Republican convention ended; he had to prepare for his Choate examinations, Lewis now insisted. But he followed what happened in St. Louis with close attention, and what happened afterward, too. It was "right" in terms of pattern that Hughes, despite his allegedly "progressive" tendencies, should in July begin to sound like a restrained Mark Hanna; Adlai was quite possibly less surprised by it than were Hughes's long-time personal friends. It was equally "right," in terms of pattern, that the Wilson administration should advance the New Freedom, through governmental action, even while the campaign was going on: the Federal Farm Loan Act on July 17; the Jones Act, guaranteeing ultimate Philippine independence, on August 29; the Adamson Act, establishing an eight-hour day (instead of the prevailing ten) for interstate railroads, on September 3.

The latter, which caused the four railroad brotherhoods to call off a nationwide strike scheduled to begin at midnight September 4, was at once a major campaign issue, being bitterly denounced by candidate Hughes. Hughes termed it a "force bill" whose passage, in the face of threats, rendered contemptible the government of the United States. The charge, to which Wilson eloquently replied in terms of the "general welfare," disturbed Lewis Stevenson not at all. This was a "good" issue for Democrats, he explained. It made the labor vote secure, and it must drive into Democratic ranks those former Bull Moosers who might still be wavering between the parties.

With this, Carl Vrooman agreed. The Assistant Secretary of Agriculture came to Chicago in mid-September to confer with U. S. District Attorney Cline as to what action, if any, the federal government should take to avert a threatened milk strike in that city; he came down to Bloomington afterward for a brief visit.

And Josephus Daniels agreed, also. Wilson's Secretary of the Navy came to Bloomington in September as keynote speaker at a giant Wilson rally in the Coliseum; he stayed as house guest at 1316 East Washington, where his presence raised to its highest pitch the Stevenson family's personal involvement in the national campaign. Lewis was unable to come over from Springfield on the great day, so Buffie—at a large dinner given in Daniels' honor—sat proudly in her father's place. Moreover, she took charge of decorating the Coliseum with banners and flowers, many of the latter coming from Helen Stevenson's flower beds. Both she and Adlai sat on the platform at the rally—"and *that* time," as Adlai would say long afterward, "I stayed wide awake!"

Nor was Adlai's personal involvement in politics during those weeks merely a passive one of listening and reading. Lewis Stevenson was running for his first elective office, that of secretary of state, to which Governor Dunne had appointed him. He had exercised the powers of that office with such even-handed efficiency that many a Republican voter and newspaper, including the Chicago *Tribune,* now supported his candidacy, but for some reason, Roger Sullivan, the powerful Democratic Chicago boss, opposed him. In consequence the primary campaign became a hard and dirty one. Several unknown men, whose names just happened to be closely similar to Lewis's, filed for the nomination in competition with him; he had to hire private detectives, at considerable personal expense, to ferret out the skulduggery and protect his name on the ballot. But on September 13 he won the primary. He won by a big majority. He even carried Cook County, to everyone's surprise and Roger Sullivan's acute discomfiture. . . . Adlai made several trips with his father, to political rallies and such. He helped his father pass out cards on the streets; he also drove the family Hudson through the country roads around Bloomington, pausing every few hundred yards to tack a Lewis Stevenson placard on a telephone pole.

But despite these distractions, plus a camping holiday in northern Michigan with some Bloomington boys, Adlai managed to make up his French deficiency. In September he was notified, through his parents, of his acceptance by Choate.

IV

He left Bloomington on a golden autumn day when trees arched red and yellow over the quiet streets. Gaudy leaves skittered on a frost-edged wind in the gutters, and pillars of bluish-white smoke rose in the back yards as if in solemn ritual: funeral pyres for the dead summer. He left with some thousands of words of advice poured into his ears by his mother, and some dozens of bottles of medicine packed by his mother into his suitcase, and with an earnest desire to do well enough in his new life to realize at least a few of the great hopes his mother (and to some extent his father, too) seemed to have for him. Beyond that, which was more a sense of obligation than a personal ambition, his will was as relaxed as his gaze across the flat Illinois prairie. He saw bright woods tinged with powder-blue mists on the far horizon; he saw the same powder-blue tinge on the tall brown bluestems growing along the railroad right of way, a last vestige of the virgin prairie; and this soft blue haze, falling like a transparent curtain from a sky of aching blue, was an image of his mood all the way to Chicago, where he boarded a Pullman on the New York Central and rode eastward into night. Even as night fell and he gazed out into it from the dining-car window, this mood continued. He felt a mild regret for the receding past, a mild eagerness for the approaching future, and almost no anxiety at all.

Yet he moved toward awful hazards.

At the far eastern edge of night, where the sky would soon glow into another bloody dawn, weary Allied soldiers prepared again to attack and conquer another patch of shell-torn earth which had no value tactically, or strategically, or even symbolically. Sixty thousand British had fallen on July 1, when the vast stupidity of the Somme was launched; nearly a million would fall before November rains made further murderous advances impossible. Nearer at hand, on the black Atlantic, German submarines were abroad, and every ship they sank would make American involvement in the war more certain. Still nearer at hand, in Washington, while Wilson's campaign managers harped on the "Peace and Prosperity" theme, certain administration officials lay sleepless as they sought to brace themselves for what seemed to them a virtually inevitable declaration of war. Death—death in war—lay in the immediate future of thousands of teen-aged Americans that year. Sixteen-year-old Adlai Stevenson might have wondered if he were one of them.

Instead he was concerned (though far this side of anxiety) with questions of his fitness for the life he now entered. He was coming to Choate at a disadvantage. He was late, for one thing, and he was not particularly well prepared, by his schooling thus far, to compete with such boys as Choate enrolled.

He was concerned, too, about the outcome of the political campaign. As he rode eastward that night, his father's chances for election, though doubtful, seemed to him considerably greater than Wilson's, and while he was certainly eager for his father's success he was dismayed by the seeming probability of Wilson's failure. Wilson seemed to him so great a man, one who really *cared* about human freedom. Yet almost everyone, including Hughes, was convinced that the Republican candidate was so far ahead in the race that all he had to do was mouth platitudes, coasting to victory.

Next morning Adlai bought a Cleveland paper from a newsboy on the train and read it at breakfast as his father would have done. He found the world which the paper reported to be challengingly various, endlessly interesting. Then he folded the paper and looked out the dining-car window. Morning sunlight glinted on the waves of Lake Erie. He took a deep breath and squared his shoulders.

And smiled.

CHAPTER SIX

From Choate to Princeton

The town of Wallingford, Connecticut, lying a dozen miles northeast of New Haven, contained in 1916 some ten or twelve thousand people. It was, by American standards, an ancient town, dating from 1670, a center of silver manufacturing surrounded by a rolling countryside over which great orchards and vineyards had spread for generations. The Choate School, with a campus of several hundred acres dotted with handsome buildings, lay at the town's eastern edge.

Though founded by Judge William Gardner Choate in 1896, the school was, for the most part, a creature of Dr. George St. John, headmaster since 1907. The two hundred-odd boys of whom Adlai Stevenson became one were recognized as distinct individuals, and to each, in terms of his individual needs and nature, was given the kind of liberal education through which English public schools had developed the British governing class. "Habits of efficiency and industry" and "an understanding of the enduring values and of the spirit of public service" were instilled. Grade standards were high. So were the standards by which general conduct was measured. Morality at Choate was considered to be firmly rooted in Protestant religion, and church attendance on Sunday mornings 'was a rigid requirement.

In this environment Adlai flourished, by the standards of formal schooling, as he had never done before, but he made no outstanding scholastic record. When he again took College Board examinations in May of 1917 he did approximately twice as well as he'd done the year before, passing a few of the ten to fifteen different tests which were required. In the autumn his examination record helped determine his course for his second Choate year. "I find that I can get into Princeton without taking Physics, Solid Geom., and Trigonometry by substituting 2 years of Spanish or German," he wrote his mother. "I expect to do this as it makes it much easier and Spanish is a coming language." In another letter he wrote that "Solid and Trig are worthless subjects anyway." Science courses were almost meaningless to him, then and later. He had had no grounding in the mathematical language; both University High and Choate placed their emphasis on "literary" subjects. Nevertheless, in early June of 1918 he reported to his mother that on his final examination he received the second highest mark in his "Trig" class; it was "88 percent and Mr. Mc-Ormond wrote *splendid* on my book." "I got 82 in Spanish," he went on. ". . . My other marks were 78 in French, 74 in Algebra and 69 in Latin."

That same spring, Dr. St. John wrote a letter to Helen Stevenson saying that Adlai was to have a month's drill in the taking of examinations. The headmaster had observed that examinations "never do him justice," the boy having far more knowledge and a far greater intelligence than the results of formal tests would indicate. In the spring of '18, playing "third man" on the Choate tennis team, he was defeated by the captain of the Taft team 7–5, 6–1. "I was rotten and should have beaten him," he reported to his mother disgustedly, "but was a little nervous I guess." Did a classroom test have, sometimes, the same effect?

At Choate, as at University High, Adlai's vital interests centered on extracurricular activities, and he might well be proud of the successes he made of these, for he began under some serious handicaps.

As a latecomer in the fall of '16 he was assigned a single room and he lived alone through all that school year. He was one of the few students who did. To his physical isolation was added, at the outset, a rather acute spiritual loneliness: he discovered that he was one of only three Democrats in all the student body and that neither of the other two had a personal stake in the outcome of the elections. Alone, then, he must defend his political position against great numerical odds. Most Choate boys had inherited from their fathers a faith in the sanctity of private property and in the divine right of businessmen to rule the country, which had been rendered all the more vehement by the attacks of Populists, Muckrakers, and Bull Moosers. Some of them looked upon Adlai's Democratic loyalties as actually subversive. They were not loathe to say so. "We used to argue politics by the hour," said Harry Stearns, one of his classmates, long afterward, adding that the arguments often generated far more heat than light. "But," Stearns concluded significantly, "I never saw Ad lose his temper or act bitter."

Surely he might have been excused for doing so in October, when all looked dark for the national Democratic ticket. And his psychic wounds could have been only partially assuaged by the results of the balloting on November 7. By late evening of that day, Adlai knew that his father had lost his race for secretary of state. Governor Dunne had lost, too, to Frank Lowden. The boy might take some comfort from the fact that his father had run thirty thousand votes ahead of anyone else on the state Democratic ticket, had received more votes in Cook County than Frank Lowden, and had run thousands of votes ahead of Woodrow Wilson in Illinois as a whole. Nevertheless it was a defeat. To the news of it, that night, was added the news that Woodrow Wilson had also lost. Adlai went to bed convinced that Hughes was the next President of the United States. Not until next day, when the close California vote was at last tabulated, did he learn that Wilson, after all, had won, with 277 electoral votes to Hughes's 254, and with 9,129,606 popular votes to Hughes's 8,538,221. Moreover, the Democrats retained control of both houses of Congress.

Reading this news, Adlai might feel somewhat less lonely than he'd felt twenty-four hours before. And he might learn lessons of character from the gallantry with which both his father and Charles Evans Hughes accepted their defeats. On election day Buffie and Helen Stevenson were in Lakewood, New Jersey, where they had been encouraged to remain by Lewis Stevenson, for he did not want his family to suffer the last nerve-racking days of his campaign. Next day they received from him a bright, cheerful letter which buoyed their spirits. A little later Charles Evans Hughes and Mrs. Hughes came to Laurel in the Pines, where Buffie and Helen were staying, and if he were at all embittered by the manner in which his hopes had towered to the skies, only to crash to the ground, they saw no sign of it. They reported to Adlai that Hughes was quietly dignified, a bit aloof perhaps, but wholly admirable. . . .

The boy might learn, too, from the historic events which followed hard upon Wilson's re-election, considering these in terms of the campaign slogan, "He Kept Us Out of War," to which the President had given at least a tacit consent. The clearly implied promise was, "He Will Keep Us Out of War"—and it proved acutely embarrassing to the administration as history, no longer a flowing process, advanced with martial tread from 1916 into 1917, carrying the United States inexorably toward armed intervention.

Mid-January 1917 saw the collapse of Wilson's attempt to negotiate a "peace without victory" in Europe. On January 31 Germany announced that all ships, including those of neutral nations, would be sunk without warning by her submarines if they entered a broadly designated "war zone." On April 2, after six unarmed American vessels had been sunk within a few weeks, Wilson asked the Congress for a declaration of war, using those eloquent phrases which would ring so hollow a few years later: "The world must be made safe for democracy. Its peace must be planted upon the tested foundations of political liberty." On April 6, the war declaration, having passed the Congress overwhelmingly, was signed by the President. . . .

The lesson was clear. Adlai Stevenson would express it again and again in the 1950s. "We cannot afford to forget," he would say, "that *how* you win in politics is as important as *what* you win." The "what," after all, is largely determined by the "how."

But of course this lesson was not one which the boy could have stated in 1917 and '18. His letters made no reference to the stupendous historical events of that spring, save that older boys were enlisting and that next fall's football team was being "ruined." For him as for others, however, the war was an intense present excitement: flags, parades, martial music, much talk of honor and glory and sacrifice, an outburst of passionate idealism which would seem, in retrospect, incredibly naïve.

In the summer of 1917 he and Buffie spent a long vacation on the H F Bar ranch, a famous "dude" ranch near Buffalo, Wyoming, to which they had first gone in 1915. They arrived in Buffalo on July 4, witnessed there a "gala celebration" featuring broncobusting and auto racing, then rode eighteen miles by auto to the ranch whose setting, amidst the mountains, stirred Adlai to ecstatic comments in a letter to his mother. During that summer he was supposed to combine pleasure with further tutoring in French: his parents had hired as chaperone one Nora Caroe, who had been Buffie's French teacher at Miss Wright's school: but the arrangement did not work out as planned. For the one hundred guests at the ranch, a crowded schedule of "activities" was worked out, and Adlai missed so few of them that he had little time for scholarly pursuits. He bought himself a pair of bearskin chaps and spent hours every day in the saddle; he took part in the cattle roundup, riding as one of the back guards; on "Frontier Day" he won a prize in the gymkhana contest, spearing potatoes while riding pell-mell; he went on a ten-day pack trip into the Big Horn mountains with Frank Horton, owner of the ranch; he did a great deal of fly casting for trout in icy, rushing mountain streams; he climbed mountains.

His chief companion in these exercises was a boy his age named Ralph Goodwin, from Cleveland, who loved the West as Adlai did. Lying under twinkling cottonwoods beside the little stream which flowed clear and cold behind his cottage, he and Ralph dreamed of coming West after college and becoming ranchers. Theretofore he'd thought rather vaguely of journalism as a career, but by that summer's end he was convinced that ranching in the mountains—a vigorous life in a setting of great natural beauty—was what he *really* wanted.

He retained his interest in journalism however; when he returned to Choate the interest became intensely active. Within a day or so after the fall term opened he was "heeling" for the *Choate News* board, engaging in what was apparently a stiff competition. At first he seems to have felt inadequate to solicit advertising and indicated as much to his mother, but by the end of two or three weeks he had sold several hundred dollars' worth and was trying to enlist the support of his father for a final "push." "I am writing you on a matter of great import, i.e., import to me," he said. "You see the *News* competition ends this Saturday and I am now fourth man in the competition. Furthermore I think (and have been told so) that the board is only going to take on three men. Now an 'ad' will help me greatly and I might possibly get taken on . . . if I get a good one . . . as I am so near to third place anyway. The *News* is considered the second biggest thing in school after football and Mr. St. J. thinks it the first. . . . Do you know of any firm, co., etc. that might advertise? If you do know of one please let me know immediately." A week later Adlai won his place on the board. Soon he sent his mother "the best first issue the *News* has ever had—all the masters say so," and in the spring he became the paper's editor in chief. No triumph of his later years gave him greater pleasure than this. Proudly he wrote home on *Choate News* letterhead stationary: "pretty hard last week getting out my first *News*," but that "my efforts were well rewarded because the general opinion is that it is about the best issue of the season. When you receive it look at the picture on the right side of the front page and see if it resembles any one you ever saw before. Also read the article about the 1918 board as I wrote most of it. Also read the editorial, which is another product of my pen. Furthermore notice my name in the headlines on the Loomis Tennis match."

The latter story reported that Choate had defeated Loomis, the preceding Wednesday, 4–2, and that A. E. Stevenson had beaten his man in straight sets, 6–1, 6–3.

He shared a room, that second year, on the top floor of Hill House with Harry Stearns and Jim Milholland, "the best room in the School," he wrote his mother, with a huge dormer window looking far out across the rolling Connecticut countryside. His letters spoke of "select feeds" in various rooms, of dances ("we are going to have a dance after the Taft [football] game, and Harry is going to have a girl up from Hartford for me"), and of visits in New Haven—happier letters than those of the preceding year. "I am never going to room alone again," he vowed.

His social life became quite brilliant during the Christmas holidays, which he spent in Washington with his family. On December 22, 1917, Lewis Stevenson was appointed Chief Special Investigator of the U. S. Navy by Secretary Daniels, his job being to prevent frauds in Navy food contracts. Immediately Lewis, Helen, and Buffie moved into an apartment in the Hotel La Fayette, and when Adlai joined them for the holidays he found them plunged into society. Ellen Bruce, daughter of a friend of his parents, undertook to "float" him, getting him all manner of invitations to dances and receptions. It was all so exciting that upon his return to Choate he found it hard to concentrate on his studies; he ordered Buffie to write him "all the dope" on the capital's society.

The following spring, 1918, when he became editor of the school paper, was for him a season of honors. He was elected captain of next year's tennis team. He was elected vice-president of the senior class. "By some strange freak that I can't understand," he was elected secretary of the Athletic Association, which was the student athletic governing body; "[this] strikes me as very amusing when the other two officers are the two biggest athletes in School," he wrote his mother. And, as a crowning honor, in his view, he was elected president of St. Andrews, the school's religious society for all denominations. "You didn't know your son was a young evangelist, did you?" he chortled. "If I come back [to Choate] next year, it looks as tho' I'd be a pretty big dude." Reporting these triumphs to his mother gave him great pleasure, because *she* obviously derived such pleasure from them. "How you keep your equilibrium with so much glory being thrust upon you, I do not see," she wrote him. "Certainly you have made good with both faculty and students and our pride knows no bounds!"

And the phrase, "made good," seems an apt description of his effort and of its motivation. His letters show that he was not driven to his successes by prideful ambition so much as led to them by a sense of duty. He was obliged to be successful, making moral "good" in the process, in order to be worthy of his family, his ancestors, his Christianity. He had no desire to overawe his contemporaries, nor to dominate them; no boy could have cared less for power per se. His prevailing attitude toward the world was one of uncritical acceptance; his attitude toward himself, in so far as he was self-conscious at all, was a compound of objectivity and wry humility. Every triumph came to him as a pleasant but slightly absurd surprise.

Of negative judgments of people his letters were wholly devoid. He wrote:

"I met [Pomfret's] star halfback. He's an awfully nice fellow. . . . The new fellows are a fine looking bunch. I found 4 or 5 especially that I like awfully well. . . . An alumnus from Harvard has been down here this week and he says Dave [Merwin] has the Lampoon clinched. We certainly hope he makes it. . . . Tell Buff there is a fellow here from Boston who knows Jack Churchill, Nichols, and Pete Gunner very well. His name is Goddard and he is an awfully nice fellow."

Similarly of the talks he heard, the shows he saw:

"Dean Brown of Yale had the services today and was awfully good. . . . Last night we had movies, *Joanne the Woman* with Geraldine Farrar. It was a wonderful picture. . . . Last night, Mr. Seymour, Mrs. St. John's brother, gave us a very interesting talk on the Kaiser. . . ."

Meanwhile his mother's letters to him were full of advice that mingled Christian piety with a kind of Chesterfieldian worldliness.

"We are so pleased that you are so happy in your new room and in being an 'old boy,'" she wrote him in October of '17. "Of course

your connections with 'News' . . . make you a big factor and I think
it is splendid experience for you. You will learn how to handle men,
etc. etc. . . . I hope it will show you how necessary it is to gauge
your strength, to allot your time, and not give of both too ceaselessly.
This is just as important in becoming successful as talent. And another thing, never be annoyed or anxious. *Worried* is the common
way of expressing it. It *never* helps and slowly and insidiously it
ruins your mind and body. 'Sufficient unto the day is the work
thereof' the Bible says and you must learn never to go to bed with
a business thought in your mind! Just think, you have already $500
worth of ads and while you were in C. you were a little anxious
about them. Now you see it was unnecessary to be the least troubled.
Please keep these things in mind and see if you can't get steadier
by the discipline this work affords. To keep placid and cheerful,
know all things come to those who love the Lord and doeth His
works. . . . May God be with you always."

II

In late June 1918 he joined his family, who had returned from
Washington to Bloomington. He had learned that if he passed the
Navy physical examination and the college-entrance examinations,
he might be enlisted in the U. S. Navy as an apprentice seaman,
stationed at Princeton as a student trainee. He spent the summer
"cramming" for the College Board, concentrating on Virgil, while for
relaxation he rode horseback with Buffie along the side roads around
the town. Avidly, in the *Pantagraph* and Chicago papers, he read
of American forces fighting in France, of Lenin's Bolsheviks in Russia, of the German occupation of the Ukraine. In the last week of
August he returned to Wallingford, Connecticut, there to complete
his "cramming."

"I am each day gaining in erudition and sincerely believe that you
will not recognize me in my present intellectual disguise when next
we meet," he wrote his mother. "I think, if the Gods are with me,
that I may pass my exams. The Virgil is, I find, an enormous task for
so short a time but, as I said before, if the Gods are with me, *very
close by*, I may pass." Meanwhile he had registered for the draft, as
all men between the ages of eighteen and forty-five were required
to do, and spent what little time he had free trying to collect *Choate
News* advertising money. Before he left Wallingford for Princeton

he'd collected some $550, of which his personal share was $130. "Not so bad, eh?" he asked.

On Sunday, August 31, with a Choate friend, a "corking fellow" named Eldridge Snyder, he moved into a room in the Nassau Inn in Princeton, directly across from the university campus. The two boys spent that day wandering around the town and campus—through Nassau Hall, past the big cannon (it had been used by Hessians in the Battle of Princeton during the Revolution) and the library, and under the great elms of McCosh Walk to Washington Road. They passed a dozen impressive Gothic edifices on their way to Palmer Stadium and back. They wandered through the grounds and formal garden of Prospect Mansion, the president's house.

Next morning Adlai entered the examination room to begin three grueling days of tests from which he emerged tired, dispirited, convinced of his failure. . . .

Three weeks later, on the morning of Monday, September 23, he again awoke in Nassau Inn. Turning to look through the window, he found himself too tense to enjoy the beauty of morning light upon leaves that were just beginning to turn into the colors of autumn. He was too tense to enjoy his breakfast. With shallow breath and pounding heart he walked into the corridor of Nassau Hall where a small crowd of boys stood before the bulletin board, peering at a sheet mounted there—a typewritten list of those eligible for admission to Princeton as regular freshmen. His own gaze ran anxiously down that list: "Stearns, Sherman D. . . . Stecker, Philip J. . . . Stephan, Audley H. F. . . . Stevens, Richard K. . . . Stevenson, Adlai E. . . ." He let out his pent breath in a long whistling sigh, and grinned. "*Stevenson, Adlai E.*"

He had made it!

The rest of that crowded day was suffused with a glow of happiness. He went at once to the registrar's office and enrolled in the university. Then he went to the gymnasium, below McCosh Walk, where he filled out a Naval Reserve Force enlistment blank and cheerfully submitted to the orders, the poking and prodding, of brusque naval doctors and their even more brusque assistants. Stripped, he weighed 137 pounds—just a little less than normal for his age and height of five feet, nine inches. His chest expansion was four inches. His vision was normal (he was astounded by the number who were rejected because of color blindness), and so were his heart, his blood pressure, his lungs, his muscular co-ordination. By midaft-

ernoon he was officially deemed acceptable by the Navy. ("Thanks
to your unceasing care I passed . . . pretty high," he wrote his
mother.)

He was assigned to No. 64 Stafford Little Hall, a suite consisting
of a study and two small bedrooms; he was assigned a bureau, desk,
bed, and chair and was told he could not mount a Choate banner
nor any other "decorations" on his bedroom wall. He had three roommates: Hendrik Terry of New York City ("a very nice fellow"),
William E. Hale, and the Ralph Goodwin with whom he had formed
a close friendship at the H F Bar ranch the previous summer.

For the first few weeks thereafter, his half-comic role as apprentice
seaman was dominant over his role as a Princeton man. He was ordered out of bed at 5:55 each morning, must be properly dressed in
his company's ranks outside Little Hall a few minutes later, and then
must march to commons, where breakfast was served promptly at
6:15. He marched to lunch at 12:15, to supper at 6:15, to chapel on
Sunday, and in the hours between he marched and drilled for hours.
When classes opened the following week, he was assigned courses in
naval instruction, Spanish, law, history, and chemistry, and to these,
too, he was marched in formation. He bought, for thirty-five dollars,
"a good uniform to wear on liberty . . . as the Gov. stuff is not very
good" and became "believe me . . . one hot looking little 'jack.' You
will just about split when you see me," he predicted to Buffie and
his mother. He helped organize a brass band for his naval unit, despite the fact he himself played no instrument but a mandolin. Occasionally he "put to sea" with his fellow seamen on Lake Carnegie,
an artificial lake eight hundred feet wide and three and one half
miles long, given the university by Andrew Carnegie for rowing activities. Whaleboats were used, but there were so few of these and
so many seamen that most of the latter spent most of their time on
the lake shore, watching, and tying sailor's knots.

Meanwhile, in France, the Allied offensive roared on, with
Americans attacking through the Argonne forest, until by November
10 the Germans were retreating so rapidly it was difficult for Allied
troops to maintain contact with them. Next morning at eleven o'clock
the end came. After four years, three months, and seven days of a
war in which ten million men had been killed in action, every gun
on the western front fell silent—and Adlai Stevenson joined his fellows in a delirious celebration of the Armistice, consuming with them

a somewhat excessive quantity of beer in the taproom of "Old Nass."

In the days that followed, the relative emphasis between his two roles was reversed. No longer did the apprentice seaman dominate over the college man: he was, thenceforward, a Princetonian for whom the Navy was but a minor campus "activity," until he received his formal discharge in January 1919. The Navy discipline was at once relaxed. He had the leisure, or at least he took the time, to wander around campus and town and countryside, drinking deep of beauty. A day in early December, when the first snow of the season fell upon Princeton, became "the most beautiful winter day" he'd ever seen. "I wish you could have seen McCosh Walk and the trees around Prospect embedded in snow—about two inches on the smallest twig!"

III

Even at the height of his Navy "career," he had been acutely aware of a difference in status between himself and those of his fellows who had come to Princeton "on certificate" to join the military organizations. The latter were not members of the class of '22 and were constantly reminded that they were not. "I certainly am glad that I came in by exams and am a real Princeton man," says one of Adlai's letters. "Although it is very difficult to maintain all the old customs etc., the difference between the regular Princeton men and the others is very obvious. For instance, whenever 'Old Nassau' or any of the P. [Princeton] songs are sung the non-regular men are not allowed to sing and have to stand at attention."

Nor were they permitted to join in such joyous celebrations as the annual freshman "P-rade," on Saturday afternoon, October 27. "We P-raded around the campus singing Princeton songs . . . [and] then went to the steps of Whig Hall for the freshman picture. The fellows in the Navy Unit formed a huge 'P' on the steps and the Army and non-military fellows filled in." After that, election of class officers was held in the assembly room of McCosh Hall, a process Adlai found to be "all graft but very interesting." Since first-term freshmen did not know one another well, prep-school loyalties dominated the proceedings; such electioneering as occurred was designed to influence the vote of the non-prep, or uncommitted, freshman. In some cases "deals" were made between alumni of the smaller schools whereby they pooled their votes, school A putting up the candidate for president, school B the candidate for vice-president, and school C the candidate for secretary-treasurer. Adlai himself was one of five or six nominated for secretary-treasurer ("much to my surprise and inquietude") and was forced to stand up before the multitude and then retreat, with his fellow nominees, into an adjoining room while the vote was taken. He returned to find that Philip Strong, a Hill alumnus, had won the office, though he himself had received a great many more votes than he had expected, having come from so small a school. Everett Case of Hotchkiss was class president (about one fourth of the freshman class was composed of Hotchkiss men) and Kenneth Drummond from St. Paul's was vice-president. The election over, the class did some more "P-rading." That night they all attended a smoker.

His mention of the smoker, in a letter home, elicited from his mother a fervent argument designed to show him "the futility of . . . the tobacco habit." She urged him to "put the matter squarely" to himself and "see honestly if the one advantage (that of being companionable, one of the crowd) will offset the disadvantages." What, after all, was his "desire . . . in life"? Was it not to live "as decently, uprightly as is possible" and "be an example of every moral virtue to your fellow men"? "Please remember you had two grandfathers who never found it necessary to smoke and they were held in the highest esteem," she went on, mentioning nonsmoking Carl Vrooman as another example of "men . . . not looked down upon." She concluded: ". . . I shall pray that you be led into the light in this matter. God help you." To all this, Adlai made no reference whatever in his next letter home.

As a "real Princeton man," moreover, he had a relationship with his superior officers in the Navy which was certainly not common to apprentice seamen. The commandant was Admiral Goodrich, a very distinguished retired senior officer, who attended smokers with those of the class of '22 who were under his command, and otherwise associated with them on a basis of social equality. He was particularly cordial to Adlai, whose grandfather he remembered, and whose father had so important a position in the Navy Department and stood so high in the esteem of Secretary Daniels.

Adlai's battalion commander was a highly respected Princeton student named John Harlan, class of '20, the "high duke here," as Adlai reported home, "and a wonderful fellow." (After graduation Harlan would go to Oxford as a Rhodes scholar; by the 1930s he'd be a brilliant and successful corporation lawyer; by the mid-1950s, he'd be an associate justice of the Supreme Court of the United States.) Harlan it was who had charge of arrangements for the annual "P-rade"; he'd led the cheers, organized the smoker, and supervised the presentation of "stunts" by companies of his unit. "[He] certainly is wonderful at putting thru anything he undertakes," said Adlai, who felt "very much honored" when Harlan called upon him in his room on a September Sunday afternoon. Nevertheless, he suspected that a desire for his friendship was not the sole motive for Harlan's call, since "Harlan inquired particularly for you and Buff— when you were coming etc.," as he wrote his mother. With such mixed emotions of half pride, half disillusionment, he discovered that his hero had given Buffie a "big rush" during the Washington social whirl early in 1918, particularly at a coming-out party for Courtney Letts, and that Buffie continued to loom large among Harlan's multiple interests.

When Adlai returned to Princeton after the Christmas holidays, in January 1919, it was to a university rapidly reforging its links, partially broken by the war, to a long historical past. The "old customs" which it had been "difficult to maintain" were restored full force on the campus, and student attention, no longer distracted by enforced martial pursuits or by events abroad, again centered upon the traditional interests of undergraduates. On January 23, 1919, he began "heeling" for the *Daily Princetonian*, the student newspaper. His college career had begun.

Book Two

THE EMERGING INDIVIDUAL

CHAPTER SEVEN

"A Real Princeton Man"

Perhaps as good a way as any to assess the over-all effect of Princeton on Adlai Stevenson is to contrast it with the effect of the university upon another eager youth from the Middle West, one who had been admitted precisely five years before Adlai was and whose experience of life was to have some effect, incalculable but real, upon Adlai's own. It was on September 23, 1918, that Adlai informed "Dearest Mum" of his admission to the university. ("This has been a most successful day," he wrote.) It was on September 24, 1913, which happened also to be his seventeenth birthday, that one F. Scott Fitzgerald wired *his* mother (whom, in a complicated way, he hated): ADMITTED SEND FOOTBALL PADS AND SHOES IMMEDIATELY PLEASE WAIT TRUNK. Fitzgerald then settled into a room in a stuccoed house at 15 University Place and prepared to conquer glory.

The Princeton world which Fitzgerald entered was slightly smaller than the one Adlai was to know. It contained approximately fifteen hundred students, as compared with around two thousand in 1919 (Adlai's freshman class contained a little over five hundred) and it was yet, in physical appearance, not greatly changed from the Princeton of the 1890s. Nassau Street was yet unpaved (only six Princeton students had automobiles in 1913; hundreds had them in 1918), as were many other streets whose pavements Adlai would walk. Palmer Stadium, where Adlai was to spend so many exciting Saturday afternoons, was under construction. The Gothic undergraduate commons in the northeast corner of the campus had not yet been built (it would be opened in 1915), and several of the buildings had not yet been begun which were to shift the center of the university's physical plant to a point some one hundred yards south of McCosh Walk by the time Adlai entered.

But in most essential respects this Princeton world of Fitzgerald's was identical with that which Adlai knew. Actually, as force or influence, it was a double world, with one powerful portion of it a contradiction of the other portion, equally powerful. It therefore produced in each entering student a tension which, if sometimes creative, was always dangerous. Facing Princeton's two worlds, the undergraduate was challenged either to make a flat choice between them, rejecting one while accepting the other, or to resolve their contradictions in some "higher synthesis." The student who could do neither was certain to be badly hurt and might be wholly lost.

One of the two worlds was in many ways a creature of Woodrow Wilson, whose ideal for the college was much the same as that toward which Choate, as educational process, was aimed. Education should be a living thing instead of a cut-and-dried system of lectures, textbook assignments, and recitations by rote. It should inspire in men a passion for public service. (He wrote: "Who is 'noble' amongst us? He who spends his energy outside the circle of self-interest.") To this end he had led his faculty into a radical revision of the curriculum, introducing the four-course honors system. He had led his trustees to approve, and had himself raised much of the money to finance, a preceptorial system modeled somewhat on Oxford's. He drew to Princeton fifty outstanding young men to serve as tutors. With them he sought to transform the undergraduate college from "a place where . . . youngsters [are] doing tasks to a place where . . . men [are] doing thinking . . . conversing about the things of thought . . . eager and interested in the things of thought."

But as Wilson led Princeton along the path of his purpose, he inevitably came into conflict with the second of the Princeton worlds, one which was essentially anti-intellectual and hostile to his concept of a college community. This second world was divisive in its effect on the student body. It sought to perpetuate attitudes and ways of life that made unyielding distinctions between men, not primarily on a basis of individual worth as measured by intellect and moral character, but on a various categorical basis of birth, wealth, social grace, and extracurricular achievement. Wilson came to regard this second world as intolerable by the university he was making. Boldly he set out to eliminate it. Instead, he was himself eliminated, having raised such a storm of opposition (involved in it was a question as to the location of the Graduate College) that he was glad to escape from his college presidency into New Jersey's gubernatorial race in 1910.

The capital of this second world, so to speak, was Prospect Avenue, lined on both sides by the beautiful and luxurious homes of upper-classmen's clubs: Ivy, Cap and Gown, Cottage, Colonial, Tiger Inn, Quadrangle—some seventeen of them by the time Adlai Stevenson came to Princeton. These were the end products of a process that had begun in the late 1870s, in the social vacuum resulting from President McCosh's firm suppression of Greek-letter fraternities. Small eating clubs were formed at that time, perfectly innocent and innocuous. They did not even have names at first: each was simply a group of students having like interests and congenial tastes who took their meals together in one of the boardinghouses scattered around the town. Then, in the early '80s, one of these groups rented a small building to be used as a clubhouse. Ivy Hall, it was, on Mercer Street, built originally for the Princeton Law School. Thus the Ivy Club was born. Soon its example was followed by other groups, and the custom was established of choosing second-semester sophomores each February to replace seniors lost by graduation. Within a decade the Princeton club system was deeply rooted in the college life; and as their alumni prospered the clubs became more exclusive, their houses more elaborate, their arrangement more precise in a hierarchy of snobbism. They generated loyalties and values and codes so pervasive that no student could be entirely unaffected by them. For their members they also provided places of relaxation and social activity so luxurious as to justify, in part, a widespread designation of Princeton as "the finest country club in the East."

The whole of this process was strongly influenced by the fact that Princeton has always been the most "southern" of northern colleges. Before the Civil War, it often happened that half the student body came from below Mason and Dixon's line. They made integral to the developing Princeton tradition—the tradition in which the club system grew—many of the manners and prejudices, and even some of the social philosophy, of the southern planter aristocracy.

One result was the production of a "Princeton man" who could be quite sharply distinguished from, say, a "Harvard man" or a "Yale man." (Of course such sweeping categorical generalizations are always inaccurate in detail: they ignore the real differences between the real men who are categorized: but as summings up of dominant characteristics they serve a useful descriptive purpose.) It was of the essence of the "Harvard man" that he be not a type at all but a strong individualist; Harvard seems always to have encouraged intellectualism and individualism, the latter sometimes to the point of eccentricity. Contrariwise, it was of the essence of the "Yale man" that he *be* a type: athletic, hearty, extroverted, ambitious, and intensely competitive. The Yale fraternity and senior-society system generally encouraged a frank and open pursuit of "success," and everyone "knew" that he who was tapped by Skull and Bones had his financial security virtually assured. But the "Princeton man" was different from these. It was of his essence that he be neither a strong individualist (to be at all eccentric was to risk being tabbed a "bird") nor a conformist whose conformity was molded by an openly confessed ambition. He was, above all, "smooth"—that is, socially adroit and graceful. ("I think of Princeton," Scott Fitzgerald would have one of his fictional characters say, "as being lazy and good-looking and aristocratic.") He dressed well, talked well, danced well; he had a casual, insouciant charm, he looked upon "bourgeois" manners and values with amused contempt, as an aristocrat should, rather than with angry hatred, as proletarians are supposed to do.

The "Princeton man," as a matter of fact, avoided all extremes like the plague: to express strong commitments or aversions on any subject save an admittedly trivial one, like sports, was to be accused of "running it out," and to "run it out" was the deadliest of social sins. Thus, while Princeton's competitions in Adlai Stevenson's day were as fierce as any in the Yale system, it was necessary that the competitor *seem* not to be seriously competing at all. He must, above everything, maintain good form. To make one of the "best" clubs, for instance, was the major ambition of a great majority of freshmen and sophomores; but for that very reason one seldom saw a freshman or sophomore sauntering down Prospect Avenue. A club membership, like virtually every other ultimate reward of Princeton success, must be approached indirectly, with a careful concern for the aesthetic quality of the acts through which the approach was made.

Upon this glittering world the seventeen-year-old Scott Fitzgerald bent a gaze that was at once far more sophisticated and far more naïve than that which the eighteen-year-old Adlai Stevenson looked upon it five years later. Though abnormally conscious of class distinctions, he was unable to determine to which class he himself belonged—and his upbringing (his mother had spoiled him badly) had encouraged his belief in the injustice of a world that so often refused to defer to *his* feelings, *his* wishes. Hence his view of Princeton was colored by such personal insecurities as Adlai Stevenson had never known.

But it was also sharpened by these. The outsider who longs to get in is always aware of things which the insider, taking them for granted, doesn't really notice at all, and Fitzgerald was a sensitive observer. His vision, if badly distorted in some ways, saw at once in the Princeton landscape many subtle variations of which Adlai Stevenson (as freshman and sophomore, anyway) remained blandly, cheerfully unaware. Fitzgerald's was a calculating look. Princeton was a world he meant to conquer: he *had* to conquer it if he were to feel secure in it: and as he closely studied the terrain over which he must advance, he shrewdly assessed the various routes by which he might achieve those heights occupied by the "Big Men" of the campus. He also assessed the relative value of the weapons others had used and that such as he might employ for conquest.

Football was of course the surest way to distinction, but a single afternoon on the freshman squad was enough to convince him, and the coach, that this way was closed to him. (He weighed just 138 pounds, as compared with Adlai's 137, and his height of five feet, seven inches, was two inches less than Adlai's.) Next in the hierarchy of prestigious activities was the Triangle Club, annually producing a student-written musical comedy which toured major cities during the Christmas holidays. Only slightly below Triangle, and perhaps even equivalent with it, was the *Daily Princetonian;* certainly a "Prince" board member had a considerable persuasive power, and if he did not use it to command an equivalent social prestige, the fault was his alone. (One "Prince" editorialist was to arouse Fitzgerald's awe by boldly attacking the club system itself!) After the student newspaper came the student humor magazine, the *Tiger,* and on approximately the same level with this was the Philadelphian Society, which was Princeton's equivalent of the Y.M.C.A. whose officers were invariably men of weight and influence. Considerably below all these, but still possible if one were brilliant enough, was the *Nassau Literary Magazine.*

Alas for Woodrow Wilson's dream, high scholarship never presented itself to Fitzgerald, nor to Adlai Stevenson five years later, as a possible avenue to glory; it did not even appear particularly valuable in itself. But success in any of the other above-named endeavors would assure a bid to a good club in the middle of the sopho-more year. Major success would assure a bid from one of the "best" clubs. Accordingly, Fitzgerald concentrated on Triangle, spending much of his freshman year writing the libretto for a show which Triangle accepted the following September and produced at the end of his first sophomore semester. He also contributed to the *Tiger* and the *Nassau Lit*, and wrote a farce produced by the Elizabethan Dramatic Club in September of 1914. The following February he was elected secretary of the Triangle Club; a little later, having rejected bids from Cannon, Quadrangle, and Cap and Gown, he went into Cottage, a very prestigious club indeed, "Though," as he confessed later, "I might have been more *comfortable* in Quadrangle . . . where there were lots of literary minded boys." He was elected to the edi-torial board of the *Tiger* in May. He could look forward with con-fidence to the presidency of Triangle and, in his last year, to election to the Senior Council, the latter being the ultimate of Princeton glory.

(His confidence was curiously sustained by the fact that his strik-ingly handsome person was topped by blond hair. He went through the Princeton yearbooks for the ten years preceding his entrance and found, from a study of pictures of the Senior Council, that two thirds of its members were light-haired men despite the fact that "only about thirty-five percent of every class here are blonde."[1] This meant "that out of every *fifteen* light-haired men in the senior class *one* is on the senior council and of the dark-haired men it's only one in *fifty*." There is no evidence that Adlai Stevenson, reading this "sci-entific" analysis at the end of his sophomore year, was particularly disturbed by the fact that his own yet abundant hair was dark.)

It was a brilliant career. It contained, however, a fatal flaw. If scholarship was no path to glory, a minimum of it was required by the college authorities. Fitzgerald, completely absorbed into extra-curricular activities, failed to achieve the minimum. In November of his junior year, having been declared ineligible for further extra-curricular enterprises and fallen ill of malaria, he dropped out of college to avoid being flunked out (as he would certainly have been) at the term's end. He came back the following year and completed his work as a junior, but he had forever lost his chance to become a "Big Man." In October of his senior year he went into the Army

[1] *This Side of Paradise* (New York: Charles Scribner's Sons, 1920), p. 140.

as the "world's worst second lieutenant," spending all his free time in the Officers' Club, first at Fort Leavenworth and then at Camp Taylor in Kentucky, writing a novel whose subject was himself, and Princeton. . . .

The whole experience hurt Fitzgerald badly as a human being. As Mizener has said,[2] it fixed permanently in him his sense of social security, and it caused him all his life long to overvalue the "badges and medals" of a "success" he had almost, but not quite, achieved.

II

The contrasts between this career and Adlai Stevenson's, amidst the same scenes and under the same external pressures, can of course be partially accounted for by differences in background, social status, and past experiences. Adlai began his race for those honors Fitzgerald prized so highly with advantages that Fitzgerald wholly lacked. He had family. He had economic security. He came from a prep school which, though small, was recognized as in all respects first rate. From the day of his enrollment he was a member of that "in-group" to which Fitzgerald, for all his striving, could never quite penetrate. John Harlan, the "high duke" of the campus, president of the class of '20, and full of other honors, was Adlai's personal friend. So were many of the other "Big Men." When the Choate Club of Princeton was organized in early February, he was elected secretary. ("The rub regarding the officers is that the president and vice-president must be from the upper classes and the Sec. from the freshman class," he explained to his father. "In other words, I got elected, by some miracle, over the other freshman.") There was never any doubt that he would receive bids from the best clubs, and of these it might have been predicted that he would choose (as he did) the Quadrangle.

But such external differences in initial advantage are by no means the sole explanation of the fact that Adlai Stevenson made a success of Princeton by the standards Scott Fitzgerald employed, whereas Fitzgerald himself failed by almost any standards one might apply. Far more important, as explanation, were internal differences—those of mind and character. Fitzgerald's was a divided nature, Stevenson's an integrated one.

[2] Arthur Mizener, *The Far Side of Paradise: A Biography of F. Scott Fitzgerald* (Boston: Houghton Mifflin Company, 1951), pp. 54–55.

At the very beginning, as a precocious youngster just turned seventeen, Fitzgerald looked upon Princeton's double world with what Malcolm Cowley,[3] in a somewhat different sense, called a "double vision," aware in the upper reaches of his mind that the glittering objects of the club world were really only brightly colored bubbles, fun to play with and for, but not worth a truly vital commitment, yet at the same time emotionally involved in the pursuit of those objects to a degree Stevenson would have found absurd. The tension between the two views was, as Mizener indicates, the chief determinant of his art. With a terrific effort of the imagination, employing the full forces of a major literary talent, Fitzgerald would strive to give depth to the superficial and meaning to the essentially meaningless, creating in the process much of the consciousness of a whole generation—the "Jazz Age" which he named.

By contrast, Stevenson's approach was far more innocent, far less complex—and far more wise. Stevenson engaged in no such shrewd appraisal of terrain as Fitzgerald made; there's no evidence that he consciously set out to be a "Big Man" at all; he merely accepted the double world as it was, uncritically, and sought to do his "duty" within it (fulfilling felt family obligations) to the best of his ability. If he chose as his major activity precisely the one which, given his special aptitudes, was most likely to lead him into the "Big Man" category, it was only because those same aptitudes caused him to regard journalism as an interesting career possibility. The nature of his hero-worship was significantly different from Fitzgerald's. What Fitzgerald most passionately admired was the glamor, the popularity, the power which surrounded the "Big Man" like a halo. What Adlai Stevenson most admired was sheer ability—the ability to "get things done" and done well. John Harlan, his greatest hero of those years, made things "work" superlatively, and it was this capacity, in Adlai's view, which caused Harlan to be twice elected president of his class, to be made chairman of the board of the *Princetonian* ("he is an excellent chairman, and works awfully hard at it himself"), and to be elected not only to the Senior Council but to the chairmanship of that august body in the fall of 1919. This over-all ability of course involved a measure of popularity; one could not lead men to work well together toward common goals if one were not personally liked; but the solid core of this liking must be a respect earned by ob-

[3] In *The New Yorker*, January 30, 1945, p. 54. Quoted by Mizener, ibid., p. 60.

jective accomplishments. To pursue popularity as an end in itself seemed to Adlai Stevenson, even as an eighteen-year-old, a senseless enterprise. (He was realistic, however, in his appraisal of the advantages he gained from Harlan's friendship—and since he had a shrewd notion that this friendship was at least partially motivated by Harlan's interest in Buffie, he was not averse to encouraging his sister, now and then, to accept Harlan's invitation to club dances and the like. In one of his letters he mentioned, as a passing remark buried in a closing paragraph, that Harlan had asked him "if Buff was going to be up here at the time of the Junior Prom" on March 15. "I think he is going to ask her," he went on, "and I think it advisable that she be here as he will probably head the Prom, if he is reelected Pres. of the class"—which Harlan was. . . .)

His career attitudes at Princeton, essentially the same as those with which he had become a "pretty big dude" at Choate, are clearly revealed in his letters. "Thus far I have written 2 stories for the 'Prince' and both were printed," he reported home on January 29, 1919, just a week after he'd begun to "heel" for the *Princetonian*. "It is awfully hard work but quite worth while and interesting. I was talking to Jim Douglas the other day and he urged me to stay out for it. I have to write a story a day from now on." Yet when he feared that his *Princetonian* activity might dangerously impair his scholastic standing, he was perfectly prepared to sacrifice the former to the latter. "The freshman uniform tests begin tomorrow and if I fail any of them I think I will drop the 'Prince' as it takes a great deal of time and I haven't much chance of making it this competition anyway," he reported on February 8, just three days after his nineteenth birthday. By that time he was one of only thirteen men who had been retained in the competition out of the thirty-seven who had started it, but, as he pointed out, only two men were to be taken on the board. Since "several fellows are way ahead of me," he felt that his own chances were slim. But he failed no subjects in the examinations, and John Harlan joined Jim Douglas in urging him to stay out. He decided to do so "for awhile longer, as I hate to be a quitter."

In the end, having produced an exceptional quantity and quality of copy, he won the competition. By the close of his freshman year he was a member of the newspaper's board and well on his way toward a top editorial position.

The whole of this experience he made an integral part of himself

—he grew into it and absorbed it into his total being—in a way Fitzgerald was unable to do either with his college experience or with his later ones. As a result, the Princeton which corrupted Fitzgerald, fixing in him his sense of insecurity, would have an opposite effect on Stevenson. The latter's college career speeded the process of continuous balanced growth (mind-body-spirit progressing as organic unit) which, from the outset, had been characteristic of him. Fitzgerald lost poise, Stevenson gained it, and that which drove sharp wedges into Fitzgerald's psyche, further splitting it, merely gave to Stevenson a wider range of possible attitudes (he would learn to employ them quite consciously, like an actor), plus a higher social polish. Princeton encouraged in Fitzgerald that fiscal irresponsibility for which he became notorious ("All big men have spent money freely," he told his mother petulantly when she remonstrated with him) and which kept him continuously in debt during the years of his highest income. Upon Stevenson's attitude toward personal finances Princeton's club world had no effect whatever. He continued to be "frugal as only the rich can afford to be," in the words of John Bartlow Martin.[4]

And of all the influences that played upon Adlai Stevenson at Princeton, not the least was that of Scott Fitzgerald himself. During the early months of 1919, while Stevenson was "heeling" so industriously for the *Princetonian,* Fitzgerald in New York was writing short stories and garnering with them 122 rejection slips which he "pinned in a frieze around my room." In the summer of 1919, while Stevenson was again at the H F Bar ranch in Wyoming, Fitzgerald was rewriting the novel he'd first drafted while in the Army. In the fall of 1919, when Stevenson's greatest anxiety was over the fact that his mother insisted on renting a house for Buffie and herself in Princeton ("I thought it was the cruelest thing a parent could do—coming to live at a son's school," Adlai told Buffie later), Fitzgerald's novel was accepted by Scribner's. In March of 1920 Fitzgerald and Stevenson must actually have brushed elbows, though the latter had no remembrance of it in the 1950s, for Fitzgerald was living at Cottage that month, awaiting the publication day of his novel. He attended the prom. And on March 26 the *Princetonian,* which was continuing to absorb most of Adlai's extracurricular energies, carried a small advertisement that aroused some excitement in him as it did in nearly

[4] *Adlai Stevenson* (New York: Harper & Brothers, 1952), p. 154.

every other undergraduate. It announced the publication that day of *This Side of Paradise*, "the First Novel of F. SCOTT FITZGERALD, '17. . . . A Story About a Princeton Man."

According to Mizener, Fitzgerald was distressed by the small size of the *Princetonian* ad, but he could hardly have been distressed by the effect it produced: there was a gratifying rush of buyers of his book at the Princeton University store. Among them was Adlai Stevenson, who read it avidly through two or three soft April evenings. Though he refused to remember, in his later years, that it "really influenced me very much," the evidence that it did influence him is in his letters which, almost immediately, began to have a somewhat different tone. His habitual self-deprecation—an attitude so different from Fitzgerald's outward pose, yet so consistent with Fitzgerald's inward feeling—began to wear a gloss of wry wit, and there were turns of phrase which echoed, if faintly, the Fitzgerald style. Always he had been remarkably sensitive to landscape beauty, and the lyric evocations of the Princeton landscape, which were among the best things in *This Side of Paradise*, touched a deep answering chord in his nature. (A year later he wrote to his mother, who was in Europe, agreeing with her that Montreux in April was lovely. "However," he added, "in my estimation Princeton is almost supreme at this . . . time of year and it is difficult for me to conceive of anything more beautiful than the view out toward the Junction in early morning while the grass is still damp and a mist envelopes everything.") He *would* remember, characteristically, that he was immensely impressed by the fact that "a young man, scarcely older than myself, had written this book and made such a success."

"I also remember saying, to girls on dates, about the book, 'It's a great human document,'" he told a friend, laughing, early in 1956. "'A remarkable human document,' I'd say, and look very wise and sophisticated of course. It was the thing to say that spring about that book."

Saying it gave him an exhilarating sense of "emancipation," as though he had gone above and beyond those of his generation, and of the elder generation, who found Fitzgerald "shocking" and "wicked." Saying it to girls increased the exhilaration in a year when kissing and "petting" were widely equated with an absolute "breakdown of moral values." One of the girls he said it to was a dark-haired and lovely Vassar student who might herself have come from a Fitzgerald story; he loved her for a brief season, but she quickly passed out of his world and on to marriage and life in distant parts and he was astonished by the promptness with which he "recovered." But he never quite forgot the Fitzgerald mood of the spring of 1920, nor the haunting feminine beauty which, for many weeks, pervaded his world. . . .

Thirty-six years later there were echoes of that lost mood in a note Adlai Stevenson wrote, in the midst of a particularly grueling primary campaign, to a friend who had been visiting with him, about his Princeton years. "I haven't the remotest idea where I stood in my class scholastically," he wrote. "My greatest pre-occupation was with extra-curricular activities and I think I was content with what we generally called 'a gentleman's third group.'[5] Certainly I was never threatened with Phi Beta Kappa, nor, I fear, even tempted. It was a different time [with] different mores and there are those of us who still shed a salty tear for F. Scott Fitzgerald and the departed glories of the Princeton Country Club.

"But, oh," he added, "what a *Daily Princetonian* was produced under my mothering eye!"

III

Though he had dreaded his mother's coming to Princeton and had done all he could to dissuade her from doing so (he kept insisting that he'd be much "too busy" to see her often), he was forced to admit, as the sophomore year advanced, that the arrangement was "not so bad." In October of 1919 Buffie and Helen Stevenson moved into a beam-and-brick Tudor mansion in Library Place, owned by Dean Fine. It had mullioned windows looking out over a sweep of lawn in which grew ancient gnarled apple trees and huge pines. It had a large living room with a great fireplace in which a log fire blazed cheerfully on every winter evening. And it had a garage housing the Hudson Super-six which Adlai had chosen and which he found to be very useful to him.

Soon the house became as much a center of his social life as the Quadrangle Club would be in his junior and senior years. Mrs. Stevenson engaged an efficient local Negro couple as servants, and

[5] In Princeton's peculiar grading system, the usual A, B, C, D, F (for failure) were replaced by seven groups, with group one being the highest grade. Groups one to five were passing, groups six and seven were failures. The third group, above which no gentleman need aspire, was equivalent to a C.

maintained a kind of open house for Adlai's and Buffie's friends, all of whom remembered her as a very gracious hostess, "serenely charming" in the words of Francis Comstock, later a professor of architecture at Princeton. When Adlai took his Sunday dinner in Library Place, as he usually did, he often brought with him his roommate, William E. Hale, or some of his many friends. Sometimes they called him "Rabbit" Stevenson, Buffie was amused to learn. He had, they claimed, two distinctive qualities of a rabbit. One was a passion for raw vegetables and salad (a vestige, no doubt, of his parents' vegetarian periods). The other was his habit of dashing from place to place at a half trot, "swift as a hare." . . . He put up his girls from out of town for weekends at the house, and occasionally some of his friends' dates were put up there, too. John Harlan was a very frequent visitor in Library Place—he was Buffie's chief beau that year —and Weldon Funk, Buffie's long-time Bloomington beau, came several times. Yet another frequent visitor was Dick Cleveland, whose father, Grover Cleveland, had settled in Princeton and been a trustee of the university for a decade before his death in 1908, and who had led a revolt against the club system in 1917 when he was a sophomore and Scott Fitzgerald (who was much impressed by this revolt) was a junior.

There were quiet times, too, in Library Place, when the family was alone—evenings when Adlai reclined on the floor before the fireplace, watching the bright flames curl around the logs while Buffie or her mother read aloud; sometimes Buffie, whose interest in the theater remained unabated, did imitations, a particular favorite of hers (and Adlai's) being a take-off of Irene Bordoni singing "Why Do You Make Zose Eyes at Me?" From the house they went out for family drives through the lovely countryside, picking great bouquets of colored leaves in the autumn, and Adlai and Buffie went for long tramps through the snow on winter Sundays.

But though Adlai spent far more time in Library Place than he had said he would do, this did not belie the fact that he was, as he'd said, "very busy." He was always "on the go"—to classes, to Choate Club and other organization meetings, to the *Daily Princetonian* office—and when he came to his mother's house he usually carried with him a brief case loaded with books and papers. He worked at them, too, conscientiously.

"I didn't like mathematics or the physical sciences," he explained long afterward, talking of his college days. "But I enjoyed geology so much—and not because it was easy!—that I well remember regretting that I had not had more of the natural sciences. But certainly my tastes were largely humanist and I loved the history and English and literature courses—*all* history and all literature. I suppose, actually, it has been the same ever since. A page of mathematical equations makes me shudder and the books mounting around me make me angry that there is so little time for reading."

When the Christmas holidays came Adlai spent them in Library Place, where the family was joined by Lewis Stevenson. It was a happy family time. December 25, Buffie reported to her diary, was "one of the happiest days I've ever spent." She listed her reasons for thinking so, of which the first was, "not a single family row!"

Lewis Stevenson had returned to his farm-management duties in Bloomington early in 1919. Most of his energies were focused, however, upon a very different enterprise. In Washington he had become interested in German Zeppelins, which, he thought, might become almost as important to the travel of the future as railroads were to the travel of 1918. Accordingly, when released from his Navy duties, he had organized a syndicate to acquire the American rights to basic patents for German lighter-than-air craft, and had managed to interest Dr. Johann Schuette, a German inventor and engineer who had built twenty-two dirigibles, in the leasing of such rights. He had lined up as investors a most distinguished list of men, including Owen D. Young, David Goodrich, William Wrigley, Jr., Marshall Field, R. B. Mellon, and Franklin D. Roosevelt. The plan was to establish a Zeppelin line between Chicago and New York, and of this plan he was full of sparkling talk that Christmas season. Adlai listened with avid interest.

IV

They talked, too, of politics. . . .

Woodrow Wilson, whom all of them so greatly admired, was now a tragic figure. Republicans, by a narrow margin, had gained control of the Congress in 1918, and Wilson, as Lewis Stevenson admitted, had made a grave error when he had appointed no Republican leaders to the U.S. delegation which he personally headed at Versailles. The President had managed to have the Covenant of the League of Nations incorporated in the Treaty of Versailles, but he had returned to find key Republicans in the Senate, notably Henry Cabot

Lodge of Massachusetts, bitterly hostile to the ratification of that treaty. Lodge, chairman of the Senate Foreign Relations Committee, introduced reservation after reservation when the treaty was before the Senate in the summer of 1919; these, or any other reservations, the equally implacable Wilson refused to accept; and when a joint resolution of the Congress was adopted, declaring the war with Germany at an end, Wilson promptly vetoed it. At this crucial juncture the President, despite the warning of his physician, decided to carry his case directly to the people. In September he set out to make thirty-seven speeches in a three-week swing through the Middle and Far West. He got as far as Pueblo, Colorado. There, on the speaker's platform, he collapsed; he was brought to Washington partly paralyzed.

An invalid in the White House, he must now watch in action that "Congressional government" which he himself had once advocated in a book bearing that title. In practice, government by Congress proved to be irresponsible government, as it had always done before in our history, most tragically in the decade preceding the Civil War. Lodge, Borah, Hiram Johnson, La Follette—these were bent (if from different motives) on frustrating what they knew to be the will of the national majority. In the absence of strong executive leadership they had thus far been able to do so.

And it was in the shadow of these events that Lewis and Adlai Stevenson discussed the political situation that Christmas of 1919. If the issue were placed squarely before the American people, there was still little doubt that the United States would sign the Versailles Treaty and become a member of the League. But Lodge had it in his power to delay final action until such time as his view gained a wider, solider support, and there was no doubt that his side *was* gaining.

After the long creative excitement of Populism and Progressivism and the New Freedom, after the enormous effort of war, the people seemed to want a rest. They seemed to be tired of reform, tired of idealism, tired of heroics, tired even of the responsibilities of self-government—and with this gathering mood of irresponsibility, an irresponsible government was perfectly consistent. When the people want a rest, said Lewis Stevenson—when they want a do-nothing government—they vote Republican. In terms of their want, they were right to do so—for though mediocrity was no Republican monopoly, God knew, there being plenty of it in Democratic ranks, it was only the Republican party which made of mediocrity a political principle. Not once since the Civil War had the Republicans put into the White House a man who approached the first-rate—with the possible exception of Teddy Roosevelt, who got in by accident—and they certainly would not do so in 1920.

"If they win," said Adlai.

"If they win," agreed his father—for it did not "pay" to be defeatist.

Adlai, who'd been arguing the League issue and politics in general at Whig Hall meetings, and at the *Princetonian* office, too, was forced to agree about the gathering mood of the times. Certainly the mood at Princeton was far different from what it had been (or so he had been told) in the days of Woodrow Wilson's university presidency. A high proportion of Princeton's student body was Democratic, but this was due more to Princeton's southern traditions than it was to a belief in Wilsonian idealism or in the domestic policies of the New Freedom. Princeton students *did* seem to want to "take it easy" and "have fun" to a greater degree than they had formerly done. Not that Adlai himself objected strongly. He "went along," and had fun too. But he could see, as one example of the new mood, that no such movement as that which Dick Cleveland had led against the club system would have the slightest chance of success in the school year of 1919–20.

Well, anyway, said Lewis Stevenson, he himself was definitely going to attend the Democratic National Convention in June. He was also planning a business-and-pleasure trip to Europe during the summer, but the trip would have to wait until the convention was over. And why didn't Adlai plan to come to the convention too?

But Adlai shook his head. He and a group of his friends were planning a European trip themselves that summer, and they'd want to spend as much time overseas as possible before the fall term opened.

CHAPTER EIGHT

Educative Interlude:

Europe, 1920

It was in late June—after Republicans in the notorious "smoke-filled" room convention had given the presidential nomination to Warren G. Harding with Calvin Coolidge as running mate, and while the Democratic convention was fighting its way through ballot after ballot toward the nomination of James M. Cox for President and Franklin D. Roosevelt for Vice-President—that Adlai Stevenson sailed with a party of Princeton friends including Bill Tucker, Tom Matthews, Jack Wainwright, and Monk Hackney. They sailed on the S.S. *New York*, docking in Southampton in early July.

There followed weeks of that indefatigable sight-seeing which was already characteristic of Adlai Stevenson's travels and which, in later years, would arouse in exhausted traveling companions both awe and dismay. His curiosity was as insatiable as his physical energy seemed limitless.

Sometimes with his friends, sometimes alone, he wandered for hours through London's streets and parks. He went through Windsor Castle and Westminster Abbey, where the "contemplation of the tombs of ancient kings" had upon him an awesome but incommunicable effect. He visited Limehouse at night and found it disappointingly tame. He spent five wonderful days in Oxford where he visited all the colleges—and, one golden day, went punting up the Isis into open country to eat a picnic lunch in a green rolling meadow under an ancient oak, looking out across a landscape dotted with thatched cottages. He and his companions walked twenty-four miles from Oxford to Banbury. They saw Kenilworth, Warwick Castle, and *Cymbeline* in the Memorial Theatre at Stratford-on-Avon. Back in

London he attended the opening of a new comedy, *I'll Leave It to You*, and next morning, with Bill Tucker, "left for Paris by *Airplane!*"

The plane passage, he reported to his mother, cost forty-two dollars—about two and a half times as much as the cost by boat and train. "It sounds pretty extravagant but it was, I think, altogether worth it for the experience was wonderful and the trip across the channel is beastly and [there is] an awful lot of trouble with customs, etc." Sitting in a wicker chair in what he described as a "huge" Handley-Page, he—who was to spend so many hours in planes—saw the world for the first time from the air: the "toy boats" in the channel, the fields of France looking "like a vast puzzle composed of pieces of wood and in straight geometrical figures and painted all shades of browns and greens."

He "did" Paris as all American tourists "do" Paris, albeit with a heightened awareness of historic significances: Notre Dame, the Louvre, Montmartre, Versailles, including the now thrice-historic Hall of Mirrors. With Tucker and Frank Murray, another classmate, he went to Coblenz on the Rhine, in the American Occupied Zone of Germany and managed somehow to get across the bridge into unoccupied Germany and thence to Berlin, where they were befriended by some now "unemployed" Prussian officers, older than they and, oh, so much more experienced! The officers talked sadly of the war and cynically of the future, leaving the ever inquisitive student with much to ponder. And the officers enabled them to see Berlin as few Americans might then see it; they saw Potsdam, too, with its arrogant grandeurs.

Back in Paris he and two companions obtained a room together in the Oxford and Cambridge Hotel and, that night, joined nine other friends in a tour of the city which was climaxed by a visit to the Folies-Bergère. "Imagine my astonishment to see Father walk in all of a sudden!" he wrote home. "Of course he *said* he was looking for me but it certainly looked as though he had started out on a little party of his own and I had accidentally interrupted it. I met Father and Buff for lunch the next day and hung around with them most of the time for the next few days until [Buff and I] started for Switzerland." Lewis Stevenson went to Berlin on Zeppelin business, and Buffie and Adlai, though they had "a delightful if quiet stay in Zermatt," rather wished they'd gone to Berlin, too, where their father "from all his accounts . . . must have had an intensely interesting and valuable time—hobnobbing with German capitalists, etc."

Adlai, with a guide and a party of strangers, climbed the Breithorn, in what he proudly announced to his mother was remarkably fast time, but was so footsore upon his return that he could not do the Matterhorn next day as he had planned.

He came down from Zermatt to Montreux instead, moving into a luxury hotel with Buffie and his father and meeting the wealthy Mrs. Stanley McCormick "of Chicago, Washington, New York," who was to be the means through which a great influence was exerted on Buffie's life. For on the evening before Adlai was to leave Switzerland, Buffie had a long visit with Mrs. McCormick who, learning of Buffie's interest in "psychology" (for Buffie it was a quest for the meaning of life), "fairly shouted" that the place for Buffie to go was Zurich and that the man with whom she should study was her own friend and teacher, Dr. Carl Jung. On the day after she'd said goodby to Adlai, Buffie motored with Mrs. McCormick in her Rolls-Royce to Zurich; and on September 18, the day Adlai sailed from Cherbourg on the *Mauretania,* Buffie wrote her brother a long letter from the Hotel Baur au Lac in Zurich, reporting her first glowing impressions of Jung. Adlai read her letter in Princeton, as he plunged into the classwork and, especially, the extracurricular activities of his junior year. . . .

II

To review the summer of 1920 in terms of Adlai Stevenson's education is to gain interesting insights into that which was fixed or static in his character and that which was changing through continuous growth. Both elements of himself were highlighted in his accounts of his experiences, in letters to his mother, and by the memories he retained of the trip thirty-five years later.

Permanently fixed in him, and unchanging, was his careful attitude toward money. No one could read his letters from Europe without being impressed by his numerous precise references to the prices of things. Arriving in London, he sent his mother a post card with three sentences hastily scrawled upon its face. "Everything is much cheaper here than in N.Y.," said one of the three, "and they say Paris is *very much* cheaper than London." A few days later he and his friends were fitted for suits by one of the best London tailors. "I was very well satisfied with mine," he reported, "but was sorry we couldn't get them any cheaper." He was more than satisfied, however, by the price of board and lodgings in a "very quaint old private house" in Oxford; though "it seems impossible it is the truth" that the price was only two pounds and sixteen shillings (or ten dollars) a *week*.

This fiscal concern was in part dictated by his realization that the money he spent was unearned by him; conscience bade him make sure that every cent he spent of money not his own be wisely spent. But this fact is countered by the fact that his mother, in her copious written advice to him, often urged him to be *less* prudent, *less* thrifty. Moreover, his attitude toward money, which contrasts so sharply with Scott Fitzgerald's, seems consistent with his apparent attitude toward the people he met upon his travels— an attitude also sharply contrasting with that which Fitzgerald would have had in the same circumstances. There is even a sense in which the two attitudes, in each man, seem continuous with one another, being merging aspects of the same strand of character. Certainly Fitzgerald, who was so extravagant in his expenditure of money, was equally extravagant in his expenditures of personal emotion: he was passionately attracted and repelled by people, sometimes attracted and repelled simultaneously by the same person: and the result was that his fiscal insolvency was matched, in depressed periods, by a bankruptcy of the emotions. That the latter would become a permanent condition was the greatest fear of his life. Adlai Stevenson, on the other hand, seems to have been as instinctively prudent in his paying-out of personal feelings to others as he was in his payments out of pocket.

He was seldom solitary that summer. He never traveled alone from place to place. Always he was with people, and often his companions formed a sizable group with whom he shared rooms, meals, sightseeing expeditions. In such circumstances there are inevitably many opportunities for personal irritations, for the development of strong likes and antipathies, and for the making of invidious comparisons among one's associates. There is no evidence in his letters, however, that any of these opportunities were realized in him. His associates all belonged to that class of men—a very large class, from his point of view—known as "fine fellows." He made no effort to characterize them as individuals. Nor did he achieve this benign attitude through any apparent personal aloofness. On the contrary, he was, to all appearances, very much a member of his group. The pronoun "I" was infrequent in his letters home: generally it was "we saw this" or "we went there" or "we did that": and at least one of his companions would recall that "Steve was the one you imposed on, the one you got to do everything," because he was so willing and conscientious, if sometimes quite notably inefficient. No, there was no noticeable withdrawal, no obvious refusal to become emotionally engaged. There was simply a prudence, a thriftiness in his handling of vital coins, as though he chose not to spend his passions and critical energies upon immediate personalities when he might buy so much more with them in *generalized* human situations and from scenes that were new to him, and strange.

In all this he remained essentially the same as he had been in Choate, or in Bloomington as a boy. But in another element of his character, as has been said, he was changing that summer, growing steadily and rapidly. Obvious in his letters was a sharpening and an enlargement of his critical faculties, his capacity to define and weigh and judge.

On his first Tuesday night in London, for example, he and his friends dined well at a restaurant off Shaftesbury Avenue, then started back to their hotel, encountering on the way a couple of the Yale boys who had been ship companions. They were "well under way to getting uproariously tight so we went along to keep them out of trouble." One of the Yale men was on the Yale *Record* and, because he and Adlai thus had a common interest in college journalism, he became Adlai's charge after the pubs had closed at ten o'clock. The two became separated from the others on the way to the hotel and the Yale boy was so very loud that Adlai felt it advisable to walk him around the block a couple of times to sober him a bit before putting him to bed. What the Yale boy revealed about himself, in his alcoholic talk, was rather shocking to Adlai. "I could not help [but] observe that the senior society system must be awfully bad at Yale," he wrote, "if it occupies such a prominent place in a Yale student's mind that he should talk about it constantly when drunk [and] . . . in a foreign country. . . . From what he said it was obvious that, although he was in Europe and experiencing altogether novel sensations, the thing which was uppermost in his mind . . . [was] the senior societies and his chances of making one. I fully believe that had he been with anyone else, an Englishman say, who

. . . had never heard of Yale, he would have talked about the same thing."

In France he was impressed by the fact that the men were unprepossessing and the women attractive ("very good-looking and awfully well-dressed") while in Berlin almost the reverse was true: German men were much more attractive than German women, the latter being, in fact, "quite unattractive" and very badly dressed. At the race track in Berlin, "there was an enormous crowd . . . and it appeared an excellent opportunity to study the German people" en masse. He took note of a phenomenon many others have noticed, namely that "individual Germans I have met have . . . impressed me very favorably, in fact I like them very much," but that the impression produced by Germans in a crowd was definitely "unfavorable." In a crowd the Germans seemed to take on the dominant characteristics of their language, which seemed to Adlai remarkably harsh and assertive and ugly. He was impressed, too, by the fact that the Germans he talked to neither admitted nor felt any "war guilt" and bitterly resented the entrance of the United States into the war.

He was also able to stand somewhat outside, and make assessments of, his experience of the German officers who befriended him and his companions in Berlin. One of them was a captain of uhlans who claimed that his unit got closer to Paris in 1914 than any other in the German Army. Another was a handsome young aristocrat named Freidrich Wilhelm von Lertz whose family had once owned a large racing stable; indeed, it was to "see the last of the Von Lertz stable" in action that Adlai and his friends had gone to the races. Still another had owned, he said, a castle on the Rhine, now occupied by the commandant of French occupation forces.

"All is now lost to me," said the latter young man. "There is no longer a place for me in my own country. All I can do is go to Japan and help to train the Japanese army."

These young men were glamorous figures: they'd lived so much, been through so much: and Adlai was impressed by their graceful, arrogant manners. He would particularly remember, thirty-five years later, how these young Prussians drank champagne with a peach in it. He did the same thing himself, to impress girls on dates, when he returned to Princeton, the gesture being made all the more "sophisticated" by the fact that the Eighteenth Amendment had by then been ratified and the Volstead Act passed over Wilson's veto.

While on his way from Paris to Coblenz he'd had a vivid sense of the price which had been paid for the carrying over of mid-nineteenth-century romanticism into an era of machine guns, and high-explosive shells, and poison gas. With it had come something else, something deeper. . . .

He, Frank Murray, and Bill Tucker had obtained their military passes into the occupied zone from a colonel Frank knew at the American military legation in Paris. They'd left Paris at nine o'clock on the night of July 29, the sixth anniversary of the declaration of war between Serbia and Austria. The night was clear and the moon was full. Soon the train was running through the shell-torn landscape, the ruined towns along the Marne. Two miles outside of Château-Thierry, Adlai gazed out through the compartment windows across the miles of churned earth, with ruined walls standing up black on hills against the brilliant moon-washed sky. A little farther on the train passed a great field of white crosses, the American cemetery where some thirty thousand soldiers and marines were buried. It was borne in upon him, as he said in a letter home, "that it was almost exactly two years and one week ago" that the battle of Château-Thierry was fought (actually American troops helped to break the German advance there in early June of 1918). And as he looked out upon the desolate scene—weirdly beautiful in silver light—a girl in the next compartment, an accomplished violinist, began to play her violin. The haunting melodies she played, the moonlit landscape of heroism and death, the consciousness that this was the anniversary of the war's beginning—these mingled to stir him to the point of tears. Thirty-five years later, when he spoke of it to a friend, he revealed almost unwittingly that this night of July 29, 1920, had been one of the great emotional experiences of his life. He revealed it in his tone of voice, and in the flippancy he suddenly employed when he feared he might be showing himself as a shallow sentimentalist.

"I was very young, you know?" he said, on a rising inflection, his lips twitching into a swift self-deprecating smile. "I'm sure that girl ended her serenade with 'The Marseillaise.' She could do no wrong."

And on his return to France from Germany he again experienced vividly the aftermath of war. He and Frank Murray arrived at midnight in a ruined town on the Belgian frontier. Having cleared customs, they walked among the ruins, seeking a place where they might sleep until the train left at five-thirty in the morning. They stretched out for a time upon a gravestone in the cemetery, then went back to the station platform where, at last, they managed to sleep a little. They were on their way to Reims and the battlefields around it; they had to change trains eight times before reaching that smashed city; and one of their stops was at Soissons. Here they hired a car and drove along the Chemin des Dames, where so many thousands had died in attack and counterattack. They also stopped at Laon, from which the German Big Bertha had shelled Paris. From Laon to Reims the train ran "over a newly constructed bed through an almost totally barren country, with trenches and barbed wire stretching away on both sides of the track." The battlefields around Reims were "practically paved with iron and, although it had been cleaned up, I found lots of unexploded shells, hand grenades, etc." In September 1914 there were some sixteen thousand houses in Reims, he learned; on November 11, 1918, there were exactly fourteen that remained intact.

Truly the price of Wagnerian glory came high. Too high. . . .

He was impressed by the contrast between the Europe of his present vision and the Europe he had seen in 1912; as the years passed, this contrast would feed his growing sense of the importance of social order and of deeply rooted historical tradition as the core of progress.

With the sharpening and enlargement of his critical faculties, that summer of 1920, came a marked improvement in his abilities as a writer. The letter in which he described his climb up the Breithorn, for example, contained an unprecedented lyricism. One paragraph of it told of the night he spent in a shelter cabin perched on a great rock five hundred feet above the Théodule Glacier, just prior to the final stage of the ascent.

"I shall never forget that night," he wrote. "It was intensely cold, the moon full and brilliant and not a cloud in the sky. . . . My window faced the Matterhorn which rose like a jagged column of granite out of a sea of sparkling white. Down below me, glittering in the moonlight, lay a vast glacier which occasionally uttered a reverberating groan as the ice cracked or moved slightly.

"In every direction great jagged peaks shot up and stood black against the unearthly blue of the sky, and over all was a choking, maddening silence. The intense cold and clearness of the atmosphere made the stars unbelievably brilliant and everything seemed magnified and brought closer while the real vastness of the scene was inconceivable. It was a sight that I shall never forget and I know hardly whether to call it beautiful or horrible for there was some-

thing about it that was awe inspiring and at the same time . . . fright-
ful and supernatural. I could not determine whether . . . I should
thank God or Satan and in fact I feel sure that there was more of
the latter in it—an awful grandeur. . . ."

III

He had predicted that Buffie, scaling Alps of the spirit in Zurich,
would "go nutty," and perhaps it seemed to him that she had done
so as he read her excited letters that autumn. "I bury myself in huge
books on psycho-analysis all the morning," she wrote in late September, "and in the afternoon I have lessons with Mrs. [Edith Rocke-
feller] McCormick. She is a Christian woman, kind, gentle, with
high ideals. . . . I am so enormously interested that all ideas of suitors and society have flown out of my head." She was, she said, learning that her "real nature" was revealed "through dreams." When
Jung returned from three weeks in London, she began her studies
under him, and her letters to Adlai became full of sage advice, studded with references to "complexes" and "persona" and the "unconscious self."

"You know your persona, Adlai Stevenson dressed in a brown golf
suit," she wrote him in late October, "but you probably have not
much idea who it is that is prompting you to say that you want to
go to Oxford & be a writer, or a diplomat or whatever you want
to be. The person who says all this is YOU—your soul or the bit
of God in you or whatever you want to call it. You have to encourage
the acquaintance of this unconscious you & learn to listen to it. . . .
Of course you must face the facts of reality, but facing them squarely
and your*self* at the *same time*—you can't be at a loss."

What Adlai thought of all this at the time is now lost to history,
for his letters to Zurich have been lost, but there can be little doubt
that he found all this emphasis on *self* to be more than a little mor-
bid. Certainly he found his sister's "babbling about psychoanalysis"
to be acutely embarrassing, sometimes, at Princeton parties in the
months that followed. Buffie herself laughingly recalled, thirty-five
years later, that "he used to get crimson" as she talked.

CHAPTER NINE

A Princetonian
Goes to Harvard

In Princeton that autumn of 1920 Adlai Stevenson's major interest for some weeks was national politics. He was one of the organizers of Princeton's Cox-Roosevelt Club; he wrote several articles for the pro-Cox *Princetonian;* he was a member of the committee which brought Governor Cox to Princeton, where the Democratic candidate spoke at Alexander Hall; he was an usher at the great student Cox rally. The central issue of the campaign, as he saw it, was presented by the League of Nations. World peace, he argued, required a strong League, and a strong League was impossible if the United States refused to join it. Since the Democratic platform and candidates were unequivocally pledged to United States membership in the League, while a hard core of the Republican party was flatly opposed to membership, surely a majority of the American people in their wisdom would cast their ballots for James M. Cox and Franklin D. Roosevelt.

His hopes may have been buoyed by the fact that Cox's speeches were well organized, forthright appeals to the intelligence of the electorate. To Adlai, Cox's arguments in favor of the League seemed unanswerable. Nor did the handsome Senator Harding attempt to answer them. Harking back to the days of William McKinley, Harding conducted a "front-porch campaign," reading to visiting delegations speeches deliberately designed to obscure his position on the League, and demonstrating in general a veritable genius for platitudinous mediocrity.

But something sick and tired in the American people responded to Harding's declaration that what the country needed was "not heroism but healing, not nostrums but normalcy, not revolution but restoration, not agitation but adjustment, not surgery but serenity, not the dramatic but the dispassionate, not experiment but equipoise, not submergence in internationality but sustainment in triumphant nationality." Few political statements in all our history can have been more hilariously absurd than this, considered merely as rhetoric (surely the Harding-coined "normalcy" was no more original than his balancing of "surgery" with "serenity"!). Yet few statements have proven more persuasive of the electorate.

Harding's victory was of landslide proportions. Only after the votes were counted did Harding discover that the central issue of the campaign had been, after all, membership in the League, and that in voting for him the people were voting against the League. The League issue, said he, was now dead.

Said Woodrow Wilson: "The people of America have repudiated a fruitful leadership for a barren independence. . . ." In doing so they had turned away from their historical and moral obligation. Soon, he predicted grimly, "we will see the tragedy of it all."

II

No such profound despair, no such premonitions of tragedy, oppressed Adlai Stevenson's spirits as, turning from the unedifying spectacle of national politics, he again devoted his abundant energies to the activities of Princeton's double world. The mood of irresponsibility which now swept the country, however costly in the long run, was remarkably enjoyable in the short run for those who did not too much resist it with moral qualms, and if Adlai's unabated conscientiousness kept him from such experiments in sex and alcohol as many of his classmates made (he would be remembered as "rather conservative" in his fun), it did not prevent his active enjoyment of that "new freedom" which, in the opening 1920s, was so different, so very different, from Woodrow Wilson's.

He managed to maintain his standing scholastically in the "gentlemanly third group," but his interest in his studies was peripheral. Practically never did he mention his classwork in letters to his parents or to Buffie. His sister, viewing his activities from Jungian heights, protested that he was wasting too much time with "the debs of Philadelphia, etc." She said, "You seem to be quite outdoing us all in the social line" and "how frothy and futile it seems." She con gratulated him upon his election to the secretary-treasurership of the Quadrangle Club, but only because "you can have a great and good influence through your position of power." She now looked upon Princeton's club system with a critical eye, being encouraged to do so by young Fowler McCormick, who was also studying at Zurich. "How about your lessons?" she asked Adlai. "Remember, this is a good time to learn!"

In February he was advanced to the second highest editorial position on the *Daily Princetonian,* a triumph his father promptly reported to the *Pantagraph* but, alas, inaccurately. Soon, an irate Adlai wrote his father that he was "assailed from all sides with clippings from the Chicago *Tribune* to the effect that I am head of the *Princetonian* [when] as a matter of fact [I] am only second." Particularly galling to him was the gloating tone of the story: "The position . . . is the highest on the paper and the most sought after honor in Princeton literary life. Young Stevenson is a junior and is not yet 21 years old." Actually the story was printed on his twenty-first birthday, and "Young Stevenson" was furious. "Once more may I protest (as usual in vain I suppose) against your assumption of the duties of my publicity manager," he wrote his father. "As in the past, when I have strenuously objected, you have . . . gone ahead and, with the apparent intent of pleasing a mere child, put things in papers which were altogether wrong in point of fact and most embarrassing to me. . . . Please desist and do me a real favor."

His anger may have been soothed by the birthday letter he received from his mother, though this too became a source of some embarrassment to him when, thirty-five years later, it was published in books and magazine articles about him. It was a typical example of the kind of influence his mother sought to exert over his growth. She wrote:

21 years old, 21 years young, 21 years wise, 21 years beloved!

Your babyhood, boyhood, and young-manhood have been a natural sweet unfolding and gradual development! Round upon round. There are no dark muddy spots thus far in your career. Since you have become a reasoning being, you have made always an earnest, honest effort towards high living. This effort is character-building. The rewards are secondary in importance. . . .

You have never wanted something for nothing, nor anything that was not rightfully yours. And so whatever in rewards come to you,

you can rejoice over Right for the sake of Right! These, my dear,
are the only principles that make for permanent success or happi-
ness, and better never be rewarded or successful than to allow these
to be forgotten for one moment. Character is better than all success
and it will bring success more certainly than friends, fortune or
talents.

A few weeks after writing this, Helen Stevenson and Buffie were
again in Europe, and as they traveled through France to Montreux,
and from Montreux to Florence and Rome, letters from Adlai informed them that the spring of 1921, like the springs of former years,
was for him a season of triumphs. In April he was elected secretary
of the board of trustees of Quad, though he "wasn't too keen for the
job." However, it wouldn't take much time, he said, and he much
preferred it to the presidency of the club, an office for which he had
been considered. At the same time he was working on an all-
university committee which, with a member of the faculty, was
drafting the constitution of a new student organization to control
"all matters pertaining to the clubs"—the administration, methods of
election, and so on. All this was in addition to a heavy load of work
on the *Princetonian.*

Nevertheless he found time to play tennis on the club courts every
afternoon, he was a fervent rooter at every baseball and track and
rowing event, and his social life had not been noticeably abated by
Buffie's strictures upon it. His principal girl that spring was Harriet
Cowles of Vassar; she was his date at the house parties in mid-May.
Coupled with his social activities was a certain anxiety concerning
his hair. It was beginning to thin, he feared, and threatened to go
ultimately the way of his father's hair and his grandfather Stevenson's. He gazed closely at himself in a mirror, tried to imagine how
he'd look bald, shuddered, and went down to Bank Street where one
Miss Green gave him a hair and scalp treatment every week until
the spring term ended.

By that time he had achieved the office his father had announced
for him in February: he was managing editor of the *Princetonian:*
and during the second week of June he represented the "Prince" at
a convention of the Eastern Intercollegiate Newspaper Association,
of which he was elected vice-president for the coming year "with
the provision, however, that I would not have to do any work!"

His greatest triumph, however, was his nomination by the Senior

Council as a candidate for the Council next year. Each spring, the twelve "most prominent" men in the junior class were nominated ("that I should be considered in that category was most unexpected"), and, of these, five were elected by vote of the entire junior class. The remaining members of the fifteen-man Council would be elected in the fall. "Of course I will not be elected among the five taken on this spring but now I at least have hopes of making it next year," he wrote his mother and sister.

His prediction came true. He was not elected that spring, but he received a very respectable number of votes.

Meanwhile he again toured Europe. With Bob Brooke, Everett Case, and Ogden West of Chicago, he sailed from New York on the *Finland* on June 25. There, in early July, he met Monk Hackney and went down with him into Spain, where Ed Hackney and John Harlan were studying through the summer at the University of Madrid. Adlai and Monk traveled back and forth across the whole of Spain for weeks, so that by the time Adlai joined his mother and Buffie in Lausanne he had much to tell of bullfights witnessed (he disliked them) and other adventures, including sleeping in a park to witness a fabulous ceremony in the great Cathedral of Burgos, on the seven-hundredth anniversary of the death of the Cid. He and two Princeton friends took Buffie with them to Venice, where Buffie, as she confessed long afterward, "was exhausted trying to keep up with my brother's appalling standards of sight-seeing." The art galleries, the doge's palace with its dungeons, St. Mark's, the Lido beach, Murano and the glass blowers—none was missed by Adlai nor, perforce, by his sister.

Back in Princeton, in September of 1921, he plunged into the last and busiest of his college years. His classwork was heavier than it had been in earlier years, and every issue of the *Princetonian* was a challenge, a problem he spent hours helping to solve. Thirty-five years later he'd remember with acute nostalgia the long nights at the printers' (the paper was printed in town), working on make-up, writing heads, supervising the staff, and dealing with "Doc" Eberlein who was the print-shop foreman. "Doc" was a typical printer, sure that the editorial staff delighted in making things hard for him: he was gruff, and acid in his remarks: but underneath all that he was very kind and gentle, and Adlai formed for him a deep affection.

"He was so amazingly patient with us," Adlai recalled long afterward. "It really must have been maddening for him at times—we changing headlines and stories at the last minute."

One headline which, alas, was not changed dealt with the return to Princeton of Professor Henry Norris Russell after a year as visiting lecturer in England. WORLD FAMOUS ASTROLOGER RETURNS TO PRINCETON, the headline said, and Adlai read it with horror the morning that issue appeared. He'd not gone down to the print shop the night before; Byron Dexter of the editorial board was make-up editor for the issue, and Adlai had left things in Byron's hands. But when Byron, tired (he'd worked till 3 A.M.), appeared at the managing editor's office Adlai treated him gently. Complimenting Dexter on a "very good" issue, Adlai added that there *was* one little thing, and pointed to the headline. The word, said he, was "astronomer."

"And that was all," Dexter told Buffie many years later. "No lecture on my awful boner. Naturally, I became your brother's devoted slave from then on!"

From time to time the *Princetonian's* editor was himself in the news. In early autumn his hope of being elected to the Senior Council was realized. As a matter of fact, he received the largest vote of any among twenty-three candidates. In the spring he was appointed to two commencement committees. In the voting for "biggest politician," he received eight votes from his classmates and placed third, the winner receiving 124 votes and the runner-up nine. He was second in the voting for the man "who *thinks* he is the biggest politician," receiving 28 votes as compared with 41 for the winner. He received two votes as "the man most likely to succeed," placing eighteenth on that list, and he was ninth on a nine-man list of those receiving votes for "best all-around man outside athletics."

During the second semester of that year his mother and sister again lived in Princeton, despite Adlai's effort to discourage their coming. In late autumn he received a letter from his mother asking him to look for a house they might rent furnished; some days later he received a special-delivery letter from his father angrily demanding that he take care of this business at once. Adlai replied: "I don't believe you would have been so peremptory in your demands . . . if you fully appreciated the exacting demands for time on an active student in the two big game weeks of his senior year. . . . Personally I can see no reason for coming to Princeton—if you want to come at all—until after Christmas—about the first of February. There is nothing doing here now and I thought perhaps the family would like to go south somewhere for Christmas—Pinehurst, Southern Pines, Camden, or some other place where mother could enjoy the weather." He hoped that she would enjoy the weather so much she'd want to stay in the South, but he hoped in vain. Helen and Buffie Stevenson were residents of Princeton in February.

June came, as it seemed, with a rush, hard on the heels of February, so busy was he. Commencement Week came: President Hibben's reception in the lovely gardens of Prospect, the last club parties, the commencement exercises themselves: and, all at once, he was a Princeton alumnus. . . .

He would be a very loyal one, returning whenever possible to class reunions and keeping close track of university affairs. Thirty-two years later—on March 22, 1954—he returned to address the Senior Class Banquet. Bits of that speech would be often quoted, and he concluded it with some extemporaneous remarks about what Princeton had meant to him personally. He said:

"Let me add a final word, gentlemen. I came here last night in darkness, after an absence of four or five years. I came with an old friend, an old classmate. We drove a little through the campus, after dusk. It was soft, the air fresh with the beginning of spring. I thought of some words that I read here long ago, written by the English poet, Alfred Noyes, who stayed for a time on the Princeton campus. They were something like this if I am not mistaken:

> *"Now lamp-lit gardens in the blue dusk shine*
> *Through dog-wood red and white,*
> *And round the gray quadrangles, line by line,*
> *The windows fill with light,*
> *Where Princeton calls to Magdalen, tower to tower,*
> *Twin lanthorns of the law,*
> *And those cream-white magnolia boughs embower*
> *The halls of old Nassau.*

"Sentimental? Yes. Nostalgic? Perhaps. Yet beautiful, true. Your days are short here; this is the last of your springs. And now in the serenity and quiet of this lovely place, touch the depths of truth, feel the hem of Heaven. You will go away then with old, good friends. And don't forget when you leave why you came."

Two months later he would return to Princeton to receive her highest recognition, the honorary degree of Doctor of Laws.

III

During this same address to the seniors, Adlai Stevenson remembered that the world into which he and his classmates graduated was "happier and more hopeful" than the one into which Princeton seniors would graduate in 1954. "A terrible war to make the world safe for democracy had just ended victoriously," he said. "A noble concept, the League of Nations, had emerged from the chaotic aftermath of that elemental struggle. It was the twilight of kings, the dawn of world-wide democracy. Optimism was boundless and people proclaimed that we were on the threshold of the new era of universal and perpetual peace and prosperity."

This memory of the prevailing mood was, no doubt, an accurate one. A "golden glow" (the phrase was Charles Beard's) emanated from a press increasingly dominated, not by professional journalists, but by business interests who imposed upon the communication of news and opinion a subtle but highly effective censorship. Nevertheless, there were dark and ugly spots in the generally bright scene, and those who saw them and assessed their significance for the future were by no means as confidently happy as Adlai remembered America to have been in that summer of 1922.

Nor was he himself carefree that year. He could not decide what he wanted to do with his life.

His major interest was journalism. It was in his blood. In the years before he went off to school he spent much time during his vacations at the *Pantagraph*, doing odd jobs for the love of it. "I have many happy recollections of trips in the neighborhood with reporters to county fairs, preparing lists of ribbon winners, etc.," he wrote in a reminiscent letter in the 1950s. "In fact, I think I knew every nook and cranny of the old *Pantagraph* building and sat at linotype machines before I had long pants." If that paper had been wholly Stevenson property he would have returned without a qualm to his home town and made his career there, perhaps emulating William Allen White whose town of Emporia, Kansas, was remarkably like Bloomington in several respects. His experiences with the *Choate News* and the *Princetonian* had convinced him that he was not without ability as a newspaperman. Like White, he might be led through journalism into creative writing, for sometimes he was quite sure that what he really wanted to be was a writer. But the *Pantagraph*, as his father pointed out, was *not* Stevenson property. Uncle Bert (Hibbard O.) Davis was the paper's publisher and active manager, and there were cousins. The political editorial policy, which was so conventionally Republican, might prove distasteful. The town was not very large. The situation *could* become unhappy.

It would be wise, Lewis Stevenson insisted, for Adlai to attend law school and have a profession. How he wished that he himself had done so! His own father, and Adlai's great-grandfather Jesse Fell, had started their careers as lawyers. Such training would be useful "no matter what you do later." Adlai himself could see that this was so: the whole of human experience—economic, political, moral, even aesthetic—was reflected in the law, and from the law careers in a score of fields seemed to radiate like spokes from the hub of a wheel. Accordingly, Adlai had agreed to enter the Harvard Law School and by the time he received his undergraduate degree he was not only entered at Harvard but had also arranged to room in Cambridge with two classmates, Charles Denby and William B. McIlvaine, Jr., and a Choate School and Harvard friend, Norman Davis, Jr., whom everyone called "B."

He had agreed, however, reluctantly. If he were not to be a newspaperman, he preferred to be a rancher in the West. Ever since the summer when he and Ralph Goodwin had first met at the H F Bar, the desire to become a rancher had competed with his desire to go into journalism, and in that summer of '22 the lure of the West was so strongly renewed that it led him into a conflict of wills with his father. Ralph Goodwin, driving his Jordan roadster from Cleveland to Wyoming, picked up Adlai in Bloomington, not long after graduation.

They went together to the T A T ranch in Wyoming, not a dude but a working ranch owned by Goodwin's sister and brother-in-law, and as the two shocked barley, stacked hay, rode the range, mended fence, and camped and fished in the mountains, they decided to try ranching together. They went so far as to look for a suitable property and notified their parents of their plans. The effect on Lewis Stevenson was explosive. Not only did he flatly refuse to give financial backing to any such venture, he also proclaimed that if Adlai were not home in time for law school he, Lewis, would come to Wyoming and bring him back!

Thus Adlai entered upon his career as a law student in a rebellious mood. The law school, he reported to his mother on September

22, "is the hardest graduate school of any kind in America" and "the most feverish place I've ever seen—everyone works *all* the time and still about 25–35 percent get dropped every year." All he'd heard since he arrived were "gruesome tales of . . . astonishing hours of work when the big reviews begin in March." Until then, he added sarcastically, it was a "comparative loaf" requiring only eight full hours of work every day. "We have so many enormous books and notebooks that we have to carry them back and forth to class in satchels," he concluded. "More bad news later." The only happy news he could report in those first weeks was that his room in Claverly Hall was "very comfortable, large, sunny, etc." and that he and his roommates had been the first new students to be taken into Lincoln's Inn, "the best of the Law School eating clubs" where there was a "splendid bunch of men" and where the food was excellent.

Cambridge seemed to him a "most unattractive place"; he doubted if he could ever "reconcile" himself to it. "Haven't seen a blade of grass, except a few square ft. on the campus [the word betrayed his assertive Princetonianism; at Harvard it's the Yard] . . . but I'm still searching," he reported in mid-October. On the following Sunday afternoon he found some. B. (Norman Davis, Jr.) borrowed a Ford and Adlai road with him out to Milton where B.'s young sister was in school. They had tea "in the demure and chaste confines of the young ladies seminary" and drove back along the Charles River as the sun went down. The blaze of sunset, the blaze of autumn leaves reflected in the river were as wine to his drooping spirit "after being cooped up in this god-forsaken city" for weeks. As for Harvard University itself, "the thing that impresses me particularly is that no-body seems to know or care to know *anyone* else." The atmosphere was "entirely different . . . from Princeton—a city club rather than a country club." He infinitely preferred the country club. "Everything," he added in bitter resignation, "is concentrated, work, play and exercise." He himself took up squash and played it every afternoon because it was "splendid exercise and doesn't take long."

By November he felt that he was gradually becoming adjusted to the hard, monotonous routine, though "we all continue to go to bed with a tacit cheer for Princeton and wake up with a groan for Harvard." (He and his roommates were overjoyed when Princeton beat Harvard in that year's football game. So was Buffie, who came up to Cambridge for the event and was taken to a tea dance at the

Hasty Pudding Club by Dale Warren and her brother.) He was even discovering that "parts of the law are quite interesting" and was encouraged, very tentatively, to believe that "I may learn to enjoy it." The belief was strengthened when, on November 7, he won his first club law case.

In December he won his second case by a point score of 25 to 15, and with a sigh of relief packed his bags and went home for one of the happiest of his Christmas holidays. Buffie would remember that Adlai and his father had a "fine time" talking over legal problems during those few days and that her brother, for all the load of work he'd been carrying, had been doing a good deal of general reading. Particularly she remembered that he'd been absorbed by Sir Arthur Quiller-Couch's *Literary Studies* and that he repeatedly urged her to read the lecture on Byron. She herself had just discovered Emerson's essays, her mind being well prepared for New England transcendentalism by her experience of Jungian psychology, and she read aloud from Emerson during the evening gatherings before the fireplace. Shortly before New Year's Adlai left Bloomington for Lake Placid where he joined some law-school friends and Boston girls and celebrated the birth of 1923 and was introduced to the delights of skiing. A month later, between semesters, he went skiing again, in New Hampshire, with a gay party of fourteen, including chaperones. "[The] whole thing, my fare and all, cost only $32 for 4 whole days," he reported.

His second semester at Harvard was somewhat happier than his first had been. Cambridge under a blanket of fresh snow became, he found, almost beautiful (soon, of course, the city snow became gray with soot, and as dully ugly as the New England winter sky), and he met some local people whom he liked very much. Especially he liked the Underwoods, whose home in Belmont became his favorite haunt on Sunday afternoons. Through all the long, hard week he looked forward to horseback rides and cross-country tramps through the snow with Lorna and Nina Underwood, and tea with all the Underwoods, and supper and bridge on Sunday evening. Lorna was so *alive!* One of the memorable nights of Adlai's life stemmed from one of Lorna's "original ideas." In the early spring, on a warm balmy Saturday evening, a fellow law student named Francis Plimpton (he would be one of Adlai's roommates next autumn), Charles Denby, and Adlai went down below Scully Square in Boston to the open-air market, accompanied by Cornelia Hallowell, Pauline Ames and, of course, Lorna. The market, stretching for blocks along a narrow, crooked street, lighted by gas flares, its crowd noises threaded through by hurdy-gurdy music, made Adlai feel that he was in southern Italy; he was enchanted by "an old and villanous oyster bar" which they all "boldly entered" and where, sitting in little alcoves on hard narrow benches, they ate "a tremendous sea food dinner." Next morning, Sunday, he went as usual for a horseback ride with Lorna—three hours in the bright early spring sunshine through mud which spattered them from head to foot. That evening (the Sunday was a typical one) he went to a Boston friend's house for supper. He enjoyed the evening, "but I must say I don't get much kick out of the parlor games—consequences and the like—which seem to be such a prevalent form of entertainment in Boston society." Lorna Underwood was vividly interested in the arts: she painted and modeled in clay: and with her, Adlai attended exhibitions in the Boston Museum of Fine Arts.

There was a miraculous quality to the coming of spring after the long rigors of a New England winter. He found himself looking upon the greening grass (there *was* some after all, under the great elms of Brattle Street) and upon the budding trees and flowers with "an air of complacency." Through much of that spring he was working a fifty-hour week, forcing his way through heavy books "and their appalling contents of undigested knowledge": he called his experience the case of "Blackstone vs. Stevenson." "We [have] a regular schedule now—from 9 to 1 each morning, from 2 to 5 in the afternoon, and from 7:30 to 10:30 at night." But he managed to survive the spring examinations—and this, like the New England spring itself, seemed to him miraculous.

One weekend he went to New York to bid bon voyage to Buffie, who was sailing for England to visit with Cousin Millie Bromwell, who had now become Millie Bromwell Bailey (she'd be Lady Bailey by the 1930s), having married the British naval attaché in Washington. Aunt Letitia Stevenson was in New York, too, having just returned from a trip around the world—gay, witty, and yet-lovely Letitia. "Did you have a good time?" she was asked. She smiled. "Do you want my advice?" she said. "Just plan your trip down to the last detail—and then cancel your ticket." But Buffie would never do that. Adlai arranged for her deck chair, and Dale Warren went aboard, too, plying Buffie, as she would always remember, "with flowers and sentiment."

Buffie, in those years, continued to fall in and out of love with quite amazing facility, rejecting proposals of marriage with a recklessness which prudent Adlai found rather breath-taking. Was she, like Aunt Letitia, to continue rejecting them? Would she, after all, give up marriage for a "career"? She seemed still so restless, so unfulfilled, and she still talked, sometimes, of a stage career.

In the fall of 1924, just seven weeks after Harding had died under mysterious circumstances in San Francisco and Calvin Coolidge had become President of the United States, Adlai with five companions moved into a dilapidated old wooden house just down Mount Auburn Street from Claverly Hall, where they rented eight rooms, two baths, and a sleeping porch. He was happier in Cambridge his second year than he had been in his first. Outside the hard grind of his studies, his life was a pleasant one: football weekends at Princeton as well as Harvard; visits to New York where he saw Pavlova dance, saw a World Series game, and had an exciting talk "about democracy etc." until after midnight one night with B.'s father, the famous Norman H. Davis who had played so important a role in international affairs during Wilson's administration; weekends on Lewis Farm, Walpole, Massachusetts, the country place of Francis Plimpton's father, who was president of Ginn and Company, publishers, and chairman of the trustees of Amherst; squash in the afternoon; a good many parties in Cambridge and Boston, though he continued to regard Boston society satirically; long walks through the Cambridge residential sections which, draped in vivid autumn foliage and bathed in sparkling frostbit autumn air, no longer seemed to him wholly ugly and depressing.

He particularly enjoyed the weekends at Lewis Farm, in a house built in 1742, surrounded by rolling woodlands full of unexpected cigar-store Indians, and interspersed with meadows for the dairy herd. The elder Plimpton struck him as a rather rigid Puritan gentleman, of long and distinguished ancestry, and the household was even more formal than Grandfather Stevenson's had been; but there were scores of colonial relics in the old house to whose stories Adlai listened avidly, and there were golf at the nearby Brookline country club and tennis on the farm itself during the fall and spring. He weekended, too, with other friends and at Haven Parker's at Lancaster, dined on "succulent pheasants" which, he was informed, abounded in the woods thereabouts.

But his favorite haunt continued to be the Underwood home,

which seemed to be always bursting with young people, his favorite companion Lorna Underwood, with whom he hiked, and supped, and danced, and rode, and golfed. One weekend in New York, during which he saw Owen Davis's *Outward Bound* (Buffie went to see the new play by Bloomington's Rachel Crothers), he purchased at Dutton's a magnificent and expensive eighteenth-century book on riding which he hoped, as a gift, "might in some measure help to discharge my colossal obligations to the Underwoods." The Underwoods were such a *natural* and joyous family; when Adlai was there the rooms rang with laughter.

And yet, deep down, he was not wholly happy. He continued to find the law "a jealous mistress and not a particularly attractive one," requiring at examination times ten or twelve hours of concentrated work every day for a week at a time. And examinations continued to terrify him. It seemed always miraculous to him that he could pass any of them. Moreover, he continued to feel that his life, as yet, had no clear purpose, no defined goal. Assuming that he received his law degree and were admitted to the Bar, what then? Did he really *want* to be a lawyer, devoting himself exclusively to abstracting property titles and drawing up prospectuses and helping to organize and reorganize corporations? He didn't think so. He still much preferred journalism. He was watching with close attention the exciting new venture in journalism, *Time* magazine, launched in 1923 by two Yale men of the class of '20, Briton Hadden and Henry Luce; he was impressed not only by the commercial possibilities but also by the social idealism which the youthful founders of *Time*, as yet uncorrupted by power, espoused. Last year he'd even toyed with the idea of investing some of the money he had made on the *Princetonian* in the project and going himself to work upon it, and he sometimes wished now that he had done so. . . . No, the only justification that the law had for him personally was that, as his father had said, it could lead him into something else, something more active, with a stronger appeal to his whole nature. The fact that he did not know what this "something" would be made him more than a little restive, and even anxious, under all his day-by-day busyness.

Then, suddenly, there occurred an event which put an end to his Harvard career and, for a time, took his career decisions, or indecisions, out of his hands.

CHAPTER TEN

An Interlude of Journalism

Uncle Bert Davis, son of W. O. and successor to him as *Pantagraph* head, had been in failing health for a year or more. In the spring of 1924, in California, he died. Adlai returned to Bloomington for the funeral. He found that grief over the passing of his uncle was not the only grief that descended upon the Stevenson and Merwin families while he was yet in Bloomington.

Grandfather Davis's will, under which Uncle Bert managed the paper, had been drawn up by Davis's great and good friend "Private Joe" Fifer, former governor of Illinois. Due to an unlikely series of deaths, and to a lack of legal precision, the terms of this will now became ambiguous. The will had provided that the shares in the *Pantagraph* be held in life estate by W. O. Davis's children, then passed to their children. Uncle Bert had had two sons, William and Louis. William had died of illness while at a military school; Louis had been killed while training as an Army Air Force pilot at Ellington Field, in Texas, in May of 1918. Surviving, then, were five grandchildren, three Merwins and two Stevensons. The question now arose as to how the estate was to be divided between the two families. By the reading which the Stevensons favored, the will stated that the eight hundred shares of *Pantagraph* stock less ten shares which had been bequeathed to a long-time employee of the paper, would be equally divided between W. O. Davis's two surviving children, Helen Stevenson and Jessie Merwin. By the reading which the Merwins favored, the will stated that the stock was to be divided between the two families in proportion to the number of grandchildren in each—that is, in such a way as to give each grandchild the same number of shares. The former reading meant that the Stevensons and Merwins would each receive 50 per cent of the property, or 395 shares. The latter reading meant that the Merwins would receive 60 per cent and the Stevensons 40, or 474 and 316 shares respectively. (Lewis Stevenson fumed that he'd have had six children if he had known the will could possibly be interpreted in the latter way.)

As might be expected, the situation was not clarified by long and somewhat heated family conclaves. The stakes were large, for the *Pantagraph* was a major power in central Illinois, and in all cases of this kind the human mind becomes remarkably fertile of plausible rationalizations. Certainly there was room here, too, for honest disagreement.

Finally the two families decided to institute a "friendly suit" so that the courts could decide the matter in terms of law. But of course the suit was not wholly friendly. Inevitably a good deal of acrimonious feeling was involved, and Adlai, having missed more classes than he could adequately make up, returned to Harvard in a disturbed emotional state. His mother, even more disturbed, fell ill and went to Battle Creek Sanitarium for a rest cure. "I hope and feel sure it will do you a lot of good, but nothing but *mental* peace will ever make your physical condition what it should be," Adlai wrote her out of his own travail. "Of this I feel sure, and it's all in accord with your theories anyway. So I hope you are trying to look at things as dispassionately as possible." As for himself, he was going through "the hardest weeks on record," weeks during which he put in between fifty and sixty hours of concentrated mental work, trying to catch up in time to pass the term finals. ("I do hope *I can* keep my mind functioning. . . . If I can [only] keep my spirits and my physical well-being intact. . . .") Desperately, all too aware that he was inadequately prepared, he plunged into examination week —and failed two courses.

But it had been decided that he and his cousin and boyhood companion, Davis Merwin, should both go to work on the *Pantagraph*, while the lawsuit ground its ponderous way through the court. Accordingly, Dave Merwin became a business manager and when Adlai returned to Bloomington he became an editor of the paper, an arrangement which was maintained for almost two years. . . . There is no evidence that Adlai was dismayed by this interruption of his legal education in favor of working journalism.

He entered upon this new phase of his life after a brief, hectic interlude during which he was totally immersed in national politics.

On Thursday, June 20, 1924, he and Francis Plimpton motored to New London to see the Yale-Harvard boat races. The two spent all day Friday aboard the *Alido,* a yacht on which Lorna Underwood and Elizabeth Meeker were guests. It was at Lorna's invitation that the two came aboard for lunch on the yacht, but their host was so taken by them that he insisted they stay all afternoon, and for dinner, and come back for supper after the dance that night at the Griswald. ("The two men who were cruising with the girls looked a little bored with us," Adlai reported—and no wonder!) Next day, after the races, Plimpton and Adlai motored to New York, to the Plimpton's home on Park Avenue, in whose library, "surrounded by the greatest collection of *mathematica rara* in the world," Adlai, on Sunday afternoon, wrote a newsy letter to his mother. The Democratic National Convention would open Monday morning. Adlai—with B. Davis, Francis Plimpton, and Bob Finley—was to be an assistant sergeant at arms. The assignment had been secured for him by his father.

Lewis Stevenson was a figure of definite if minor importance in that interminable and disastrous convention. Long before the convention opened it was quite obvious to the knowledgeable that the two leading candidates of the party, William G. McAdoo and Alfred E. Smith, would eliminate one another in the balloting, neither being able to achieve even a majority of the votes, much less the two thirds then required. It was, therefore, a foregone conclusion that a dark horse would be named, and Lewis Stevenson's dark horse was David F. Houston, the Secretary of Agriculture in Wilson's administration with whom Carl Vrooman had served. Lewis Stevenson, as a matter of fact, was the guiding spirit of the Houston campaign, whose headquarters were at the Hotel Saville.

But Houston, alas for Stevenson hopes, was so dark a horse as to be almost invisible against the background of gloom in which the Democratic convention was held. Houston was a most able mind but he lacked fire; he lacked the capacity to inspire others; he could administer, but he could not lead. And Adlai Stevenson himself, writing his mother on the day before the convention opened, said that "frankly" he didn't think Houston "has much chance of getting the nomination." It looked to him "more and more as if John W. Davis was the man."

Davis had immense personal superiority, by every sane criterion of value, over Silent Cal Coolidge. The great trouble with him as a candidate was that he seemed to represent the same big-business interest as Silent Cal represented: he was a corporation lawyer, he had "Wall Street connections," being affiliated with the United States Rubber Company, the New York Telephone Company, and (worst of all) the House of Morgan. Thus his nomination would blunt the only issue, that of business domination of government, on which the Democrats might conceivably win.

Certainly this last was an issue on which the Republicans in that year were more than usually vulnerable. Only a little over two months after Harding's death, Senator Thomas J. Walsh of Montana had demanded a full Senate investigation of the mysterious circumstances surrounding the leasing of two naval oil reserves, Teapot Dome in Wyoming and Elk Hills in California, to Edward L. Doheny and Harry F. Sinclair, respectively. Soon the public was hearing a sordid tale of graft and corruption, the like of which had not been heard in the land since the administration of U. S. Grant.

One thousand and ninety-eight delegates assembled on June 24 in Madison Square Garden. This was the old Garden (soon it would be replaced by a skyscraper) on whose roof Harry Thaw shot Stanford White. On its floor Democrats now seemed inclined to shoot one another, for it is literally true that, one terrifying night, a riot would certainly have occurred if the aisles had not been patrolled by extra scores of special-detail policemen.

The issue that night lay between two planks of the party platform dealing with the Ku Klux Klan. One plank, drafted by a cautious majority of the platform committee, deplored racial and religious intolerance in general terms. The other, drafted by a bold and morally outraged minority, flatly condemned the Klan by name. McAdoo forces favored the former plank, Smith forces favored the latter, and for dangerous hours the result of the battle was uncertain. (It should be noted that no such dispute had disrupted Republican deliberations; in Cleveland, where Calvin Coolidge had been nominated by acclamation, with Charles G. Dawes as his running mate, the Klan was not mentioned aloud.) The final vote was very close. Fractional votes being allowed some of the delegates, 546.15 voted for the cautiously worded plank while 542.85 voted to condemn the Klan boldly, unequivocally. Then the weary delegates, some of them more embittered than ever, others of them relieved, went back to their sweltering hotel rooms for a few hours of sleep.

Adlai Stevenson—scurrying between convention floor and hotel suites with messages to and from delegates and wire-pulling managers—saw and heard and felt it all. He sat in on strategy conferences during which every facet of the Houston candidacy was argued out. He learned thus how much shrewd planning, how much complicated thought, goes into a political campaign. But he learned, too, how crucial a role sheer chance often plays in political success or failure, and that nervous control and a quick wit in moments of crisis may be more decisive than a long-range thoughtfulness.

For instance, on the night his father was to make the speech nominating David Houston, the taxi in which his father rode from the Hotel Saville to the Garden was immobilized in a crosstown traffic snarl. Precious minutes passed during which Lewis Stevenson grew desperate, for if Houston were not presented that night he might never be. Finally he leaned his head out the window and called to a traffic patrolman. "Officer!" he cried. "I've got to be at Madison Square Garden in five minutes to make the nominating speech for *Al Smith!*" The effect was magical. Immediately the cop's whistle shrilled; he leaped on the running board and, blowing his whistle and waving his arm, cleared the taxi's way through the jam and all the way to the convention hall. He even escorted Lewis Stevenson through the crowd into the hall itself, a way opening for them miraculously whenever Smith's name was pronounced.

Actually the speech nominating Smith was given by Franklin D. Roosevelt, who hobbled gallantly to the platform on crutches and, following the long demonstration set off by the first syllable of "Alfred" to fall from his smiling lips, spoke very well indeed. But Adlai believed, and many others shared his belief, that Lewis Stevenson's speech for Houston was better written and at least as well delivered. Adlai was proud of his father, proud of the fact his father was being mentioned here and there among the delegates as a possible vice-presidential candidate, and while his father spoke it was even possible to believe that Houston, after all, might have a real chance. . . .

The belief remained alive for several days—though as those hot angry days wore on it appeared likely that the party itself was on the point of total dissolution. On the first ballot, McAdoo had 431½ votes and Smith had 241, whereas 732 were necessary for nomination. Both men gained votes on succeeding ballots. These followed one another in swift, endless succession—the tenth, the twenty-fifth, the fortieth—with Governor Brandon of Alabama standing on his chair at the beginning of each of them, screaming: "Alabama casts twenty-four votes for Oscar-r-r W. Under-r-wood!" As the number of ballots soared above fifty, with no decision in sight, fearful men recalled that the largest number of ballots ever taken in a Democratic convention had been at Charleston, South Carolina, in 1860, where after fifty-seven ballots the party had split in two, with the southern faction nominating John C. Breckenridge and the northern one Stephen A. Douglas. Yet when the fifty-eighth ballot was taken in the 1924 convention, Smith had only 221½ and McAdoo only 495; a decision was as far away as ever. McAdoo forces angrily demanded that Smith withdraw in order that the front-runner might achieve nomination, a demand they could support on every ground of "practical politics." But this was not the determining factor in this situation; the ultimate determinant was a moral feeling. Those delegates who had fervently supported the anti-Klan platform plank and were outraged by McAdoo's refusal to disavow Klan support flatly refused to agree to Smith's withdrawal unless McAdoo also withdrew. So the balloting went on hopelessly, until at last, on July 9, McAdoo gave up. He and Smith released their delegates. Four hours later, on the hundred and third ballot, John W. Davis was nominated. . . .

There would follow a campaign in which Cal Coolidge pitched hay, carried maple-syrup buckets, and held up long-dead fish for the benefit of cameramen, while saying very little; and in which Davis attempted to capitalize on the issues presented to the country by the Republican record. When the votes were counted in November, it was found that Coolidge had won 382 electoral votes as compared to Davis's 136 and La Follette's 13, and had received nearly 58 per cent of the popular vote.

III

On the whole, Adlai Stevenson enjoyed his work on the *Pantagraph*, despite the fact that the circumstances in which he worked were by no means of the happiest. He bore the title of "managing editor." He supervised reporters and helped make up the paper. In the summer of 1925 he wrote a series of editorials concerning the trial of John T. Scopes in Dayton, Tennessee, for teaching evolution in the Dayton high school in violation of Tennessee law. This was the famous "monkey trial" during which William Jennings Bryan was special prosecutor and Clarence Darrow the lawyer for the defense. It became, of course, the trial of Bryan the Fundamentalist before the Bar of public opinion on charges of fanaticism, ignorance, and a bigoted censorship of education. On these charges, with Darrow as his prosecutor, Bryan was convicted. Soon he would die. To Adlai, whose grandfather had been Bryan's running mate in 1900, the spectacle, for its hilarious trappings, was sad, and his editorials were sober defenses of the principles which Bryan and the Fundamentalist party attacked: free inquiry, free speech, the separation of church and state.

Adlai was not, however, exclusively an editor during those years. He was also a reporter, being often on the street or in the country-side in quest of news.

His biggest story, or stories, concerned the great tornado which swept through southern Illinois ("Egypt," as it is called) on Wednesday, March 18, 1925. Some eight hundred people were killed, more than two thousand were seriously injured, and estimates of property damage soared over fifty million dollars as survivors looked over the ruins of Murphysboro, West Frankfort, De Soto, Carbondale. Adlai went down on a relief train from Chicago to write eyewitness reports of the tragedy, taking with him Joe Bohrer. At Murphysboro, where one hundred and eighty-seven had been killed, he saw a "bleeding, smoking world." At West Frankfort he visited one morgue where lay the bodies of thirty children varying in age from two months to two years. His reports rather strangely combined classical allusions with vivid sense impressions, but Joe Bohrer (who continued to see nothing "very remarkable" in his friend) was impressed by them and a little surprised that Adlai was capable of writing them.

In August of 1925 Adlai took a two-week vacation with Joe Bohrer, Charles Agle (later a New York architect), and M. Scott Bromwell (grandson of Mrs. Julia Scott and later connected with the financial firm of Halsey, Stuart, and Company, in Chicago). They went on a canoeing and fishing trip, outfitting in Ely, Minnesota, and making a great circle of one hundred and twenty miles in southern Ontario, carrying their canoes over the narrow portages between one lake and another.

The lawsuit at last came to trial in the circuit court and was lost there by the Stevensons. Naturally the Merwins were satisfied with the lower court's decision, but Adlai's family insisted on appealing the case. When the Illinois Supreme Court finally ruled, it sustained the appellate court in the Stevensons' favor: the *Pantagraph* stock was to be divided equally between the two families.

But while the case was pending on appeal the Merwins quietly acquired ten shares of stock that W. O. Davis had given to a valued employee many years before. With them went voting control of the company, despite the court's later decision in favor of equal treatment, and with them also went Adlai's vision of a career as a newspaper editor.

Lewis Stevenson and Adlai had discussed Adlai's future while the case was still in the courts. Lewis pointed out how much time and effort and money had already been invested by and for Adlai in the law. Surely it was the part of wisdom to finish law school, since his future at the *Pantagraph* was uncertain. Adlai agreed, and he stuck to this conclusion despite the offer of an instructorship in English or history which came to him from the Lawrenceville School, near Princeton—a most attractive offer, declined with regret. Accordingly, in the autumn of 1925 he was again a law student, spending his weekdays at the Northwestern University Law School in Chicago and coming home weekends to look after *Pantagraph* matters.

At Northwestern his interest in the law quickly grew, perhaps under the influence of the dean, the famous John Henry Wigmore, who became Adlai's fast friend. Perhaps, too, he caught an expanding vision of the advantages of life in a mighty city and felt challenged by the stern competition at the Bar. Certainly he was strongly influenced by a trip he made to Washington during this period to serve as an usher at Charley Denby's wedding to Senator David Reed's daughter. Charley was finishing a year as secretary to famed Supreme Court Justice Oliver Wendell Holmes, who had been a good friend of Adlai Ewing Stevenson I, and who gave to his old friend's grandson one of the unforgettable afternoons of the latter's life. Before the fireplace in Holmes's Washington home the old man talked to the young one about the law, legal education, the Civil War, and all manner of things—and as he talked, Adlai gained a larger, more exciting view of the law as a career than he had ever had before. . . . In June of 1926 Adlai took his J.D. at Northwestern and immediately thereafter passed his examination for entrance to the Illinois Bar.

Then, before he settled down to a law practice for which he still had no real enthusiasm, he decided to take what he called "one last fling" at journalism. . . .

IV

The idea was born at a convivial bachelor dinner following the wedding of one of Adlai's friends in June. The young men talked of Russia, and three of them—Adlai, George Norton, and Bob Page —expressed their eagerness to visit that enigmatic land and to observe, at first hand, the workings of the great Communist "experiment." But foreigners were barred from Russia by the Soviet government, and even if they had not been, the American State Department would have denied to private citizens permission to travel there under American passport protection. How, then, could the young men gain entrance? By becoming foreign correspondents of American newspapers, replied Adlai promptly. Immediately he grew excited about an idea which itself grew large as he talked of it.

One of the most newsworthy figures in the world that year was Grigori Vasilievich Chicherin, Soviet Foreign Minister. It was with him that American diplomats had endeavored to negotiate over the Czarist debts repudiated by the Bolsheviks, and over the compensation of Americans for their confiscated Russian property. Those negotiations had now broken down completely. But Chicherin was as silent and invisible as he was newsworthy—he refused to see any of the handful of American correspondents then stationed, or marooned, in Moscow—which meant that anyone who obtained a private interview with him would have a great news "scoop."

Why not make this the object of a Russian expedition? asked Adlai. With it, one might not only gain the newspaper accreditation necessary to the securing of a Russian visa but might also help pave the way for a settlement of some of the outstanding issues between the U.S. and U.S.S.R. Admittedly this last was a farfetched possibility.

"But why should Chicherin see *you*," Adlai was asked, "when he won't see the *experienced* correspondents who are already there?"

Adlai grinned. "He might see me precisely because I'm young and naïve. He might think I'd be more sympathetic to new ideas than older and more sophisticated men. At least, it's worth a try."

George Norton and Bob Page agreed that it was. Lewis Stevenson, too, was intrigued by the audacity of the idea when Adlai explained it to him: he helped Adlai obtain the necessary credentials as a foreign correspondent for the Chicago *Herald-American* and Hearst's International News Service. George Norton, meanwhile, obtained credentials as a representative of his home-town newspaper, the Louisville *Courier-Journal,* and Bob Page, unaccredited, decided to come along anyway on the off-chance that he could accompany his friends across the forbidden border.

Nor was this the only "plot" in which Adlai was involved that summer. He was also active in an attempt by Lewis and Helen Stevenson to "save" Buffie from the theatrical career on which she was now embarked, a risky career that was looked upon, by Adlai and Helen especially, with disapproval. She was with Gilbert Miller's stock company in Rochester, drawing fifty dollars a week and working under the direction of George Cukor, with Rosamund Pinchot, Glenn Hunter, Ilka Chase, and Louis Calhern. There seemed every chance that she would be caught halfway between success and failure in the theater, wasting her youth in that gray land of in-between, and waking up some gloomy morning to find herself a middle-aged spinster with a scattered, meaningless past and with no future at all.

Accordingly, it was decided that Adlai, on his way to New York, should stop off in Rochester and attempt to persuade Buffie to go to Italy with him and their mother. He did so. He saw Buffie "act." Her role, that hot night, was a brief scene in which she entered, sat upon a bench, and spoke one line. When he took her to supper afterward he managed gently and tactfully to let her know that her work, if that night was a fair sample of it, didn't seem to him especially exciting, or glamorous either. The Italian trip would be much more exciting, much more glamorous. . . .

And so it proved.

On July 24, Adlai and Buffie sailed with Helen Stevenson on the *Conte Biancamano.* A huge crowd was at the pier as the ship cast off, for on board was Generale Umberto Nobile, the hero of the hour, he having just flown over the North Pole in a dirigible. "Even Rudolph Valentino was there to see him off," wrote Buffie, long afterward. Moreover, she became a good shipboard friend of the heroic general. When the ship steamed into the Naples harbor, where a great triumph awaited him, he asked Buffie to stand beside him on the bridge of the ship! Surely this was enough to drive thoughts of a stage career at least temporarily from her mind.

Excitement continued. On her very first day in Italy she tucked her feet under her as their train rolled northward, and went to sleep. She was awakened by a screaming Fascist guard who put her under arrest for "defiling the upholstery"! If Adlai, pale with rage, had not kept his temper, a really unpleasant incident would have occurred.

Buffie had always found travel with Adlai to be a stimulating and educative (if exhausting) experience, and on this trip it was especially so. He viewed Fascist Italy through a journalist's eye, storing away facts and impressions for use in future writing.

He would use this material, too, not for Hearst but for two long articles which would be published in the Bloomington *Pantagraph* after he had returned. Those who became interested in the development of his mind, in the 1950s, would study these articles with a considerable interest. He himself would remember them as "very critical" of Mussolini and of fascism; those who viewed them across the years of bloody chaos which Mussolini helped to produce would not see them so. He was obviously influenced by Fascist propaganda, a thing wholly new to a young American of 1926.

But he was far more critical than most Americans who, traveling in Italy at that time, were inclined to praise Mussolini to the skies because "the trains now run on time." He noted with "surprise" the inconsistencies between Mussolini's pronouncements of 1921 and those of 1924 and after. In 1921 Mussolini had said: "The nation turned to us when our movement appeared as a liberator from tyranny; the nation will turn against us if our movement takes on the guise of a fresh tyranny." Yet in 1926 Mussolini had utterly stamped out free speech and was insisting that "liberty" in the Fascist vocabulary should be replaced by "order" and "discipline." Wrote Adlai, "It is evident that to insure its position and the safety of its chief, Fascism has adopted the same tactics that communism has in Russia, though under considerably different circumstances. Historically, suppression leads to violence. Taking away free speech is taking away the safety valve. . . ."

He said good-by to his mother and sister in the Tirol and hastened to Vienna to meet Bob Page and George Norton. All three had applied for Russian visas before leaving New York and hoped to find these waiting for them in the Soviet consulate in Vienna. Their hopes were not fulfilled. For days they haunted the consulate, being continuously put off by officials who claimed to have communicated with Moscow on the matter. After a precious week had passed, Bob Page gave up and departed, while Adlai and George Norton went down the Danube to Budapest, having arranged for the visa (if permission arrived) to be issued there. Adlai visited a college friend[1] in the American legation at Budapest; he and Norton had a good time there, but the friend's efforts to facilitate the visa were unavailing.

"It's hopeless," George Norton asserted one evening, adding that he knew of a delegation of southern religious leaders who were going into Russia via Poland. "I'm going to join them. We'll be sure to get in that way."

But Adlai shook his head. He was going into Russia as an accredited foreign correspondent if it could possibly be done. So George Norton left him (incidentally, the religious group, with Norton among them, were halted at the Polish-Russian border), and Adlai pushed on alone to Belgrade. No visa. He pushed on to Bucharest. Here again, no visa, though his stay in Bucharest seemed to him profitable as education: he became the guest of an officer of the Rumanian Standard Oil Company, a fact which, as he reported to the *Pantagraph* upon his return, "materially facilitated my investigation into economic and political conditions in the Balkan states." He paused in Sofia. No visa. He went on to Constantinople. Still no visa. But in Constantinople he stubbornly spent two solid days in the outer office of the Soviet consulate, ostentatiously waiting, before at last he virtually gave up hope and went out to explore the fascinating city. Two days later he went back to the Soviet consulate, where officials rebuked him for his absence. Didn't he want his visa? they asked. It was ready and waiting!

If he thought this the end of his difficulties, however, he was promptly disillusioned. There remained much more severe tests, not only of tenacity but of ingenuity and physical stamina as well. The visa granted, Soviet consular officials considered their duty wholly done; no suggestions were forthcoming as to how one might travel from Turkey to Moscow. So Adlai went down to the water front, where he learned that a small Italian freighter, the *Diana*, was about to sail up the Asiatic coast of the Black Sea to the Russian port of Batum, at the western end of the Caucasus mountains. He hired a

[1] H. Freeman Matthews, U. S. Ambassador to the Netherlands in 1957.

man to row him out to the *Diana*, where he managed to talk the captain (in very broken Italian) into taking him as a passenger. The voyage required five days, for the little ship seemed to put in at every port along the way. Also on board was an Italian diplomat, an interesting old man on his way to Persia, with whom he joined in the ship's officers' "sport" of shooting sea gulls with a rifle. At Batum his troubles began. All his papers, all his books, including his French-Russian dictionary and Bernard Pares' *History of Russia,* were taken away from him. Without knowing any Russian at all, he must now make his way. . . .

Afterward it would seem to him almost miraculous that he had done so. No one spoke English; almost everyone regarded him as a suspicious character. Never had he felt more utterly isolated, nor more miserable physically. He was almost always dirty and tired and hungry; it was borne in upon him that he might easily fall ill in this strange wild land, and if he did he might die untended among half-hostile strangers, for the individual life, he quickly realized, was not deemed sacred here. Yet it did not occur to him to turn back. Somehow he managed to travel along the mountains to Tiflis, capital of that Georgian republic of which Stalin was native, and from Tiflis to the oil city of Baku on the Caspian. There he obtained a train ticket for a journey northward. For five days he shared a train compartment in an old gaslit *wagon-lit* with an extremely bearded Russian who spoke not a word, creeping through Rostov, Kharkov, and Kiev, across an endless flat plain on which the works of man were far less various and interesting than those of the prairies of Illinois. He arrived at last in Moscow, tired and dirty, and none too certain of what to do next. The poverty of the people was everywhere apparent, and it was, as he immediately saw, intensified in Moscow. His first sight, when he stepped out of the railroad station, was of a group of "wild children," "wolf children"—the homeless, hopeless orphans of war—crouched upon the cobblestones where someone had dropped and broken a jar of jam: the children scraped the stones with their fingers and licked their fingers ravenously, and fought among themselves like mangy animals.

In Moscow he stayed in a house run by the Friends Service Committee, directed by two kindly and efficient ladies to whom he was always afterward grateful—a Miss Graves of Baltimore and a Miss Higgins from England. Most of the American newspapermen ate there every day, and Adlai was thus daily associated with such famous journalists as Walter Duranty of the New York *Times*, Junius Wood of the Chicago *Daily News*, William Henry Chamberlin of the *Christian Science Monitor*, H. R. Knickerbocker of the INS, and often their few British colleagues. These men were inclined to regard Adlai's project with amused skepticism, but they admired the young man's audacity and did what they could to help him. He learned from them most of what it was then possible to know about the workings of the Kremlin and about the great crisis through which the Soviet Union was then passing. Lenin had died two years before and the bitter struggle for his succession between Stalin and Trotsky was being won by the former. Lenin's "new economic policy" (the N.E.P.), which had seemed to point toward a liberal socialism that mixed state ownership with private enterprise, was now abandoned by Stalin who was taking steps to "liquidate" the kulaks and every other vestige of capitalism. He was doing so with utter ruthlessness.

"The atmosphere of fear was palpable," said Adlai Stevenson long afterward, "as palpable as the abject poverty of the masses. I never knew whether or not I was being followed, but I did know that people were afraid to be seen talking to me. One of the Russians I talked to," he added, "was Karl Radek, the old Bolshevik theoretician, who was later killed in the Purge. He was head of Intourist, which was in the planning stage when I was there."

His chief Moscow guide, however, was the Countess Sophia Tolstoi, who as a relative of the great writer and curator of the Tolstoi Museum was tolerated by the Communists. Several Russian refugee friends in America—Prince Rostislav, Colonel George Voevodsky, Prince Galitzin, and Ilya Tolstoi, among others—had asked him to communicate, if possible, with relatives, and Countess Tolstoi helped him to do so.

Every afternoon he called at the Foreign Office; he went there, as a matter of fact, before he'd unpacked his bag on his first weary day in Moscow. He talked with Chicherin's press secretary, who sat with his back to folding doors behind which, Adlai suspected, sat Chicherin himself, closely listening to every word that was said. Adlai, therefore, said many words. He was eloquent in his presentation of ideas concerning the Czarist debts and the expropriations, he was "sympathetic" and "open-minded" concerning Soviet problems, he admired Chicherin's proven abilities, he was convinced that a full-dress interview with the minister would be of immense value to "both our countries." The press secretary listened politely, then smilingly advised him to return next day. This continued for a month. At the end of that time the persistent young American, his money running low, was forced to give up what he finally concluded to be, in any case, a hopeless enterprise. He left Moscow without his story.

"But I've always been very thankful for that trip," he said in the 1950s. "After what I saw there, I could never believe, as so many did in the early 1930s, that Soviet Russia's way was a good way for any state to go. Some men, from the highest humanitarian motives, became Communists or fellow-travelers during the Depression, but I felt that I had seen at first hand what communism really meant, in terms of terror and brutality. All that terror and brutality breed are more terror and more brutality, and so it was in the Russia I saw."

He went to Leningrad, where he spent a fortnight. Then he went to Stockholm by way of Helsingfors, Åbo, and the Baltic Sea, sailing for the United States from Gothenburg, Sweden. He returned to Bloomington on October 12, 1926.

There he discovered, through letters from Switzerland, that the failure of his "plot" concerning Chicherin had been more than offset by the success of the "plot" against Buffie's stage career. The latter success, in fact, was almost *too* complete, in Helen Stevenson's view.

In a hotel in Valmont, above Lake Geneva, Buffie had met a handsome young Virginian named Ernest Ives, first secretary at the American Embassy in Constantinople, who had come to Switzerland on leave. Within three days after they'd met they were planning to honeymoon in Egypt. (He'd formerly been consul in Alexandria.) Their idea was that they marry at once, while he was still on leave, but this precipitance was successfully opposed by Mrs. Stevenson who argued that a two- or three-month separation was required by wisdom. It was finally agreed that Buffie and Mrs. Stevenson would return to Bloomington until early in 1927, when Buffie would return to Europe for a wedding in Naples.

Minor complications arose when all this was explained to Lewis Stevenson. As a matter of fact, he exploded in characteristic fashion, flatly refusing to permit his daughter to marry a man he'd not even met. He would go to Naples with Buffie; he'd look this strange young man over carefully; and *then,* if he liked what he saw, he would permit the wedding to go forward. As usual in family crises, he faced a united front formed by his wife, his daughter, his son.

As usual it was Adlai who smoothed things over. On the eve of the fateful voyage he sent his father a long letter for which Buffie, though she never saw it, was especially grateful. "You can't imagine what an effect your splendid letter had on Father," she wrote from mid-ocean. "He has done everything possible to help me and not fret me, and I do appreciate your tact and understanding. . . . You should hear OLD PAPA tell me he thinks you have a 'master mind, and altho' a boy, one of the great men he has ever known.' He has utter awe of you, as I have love and confidence."

On February 4, 1927, Elizabeth Stevenson and Ernest Ives were married in Naples. In accordance with Italian law, there were two ceremonies, a civil one at twelve noon and one in the Presbyterian church at three in the afternoon. Bride and groom departed at once for Egypt, to honeymoon until March 1.

v

By that time Adlai Stevenson was drawing $125 a month as law clerk in the old and highly respected law firm of Cutting, Moore and Sidley, with offices on La Salle Street in the heart of Chicago's financial district. He had obtained the job through his Princeton friend, M. Ogden West, with whom he had traveled in Europe in the summer of 1921. Ogden West had a brother-in-law in this firm and would himself become, in later years, a partner.

Soon Adlai found that he was working harder as law clerk than he had ever done as a law student. He was stubbornly, conscientiously determined that he would become a first-rate lawyer, always an asset and ultimately a partner in the firm.

CHAPTER ELEVEN

Bachelor Days End
in Fashionable Marriage

Chicago's celebrated Gold Coast extends southward for a mile or so along Lake Michigan from Lincoln Park to approximately Delaware Street, itself a mile north of the Loop, and inland perhaps a quarter of a mile. In geographic terms, therefore, it is a tiny segment of the great city. In terms of power and prestige, however, its dimensions are vast, and they were even greater thirty years ago when Adlai Stevenson became a member of the community they bounded: here dwelt the rich, here were the city homes of society. The Coast's glittering façade was rapidly changing. Skyscraper apartments for the wealthy were rapidly rising along the Drive itself, replacing the grandiose mansions of former years, and along the side streets— Oak and Cedar and Elm—many of the substantial dwellings were being made over into apartments and let out piecemeal to young single people who were just beginning their careers. It was into one of the latter, a brick building at 70 East Elm, that Adlai Stevenson moved early in 1927.

Elm Street was remarkable in that it did actually have, in its narrow parkings, some puny specimens of the tree after which it was named. (Maple, alas, had no maples, nor did Cedar have cedars.) If they were slender plants scarcely taller than a tall man's head, if their crowns were but scraps of foliage during the warm seasons, they nevertheless brought green information of the world of nature into this man-made world of pavements and walls. Stevenson was grateful for them. He moved in the autumn into a small apartment on East Delaware Place, where he had a view of the lake from the front windows of his room. From them, at an angle, his view caught be-

tween towering walls, he could look far out across the inland sea to
a watery horizon, often shrouded in mists, out of which the full moon
rose on clear nights with a magical radiant beauty. On Sundays he
often walked along the lake from Oak Street beach to the breakwater
at North Avenue, his senses drinking deep of the seascape's beauty
bounded by the grass and trees of the park. He needed thus to renew
himself after a week in the gray smoky canyon of La Salle Street.

The workaday fare on which a beginning law clerk feeds is no
more fattening to his ego than his salary is to his pocketbook, nor is
it of such a nature as to engage, very often, the clerk's fascinated
attention. Most of it is drudgery; much of it is menial. This is especially true in such financial law firms as Cutting, Moore and Sidley.
A relatively small portion of the work there involved anything so
dramatic as a court trial. Most of it, as a matter of fact, was designed
to keep court trials from happening. Young Stevenson, therefore,
had little opportunity in his law work to display that skill in oral
argument, that ability to project his personality over a group of people, which he had begun to develop at Princeton.

He was, in effect, a servant of the partners, to whom those tasks
were assigned that were too time-consuming and routine for a partner's close and expensive attention. Yet a great deal depended upon
the efficiency, the precision, with which these tasks were performed.
He looked up the law as it pertained to a case a partner was handling. He wrote memoranda on questions of law. He kept a docket
for a partner or for partners. He drafted simple wills and contracts.
He ran all kinds of errands. And all the time he was acutely aware
that he was in competition with other young men, and that there
were more of these than there were future "successes" to reward
them.

The yardstick by which the competitions were graded was, in his
firm, a tradition of legal work of the highest quality, extending un-
broken to the year following the Civil War—the longest such tradition in Chicago. The firm had begun as Williams and Thompson in
1866; it became Williams, Holt and Wheeler in 1888; in 1889, it became Holt, Wheeler and Sidley; in 1913, it became Holt, Cutting and
Sidley; in 1919, it had become Cutting, Moore and Sidley. This information was printed in the upper left-hand corner of the firm's
stationary, a constant reminder to young law clerks that they had a
great deal to live up to and that few futures could be more honorable
than one in which their own names were listed, as senior partners,

on the office door. Much of the financial history of the entire Middle West had been written in such narrow rooms as that at 11 South La Salle in which Stevenson now sat from early morning until (often) late in the evening. He himself, he could legitimately feel, was continuing that writing, if in a very minor capacity.

He was immediately well liked personally in the firm, both by his superiors and by his fellow clerks. He was uniformly cheerful, even-tempered in times of pressure, conscientious in the performance of his duties, generally sound in his judgments. His presence was no obvious threat to anyone. If he had success-anxiety (and he did have some), he hid it well under casual, pleasant, unassertive good manners. If he had any brilliant potential either as lawyer or as man, it was not recognized by his superiors. They noted, however, that he steadily improved as a lawyer and that he was better at any given moment than he seemed to think he was. He claimed far less than his due: he seemed to feel that, given his heritage and initial advantages, he should do far better than he was doing.

Conscience thus deprived him of self-satisfactions that others in his circumstances would have enjoyed. But it also ensured his future growth. And growth was ensured, too, by the fact that he was involved, as he had been at Choate and Princeton, in a great deal of extracurricular activity. He followed the pattern established in his school and college days. A fifty-hour week devoted to the law by no means used up all his energies. Most of these, it sometimes seemed, were held in abeyance while he performed his hired duties, to be released after hours in a great number and variety of social engagements and civic enterprises.

II

The social engagements, joined with recreational activities of many kinds, were at first predominant. He at once became a member of the Harvard-Yale-Princeton Club[1] and played squash there two or three times a week; he was also active in the management of the club, constantly enlarging through it his circle of friendly social acquaintances. He was, of course, no stranger to Chicago's society when he first came to the city: many of the fashionable and wealthy citizens were long-time friends of his family. Their sons and daugh-

[1] The club ceased to exist in the 1930s.

ters were, often, his own personal friends, some of whom he had known since his boyhood summers at Charlevoix and others of whom he had known in the West, or on his travels, or at Princeton or Harvard.

One long-time acquaintance, for instance, was Hermon Dunlap Smith, whom everyone called "Dutch." The Smiths had had a place across the lake from the Davis cottage at Charlevoix, and the two boys (they were almost precisely the same age, Dutch having been born on May 1, 1900) had sometimes, though seldom, played together during those idyllic summers. During their college days the two had also sometimes met. Dutch had gone to Harvard, graduating with the class of '21, and at Harvard he had been president of the *Crimson;* as a result, he and Adlai had met sometimes at conferences of eastern-college student-paper executives. The acquaintanceship had been slight and casual, however, until Adlai moved to Chicago. Thereafter it quickly grew into a very warm, close friendship and would remain so.

By the spring of 1927 Dutch Smith was already very solidly established as a business executive and a member of Chicago's social elite. He had gone to work for the Northern Trust Company in 1922. In 1926 he had become a second vice-president of the company. In 1928 he would join Marsh and McLennan, insurance brokers, advancing ultimately to the position of president of that large and prosperous enterprise. In 1923 he had married Ellen Catherine Thorne, daughter of the president of Montgomery Ward & Company, with whom Adlai had had a slight acquaintance ever since the summer of 1919, when she and Adlai had met at the H F Bar ranch.

Ellen Smith seldom gave a party to which he was not invited, for, somehow, he helped to make things "go" and to do this without being, in any obvious sense, the "life" of the party. He never dominated the group, nor displayed an intimidating brilliance, nor did he have (people felt this) any desire to do so. With his steady good cheer, his genuinely interested questioning, his close listening to answers, he helped others to put their best selves forward. Their attitude toward him was warmly affectionate, if often a little patronizing. He claimed so little for himself that they would like to have claimed a great deal for him, but there were not many who felt they could honestly do so.

"There was a very general tendency to underrate Ad," Dutch

Smith would say, long afterward. "I sometimes think the tendency persists among those who knew him in the old days. He seemed just a charming, affable fellow who'd get along all right but never amount to a great deal, never have much real force, and this past view—which I thought was inaccurate at the time—keeps them from seeing him as he is today."

There were a great many parties in those years, both formal and informal; it was the very height of the Jazz Age, when the pursuit of pleasure absorbed a greater proportion of youthful energies, perhaps, than it had ever done before in America or has ever done since. Stevenson became one of a loosely organized "set" composed of young married couples, as yet childless, and young bachelors and unmarried women of approximately the same age and social class and future prospects. They were constantly encountering one another at clubs and theaters and private homes—mostly the latter—and came to know one another almost as well as the residents of small towns know one another (indeed they formed a kind of small-town community superimposed on the sprawling city), though this knowledge was filtered through a far greater sense of privacy than prevails in small towns. Many of them had a background of money; few were wealthy in their own right, most of the men earned meager salaries, but none was really economically insecure. Many had family prestige; all would inherit a substantial property. The young men had gone to Ivy League colleges, almost invariably one of the Big Three though, now and then, one encountered a man from Williams, or Amherst, or Dartmouth.[2] The girls had gone to Westover, or Dobbs Ferry, or some other fashionable finishing school; rarely had one of them attended a university. Doing so was not considered a necessity for girls in the upper income brackets at that time.

Among the men were Harry Wilmerding, Bill Lauderback, Ogden West—all of whom would make considerable successes in business and the law before their early deaths—and James F. Oates, Jr., who would become chairman of the board of the Peoples Gas, Light and Coke Company; William B. McIlvaine, Jr., who became a leading Chicago lawyer; Stephen Y. Hord, later a partner in Brown Brothers, Harriman and Company; Walter Paepcke, later chairman of the

---

[2] Significant of a prevailing attitude in Stevenson's "set" is a remark quoted by John Bartlow Martin in his *Adlai Stevenson*, p. 47. One of the former members of the Harvard-Yale-Princeton Club told Martin that the club, in its dying days, "even took in people from Dartmouth."

board and chief executive of the Container Corporation of America; John Paulding Brown, later a prominent Washington lawyer. Oates was a fellow law clerk in Cutting, Moore and Sidley. So was Edward D. McDougal, Jr., who, in the 1950s, would be vice-president and general counsel of International Minerals and Chemical Corporation. These young men were not, in 1927–28, a frivolous group. They worked harder than most of their contemporaries were doing and most of them were developing, like Stevenson, a driving sense of civic responsibility.

Among the girls were Margaret Willing (later Mrs. John V. Farwell); Rue Winterbotham (Mrs. Alfred Shaw); Ruth Elting (Mrs. Edwin Winter); Jane Warner (Mrs. Edison Dick); and Alicia Patterson (Mrs. Harry Guggenheim of New York). Among Stevenson's slightly older women friends was Harriet Welling (Mrs. John P. Welling). Both Harriet Welling and Jane Warner would remember that Adlai Stevenson was considered one of the most attractive, one of the most eminently eligible in all respects, of the young men they knew. They talked about him a lot and considered him a "catch" of whom any girl might be proud.

Among the closest of these women friends, destined to play a role of some importance in his future life, was Jane Warner. (She would marry Edison Dick in 1930; in the 1950s he would be chairman of the executive committee of the board of directors of the A. B. Dick Company.) Her father was Ezra J. Warner (Yale, '99), president and treasurer of the great wholesale-grocery firm of Sprague, Warner and Company. It was Warner, a Republican, who urged Stevenson to become a Democratic candidate for the legislature in 1928—the first time anyone suggested that Stevenson become a candidate for public office. The young man toyed with the idea for some weeks, then gave it up as unfeasible in his circumstances. Distracted by active politics, he would never "make the grade" at Cutting, Moore and Sidley. . . .

In the summers of 1927 and '28 Stevenson was one of a group of young men who rented a house in Lake Forest, that most famous and fashionable (at least at that time) of all the string of north-shore suburbs. They dubbed their house "The Château," commuting from it to their city offices (many of them rode bicycles to the station) all through the summer. Most if not all of them became members of Lake Forest's fashionable Onwentsia Club, where dances were held every weekend and where Stevenson played a great deal of tennis during his hours off, and a good deal of golf. He rode, too. He was naturally good at games, his friends would remember. When he was playing regularly he golfed in the lower eighties. He still played a very tough tennis game and was a good shot and a fine horseman.

Concurrent with all this informal social life was an intermittently glittering formal one, particularly during the Christmas holiday season and the weeks following it. The Jazz Age, like the Gilded Age, was one of particularly conspicuous consumption among the wealthy. During it, Chicago's debutantes were launched, not en masse as they later were, but one by one at balls costing their parents anywhere from three to five thousand dollars apiece, and sometimes more. On occasion two orchestras were employed at these affairs to ensure continuous dancing into the wee hours, and always a long stag line was required to assure each girl of a number of dancing partners in gratifyingly swift succession. No hostess could be personally acquainted with all the people required to fill huge hotel ballrooms; particularly was it impossible for her to know all the young men whose presence, in droves, was demanded. Hence "Miss Campbell's List," from which Miss Eliza Campbell, the social secretary employed by Chicago's society mothers, made up guest lists for her clients. Stevenson and his "Château" friends were on the list, as a matter of course.

But Adlai Stevenson was not deeply susceptible to the prevailing mood of the Jazz Age, then approaching its climactic moments. On Chicago's Gold Coast no more than in Princeton's "country club" was he likely to devote a major portion of his energies to a pursuit of sensual pleasures, nor was he likely to be hypnotized by those glittering baubles which were so stimulating to the Fitzgerald imagination, so corrupting of the Fitzgerald character. He seemed to have been born knowing that, in the total scheme of things, there *are* no privileges: everything truly possessed must be paid for sooner or later, either through a conscious fulfillment of the obligations which "privilege" imposes or through a loss of personal quality, a cheapening and coarsening of personality. Even conscience—a felt knowledge of obligations, an acute sensitivity to moral values—may be a "privilege" in this sense. Certainly no one can live well without it, and certainly it must be paid for; it carries with it vital dangers of which Stevenson's remarkable mother was well aware.

Excessive conscience, she realized, could breed life-negating fears;

it might become a kind of cowardice which kept a man from realizing that greatness which Helen Stevenson believed to be potential in her son. "Free yourself of all fear," she earnestly advised him in a letter written in April, 1927. "Fear of *anything* is devastating. . . ." It would be a "good sign" if he wanted to be "very elegant in appearance, and if you blow a little money, it will kill off scare-cat fear." Buffie, she pointed out, had "bought more finery" in her "enthusiasm in feeling well and free." Buffie might "go too far that way, but better that than an attack of fear." She urged him to "get a true knowledge" of himself and of what he really wanted out of life, and she begged him not to "be hurried" and harassed. "What is best for you to do about life will have opened up to you as time goes on." (She was also concerned, in that letter, lest her husband sap Adlai's self-confidence by "passing on his worries and fears." Poor Lewis Stevenson, certainly, was having his troubles that year, what with the continuing farm depression, Coolidge's veto of the McNary-Haugen Bill on which Lewis had worked with George N. Peek and Hugh S. Johnson of the Moline Plow Company, and the collapse of the Zeppelin project for which Lewis had had such high hopes. That spring, for the first time, he sometimes impressed his son as a tired, harried old man.)

Thus Adlai and the kind of friends he made were as an island around which the stream of sensationalism flowed downward through the Roaring Twenties toward the Depression. On this island the old-fashioned virtues were sustained in full vigor. Those sober qualities of "good judgment," "sound morals," "industry," and "common sense" —damned by the Jazz Age with faintest praise—were deemed superior, though by no means antithetical, to wit and gaiety, spontaneity and sophistication and personal charm, qualities which the Jazz Age exalted. Adlai Stevenson continued to admire, above all, competence and character, and even among his own relatively sober group he was by no means the gayest.

"I always think of Ad as a terrific worker," one of the old "Château" group told John Bartlow Martin in '52.[3] "Of course, nearly all the young lawyers were. More so than the bankers. The lawyers were getting the seven-sixteen train in the morning and weren't coming back till after six in the evening. No young lawyer caught the five-ten

[3] Op. cit., p. 49.

from the city. I remember a skiing weekend at Charlevoix with Adlai—he worked all weekend."

But if Stevenson's group formed a cultural island, the stream *did* flow around it and did affect its climate and, to some extent, its shape. Fitzgerald in Chicago, like Fitzgerald in Princeton, touched young Stevenson's life at many points. Everywhere were the vital echoes, the living images of *This Side of Paradise*. . . .

It is perhaps an unanswerable question whether art is more an imitation of life than life is of art; the two interact and modify one another profoundly. To what extent did *Paradise* reflect a certain kind of glamorous girl who emerged during the war? To what extent was that girl created by *Paradise*? No one can say. But it is a fact of literary history that the living model for the Isabelle Borge of Fitzgerald's first novel was the beautiful Ginevra King of Chicago and Lake Forest. Among her neighbors and contemporaries in Lake Forest were Peggy Carry, Edith Cummings, and Courtney Letts. These three had been the "great belles," as Buffie put it, of that social life in Washington in which she was so much involved in early 1918; it was at Courtney's coming-out party in Washington that John Harlan, with Allister McCormick and several Princeton men, had given Buffie "such a rush."

Ginevra King would become the wife of John Pirie (it was the second marriage for both of them), who would be president of Carson, Pirie, Scott and Company, the large department store on State Street, by the 1940s. Courtney Letts, having at her first wedding become Courtney Letts Stillwell, would at her second become the wife of John Borden of Chicago, in March 1925. By his first wife John Borden had two daughters. The youngest would marry Robert Pirie, brother-in-law of the former Ginevra King. The eldest was destined to marry Adlai E. Stevenson, who thereby, for a brief period, became a son-in-law of the former Courtney Letts.

The event was being prepared in the spring and summer of 1928. . . .

III

Her name was Ellen, and to a superficial view it seemed that she too might have stepped from the pages of a Fitzgerald novel. At eighteen, she was a slender, vivid, dark-blond-haired girl, with plump cheeks, a firm and even stubborn jaw, heart-shaped lips, and hazel eyes through which she habitually looked out upon the world with a bright, smiling, wide-lidded stare.

She was very pretty and very rich, but these attractive qualities by no means accounted for the whole of the fascination she seemed to have for the young men who thronged around her at parties. Her attitudes mingled a childish innocence with worldly sophistication in ways that were confusing but delightful to most people. She was, some thought, rather birdlike. One tended to describe her with the adjectives one applies to the actions of birds—perky, flighty, fluttery —for though her movements were graceful and seemed, when one was with her, to flow smoothly together, one was likely to remember them as jerky, disconnected, hopping from here to there like a brilliant bird who pauses now and then to preen and to stare. The same was true of her conversation. It was very quick and gay and witty: it was, most people agreed, wholly charming: but it did have a tendency to break into pieces when one handled it with the fingers of memory. It became a clutter of impressions, a scattering of moments vivid and even brilliant, but without evident relation to one another. One sensed obscurely that she was dangerous—dangerous to others but above all to herself—and one longed to *protect* her. She was so eager for life! So anxious to grasp and shape the world into forms that expressed, beautifully, herself! She might be terribly hurt by it!

She lived, as a princess should, in a palace—a turreted sixteenth-century French château built of smooth gray stone in the latter part of the nineteenth century by her grandfather, William Borden, who had inherited and also made a fortune out of Chicago real estate. It stood at 1020 Lake Shore Drive, on the corner of the Drive and Bellevue Place. Directly across Bellevue from it stood Edith Rockefeller McCormick's great limestone mansion, for whose architectural ugliness the Borden château helped somewhat to compensate. When Ellen was a little girl she used to write verses as she lay in her bed at night, scribbling them on smuggled sheets of paper by the light of a street lamp that shone into her room. She also early evinced a taste and talent for interior decoration. She was very sensitive to colors and their relations to one another, and to the balancing of a room's furnishings.

She could feel that she came naturally by her interest in writing, and in the arts in general. Her mother, the former Ellen Waller of an old and distinguished Chicago family, from whom she inherited her beauty (mother and daughter looked much alike), was among the city's patronesses of the arts, with a particular interest in music. Her father's sister, Mary Borden, was a famous novelist. Aunt Mary was now Lady Spears, for in 1918, a year before she published her first novel, she had married the famous soldier and diplomat and author, Brigadier General Edward Louis Spears, now a knight of the British Empire.

As for Ellen's father, John Borden, from whom she inherited many of her salient characteristics, he too possessed qualities which might have led him to success in the creative arts had he chosen to channel his energies in that direction. He had not so chosen: he was not, as a matter of fact, much interested in the arts at all. After receiving his B.A. from Yale in 1906, he had entered the Northwestern Law School (it was while he was a law student that he had married Ellen Waller in 1907), receiving his LL.B. and being admitted to the Illinois Bar in 1908. In the years since, he had demonstrated a restless imagination, remarkable courage, and great physical vigor. He had also revealed a penchant for daring speculations. These qualities had led him to dramatic business successes. They would later lead him to equally dramatic failures, for in him they were joined (they often are so joined) with an impatience of procedural rules, a boredom with routine, and a careless bravado. In 1928, however, he was at the very peak of his success. Having inherited a fortune, he, too, had added another to it as an associate of John Hertz in the Yellow Cab Company; then he had gone into Southwest oil and added yet another. Simultaneously he had so distinguished himself as an Arctic explorer that he was listed as one in Who's Who.

And not only was he explorer, sportsman, clubman, financier. On his Glenwild Plantation near Granada, Mississippi—an estate of baronial proportions—he raised purebred Shorthorn and Hereford beef cattle, and Duroc-Jersey hogs, entering outstanding animals in the great livestock expositions in Kansas City and Chicago and winning with them an occasional ribbon. At the age of forty, after seventeen years of a marriage most observers had thought to be a very happy one, he had divorced Ellen Waller Borden in order to marry, barely three months later, the glamorous Courtney Letts Stillwell. To Ellen and her younger sister Betty, in the divorce settlement, went the mansion at 1020 Lake Shore Drive, and other riches, the house to be used by Mrs. Waller Borden so long as she wished to do so. But with these came a great deal of pain and bitterness, a breaking of vital strands from which the eldest daughter suffered only slightly less than her mother did.

Ellen was educated at St. Timothy's, Catonsville, Maryland—a school famous for its exclusiveness and its devotion (under Louisa McE. Fowler and Jane R. Heath) to very conservative educational values. Even at school the teen-aged Ellen had an unlimited expense account, thanks to her father, who may thus have attempted to "make it up to her" for her broken home. After leaving St. Timothy's, she had gone for a year to Miss Sheldon's and Miss Nixon's in Florence, Italy. Then, in December of 1926, she was presented to Chicago society and became one of the most popular debutantes of her year. She was presented at the Court of St. James during one of the levees of the spring of 1928.

By the time the latter event occurred she had virtually decided that, from her many suitors, she chose Adlai Stevenson. She had met him again and again at parties. He had become the most frequent of her escorts. He was obviously devoted to her as a *person* and not just as the leading deb, or as an heiress. She enjoyed his sparkling conversation, his good dancing, his charming manners; and life with him, she decided, would never be boring. These things she would say to interviewers in later years. She would deny, in these later years, that she had ever really loved him. . . .

But if she did not, appearances deceived the most intimate of their friends at the time. They seemed so very much in love, so wholly delighted with one another. Her mother was delighted with Adlai, too, and encouraged the match; and when Lady Spears met him she became wholly committed to him. As for Adlai, by the spring of '28 he was writing glowing letters to his mother about this completely captivating girl who, for all her wealth and beauty, was very far from having had a happy life. He was profoundly moved by her yearning toward beauty, and very proud of her manifestations of literary talent. When the Chicago *Tribune* printed one of her verses on its editorial page, he bought extra copies of that issue and sent a clipping of it to Bloomington for mounting in the family album.[4]

---

[4] The verse, entitled *It Must Be Mad*, was as follows:

I watch my shadow slide about　　　　*I watch it raise its fist and know*
And O, I know without a doubt　　　　*There's no one there to take the blow*
It must be mad!　　　　　　　　　　　*I see it going out the door*
I watch it pick up things with care,　　*And wonder what it's going for:*
When I can see there's nothing there,　*It must be mad!*

One of the points he referred to, as he spoke of her to his family, was her *spontaneity*. She seemed to him so fully and freely and charmingly self-expressive, and she did things on the spur of the moment, in defiance of schedules and plans.

"You know," he said to his mother, "I've always planned things, and considered consequences. But she just does things as she *feels* like doing them." Together they might balance one another, he felt, making up for each other's deficiencies.

Moreover, by marrying him Ellen would become a member of a family, and would partake of a family life, such as she had never known before. In later years she would make a much-quoted remark to the effect that the Stevensons "must have Chinese blood in them, they all worship their ancestors so." The remark would be considered a jibe at her husband's people. But at the outset she was intrigued by the intense family feeling which all of them had, and was herself sustained by the sense of belonging to a living tradition, deeply rooted in history and growing through her husband and herself toward the future. If this "ancestor worship" seemed to her ridiculous in some respects, she could not but realize that it gave to every present Stevenson life a richer, deeper significance.

And this sense of vital continuity was particularly strong through the spring and early summer of 1928, for in March of that year Mr. and Mrs. Ernest Ives returned to the United States for the birth of their son, Timothy Read. He was born in Chicago on April 9. Ellen and her mother were impressed by the intense family feeling which focused on this event. So much warmth and joy surrounded it! Joy glowed in the proud father and mother scarcely more than it did in the baby's grandparents and uncle! Obviously, then, the family feeling was far more than "ancestor worship"; it was concerned more intensely with the future than it was with the past.

That year, as a matter of fact, it looked for a time as though new luster might be added to the Stevenson family name in the very immediate future. Almost simultaneously with the birth of Timothy Read Ives came the birth of a vice-presidential boom for the baby's grandfather Stevenson. The Democratic National Convention was to be held in Houston, Texas, in July, and as July approached, Lewis Green Stevenson was deemed an increasingly strong contender for nomination as Al Smith's running mate. Several leading Illinois newspapers editorialized on the subject, pointing out that Lewis Stevenson's nomination would greatly strengthen the Democratic appeal to the farm vote, a vote which should certainly have been lost to the Republicans when they, at their convention in Kansas City, rejected the principles of the McNary-Haugen Bill and proposed as a "solution" to the farm problem a farm board which would encourage co-operative marketing!

Buffie remained in America until July, while Ernest Ives returned to his post in Ankara, Turkey. She attended the Houston convention with her parents. And there she saw her gallant father's boom die swiftly as Al Smith, nominated on the first ballot, threw his support to the liberal Senator Joseph T. Robinson of Arkansas. Robinson was of course nominated: the campaign became one of Smith-Robinson versus Herbert Hoover and Kansas Senator Charles Curtis. Lewis Stevenson was not uninfluential at Houston, however. He had a hand in shaping the farm plank of the Democratic platform.

For Adlai, Lake Geneva, Wisconsin, held a greater vital interest than Houston, Texas, did that month. Mrs. Waller Borden and her daughters Ellen and Betty were living there, at Ceylon Court, the luxurious estate of the late Mr. and Mrs. John J. Mitchell. Adlai was a frequent weekend visitor. By the latter part of the month, he and Ellen were engaged to be married, though the formal announcement would not be made until late September. One particularly "beautiful weekend" with "the 'wife' and in-laws" began on Saturday, July 28, and when he wrote his mother about it the following Monday he said that "Mrs. Borden expects you & father whenever you can come & wants you to understand that you won't be visiting, just 'staying.'"

Three days later, on Thursday morning, he called upon Ellen's father at the latter's office, 6 North Michigan Avenue, for an interview he had dreaded but which "turned out most pleasantly." He found the elder Borden to be really "a most pleasant" man, if perhaps a bit arrogant and willful, and received from him a great deal of advice as to how and where they should live, the size and nature of Ellen's property, and so on. That afternoon, Mr. McPherson, a senior partner of Cutting, Moore and Sidley, summoned Adlai to his office. "[With] quaking knees I responded, but, wonder of wonders, instead of firing me he raised my salary beginning August 1 to $200 per mo!" Adlai wrote his mother that evening. Thus emboldened, he told McPherson that he was engaged to be married and would like to have a month or six-week vacation. "To the month he acquiesced eagerly—to the 6 weeks he hesitated on the ground of example to the other young men but said he would take it up with his partners. Hereafter, August 2 will always be my lucky day."

Autumn came and passed for him in a delirium of happy, hectic activity. Everything seemed to be breaking his way, including his modest stock-market speculations—though they, of course, were apparently breaking in favor of *everybody* who was in the market that year, else the prudent Stevenson would not have bought stocks at all.

On a typical weekend in early October he and Ellen motored up to Lake Forest on a Saturday afternoon, played some tennis there, then drove over to Lake Geneva for a Saturday night and Sunday at the country home of the Kellogg Fairbankses. Mrs. Fairbanks was almost equally famous as hostess and as Janet Ayer Fairbanks, the novelist, and Ellen and Adlai had a marvelous time with her. She and Adlai got along particularly well because she was that rare creature in her stratum of Chicago society, an ardent supporter of Al Smith.

The only cloud on the bright skies of his happiness was the defeat, in early November, of Al Smith and of most of the Democratic candidates for House and Senate. Once again the Republican victory was of landslide proportions—due in part to a "smear" campaign against Al Smith's Catholicism and his alleged determination to "bring back the open saloon," but due mainly to the continuing "Republican prosperity." (Said Herbert Hoover, as he accepted the nomination: "We in America are nearer to the final triumph over poverty than ever before in the history of any land. . . . We shall soon . . . be in sight of the day when poverty will be banished from this nation.")

IV

At four-thirty on Saturday afternoon, December 1, 1928, in the small chapel of the fashionable Fourth Presbyterian Church on Upper Michigan Avenue, with the pastor, Dr. John Timothy Stone, officiating, Ellen Borden became the bride of Adlai Ewing Stevenson II. The bride wore a white velvet gown, with collar and full-length panels of a rose-point lace that had been worn at their weddings by her mother and her grandmother and her great-grandmother. Her only ornament was an antique necklace of uncut emeralds. She was given away by her father. Her younger sister, Betty, was her only attendant. William B. McIlvaine, Jr., was the bridegroom's best man. Only the immediate families and a few intimate friends, some twenty-five in all, attended the ceremony. Among these were Mrs. Louis B. Merwin, Mr. and Mrs. Davis Merwin, Mr. and Mrs. Ralph C. DeMange, and Mrs. Davis Ewing, all of Bloomington. From Chicago were Mr. and Mrs. Chauncey McCormick, Mr. and Mrs. Chauncey Blair, Mrs. Edith Rockefeller McCormick, Mr. and Mrs. John Paul Welling, and Colonel and Mrs. George Langhorne.

After the wedding Mrs. Waller Borden was hostess at a large reception for the bridal couple at 1020 Lake Shore Drive, and on the following Tuesday, December 4, Mr. and Mrs. Adlai E. Stevenson sailed from New York for the Mediterranean, where they honeymooned for six weeks (Mr. McPherson and the partners had decided to grant the extra two weeks), motoring through Tunisia, Algeria, and Morocco.

When they returned to Chicago in mid-January 1929 they moved into an apartment in a remodeled brownstone house at 76 East Walton Place. Here, on February 5, Adlai Stevenson celebrated his twenty-ninth birthday. His bride was barely twenty.

Book Three

YEARS OF GROWTH

CHAPTER TWELVE

Change of Phase:
A New Stage of History Is Set

Early in 1929, Lewis and Helen Stevenson were in Europe, where they visited Buffie and little Timmie and Ernest Ives in Constantinople. Helen Stevenson remained in Constantinople for several weeks, then went to the Riviera with Buffie, while Lewis traveled extensively through central and western Europe. Everywhere he encountered a bitter resentment of America's failure to join the League of Nations, or even the World Court. He spoke of this in a newspaper interview when he returned in March to Bloomington. He spoke also, to friends, of the wave of social unrest which seemed to be sweeping Europe. There could be no doubt that in Austria and Germany the failure of the United States to ratify the Versailles Treaty gave a persuasive political power into the hands of weird figures—a "crazy demagogue named Hitler," for instance—who denounced that treaty and termed it a piece of treachery by "the Jews."

On the evening of March 26 Lewis Stevenson sat at a little desk in the Bloomington Club, writing a letter to Buffie—a "very sweet, loving letter"—all the more poignant to her because it was destined to remain forever unfinished. In the very midst of it he became aware that he was unwell. Then, abruptly, his body was racked by an overwhelming pain of a kind he had never known before: he called for help and collapsed. He was rushed to Brokaw Hospital. His young cousin, Dr. E. M. (Ed) Stevenson, was summoned. The doctor's diagnosis was instantaneous: Lewis Stevenson had suffered a severe heart attack and was in imminent danger of death.

Examining him with a greater care than he'd been able to do before, Dr. Ed was astonished to discover that the Lewis Stevenson he had known, a witty, active man who seemed younger than his sixty-one years, actually lived in a very old man's body. Heart, arteries, muscular tone—all were such as a doctor would expect to find in a man in his late seventies. And as Dr. Ed reviewed his patient's life in the light of present evidence, he was struck by the gallantry with which Lewis Stevenson had lived through what must have been long periods of intense pain. Only extreme tensions long continued (of these the migraine headaches had probably been a symptom) could have ravaged a body as this beneath his hands was ravaged. Yet courage, buoyant courage, had certainly been one of Lewis Stevenson's salient characteristics in politics and business, where he had taken many a bitter blow without whining and without giving up.

Messages radiated from the sickbed—north to Chicago, east to Ithaca, New York, far eastward to Buffie and Helen Stevenson in the South of France. . . .

Adlai, with Ellen, came down from Chicago. When it became apparent that Lewis Stevenson, after all, might survive for a time, they returned to Chicago for a few anxious days.

Once, when he was alone in the hospital room with his father, it was borne in upon Adlai with special force that his father lay upon his deathbed, for on that day his father himself obviously believed that the end was near. Lewis Stevenson, in great pain, could hardly talk above a whisper, but he looked at Adlai in a peculiarly penetrating way as he gasped that "politics is a hazardous life, full of ingratitudes"—and it seemed to Adlai, at that instant, that his father was trying to warn him against a political career. But why? Apart from his brief and not very serious consideration of Mr. Warner's suggestion that he run for the legislature, Adlai had hardly considered politics as a career. Afterward Adlai could not remember precisely what his father's words were.

"Memory plays tricks on you when you recall moments like that," he said, many years later. "You're emotionally wrought up and later, out of all your later experience, you're likely to ascribe a greater significance to words and gestures than they actually had at the time."

But he did remember, beyond power of doubt, that his father murmured something about an "obligation" and "doing what you must" along with his warning. It all seemed very strange to Adlai at the time. Later it was one of the memories which convinced him that his father had always had undisclosed ambitions for him, had always known that Adlai, with his heritage and background and personal character, was destined (or "doomed," as Adlai would sometimes feel in later years) to follow a political career.

Shortly after one o'clock on Friday, April 5, Adlai and Ellen in Chicago boarded a train for Bloomington to spend the weekend at his father's bedside. At approximately the same time Lewis Stevenson, after a light lunch, dropped off to sleep. Lewis's sister Julia, Mrs. Martin D. Hardin, sat watching him. He slept quietly. But at five minutes before two o'clock he awoke and fixed upon his sister a puzzled gaze.

"Is everything all right?" he asked.

Mrs. Hardin, surprised, nodded and smiled reassuringly.

"Yes," she said. "Everything's fine."

He closed his eyes. He heaved a great sigh. He was utterly still. His sister stared at him, touched him. She called frantically to the nurse. . . .

The funeral sermon, in Bloomington's Presbyterian church, was preached by Lewis Stevenson's brother-in-law, the Reverend Martin D. Hardin, now of Ithaca, New York.

Immediately after the funeral Adlai Stevenson went to New York to meet his mother, who had sailed from Europe on the S.S. *Homeric* and was on the high seas when her husband died.

II

An ending. . . . Six months later it might have seemed to Adlai Stevenson that his father's death acquired, through its timing, a symbolic historical significance. In the gloomy canyon of La Salle Street, it seemed to many that the world itself was ending as, day after day, banner headlines in newspapers proclaimed the death of the great bull market. Lights burned all night in brokerage offices as calls for more margin went out, and through the panic-stricken days wild rumors swept the crowded sidewalks and offices, agitating even such islands of relative calm as the offices of Cutting, Moore and Sidley.

Adlai Stevenson suffered no real personal hardship from the deepening Depression. His wife's fortune, and his mother-in-law's, shrank in proportion to the prevailing decline in values. His father-in-law would lose millions and with them his formerly high position in

Chicago's financial world. His father's estate was not large, but Stevenson retained his interest in the *Pantagraph,* of which he was a director and vice-president, and a large interest in that property would come to him and his sister upon his mother's death. He seemed to be making satisfactory progress toward a partnership in his law firm. He knew well that he was among the very fortunate ones.

The realization of this was heightened in him whenever he walked to and from his work, as he sometimes did; he liked to walk. Invariably, even on fashionable North Michigan Avenue, he encountered ragged, hungry, humiliated men begging in one form or another for nickels and dimes. Both pity and terror arose from the sight of long bread lines, of men sleeping under bridges and on the benches of Grant and Lincoln parks, of jungles of shacks ("Hoovervilles," they were dubbed) on the outskirts of the city, and of war veterans selling apples on street corners. The contrast between these miserable people and those with whom he associated professionally and socially was so great as to stab any fortunate one, and especially one so conscientious as he, with guilt feelings.

He could hardly feel *personally* guilty, however, and despite such anxieties as he may have felt concerning the public welfare, his own life entered smoothly upon what, in retrospect, might seem its happiest decade. As always before, it was a very full, active life, containing a great variety of interests.

His work in the law office naturally continued to absorb the bulk of his time and energy. The over-all effect of the Depression upon Cutting, Moore and Sidley was to expand its practice almost in proportion to the contraction of Chicago business in general, and to change its character. Probate work grew relatively less important as the firm became involved in the enormous job of picking up and trying to put back together the shattered pieces of financial structures which it, if to a lesser extent than some other firms, had helped to build in the '20s. Hence fifty-hour work weeks continued to be Stevenson's common lot, and he had difficulty breaking away for weekends or vacations.

On his thirtieth birthday he was in a courtroom trying an extremely difficult jury case and was dismayed when, at six-thirty that evening, the jury brought in a verdict against his client. "It was the hardest birthday I ever put in and ever will, I hope," he wrote, thanking his mother for her birthday letter.

He had energy left over, however, for an extremely active social life. He and Ellen had multitudes of friends. Being everywhere regarded as one of the most attractive couples in the city, they were invited everywhere: and when in 1930 they moved from East Walton to a larger apartment on Lake Shore Drive, they increased the modest amount of entertaining they did. At every party Ellen sparkled, with her beauty and gaiety and quick intelligence, in a way that made her husband immensely proud—and some of their friends would remember in later years that he had been perfectly content to let her be the focus of attention, remaining himself in the background, enjoying her with the others.

He began to take part in civic activities. Conscience led him to work with the Lower North Side Community Council; it became for a time a principal one among his nonsocial "extracurricular" activities. Through this activity, and through work with Hull House, of whose board of trustees he became later a member, he saw the darker side of that economic crisis which he viewed topside through his work as a financial lawyer.

But by far the most important of his civic activities, in its effects upon the city's future and upon his own, was his work with the Chicago Council on Foreign Relations. Organized in 1922, the council was an educational enterprise designed to infuse the capital of midwest "isolationism" with some knowledge of, and active interest in, American foreign policy. Most of its members were League of Nations advocates whose local aim was to counteract in part the influence of Colonel Robert McCormick's reactionary nationalism as expressed through the Chicago *Tribune*. The membership was a highly prestigious one. Stevenson's mother-in-law was on the council's executive committee in the early '30s; so were William Pratt Sidley, the head of Stevenson's law firm, and Mrs. Harriet (John P.) Welling, Stevenson's good friend. Stevenson himself was on the committee by 1930 when the council hired, as its executive director, a brilliant, articulate young man named Clifton Utley whose leadership would help to make the council a major influence upon Chicago's intellectual life.

Utley's introduction to Adlai Stevenson took place at four o'clock on a winter afternoon in 1930, in the office of George Richardson, manager of the Marshall Field estate and then president of the council. It was a meeting of the executive committee. Utley would not remember that Stevenson made any particular impression upon him, however—then or for many months thereafter. Stevenson was considerably younger than the other committee members, who were all very distinguished people, and he said very little at these early meetings. Utley was perhaps more impressed by Ellen Stevenson, who, with her mother and younger sister, Betty (Mrs. Pirie), became a member of one of the three classes in foreign affairs which Utley taught at Lake Forest during those early Depression years.

A natural correlative of council work was an active interest in International House when this was established, with Rockefeller money, at the University of Chicago in 1932. Stevenson became a member of International House's board of governors.

III

On October 10, 1930, the Stevenson's first child, a son, was born. They named him Adlai Ewing Stevenson III. Three days later the proud father informed his mother that "family matters are progressing satisfactorily—the young man is losing some of his enchanting birthday appearance—in short, he's beginning to look more human tho he still has some distance to go." Ellen was still "terribly weak." The baby, who weighed ten pounds at birth, was promptly dubbed "Big Boy" or "Goliath" and soon became, in his father's opinion, the "funniest one-man show in the world," so much loved and enjoyed by his parents that they had difficulty making up their minds to follow through on long-laid plans for a vacation abroad in the late spring of 1931. Stevenson badly needed a vacation, however; he felt that he was going "stale," and his eyes were beginning to bother him.

He and Ellen sailed for Europe, leaving Big Boy in the hands of Alverta Duff in Bloomington. They visited Buffie and Ernest Ives in Copenhagen. Ives, having been transferred northward from Constantinople, was approaching the end of his tour of duty in the capital of Denmark. He'd soon be transferred to Pretoria. He and Buffie had insisted that Adlai and Ellen, and Mrs. Helen Stevenson, must visit them in Copenhagen before the Pretoria transfer was made, for Denmark, they said, was "wonderful." It was, too, as they presented it to their guests. Adlai called it an "epic experience." He also said, in a letter written to Buffie, Ernest, and his mother from Stockholm, that "Cutting, Moore, and Sidley seems charmingly remote now and I haven't worn glasses for two weeks."

In Stockholm they were lavishly entertained by American legation friends of Ives's. Even the "horrible news" he heard there about the "current condition of the stock market" failed to dampen their spirits, though it sharpened Adlai's awareness that Sweden, with its mixed economy of co-operatives, and of government and private enterprise, seemed remarkably immune to the world-wide economic collapse.

In Norway they also traveled widely and climbed for long happy hours in the mountains around the fjords, whose grandeur they found breath-taking. Ellen, Adlai reported to his mother and sister, had blistered feet, which were "taped up like a Napoleonic trooper's"; his own, he said, were flat, "but we are burned brown and simply spurting with health and happiness."

In late June they were back in Chicago, refreshed and renewed. Adlai plunged again into a busy, various life, and if he had any personal anxiety, it may have been over the question of whether or not he was, in actual fact, to gain a partnership in Cutting, Moore and Sidley. Five years had passed since he joined the firm, as 1932 came on, and he was well aware that six years was about the average elapsed time for this firm between the hiring of a clerk and his acceptance, if successful, into partnership. He had no hint from the senior partners concerning his own acceptability. . . . But if he had such anxiety, it was more than balanced by a new strand of happiness which wove into his life in the autumn of 1931. He was again to become a father. . . .

The second Stevenson son was born on July 7, 1932. He was formally named Borden, after Ellen's family. Informally he was dubbed "Squeak." Both children gave their parents immeasurable delight. "If laughter is an intoxicant," said the father, "I am perpetually tight." He'd remember particularly that when "Goliath" was a year and a half old he suddenly took to making imaginary snowballs under the table, then rising up and throwing them hurriedly at his mother, who dodged them laughingly, or pretended to be hit by them and dismayed. "Goliath" had also developed a strategy for dealing with admonishment or threatened correction. "If you ask him to do *anything* he finds uncongenial . . . he takes on an injured expression and says, 'Addie got a cold!'" wrote Adlai to his mother. By that time, Squeak had become "very large and handsome" and said "ga, ga," and laughed out loud at his elder brother all the time.

They were gloriously happy. . . . But their bright, cheerful private lives—and the lives of the fortunate social class—stood out in stark contrast to the gloom that spread and darkened throughout the country as America sank deeper and deeper into the slough of Depression. Even if Stevenson were not (as he would insist he was not) a "very thoughtful person" at that time, the contrast could not but impress him. Later, coupled with his view of Republican Depression policies, it would become one of the major determinants of his political feeling and thinking.

As the months passed he was forced to recognize that organized class conflict of a kind theretofore regarded as a unique European phenomenon was by no means impossible in America. Others seemed to welcome this fact; it horrified him and would have even if his class status had been less privileged, for he remained by temperament and philosophy a peacemaker, committed to reasonableness. Reasonableness itself, however, was outraged as the spring of 1932 came on. By that time 40 per cent of the possibly gainfully employed were unemployed in Chicago. Hunger stalked the food capital of the world, while a "surplus" pressed livestock and crop prices down to, and below, the cost of producing them on Stevenson farms and those other farms his father had managed!

Surely the only power great enough to challenge successfully the Great Depression was the power of the federal government. Yet government presented, to a politically minded young man, a spectacle of confusion and impotence as educative as it was unedifying through those dismal years.

Hoover's tragedy was not that he was coldhearted, indifferent to human suffering. Rather was it that he and his colleagues remained helpless prisoners of rigid, economic fatalism. The President had apparently invested most of the moral energy of his highly moralistic nature in the belief that prosperity "depends" upon the activities of businessmen, that jobs are "created" or "provided" by businessmen, and that such direct economic aid as the federal government gave in this emergency should therefore be limited to businessmen. He displayed no awareness of the fact that total national income must be so distributed as to be effective in the market place, that mass purchasing power must match mass productive power, if economic disaster is to be avoided. Adlai Stevenson laughed when someone, in a vulgar but remarkably apt metaphor, said that Hoover's economic policies were based on the theory of "feeding the sparrows by feeding the horse"—but he could not laugh at the effect these policies produced. And Hoover's was one of the examples he would have in mind when, in later public speech, he repeatedly inveighed against the dangers of stereotyped "political thinking,"[1] the "lazy preference" for "slogans" and "labels" and omnibus "isms" over the "rigors of rational thought" and direct, clear-eyed observation. As for himself, "I have no fixed principles by which every issue is to be *automatically* resolved. . . ."

Nevertheless the Republican party, its Old Guard firmly in control, in June nominated Herbert Hoover for a second term and mapped a campaign strategy which stressed the "international causes" of the Depression and blamed the obstructive tactics of a Democratically controlled Congress for the administration's inability to act effectively in the growing emergency.

The Democratic National Convention met in the Chicago Stadium the last of June. The meeting was remarkably harmonious. Adlai Stevenson, who observed a good portion of the proceedings from the gallery, felt no such excitement and witnessed no such displays of acrimony as had marked his last Democratic convention (that of 1924), for there was not, this time, a really close competition among the top three candidates for the presidential nomination.

Speaker John Nance Garner of Texas was one of the three, but the fact that he was William Randolph Hearst's choice indicated personal qualities which made him unacceptable to the decisive liberal wing of his party. Al Smith was still in the running, but could be nominated only if there was a deadlock between Garner and the front-running candidate. The latter was fifty-year-old Governor Franklin Delano Roosevelt of New York, who received a majority of the delegated votes on the first ballot and was nominated on the fourth, with Garner as his running mate.

It would seem strange to Adlai Stevenson, later on, that Franklin Roosevelt at the time of his nomination was widely regarded as an amiable weakling, so eager to please everyone, so needful of being personally liked, as to be incapable of truly bold, decisive action.

Of his personal charm, Stevenson had direct experience during the campaign. The Democratic candidate for governor of Illinois that year was Henry Horner, the probate judge of Cook County. Since much of the practice of Cutting, Moore and Sidley had been probate work, Stevenson had had many professional contacts with Horner

---

[1] See, for example, Adlai Stevenson's address to the New York *Herald Tribune* Forum, New York City, October 24, 1949.

and the two became good personal friends. They shared a passion for Lincolniana, of which Horner was an avid collector, and often discussed the role of Stevenson's maternal ancestors in early Illinois history. Particularly did they talk about Jesse Fell. Horner was intensely interested in the three-page autobiography in Lincoln's handwriting, now in the possession of Adlai's cousin Emmett Richardson, executor of the estate of Adlai's great-aunt Fanny Fell. Through Stevenson, Horner hoped to obtain the priceless document for the State Historical Library in Springfield—and perhaps it was in the nature of a "bribe," in part, that Horner took Stevenson with him to call upon Roosevelt in the latter's campaign train that autumn.

A long line of politically important men was passing through the car in which Roosevelt sat, and as Stevenson joined the line with Horner he expected no more than a perfunctory handshake from the candidate. Instead, Roosevelt "placed" the young man as soon as Horner pronounced his name, recalling that F.D.R.'s father, James Roosevelt, had been a friendly acquaintance of the first Adlai Ewing Stevenson and that he had known Lewis Stevenson well in the Navy Department during the war, when both worked for Josephus Daniels. The zest and magnetism of the man seemed to Stevenson almost irresistible.

When election day came, Roosevelt's victory, though decisive, was less overwhelming than might have been expected under the circumstances, and during the four months intervening between election day and the inauguration of March 4, there was a rising tide of financial panic. A wave of "banking holidays," declared by state governors, swept the country in February. Trade was reduced to a barter basis in hundreds of communities. A virtually complete economic paralysis, wholly unprecedented, wholly terrifying, gripped the country as the fateful month of March came on.

IV

Saturday, March 4, 1933. . . . This morning the banking system of America ceased to function. This morning the Democratic party—that loose collection of dissident elements, flawed by a score of self-contradictions—is to assume control of both the legislative and executive branches of government, for the first time since 1918. What will it do? What will the new President do? What can anyone do . . . ?

Adlai and Ellen Stevenson are in Washington that day. They have obtained tickets to the inaugural festivities through their good friend James H. Douglas, Jr., who in March of '32 had accepted appointment as fiscal Assistant Secretary of the U. S. Treasury, and through Senator J. Hamilton Lewis, Democrat and Stevenson friend from Illinois. Buffie and Ernest Ives are also in Washington. Ernest has completed his tour of duty in Africa and is to be stationed for several months in the capital, between assignments abroad. But Adlai, alas, suffers that day from an ear infection; he dare not take his seat with the others on the great square, immediately below the flag-and-bunting bedecked platform at the Capitol's east front, for it is yet winter in Washington and exposure to it would be dangerous to him. Instead, he listens to the ceremony, huddled beside a radio, like millions of his fellow Americans.

Those millions are gripped by a fear as gray and chill as the sky above the Capitol dome that day. The oath is administered by Chief Justice Charles Evans Hughes, whose bearded dignity remains as glacial as it had been on that day in 1916 when Buffie first saw him. Then, in a ringing, confident, mellow voice, the new President of the United States addresses his fellow Americans.

First, he says, "let me assert my firm belief that the only thing we have to fear is fear itself—nameless, unreasoning, unjustified terror which paralyzes needed efforts to convert retreat into advance." What caused the present crisis? Not a blind impersonal force, but living and all-too-fallible men, says Franklin Roosevelt; the trouble flows from the grasping actions of "the rulers of the exchange of mankind's goods." And such men, in control of government, have proved their inability to cope with the evils they have produced. "True, they have tried, but their efforts have been cast in the pattern of an outworn tradition. . . . The money changers have fled from their high seats in the temple of our civilization."

Adlai Stevenson glances down quickly at his clasped hands, with a smile and a quick shake of his head. In later years he will deplore the antagonism between business and government which New Deal sloganeering, and big-business sloganeering, will help to produce. But on this March day there is, perhaps, the necessity to restore a balance by such harsh thrusts as the new President is making—and it can hardly be denied that the great financiers have, at least for the time being, forfeited their right to public confidence. Anyway, thinks

Adlai Stevenson, this new President is obviously no weakling. Here is a fighter!

If necessary, the new President declares, he will not hesitate to ask the Congress for "broad executive power to wage a war against the emergency, as great as that which would be given me if we were in fact invaded by a foreign foe." The declaration rings in ears which, for three stagnant years, have heard mostly from government abstract moralistic reasons for not doing what the people want it to do. The people, this new leader says, "have registered a mandate that they want direct, vigorous action. . . . They have made me the present instrument of their wishes. In the spirit of the gift I take it."

Speech like this, in these circumstances, is itself action—passionate action! And by action it will be swiftly followed. Adlai Stevenson has had a sense of this from the moment he set foot in Washington: there is a new excitement in the air, an electric energy, which makes him long to have some part in the history about to be made. He had hinted as much to an old family friend, Harold Ickes, who is the new Secretary of the Interior, and had been surprised when Ickes pounced on the vague suggestion. The New Deal will need bright, eager, energetic young men—men able to plunge boldly into new, uncharted country. Like a magnet, the administration will draw such men to Washington. . . .

Action! Action in overwhelming quantity and bewildering variety!

On Sunday, March 5, the banking holiday will be made national; the Congress will be called into an extraordinary session; and the export of gold and all dealings in foreign exchange will be prohibited. Thus will the country go part way off the gold standard—and this is but a slight shadow of coming events. Soon the country will go all the way off gold into a managed currency, which will be promptly inflated. In orderly fashion, and with no renewal of panic, the banks will be reopened, their individual deposits soon insured up to ten thousand dollars through a Federal Deposit Insurance Corporation.

Adlai Stevenson thereafter will live his life against a background of positive government, some of his life in the midst of that government.

CHAPTER THIRTEEN

A Civic Leader Emerges

To the amazingly symptomatic Scott Fitzgerald, the Depression meant the utter repudiation of values to which, despite himself, he had committed most of his ardent nature. "[We] will never feel quite so intensely about our surroundings any more," he wrote, sadly, in 1931. Perhaps to Ellen Borden Stevenson, too, the Depression meant the destruction of a world in which she felt more at home than she could feel in any that succeeded it. At least, there would be observers who in the 1950s saw her as in many ways still committed—perhaps willfully, perhaps helplessly—to the attitudes of the 1920s. But for Adlai Stevenson the Depression meant only the addition of another growth ring to his organically developing character.

Perhaps it was a larger growth ring than had been added in any preceding period of equivalent length since he achieved his majority; but there was no radical difference of substance between it and the earlier growths. It was permeated by many of the same basic values, most of the same essential attitudes. Though there was inevitably a change of emphasis among them as his total self enlarged through experience, all his former selves remained alive in him, organically joined, including the "saintly" little child, the overmothered schoolboy, the insouciant Princeton man, the Chicago man about town, the reluctant lawyer. The viability of these several selves widened the range of his possible reaction to stimuli. It provided him with multiple levels of response; and he would become able to shift from one to another of these with a smooth ease baffling to those who, knowing him well in some one of his aspects in the 1950s, believed that they knew *him*, totally, intimately. The latter knowledge, in so far as it could be achieved at all, depended upon an intimate knowledge of his ancestors and of their effects upon him—for his ancestors, too, remained alive in him. Especially Jesse Fell.

Hence the symbolic aptness of the fact that Jesse Fell's friendship with Abraham Lincoln provided one of the chief means of Adlai Stevenson's friendship with Henry Horner, who was inaugurated as governor of Illinois in 1933; and that this in turn led to a meeting with Franklin Roosevelt, whose historic role was to prevent that utter break with the American past which political upheaval might otherwise have produced. Historical tradition, personified by Jesse Fell, was vital to Adlai Stevenson. It was a main source of his innate conservatism, that "moderation" which, in the 1950s, would make him unacceptable to the "give 'em hell" type of politician in his own party. In the 1930s, coupled with his personal observations of the Soviet experiment in 1926, it prevented his seeking primary cues where so many American intellectuals were seeking them, in Moscow.

Not that he was wholly unsympathetic with the motives which prompted other young men—some of them in his own economic and social class—to don the red cap and the moujik blouse.[1] He might even honor those who suffered and died (brave and honorable young Americans did die in Spain in '36) for their belief that communism was infinitely preferable to fascism, on humane grounds, and was fascism's only alternative. But he was not himself tempted nor conscience-driven in that direction. No descendant and emulator of Jesse Fell, that firm defender of free speech in Bloomington during the Civil War, was likely to regard the sacrifice of essential civil liberties as a legitimate means to any political end; these liberties, he would say, *were* an end of government as well as a means. Nor would he admit, in the Depression's darkest hour, that the sacrifice was necessary to the cure of economic ills. On the contrary, he insisted then and always afterward that a full and free expression of all ideas, attitudes, even prejudices on public questions is an essential of political stability and progress in any society. Out of this freedom, as he clearly saw—out of this ferment of controversy—the Roosevelt programs emerged, giving the lie to Marxist predictions of an immediate total collapse of American capitalism.

Thus the New Deal was, for him, a continuation of the American Way as envisaged by such diverse American leaders as Jefferson and

[1] The phrase is from Scott Fitzgerald's *Echoes of the Jazz Age*, published by *Scribner's* magazine, November 1931.

Jackson and Lincoln, Bryan and Wilson, George Norris and La Follette. He watched its development with an avid interest after he
returned from the inauguration, and the brief holiday following it, to
a Chicago desk piled high with work. "The routine of life here quickly
dispels holiday memories, and by this time I hardly feel I've been
away," he wrote his ailing mother rather wearily in early April, "except for the children, who surprise me every night." The routine
seemed to him particularly monotonous and dull after the excitement of Washington, an excitement which rose steadily higher as the
Congress, applauded for doing so even by a good portion of the
Republican press, rubber-stamped one after another of Roosevelt's
"revolutionary" proposals.

True, Stevenson's own life continued very active through the
spring. In early April he and Ellen believed they had found their
future home—an "old wreck" of a farmhouse, with barn and other
outbuildings, on thirteen acres of the highest ground in Lake
County; it was just four miles from the Lake Forest station, had a
lovely view in all directions, and could be bought for approximately
fifteen thousand dollars. (They were destined never to buy it.) During that same month, he concurred in Dave Merwin's decision to cut
Pantagraph dividends by 25 per cent, because of declining revenue,
and advised his mother to reduce her expenditures accordingly. During preceding months, he had been repeatedly "tried out" as a chairman of meetings of the Council on Foreign Relations, and had not
been found wanting by Clifton Utley and fellow members of the
executive committee; as a result he was nominated to be president
of the council, and was elected in May.

But these activities did not suffice to stifle his yearning for a part
in what Ernest Lindley was soon to call the "Roosevelt Revolution."
This yearning was soon satisfied. He was summoned to Washington
by George Peek, whom the new Secretary of Agriculture, Henry A.
Wallace, had called to the capital as organizer and first head of the
Agricultural Adjustment Administration. Peek had taken with him a
friend of Stevenson's named Wayne Chatfield-Taylor of Chicago, with
whom Stevenson had often discussed the farm problem—so when Peek
began recruiting lawyers for the AAA staff, Wayne Taylor reminded
him about Stevenson.

"From Bloomington, you say?" Peek looked at Wayne Taylor, who
nodded. "Why, that is Louie Stevenson's boy—and he ought to be

well backgrounded in farm problems, all right. Let's get him if we can."

Thus, within four months after the New Deal's initiation, Adlai Stevenson was a working member of it. He obtained a leave of absence from the law firm—though Sidley warned that, upon his return, he might not be given the same position he then held. In the hot Washington July of 1933 he became an assistant to Jerome Frank, General Counsel of the AAA, with the formal title of Special Attorney and a salary of sixty-five hundred dollars per annum, less the 15 per cent deducted by the Federal Economy Act of March. Ellen and the boys remained for the summer in the house Adlai and she had rented in Lake Forest, while Adlai "batched it" with Ernest Ives and John Kennedy in the Kennedy home at 2121 Bancroft Place. (Mrs. Kennedy, the former Ellen Bruce Lee, who had undertaken to "float" Adlai in society during the youth's holiday visit with his family in Washington in 1918, was spending the summer at Gracelands, her family estate in West Virginia. Buffie was staying with Helen Stevenson at Charlevoix.) Immediately he was plunged into such a fever of work that he saw little of Ives and virtually nothing of Kennedy.

"The work is complicated but interesting and vastly important," he explained in a letter to Ellen. "In essence, we're creating [what amounts to] gigantic trusts in all the food industries, to raise prices and eliminate unfair competition, thereby increasing returns to the farmers ultimately. Everyone from flour millers to mayonnaise manufacturers are here and each day I hear all about the troubles of a different industry in conferences, then spend the night drafting a remarketing agreement to correct them. Then the objections begin to flow in from all over the country. Finally we hold public hearings, and at last the Sec'y of Ag. signs and approves the agreement, etc., etc. The procedure is complicated—too complicated. I would like to tell you about it but it would take forever. Furthermore, it is changed almost daily! If anything, my complaint would be that there is too much drafting done by the legal division and too little administering —but I hope that situation will be corrected when we get a better background of experience."

(Not until later would it occur to him that this formation of "giant trusts," mingling government and industry in corporate enterprises for price-fixing purposes, with a very tenuous line of responsibility between them and the public at large, was a radical departure from the American Way.)

Most of his work, which later involved a good deal of travel for the purpose of holding public hearings, had to do with special crops —particularly tree crops on the West Coast. Oranges were ripening in California's orange groves by the time the Agricultural Adjustment Act was signed into law: there was enormous pressure upon the legal division to execute swiftly the marketing agreements covering them: and Stevenson probably drafted more of these than anyone else. The work was so frenzied that he had no time for casual friendly intercourse with fellow staff members, one of whom was an attractive, thin-faced young lawyer named Alger Hiss. Felix Frankfurter had sent Hiss down from Harvard in 1929 to serve as secretary to the ancient and honorable Justice Oliver Wendell Holmes—the highest honor Frankfurter bestowed upon his students—and he now embarked upon a career in the federal service. Under other circumstances the two young men might have enjoyed arguing social and economic philosophy; under circumstances actually prevailing, they saw one another in the corridors and at staff conferences, and that was all. . . .

Ellen and the boys came to Washington in September ("and am I happy!" Adlai wrote his mother, now returned to Bloomington). They moved into rather too large a house in Georgetown. ("We may rattle a bit," wrote Adlai.) He continued to work ten-hour days. But it renewed him to come home at night to his family. Watching the daily growth, mentally and physically, of Big Boy and Squeak was literally re-creative.

As 1933 drew to a close, the emergency pressures upon the AAA legal staff slackened somewhat. By that time a temporary Federal Alcohol Control Administration was being set up to exercise some control over prices, production, and distribution of alcoholic beverages when repeal of Prohibition became effective in December. There was an immediate demand by the control committee (Joseph L. Choate, Jr., of New York was its director: Willard L. Thorp was among its other four members) for men to staff its legal division. Since the FACA was a subsidiary of the AAA, its staff could be most easily recruited through transfers from the AAA legal division, and Adlai Stevenson was asked if he would accept such a transfer. He said he would. So in January of 1934 he became assistant general counsel of this newest of the fifteen major special agencies thus far established by the Roosevelt administration—and was again working ten-hour days.

His tour of duty with the FACA lasted eight months, during which he had a good deal to do with establishing the administrative structure of the agency as well as with the regulation of the industry. Perhaps the most pleasant episode of the period was an official trip to the Hawaiian Islands, to restore some order and organize regional boards to administer codes. Ellen accompanied him on this trip. She was photographed with him as they were about to disembark from the *Lurline* for their nine-day stay. The photograph, printed in a Honolulu newspaper and later mounted in a family scrapbook, showed both Ellen and Adlai wearing leis and wearing, too, rather wan sheepish smiles. . . .

He resigned his government position in September and returned to Chicago, resuming his law practice with Cutting, Moore and Sidley. A few weeks later he was appointed to two positions on governmental bodies. By the NRA, he was appointed government member of the code authority for the flour-milling industry; by the FACA, he was appointed government member of the code authority for the wine industry. Stories and photographs of him appeared in the press, as the appointments were announced. He was rapidly becoming one of the best-known young civic leaders in Chicago, and this fact was of course an asset to his law firm. It helped overcome whatever reluctance some of the partners may have had to accepting him as one of them, with the result that, early in 1935, small news stories in the Chicago press announced that Adlai E. Stevenson had become one of eleven partners (there were by then sixteen associates also) in the firm of Cutting, Moore and Sidley. He thereby gained not only added prestige in his profession but also a marked increase in his annual income: his share of the firm's profits soon amounted to between eighteen and twenty thousand dollars a year.

Soon after Adlai and Ellen returned with the boys to Chicago, in the autumn of 1934, Mrs. Helen Stevenson came there, moving into the Churchill Hotel at 1255 North State, just a block from the house where her son lived. She was unwell; her health had steadily deteriorated since her husband's death. Dr. Ed Stevenson, for one, was convinced that her physical ills were due in part to her state of mind, and certainly she was profoundly depressed.

Now that both children were wholly independent of her, having outgrown even their need for her loving advice, her life seemed pointless to her; sometimes it seemed worse than that, for sometimes her son or daughter seemed actually to resent a little her attempts to advise them, help them. Restlessly she had moved about the country and gone abroad, seeking in vain for that vividness of experience she had formerly known. The world had gone stale—and she was tired. More and more she found herself turning toward the past, toward older members of her family who had known her parents and herself as a little girl. She strove to renew herself through these living repositories of the family tradition; sometimes she *was* renewed, but at other times, measuring herself against the past, she seemed more than ever diminished. She measured, she felt, so very small!

"Who would ever think I was a Fell!" she wrote her aunt Rachel, from the Churchill. How she would love to see again her aunts! "But beautiful, patient Adlai has wanted me near him, and so this tiny apartment, and he has come in mornings and evenings with always the same good cheer." She wrote this. Yet she knew that her son wanted her near him, not primarily for his sake, but for hers. He did not really *need* her; he exercised, with her, "patience"!

After a while she felt a little better. She traveled. The doctors said it did not harm her to travel: her blood pressure was a little high, but not alarming, and though there were vascular changes, these were not alarming either.

She died very suddenly in November of 1935. She had been on a trip; she stopped in Milwaukee in order to be near Cousin Harriet Richardson.[2] There she became ill and went to a hospital. . . . Down in Bloomington a new building was being erected to house the *Pantagraph*, and one of Helen Davis Stevenson's last acts was to pen a public message to the newspaper, congratulating it on the laying of the cornerstone.

The funeral service, in Bloomington's Unitarian church, was preached by the Reverend Rupert N. Holloway, of Madison, Wisconsin. She was buried beside her husband in the Bloomington cemetery.

Yet in her son, much of her essential self lived on, helping him to grow steadily toward that recognized greatness she had long believed would be his. Her influence upon him was greater by far than any other person's had been, or could ever be. Though it

[2] Harriet Fuffe Richardson would publish in 1930 a little book, *Quaker Pioneers*, in which she told the story of Jesse W. Fell and his descendants.

seemed overly aggressive to some observers, the love she had given him was of a kind he apparently needed to ensure the inner security, the serenity of spirit, which was so strongly characteristic of him, enabling him in later years to bear with grace, with apparent gaiety even, strains and disappointments severe enough to break most men. There was a fortunate balance between reticence and expressiveness in his handling of emotions, and for this his mother's influence may have been largely responsible. She always expressed so freely, even extravagantly at times, her love for him, forcing him to respond at least somewhat in kind and thus keep liquid emotional assets which might otherwise have frozen in the reserves that seemed natural to him. . . .

Again there was a balance of death with new life in Adlai's immediate family. New life grew in Ellen as her husband's mother died, and on February 7, 1936, she gave birth to her third son. He was named John Fell, after Ellen's father John and Adlai's great-grandfather Jesse Fell.

The future seemed by then to be rushing into the present, ruthlessly shoving the past farther and farther back. Aunts, uncles, cousins in swift succession followed Lewis and Helen Stevenson into the grave. "Aunt Lizzie and Cousin Charlie passed away within a week of each other, and I wasn't able to get down for either funeral," wrote Adlai to Buffie early in 1937. "Our family is vanishing rapidly and it gives one a wistful, lonely feeling. But I suppose it happens to everyone and that we must realize that we've suddenly become the older generation now."

II

On January 1, 1937, the law firm became Sidley, McPherson, Austin and Burgess ("Sounds like a trunk falling down stairs, doesn't it?" commented Adlai in a letter written to Buffie, who, with Ernest and Timmy, had just transferred from Algiers to Stockholm). And, as a partner, Stevenson was given increasingly difficult and important assignments. He often complained, in brief and hurried notes to Buffie, that he was "on a day and night shift at the office," so that he saw John Fell but once a week, on Sunday, during most of his youngest son's first years. ("Ho hum!" he wrote in January of '37. "It's Saturday night and I'm still at the d—— office. John Fell thrives—tho I haven't been home in time to see him since last Saturday.") But his complaints were mild responses to extreme provocations. Actually the intense pressure of work upon him failed to crush his cheerful good humor; this continued to be one of the most attractive and remarkable things about him, his associates later remembered.

In the summer and fall of 1938, for instance, Commonwealth Edison Company, with some of its subsidiaries, including the Public Service Company of Northern Illinois, was preparing to issue something over forty-two million dollars' worth of debentures, some thirty-three million dollars of first-mortgage bonds, plus other series of bonds that brought the total new financing up to approximately eighty million dollars. At that time the SEC was a recent development; there were few precedents to guide the performance of a huge, complicated job. Involved was the preparation of the prospectus and the registration statement which must be filed with the SEC. The latter was a lengthy document, one hundred or so typed legal-length pages, detailing the history of each company, its earnings, its organization structure, and so on. The most scrupulous detailed accuracy was required, and every word was reviewed by countless officials of both Commonwealth Edison and Halsey, Stuart and Company, the investment firm underwriting the financing. In such cases, the underwriters press for as early a completion of the securities issuance as possible, since they stand to lose a great deal if the market fails to hold up. Hence the time pressure on those doing the work is immense.

The law firm, representing Halsey, Stuart, assigned Adlai Stevenson to work on the project with Edward D. McDougal, Jr. (McDougal, a Princeton graduate of the class of 1918, had become a partner in the firm in 1930.) The two worked literally night and day with Willis Gale, who was then financial vice-president of Commonwealth Edison and its subsidiaries (in the 1950s he would be chairman of the board), in the Commonwealth Edison offices at 72 West Adams. They'd go down at midnight to a restaurant, for coffee and a sandwich and a breath of fresh air, returning often to work hours more. McDougal would remember that he became brusque and short-tempered under the pressure, and that others became even more so, but that Stevenson was unfailingly cheerful.

"He did his work well, too," McDougal would say. "He was a thoroughly competent lawyer. I wouldn't say he was brilliant at that time, but he certainly had the potential. These things you hear from his political enemies about his being an indifferent lawyer—they're simply not true. He was hard-working and conscientious and highly intelligent on the job. If he hadn't been, Mr. Sidley and the others would never have given him a partnership. It was almost unheard of for an associate to interrupt his career with that firm as Adlai had done. To be with Cutting, Moore and Sidley was itself a career, and I know that some of the men there looked a little askance at the 'outside' activities that Adlai kept engaging in."

For his "extracurricular" activities continued. It was as if there was always at the back of his mind the need and desire to engage in public service—the kind of public service which might lead him into politics. One noon in late '34 or early January of '35 he and Dutch Smith went to a luncheon given by the Illinois Children's Home and Aid Society. This was a philanthropy with an annual budget of many hundreds of thousands (the budget would be over a million by the 1950s) which cared for orphans and children from broken or impossibly bad homes, placing these in foster homes where their care was paid for by the society or, in many cases, arranging for their legal adoption. Would Smith and Stevenson accept membership on the board of directors? They agreed to do so—both were convinced that this was a particularly worth-while enterprise—and Adlai Stevenson became a vice-president (he was fourth vice-president, then third, then second), serving in this office from January of '35 to January of '45 and remaining on the board of directors into the 1950s. He also continued as a member of the Hull House board of directors into the 1950s.

Shortly after going on the Home and Aid board, he was asked by Governor Horner, the Illinois State Liquor Commission, and State Senator James O. Monroe (Democrat of Collinsville) to draft a bill which would separate wine and beer legislatively from distilled spirits, making the former subject to lower taxes and more liberal regulations of sale and distribution. There were several reasons why doing so seemed to Stevenson sound public policy and, drawing upon his experience with the FACA, he wrote the bill which Monroe introduced into the state Senate the last of May and which was passed.

During the same spring Stevenson's name appeared for the first time in a major headline on the front page of a metropolitan daily.

Above a by-line story by Charles N. Wheeler, political reporter, the Chicago *Herald-Examiner* placed the head:

DWIGHT GREEN POST MAY
GO TO A. E. STEVENSON

———

Walter J. Cummings Supports
Grandson of Ex-Vice-President;
Attorney for Utilities

Cummings was chairman of the board of the Continental Illinois National Bank and Trust Company and treasurer of the Democratic National Committee. The post for which he was reportedly supporting Stevenson was that of United States District Attorney. Stevenson was identified as a "practicing Chicago lawyer" who "heretofore has not been identified with local politics," and it was deemed certain that the Cummings endorsement would carry considerable weight with the administration. However, "the political experts point out that [Stevenson] is connected with a Chicago law firm that represents the Illinois Bell Telephone Company, which Congress is about to investigate as a subsidiary of the A.T.&T." It was the "expert's" notion that "the government would not be likely to select its chief legal representative in Chicago from among lawyers close to the telephone company under present circumstances." At any rate, the post was not offered to Stevenson—and more than ten years would pass before his name was again linked, in headlines, with that of Dwight Green.

Shelby Singleton ("that grand old man," as Stevenson always called him) furthered the young lawyer's political education by persuading him into the Legislative Voters' League. The League's mission was "to promote good government through the agency of the State legislature." It watched the Illinois legislature with a critical eye. It prepared reports on the actions of individual members of the two houses and graded these according to its own high standards of government. It also endorsed candidates, though it was strictly nonpartisan.

When Stevenson became involved in it the organization was on the point of dissolution for lack of financial support (the Depression had hit it hard), but public announcement of this fact evoked what the Chicago *Daily News* termed (in November of 1937) an "overwhelming popular protest." In this crisis, when a man of prestige and vigor was required for the job, Adlai Stevenson was persuaded to accept the League presidency. Said a *Daily News* editorial two days later: "Mr. Stevenson accepted leadership under the compelling conviction that the opportunity for a necessary service constituted a civic obligation. He is admirably qualified to maintain the record of his able predecessors for vigorous and impartial direction of this 'first aid for a bewildered electorate.'" Promptly Stevenson initiated a fund drive which was sufficiently successful to enable the League to continue effective operation for a time.

This work with the L.V.L. undoubtedly helped Stevenson's political career later on; it gained for him the further respect and friendship of influential, public-spirited men. But it also proved to be, on occasion, a mild political embarrassment in later years. Some of the politicians attacked by the League while Stevenson was president of it were later involved in Stevenson's political career.

"William J. Connors, for instance, in Chicago's Forty-second Ward," Stevenson would say, grinning a bit ruefully, in the 1950s. "While I was head of the League, I'm afraid we had few kind words to say about Bill Connors—and he reminded me of this, later on. But I really think Bill might agree that the League helped him to improve his performance. Anyway, he became a good loyal political friend of mine, and a very useful one. Useful not only to me personally but also to the people of Illinois."

As if these activities were not enough, piled atop his law practice, he had other special assignments that drew heavily upon his time and energy. He became, in the late '30s, a director of the Personal Loan and Savings Bank, later to become the Chicago National. In January of 1937, when he was frantically busy with office work, he was "commanded to act as General Chairman of the President's Birthday Ball for Chicago." ("Ain't that hell!" he complained.) He was also involved, in '36 and '37, in attempts to salvage as much as possible for Ellen and Betty from the wreckage of certain Borden enterprises.

During the presidential campaign of 1936, when Governor Alfred M. Landon of Kansas was the Republican candidate, Stevenson served as finance director of the Democratic National Committee and state chairman of the National Council of Roosevelt Electors in Illinois. He also made his first major political speech, at Carlton College in Minnesota. Never in his life, he later confessed, did he work harder on a speech than he did preparing for this occasion. In terms of historical principle he developed what he believed to be a clear, unanswerable case for Roosevelt over Landon. The speech held the large crowd's attention and was well applauded. Afterward, Adlai, walking along a corridor of the auditorium building beside the college president, accepted the latter's congratulations in the rather smug belief that he had, indeed, earned them. In front of the two, however, walked a couple of students whose conversation they overheard. The students agreed that it had been a fine speech, "But," asked one of them, "who was he *for?*" After this, Stevenson could hardly believe that his effort was particularly helpful to Roosevelt, who, as a matter of fact, seemed not to need much help that year. The President was overwhelmingly re-elected, carrying every state except Maine and Vermont. . . .

Repeatedly during these years Stevenson was requested to return to government service in Washington. In early May of 1937, for example, he was called to Washington by the Secretary of Labor, Frances Perkins, who offered him the position of Commissioner General of Naturalization and Immigration. He was then, and had for some time been, a director of the Immigrants Protective League of Chicago. He was therefore actively interested in the problems he would have handled as a commissioner, and the offer flattered him. He turned it down, however, without much hesitation. Thereafter, the trip was chiefly memorable to him, not because of the job offer, but because of a two-day tour which he and Ellen, who had accompanied him to Washington, made of the Charlottesville district of Virginia.

They borrowed a car from the Wayne Taylors for the expedition. "The country was glorious," he wrote to Buffie two weeks later. "Fruit trees in bloom! Woods spattered with white dogwood and purple Judas trees! And as we rolled along the road a few miles from Monticello, we passed a historical sign saying that the house (to which the sign referred) was the oldest in Albemarle County and was built by Col. Joshua Fry, our ancestor! We stopped and walked in across the blood-red fields, and there stood an ancient frame house of spacious proportions—but not 'grand'—weather-beaten and neglected these many, many years. It is occupied by a tenant farmer, who showed us around. [We saw] the old oft-painted wainscoting, the ancient locks on the doors from England. The heavy blacksmith-made nails. It's all dreadfully run down, but the property—300 acres —is beautiful and the location perfect. Just nine miles from Char-

lottesville on the main road south, with fine views, a stream, woods—
and, of course, worn-out soil. There are chimney ruins of old slave
buildings, etc., and the place could undoubtedly be reconditioned—
tho at considerable expense. We made enquiry when we got back to
town and were told it could be bought for $6,000! It looks to me
like a great possibility, and when you come back this fall you better
run down there and look it over. Good hunting and horse country. . . ."

He had barely returned to Chicago from this trip when Senator J.
Hamilton Lewis tried to persuade him to accept appointment as
Assistant Attorney General. He found it "easy to resist." A few weeks
later he attended his fifteenth class reunion in Princeton.

In that crowded summer of '37 Ellen was looking forward eagerly
to a trip to Ireland. Her great-aunt Lucy, Mrs. Kingsley Porter,
owned Glenveigh Castle in County Donegal, and the plan was that
the Stevensons sail from New York on July 9, spend a week at the
castle and another week motoring through southern Ireland, then
sail home, returning to Chicago just one month after leaving it. Alas,
when July 9 came, pressure of work forced Adlai to postpone sailing
till July 23; when July 23 came, work pressure forced postponement
till late August; and in early August Mrs. Porter cabled that she was
renting the castle beginning August 5. There ceased to be any good
reason for going to Ireland at all. Not until mid-August did he have
his work enough under control so that he and Ellen could arrange a
brief vacation in Bermuda, leaving New York on August 24, on the
Monarch of Bermuda, and returning to Chicago September 11.

"There doesn't seem to be anything but emergencies in my life any
more," he had complained in a letter to Buffie, "and though I'm fed
up with this unremitting pressure I don't seem to be able to do anything about it." But Ellen was by no means convinced that her husband was, in fact, a wholly helpless victim of circumstances. He
himself was responsible for many of his "emergencies," she pointed
out with asperity; he habitually undertook many more assignments
than were actually required of him. "I've been in the dog house again
for working most every night for the last three weeks," he reported to
Buffie wearily, in another typical letter.

But despite their occasional disagreements over his excessive busyness, he and Ellen were happy through those years. They delighted
in their sons, who passed safely through the usual ills, had their

tonsils and adenoids removed, and grew remarkably handsome and strong, quarreling less with one another than most brothers do. Then, too, the family had, in the midst of his frenzied work, some glorious, recreative interludes.

In the summer of 1935 Adlai and Ellen with the boys went to what was to become, in later years, his favorite vacation spot. Dutch and Ellen Smith, with their three children, had their summer home at Thorne Camp, Desbarats, Ontario, Canada. The camp stood on the shore of the north channel between Lake Superior and Lake Huron, and the life there was completely informal and relaxed. Motion pictures taken by the Smiths in the summer of 1936 showed Adlai lolling in a canvas chair, grinning. Then he and Ellen, in swim suits, tried out a bending exercise designed to strengthen the abdominal muscles. Ellen—slender, graceful, gay, and very pretty—did the exercise with ease, Adlai with more difficulty, and the two laughed uproariously at something someone had said while he patted his stomach. . . .

But undoubtedly the happiest of their family activities was their development of a country home near Libertyville, only a few miles west from Lake Forest. There lay seventy acres of field and forest on the Des Plaines River—gently rolling land dotted by the tallest, finest, oldest hard maples in all that region: there was no road into it; they could reach it, then, only on foot, by canoe up the river, or on horseback. Paddling to see "their property" gained significance for Adlai from the fact that the Des Plaines in centuries past had been a principal Indian and French highway through the wilderness. They bought the land. They built upon it a flat-roofed house designed, mostly by Ellen herself, somewhat like a ship riding a gently rolling sea of grass. It had picture windows framing lovely views, and second-floor porches like a ship's sun decks, and spacious rooms in which Ellen displayed her talent for interior design. Family heirlooms were moved up from Bloomington—relics of the Fells, the Osbornes, the Ewings, the Stevensons, which Adlai regarded as priceless. The house and adjoining garage-stable cost some forty thousand dollars in what was yet a Depression year; there was an enormous amount of work to do around the place; but the investment of work and money was, they were convinced, more than compensated by dividends of happiness.

"The 'farm' is developing rapidly and expensively," Adlai wrote his sister late in that crowded summer of '37. "I get up every morning at six and ride before breakfast! It's delightful and the rural life is definitely congenial to me." Ellen, he added, had "taken a job doing some experimental decoration for the Stevens Hotel" (this would become the Conrad Hilton by the 1950s) and "what with new servants, the farm, the children, etc., is busy as a bird dog."

Then came catastrophe.

That autumn the Stevensons moved back into town for a few months, and one January evening the house on St. Mary's Road caught fire. A disagreement between two local fire companies as to which was responsible for this new place delayed the arrival of the engines and promoted confusion among the engine crews when they did, at last, arrive. By the time Adlai and Ellen had driven forty miles to get there, the house of which they were so proud was beyond power of rescue. All that its owners could do was stand helplessly with their neighbors in the snow and watch the flames burst through windows and roof. Stevenson was heartsick, not so much because of the house itself, which was insured, as because of its furnishings, which were not. Especially was it agonizing for him to watch the destruction of family heirlooms. They were irreplaceable; he felt himself convicted of a breach of trust. . . .

But when a neighbor came over to express his sympathy Stevenson merely shrugged, and smiled ruefully, and stuck a cigarette between his lips. At that instant, a piece of burning debris arched through the air and landed at Stevenson's feet. Calmly he picked it up, lit his cigarette with it.

"Oh well," he said, "as you can see, we are still using the house."[3]

Within a few months the house had been rebuilt; it would remain, for all the years to come, his home, taking precedence in his affections even over 1316 East Washington, in Bloomington. "And it is very much home because I built it out of field and forest," he was quoted as saying in a Chicago newspaper in 1950. "I love it because I worked over every inch of it and so have my boys from their infancy."

III

"We talk about war in Europe constantly," wrote Adlai to Buffie early in February of 1937. "Do you?" Six months later he wrote: "I

[3] The first published account of the episode was by Noel F. Busch in his *Adlai E. Stevenson of Illinois* (New York: Farrar, Straus & Young, 1952), p. 4.

saw in the paper that a vice-consul from Barcelona has been transferred to Stockholm, so I guess you'll be hearing some gruesome tales
before long." Emboldened by the impotence of the League of Nations, demonstrated when Japan invaded Manchuria in '31 and
contemptuously withdrew from the League at the first sign that sanctions might be imposed on her, Hitler had reoccupied the Rhineland
while France stood idly by. Mussolini had conquered Ethiopia. And
now there raged in Spain a bloody civil war which many recognized
as a dress rehearsal for World War II.

Against the background provided by these dark and bloody events,
the Council on Foreign Relations, of which Stevenson again became
president in May of 1935, stood out more prominently every year as
an important civic activity in Chicago. It was Clifton Utley's impression that Stevenson quite consciously used the council presidency to
develop himself, improving his techniques as a public speaker and as
a leader in group enterprises. As presiding officer, he was not, at first,
outstandingly effective, but he quickly developed into an excellent
public speaker, continuously called upon to address professional
societies and businessmen's organizations. Thus the "Stevenson style,"
which was to become nationally famous, became locally famous
in the 1930s. A natural response to Princeton's double world, the
style seems, at least in part, to have reflected the council's manner
of conducting business. It *seemed* offhand. Actually it was carefully
studied, as Utley well knew and as those who later disliked it suspected. But it was a form of humility rather than egotism, being
motivated by the conviction that it would be presumptuous of him,
who was but a single fallible mortal, to present his wares to the multitudes as though they were solemn dicta from on high. Moreover, as
Stevenson might have said, it is fallacious to assume that truth is
always homely and honesty always blunt. It is an even greater fallacy
to assume that inarticulate speech coupled with crude earnestness of
expression is prima-facie evidence of deep sincerity and noble purpose. To be earnest gracefully, to make an aesthetically pleasing gesture of the quest for truth—these are the marks of a truly civilized
man. . . .

But "style" was not all he learned from council work. He learned
a great deal from the subject-matter presentations of the famous
speakers he introduced at public meetings, and even more from his
personal conversations with them. Particularly did he learn from
foreign correspondents of the Chicago *Daily News*. In those days the

News had a brilliant foreign staff, and rarely did a correspondent return to Chicago without being called upon to address a council meeting. Thus, the meeting at which Stevenson was re-elected to a second term as council president was addressed by Wallace R. Deuell, who had just returned from two years in Berlin. Deuell spoke that day on Hitler and Nazi Germany, stressing what he termed the "dangerous integrity" of the dictator.

Perhaps it was while Deuell was speaking that Stevenson shaped certain of the ideas he expressed, in October of 1939, when he was principal speaker at the celebration of the eightieth anniversary of Bloomington's Unitarian church.

"There is nothing a jellyfish wants more than a rock," he said on that occasion, "and authoritarian political systems have gained a foothold in Europe because well-intentioned people had no program and little courage to carry a program through. In the Unitarian church we believe we can achieve necessary standards through free discussion and free inquiry." He remained sure that the totalitarian states, for all their seeming monolithic strength, must ultimately fail for lack of "wisdom." But he stressed the dangers which a questing, self-critical society faces when opposed by dictatorships. "Liberals tend to say we should suspend judgment until all the facts are in. The trouble with this attitude is that *all* the facts will never be in, and while 'good people' are withholding judgment the practical affairs of politics are taken over by those lacking social wisdom."

By the time he made this speech Stevenson was deeply involved with the problem of defending American civil liberties against the manifold pressures which a war-racked world brought against them. As the year 1939 opened, he had accepted the chairmanship of a twenty-nine-member Civil Rights Committee of the Chicago Bar Association. "What is happening elsewhere in the world reminds us again of the importance of constant and vigilant protection of our own liberties," Stevenson had said in a public statement, as his chairmanship was announced.

It was as a result of this chairmanship that Stevenson first formed a working relationship with a young man who was to have a considerable role in the Stevenson future—a sandy-haired, lean-faced, rather dour-looking Scotch-American, thirty years old, named Carl McGowan.

McGowan had gone from the public schools in Paris, Illinois, to Dartmouth, graduating in 1932. After a year or so of odd-jobbing around his home town, he'd gone to Columbia Law School, receiving his degree in 1936. He'd then entered the law firm of Debevoise, Stevenson, Plimpton and Page, in New York—a young firm, two of whose senior partners, Francis Plimpton and William Stevenson, were, as we have seen, old friends of Adlai Stevenson. When Mc-Gowan came to Chicago as an assistant professor in the Northwestern Law School, Stevenson, informed of McGowan's coming, asked him to lunch.

"He had forgotten, when making the date, that there was a Council on Foreign Relations luncheon that day, so when I showed up at his office he asked if I'd mind going there with him," McGowan would remember. "It was at the Palmer House, of course, and of course I did go with him."

A little later Stevenson asked McGowan to help him with the civil-rights committee work, preparing compendiums of the laws and the interpretations of the bill of rights in the various states.

In May 1939 Adlai and Ellen visited Ireland and England during a vacation of some six weeks. They landed at Cóbh, motored around the coast of Ireland to Belfast where Ernest and Buffie Ives were then stationed, and visited Sir Basil Brooke, later to be prime minister of Northern Ireland. In England they visited with their long-time friend, Jan Masaryk, then with the Czechoslovakian government in exile, and, of course, with Ellen's uncle and aunt, General Sir Louis Spears and Lady Spears, the former Mary Borden.

Stevenson was vividly impressed by what he later described as the "infinite difficulty with which a democracy, loving peace, prepares to defend herself under threat of war." He was "deeply struck" by what seemed to him the almost fatuous optimism of many of the British who lived, unprepared, in the deepening shadow of Hitler's Germany. Nine months after the Munich Conference, less than three months after the Nazis had occupied all of Czechoslovakia, little more than a month after Franco Spain had signed the anti-Comintern pact, and at the very moment when Hitler and Mussolini were threatening aggression against Poland and Greece and Albania, much of England, under Prime Minister Chamberlain's government, still seemed to believe that war would not come, or that, if it did, Britain was now well prepared not only to defend herself but to fulfill the commitments she was making to the small nations immediately threatened. Stevenson heard high British officials indicate as much when he witnessed weapons testing at an English proving ground. He was himself impressed by the newly unveiled Spitfires, but he was even more impressed by the pacifism, of the extreme Oxford Oath variety, which continued to characterize so many British youths, and by the fact that business leaders continued to oppose military conscription and the vast increase in the military budget. Others, however, were somber as they viewed through disillusioned eyes the darkening scene. Among these was Harold Nicolson. One of the most memorable events of the visit, for Stevenson, was a long conversation he had with Nicolson one afternoon as they sat on a terrace overlooking the Thames, each acutely aware that the very concept of individual liberty which had been a central theme of Western civilization might soon be crushed to death under the iron heel of the totalitarian states.

From England, Adlai and Ellen went to Scotland, across which they motored from Edinburgh to Glasgow. They sailed from Scotland on a Canadian ship, landing in Quebec in late June.

IV

On August 21, 1939, Adlai, Ellen, and their three boys were with the Dutch Smiths at Desbarats, Ontario. That day Stevenson, like virtually every other student of foreign affairs in the Western democracies, was stunned by the radio news that Hitler and Stalin had signed a nonaggression pact, hard on the heels of an announcement by the Nazi leader in Danzig that the hour of "deliverance" was at hand. One of the few constants in foreign affairs had been the implacable hostility of Nazi Germany and Communist Russia. . . . Ellen Smith would never forget how profoundly Adlai was disturbed by the news, nor how they all huddled beside the radio on September 1, listening hour after hour to news bulletins of Nazi bombs raining upon Warsaw and Nazi panzer units roaring across the Polish plains. The contrast between the news they heard and the quiet beauty of the lake, the wilderness, cut into them like a knife.

On September 3, Britain and France declared war on Germany. . . .

Stevenson could at least be glad that Buffie, Ernest, and young Timmie were no longer in Europe. The year 1939 marked the retirement of Ernest Linwood Ives, after thirty years, from the Foreign Service of the United States. At a gay dinner in his and Buffie's honor, in Washington, he was presented with a silver cigarette case engraved with the names of nineteen far-spaced stations at which he had served. They were ready for a settled life.

They would establish two homes. In the summers, thereafter, they would live at 1316 East Washington, in Bloomington, where Buffie would keep the house as it had been when she and Adlai were growing up—the same furniture, carpets, window curtains, color scheme. In the winters they would live in an early nineteenth-century log house, unpretentious but very comfortable and picturesque, on a 115-acre farm they purchased near Southern Pines, North Carolina.

CHAPTER FOURTEEN

The Fight against Isolationism

In September 1939, Clark Eichelberger, director of the League of Nations Association and the Union for Concerted Peace Efforts, had asked William Allen White to head a national Non-Partisan Committee for Peace through Revision of the Neutrality Law. The famous editor of the Emporia (Kansas) *Gazette*, whom Stevenson had admired from boyhood and had once hoped to emulate with the Bloomington *Pantagraph*, acceded to Eichelberger's request with some reluctance. But he threw himself with characteristic energy into his task and was supported in this effort by two other leading Republicans, former Secretary of State Stimson and Colonel Frank Knox, publisher of the Chicago *Daily News* and Alf Landon's running mate in 1936. It can hardly be said that these three, or the committee as a whole, were particularly effective with Republican politicians (only 20 Republican House members voted for the revision; 140 voted against it), but they were certainly helpful to the Democrats in the country at large. The arms embargo was repealed, permitting exports to Britain on a cash-and-carry basis, and the move was supported by American public opinion partly as a result of the White-Eichelberger enterprise. The experience encouraged these two, in April 1940, to plan a new committee with wider terms of reference: they called it the Committee to Defend America by Aiding the Allies.

The need for it seemed urgent that month, as the Nazis occupied Denmark and invaded Norway; it seemed imperative in May, when the "phony war" ended on the western front with the lightning attack upon the Low Countries and France. A few days later White sent out dozens of telegrams from Emporia to influential men all over the country, asking for and receiving pledges of support for the new organization. Special attention was paid to Chicago, for it was clear that this city would be a major focus of the coming fight for public opinion, since it was the home of the archreactionary Chicago *Tribune* and the capital of midwest isolationism. Quincy Wright, Clifton Utley, and Paul Douglas (he was then a city alderman as well as a professor of economics at the University of Chicago) agreed to serve, and strongly recommended that Adlai Stevenson be asked to become chairman of the committee's Chicago chapter.

Immediately both White and Utley called Stevenson, who, after consulting with his law partners, accepted the chairmanship. He then plunged into the most hectic and important public activity in which he had ever engaged up till then.

It was, to begin with, a big job of organization. Money must be raised, subchapters established, outstanding speakers obtained for giant rallies, and means developed for effective presentation of the committee's case through press and radio. Clifton Utley became the "radio voice"; the *Daily News* became the chief "newspaper voice"; and the Council on Foreign Relations provided informed, dedicated, and highly prestigious leaders. Upon Stevenson's own energies and talents immense and often unexpected demands were made.

Not long after the fall of France, for example, while the Battle of Britain was being fought in the air, a public meeting was arranged in Mandel Hall at the University of Chicago by the Chicago student subchapter, with Edgar Ansel Mowrer, the famous *Daily News* correspondent, as speaker. Mowrer's name attracted a large crowd, but at the last moment some circumstance prevented his appearance. Stevenson, with no time to prepare, was called upon to pinch-hit.

"He was introduced that way, too—as a pinch hitter," recalled Walter Johnson, the student committee's faculty sponsor, years later. "The man who introduced him simply said, very flatly, that Mowrer couldn't be there, that Stevenson would speak instead. You could hear the sigh of disappointment from the crowd. Few of them knew much about Stevenson, most had probably scarcely heard of him. I can imagine no more trying situation for a speaker. But within three minutes he had that crowd's attention riveted on him. And he held it. He was magnificent! Afterward he was given what amounted to an ovation."

The committee, during that hectic summer and autumn of an election year, did not take a merely general stand in favor of "all aid short of war." It focused on specific issues. In mid-June, as France collapsed and Mussolini declared war, Stevenson and the Chicago chapter sent telegrams to Washington urging the government to release war planes to private manufacturers, who in turn would sell them to Britain and France. In late June Stevenson encouraged Republican members of the Chicago chapter to join White in putting pressure on Republican Senators who opposed the confirmation of Knox as Secretary of the Navy and Stimson as Secretary of War—appointments by Roosevelt which aroused great wrath among the GOP Old Guard. The Chicago chapter joined other chapters in efforts to keep foreign policy from becoming a presidential campaign issue. This end was largely achieved when the Republican National Convention at Philadelphia nominated Wendell Willkie and the Democratic National Convention, meeting in Chicago, nominated Franklin Roosevelt for a third term, with Henry A. Wallace as his running mate. White, Eichelberger, and Stevenson appeared before the Democratic platform committee and helped persuade it to write a plank pledging aid to the Allies. The committee also helped develop public support for Roosevelt's plan to exchange old-age destroyers for naval bases in British possessions in the Western Hemisphere, and for the Lend-Lease Bill a few months later.

"It was during this period," said Stevenson years later, "that Bill Blair first came into my life. He came in one day and volunteered to work for the committee."

William McCormick Blair, Jr., was then twenty-three, was a dark, slender, attractive young man. He was a cousin of Colonel McCormick (his father, a first cousin of the *Tribune* publisher, would be the colonel's closest surviving male relative by the mid-1950s). He had long been fascinated by politics; at the Groton School, in 1932, when he was fifteen, he had worked actively on behalf of Herbert Hoover. He had developed a serious sinus infection (he would deny that his efforts for Hoover had anything to do with it) which ultimately required several operations; it had prevented his enrolling in an Ivy League college. Instead, seeking relief for his sinus trouble, he had attended a succession of colleges in warm climates—the University of Hawaii, the University of California, the University of Arizona—receiving his A.B. degree from Stanford University just a few days before he appeared at the Chicago office of the Aid-Allies committee.

As a scion of one of the wealthiest, most distinguished, and most staunchly Republican families in the city, Blair's mere presence in the committee headquarters had a considerable persuasive value to the aid-Britain campaign. His joining the committee was construed by many as a direct and effective slap at Colonel McCormick, especially so since the *Tribune* publisher was one of the few politically active Republicans whom White openly detested and consistently opposed editorially, even in election years. ("He and his paper are a disgrace to American journalism," White used to say.) Moreover, it is quite possible that young Blair may have been motivated, in part, by his own aversion to his cousin Bertie's views.

Blair did much more than lend his presence to the cause. For two months he, with one helper, manned the headquarters at 86 East Randolph Street, serving a kind of apprenticeship for the role of facilitating officer and administrative assistant which he was later to play in the Stevenson organization. His dedication to the aid-Britain campaign was profound, and became all the more effective by reason for his urbane sophistication, his rare social charm. Everyone liked him. One of the first things he did was go to a five-and-ten-cent store where he bought a number of toy model destroyers which he put on display in the headquarters' street windows, with appropriate signs pointing up the need to support the destroyers-for-Britain plan.

II

In Stevenson's view, during that summer of disaster for the Western democracies, the committee's most important job was to counteract the growing belief that Britain's cause was hopeless, now that she stood alone against overwhelming German and Italian might.

The "battle for public opinion" grew daily more bitter in Chicago, and personal attacks upon Stevenson, as local committee chairman, became numerous and venomous in the Chicago *Tribune*. Isolationist sentiment—though it remained a minority sentiment even in Chicago, according to a Gallup poll—was now well organized and richly financed through the America First Committee, headed by General Robert E. Wood of Chicago, president of Sears, Roebuck and Company.

Wood, Charles A. Lindbergh, Colonel McCormick, and other prominent American Firsters insisted that their sole motive was to keep America out of the war; they claimed to be exclusively *national* patriots, and undoubtedly most of them were. Nevertheless there was no blinking the fact that many of the most vociferous American Firsters were openly sympathetic to nazism and fascism. Though American First publicly repudiated the support of the pro-Hitler German-American Bund, it did not reject the support of Father Coughlin's Christian Front, the American Destiny Party, the Ku Klux Klan (again resurgent), William Dudley Pelley's Silver Shirts, and the notorious publicist, George Sylvester Viereck. Strangely allied with these were American Communists (now that Stalin and Hitler were allies), Socialists, and Christian pacifists.

It seemed to Stevenson ominously significant that America First steadfastly refused to publish a list of its principal contributors. His own committee published such a list periodically, and announced that its books were open for inspection at all times. Nor could he fail to resent being dubbed, with his colleagues, a "cookie pusher," a "professional bleeding heart," a "war monger," day after day in *Tribune* news and editorial columns (in Colonel McCormick's paper, "news" stories on political questions were really editorials) and from the platforms of American First rallies. He was finally goaded into writing a letter to the Voice of the People section of the *Tribune,* replying to one of the more virulent of that newspaper's attacks, in which he asserted that "the importance of the controversy warrants more sobriety" than was indicated by *Tribune* epithets, and went on to state the case of the committee whose local chapter he headed: "We think Hitler is a menace and detests democracy; he has said so. We think Britain is engaged in a death struggle to stop that menace. We think that, with our help, she can succeed. . . . We know that no more aid for Britain would be great news in Berlin—and evidently in some quarters of our country."

The *Tribune* held the letter for eleven days before publishing under the heading, "From America Second." On that same day, it published an editorial more viciously personal in its attacks on Stevenson than the earlier editorials had been. Four days later Stevenson had the dubious pleasure of seeing himself branded a coward by a *Tribune* letter writer who proved his own courage by signing his communication "Just a Veteran."

Thereafter Stevenson made no attempt to debate the issue in *Tribune* columns. He did accede to a request from the *Daily News,* in a front-page editorial, that he and the chairman of the Chicago America First Committee, Thomas S. Hammond (president and general manager of the Whiting Corporation), "get together behind the production program for a strong national defense." Hammond and he agreed that the United States must speed up its defense effort, and Stevenson seized the opportunity to plead that the debate be kept on a high rational plane.

"America does not want war, nor does it want Britain defeated," he wrote. "But Britain cannot win without our help on a tremendous scale. So we must decide in the critical weeks ahead how far we are going to help her, what risks we are willing to take. . . . I hope and pray that this issue can and will be presented to the people henceforth with the restraint and responsibility it deserves. Sincere, patriotic Americans can honestly disagree on this issue. . . . There has been too much suspicion, too many epithets, too little reason. The decisions we make this winter will affect our future for years, perhaps generations. Let us approach them in our best, not our worst, national tradition."

By the time he wrote this he had had a considerable education in the ways and means of influencing public opinion and in the hazards of controversy in areas where emotions grow strong. In early September he had helped arrange one of the largest public meetings ever held in Chicago—a giant rally of some sixteen thousand people (more than three thousand were turned away) in the Coliseum. It was held on Wednesday evening, October 18, with Stevenson presiding. As the crowd entered the great hall, it passed through lines of sign-carrying pickets: "Britannia Rules the Waves! Free Ireland and India," "Youth Needs a Job, Not a Gun," "Lest We Forget 1918–40 Million Dead." Inside, the crowd heard itself characterized by Stevenson as a "decisive answer to Chicago's active minority, well intentioned and otherwise, of appeasers, defeatists, and foes of aid to Britain." They then listened to eloquent and impassioned pleas for British aid from Maury Maverick, former congressman and now mayor of San Antonio, Texas; Admiral William H. Standley, U.S.N., Ret.; Douglas Fairbanks, Jr., the motion-picture actor; and Dorothy Thompson, author and newspaper columnist. They adopted, by roaring acclamation, a resolution calling for the extension to Britain of "all possible aid, compatible with our own defense requirements, to sustain her gallant resistance against Nazism and Fascism" and specifically urging "that 24 'flying fortresses,' as many other combat planes as can be safely released, and two mosquito boats be made available to Britain immediately."

A month later the Adlai Stevensons had been hosts to Ambassador William C. Bullitt—envoy first to Russia, then France—when he came to address a Council on Foreign Relations meeting at the Palmer House. The crowd on that occasion, as on many others during these months, more than filled the hotel's Grand Ballroom and the adjoining Red Lacquer Room; hundreds who wished to attend had to be turned away.

"It was an exciting time," Stevenson himself recalled in a later year. "It was a knock-down drag-out fight, really. The *Tribune* used to send photographers to photograph all empty seats, if any, in halls where we presented programs—and the *News* photographers photographed all the full ones. I'd be a dirty dog in the *Tribune* in the morning, and a shining hero in the *News* at night. . . ."

Nor was the fight always conducted according to the rules of fair play. As 1941 came on and advanced through spring into early summer, some America Firsters displayed an increasingly strong tendency to answer arguments with economic sanctions. Clifton Utley found his income reduced, his very livelihood threatened, through the cancellation of contracts by certain sponsors of his radio broadcasts. Adlai Stevenson himself suffered from pressures brought to bear upon him, and upon his law firm, by angry America Firsters. Fortunately for him, Donald F. McPherson, a senior partner of the firm, was president of the Council on Foreign Relations that year, and Sidley continued active in the council; but even so there were some who grumbled at the amount of time Stevenson was spending on committee work and over the withdrawal of business from the firm by clients who were bitterly hostile to the committee's activities. Moreover, some of the grumbling seemed, to Stevenson, justified. He offered to take a reduced share of the firm's profits for that year—an offer which Sidley refused.

Stevenson was hurt, too, by some of the things said to him, and about him, by men and women he'd always regarded as friends. One person said, "Adlai's trying to kill our sons." This cut him so deeply that years later, talking about those hectic months, he still cried out against it. "I was trying to *save* their sons!" he said. "I was convinced that aid to Britain was the only means, the only chance of our keeping out of the war."

III

He was convinced. . . .

Yet, as the months passed, he was forced to examine more and more critically his essential convictions. Tormenting questions grew stronger in his mind. He might say in all honesty that aid to Britain offered the "best chance" for America to stay out of war, but did he believe it actually *would* keep us out? Supposing the choice became one of entering the war or accepting a Nazi-Fascist conquest of Britain, which would he choose? When he frankly admitted to himself that, in such a case, he would choose war, he was forced to face a further, moral question: If Hitler's defeat were of such imperative importance, was it not the part of honorable men to assume the vital risks of ensuring that defeat? Was it not cowardice to hide from so terrible a menace behind the sacrifice, the valor, the fortitude of Britain and the Commonwealth? Surely no national power could be truly great who failed to play her part greatly upon the stage of history. . . .

Almost from the moment he assumed his duties as committee chairman, he had been uneasily aware that he occupied a somewhat ambiguous, equivocal position—and this sense of ambiguity had grown stronger as a result of his working relationship with William Allen White. Critical Kansans had long complained that White's great service to the state's political conservatism had been to focus "liberal" energies upon himself between elections in order to dissipate them at precisely the points (the polling booths in even-numbered years) where they might be truly effective—and he seemed determined to exercise this dubious "leadership" in the present moment of national peril.

The first instance of this occurred in the late summer and early autumn of 1940, when White was actively supporting Willkie for President while Clark Eichelberger supported Roosevelt.[1] Stevenson also supported Roosevelt. In September he contributed to the Chicago *Herald-American,* at that paper's request, a statement on "Why I'll Vote for Roosevelt" in which, while praising Willkie as a "sincere and forthright liberal," he condemned the isolationism of the candidate's "adopted party" (Willkie had been a Democrat). A number

[1] See *William Allen White's America,* by Walter Johnson (New York: Henry Holt & Company, 1947), pp. 538 et seq.

of committee members, Stevenson included, wanted the organization to publish the voting records of incumbent isolationists running for re-election to the Congress. This seemed to them a logically necessary step, determined by the committee's *raison d'être*. White, however, flatly refused to permit it. To do so, he argued, would cause the committee to oppose nearly all the Republican members of Congress, destroying the committee's nonpartisan character! Thus balked, members of the committee's New York chapter formed a Non-Partisan Committee to Defeat Hamilton Fish, New York's notoriously isolationist if not actually pro-Hitlerian congressman. (Fish had organized a well-financed propaganda campaign against lifting the arms embargo, he had fought every measure of aid to the Allies, he had visited Germany and happily accepted the feting Nazis gave him there, he had asserted that German demands upon Poland were just demands.) White then wrote to Fish, October 18, disavowing every attempt to use the White Committee's name against him and adding, "I hope as Republicans we are united in our support of the Republican ticket from top to bottom in every district in every State." The letter, White made clear, was intended for publication —and Fish did publish it. But when the storm raised by this letter threatened to destroy the White Committee altogether, the Emporia editor wired Fish's opponents: "Our Committee is nonpartisan. As such we wish to see the Republicans and Democrats elected who support a program of aid to Great Britain. Our Committee naturally wishes to see appeasers, isolationists and pro-Germans defeated irrespective of party. You may make the widest use of this you wish." Whereupon Fish was re-elected and continued to fight everything for which the White Committee stood.

In mid-November, White and Stevenson, with other Chicago chapter leaders, conferred on committee policy. They lunched at the Chicago club and retired afterward to White's room for further discussion. Stevenson was deeply concerned by the rising rate at which British supply ships were being sunk by German submarines. So was White. But the older man hesitated to advocate the only step which could now be taken to help Britain at sea, namely the convoying of ships carrying American aid. It was, White said, another long step toward actual intervention. Stevenson argued that, unless this step were taken, the whole aid-Britain program might soon be rendered futile—and in this he was supported by Utley, Wright, and others of the Chicago group. White then agreed that a new national committee policy should be determined and went on to New York to shape it with Eichelberger and others on his national committee.

The new policy statement was issued on November 26, making front-page headlines in the nation's press. It asserted that, since the "life line between Great Britain and the United States is the sea route to the Western Hemisphere," the United States could "under no circumstances" permit it to be cut and "must be prepared to maintain it. . . ." It called for "a revision of our international policy" through congressional action, including "a repeal or modification of restrictive statutes which hamper this nation . . . when it would cooperate with nations defending themselves from attack by nations at war in violation of treaties with the United States." The implications were clear: the committee favored American convoys to Britain and a repeal of the Neutrality Act: and White, like all the others at the meeting, knew that this was so. But he had barely returned to Emporia—weary and worried—before he was wavering before the blasts of isolationists who charged him with "war-mongering." Four weeks later, having been informed that the Scripps-Howard newspapers were about to launch an attack upon him and the committee, he dictated a typical White letter to Roy Howard, head of the chain, and, without consulting Eichelberger or anyone else on the White Committee, gave Howard permission to publish it. He flatly denied that he or "our outfit are in favor of sending convoys with British ships or our own ships, a silly thing, for convoys unless you shoot are confetti and it's not time to shoot now or ever." He said, "It is not true even remotely that we favor repealing [the Neutrality Act] to carry contraband of war into the war zone. . . . If I was making a motto for the Committee to Defend America by Aiding the Allies, it would be 'The Yanks Are Not Coming.'"

Stevenson read this in the papers with the same astonishment and dismay which overwhelmed Eichelberger and the New York chapter. Rebellion against this kind of "leadership"—a rebellion centered in New York but also widespread in other chapters—threatened to wreck the national organization. Mayor La Guardia of New York personally denounced White for "doing a typical Laval." White promptly tendered his resignation as chairman. Stevenson and Utley took part in a four-way long-distance telephone discussion with Eichelberger in New York and White in Emporia, striving to persuade White to reconsider. In vain. . . .

But was not this, too, an act of ambiguity?

Twice in preceding weeks Stevenson had engaged in public debate with Clay Judson of the America First Committee—once before the Hyde Park League of Women Voters, once before the Chicago Bar Association. On both occasions he had argued that the fall of Britain would inevitably mean war for the United States. "You hear it said that this is not our war," he had told the Bar Association. "I don't care whose war it is—the enemy is our enemy, and if Britain can't stop, can't defeat that enemy now, then we can confidently look forward to the day when, perhaps alone in the world, we shall have to make a stand. . . . I do not think that with tyranny in four fifths of the world, freedom can endure in one fifth. . . . Great Britain can win, but I'm not sure that she will win—and she cannot win without us."

But even as he said these words, he had felt himself and his committee to be vulnerable to precisely the attack Judson made upon it—the one point in Judson's argument which deeply disturbed him. Said Judson: "The question we must answer before it is too late is: 'Is this our war?' If it is our war, then we should be in it without delay, even though it will not be the comparatively simple job it was the first time we saved the world for democracy."

If this is our war, then we should be in it!

The point seemed to Stevenson unanswerable. And was not he himself arguing, with all the eloquence at his command, that this *was* our war? Through the winter and spring of 1941 he felt that his public position was becoming more and more badly blurred, that in essential respects he appeared as self-contradictory as White had been—and with less excuse, for White was seventy-three years old and far from well and had lifelong commitments to the Republican party, whereas he himself was young, in perfect health, and a lifelong Democrat.

One evening, as he rode a North Shore commuters' train toward the Deerpath station whence he would drive to his farm on St. Mary's Road, he read in the paper a "Letter to the Editor" which focused the matter so sharply that it probed painfully into his already aching conscience. The Committee to Defend America by Aiding the Allies continued to assert that its purpose and function were "to keep America out of war by keeping the war out of America." But this was palpably dishonest. So said the letter writer. The committee's real purpose and function were to condition American public opinion for full intervention in the war. To pretend otherwise was contemptible. For as matters now stood, the letter went on, there was no tenable "middle ground" between isolationism and outright intervention: one must choose one side or the other. . . .

And Adlai Stevenson, looking up from his paper, gazing out upon the greening April countryside, was forced to admit that, in his deepest self, he had made his choice long ago—as long ago as the fall of France. He was an interventionist. By the time his train came to a halt beside the tiny Deerpath station, he had decided that, at the earliest opportunity, whenever he could do so without letting down his committee colleagues, he would resign his position as committee chairman.

The opportunity soon came.

He stands now at another "critical point" in his career, another point from which "before" and "after" will be dated in his memory. What mark has the decade left on his appearance?

At forty-one he has less hair on his head, for one thing; he has more flesh on his middle, for another. But he still has thin strands of hair atop his skull—a lonely-looking, obviously ephemeral wedge of hair—and his middle is by no means paunchy. He continues to bend upon the world an unusually bright, blue-eyed gaze, but in his latest photographs those eyes seem darker, their gaze more narrowly lidded, than they had appeared to be in the early and middle thirties. His cheeks are perhaps a trifle fuller now than they were then, and his lips no longer seem to be twitching on the verge of a rather self-conscious smile. The "aesthetic" look of his earlier pictures remains, but it is coupled now with an appearance of firmness, self-assurance, poise.

Here is a sensitive man: one sees it at a glance. He responds quickly to stimuli; he is aware of subtle shifts of atmospheric pressure in more realms of discourse than most men ever know. Consequently he is vulnerable to more and deeper hurts than most men in his external circumstances would be. But his heightened sensitivity is matched by a heightened capacity to "take it," and smile, and go forward without malice or self-pity along his chosen path. Here, too, is a prudent man, not prone to running uncalculated risks. He shies away from extravagance of emotion, or money spending, or self-expression in other forms, yet continues to admire in Ellen precisely these qualities and the spontaneity that goes with them.

His nervous and physical energy is almost limitless, and sometimes it moves him about, restlessly, from one activity to another. But for the most part it is a controlled energy. He walks very fast, but purposefully. He talks very fast, but always in complete sentences. His movements are quick, but precise. He can be going at top speed, working under great pressure, yet relax instantaneously and completely when an opportunity for doing so presents itself. On planes or trains (latterly he has traveled mostly by plane) he is learning how to drop off to sleep in a flash, and awake in a flash, too, immediately alert as he opens his eyes from a seemingly deep sleep. A ten- or fifteen-minute nap seems to refresh and restore him completely after a period of strain which would push most men into a stupor of weariness.

Career decisions continue to be difficult for him, but they are less so than they were a decade ago whenever their objects are of anywhere near the same size as they were then. The trouble is that lately the objects have not been the same size: they are much larger, they involve more factors. Indecision, however, is no longer as deeply rooted as it once was in doubts concerning his capacities. Experience has taught him that there are certain natural limits beyond which he cannot go, but that these limits are fewer than he had once believed they were. For instance, he had once had none too high an opinion of his mental abilities; now he knows that these abilities (though he will never say so out loud) are superior and that they grow constantly through experience. He had once felt nervous, inadequate, as he faced the brilliant people who attended Council on Foreign Relations meetings; now, before such audiences, he feels perfectly at ease, provided he is prepared. He must be prepared, though; he is not, at this point in his life, a man who can stand up before an audience and give a good speech "off the cuff" easily. . . .

There is another change in him—one of which he may not be aware. A dozen or so years ago he was by no means a social snob: he lacked wholly the malice which lies at the core of snobbery: but when he came to the city to live and work he was more impressed by wealth and power, more flattered by associations with the wealthy and powerful, than he now is. He is no longer as prone as once he was to accept privileges as rights or to assume the prejudices, the exclusive attitudes of his own social class. Naturally his closest personal contacts and companions are all of the upper income group. This will continue to be so. But from now on this fact will be more a function of past circumstances than of conscious personal choice.

Book Four

OF WAR AND INTERNATIONAL ORGANIZATION

CHAPTER FIFTEEN

Washington in Wartime

May 1941. . . . Greece, who had been able to hold her own against the Italians, has fallen swiftly under the onslaught of German troops; shattered remnants of a token British expeditionary force have been rescued from Greek shores in another, smaller Dunkirk. Still more frightening has been the lightning conquest of Crete by German airborne troops.

After a bitter battle with Republican-led isolationists the administration has been able to push the Lend-Lease Bill through the Congress (Republicans in the House voted 139 to 24 against it, in the Senate 17 to 10 against), but Secretary of the Navy Knox is now well aware that Lend-Lease will not be enough to prevent Britain's fall, even if the shipping gets through—especially so since American industry, in the absence of profit guarantees, continues naturally reluctant to convert itself to war production on anything like the needed scale. Nor are the voices of isolationism noticeably muffled by the impending Nazi-Fascist victory: on the contrary, they seem strengthened by the fact that all Western Europe—with the dubious exceptions of Franco's Spain, Salazar's Portugal, and Vichy France —is now a Nazi-Fascist empire. The war, say such men as Lindbergh, is already virtually over. Hitler has won. We should accommodate ourselves to that fact. . . .

On May 27, President Roosevelt proclaims that "an unlimited national emergency exists. . . . Our patrols are helping now to insure delivery of the needed supplies to Britain," the President says. "All additional measures necessary to ensure delivery of the goods will be taken. *Any and all further methods or combinations of methods which can or should be utilized are being devised.*" Surely this means that the President will soon appear before the Congress to ask for a declaration of war against Germany. But does it? Next day at his press conference the President denies any intention of using the U. S. Navy for convoy duty or of asking the Congress for revision or repeal of the Neutrality Law. . . .

Nevertheless, the proclamation can only mean further pressures upon the Navy and the Navy Secretary. Stocky, sandy-haired, sixty-seven-year-old Frank Knox is a strong and brave man. He has proved his physical courage time and again: as one of Teddy Roosevelt's Roughriders in 1898 (Teddy remains his idol, upon whom he models himself); as a weekly newspaper editor crusading against vice and corruption in tough Sault Sainte Marie; as a private who became a major of field artillery in France during World War I (he is now a colonel in the reserves, ret.). He abundantly proves his intellectual and moral courage by being in the position he now occupies. All his mature life he has been the most rugged of "rugged individualists," a laissez-faire economist who was outraged by the New Deal: he condemned the AAA, the Social Security Act, the Wagner Act, the federal administration of relief, and as Republican vice-presidential candidate in '36 he had fought Roosevelt far more effectively than Alf Landon had been able to do. His acceptance of a cabinet post under Roosevelt, therefore, had been an act of patriotism that cost him many long friendships and a terrific struggle with himself. Ever since, he has heard himself damned as a traitor and turncoat by Republican leaders he has long admired; daily he sees and hears himself vilified by isolationist newspapers and radio broadcasters. But he stands firm in his conviction that the republic is in mortal danger, having been "educated," as he himself admits, by the superlative foreign staff of the *Daily News,* which he had acquired in the early '30s.

A strong man. . . . Yet the mounting pressures of his rapidly expanding job in the gathering crisis call for a strong and able personal assistant with legal skills and strong convictions. He knows, too, whom he wants as assistant. He wants Adlai Stevenson.

He had become interested in the work of the Council on Foreign Relations at about the time that Stevenson became president of it; besides sharing Stevenson's views, he had soon developed an admiration for Stevenson's quality of mind and leadership, and a personal liking for him. This liking and admiration have grown since

Stevenson assumed the chairmanship of the local aid-Allies committee. About once a month Knox has been in Chicago since becoming Secretary of the Navy, and on each occasion he and Stevenson have conferred. Occasionally, when Stevenson has had to go to Washington on committee business, Knox has given him a ride in his Navy plane and they have talked some more of dark events. He has told Hopkins and Roosevelt about this "young man, a terrific guy"—and it is only because the aid-Britain work has seemed so important that he has thrice changed his mind and asked Stevenson to stay in Chicago after first suggesting that he come to Washington "to help him."

"I go to all these meetings," Knox grumbles to Stevenson. "Every day, important meetings with important people. There sit Hillman and Knudson and Stimson, and the others—and every one of 'em has his own personal lawyer. Even Jim Forrestal has his own lawyer" —James Forrestal is Knox's Undersecretary—"and I don't have one."

But it is not until a day or so after the "unlimited emergency" proclamation that the request becomes specific. On an afternoon near the end of May he puts through a telephone call to Stevenson in Chicago.

"When are you going to be in Washington again?" he wants to know.

Stevenson says he has no definite plans for coming at all.

"Well, you'd better plan to come as soon as you can. Bring a big suitcase, and plan to stay."

The public announcement of Adlai Stevenson's appointment as personal assistant to the Secretary of the Navy was made on July 6, 1941, two weeks after German armies had invaded Russia. He accepted the appointment on a strictly temporary basis, having been granted a three months' leave of absence by Sidley, McPherson, Austin and Burgess—and when he arrived in Washington some ten days later, he came alone. Ellen and the three boys remained on the farm near Libertyville. If things "worked out that way" the family would join him in the autumn. He moved into the Hay-Adams House on Lafayette Square across from the White House, and was given an office next door to Knox.

"I've a grand job," he wrote Buffie on the first Sunday after his arrival, "tho I confess I don't know yet precisely about my duties. Apparently most anything the Secretary wants to unload." It was already clear to him that he was to be Knox's intimate, confidential assistant, sharing much of the Secretary's private life as well as nearly all his public life. "I've played golf with him," Stevenson wrote Buffie, "been down the river for the evening on his beautiful yacht with a company of distinguished guests, lunched with him in his private dining room at the Dept. most every day, and heard all the lowdown on what's going on and his troubles in the Dept. in a very confidential and disarming way. So I feel I'm in an interesting spot and only hope I'll be able to be of some real service to him."

A test of his usefulness soon came—and it was a major one.

At Kearny, New Jersey, in the huge shipyard of the Federal Shipbuilding and Dry Dock Corporation, some 16,000 employees worked on $493,000,000 worth of fighting ships for the Navy and of merchant vessels for the Maritime Commission. It was of crucial importance to the national security that this yard's production be uninterrupted. When Stevenson arrived in Washington, however, a work stoppage at Kearny was imminent. Negotiations between the company and the CIO's Industrial Union of Marine and Shipbuilding workers were breaking down over a union "maintenance of membership" clause which the union insisted must be in the contract in exchange for a no-strike pledge during the emergency. Under this clause, present and future union members would be required to remain in good standing as a condition of employment, though non-union workers would not be required to join.

Stevenson sat in as Knox's assistant at meetings with the Defense Mediation Board, the Maritime Commission, the Attorney General, and the Office of Production Management, during which the deepening Kearny crisis was discussed. It was decided that the government must be prepared to take over and operate the shipyard if a strike occurred. Stevenson was asked to draft the plan, devising necessary legal machinery, for carrying out this decision: it involved such matters as management responsibilities, contractual continuances, and other intricate and, for the most part, unprecedented legal problems. It also involved an executive order for the President's signature, for this would be the first peacetime seizure of a great private plant by the government in the interest of national defense. The assignment was by far the most important given Stevenson up to that time, and he plunged into the drafting and negotiating job with tirelessness and also trepidation. He emerged days later, however, with plans and documents which the services, the Department of

Justice, the Office of Production Management, and all others concerned found satisfactory.

On August 7, the union struck. The Kearny yard closed down. Again Stevenson sat by Knox's side, or as Knox's representative, at long and fateful meetings as the Mediation Board held negotiations with both the union and the management, but the company flatly refused to accept the Mediation Board's recommendation. And after ten days of shutdown it was deemed imperative to resume work on the ships at once, and that the President must immediately issue the executive order for seizure of the plant. To a feverishly excited Washington officialdom even another twenty-four-hour delay seemed fraught with mortal danger to the Republic.

But the President was not in Washington. On August 9, the British Prime Minister, Winston Churchill, on H.M.S. *Prince of Wales* and the American President on the cruiser U.S.S. *Augusta* had met at a secret rendezvous off Newfoundland. There they reached agreements concerning American aid to the Allies, now that Soviet Russia was one of them (Hopkins, just back from Moscow, was present), and drafted the Atlantic Charter with its historic pronouncement of the Four Freedoms as the basis of future peace. The President, therefore, would not be back on United States soil until August 16, when he would debark at Rockland, Maine. It was decided that Adlai Stevenson must fly out to meet the *Augusta*, brief the President, and secure his signature to the executive order. Hurried arrangements were made for his flight to Quonset Point, Rhode Island, whence a Navy seaplane would fly him to the cruiser at sea.

Just as he was about to depart, he was called again into Knox's office. A solemn-looking senior admiral was there. Knox, too, looked solemn and worried.

"The admiral has a message he wants you to take to the President and deliver to him in person," the Secretary said. "Go ahead, Admiral."

"You are to deliver this message to the President, and *to no one else!*" the admiral said with stern emphasis. "Tell him I have learned today, from a heretofore reliable source, that Stalin has opened negotiations with Hitler."

Stevenson stared, and gulped, as well he might. If the information were true, every plan based on the assumption that Russia, for weeks or months to come, would absorb much of Germany's offensive strength was rendered futile. Moreover Stevenson could see that both Knox and the admiral were not dismissing the report lightly.

"May I write the message down, sir?" he asked.

"Better not!" the admiral said. "Better nothing on paper about this on your person."

Stevenson then repeated the message aloud, to make certain that he stated it correctly, and asked some questions about the source of the report. Again he was warned that the President *alone* must receive it, and as quickly as possible. He departed.

All the way to Quonset, Stevenson pondered the implications of his mission and the message he was carrying—and the more he pondered the more solemn and urgent his journey became for the smiling summer land over which he winged. Germany would be free to turn westward again, perhaps in time to invade Britain in the autumn—and her westward-driving power would be greater than ever before because her eastern frontiers would be secure. That Britain could long withstand the onslaught seemed unlikely. She would have to stand alone. The United States was not ready to give aid on a scale large enough to be effective; she was even more unprepared psychologically. Another moment's delay at the Kearny yards seemed intolerable, for after Britain *we* were next.

At Quonset, Stevenson's trip began to take on nightmare qualities. Bad weather had closed in. All planes were grounded. Desperately he tried to impress upon the admiral in charge the crucial importance of time. Emphatically the admiral refused to permit his plane to take off in search of a cruiser at sea in weather like this. Hours passed. Finally the admiral agreed to permit a small plane to fly Stevenson to Rockland, Maine, though to do so was risky.

"You can get there by the time the President's ship docks," he said.

The plane got through to Rockland all right, but as it circled over the port, Stevenson looked down to see the *Augusta* already at the dock and a huge crowd gathered around a train alongside. The pilot, urged by Stevenson, set the plane down in a primitive grass field. Stevenson, lugging his precious brief case, ran to the highway and flagged down a car driven by an elderly lady. She was startled, even a little frightened, but Stevenson, turning on all his charm, reassured her; she kept a heavy foot on the gas pedal as she drove to town. There, six blocks from the station, they were halted by a traffic jam. Jumping from the car, Stevenson ran as hard as he could to the station. But as he drew near he could hear the shouting and see the puffing smoke above the housetops as the President's special train pulled out. Hitchhiking back to the airport, he and his pilot took off for Portland, which was the first stop the train would make—hours from Rockland by rail but a short distance by air.

In Portland, Stevenson nervously whiled away a couple of hours at dinner and in a motion-picture theater, though he had difficulty keeping his mind on the picture. He then went to the Portland station where he discovered, to his dismay and self-disgust, that a crowd had gathered which was many times larger than the Rockland crowd had been. Every approach to the tracks was blocked by a solid wall of humanity. Portland's policemen were wholly unimpressed by Stevenson's insistence that he had a message of crucial importance to deliver to the President personally; they merely looked at him wearily—they'd heard *that* one before—and curtly ordered him to stand back. At last a slight acquaintance, Senator Claude Pepper, appeared, accompanied by two other gentlemen and two policemen. The gentlemen turned out to be the mayor and former governor, and, thanks to them, Stevenson stood at last in the front line by the station platform.

With some embarrassment he explained to the senator the imperative importance of his getting on the train when it came: he had papers relating to the Kearny shipyard case which required immediate presidential signature. (He did not, of course, mention the secret message.) Pepper promised to see what he could do. The train pulled in. Pepper and the others promptly boarded it. Stevenson, however, was held back by Secret Service men. For fifteen agonizing minutes thereafter he waited on the platform, painfully aware that his predicament had made him an object of amusement for the crowd pressing around him. At last General "Pa" Watkins, presidential aide, came out the door of the presidential car, spoke kindly to Stevenson, and asked him to hand over the necessary papers. The President, explained Watkins, was at dinner. Stevenson refused to hand the papers over; he must, he insisted, see the President personally. Watkins, puzzled and a little annoyed by Stevenson's obstinacy, at last withdrew into the car—and for five more minutes, Stevenson, now red-faced with embarrassment before the snickering crowd, waited helplessly. He more than half expected the train to pull out and was pondering what to do next when Pa Watkins returned and said that the President would see him.

Roosevelt was still at the dinner table as Stevenson entered the car. With him were Marvin McIntyre, Harry Hopkins, Mrs. Roosevelt, and Grace Tully (the President's personal secretary).

"Well, Adlai," said Roosevelt, smiling, "I'm glad to see you again. Glad to hear you're working for Frank Knox."

Astonished by such a warm and personal greeting, Stevenson mumbled an incoherent reply, rushing on to say that he had emergency papers for the President's signature.

"Let's have a look at them," said Roosevelt.

Stevenson's own written account of what then transpired, an account he would always swear was literally accurate, follows:

"I opened up my brief case clumsily and fished out the Kearny shipyard papers, I explained the intricate situation as best I could, as the President's dinner got colder and the others more restive, and pointed out where he was supposed to sign the order. He looked it over for a minute and then said:

"'Well, now, Adlai, you just leave all these papers in your folder with me, and I'll read them over tonight. We'll have a meeting at the White House in the morning. You fly back to Washington and arrange it. Tell Secretary Knox I'd also like to see him and Myron Taylor and the Attorney General at nine o'clock—and you be there, too.'

"'But, Mr. President,' I said, 'this executive order should be signed right now!'

"'I think it will work out all right this way,' said the President.

"'Well,' I said, 'if you say so I guess it will be O.K.!' I marvel that I could have talked like such a fool but I was so nervous I hardly knew what I was saying—mostly, I suppose, because I hadn't yet said the really important thing—the message—and I didn't know how to deliver it with all those people sitting around. I could see he was waiting for me to leave, and I had to come out with something. The talk went about like this:

"'I have something else to tell you, Mr. President.'

"'Do you, Adlai? What is it?'

"'Well, Mr. President, it's a message from Admiral ——. He said to tell you . . . alone.'

"'Oh, I think you can tell me here, Adlai.'

"'No, sir, I can't.' I had a feeling that everyone was doing his best to keep from laughing! I had an idea, just in time. 'Can I write it down, sir?'

"'Why, certainly.'

"I took the menu and I wrote on the back of it, 'Admiral ——
has heard from a heretofore reliable source today that Stalin has
started negotiations with Hitler.'

"Then I gave him back the menu. He read it carefully and then
looked up at me.

"'Adlai,' he said, 'do you believe this?'

"That was too much! I didn't know what I thought. 'Why, I don't
know, Mr. President,' I stammered.

"'I don't believe it,' said F.D.R. 'I'm not worried at all. Are you
worried, Adlai?'

"I said I guessed I wasn't so much worried after all. Then, mission
completed after a fashion, I took my departure, and in my embarrassed confusion, I wheeled around and crashed right into a closed
door, thus bending my crooked nose some more. I flew back to Washington, woke Secretary Knox to tell him about the meeting at the
White House, and we all went over there at nine o'clock. My crowning mortification was that the President hadn't even opened the envelope containing my precious Kearny shipyard papers. He pulled
them out and settled the whole business in fifteen minutes and
signed the executive order. As for the negotiations between Stalin
and Hitler, the President was, of course, right, and the admiral's
source was unreliable that time—thank God!"

Thus Stevenson's account, deliberately designed, it would seem,
to create an impression of fumbling foolishness. Actually, of course,
he had displayed courage, tenacity, and ingenuity, a fact well realized by Knox, and Roosevelt too, when the full story was known.
Even at the time, the President expressed to Secretary Knox appreciation of the manner in which the critical Kearny case was handled.
Perhaps from that moment forward Stevenson's position as Knox's
assistant—a position somewhat analogous to that which Harry Hopkins occupied in relation to Roosevelt—was secure.

The seizure of the shipyard on August 23 (work resumed there
on August 26) by no means ended the Kearny matter. The case was
a test of the emergency powers granted the President, and there
were all sorts of complicated problems whose solutions required
creative and legal intelligence of a high order. "It was very tough,"
said Stevenson years later, "and I worked very hard on it off and on,
all that fall of '41." He worked closely with Admiral Harold G. (Hal)
Bowen, technical aide to the Secretary, who took over the management of Kearny and did, as Stevenson always said, "a really terrific

job—I think of Hal Bowen as one of the great unsung heroes of the war." In the end, the legal machinery through which the Kearny problem was solved became the pilot plan for scores of plant seizures which the war effort later made necessary.

But the Kearny matter was by no means the only one with which Stevenson dealt even in those early months of his new assignment. For many purposes he became, in effect, Knox's alter ego, intimately involved in problems of Navy administration, public relations, and relations with other departments. As Knox's assistant, often as his deputy, he attended virtually all the top-level policy meetings of the interdepartmental agencies which, as the defense effort grew, sprang up in bewildering quantity and variety. He himself had no small part in the shaping of executive policy, particularly in liberalizing the Navy's public relations in the interests of fuller disclosure of news about the Navy's infinite activities and problems. In labor relations and in enlarging opportunities for Negroes in the naval service, he also played an important part.

As time went on and their trials and travels together multiplied, Stevenson became an even closer and more intimate personal friend of Knox. The two complemented each other in many ways, and learned from one another. Knox was bluff, hearty, forthright; he liked to think of himself as a tough, hard-driving, ruthless patriot and super-administrator. In actual fact, he was a simple, kind and gentle man who enjoyed Stevenson's wit, respected his judgment, and admired mental qualities which he himself lacked. As for Stevenson, he more than admired Knox.

"I loved that man," he said, long afterward. "He was brave, and honest. And he made a very great contribution to his country in her hour of greatest need. It cost him a lot. I'm sure it shortened his life. He was no intellectual, God knows, but he was highly intelligent—which a lot of 'intellectuals' aren't you know—and he knew his fellow man from a rough and crowded life. His loyalty to President Roosevelt, his political adversary in 1936, had a defiant quality, and his admiration and respect for his chief seemed to grow as the going got tougher. He had the ability to simplify complex problems. He and I saw eye-to-eye on foreign policy. On domestic policy we often disagreed pretty radically. But he never held that against me. We belonged to different generations, and I really think he became a lot more tolerant as a result of his Washington experiences. Although he continued to regard himself as violently anti-New Deal, of course, he liked to call me *his* New Dealer. He used to say, 'I have to have a New Dealer next to me to protect me from the New Dealers around here.' And he'd turn to me and say, 'Adlai, you're not letting any of 'em creep in here, are you?' Yet I can't recall that he ever vetoed an appointment I wanted made or ever asked me more than perfunctory questions about it."

II

In early September 1941, Mrs. Ellen Borden Stevenson—with Adlai, Jr., Borden, and John Fell—moved into a large old Washington town house which her husband had rented furnished. It stood at 1904 R Street, just off Connecticut Avenue. According to a Chicago society reporter, "Washington society is charmed by Ellen's Greuse-like beauty and Adlai's witty sayings," and during the months that followed, Ellen's name and photograph continued to appear with frequency in the society sections of Washington and Chicago papers. The impression this may have given of a full and gay social life was misleading, however, for Stevenson was working night and day and over the weekends all that autumn. He had little time even to be with his family and virtually none for parties that were not directly in the line of duty.

To his shipyard worries were added, in October and November, numerous other anxieties. He helped draft ideas for Roosevelt's annual Navy Day speech on October 27—the strongest speech the President had yet given on America's relation to the war. (It followed an attack on the U.S.S. *Kearny*, a destroyer, by a Nazi submarine, in which eleven Americans were killed, and a public statement by General Wood of the America First Committee daring the President to ask the Congress for a declaration of war.) He was involved in the stupendous logistical problems incurred by the granting of a one-billion-dollar Lend-Lease credit to the Soviet Union in November, in so far as these problems affected top policy-making levels. And then there were the endless committee and interdepartmental meetings about industrial production, controls, manpower, foreign trade, government information, and all the policy questions precipitated by the war that was creeping ever nearer. He was of course kept *au courant* of the situation in the Far East where Japan, according to British and American intelligence reports, was preparing to attack Indo-China and the Dutch East Indies. He shared to the full Knox's concern over this: a Japanese conquest of these areas would forge a sword pointed directly at the throat of a United States whose hands now seemed tied more securely than ever behind her back by bonds of apathy, confusion, and isolationism. By the narrowest of margins, in early November, after the U.S. destroyer *Reuben James* had been sunk, the Congress permitted the administration to begin arming merchant ships. . . .

On Friday, December 5, Mr. and Mrs. Hermon Dunlap Smith arrived in Washington to spend the weekend as guests of the Adlai Stevensons. That evening they were the guests of honor at a dinner party in the R Street house. Among the other guests were Ted Weeks of the *Atlantic Monthly* and Henry S. Morgan, the banker son of J. P. Morgan, whom Dutch Smith had known since his Harvard days. Ellen was the same superb hostess she had always been, very pretty and gay, and her husband was as witty and stimulating as always before. After the other guests had left, Dutch and Ellen Smith planned with their host and hostess a picnic for the following afternoon. The Stevensons knew of a wonderful picnic spot some fifteen or twenty miles from Washington, along the Chesapeake and Ohio canal on the Maryland side of the Potomac.

When Adlai went to the office next morning, however, he found that new problems had arisen in the Kearny shipyard matter. The Smiths, with Ellen Stevenson and the three Stevenson boys, picnicked without him. They returned with glowing accounts of their afternoon.

Next morning, Sunday, December 7, the Smiths left Washington for Chicago. Adlai and Ellen Stevenson drove them to the Union Station, with Dutch sitting beside Adlai in the front seat and the two Ellens sitting in the back. In the back seat the talk turned to Washington life and Ellen Stevenson's dislike for it—a reaction, as Ellen Smith discovered, actually stronger than dislike—and to her feeling that she was being increasingly alienated from Adlai, who had no time for her. . . . In the front seat the talk turned to Illinois politics.

The old Horner group remained a major power in Illinois politics, despite Horner's bitter primary fight with the Kelly-Nash machine in 1936, his death in October of 1940, and the election of Dwight Green, Republican, to the governorship on a reform platform in 1940. Some of this group, Stevenson told Dutch Smith, were "after him" to run for the Senate against the Republican isolationist incumbent, C. Wayland (Curly) Brooks, darling of the Chicago *Tribune*, who was up for re-election in the fall of '42. The issue, of course, would be foreign policy, and on that issue Stevenson would be a strong candidate, according to the people who had talked to him about it. What did Dutch think? Smith was surprised. His friend, so far as he could recall, had never before mentioned to him the possibility of running for public office—at least not seriously.

"Why, Adlai," Smith said, "I just don't know anything about it. Besides, as you well know, I'm a Republican."

"Well, it probably doesn't make any sense. You might ask around about it, though, and try to find out if there's anything to it. And let me know."

Smith said he'd do that.

On the train Smith reviewed his weekend with his friend, and it was then, as he said years later, that he first realized that Adlai Stevenson was becoming a great man. He had sensed in his friend a greater weight and balance of judgment, a firmer grasp of problems, a wider and deeper vision than he had ever noticed in him before. He had always had a high opinion of his friend's abilities. He had admired him for his nimbleness of wit and loved him for his sweetness of character. But it had not occurred to him before that Adlai might play a major role in history.

He spoke of this to his wife.

"This political business—it opens up possibilities for him I'd never thought of," Smith said.

"Politics?"

"Yes. Didn't you hear what he was saying?"

Ellen Smith shook her head. "I was too busy with Ellen," she said, frowning a little. After a pause she added, "She seems so—discontented——"

Had Ellen Smith been able to spend that afternoon with the Stevensons, her concern about impending trouble would surely have been lessened.

On the way back to R Street from the station Adlai suddenly decided that, despite the work which piled up around him, he'd take the afternoon off. It was Sunday, after all; he'd had no time alone with his family for weeks. . . . They decided to go on a family picnic, to the same spot where Ellen and the boys had gone with the Smiths the preceding afternoon.

They had one of their happiest times together. They picnicked on a high rock bank overlooking the Potomac. They canoed on the river. On the way back to Washington they stopped at the falls of the Potomac, a particularly beautiful spot, where Adlai romped with the boys for some time. They returned in the winter dusk to R Street where the maid informed them that the phone had been ringing constantly; beside the phone was a stack of messages requesting Adlai to call back. Undoubtedly it was the Kearny business again, he told Ellen; they could wait until he'd had a shower.

While he was showering the phone rang again, and Ellen answered. A newspaperman was on the line, an acquaintance of theirs. He demanded to speak to Adlai, overruling Ellen's objections to calling her husband at that moment. Of Stevenson he requested a statement for the press.

"About what?" Stevenson asked.

The newspaperman was at first irritated by what he deemed Stevenson's tasteless facetiousness, then astonished by the realization that Stevenson really didn't know what had happened. The Japanese had bombed Pearl Harbor; they were attacking the Philippines, Guam, Midway Island. . . .

Stevenson rushed to his office adjacent to Secretary Knox's. He spent most of that night in Knox's outer office as Admiral Stark, Chief of Naval Operations, and other senior officers came in for conferences, and ominous tidings continued to roll in from the Far East.

Next morning, before a joint session of the Congress, the President of the United States asked for and promptly received a declaration of war against Japan, Germany, and Italy. A little later Stevenson drafted and sent a message which Knox signed and released to the Navy and the press.

"The enemy has struck a savage, treacherous blow," the message said. "We are at war, all of us. There is not time now for disputes or delays of any kind. We must have ships and more ships, guns and more guns, planes and more planes, men and more men—faster and faster. There is no time to lose. The Navy must lead the way. Speed up—it is your Navy and your Nation."

When Knox returned from his inspection trip to battered Pearl Harbor, Stevenson asked if he could have a commission and a uniform. Knox said he could if he insisted, but he hoped he would not insist; Knox would not be able to give him sufficient rank under the Reserve rules then in effect, and felt therefore that Stevenson would be more useful to him as a civilian.

The possibility of Stevenson's running for the Senate next fall was, of course, shelved if not actually forgotten. In November the egregious "Curly" Brooks would be re-elected as Republican senator from Illinois.

The Stevensons had long planned to spend the Christmas holiday of 1941 with Buffie and Ernest Ives at Southern Pines. For many days following Pearl Harbor it seemed impossible that Adlai could get away. He managed to do so, however, just for Christmas Day itself, taking a night train down from Washington on Christmas Eve and a night train back to Washington on Christmas night. Ellen and the three boys, who had grand times with Timmie Ives, remained for nearly two weeks.

To Buffie, as to Ellen Thorne Smith, Ellen Stevenson revealed her unhappiness in Washington, her dislike for the hectic Washington life with its demands and its constantly recurrent crises. Everyone was so full of self-importance, so sure that the fate of the world rested on his shoulders. She loved the quiet, the solitude, the freedom from "plans." She rebelled against the "planning-out" of things; it destroyed the element of surprise, it kept the planned things from *really* happening.

"*This* is the way I'd like to live," she said again and again, as she looked out across the winter-green fields and hills of North Carolina. "You have the perfect life!"

III

During the war Stevenson traveled with and for the Secretary extensively. In three years he flew some two hundred thousand miles throughout the United States, into the Pacific theater, across the Caribbean, across the Atlantic to North Africa and Europe.

The longest of his numerous trips with Knox was an inspection tour made in December of 1942 and January of 1943, covering the entire Pacific theater. It was not without its hazards. One of the engines of the big four-engine flying boat in which they took off from Pearl Harbor at dawn quit when the plane was barely seventy feet above the water. In the violent landing Admiral Nimitz's scalp was cut, and one wing went under the water. To right the plane the party had to crawl out of the hold through the escape hatch and out onto the high wing, a procedure somewhat complicated by the portliness of the Navy Secretary, who was squeezed through the narrow hatch by pulling from above and hearty shoves from the rear by his "personal lawyer." ("To see the rotund Secretary pulling himself up that steep wing on his stomach followed by the commander of the Pacific Fleet is my most vivid and amusing memory of that memorable trip," commented Stevenson in a speech before the Maryland Council of the Navy League two months later.)

At Midway Island, which had been badly battered by the Japanese in the Battle of Midway, the plane in which they rode smashed a pontoon while landing, and their departure was delayed. At Espiritu Santo in the New Hebrides Islands the party slept on the decks of a Navy ship. Never before bombed, the enemy chose the time of the Secretary's visit to send over a bomber which missed the target but gave rise to the suspicion that enemy intelligence might be cognizant of the party's composition and itinerary.

During those years Stevenson wrote or edited most of the Secretary's public statements and formal speeches, and it was perhaps in this role of ghost writer that he earned Knox's most fervent admiration and gratitude. It cannot be said, however, that he succeeded in such attempts as he may have made toward tailoring his eloquence to Knox's natural style of public speaking. The speech drafts employed a longer period, a greater vocabulary range, and a much more intricate rhythmic balance than earlier writings bearing Knox's name had done. Their creator might be embarrassed by the purple passages they contained when, a few years later, after the fever of the war had subsided, he re-read them. Knox, he then opined, must have had the devil's own time giving some of them.

He was also called upon by the Navy to give some speeches of his own—and if he never wholly mastered the art of writing a speech that sounded like Frank Knox, he became during these years a master of speeches that were uniquely Adlai Stevenson. He did not do so easily. Never a swift and facile writer, always pressed for time, he now composed more painfully than ever. But he knew that, in large part, the difficulty of his drafting stemmed from his refusal to accept easy ways. If he aimed for clarity and simplicity, he aimed also for an eloquence increasingly rare among the public speakers of his time, knowing well that a formal eloquence has its own message, enhancing the meaning of all that is said through it. Determined to do this work in the grand tradition, he must risk the ridiculous continuously in an effort to achieve the sublime—an effort which succeeded more and more often as he learned through experience.

The style he was developing was not, in his own view, consciously influenced by any other one style. "My object," he would say, "has merely been to talk as well as I can—to honor the language and elevate the listeners if I could." Inevitably, however, whether consciously or not, he was influenced by others who had "honored" the language, notably Abraham Lincoln and Woodrow Wilson, with echoes here and there of Winston Churchill.

In mid-February of '42 he electrified a large crowd at a Chicago Council on Foreign Relations luncheon in the Palmer House with a passionate, fighting speech aimed at "complacency." Said a feature story in a Chicago paper next day: "The talk which Adlai Stevenson gave . . . was sufficient to make him one of the most celebrated men of the times." He spoke before the Princeton Club in New York, before the Real Estate Board in Chicago, before a huge Navy Day celebration in Bloomington, before a dozen other large audiences, and with each address his power as a speaker, he felt, was increased.

It was, he admitted to himself, a thrilling power; it was also a sobering one, counseling humility. One could become addicted to this kind of power. And one could misuse it to disastrously egotistical ends, as Hitler had done, if one let it slip the leash of logical rigor and moral responsibility. He therefore strengthened the leash. He began, more and more, to weave strands of humor into it—a wit which not only leavened his serious message, making it more palatable, but also illumined the points he wanted to make. It was himself he most often laughed at publicly. He presented himself in the role of Everyman, whose individual fate is tragic, certainly, since the grave inevitably awaits him, but who is also a comic character as he fumbles and stumbles along his path, striving to hide his woeful inadequacy behind a thousand ridiculous pomposities.

In May of 1943 Stevenson became involved in a legal problem which, in some ways, was even more difficult than the Kearny shipyard case had been. What's more, as the devoted assistant saw it, it was fraught with greater peril to Frank Knox's personal reputation.

It had to do with the naval oil reserve at Elk Hills, California—a focus, it will be remembered, of the greatest of the Harding regime scandals in the 1920s. The reserve contained approximately forty-three thousand acres, but not all of these were government-owned.

Some nine thousand acres belonged to Standard Oil of California. Standard was under pressure to fill huge war orders for oil, but if the company operated its nine thousand acres independently of government control it would drain off oil which the Congress, in the Naval Reserve Act as amended in 1938, had sought to guarantee as reserved. Accordingly, Knox had entered into a contract with Standard for unit operation of the pool by Standard under Navy supervision, in November of 1942. Soon there were published rumors that the contract was illegal and that graft and corruption were involved in it. Pressure developed in the Justice Department and in the Congress for immediate condemnation of Standard's nine thousand acres.

It was at this point that Knox called in Stevenson and assigned him the problem. Stevenson's paramount consideration was to ensure uninterrupted production of the fifteen thousand barrels of oil a day which the war effort required of the Elk Hills pool. Only Standard, it appeared to him, could get the needed oil out. Accordingly he recommended to Knox that a temporary operating agreement be executed with Standard to remain in effect while the Navy Department drafted amendments to the 1938 Act for presentation to the Congress. Knox accepted this recommendation; the temporary agreement was signed on September 8, 1943, after approval by Attorney General Francis Biddle and the President.

Associated with Stevenson in this task was his younger friend, Carl McGowan. Shortly after Pearl Harbor Day, McGowan had written to Stevenson, asking if there were a spot for him in the Navy Department; Stevenson, having high regard for McGowan, said to come at once, and early in '42 McGowan had become a civilian lawyer in the Bureau of Ships and later, after the war began, an officer on Stevenson's staff. Out of their work together in the terrible urgency of wartime Washington, Stevenson and McGowan became close personal friends, with a profound respect for each other's abilities. A foundation was firmly laid for their future working relationship.

CHAPTER SIXTEEN

Journey to War, with a Postscript on
Journalism in Chicago

In late 1943 and early 1944 Adlai Stevenson was "borrowed" from Frank Knox by President Roosevelt to head an emergency mission to Sicily and Italy. The assignment was by no means an easy one; it was, indeed, "one of the most difficult" possible under the prevailing circumstances, as an unnamed official of the Foreign Economic Administration was quoted in the national press as saying. There were no real precedents for the job Stevenson had to do.

By late 1943 Allied forces stood on a bloody line reaching from sea to sea just south of Cassino, less than a third of the way up the Italian boot, their position made all the more difficult by the chaos, the human misery behind them. Cut off from the industrial north and devastated by war, the southern Italian economy was at a standstill, transport paralyzed, the people hungry and demoralized, the specter of disease and famine looming over the land. Stevenson's mission was to study and report on how relief should be given the Italian people while the country was rehabilitated; the ways and means by which a working economy might be re-established; and the economic aspects of the problem of re-establishing local governments in areas where every experienced administrator was *ipso facto* a Fascist or Fascist supporter.

All this was difficult enough. It was further complicated by what seemed to many close observers a hopelessly tangled administrative setup. The Foreign Economic Administration had been created by presidential edict in late September in an effort to reduce interagency squabbles which were sadly reducing the effectiveness of the whole economic warfare effort. In FEA had been consolidated the Office of Economic Warfare, the Lend-Lease Administration, the Office of Foreign Relief and Rehabilitation, and other foreign economic agencies. But this nominal "unification" had not, in actual fact, removed the causes of interagency strife: to some observers strife seemed to be the very essence of the FEA; and it was even more severe in the Mediterranean theater, at the end of long lines of communication, than it was in Washington itself.

The mission included an industrial engineer, an agronomist, and an economist who spoke Italian. They took off at nine-thirty on the morning of December 7 (Pearl Harbor Day), 1943, being "herded into bucket seats in the luggage compartment of an old converted TWA stratoliner," as Stevenson noted in the diary he kept of his trip. They arrived in Georgetown, British Guiana, at eight next morning, breakfasted there at the airport officers' club, then took off for Belém on the Rio Pará in Brazil, flying over "everlasting jungle —flat—broken by patches of open country. (God, what vast areas of unused and useless land I've seen in the last couple of years!)" to Natal, where they arrived at midnight. "Full moon, gorgeous night, soft wind from the sea. . . . Comfortably bunked in barracks. Supper, shower, and bed at last."

After a dull day in Natal ("hideous . . . town") they took off for Dakar, winging across the Atlantic in the silver light of the full moon, riding this time in a "modified Liberator" bomber. Opposite him sat the "Assistant Commissioner for colonies of the French Com. of Liberation, en route to Algiers," whose preparations for the night fascinated him. "I was reminded of all my earlier experiences with traveling Frenchmen and their horror of cold," he wrote. "First he took off his elegant shoes and put on slippers, then his coat and put on a heavy wool sweater, then a sheepskin-lined jacket, then a camel's-hair greatcoat, then a knitted contrivance over his head and ears, then a ski cap emerged from somewhere, finally a muffler around his neck and another wound around his legs. I've omitted the Mae West lifebelt we all had to wear! All this went on in a blacked-out plane that was crowded beyond description. I watched him emerge in the morning with wonder." At noon, December 10, "we hit Dakar right on the button."

Next morning, at seven-thirty, the mission took off for Morocco, flying hour after hour over the great desert. "As we approach the Atlas Mountains little circular . . . villages and patches of palms begin to appear. We climb to 12,000 into the rugged snow moun-

tains—now there's water shining in the streams and fertile little valleys with terraced fields up the hillsides and many villages hanging
precariously. They must be thrifty farmers—these Moors. Over the
pass with snow at arms length off each wing and down into the fertile
valley of Marrakesh." He noted that, whereas "Tunis and Algiers
were white when Ellen and I were there 15 years ago this month
. . . Marrakesh is pink." He spent the night in Marrakesh, seeing
the sun set "in fire over the pink city behind the minaret on the
great mosque" and wandering "through the crooked side streets
canopied with matting and lined with stalls and shops."

The following day came close to being Stevenson's last. They were
"up and off in darkness" on the morning of December 12. "As we
approach Oran and the sea, the weather gets worse—bumpy, high
wind, white fog rolling in from the sea. All of a sudden we're over
the water and then there followed the worst hour I've ever had. The
pilot was lost. The coast is dangerous flying—mountains and valleys.
He had to pull her nose up sharp several times and almost turned
me inside out, and all the while the big plane was shaking like a
leaf and the wind was howling as I've never heard it. It was raining
torrents and the ceiling was zero. They put up a smoke screen on
the ground that finally gave the pilot a fix and at last we landed
on instruments. There was no going on. . . ." Next day the weather
was still wild—windy and rainy—with all planes grounded, and Stevenson "foolishly" decided to motor to Algiers, leaving his party in
Oran, to come on when flying was again possible. "What a [trip]
300 miles. First we break a fan belt—repairs at a French Army camp,
thanks to my French. Thousands of . . . army trucks on the roads.
Through the mountains just before dark—then a flat tire and repairs
by a French soldier under a street lamp in Blida, again thanks to
my French! I wish Ellen could have heard me giving technical directions. Finally reached Algiers after 10½ hours of beating. . . ."

On the morning of the fourteenth he went to the Hotel St. George,
where the Allied GHQ was located—the hotel where Adlai and Ellen
had stayed during their honeymoon. Here he presented his credentials, including letters from President Roosevelt, Secretary Knox, and
Secretary of War Stimson. He did not, however, present them personally to General Eisenhower. Instead he was "ushered into Gen.
[Walter Bedell] Smith, the chief of staff." "Long talk, very cordial,
much about the Italian political situation and plans to force the king's
abdication, military gov't, etc., and then to Brig. Gen. Julius Holmes,

the Civil Affairs Officer. [Holmes] very cordial, suave, self-confident, State Department type. . . . To billeting officer and sent to 4th rate Hotel Feminie! No sheets, no hot water, tiny cell, dirty. . . . Lunch downtown with Wesley Sturges. . . . Much talk, Communism in Italy. . . . Back to talk with Holmes's staff, and there are my lost colleagues!" They had just landed in the plane from Oran. He dined that night "with Holmes and Murphy [Robert Murphy, the State Department French political expert, still under heavy fire at that time for his North African political arrangements] in their fine villa opposite St. George" which "turned out to be villa Buffie had for a year . . . Holmes much disturbed when he heard I was poorly quartered—somebody had slipped, please forgive, all would be corrected tomorrow." And it was. Others of Stevenson's party were taken to the Aletta, the best Algiers hotel, while Stevenson himself was taken to "beautiful Villa Bel Air—reserved only for generals, admirals, and the most distinguished guests of Gen. Eisenhower." He added in his diary, "All is forgiven!"

He was mistaken, however, in his belief that his mission thereafter would be efficiently facilitated by the Army. Abruptly and painfully he was introduced to the situation which had frustrated other civilian missions in the war theater: the Army was indifferent if not actually hostile to such visitors. Not until Stevenson turned to the Navy, where he was well known as the Secretary's confidential assistant, did he obtain adequate transportation, and facilities for his party to do their job. The naval commander at Palermo, Sicily, assigned him a command car and two bluejackets, sent word of his coming up the line, and from then on the mission proceeded relatively smoothly.

In the command car, with blanket rolls, gasoline cans, and K rations, the party toured Sicily and Italy for six weeks, accumulating huge piles of notes on market, transportation, the agricultural situation, industrial destruction, housing, rehabilitation of all kinds, and the problem of re-establishing a maximum possible civilian control of local government. Stevenson's diary was filled with vivid impressions of the scenes and people he encountered. Typical were his jottings for December 23, when the party was near Nicastro: ". . . off without breakfast in a cold gray dawn. K rations on a deserted road in the country, but somehow the children showed up accompanied by a cheerful young philosopher driving a donkey who pointed to our car and said, 'American car' and to his donkey—'Italian car'; to our shoes, 'American shoes'—to his bare feet—'Italian shoes'; to our K rations—'American food,' to a small crust of black bread in his shirt— 'Italian food'—and then laughed merrily. He got his reward and I some phrases that summarized my whole experience in Italy—and also an uneasy feeling that such contrasts won't endure forever. But how is the American taxpayer to be persuaded that to help Italy at his expense is to help himself? 'Perhaps his grandchildren. . . .'"

In Naples, in a corridor of the headquarters building, he at last and by chance met Eisenhower. The two had a brief, pleasant chat and parted, not to meet again for many years.

"I spent a day at the front," Stevenson wrote later, in some desultory memoirs of the trip. "We stopped first at 5th Army headquarters in the great Bourbon palace of Caserta . . . ; then on to Capua and across the bloody Volturno River, past Mignano, 98 percent destroyed, and after a wild dash of several miles where the road to Rome was exposed to enemy fire . . . we climbed up a hillside into a pile of rubble that was once the ancient town of San Pietro. From there we had a fine view of Monte Cassino Monastery a few miles north. . . . That day our patrols were in the olive groves on the hillsides around San Vittore. . . . I wish I could describe that mud that has to be shovelled off the roads like snow and the cold penetrating rain, the stench of those ruined towns with their unburied dead in the rubble, the conditions in which the doughboys live and stand sleepless watch over their guns—and fight, up and down those stony rugged mountains, supplied by donkeys, with the Germans and their machine guns and screaming mortars always above you on the next hilltop.

". . . I saw Ernie Pyle in Naples a few evenings later and asked him what the doughfeet, as they call the soldiers, were thinking about up there in the Liri Valley and he said: 'They are thinking of only one thing, and that's where they can find a dry place to sit on so they can wring out their socks.'"

On his return trip to the United States he stopped again in Dakar, where Admiral Glassford suggested that before flying home he go down to Liberia for a quick look-see in connection with a port development and submarine base which the Navy was considering. Although some familiarity with the harbor at Monrovia, Liberia's capital, and a talk with some of the officials would be helpful back in the department, Stevenson's mission was behind schedule and he might not have made the trip (he took Wesley Sturges with him) if he had not long had a curiosity about this remote Negro republic. His great-grandfather Dr. Lewis Warner Green, it will be remembered, had been one of the leading sponsors of the Liberia project in the decades immediately preceding the Civil War. . . .

The official fruit of the FEA mission was a hastily prepared report of some one hundred and fifty printed pages which became a model of its kind. Not only did it provide a firm factual and interpretative basis for top-level decisions about Italy, it also served as a guide for the solution of similar problems in other liberated areas as the Allied armies forced the Nazi hordes back step by reluctant step into the bloody ruins of the Third Reich. Partly as a result of it, the effective co-ordination of economic, political, and military activities in the areas liberated by the Allies was greatly increased.

II

In the late summer of 1943 it had been decided that Ellen, who had gone to the Libertyville farm with the boys, would not come back to Washington in the fall.

Her dissatisfaction with wartime capital life had become a chronic unhappiness, and her conclusions as to how she wished to live had been confirmed for her by her experiences of what seemed to her the idyllic country life of the Ives's in North Carolina. On one visit to Southern Pines, Ellen, Adlai, and the boys had stayed in a house owned by Struthers Burt, the novelist, just a little way from the Ives's farm. When they returned to Washington, Burt wrote to Ellen in high praise of her poetry. "She *must* find time or *organize* her time to write more," Stevenson noted in his diary. "Her quality is so high and her output so low." At Libertyville she was free of schedules. She was free of servants, too, that year; she cooked and kept house and gardened, with the help of the boys. It was, she laughed, her "war effort," and she loved it. She wrote light verse and satires, including a playlet in verse which "took-off" the Great Books program developed by her friends Robert Hutchins and Mortimer Adler at the University of Chicago.[1]

[1] This playlet was later presented by Ellen and others at a meeting of the Friday Club in Chicago, where it made a great success. Louise Wright would remember that, though men seldom attended meetings of this club, Adlai slipped in at the back of the room and stood beside her as the playlet was presented. He enjoyed it hugely, and enjoyed too the "hit" it made with the audience. "That girl is so clever!" he said proudly to Louise.

So from September on into the spring of 1944, Stevenson lived in a small bachelor apartment above a bookstore in Georgetown, sharing it with his old Princeton friend, Francis A. Comstock, now a commander in the Navy. The apartment consisted of a small sitting room, a small bedroom, and a tiny kitchenette where Adlai sometimes cooked for his guests at dinner. Ellen came for infrequent visits during that winter and spring. Adlai came even more infrequently to Chicago, once on February 18, when he accepted on behalf of Frank Knox the 1943 Award of Merit of the Decalogue Society of Lawyers, presented to the Secretary of the Navy for distinguished service to the nation and "unselfish work for a better community." Knox had been unable to attend the great dinner honoring him because of ill health.

As ardent a devotee of the "strenuous life" as ever Teddy Roosevelt had been, Frank Knox had refused to admit in practice that, at seventy, he was not so fit and vigorous as he had been at fifty. He looked easily ten years younger than his actual age, and as he strode over the golf course he displayed a young man's strength and endurance. He laughed at the advice of friends to "slow down." But on Sunday, April 23, he had a clear intimation of his own mortality. He had come to his old home in Manchester, New Hampshire, to attend the funeral of John A. Muehling, his publishing partner for forty years. There he suffered a "slight" heart attack. He treated this infirmity with contempt, returning to Washington on Monday and going to his office Tuesday morning, intending to hold his regular press conference. He was unable to do so, however; he became ill and was forced to go home and to bed.

He died at his home at 1:08 o'clock on the afternoon of Friday, April 28, 1944. Ellen, Buffie, and Ernest Ives were with Adlai in the Georgetown apartment when the news came. None of them would forget how profoundly the news affected him. . . .

James V. Forrestal, then Undersecretary, was appointed as Knox's successor, and there was newspaper speculation that Stevenson would be named to succeed Forrestal as Undersecretary. Roosevelt, it was reported, wished to do so. Stevenson himself believed, however, that Forrestal should choose his own second-in-command and that Ralph A. Bard, an old Chicago friend of Knox, who had served as Assistant Secretary during the Knox regime, had earned the post. Stevenson therefore decided to "get out of the way" and resigned his position in June, returning to Chicago.

III

By that time he was deeply involved in an enterprise which might well have determined the whole of his future career, had it succeeded, removing him altogether from active political life.

Knox's funeral was at the Mount Pleasant Congregational Church in Washington, and virtually all of the key people of the Chicago *Daily News* were among the mourners. Afterward a group of them called on Adlai Stevenson to discuss with him the future of their newspaper. They wished to form a syndicate, with others, to purchase Knox's controlling stock from his estate; they wanted Stevenson to head the group, and to be publisher of the paper once the property was acquired. By the terms of the will the entire estate was left to Knox's widow, Annie Reid Knox, who was named as one of the three executors, the other two being Holman D. Pettibone, president of the Chicago Title and Trust Company, and Laird Bell, Knox's attorney. These were given great powers of discretion; they could sell to anyone at whatever price they desired, though the will asked them to do all possible to perpetuate the personnel and policies of the paper. Knox had often indicated, orally, that he would like to have the paper become employee-owned when he died. . . .

The idea was more exciting to Stevenson than any earlier career opportunity had been, awakening all those ambitions for a career in journalism which had formerly been so strong in him. He immediately had dreams of making the *Daily News*, then a distinguished paper, into one of the greatest newspapers in the world—dreams that were shared and embroidered by his old and dear friend, Paul Scott Mowrer, the famous foreign correspondent who was then the editor, and by another intimate and beloved friend and Libertyville neighbor, the celebrated critic and biographer, Lloyd Lewis. (The colorful Lewis, who had been the managing editor during the last year of Knox's life, would often say to Stevenson during this period: "We'll ride down the street, shooting the varmints as we see 'em from *both* hips!") To build such a paper on foundations laid by the great Victor Lawson, and to save the incomparable foreign staff so respected by Frank Knox would honor the memory of the man Stevenson had so greatly loved and admired, and would give Stevenson himself something more "useful" to do and perhaps more profitable than practicing law.

Through the rest of that summer and fall of 1944 he devoted all his time and energy to the project. He managed to "scrape up" (as he put it) two million dollars. A small part of this was money of his own and that of *Daily News* employees; the bulk of it came from people who had confidence in the *News* and in Stevenson's management. He had in addition an offer from Marshall Field, then publishing the morning Chicago *Sun* in competition with the *Tribune*, to make up whatever balance Stevenson needed for a fair, acceptable bid. Also, Jesse Jones, the Texas millionaire, who had been a wartime admirer of Stevenson's in Washington, had made it clear that he was available if needed. After elaborate professional appraisals, Stevenson felt justified in bidding twelve dollars a share for the 149,941 shares of common stock held by the estate. This bid, however, was considerably lower than those made by several others. One of the others approached him with an offer to make him publisher at a large salary if he would facilitate the acquisition of the property, an offer he promptly refused. As the executors wanted to give Stevenson's group another chance, he raised his bid to thirteen dollars per share after consulting his investors. This, he felt, was as high as he should go in view of his representations to the investors about value based on the appraisals. Actually he could legitimately have gone high enough to outbid the others had the money been available. Even at twenty dollars a share, as it turned out, the *Daily News* would have been a bargain. He could have outbid his competitors, too, if he had been willing to accept Marshall Field's offer to him, but he was uneasy about having a competitor, however friendly personally, with a large stock interest.

If Mrs. Knox considered any other factor than her desire to obtain as much money as possible for the property, it may have been one which worked against the Stevenson group. As one Chicago paper's gossip columnist put it: "Mrs. Knox has indicated that she prefers to sell to a purchaser with Republican leanings." It was said that Laird Bell felt that the Stevenson group should be preferred, even at some sacrifice in price, which, after all, was within the executors' discretion. But apparently he felt he could not insist upon his view in the circumstances. The Stevenson bid was rejected.

It was a great disappointment to him, though he had had misgivings about the difficulties of management under a voting trust. Few if any career dreams had been as vividly desirable as this of a creative metropolitan journalism. And it was little consolation to be asked by at least one of the executors which of the higher bidders, in his view, they should favor as most likely to carry on a paper at least somewhat in the tradition of Knox and Lawson. Stevenson expressed a preference to John S. Knight. To Knight the paper was sold—just in time to ensure its support of Dewey in the 1944 campaign.

CHAPTER SEVENTEEN

Of International Organization

Adlai Stevenson was so immersed in the negotiations for the *Daily News* that he took little active part in the presidential campaign of 1944. He watched from the side lines as the Republican party nominated Governor Thomas E. Dewey of New York as its presidential candidate, and he did no more than attend the convention at which the Democrats nominated Franklin Roosevelt for a fourth term, with Senator Harry S. Truman of Missouri as running mate. This was the campaign in which Roosevelt, fearful that overconfidence would reduce the Democratic vote, made a talk to the Teamsters' Union about "my little dog, Fala" ("I am accustomed to hearing malicious falsehoods about myself but I think I have a right to object to libelous statements about my dog"), whereupon the campaign became, as some contemporary remarked, a "contest between Dewey and Fala." Fala won the contest, with Roosevelt picking up the winnings in November. The Democratic victory, though no landslide, was substantial.

In Europe, World War II was approaching its final phase. Germany was being subjected to unprecedentedly powerful and continuous air bombardment focused on her factories, power plants, transportation centers—and such air-power proponents as General Henry H. (Hap) Arnold, commanding general of the United States Army Air Forces, were claiming that strategic bombing was more decisive of victory than any other part of the war effort. Others had long asserted that air power alone, if adequately employed, could win the war. Were such claims and assertions valid? Precisely how effective was strategic bombing in general, and in what particular areas and respects was it most effective?

It was an attempt to answer such questions which called Adlai Stevenson back into war service from his law office whence he returned following the *Daily News* affair. He became a member of the United States Strategic Bombing Survey, dispatched by the War Department to determine the physical damage to the enemy, the psychological effect upon him, and the aid given Allied ground forces by the massive air attacks. "The methods of warfare may change," Stevenson explained to Bloomington friends when he returned from his mission, "but the fundamental theories of both ground and sea power remain the same. It is hoped that out of our experiences in this war some basic theories of air power may be evolved." He spent two months in England, France, and Belgium. He toured the western front from northern Germany to Metz in France, where he met General George Patton. He was at General Courtney Hodges' First Army headquarters at Spa in Belgium on the day before the Germans launched their last desperate attack of the war, into the Ardennes forest. Ignorant of the fact that the Battle of the Bulge had begun, he drove back to Brussels with an Air Force general and flew from there to England in a Canadian Air Force plane, in weather so bad that an emergency landing was made miraculously in a forbidden field many miles from London. By this time the organization was established, and because he was unable to do much survey work because of stubborn German resistance, he left bomb-blasted London and flew back to America. He arrived at his Libertyville farm on Christmas Eve.

Less than two months later he was again called into government service, this time in a field for which he was unusually well prepared and upon which his major interest had long been focused. On February 23, 1945, Joseph C. Grew, Undersecretary of State, announced the appointment of Adlai Stevenson as special assistant to Secretary of State Edward R. Stettinius, Jr. "He will work with Archibald MacLeish, Assistant Secretary of State, in matters relating to postwar international organization," the announcement said. Actually his role was to assist MacLeish in pioneering a "popular-education" program being initiated by the State Department in an effort to narrow the gap which had theretofore existed between ordinary citizens and the "striped-pants boys." It was a job of particular importance at that time because of the upcoming international conference at San Francisco where the United Nations Organization was to be formally developed out of proposals originally discussed, months before, at Dumbarton Oaks.

Ellen Stevenson remained on the farm with the three boys when her husband departed for Washington. "She's seen a terrific lot of that farm these past three years since her husband has been in Washington and all over the globe besides," wrote a Chicago society columnist. "And after Mr. Stevenson was released from his job with the Navy Department last summer they were settling down, as they supposed, to the quiet life in the country. Now with the new State Department appointment, Adlai Stevenson is back in Washington, probably until the war is over." In Washington, until he went to San Francisco in May, he lived with his old friends, Mr. and Mrs. Benjamin W. Thoron, in their large old Georgetown house at 2900 N Street, N.W.

His office was next to MacLeish's in a first-floor corner of the old State Department building, and in his daily contacts with the distinguished poet he cemented a permanent and mutually admiring friendship. It was, for him, a highly educative friendship. One of the things he learned was abundantly confirmed by his own later experience, namely that, in the political life of our time, *"dura est ovicipitum via"* or, freely translated, "the way of the egghead is hard."[1] The word "egghead" as a synonym for "intellectual" had not yet enriched the American language—it would be one of the products of Stevenson's future career[2]—but MacLeish certainly belonged to the category it named. He suffered for it. "For some reason hard to fathom, the fact that he is a poet has been treated by hostile editorialists as though he had a record down at the Bureau of Identification," wrote Edwin A. Lahey, Washington correspondent of the Chicago *Daily News,* in his column of April 12, 1945. ". . . MacLeish is . . . a man's man, a World War I flier, a scholar, a distinguished journalist . . . who believes in what he is doing." What he was doing, "with the valuable assistance of Adlai Stevenson," was "making the people of this country State Department conscious." Lahey added that "letters of comment and inquiry have been coming to the State Department at the rate of 600 a day in recent weeks.

[1] The phrase was coined by Professor Madison Priest of the University of Virginia and was made famous in a speech by Stevenson in 1954.
[2] The word "egghead" as a synonym for an "intellectual" was popularized in a nationally syndicated column by Joseph Alsop during the 1952 campaign.

. . . This kind of mail," he added, ". . . is no small tribute to the performance of MacLeish and Stevenson."

By the time this column was written MacLeish and Stevenson had been placed in a particularly unhappy position.

When the announcement of Stevenson's appointment was made President Roosevelt was on his way to Washington from the Yalta Conference, at which the British, Russian, and American heads of state had, among other things, endorsed the United Nations Conference, which was to assemble in San Francisco on April 25. On March 2, Roosevelt had addressed the Congress in a bid for support of the Yalta Agreement, mentioning in passing that "it is not yet possible to announce . . . publicly" the terms of the voting procedure for the Security Council of the proposed UNO, but that the announcement would be made "in a very short time." Why could not the announcement be made now? people asked, suspiciously. Four days later, from Mexico, where the Chapultepec Conference was in progress, Secretary of State Stettinius made known the veto provision which had been agreed upon for the Security Council at Yalta—a provision which was immediately interpreted by many as a "sellout" to Stalin (though in point of fact the United States would have insisted upon it if Stalin had not done so). It began to look as though the true relationship between the three great powers was far different from that which the American and British leaders had represented to their peoples.

All of this complicated the task of preparing a knowledgeable popular support of the proposed United Nations Organization, but MacLeish and Stevenson went forward with an "educational" program emphasizing that Big Three solidarity was indispensable to the peace and that the basis for this had been well laid at Yalta. Particularly did they seek to scotch the rumor that unknown arrangements had been made for voting in the proposed UN's General Assembly. In printed materials and radio broadcasts they repeatedly emphasized the "absolute equality" of the UN voting procedure, giving to the "little fellow" the same voting power as the "big fellow" within the Assembly. They did this in the perfect assurance that they spoke the truth.

One can imagine their dismay, therefore, when a "leak" to a New York *Herald Tribune* reporter revealed that an arrangement had indeed been made at Yalta whereby Britain and the United States would support Russia's request for three votes in the Assembly in return for Russia's support of the U.S.'s request for three votes, if the latter request were made. (It never *was* made, of course. The "leak" had come from a supposedly "off-the-record" meeting between Roosevelt and newly appointed members of the U.S. delegation to the San Francisco Conference.) Roosevelt was on his way to Warm Springs, Georgia, when this news was published; from there he planned to go to San Francisco to open the great conference. Harry Hopkins lay ill in a hospital at Rochester, Minnesota.

Fortunately Stevenson and MacLeish had been thoroughly briefed concerning the Yalta decisions. Stevenson had spent all of Easter Sunday (April 1 of that year) reviewing with James F. Byrnes the latter's shorthand notes on the Yalta Conference and drafting with MacLeish an "official explanation" of the situation. Roosevelt had been made acutely aware of the Russian mistrust of democratic procedures within the proposed international organization, a mistrust grounded in the fact that the Soviet Union was faced with an apparently solid coalition of western Europe, the British Commonwealth, and all the countries of North and South America. From his review of the evidence Stevenson concluded, tentatively, that Roosevelt had assented to the Russian demands only because (a) this was necessary to ensure Russia's participation in the new organization and (b) he had believed that he could persuade Stalin to abandon his insistence upon votes for the Ukraine and Byelorussia before the conference finally convened.

Then came the fateful day of April 12, 1945, a day whose event dwarfed to insignificance the MacLeish-Stevenson job anxieties. . . . On that day, the American Ninth Army stood on the Elbe River in Germany, where, two weeks later, American and Russian troops would meet in a show of fraternal affection which would seem incredible before many months had passed. On the other side of the world, air bases were established on Okinawa just 325 miles from Japan, though bitter fighting would continue on portions of the island for many weeks to come.

In his cottage at the Warm Springs Foundation in Georgia, the President of the United States sat for an artist's sketches from which a portrait of him was to be painted. His spirits were buoyed up by the news of victory in war, his mind filled with hopes for victory in peace and *for* peace in San Francisco. Suddenly he felt great pain at the back of his head.

"I have a terrific headache," he said.

He collapsed into unconsciousness. It was one-fifteen in the afternoon.

At four thirty-five he was dead. He had suffered, said his doctor, a "massive cerebral hemorrhage. . . ."

Archibald MacLeish was asked to write the official proclamation of the President's death, and he and Adlai Stevenson sat together in the State Department late and alone that night. Stevenson's contribution, however, was a modest one, as he himself always insisted. It consisted of looking up proclamations that had been issued when earlier Presidents died in office. MacLeish did the actual writing.

II

To millions of mankind, in that hour, it seemed that a rock indispensable to the foundation of world order had crumbled into dust. It still seemed so to very many when the delegates of fifty nations formally assembled at San Francisco on April 25 to write a charter for the United Nations Organization. Roosevelt, as everyone knew, had been his own foreign minister on every crucial matter; in his administration the Secretary of State had become increasingly an instrument rather than a maker of policy, and this had been particularly so since the retirement of Cordell Hull in the autumn of 1944. His successor, Stettinius, a rich and handsome man who had served as Lend-Lease Administrator, was ex officio head of the United States delegation in San Francisco; and it was soon evident that he lacked the prestige if not the natural ability to lead his own delegation with its large staff of experts, including as it did some very strong-willed and senior political leaders of both parties as well as the foremost international experts in the country. The U.S. delegation included John Foster Dulles and Harold Stassen; Senators Tom Connally of Texas, Chairman of the Foreign Relations Committee, and Arthur Vandenberg of Michigan, senior Republican member of that committee; and Congressmen Sol Bloom of New York and Charles Eaton of New Jersey. Of these, only one was younger than the Secretary of State in years (Stassen had just turned thirty-eight; Stettinius was forty-five) and all were far older than he in governmental experience.

Particularly was it difficult to handle the delegation's public relations with so many prima donnas and conflicts within the delegation.

Other delegations, notably the British, were clever at managing their press relations in such a way as to strengthen their hands in conference negotiations. They skillfully "leaked" to newsmen such items of information as would enhance the popular prestige of their delegates and further their national policies. The United States delegation, on the other hand, could seldom agree on what to give out to the press and on who was to do it, with the result that it gave out little and that little was often garbled and soon contradicted.

American correspondents were reduced to getting much of their information about the conference from the members of other delegations, and as public pressures increased upon them—there was of course an avid popular interest in the historic conference—they grew wrathful. Editorials attacking the U.S. delegation's handling of news began to appear, notably in the Washington *Post*, whose publisher, Eugene Meyer, lived on the same floor of the Fairmount Hotel as Stettinius did. The *Post* editorial so enraged the Secretary of State that he and the *Post* publisher came close to blows one day when they met in a hotel corridor. It was at that low point that Adlai Stevenson was sent for, reportedly[3] at the suggestion of Arthur Krock of the New York *Times*.

"What are you doing here, exactly?" asked Louise Wright when she encountered Stevenson in San Francisco in early May.

"Why, haven't you heard?" Stevenson whispered, laughing. "I'm the official 'leak'!"

And this was, precisely, his function. It was, in his opinion, one of the most difficult assignments of his life—to keep the press as fully informed as his good judgment indicated and to educate the American press as to the background of all the language and controversies —and do it all unofficially and largely unknown to the delegation itself. To assist him he recruited Edward G. Miller, later Assistant Secretary of State for Latin-American Affairs, and Thomas K. Finletter, later Secretary of Air. He quickly grasped the necessarily complex organization of the conference, defining the issues involved in all the strategies and tactics of all the delegations. He attended all the meetings of the United States delegation—meetings closed to newsmen, of course—and thus kept himself intimately informed of what the U.S. was doing, and trying to do, and why. He established an unpublicized headquarters in a room of the Fairmount, where

[3] Noel Busch, op. cit., p. 78.

the wholly new and very welcome experiment by the State Department was dubbed Operation Titanic. He became the cheerful focus of the top correspondents' close attention. Inevitably he became a focus, too, for some criticism by some of the U.S. delegation members. When anything went wrong in the newspapers the delegates could conveniently disclaim both the accuracy of the report and responsibility for it, blaming him. But his arrival marked a turning point from impossibly bad to excellent press relations, and his methods established a precedent which has frequently been followed. The correspondents were grateful to him, and so, ultimately, were all the members of the U.S. delegation.

The conference ended on June 26, having drafted the United Nations Charter. The new organization was very far from being a "world government" of the kind many philosophers of history now deemed essential to a permanently peaceful world order, but in several respects it went farther in that direction than the League of Nations had done. Perhaps its greatest hope for the long run lay in the Economic and Social Council, with the attached agencies through which a closer, more fruitful international collaboration than ever before was provided in a number of fields of common interest.

Stevenson himself did not deplore, as many idealists did, the fact that national sovereignty was the stuff out of which the new edifice was being built. How could it be otherwise, in the prevailing circumstances?

"Everything depends on the active participation, pacific intentions, and good faith of the Big Five, and particularly the United States, Russia, and Britain," he admitted. "Everything we hope for depends on their collaboration in peace as in war; and I risk the estimate that in the United Nations Organization that collaboration is based on the most solid of all foundations—national self-interest."

He made these statements in an article contributed to the Bloomington *Pantagraph* just two weeks after the conference had ended, an article in which he asserted that the Charter represented a "long stride" toward world peace.

A few weeks later the crucial importance of that peace would be emphasized by the dropping (on August 6 and August 9) of atomic bombs upon the Japanese cities of Hiroshima and Nagasaki, swiftly followed by the surrender of Japan, the end of World War II. It would then appear that a totalitarian age had now produced a total weapon and thereby presented all mankind with the ultimate, total choice: "to be, or not to be . . ."

Stevenson may have been reminded of thoughts that had come to him as he gazed up the sheer rock over which the Yosemite plunged —white, foaming—in the sunlight of a California June, when he and MacLeish had taken a brief respite from their San Francisco labors. If he had then measured his work small against the immensity of the rock, if he had deemed the rock eternal and his work of ephemeral importance, he could now no longer do so. Men had the power, now, to dissolve the whole of the earth into dust. Thus the "eternal mountains" and all the seas and plains and valleys of the world could depend for their existence upon the doubtful wisdom, the flawed greatness of the human soul. If mankind was to survive, political intelligence must be organized and applied on a scale and at a speed never before contemplated by men of practical, sober mind. . . .

With the San Francisco conference expired Stevenson's "term of enlistment" (as he called it) with the State Department. He agreed, however, to go back to Washington to help present the Charter to the Senate for ratification, eager though he was to return to his family and the "business of earning a living." He continued for some weeks as special assistant to the Secretary of State, a post to which James F. Byrnes was appointed after Stettinius resigned in early July—and on July 7 he himself was publicly honored for his wartime service in the Navy Department. On that day, at a ceremony in the Navy Department, Adlai Stevenson was awarded the Distinguished Civilian Service Award, the Navy's highest civilian award.

Next morning the Washington *Post* illustrated its story of the award with a photograph of the first Adlai E. Stevenson in his last years. Mildly irritated, Stevenson clipped out the story and mailed it with a brief note to his friend Wayne Coy of the *Post's* editorial staff. "Ho hum," he wrote, "I've a white mustache and a wing collar and I'm 70, and all the time I thought I was a young man and in the very mould of fashion. But then perhaps it's just as well we see ourselves as 'ithers see us,' and the resemblance would be very surprising to grandfather, dead these 35 years."

In late July, after Senate ratification of the UN Charter, he resigned his State Department post and returned to Chicago.

III

The Laird Bells loaned him a cottage they owned on Lake Superior, and to that cottage Stevenson took Ellen and the boys for a vacation—his first since 1940. While he was there he received separate phone calls from Secretary of State Byrnes and Stettinius. The latter had been named the chief American delegate to the Executive Committee of the Preparatory Commission of the United Nations Organization; he and Byrnes, and the President, too, wanted Stevenson to serve as Stettinius's deputy. The committee's work, they pointed out, was of major importance. Meeting in London, it would draft recommendations concerning the structure of the UN—"putting flesh on the bare bones of the Charter," as Stevenson would describe it—and on the location of UN headquarters. These draft recommendations would be acted upon by the Preparatory Commission as a whole, which would meet in London in November, to be followed by the first meeting of the UN's General Assembly in January.

"We need you badly," said Byrnes.

"I need your help," said Stettinius.

The pressure they exerted overcame Stevenson's reluctance to postpone, again, the "business of earning a living," but he flatly refused to be again separated from his family. "Bring your family along," said Stettinius. "We'll arrange transportation for them." So Stevenson discussed the matter with Ellen. It was decided that she would follow him to England, bringing with her the thirteen-year-old Borden and the (as he would be on October 10) fifteen-year-old Adlai III. The two boys would be entered as day students in the ancient and famous public school, Harrow. The whole experience would be "highly educational" for them. The nine-year-old John Fell, however, was considered too young to profit much from the months abroad and Ellen disliked removing him from his school at Lake Forest. The problem of caring for him was solved by Buffie and Ernest Ives agreeing to come to live on the Libertyville farm, with John Fell, until Ellen and the others returned. "I'm so glad you can take [him] while we are away and I hope it won't be too inconvenient," Stevenson wrote Ernest Ives on the evening before he flew to Washington, en route to New York. "I hope he won't be too much of a burden for you. Please take care of his tuition, travel, etc., and I will repay you when I return."

Stevenson sailed on the *Queen Elizabeth* on September 5 with a party that included Secretary Byrnes, Charles Bohlen, Ben Cohen, and John Foster Dulles, as well as Ralph Bunche, Dorothy Fosdick, and other expert "San Francisco veterans." Byrnes and his group were going to the first and far from successful meeting of the Council of Foreign Ministers in London. The others, assigned to the Preparatory Commission, met Stettinius in London. He was, they discovered, a sick man. By the time Ellen and the boys arrived in late September, doctors had diagnosed Stettinius's trouble as gallstones and he had flown back to the United States for the needed surgery, leaving Stevenson in charge of the American delegation, with its large staff of workers and advisers. Stevenson also replaced Stettinius as chairman of the conference.

Said the Chicago *Tribune:* "Mr. Stettinius has pulled out of the conference of united nations architects in Europe, leaving American interests in the hands of Adlai Stevenson, the boy orator of Bloomington." Said the Chicago *Daily News:* "This step brings an able man to a bigger job than he has previously held. . . . To date Mr. Stevenson has been one of those government servants 'with a passion for anonymity.' He has not been much in the public eye. Henceforth he may be."

The Stevensons, mission completed, expected to return by Christmas. As it turned out they did not do so until the spring of 1946. And if the presence of his family helped to keep Stevenson on even keel as he sailed stormy seas of international negotiations—seas in which many dangerous reefs were as yet uncharted—the fact was fortunate for the United Nations as well as for himself.

When he took over as chief of the U.S. delegation, difficulties with the Soviet delegation, headed by Andrei Gromyko, were accumulating. One was a basic disagreement as to the proper relationship between the Security Council, the General Assembly, and the Secretariat of the United Nations Organization. In the Soviet view the Security Council was the only really important organ of the United Nations, and to it alone should all real powers be reserved: the roles of the Assembly and of the Secretariat should be wholly secondary. To this end, Gromyko, supported by Czechoslovakia and Yugoslavia, pressed stubbornly for a departmental rather than a functional organization of the UN's Secretariat. In other words, the Soviets wanted a separate secretariat to be established for each of the UN's major departments—the Security Council, the Economic and Social Council, the Trusteeship Council, and the General Assembly—under the Secretary-General. The United States and other Western powers desired a Secretariat which, under the Secretary-General, was organized in terms of economics, social problems, trusteeship, legal operations, personnel management, and so on. Between these two positions there was no possibility of compromise; one side or the other must yield; and in the end it was Russia which did so. Other crucial problems arose from the Soviet delegation's iron concept of all the world divided, like all Gaul, into three parts: Russian, British, American. The Soviet delegates insisted that Russia and her satellites have one third of the total representation on every UN body. They shuffled around their satellites—Yugoslavia, Poland, Czechoslovakia, the Ukraine, and Byelorussia—like chessmen, displaying a profound contempt for the idea that each sovereign state should have one vote. To the Russians as (it must be admitted) to many others it seemed ridiculous that San Salvador and the U.S.S.R. should have an equal voice in the determination of any major UN policy.

Stevenson was chairman of the Executive Committee sessions in which the draft recommendations were finally acted upon. His general strategy was to avoid showdown votes on which the outcome was perfectly predictable, namely eleven to three against the Communist nations, since repeated defeats only made the Russians more stubborn. He tried constantly, during these trying weeks of night-and-day negotiation, to accent the areas of agreement. Someone remarked that while the world was falling apart at Lancaster House, where the Council of Foreign Ministers was meeting, it was being put together again at Church House, where the Preparatory Commission met—and for the latter, Stevenson was largely responsible. He was endlessly patient, and resourceful as a parliamentarian. But when firmness was necessary he was as stubbornly inflexible (if much more pleasantly "smooth") as Gromyko.

Newspaper correspondents covering the meetings (they included Herbert L. Matthews and Sydney Gruson of the New York *Times*, William H. Stoneman of the Chicago *Daily News*, Frederick Kuh of the Chicago *Sun*, and Carl W. McCardle of the Philadelphia *Bulletin*) were unanimous in their praise of Stevenson's over-all operation. Said one observer, "I never saw a man handle the Russians like he did."

He did so through patient personal negotiation and, in the committee sessions, by moral suasion, everlasting good humor, and a wit that relieved many tense moments. At one point, for example, Gromyko bitterly protested the form in which Stevenson, as chairman, had phrased a question for a vote. "I'm surprised at you," the Russian snapped angrily. Stevenson "politely but firmly" (as one reporter wrote) reminded the Russian that he was chairman. "I don't think we should alter our procedure item by item," he commented mildly. "At least I don't propose to do so while I am chairman." Gromyko then said quickly, "I have a very great respect for the chairman." And the difficulty was smoothed over.

Clifton Utley, the radio commentator from Chicago, visited briefly in London during this period. He spent some hours one evening in the Stevenson home, and he would never forget how continuously and happily busy his old friend was during those hours as he conducted negotiations by phone with the Russians, the British, the French, the Poles. Utley, himself a master of communications "technique," observed with an admiration bordering on awe the manner in which Stevenson adapted his conversational strategy to the temperament and point of view of the man with whom he talked.

"His approach to the Russians was wholly different from his approach to the French, and his approach to the British differed from his approach to, say, a member of his own delegation," Utley would remember, years later. "He changed his word choice, the structure of his argument—even to some extent his tone of voice. But he did this without any sacrifice of sincerity. He was calm and reasonable, often witty and always sincere. It was a virtuosity I had not before appreciated in him."

The Executive Committee completed its agenda on October 27, having arranged for the full Preparatory Commission to open its session on November 23 and for the first United Nations General Assembly to convene during the first week of January 1946. One of the things the committee had *not* done, however, was prepare the way for the meetings of the full Preparatory Commission, beginning on November 24. "The Committee's last sessions were so rushed and were held in such an atmosphere of nervousness that no one apparently wanted to take the responsibility for smoothing the way for the Preparatory Commission," reported Herbert L. Matthews from London on November 15. "As Mr. Stevenson was the last chairman, he felt it incumbent on him to do something about it. Otherwise the . . . Commission would spend its first days wasting valuable time on purely procedural questions." Accordingly, Stevenson and Gladwyn Jebb, British general secretary of the committee, worked out proposals for the commission's agenda, election of president, and so on, calling a special meeting of the Executive Committee to pass on these. As a result, the full commission, with delegations from fifty-one nations, organized itself swiftly and with a minimum of disagreement within two days after its session opened.

The most newsworthy item on the agenda of the Preparatory Commission meeting was the location of the permanent headquarters of the United Nations Organization. Some twenty-two American cities had deputations in London, lobbying for their respective municipalities as UN sites. Chicago was among them. Early in the sessions, Stevenson, continuing as chief of the United States delegation, felt called upon to divorce these lobbying activities, publicly, from official U.S. delegation policy. In a strong statement issued through the American Embassy, he pointed out that the United States had consistently emphasized that she was not seeking the permanent UN home, though she would welcome it if the commission voted to locate in this country. The deputations from American cities were composed, he stressed, of private citizens who had come to London on their own initiative "with the best will" and whose arguments should be considered on their merits and in no sense as expressions of official American views.

This prompted a typically inaccurate Chicago *Tribune* editorial, entitled MR. STEVENSON VOTES FOR EUROPE. He did so, it said, by "gratuitously" informing his international colleagues "that this country is not seeking the world capital.

"It is easy to understand why he does not want the international capital in America," the *Tribune* went on. "He and his kind profess an interest in foreign affairs only because they wish to get away from America and associate with foreigners, to whom they pay fawning obeisance. . . . Mr. Stevenson . . . evidently is ashamed of the fact that his roots until recently were in such a typical American community as Bloomington, Illinois."

This was neither the first nor last of such items of journalistic intelligence and integrity focused on Stevenson by the *Tribune*—items of intemperance and deceit that would concern him less and less as time passed, though, as he later said, he "bemoaned the fact" that he lacked "both the indignation and the vigor of Colonel Knox's contempt for that journal."

A Philippine delegate, Pedro Lopez, opened the debate on the UN home, asserting that "the best way to keep the United States in the United Nations is to put UNO's feet in the United States." The danger of American isolation was "as great today as ever," Lopez asserted. The United States "behaved like an elderly excited lady about to become a grandmother at San Francisco when she observed the birth pangs of the UNO," he continued. "She threw out her arms in hysterical hospitality to the delegates. . . ."

To this Adlai Stevenson made reply. He was, he said, "shocked" to hear his country referred to as an excited grandmother. He had always considered the U.S. position to be more similar to that of "an agitated, blushing debutante. . . . But the young lady is not sensitive," he assured the delegates, as gales of laughter swept the hall, "and she wishes you to converse as freely as possible about her, in connection with the UN site—and not only about her, but about all the other ladies in the block." After days of debate and maneuvering, the commission voted 30 to 14 for the United States as the UNO headquarters with the U.S. abstaining.

On December 20, 1945, after the Preparatory Commission meetings had ended, Stevenson gave a lengthy interview to C. L. Sulzberger of the New York *Times*, in which he expressed his sense of United Nations progress thus far and of the organization's possible future. America, he said, had become the "new center of world policy for peace" and by establishing its headquarters in this country, the United Nations Organization would learn much from the example of "vibrant democracy" presented by the U.S. Significant, in view of a basic developing issue of his time, was Stevenson's carefully worded comparison of the United Nations Charter, as a historic event, with the United States Constitution. The Charter "of course cannot go nearly as far as the Constitution did in the delegation of sovereign powers by the States," he said, and the analogy between Charter and Constitution "cannot be carried too far. . . . We are at a much earlier period of development in international organization, law, and government than were the thirteen colonies in the organization of a national government in the United States in 1787." The great problem now was to make the United Nations work so well within its present limitations that individual governments might be willing at some future time to cede to it more of their sovereign powers. His implicit recognition of the analogy which "cannot be carried too far" was further expressed in his warning that the "members . . . must never permit the organization to be divided into two camps, as the issue of slavery divided the Federal Union before the Civil War."

The historic General Assembly opened its first session in Central Hall, Westminster, on January 10, 1946. The U.S. delegates were Secretary of State James Byrnes, delegation chairman; Edward R. Stettinius, Jr., who had sufficiently recovered from his illness to assume this duty; Senator Connally; Senator Vandenberg; and Mrs. Eleanor Roosevelt. "Foreign diplomats were slightly surprised when Stevenson was made senior adviser to the American delegation to the Assembly, instead of being made a full delegate or an alternate," reported Stoneman of the Chicago *Daily News*. "Americans who had watched his work during earlier meetings were not only surprised, they were slightly disgusted." Nevertheless, the importance and effectiveness of Stevenson's role in the U.S. contingent did not go unrecognized as the Assembly proceeded. Nor was this recognition confined to his own compatriots: delegates from all the fifty-one nations, many of whom after the long weary weeks had become his fast friends, regarded him as a key figure in the total proceedings—intelligent, trustworthy, utterly dedicated to the cause of international organization.

Two and a half days after the Assembly's opening, its entire slate of important electoral posts had been filled, with a minimum of discontent and a wholly unexpected wealth of common agreement. "Taken as a whole," wrote Saville R. Davis of the *Christian Science Monitor* on January 14, "it was a remarkable achievement." And the "hero of the elections," wrote Davis, "is Mr. Adlai Stevenson. . . . In an unguarded moment, when he was being congratulated on his achievement, he said with a laugh, 'I guess I'm just a ward politician at heart.' This modesty wholly misrepresented his talents. Mr. Stevenson did virtually the entire job of preparing the election lists for the United States delegation, and negotiating with other delegations.

"He acted, with the support of the delegation, on the principle that he was seeking a democratic agreement rather than imposing big-power dictation," this reporter continued. "He drafted with great patience and skill a list which represented not what the United States wanted but, as nearly as possible, what all delegations and groups wanted. The result was a phenomenal electoral success."

All around them lay the devastation of war and the iron "austerity" (the meager rationing, the shabby living) which was the war's long aftermath in England. Their immediate environment pointed up the gravity of the work they were doing.

The Stevensons themselves lived in a small bomb-damaged house, converted from a stable, at No. 2 Mount Row just off Grosvenor Square. (Stevenson's office on the square, during the period he was head of the delegation, was the same one General Eisenhower had once occupied.) Ellen's total domestic staff consisted of an elderly cook. They were happy there together, and the two boys were obviously and swiftly enriched by their experience. Ellen sparkled at diplomatic dinners and receptions which are the inevitable and often excessive accompaniment of international conferences; there is no doubt that her scintillating presence helped her husband in his negotiations with the representatives of other countries. She seemed not to feel, in London, that species of claustrophobia which had afflicted her in wartime Washington.

In January she returned to the United States with the two boys, enrolling them in school there for the second semester, then sailed back to England to rejoin her husband. She arrived in London almost simultaneously with tragic family news. At approximately three o'clock on the morning of January 31, 1946, a United Air Lines plane crashed into Elk Mountain, some sixty-five miles northwest of Laramie, Wyoming. All twenty-one persons aboard were killed. Among them was Robert S. Pirie, manager of the New York office of Carson, Pirie, Scott and Company, whom Ellen's younger sister Betty had married and by whom Betty had had two children, Robert, Jr., and Joan. . . .

For weeks thereafter Stevenson continued his behind-the-scenes role for the American delegation, doing "much of the leg work and no small part of the brainwork," as Stoneman of the Chicago *Daily News* put it. In early March his mission, as he said in a letter of resignation to Secretary of State Byrnes, was completed.

Secretary Byrnes replied: "I want to thank you on behalf of the President and myself for the distinguished services you have rendered. . . . You have helped greatly to get the United Nations started as a going concern."

Before this was written, Adlai and Ellen Stevenson were on the high seas, aboard the *Queen Mary*, en route for New York. In the second week of March they were back upon the Libertyville farm they both loved.

In retrospect, few if any periods of Stevenson's life would seem to him as deeply stirring and satisfying as those months in London, during which he played so large a part in the erection of the UN structure. None, certainly, was more educative of him. He met and came to know well the leaders of many countries; he expanded and tested his own powers; and he made contributions to history which were important and enduring.

For instance, he was effective in his efforts to persuade Britain and France to withdraw their armed forces from Syria and Lebanon. Later, when the Security Council first met, the Allies could come into that court "with clean hands" and insist upon the Russian withdrawal from Iran. And if such efforts were unpublicized, they were not unrecognized by Secretary Byrnes, who, before Stevenson left London, urged the younger man to accept appointment as United States Ambassador to Brazil or Argentina. The latter post, in that troubled time of Peron's emergence, was certainly one of the most difficult and delicate diplomatic posts in the world.

CHAPTER EIGHTEEN

Interregnum: From the Spring of 1946
through the Fall of 1947

There began for Stevenson what might in later years seem to him a rather anguished interregnum, during which his life seemed to lack a clear direction. No sovereign decision controlled it. Vital decisions must be made.

He was forty-six years old as this period began. Looking back over his years, he could see that each of them had marked an advance: a growth of character, an enrichment of experience, an addition of knowledge. He had never flatly repeated himself from one year to the next. He had done new things, larger things. Was this process of growth and widening activity now to end? Must he now begin repeating himself? Men did, generally, at his age—or long before they reached his age. They got into a quiet rut, with nearly all elements of their lives predictable, and perhaps they were mostly happy there, raising their families, sending sons and daughters out into the world, making money, taking longer vacations, confining their ambitions within comfortable limits. He rode with such men every day on the commuter trains to the Loop each morning, from the Loop to Lake Forest each evening.

He returned to his law firm, now become Sidley, Austin, Burgess and Harper, where he strove conscientiously to resume the law practice he had relinquished five years before. Louise Wright visited him there one day on business. She thought his office dismal and Stevenson himself unhappy, and not merely because he said things which indicated as much. "He always talks that way, deprecating what he's doing or himself for doing it," Mrs. Wright explained long afterward. "I wouldn't have based any conclusions on what he *said* if he hadn't somehow *seemed* unhappy." She sensed that he was bored with the law and the old routines, a readjustment not unfamiliar to many returning to private life from the turmoil of war.

But he worked hard at it, and competently. On one case—it had to do with an extremely valuable piece of real estate in the financial district of downtown Chicago—he worked with a young man named J. Edward Day, who had joined the firm before the war, after having taken his law degree at Harvard and, in 1941, had married Mary Louise Burgess, daughter of senior partner Kenneth F. Burgess. He was acute and witty; he amused himself, and released tensions in times of pressure, by writing humorous topical verses. He was also a hard worker. He helped Stevenson with the brief for this case, and he was impressed by the skill with which Stevenson presented the argument in court before a judge (there was no jury). Stevenson won the case. Day and Stevenson had one thing in common, a rare thing in that office: both were Democrats: and the younger man was destined to play a role of importance in the Stevenson future.

II

If he drifted, as he sometimes felt he was doing, it was in no tranquil stream. Rather was it a whirlpool. His life, however lacking it might be in a clear direction during those months, certainly did not lack busyness.

He resumed his activities in civic affairs. He did a good deal of public speaking, writing out his speeches with painstaking care as always. In early June he was awarded an honorary Doctor of Laws degree at Northwestern University. A week later he gave the commencement address at the eighty-seventh annual Illinois Wesleyan University exercises in Normal, and he was there awarded another honorary degree. On weekends he worked happily at his country home, trimming trees, pruning shrubbery, making hay, and working in the garden. He played tennis with the boys when they were home, and with old friends on the court he had built years before in a little shaded grove not far from the house.

Sometimes he wandered along the bank of the Des Plaines River with his neighbor Lloyd Lewis, who lived a mile or so away in a house designed for him by his friend Frank Lloyd Wright. Lewis and his wife, Kathryn, had with the Stevensons a friendship which had deepened through the years, strengthened especially by the struggle the two men had made for control of the *Daily News*. It was now richly satisfying on all levels of companionship. Lewis was a vibrant, happy personality, beloved of all who knew him. He was a great outdoorsman—had been a short-time sheep rancher in the West, and loved to "rough it" in the western wilderness. He was a versatile journalist and writer—had been a sports writer, a drama critic, and a political writer who found politics and politicians fascinating. He was one of the great raconteurs of his time. To his home had come many famous personages—Marc Connelly, Alexander Woollcott, Oscar Hammerstein—and the Stevensons were always included in parties which Lloyd and Kathryn gave for such guests.

Lewis's greatest literary interest was history, particularly Civil War history. The characters of our national tragedy—somber and gaudy, funny and sad, heroic and villainous—fascinated him as they did Adlai Stevenson. He had written *Myths After Lincoln; Sherman, Fighting Prophet,* and other books, and was now beginning a long biography of U. S. Grant. The two men often talked about this project as they strolled along the river. They looked down upon a stream not unlike the Sangamon and across a landscape not unlike the Springfield countryside, and they talked of the Lincoln of 1854, roused from a long lethargy by the Kansas-Nebraska Bill and impelled thereafter, often despite himself, by a moral idea. They talked of Jesse Fell, the great man of Normal, and of Captain Grant, the ne'er-do-well of Galena. They felt the long slow tides of history flowing through them out of Lincoln's Illinois, out of the wind-swept prairie past, toward what urban future? what earthly end?

It was with this question, applied to his personal life, that Stevenson's anguish began—a quiet anguish, secret, often virtually unconscious. Part of it, a growing part of it, was a private sorrow of which he did not speak to Lloyd or Kathryn Lewis, or Dutch Smith, or anyone else.

Herndon wrote of Lincoln that the latter "never had a confidant" and "never spoke of his trials to me or, so far as I know, to any of his friends." Later some of Stevenson's intimates were reminded of this testimony, seeing some slight similarity between the Lincoln of the mid-1850s and the Stevenson of the mid-1940s. Lincoln was said by some historians to have been driven into public life by private woe; others said that his domestic woe stemmed from that which gave him public greatness. Perhaps both judgments were true, the woe and the greatness being of a piece. Were the judgments true, also, of Stevenson?

If he himself was aware of any over-all similarity here, he never said so. What he could not but be aware of, and painfully, was the fact that he and Ellen had been growing apart through the last several years. A gap had opened between them which now was rarely, briefly bridged, and in this widening gap lay a ground increasingly barren of common interest and understanding. Nettles grew there. In earlier years each had *seemed* to take pride in the other. Ellen had helped him then; he had tried to help her. Freely he acknowledged the help she had given—though it is possible that (not being the demonstrative kind) he had not made her sufficiently aware of his gratitude, assuming, falsely perhaps, that she must realize it. Now, however, she seemed to take little satisfaction in his successes; she seemed almost to resent the honors and recognition which came to him.

Yet there were ties between them: legal ties, and ties of affection and memory and family. These grew increasingly painful as the two seemed increasingly to draw apart, each stubbornly refusing to yield to the other's direction. Or was it a stubborn refusal? Was either of them really free, in the deepest sense, to refuse? Human freedom, after all, is profoundly paradoxical: the very essence of this freedom is necessity, in so far as a man's character is his fate. Each man does, over the long pull, what he is impelled by his nature to do in the circumstances in which he is placed—though it is also true (deepening the paradox) that each creates much of his own nature through his acts—and Ellen, it seemed, was impelled toward the "arts," or the literary life, as strongly, as inevitably, as he was impelled toward public service. The pain came when impulse encountered external compulsion. Vital needs tugged against vital obligations, so that the ties which bound these two together cut ever more deeply into their separate spirits. Each became aware of self-divisions. Each became aware that the struggle was within as well as between them. Each feared the effects this might produce upon their sons. If worse came to worst, the boys might be torn asunder by divergent loyalties. . . . During this period, the youngest son, John Fell, entering his teens, began to stammer quite badly. . . .

Opportunities came repeatedly to Adlai for government service abroad and at home. Trygve Lie, the Secretary-General of the United Nations, offered him the post of Assistant Secretary-General

for Administrative and Financial Services. President Truman wanted
to appoint him to the Securities and Exchange Commission, with
chairmanship of that body as a sequel (he'd been recommended by
the Investment Bankers Association). In September of 1947, George
Marshall, then Secretary of State, urged him to consider the post of
Assistant Secretary of State. All these offers he refused. A newspaper
report said he had "expressed the feeling that he would like to retire
to his private career as corporation lawyer"—and hints of one element
of his inward turmoil, one major factor of his indecision, were contained in a newspaper columnist's assertion: "[Stevenson's] boys are
growing up and he wishes them to live their impressionable years in
their native environment."

III

But other calls to public service came, during this period, which
he could not in good conscience refuse. President Truman named
him one of five alternate United States delegates to the second part
of the first session of the UN's General Assembly, meeting in New
York from early September into December of 1946.

During this session, Stevenson, operating in the Hotel Pennsylvania, was in charge of "liaison," which is to say that in New York
as in London he kept in touch with other delegations and engaged
in the personal behind-the-scenes negotiations on which so much of
the outcome of the public sessions depended. He represented the
U.S. on the committee dealing with economic and social affairs. He
was Senator Warren R. Austin's alternate on the committee-of-the-
whole which decided to locate the permanent home of the United
Nations in New York. And he was often the United States spokesman in plenary sessions on major international political questions.

It was he who presented the United States position regarding the
administration of international relief, a highly controversial and
hence newsworthy item on the Assembly agenda. The United Nations Relief and Rehabilitation Administration (UNRRA) was soon
to go out of existence, and the issue before the Assembly was whether
or not a new international organization should be created to handle
UNRRA problems. On behalf of the United States, Stevenson opposed the formation of a new international relief and rehabilitation
organization.

There followed a prolonged and vigorous debate with New York's

Fiorello La Guardia, the head of UNRRA, who insisted that a new organization was needed and proposed a four-hundred-million-dollar international fund for emergency relief. Stevenson proposed, as an alternative, consultation among the producer nations and the nations still in need of assistance—a step which the New York *Herald Tribune* (agreeing with the New York *Times* and many other papers) deemed a "backward" one, since it meant a reversion to national settlements in place of international co-operation. This argument had weight, Stevenson privately conceded. He himself strongly believed that every practicable method by which international organization could be strengthened should be employed. The trouble with the present La Guardia position was that, in Stevenson's personal view and in the view of his government, it was impracticable. In the first place—as he openly stated—it would almost certainly complicate relief administration, thus delaying and perhaps reducing the actual transfer of food and goods from producer nations to hungry people. In the second place—as he could not openly state—the Congress was much more likely to vote adequate foreign-relief funds if these were administered directly and wholly by the U. S. Government.

Nat Barrows, Chicago *Daily News* correspondent, saw the La Guardia-Stevenson debate as a study in contrasts. "Stevenson is calm, dignified, and rational, appealing to the minds of his . . . colleagues. La Guardia is flamboyant, dramatically oratorical, and close to rabble-rousing, appealing to the emotions." In his final speech La Guardia looked across the oval table at Stevenson and shook his finger menacingly as he charged that the United States, supported by the United Kingdom, was "making a political football out of food." To this Adlai Stevenson next day made sober reply. There were indeed hungry people in the world, he conceded; they must and would be fed; but the situation now was very different from the immediate postwar emergency. It could be "best and most efficiently met by simple and direct means." After certain compromises had been negotiated, his view—the official U.S. view—was substantially accepted. Afterward he himself was never sure that the policy he had espoused was the best one possible. Perhaps it would have been better to handle the relief situation in such a way as to merge it with a continuing world food program, thus giving initial impetus to the UN's Food and Agriculture Organization. . . .

After the session had ended, Nat Barrows made acid comment

upon the U.S. delegation's work. "OUR SIDE FUMBLED U.N. BALL, *Only Mrs. F.D.R., Stevenson Did Job*"—so ran the headline over Barrow's story. "Mrs. Roosevelt and . . . Adlai Stevenson measured up to their jobs excellently," the correspondent wrote. "They worked hard, thought clearly, tried to make sense out of muddled directives and intra-delegation confusion, and addressed their respective committees with ideas instead of oratory. They merit return to the 1947 delegation, with increased responsibilities. Otherwise, a realistic overhaul is necessary."

The Barrows view was widely shared, and was largely acted upon in July of 1947, when Truman appointed the delegation to the General Assembly session which opened in late September. Mrs. Roosevelt and Senator Austin were re-appointed. General George Marshall, Secretary of State, was named a delegate and chairman of the delegation. John Foster Dulles was named a full delegate. So was Ambassador Herschel V. Johnson, Austin's deputy on the Security Council. Adlai Stevenson's appointment as an alternate was, as before, greeted with a chorus of editorial approval, with only the Chicago *Tribune* dissenting. During this session he represented the U.S. on the important Budgetary and Administrative Committee and also spoke for the U.S. on matters relating to the admission of new members.

When he returned to his home in December the anguished interregnum in his life was mounting toward its crisis as it approached its end. Caught up in a web of circumstances which he himself had helped to spin, he was forced toward the most important and difficult career decision he had ever made. . . .

Book Five

THE MAKING OF A POLITICIAN

CHAPTER NINETEEN

The Road to Springfield

The web of circumstance had many strands. . . .

One of them—it had run as a minor recurrent theme through all the years of his Washington and foreign service—was a simple unorganized response to the fact that he came from a political family, bore a widely known political name, and had become in his own right, through demonstrated abilities, one of the best-known and most highly respected Chicagoans of his generation. It was this which had led to his being considered for the Senate, opposing C. Wayland (Curly) Brooks, as far back as the late autumn of '41. It had led also to an abortive movement to draft him as candidate for governor, opposing Dwight Green's re-election to a second term, in late 1943 and early 1944, though he himself had never taken this movement very seriously.

It was upon the Senate that he fixed whatever political ambitions he then entertained, and it was with the Senate in view, as a vague possibility, that he spun his own personal strand into the web of circumstance which ultimately enmeshed him. By temperament, knowledge, and past experience, he was well equipped for the national legislature in an age when foreign affairs were of paramount concern. He knew that he was—and the value he placed upon his own qualifications, the sense of public duty which was naturally strong in him, could not but be enhanced by the sorry view he took of Curly Brooks's performance. Neither Brooks nor Brooks's master, the baron of the Tribune Tower, exhibited the slightest capacity to learn from direct political experience, much less from history. In every realm of domestic and foreign affairs they exhibited what seemed to Stevenson a willful obtuseness, a stubborn preference for the worse over the better way, which might have been laughable had it not been joined to governing power.

But Stevenson's senatorial ambitions were certainly not very definite, nor did he implement them with any definitely planned strategy. He merely presented himself to the public gaze, when occasion offered, in such light as would most beautifully shine upon a senatorial toga; he chose for his public speech such subjects as would befit a chairman of the Senate's Committee on Foreign Relations.

When he pled for the re-election of Emily Taft Douglas (Mrs. Paul H. Douglas) as Democratic congressman-at-large from Illinois, in a statement issued in October of '46, he did so in terms of foreign policy. When he made a speech supporting Mrs. Olive Goldman as Democratic candidate for Congress from Illinois's Nineteenth District, in 1946, when discontent with rationing was uppermost in people's minds, he asserted that "peace," not "meat," was the dominant issue in the November election and pled for support of a foreign policy "which recognizes the principle of compromise and rejects the compromise of principle." He told a University of Chicago Walgreen Lecture Series audience, in November of '46 (he flew back from the General Assembly session for this address), that many grave difficulties must be overcome before an international security force (a UN "army") could become a reality. He told a Central States Conference of the Investment Bankers Association in March of '47 that there was no "plausible alternative" to Truman's policy of military and economic assistance to Greece and Turkey save "default" which would lead to "the isolation of the United States." At the opening of the annual Jewish Welfare Fund Campaign in Chicago in June of '47, he spoke in support of the "bold" and "realistic" Marshall Plan.

By that time, another strand of circumstance was weaving with the one he himself was spinning. In consequence his senatorial ambitions were becoming more definitely focused.

The spinning of this third strand began with a dark, stocky, ebullient man named Louis A. Kohn, a Chicago lawyer, partner in the firm of Mayer, Mayer, Austrian and Platt. In 1947 he was thirty-nine years old and was but one year released from the military service. He had served for three years in the Pacific, where he had spent much time in desolate places, miserable with heat and insects, pondering through lonely hours the "why" of it all. Why are we here in this awful hole? How came the world to this sorry pass? What must we do to ensure that it never again comes to this? When he returned to Chicago in 1946 it was with the determination to do what he could to improve Illinois's representation in the Senate. This positive aim had its negative requirement: Curly Brooks, and all that Brooks stood for in public life, must be repudiated at the polls. . . .

It now occurred to Kohn, who listened wih growing excitement to Stevenson's public speech, that Stevenson would make an excellent senator. Others had had the same idea, as we have seen, but none other had devoted to it such fervent energy as Kohn at once applied. Encountering Stevenson in the Bar Association one day, he broached the idea and found Stevenson receptive to it. They lunched together. Thereafter Stevenson's candidacy became the chief (some complained it was the sole) subject of Kohn's conversation. He talked to Dutch Smith about it, at Stevenson's suggestion. These two discussed the matter through a long luncheon hour. Then he and Smith had lunch with Stephen A. Mitchell, senior partner of the law firm of Bishop, Mitchell and Burdett, who formerly had been chief of the French division of the Lend-Lease Administration and adviser to the State Department on French economic affairs, stationed in Paris and Washington. Mitchell, an Irish Catholic and a Democrat, was much wiser in the ways of politics than either Smith or Kohn; he was no less enthusiastic than they were about Stevenson-for-Senator.

It was with this triumvirate and this luncheon, in the late spring of '47, that the first real political boom for Adlai E. Stevenson began.

Kohn wrote letters by the score, to his own acquaintances and to Stevenson's friends. Dutch Smith got in touch with his friend Loring C. (Bud) Merwin, Stevenson's cousin and active publisher of the Bloomington *Pantagraph,* who in turn sent letters to twenty-five downstate newspaper publishers, presenting Stevenson's background and asking the publishers to "find out how well, if at all, Stevenson is known in your district and whether you think he might draw any substantial number of Republican or independent votes there in a race against Senator Brooks." These identical letters concluded: "Please be completely frank, as Mr. Stevenson is in no way seeking this job, and I suspect he might even prefer discouraging reactions to those which sound hopeful!" To most of these letters the reply was that Stevenson, though respected by all who knew him, was not well known downstate. In Chicago, where he was well known, the reaction was strongly in his favor.

Meanwhile the highly tentative Stevenson candidacy was receiving a considerable newspaper publicity—largely, at the outset, as a result of the Kohn-Smith operations. Smith sounded out Milburn P. Akers of the *Sun* and found him favorable to Stevenson. According to John Bartlow Martin,[1] "Kohn began contacting various newspaper and magazine writers, usually so awkwardly and with such obvious sincerity of purpose that they felt sorry for him."

But Kohn's success in "planting" stories was not due solely, nor even chiefly, to such personal sympathies as he aroused in working newspapermen's bosoms. Far more important was the fact that one Martin H. Kennelly, successful businessman and alleged reformer, had been elected mayor of Chicago on the first Tuesday in April, 1947. Kennelly had run as a Democrat, with the full backing of Colonel Jacob Arvey and the powerful Democratic organization, and his landslide victory not only plowed into political oblivion his Republican opponent, Russell W. Root, but also markedly deflated what had looked like quite a promising presidential boom for Republican Governor Green, whose candidate Root was. Professional Democrats were naturally jubilant. It was clear, however, that Kennelly's triumph (he gained a plurality of 273,354 votes while eleven of nineteen Democratic aldermen went down to defeat in runoffs) could never have grown to such proportions had it not been fed by many Republican and nearly all independent votes—a conclusion underlined by the fact he had carried wards which had long been Republican strongholds. His triumph, then, was due in large part to his proven general abilities and to his shining personal reputation for integrity and independence. The lesson was obvious: Democrats had a chance to score further victories in Illinois in '48 if they made up a slate of high-caliber men whose past was untainted by machine politics. Into this suggested pattern Adlai Stevenson fitted perfectly, and several political writers said so in print within a few days after the Kennelly victory.

Another who perfectly fitted into the pattern was Paul H. Douglas, the professor of economics at the University of Chicago, who had got into politics before America's entrance into World War II by winning election as city alderman. Douglas, though overage, had

[1] *Adlai Stevenson*, p. 63.

enlisted as a private in the Marines, had emerged an officer with a Purple Heart awarded for a combat wound in the Pacific, and was deemed by many the perfect opponent of Brooks, a World War I Marine who had used his distinguished war record effectively in his political campaigning. Douglas, however, was talked of for the governorship at least as much as he was for the Senate, and the most knowledgeable early speculation was that he would seek the former post while Stevenson sought the latter.

As always in politics, the picture was clouded with uncertainties, its outlines blurred by imponderables. For instance, there was the possibility that Senator Scott W. Lucas might decide, or be persuaded, to run against Green, though Lucas's term as senator was not up until 1950. When Stevenson went to Washington on June 5 —partly on private law business, partly to try to facilitate congressional action on the pending bill to admit four hundred thousand displaced persons to the United States—he and Lucas lunched together, then took the same train for Chicago. Immediately a "Democratic team of Scott Lucas and Adlai Stevenson to run for Governor and Senator respectively . . . appeared a strong possibility," according to Griffing Bancroft of the Chicago *Sun*.

"There is no sense in being disingenuous about these things," Stevenson told Bancroft, with a smile. "My mind is open. Naturally I'm interested."

Thereafter the Stevenson candidacy was continuously in the news, being publicized in the New York *Times* and other "national" papers, in magazines, and in nationally syndicated columns to such an extent that by October, when Stevenson was in New York for the General Assembly session, Lou Kohn's pockets continuously bulged with clippings which he pressed upon his acquaintances. On November 6, with Stevenson's blessing, Kohn, Mitchell, and Smith announced the formation of an Adlai Stevenson for Senator committee. A "vigorous campaign," including personal visits to hundreds of Illinois communities, would be waged, Mitchell said. Among those on the committee and prominent thereafter in Stevenson's political life were Mrs. Edison (Jane Warner) Dick; William McC. Blair, Jr., still a registered Republican; Walter T. Fisher, a Winnetka lawyer; and Walter V. Schaefer, professor of law at Northwestern University.

Smith, meanwhile, was soliciting campaign-fund pledges from his wealthy friends and acquaintances, achieving sufficient success to encourage continued efforts. Kohn was convinced that, once Stevenson's nomination was assured, they would have no trouble raising $250,000—and Stevenson himself was much more sanguine about money-raising possibilities than later events justified. (He relied excessively on "cocktail-party promises" made in former years by wealthy Republican friends, according to Smith. "If you ever run for office, you can count on me to back you," such people said—and proved now that they hadn't meant to be taken seriously.)

Up to this time, however, no professional politician had come out openly for Stevenson, and the problem of getting organization support was worrying Smith and Kohn and Mitchell.

It is a measure of the vast esteem in which Kennelly was then held that Stevenson's backers, and Stevenson himself, were particularly anxious to have the mayor's backing. "I have spoken to Mayor Kennelly several times about Adlai, and he asked me to arrange a meeting with him sometime," Smith wrote Bud Merwin on July 30. "That meeting is now scheduled for tomorrow afternoon, and although I do not expect any immediate results, it is obvious that the mayor could be a very helpful friend." He could have been—at that time and later. He chose not to be. He was courteous, he was mildly interested, he was aloof and noncommittal. So was George Kells, the Democratic state chairman. So were the other "big name" Democrats; all wished to wait, they said, to see what "developed." It became apparent that they waited, most of them, to see what Colonel Arvey would do. Arvey was chairman of the Cook County Democratic Central Committee. A word from him, one way or the other, would be a major "development."

Accordingly, one early November day, the leaders of the Stevenson committee called upon Arvey in the latter's Loop office. If the essence of humor is the juxtaposition of incongruous elements, that meeting had, certainly, its comic aspects. The Stevenson delegation was composed of North Shore socialites, nearly all of them lifelong Republicans and members of families which had been prominent and wealthy for generations. They were Ivy League college graduates. Their distaste for machine politics, their disdain of machine politicians were cardinal articles of their political faith. Yet here they were, calling upon a big-city "boss" and bidding for his support.

Arvey, however, was no such crude type as Hague of Jersey City or Crump of Memphis or old Tom Prendergast of Kansas City. Born of a poor Jewish family in Chicago's Twenty-fourth Ward, which was 90 per cent Jewish, he had come up in the hard way traditional

of bosses, working in his teens as a delivery boy for a tailoring firm
and attending the John Marshall Law School at night. After being
admitted to the Bar he became clerk in the law firm of John Mc-
Inerary, an associate of Pat Nash and Ed Kelly, later the principals
of the notorious Kelly-Nash machine. Of this machine, Arvey became
in time a leading member—he was smart, he was hard-working, he
was immensely likable—with a law firm of his own which was naturally on the books of every company which wanted to stand in, or
at least stand well, with the local political powers. As ward committeeman and absolute boss of the Twenty-fourth Ward, he regularly
delivered 90 per cent or more of the ward's vote to Kelly-Nash candidates. He did so even in 1936, when Horner was waging his bitter
and successful fight for re-election against the machine—and this despite the fact that Horner was a co-religionist and personal friend.

But by the fall of 1947, when Arvey was fifty-three years old, he
had gone through a widely advertised "conversion" to clean politics
and good government for Illinois. Various motives of idealism and
expediency were alleged for this conversion. Some said that Arvey,
who had served as judge advocate of the 33rd Division in the Pacific,
had returned from the war a "different man," having seen the dreadful cost of gangster politics practiced on an international scale. Others said that the elections of 1946, which swept Republicans into
power, had convinced him that the kind of machine politics he had
theretofore practiced had passed its point of diminishing returns.
Whatever his motives—and they were undoubtedly mixed as all
men's are—he used the defeat of Kelly-Nash stalwarts, in '46, to persuade Ed Kelly (Pat Nash was now dead) to step down. Times had
changed in Chicago, Arvey argued; Kelly's chances of winning re-
election in '47 were too slim to justify taking them. Thus the city
had been presented a choice for mayor between "Honest Martin"
Kennelly and a Republican party hack who was but a pawn of Mc-
Cormick and Green, with such results as we know.

They were results which naturally encouraged Arvey's friendly interest in the mission of his callers, that November day. He greeted
them cordially, and they looked up at a man who certainly lacked the
appearance of a tough city boss. Nearly all bosses are big men physically. Arvey was not. He stood five feet, six inches high and weighed
one hundred and fifty pounds. He had quick shrewd friendly eyes
behind horn-rimmed spectacles, a bald head mottled with sun-
darkened spots, and a wide genial smile which, joined to a gentle

manner, disarmed his visitors as it had customarily disarmed his harshest critics whenever these came into personal contact with him. The smile, the gentleness were obviously expressions of the inner man, and they were accompanied by slight nods of seeming agreement as Stevenson's virtues were extolled.

This, of course, was not the first time he had heard of Stevenson; he had long known of him in a general way. Nor were his present visitors the first to call Stevenson specifically to his attention as a political possibility. No less a personage than former Secretary of State Byrnes had done so as recently as late July of that year, when Arvey was in Washington consulting with Senator Lucas over the naming of a U.S. attorney for the Northern District of Illinois. The Senate Secretary, Leslie Biffle, had given a luncheon which Lucas and Arvey attended. Byrnes was there and, hearing talk of Illinois politics, gave it as his opinion that "you people out there have a gold nugget in the person of Adlai Stevenson, he is one of the smartest, cleanest, most patriotic men I know."

Arvey, however, said nothing of this to his present callers, nor did he indicate to them the depth of his real interest in Stevenson as a possible nominee. He agreed, aloud, that Stevenson would make a very good senator.

"But to become a senator, you have to get elected," Arvey said, "and your man is not as well known as Douglas, who worked all summer downstate. I feel Douglas would make a better candidate."

The question was left open, however, as the callers departed.

A few weeks later Dutch Smith encountered Arvey in the club car of the Twentieth Century Limited, en route to New York, and seized the opportunity to talk with him again about Stevenson. Arvey this time seemed somewhat more interested. He had been told, though, that Stevenson had gone to Oxford, and if that were true it was a serious political liability, Anglophobia being a disease spread widely through Illinois by Colonel McCormick's *Tribune*. Smith promptly laid this bogey at rest (he obtained a telegram from Stevenson, saying, "NEVER WENT TO OXFORD NOT EVEN ETON") and, discovering that he and Arvey were returning to Chicago a few days later on the same train, arranged to meet Arvey then in the club car. On this return trip Arvey asked about Mrs. Stevenson. Would she be an asset in a political campaign? She certainly would, Smith replied; she was very pretty, very friendly, a wonderful hostess. He offered to arrange a luncheon at his Lake Forest home, where Arvey could meet the Stevensons.

This luncheon was held soon after Stevenson's return from the General Assembly session. Arvey was favorably impressed by both the Stevensons. Subsequently, as the Christmas season approached, there were other meetings between Arvey and Stevenson, all of them pleasant, each more friendly than the last. By this time, several newspaper reports of slatemaking Democratic meetings agreed that Stevenson was the probable senatorial candidate, since Douglas had encountered labor opposition, though the strength and nature of this opposition was never made clear. Others reported an increased likelihood that Douglas would be run for governor. Douglas himself preferred the governorship; he had told many people privately that he did. Kennelly, too, was considered for the gubernatorial nomination until December 17, when he told a delegation to his office, headed by Arvey, that he definitely would not run. He declined to recommend a candidate but said, in reply to a question, that he considered Circuit Judge Thomas J. Courtney "eminently qualified for any position"—a remark which caused some consternation among party leaders since it hinted the possibility of a split between Kennelly and the Arvey group, throwing into the discard all slatemaking efforts thus far. Courtney, who had broken with Ed Kelly and Arvey to run for governor in 1944, was cordially disliked by organization Democrats.

The climax came in late December. On the day after Christmas, a Friday, Arvey, who had talked with Smith several times during the last week, announced to Smith a final decision. The organization slate for '48 was to be finally decided by a thirty-man Democratic State Committee meeting in the Morrison Hotel next week. At that meeting Douglas would be named the candidate for senator. The candidacy for the governorship, however, remained open. Would Stevenson take it? Smith, dismayed and disappointed, shook his head dubiously. He was almost certain that his friend would not be interested. He suggested, however, that Arvey put the question to Stevenson directly. Next morning Arvey did so at a meeting of the three men in Smith's office.

Stevenson's initial response was negative, as Smith had predicted. His experience had been almost wholly with the federal government. "I know the Congress like a book," he said. He was qualified for the Senate; he was interested only in the Senate. Douglas, on the other hand, was primarily interested in the governorship. Why the switch? Jack Arvey (it is an interesting if insignificant fact that Jacob Arvey was never called "Jake") said that there were reasons, not good perhaps from Stevenson's point of view, but sufficient in terms of practical politics. There was Douglas's war record, for one thing; a spellbinding orator, Douglas would be able to match Curly Brooks "wound for wound and deed for deed" in campaign speeches. In any case the matter was no longer debatable. Douglas was slated for the Senate. Stevenson, if he agreed to it, would be slated for the governorship.

"What about my appointments, if I'm elected?" Stevenson asked. "Will I be entirely free on my appointments?"

He would be, Arvey said.

"On your major appointments I wouldn't make a suggestion if you asked me to," Arvey went on. "On minor appointments—there'd be hundreds of them—you'd need help. Even there I wouldn't suggest names unless you asked me to. We would hope that you would appoint Democrats if qualified. It would be your free choice."

And who, Stevenson asked, would determine "qualifications"?

"You," Arvey replied.

Stevenson pondered. Finally he said that he'd like to think it all over for a few days. Arvey agreed, pointing out, however, that the final slatemaking session was meeting early next week.

For Stevenson there followed three and a half days of agonized soul-searching. Tramping across the snowy fields of his farm that weekend, staring into flames which danced in his fireplace in the evenings, talking the whole thing over with Ellen, he pondered a decision which, he knew, would determine the whole future course of his life. On the one hand was the safety, the assured and secure comfort of an established financial lawyer with multitudes of interesting friends, a gratifying community prestige, and no enemies. This he would have at once to renounce; he must sever completely his relationship with the Sidley firm on the day he became a bona fide candidate. On the other hand were the hazards his dying father had spoken of—the hundred chances for public failure and humiliation, the thousand inevitable frustrations and injustices, in a career wholly dependent upon an erratic, often deliberately misinformed public opinion. To accept those hazards as a national legislator, a role for which he was well rehearsed, was one thing; to accept them as a great state's chief executive, a role which he had never seriously considered, was quite another. He was not without large-scale administrative experience: he had learned much in London and while with Knox in Washington: but for large-scale political administration he was, he feared, unprepared.

Ellen made no objection to Springfield; she would prefer Springfield to Washington. She told Dutch Smith so on Monday evening, December 29, when Smith called her. Arvey had phoned Smith, worrying because Stevenson's decision had not been made and wondering if Mrs. Stevenson were persuading Stevenson not to accept. No, she wasn't doing that, Smith now told Arvey, calling back, adding that he'd not been able to reach Stevenson himself, who had gone to a "show." (Actually Stevenson was attending a performance of the Princeton Triangle Club, but Smith feared that saying so would make the prospective candidate seem to "hard-boiled" politicians a hopeless "cream puff.") Well, said Arvey, his patience near an end, he'd give Stevenson until noon tomorrow to make up his mind. The slate had to be completed. . . .

Through the corridors and suites of the Morrison Hotel that night confusion drifted and eddied thicker than the cigar smoke as Democratic politicians sought to do their work amidst repeated alarms and excursions. The evening edition of next morning's *Sun* had carried a scarifying story. John Pickering, interviewing Mayor Kennelly in his office at City Hall, had emerged with a direct quotation from the mayor: "Judge Courtney is my man for Governor and I will campaign for him if necessary." As soon as they read this, the slatemakers recessed until the following morning, gathering in little gloom-laden groups to ponder the imponderable. They worried, too, about an announcement just made by former Vice-President Henry A. Wallace saying that he would run for President on a third-party ticket. Meanwhile a *Daily News* reporter called the mayor, who said he had been misquoted, though he again praised Judge Courtney, whereupon the slatemakers, somewhat soothed by the dubious retraction, insisted that Stevenson be "rounded up" and brought to them that night.

He came at midnight from the gay foolery of a college boys' musical comedy to a serious business conducted in the atmosphere of comic opera, and he told the slatemakers what he had told Arvey on Saturday. His experience had been "largely in the Federal field" and he had "never thought of anything else than the post of Senator"; he needed more time in which to "reflect."

At nine o'clock next morning Dutch Smith came to Stevenson's office. He found his friend "in terrible shape," as he later recalled. He argued, as Stevenson had argued with himself, that it was "now or never" so far as a political career was concerned. "They need you this year," Smith said. "If you say no when they need you, they won't take you when they don't need you." Stevenson paced the floor, saying over and over, "I'm bothered, I'm bothered." Back of the decision he struggled to make, impelling him toward it, was the great inward weight of his family tradition, with all the moral obligation it imposed. Finally he said that, if he were to do it at all, he would have to have Kennelly's backing. Smith balked at that, arguing that Kennelly had "nowhere to go" except into the Stevenson camp, once Stevenson became the Democratic candidate.

"He could hardly support Green, could he?" Smith asked.

"I want his active support, at least his announced support," Stevenson said stubbornly. "If I can't have it I won't run."

So Smith tried to reach Kennelly, through a mutual friend, Edward Eagle (Ned) Brown, chairman of the board of the First National Bank. Kennelly was in a City Council meeting and would not be out until after Arvey's deadline had passed.

"Well, you've certainly shown your respect for his opinion," Smith said to Stevenson. "He'll *have* to support you. He can't do anything else."

Stevenson shook his head. He knew that Kennelly might just "sit it out," being so strongly committed to Courtney and so determined to be "above" politics, and he believed that this might utterly destroy what then seemed very slender chances for victory. (The event proved him right about Kennelly. Not until August 31, 1948, in a statement endorsing the entire Democratic slate, did the mayor publicly mention Stevenson by name.)

The clock hands moved toward noon.

"Well, I guess you're right," Stevenson said. "It's now or never." He sighed wearily. "I'll do it," he said. . . .

II

If this career "indecision" was characteristic of Stevenson, his post-decision operation was no less so. Once his mind was made up, he suffered no post-decision anxiety. He was a candidate for governor. He was utterly absorbed into that role. He was going to win if it were humanly possible, though he was realistic enough to admit, strictly in private, that it might not be possible.

For as the new year began, it certainly looked like a Republican year nationally, what with Truman's inability to dominate his own party and Henry Wallace's third-party movement which, at the outset, seemed likely to garner from five to ten million votes, nearly all of them from Democratic ranks. If the national Republican victory were of landslide proportions, it would be likely to ensure the election of a Republican governor of Illinois. Recognition of this probability, however, served only to increase Stevenson's campaign effort. Others might regard him as a "sacrificial goat" led to the slaughter by the cynical Arvey and the "machine." Why otherwise, they asked, would a man like Arvey choose men like Douglas and Stevenson as candidates? But Stevenson himself focused primarily on the weaknesses of his opponent, and would make increasing capital of these as they were more and more fully exposed. No one who watched him closely through the first nine months of '48 would ever have the illusion that this son of privilege, this society Ivy Leaguer, was not a tough man in a fight—tireless, resourceful, courageous.

On January 7 Stevenson and Douglas rode down on a train to Springfield with Arvey, to accept formally the endorsement of the Democratic State Committee. Stevenson's brief acceptance speech, which he'd written in the club car on the way down, declared that Illinois had been richly blessed with almost everything but good government. "The crude, old-fashioned spoils politics of the State Administration cannot be veiled forever by virtuous pronouncements," he said. "The people don't like what they've heard, and they will like it less and less as they hear more and more about what's been done and what's not been done in the last eight years." Arvey and Spike Hennessey, the Democrats' publicity campaign manager, looked at one another with pleased surprise as they listened. Stevenson had an accent vaguely "British" or "Eastern" (actually it reflected his wide-ranging travel during his formative years and had as its chief quality a clipped precision), but it was pleasant to listen to, riding out as it did on a voice with singing overtones. The accent might be an initial political liability, but it might also become, ultimately, a definite asset, if Stevenson in other ways identified himself with his audiences. Instinctively the average American, listening to this voice, might think Stevenson "above" him, but if Stevenson expressed the hopes and aspirations of his listeners the latter might conclude that they *wanted* their elected executive to be superior. . . .

On February 4, the eve of his forty-eighth birthday, Stevenson's withdrawal from his law firm was announced. That evening Democratic leaders in Chicago gave him a well-publicized birthday party. Thereafter he was a professional politician, though he continued to refer to himself for years to come as an "amateur."

He opened campaign headquarters on the fifth floor of 7 South Dearborn, in a large room with cubbyhole temporarily partitioned offices at one side. Wooden floors clicked and clacked as women's hard-heeled shoes came down upon them. The bare walls and ceiling echoed the noise of typewriters and voices. The lighting was poor. As a working office the place's only virtue, dictated by necessity, was that it was cheap.

The campaign, from first to last, was run on a shoestring, with outgo often exceeding income in ways maddening to Stevenson, whose acute awareness of the value of a dollar had certainly not lessened with the years and who put into the campaign some thousands of his own money. So did Dutch Smith, who served as campaign treasurer and had often to issue hurry-up appeals to contributors in order to pay cash on the line for radio time, and newspaper advertising, and billboards. Buffie put in several thousand dollars, and numbers of Stevenson's personal friends, most of them Republican, made substantial contributions. But there were many others who should have contributed, Smith felt, if their deeds were to be consistent with their long-professed concern for good government, and with their personal loyalty to Stevenson, yet who gave nothing. Of the $250,000 which Kohn had thought they could easily raise, less than $100,000 was actually obtained (Green's campaign received at least five times that much).

The financial problem could have been easily solved, of course, if Stevenson had been willing to make "deals." He wasn't. At one dark moment, when the treasury was virtually empty and Stevenson feared that his headquarters might have to be closed for lack of rent money, he wrote a long letter to Smith indicating possible money sources. It was a letter full of anxiety, but embedded in it was a casually matter-of-fact sentence: "I am, of course, trying to avoid taking any money which would leave me with any possible embarrassing commitments."

Nor was his aversion to deals limited to financial matters. Two powerful labor leaders called on him at the headquarters one day. Arvey was in the office at the time. The union men came directly to the point. They were prepared to support Stevenson, but they wanted it understood that he would appoint as labor director a member of their union. Arvey, they said, would be a witness to Stevenson's promise. As witness, Arvey's later testimony[2] was far different from what the union officials had confidently expected.

"I need your support," Stevenson said frankly. "But I haven't made any promises about appointments, and I'm not making any. I may or may not pick a man from your union. Jack, here, hasn't asked me for such commitments. If he doesn't, why should you?"

The campaign manager was James Mulroy who, in the 1920s, while a reporter on the *Daily News,* had won a Pulitzer prize for uncovering the "typewriter evidence" which helped to convict Loeb and Leopold. He was a heavily built, excitable Irishman, utterly devoted to Stevenson and incredibly energetic, who had a decided flare for the dramatic moment and seemed to operate best in an atmosphere of crisis which, sometimes, he himself created. Publicity was handled by a young man, a friend of Mulroy's, named William I. Flanagan, who had recently left a newspaper-reporting job to head the Chicago office of a national press agency. Flanagan helped out at nights and on weekends at first, then worked full time for Stevenson until the impossibility of paying him forced his resignation. The chief secretary was Carol Evans, a tall blond woman, then in her thirties, whom Stevenson had known casually for ten years. She had been secretary to Paul Harper, senior partner in the Sidley law firm when Stevenson returned to his law practice in '46, and she had worked for Stevenson for a brief period in the late spring of that year. Soon thereafter she had left the firm to return to the University of Chicago, where, while working intermittently toward a degree, she had been secretary to Louis Wirth, the famed University of Chicago sociologist.

Necessarily, a great deal of work was done by unpaid volunteers whose dedication was often far greater than their professional competence. People from Lake Forest and other North Shore suburbs came down to help. There was frequent despair among the amateur politicians because "the organization" (it's always "the organization"

2 See Busch's *Adlai E. Stevenson of Illinois,* p. 91.

when it's on your side, Bill Blair once declared, and "the machine" when it's against you) seemed to be doing nothing to help.

"We didn't know," explained Kohn to John Bartlow Martin, later, "that they *never* get going till October."

Co-chairmen of the women's division of the nonpartisan Stevenson-for-Governor Committee, formed in July, were Stevenson's longtime friend, Mrs. Edison (Jane) Dick, and Mrs. Eric W. Stubbs, wife of a Chicago businessman and long a leader in the Hyde Park League of Women Voters. Lloyd Lewis helped Stevenson with speech preparation, especially in the later stages of the campaign when the number of speeches he must make far exceeded the time and energy which any one man could give to their writing. Many others presented drafts of which portions were sometimes used.

This first of the Stevenson campaigns, however, set a speech-writing pattern from which he seldom deviated, and then only under extreme pressure, in the campaigns which were to follow. By and large he wrote his own speeches—and he seemed to need a prepared address for every major gathering, particularly in these first months of his politician's life. Then, as later, his associates complained that he spent far too much time on his speech writing. Then, as later, he readily agreed that he did. But he seemed unable to help himself in this regard. Something in him—a stubborn integrity, a literary craftsman's respect for words—rebelled against the whole system of ghostwriting, and of public-relations engineering, whereby a manufactured myth rather than the real man is presented to the electorate's decision.

He formally opened his campaign on February 23, 1948, in Bloomington, with a reception in the Ives's home—his own boyhood home—at 1316 East Washington. The reception was attended by hundreds, among them Miss Kitty Cowles, Adlai's grade-school teacher, and was very fully covered by the press. Scores of newspaper photographs showed Ellen standing beside her husband—very pretty, smiling happily; it was one of her few public appearances during what would be a very long campaign. Then, from March 1 through March 17, Stevenson toured downstate Illinois with Douglas in a Democratic campaign caravan, speaking at forty-one meetings.

At the outset he was no more than moderately effective as a speaker before political rallies. But he learned steadily and rapidly, and from the first the meetings were surprisingly well attended.

His own view of the strange new experience he was having was expressed in one of his personal letters to Mrs. Dick, written on the stationary of a motel in the little town of Carmi in the midst of this first campaign tour. "It's Sunday morning," he wrote. "I'm in an automobile driving from Danville where we spoke last night to Decatur to resume this fantastic ordeal. We've driven 1350 miles since last Sunday, and I've spoken about 20 times, shaken hands with thousands of people, and slept all too little.

"It's been an amazing experience, and I've come to wonder how anyone can presume to talk about 'America' until he has done some campaigning. Perhaps it's the secret, perhaps the curse, of American political success—the illusive business of finding your way to the heart of the average man—when there is no such thing—and, unhappily, the human heart is often an organ encased in a pocketbook, and not a Bible or a textbook.

"I've seen Illinois in a capsule—the beauty of the south, the fruit belt, the coal fields, the oil fields, the great industrial area around East St. Louis—and everywhere the rich, black fecund earth stretching away and away. . . . But I'm getting a little lyrical for a Democratic politician. . . ."

Thus his personal reaction, privately expressed. His public reaction took a wry, ironic form. When a Republican organization adopted a resolution saying that his Libertyville address was a phony one, that he actually lived in Vernon Township and claimed Libertyville as home simply because it was a "symbol of American freedom," he made a public speech which convulsed his listeners with laughter.

"People wiser in the ways of politics than I am say that it doesn't make any difference what you think or I think," he said. "The way I tie my necktie or whether I prefer jelly or jam can win or lose votes. . . . And of course whatever I say or don't say will be misinterpreted or misrepresented by the opposition. . . . Now they say I'm a fraud and impostor who doesn't even reside in Libertyville. In my innocence it never occurred to me to tell the U. S. Post Office Department its business or the correct address of my farm. I guess I am too naïve to be a good candidate. . . ."

Good or not, he was certainly different. Being so, he could not but conduct a very "different" kind of political campaign. Political reporters admitted, in print, that they had never seen anything quite like it, and their glowing reports had an effect on Governor Green, who was taking a winter vacation in Florida. Green had let it be known that he would not bother to conduct a primary campaign, but he now cut short his vacation, returned to Illinois, and began his campaign with a speech at Fairfield on March 10. In this maiden speech he identified his opponent as "a man on leave from the striped-pants brigade of the Roosevelt-Truman State Department. . . . This candidate, whose chief claim to fame is a sub-author of the UN plan—the most dismal failure in the history of American diplomacy—seeks to hold up to ridicule the men and women who grapple with our State problems in the House and Senate at Springfield." To this, Stevenson made swift reply. "The Governor has added two words to the lexicon of political damnation," said he, on the night following Green's speech. "One is 'striped.' The other is 'pants.' But, damned or striped . . . I will continue to talk Illinois, which is the business of the Governor of Illinois. . . ."

Green repeated his "striped-pants" charge in later speeches, until *Daily News* reporters found in the files a photograph of the governor in striped pants and cutaway, and printed it with the comment that they had been unable to find any such picture of Stevenson. Stevenson himself was not amused, though his responses amused voters. "He probably likes Easter parades," said he, and went on earnestly to identify himself with the cause of world collaboration. "How can any thinking man in the world today be anything but an internationalist?" he asked, intensely serious. "At this moment, we are engaged in an ideological conflict throughout the globe in the interests of democracy and decency." He pointed out, however, that he was not running against Green for the vice-presidency of the United States—a statement of penetrating point since Green was, at that time, working hard for a second place on the national ticket.

He had good reason to be thankful for Green's vaulting aspirations, however, for they led the governor into repeated and ultimately disastrous political errors. At the National Republican Convention in Philadelphia in late June, Governor Green made the keynote address. It might have been written by Colonel Robert McCormick, whose hatred of Governor Thomas E. Dewey of New York and the entire "liberal" wing of the Republican party was profound and vociferous. Isolationism in foreign affairs, black reaction at home—these were the twin themes of Green's performance, which branded him before all men as the "errand boy" (Stevenson used the phrase again and again) of the *Tribune* publisher. When Dewey won the nomination, Green's chance for a place on the ticket was gone with the wind which blew from the Tribune Tower, and his cause in Illinois was badly damaged.

Stevenson, on the other hand, helped his local cause and gained national political stature with his performance as a delegate to the National Democratic Convention, which also met in Philadelphia that year, in mid-July.

It is a measure of the depths to which President Truman's prestige had fallen that his renomination, in the spring of '48, seemed doubtful. Jack Arvey was among the astute politicians who were convinced that if Truman became the candidate, he would inevitably lead his party to disaster at the polls. He joined Mayor O'Dwyer of New York, the Americans for Democratic Action, Paul Douglas, and numerous others in an attempt to draft General Eisenhower as the Democratic presidential candidate despite the fact that the general's politics, in so far as he had any, seemed vaguely Republican. Stevenson, however, declined to join the draft-Eisenhower movement. He genuinely admired Harry Truman as man and as President, critical though he was of both. He was convinced that Truman's handling of the great crises of his first term gave the President no small claim to historical greatness and an overwhelming claim to renomination.

Accordingly, on the train going to Philadelphia on July 10, Stevenson "jumped into the Truman camp with both feet," saying to reporters that "Truman deserves our support in Illinois, and he will get it." Thus he anticipated the harmony which prevailed throughout a two-hour caucus held in Philadelphia next day, following which it was announced that all of Illinois's sixty votes would go to Truman on the first ballot. At that caucus Stevenson joined Ed Kelly in advising the delegates to "shake off the gloom about November" because "we're going to win"; he then invited the delegation to a cocktail party to "cheer up."

Two days later, at the Stevenson party, "an incipient revolt against Arvey-Kelly direction flared into the open," according to one typical newspaper account. "Angry downstaters, distressed first at Arvey's ditch-Truman-for-Ike movement, now accuse him . . . of trying to substitute a New Dealer for Minority Leader Alben Barkley, the strong favorite of most of the Illinois delegation for the Vice-Presidential nod," this account went on. "Stevenson, who did not participate in the dump Truman efforts, also did not participate in the Barkley maneuvering." He admired Barkley: at seventy-one, the senator was one of the few political leaders who had served both

Wilson's New Freedom and Roosevelt's New Deal: and Stevenson might even have some slight family feeling for the grand old man, since his paternal grandfather was a second cousin of Barkley's mother. After Truman had been nominated on the first ballot, Stevenson strongly supported Barkley for the vice-presidency, making a speech seconding the Barkley nomination.

He did this despite the fact that he and Barkley had been on opposite sides of one of the key issues of the convention. Nineteen forty-eight was the year of the Dixiecrat revolt against Truman's stand on civil rights and, as a member of the credentials committee, Stevenson led the fight to bar from the convention the Mississippi delegation which had announced in advance that it would not support Truman or any other candidate who stood for Truman's civil-rights program. Having failed to carry with him a majority of the committee, Stevenson sought to carry the fight to the convention floor—and it was there he encountered, and was defeated by, Barkley. Barkley was chairman of the session, and when Stevenson, Arvey, and Kelly rose to protest the acceptance of the slim majority action on the credentials committee, he was "afflicted with temporary deafness," as newspaper accounts put it. He was also afflicted with temporary blindness, being unable to see the commotion among the Illinois delegation whose standard was immediately in front of the speaker's stand. "Something must have been wrong with the microphone system," he later blandly explained.

The general public was, of course, neither as blind nor as deaf as Barkley seemed to be that day, and Stevenson's civil-rights role received national recognition, reducing the effectiveness of later attempts to label him an appeaser of the South's institutionalized racialism.

Adlai Stevenson III, eighteen years old, had been graduated from Milton Academy that spring. His cousin, Timothy Ives, twenty, was a student at the University of Virginia. Both served as pages at the Democratic National Convention and both were taken by Stevenson, one day, on a tour of Philadelphia's historic spots. Inevitably, news photographers trailed them. Pictures of the two youths and Stevenson at the Liberty Bell appeared within a few days in dozens of Illinois papers.

"Little Adlai," as everyone called him, though he was in fact taller than his father, toured with his father and the sixteen-year-old

Borden through the fervent Illinois summer. In September the two brothers left for school—Adlai to enter his freshman year at Harvard and Borden to enter his last year at his father's old school, Choate. Only John Fell then remained with his mother at the Libertyville farm. He was twelve and a student at the Lake Forest Day School where he organized his friends into a kind of Stevenson-for-Governor committee which reportedly addressed envelopes and distributed campaign literature.

"He keeps close track of my campaign." Stevenson laughed proudly. "He tells me my chances are very good."

III

Others did not think so. Betting odds against Stevenson's election had been reported at ten to one as the summer began; they reportedly stood at five to one in late July, after the national conventions had enhanced Stevenson's prestige while lowering Green's. Green still possessed perhaps the best-financed, most tightly organized political machine in all Illinois history, plus the inestimable advantage of an expected national Republican landslide. (To offset the latter, Republicans-for-Stevenson inserted newspaper ads urging support of a Dewey-Stevenson ticket—and most of the papers supporting Stevenson took the same line in their editorials.)

Certainly Stevenson himself did not underrate his opponent's strength. All through the August doldrums he concentrated on Green an unremitting fire—and after Labor Day this fire became even more intense. He had a twelve-point program for the state. Again and again he presented it in public speech. If elected, he would strive:

—to improve Illinois's inefficient and inequitable taxing system;
—to increase the proportion of total tax revenue going to cities;
—to abolish the present flagrant corruption in state purchasing;
—to call a constitutional convention for a complete revision of the constitution adopted in 1870;
—to overhaul drastically the state's public-welfare system, which had permitted state hospitals—particularly those for the mentally ill—to degenerate "into unspeakable horrors of sadism, inefficiency, and corruption";
—to undertake an extensive long-term road-building program, and

do away with "political engineering" in highway building and maintenance;

—to establish a state Fair Employment Practices commission;

—to strengthen the mine safety laws and take mine inspection out of politics;

—to increase state financial aid to the common schools;

—to increase the efficiency and economy of state administration;

—to take the state police out of politics and use them *as* police rather than as politicians' errand boys;

—to remove parasites, and the names of nonexistent employees, from state payrolls.

But he quite generally presented this positive program in negative terms, as an attack on the Green administration.

His campaign's effectiveness was vastly increased that fall by the fact that, of the state's most influential newspapers, only the Chicago *Tribune* yet bitterly opposed him. The *Daily News* and *Sun-Times* had supported him from the first. So had the Bloomington *Pantagraph*, which asserted that it did so "despite rather than because of" Stevenson's connection with the publishing company. (Editorially the paper explained that the Stevenson interest in the paper was a minority one and that he had nothing to say about management or policy.) So had the St. Louis *Post-Dispatch*, which had a great downstate readership and whose editorial page, under the editorship of Irving Dilliard, was perhaps the best written and certainly one of the most effective in the nation. Many another normally Republican paper deserted Green for Stevenson.

And this support gained fervor when, in mid-campaign, a *Post-Dispatch* star reporter, Theodore C. Link, sent to Peoria to investigate the murder of one of the notorious Shelton gang, was arrested and indicted by Green machine politicians. (The indictment was withdrawn immediately after the election.) It was then revealed that scores of downstate newspaper editors were actually on the payroll of the state, placed there, it was suggested, by Republican politicians in order to keep them quiet while the politicians shook down gamblers, formed working alliances with all kinds of grafters and racketeers, profited richly from kickbacks and payroll padding, and bought state materials at fantastically inflated prices in profit-sharing schemes. With "freedom of the press" thus raised as an issue, papers which usually made little effort to uncover or develop the news began to do so with a vengeance.

These scandalous revelations in the autumn augmented the moral outrage which had been inspired in the spring by revelations concerning a coal-mine disaster in southern Illinois. On March 25, 1947, an explosion in Centralia No. 5 had killed 111 miners. In March of 1948, a long article by John Bartlow Martin, in *Harper's* magazine, had exhaustively reviewed the tragedy and the investigation into its causes, revealing an appalling looseness of mine safety laws and an even more appalling laxness in state mine inspection. Included were the facts that the Centralia miners had repeatedly complained that the mine was unsafe, that these complaints had been ignored by both the operators and Green's mine inspectors, and that the latter regularly solicited campaign contributions from the former. Extended excerpts from the Martin article had been printed in Illinois papers and numerous angry anti-Green editorials had been stimulated thereby. Stevenson himself quoted the article again and again throughout his campaign. . . .

On the afternoon of Tuesday, November 2, Adlai and Ellen Stevenson voted at Half Day, a tiny village near their Libertyville farm. They were photographed as they emerged from the voting booths. He was wearing a dark suit, rather rumpled-looking, with a white handkerchief protruding well beyond the fashionable tenth of an inch from his left breast pocket. Ellen was wearing a bright plaid suit with a long boxlike jacket. Unsmiling, he looked tense and tired. Smiling, she seemed relaxed and happy. That evening the Stevensons and Dutch and Ellen Smith dined as guests of Mrs. John Alden Carpenter, Ellen's mother, in town. Then they all went downtown to 7 South Dearborn. On the sidewalk before the headquarters a newsboy was selling the early evening edition of the Chicago *Tribune*. The eight-column front-page banner headline proclaimed in huge type that Dewey had won a landslide victory over Truman. Dutch Smith glanced quickly at Stevenson whose face showed nothing and who said nothing.

The headquarters was crowded. The Edison Dicks were there. Lloyd and Kathryn Lewis were there. Everybody seemed to be there. Newspapers had reported that the Stevenson campaign, roaring through its final week, had become an even-money bet for victory among the professional gamblers, but at 7 South Dearborn the optimism was cautious as the early returns, nearly all of them from Cook County, came in. These early returns all showed Stevenson leading, but Cook County was Democratic country; he'd have to carry it by a huge majority to offset the expected Republican victory downstate. Many of those who had worked hardest in the campaign, and were now tired, let-down, expressed the belief that the Cook County margin wasn't large enough—that the election was lost. Stevenson expressed the opposite view.

"I think we've won," he said quietly.

He went into his little corner office. The returns kept pouring in, with Stevenson's leadership margin steadily widening. "Don't let 'em leave the polls," Lewis kept warning Stevenson, referring to the Democratic poll watchers, for he knew well that ballots had been stolen in the past and that this had sometimes robbed winning candidates of their victory. Stevenson knew this well, too. (In 1908, when his grandfather ran for governor, ballot boxes full of votes for Adlai E. Stevenson had found their way, somehow, to the bottom of the Chicago River and were never officially counted.)

By nine o'clock the initial anxiety had departed from the office. Stevenson was winning! *He was winning big!* The crowd grew noisily jubilant.

Stevenson sat quietly in his cubbyhole, with Lloyd Lewis beside him, rewriting his acceptance speech. (His habit of rewriting speeches up to the moment he gave them would become legendary.)

By ten o'clock it was clear that he had scored a landslide victory. Radio broadcasters were saying his margin might be as high as four hundred thousand when all the returns were in. He was leading his ticket, though Douglas was overwhelming Brooks and other Democrats on the state ticket were winning by substantial margins. More amazing was the fact that Truman remained consistently if only slightly ahead of Dewey, even after the national rural vote began to come in; nationally Truman was winning thus far! Copies of the early *Tribune* edition were gleefully displayed. . . .

Green conceded his defeat.

Stevenson spoke into a radio microphone, saying that he was "at once gratified and humbled by the size of the majority which has, today, called me to the State capital of Illinois."

Ellen, wearing a gray wool dress with fringed cuffs and a two-toned gray felt hat, came to sit beside her husband at photographers' requests. Flash bulbs flared. The resulting pictures showed Stevenson's face lighted from within by a radiant smile, white teeth gleaming as he talked into the telephone. Ellen's smile, in some of the pictures, was pleasant but withdrawn; in other pictures she wasn't smiling at all. She declined to answer newsmen's questions about herself, except to say that she was forty years old, that both she and her mother had expected her husband to win, but that the victory margin was wider than she had expected.

"I think when people have the facts they choose the best man," she said, "and I think my husband is made for this job."

"Will you enjoy the next four years?" she was asked.

She half smiled, half frowned in reply. "What a question!" she said, with a slight reproving shake of her head.

When all the returns were in, it was found that he had won the governorship by the largest plurality in Illinois history—572,067 votes. Of these, 546,424 came from Cook County, but the really incredible thing was that he had also won downstate by 25,643 votes, carrying 48 out of 101 counties in an area as monolithically Republican, most years, as Kansas or Vermont. Truman had carried Illinois by only 33,612, some 539,000 votes less than Stevenson's margin. Stevenson, it appeared, had carried Illinois for the President whose victory was the most amazing upset and perhaps the greatest personal triumph in all American political history.

CHAPTER TWENTY

"This Strange New Governor of Illinois"

By the evening of Sunday, January 9, 1949, every hotel, motel, and tourist home in Springfield was jammed to capacity. Some hotels had lined their corridors with cots, for each of which there were many bidders. The capital of Illinois had not had a full-scale inaugural celebration for eight years—Green's second inaugural, in the midst of World War II, had been a brief perfunctory ceremony—and hundreds of Chicago Democrats, with almost as many hundred Republicans came down on special trains for the occasion, many of them sleeping Sunday night in parked Pullmans.

The governor-elect, with an official party of some seventy members, came down on Sunday evening in the last two cars of the Abraham Lincoln Streamliner, crack train of the Gulf, Mobile & Ohio. Heavy rain was falling upon Springfield when the train arrived. Through it, Stevenson and his family were driven in the limousine of Governor Green, who had sent it to the station with his state police chauffeur. Stevenson remarked that this was the first time he had ever ridden in the state car with the Number 1 license plate. His party had been assigned the twelfth floor of the Hotel Abraham Lincoln, and as they entered the lobby they were greeted with cheers and applause by a great crowd. John Fell and young Edison Dick were so excited by it all that their parents couldn't get them into bed until very late in the night. . . .

At eleven o'clock next morning—a chilly gray morning through which a drizzling rain fell intermittently—the Stevensons left their hotel suite, pressing their way again through an applauding crowd which had long jammed the hotel corridors and lobby awaiting their appearance. They were driven directly to the ninety-three-year-old Executive Mansion—a plain, square, white-painted structure containing twenty-three tall-ceilinged rooms, set upon a low hill overlooking Springfield's downtown district. They were greeted in the blue-carpeted foyer by the Greens, who, with simple and gracious ceremony, gave into Stevenson's hand the keys to the mansion.

At eleven-fifteen the inaugural procession left the mansion. It was a cavalcade of thirty-eight cars, headed by eight white-gloved state policemen on motorcycles and followed by marching soldiers in white helmets. The slow ride through the business district to the National Guard Armory might have been an uncomfortable one for both the Greens and the Stevensons. It wasn't. Whatever bitterness the Greens felt was well hidden by a warm hospitality, and in appreciation of this the incoming governor decided to omit from his inaugural address a reference to "the last election in Illinois" which reflected upon his predecessor. The procession arrived at the armory, across the street from Illinois's tall-domed capitol, shortly before twelve o'clock, noon. Hundreds of people who had been unable to gain entrance to the jam-packed building stood on the sidewalks applauding as the Greens and Stevensons entered.

Halfway through the thirteenth hour of January 10, 1949, Adlai E. Stevenson was formally installed as the thirty-first governor of Illinois—the fourth Democratic governor of that state since the Civil War.

A mighty roar burst from thousands of throats, lifting men and women to their feet, surging across the platform where John Fell and Adlai III applauded wildly, stirring deep emotions in the man whom the thousands cheered, though he stood quietly, and only smiled, waiting for the ovation to die that he might begin his inaugural address. Even Ellen, whose manner had been pleasant but aloof through the inaugural activities thus far, now "permitted herself a broad smile of pride," as one newspaper reported.

Next morning, the new governor did not arrive at his State House office until eleven-fifteen. He was smiling broadly as he strode in, cheerfully greeted assembled newspapermen, and sat for the first time in the big chair behind the executive desk.

He apologized for his lateness. This was his first morning in the Executive Mansion, he explained ruefully, and already a "major crisis" had occurred. His son John Fell and the eleven-year-old Edison Dick had gone upstairs to peek into the room where Carl Sandburg, who had spoken at the inaugural, slept late. They were fully aware that what they did was reprehensible, and when the poet stirred in his sleep they scampered away into the mansion's automatic elevator, excitedly pushing buttons in such a way that the elevator got stuck between two floors. An hour passed before a repairman arrived to rescue them. . . .

A newsman was emboldened by this to tell the governor that the poll was not yet completed on his use of the word "proliferation" in the inaugural address as a description of the process by which state bureaus had become overlapping. Another newsman said he'd looked the word up and as far as he could tell it had something to do with the way coral spreads.

"That's good," Stevenson laughed. "Better than I thought."

Thus did this first of his press conferences set the tone prevailing through later ones, causing newsmen to speak with delighted surprise of "this strange new governor." His gaiety and wit did not hide from them the seriousness of his purpose nor the almost incredible energy he devoted to it. . . .

He had not been governor for twenty-four hours when he tasted to the full the awfulness of his responsibility and the loneliness it would have imposed on him even had he not been by nature and, paradoxically, despite his gregariousness, a lonely person.

Amid the festivities of his inaugural he had been forced to consider a reportedly "dangerous situation" at the state penitentiary in Pontiac. It was said that twice the normal number of prisoners were in solitary confinement there and that a riot was brewing as a result of maladministration by the Green-appointed warden, Arthur A. Bennett. T. P. Sullivan, State Public Service director and Bennett's superior, was a Green appointee whom the new governor had not replaced. He would resign a few months later, the target of considerable public criticism, but he now stood high in Stevenson's esteem and when he recommended that Bennett be dismissed at once "for the good of the service," Stevenson issued the dismissal order, being careful to announce at the same time that this action did not affect the other wardens' positions. Bennett, informed of his dismissal by phone on the morning of January 12, protested to newsmen that he had no chance to present his side of the case and that "someone had lied to the governor about me." "Charges that I collected campaign funds for Green at the prison are a damned lie!"

he cried excitedly, adding that he was "going to try to see Governor Stevenson right away" because "I'm sure he doesn't know all the facts." He did try to reach the governor, but in vain. Two days later he was dead of a coronary thrombosis.

II

Every newly elected governor has his "honeymoon" period with the press of the state. Stevenson's was unusually ecstatic and unusually prolonged. For once, the correspondents of an overwhelmingly Republican press found themselves face to face with a Democratic chief executive whom they not only personally liked but of whom they could express their liking in print, since most of their publishers had supported him. They delighted in him, and the delight came through in the copy they wrote.

"The new Governor of Illinois is a curiosity," reported a Springfield newspaper. "Powerful politicians such as once gave orders from smoke-filled rooms are now taking orders from Mrs. Bricklayer, Mrs. Breadbaker, Mr. Farmer, Miss School Teacher, Mr. Butcher, Mr. Ditchdigger, and Mr. and Mrs. Everybody interested in good government."

"Governor Stevenson ordinarily looks out on the world with a humorous, good-natured air, which is one of the reasons so many people are drawn to him," wrote Marquis Childs in a nationally syndicated column. "Seated in the Governor's chair, surveying the horrendous housecleaning job to be done, he looks grim. The old habits, the old indifference, the familiar venality may be too deeply entrenched. But you know that here is a man who is going to do his damndest to end ancient evils that benefit the few and burden the many."

"This fellow Stevenson had better look out lest he wake up some fine morning and discover he's got no one with him other than the public." So wrote Milburn P. Akers in the *Sun-Times*. "A Governor who tries to keep his campaign pledges; imagine that, this day and year in Illinois!"

Even the Chicago *Tribune* said surprisingly kind things for a surprising number of weeks after the inaugural.

More correspondents than one found similarities between Stevenson and Lincoln, for all their obvious differences. According to John

Dreiske of the *Sun-Times,* in the spring of 1949, Stevenson had "a literary flare and mode of expression that strikes many as being definitely along the Lincolnian line. . . ." (Dreiske referred to the governor's "quotability" as a "refreshing breeze" and reported repeatedly, as a newsworthy item, that Stevenson "writes his own stuff.") Such public views of Stevenson as one who moved and had his being in the Lincoln tradition were enhanced by the governor's very evident love affair with Illinois history. One of his earliest acts was to establish direct and well-used lines of communication between his office and the Illinois State Historical Library whose head, State Historian Jay Monaghan, was the author of widely read books on Lincoln and Illinois history. From the library he obtained a carefully selected group of books for his office shelves, and oil paintings by Illinois artists to hang on the mansion walls. Out-of-town visitors to the mansion were almost invariably taken, either by the governor himself or by an appointed guide, to reconstructed New Salem, to Lincoln's tomb, to the house on the corner of Market and Eighth—and these visitors spread abroad tales of the governor's total immersion in Lincolniana and of his fondness for the company of such famed Lincoln scholars as Monaghan; Benjamin Thomas, then at work on his classic one-volume biography of Lincoln; and Carl Sandburg. In conversation with a Springfield physician, he heard a theory about the causes of Mrs. Lincoln's notorious temper and of Lincoln's chronic melancholia—a theory he enjoyed expounding.

"You know," he said to a visitor at Libertyville some years later, "nobody has published, as far as I know, anything medically sound about the Lincolns' very serious physical disabilities. This doctor friend in Springfield convinced me that Abe had a duodenal ulcer. He had all the symptoms. His peculiar eating habits, for instance. He seemed to have no taste for food, seldom paid any attention to what was set before him——" Stevenson's visitor grinned a little, being aware of how sad this fact must seem to the governor, himself a very hearty trencherman. "Also his chronic depression and 'indigestion.' As for Mrs. Lincoln, she suffered from diabetes. It was a mild case, but devastating to her nerves. She had constantly jangled nerves, you know—was driven wild by sudden loud noises." Stevenson shook his head. "No one can guess what those two must have suffered!"

His close friendship with Lloyd Lewis further enhanced the public view of him as a man in the Lincoln tradition, Lewis being known to the world as a man of high Lincolnian flavor.

When the governor flew to Washington in a National Guard plane to attend the annual dinner of the White House Correspondents Association for President Truman, Lloyd Lewis accompanied him. The press reported that prior to the dinner the two men strolled in Lafayette Park, talking and laughing together in rich enjoyment of one another. Shortly afterward Leonard Lyons, in a nationally syndicated column, told his readers that Stevenson's election campaign had helped Lewis to "make rapid progress in writing his biography of Ulysses S. Grant." "Lewis," Lyons explained, "lives at Libertyville, Illinois, a Republican stronghold, and he campaigned for Adlai Stevenson, the Democratic candidate for Governor. His Republican neighbors therefore wouldn't speak to him, and this isolation gave him time to work on his book. 'If the campaign had lasted six weeks longer,' Lewis insists, 'I'd have had Grant at Antietam.'"

Stevenson smiled, and at the same time shook his head reprovingly, when the Lyons column was brought to his attention. He knew very well that his good friend had never made the statement put into quotation marks by Lyons, for Grant was never at Antietam, which was one of McClellan's bloody but indecisive battles fought while Grant, yet under a cloud for the near disaster at Shiloh, held a secondary command in the West. The governor planned to "kid" Lewis about this when next they met, pointing out how fortunate it was that the campaign had *not* lasted six weeks longer, since Grant's arrival on the field of Antietam would have marked the end of Lewis's reputation as a historian.

Alas, the two friends were destined never to meet again.

In that year, and for some years earlier, Lewis was editor of the *Newberry Library Bulletin,* coming in from his farm home to this Chicago research library for a day or so each week. On April 21, 1949, on his way home from Chicago, he was stricken by a heart attack. A few hours later he died. In his book (it was published the following year with the title *Captain Sam Grant*), he had got his hero only as far as Camp Yates on the outskirts of Springfield where, on June 28, 1861, Grant was colonel in command of the Seventh District Regiment of Illinois volunteers. . . .

Stevenson came to Libertyville for the funeral. He was unexpectedly called upon to say a few words. When he arose he spoke from a full heart, for he had loved Lloyd Lewis as he loved few people, and the words he said rang sweet bells forever afterward in the memory of Kathryn Lewis and of all the others who heard him.

"I have been asked to share in these farewells to a friend," he said. "I think it is a good day for this meeting. It is April now and all life is being renewed on the bank of this river that he loved so well. I think we will all be happy that it happened on this day, here by the river with the spring sky so clear, and the west wind so warm and fresh. I think we will all be the better for this day and this meeting together.

"He was my neighbor. He was the neighbor of many of you. He was a very good neighbor; quick in time of misfortune, always present in times of mirth and happiness—and need. . . . I think it will always be April in our memory of him. It will always be a bright fresh day, full of the infinite variety and promise of new life."

III

The sorrow over the death of Lloyd Lewis was sudden, swift, leaving behind it a long ache of loss but leaving sweet memories also. There was, however, another sorrow in Stevenson's life that spring, the secret sorrow of whose beginnings we have spoken and which, all through those crowded months and through the fervid Illinois summer, grew in a crescendo of hidden anguish until, in late September, it burst at last its bonds of secrecy. It became, then, a too public sorrow, and in it there was no sweetness. Instead was an acid bitterness which ate into the remembered past. The acid worked strongly in Adlai Stevenson's mind. It worked even more strongly in the mind of Ellen Borden Stevenson. It would keep on working, deeper and deeper. . . .

On the day after the Springfield inaugural, Adlai III began his journey back to Harvard and Ellen accompanied her husband, with John Fell, to Bloomington for the Chamber of Commerce banquet at which Stevenson and Alben Barkley were featured. She then returned to the Libertyville farm. It was reported in the press that "Stevenson will lead a more or less bachelor existence during the next six months because his 12-year-old son, John Fell, is a student at Lake Forest Day School and Mrs. Stevenson wants to be close to him rather than live in the Executive Mansion in Springfield."

The Chicago *Herald-American's* story added a cryptic sentence: "Mrs. Dwight H. Green's warning to Mrs. Adlai E. Stevenson that being the wife of the Governor of Illinois is not all everybody thinks it will be, already is being proved." It was said that Mrs. Stevenson planned to spend weekends at the mansion and to come down for "special occasions."

She spent, in fact, few weekends there. She accompanied her husband to the Truman inaugural. In early February her husband came to Libertyville for a celebration of his and John Fell's birthdays: his forty-ninth birthday was February 5, John Fell's thirteenth birthday was February 7, and Ellen, as in the past, "split the difference," holding a joint celebration on February 6. She came to Springfield in late March to preside as hostess at the first and second of the series of dinner parties which the governor traditionally gave for members of the legislature. The legislators were invited, in alphabetical order, in groups of twenty-five or thirty. After the fifty Senate members had been dined, and before the series for the lower house began, she returned to Libertyville with the mumps! (Jane Dick had the mumps, too, at about this time, having been exposed by her son Edison, Jr., who in turn gave them to John Fell, who gave them to Ellen.) At subsequent state dinners, and at other absolutely necessary social functions, Mrs. Ernest Ives was hostess, coming down for days at a time from Bloomington. Her husband moved into the mansion to be of what help he could to her brother in his terrible difficulties.

Inevitably there was a great deal of talk about the social situation at the mansion among legislators and Springfield residents, much of it sparked by a malice born of disappointment, for it had been forecast that Mrs. Stevenson, famed as a belle of the highest Chicago society, would bring to the mansion a glamorous social life such as the old house had not known since the Lowden administration of 1916 to 1920. Instead, there was for many months virtually no social life at all. State senators and their wives complained, after the first of the two Senate dinners, that the affair had been coldly formal. A single cocktail was served before dinner and the guests were dismissed promptly at nine-thirty. (During the regimes of Horner and Green these dinners had lasted sometimes until well into the following morning.) Forewarned, several of the guests of the second Senate dinner took the precaution of pausing at a hotel bar on their way to the mansion, but even this added incentive to a festive mood failed noticeably to thaw (so several guests complained) a freezing atmosphere—and again the affair ended promptly at nine-thirty. Springfield gossips contrasted Mrs. Stevenson's polite reserve at the inaugural festivities with the elation and happy pride which Mrs. Ives had displayed, and they quoted frequently Mrs. Stevenson's remark about the "ancestor worship" in "Adlai's family." They also quoted remarks allegedly made by Chicago socialites at a luncheon in the Drake Hotel, shortly after the election—remarks that "Ellen has a mind of her own," and that "she's a positive personality" who would "never live in the State mansion."

Only to the Iveses, to those members of his staff who necessarily handled confidential detail in the governor's office, and to the most intimate of his longtime friends did Stevenson himself give any hint of the impending dissolution of his marriage. Even with these few he was extremely reticent concerning his personal feelings. Several times he indicated his pride in Ellen's wit and literary talents. One day he brought to the office, and proudly circulated, a "round-table discussion" of *Modern Woman* (years later, it was printed under that title in *Chicago* magazine), which Ellen had written. It was a dialogue in verse whose scene was "any intellectual parlor" and whose characters were Plato, Aquinas, Bacon, Voltaire, Freud—and Modern Woman.[1]

He also indicated a respect for Ellen's political opinions—though his most intimate friends believed he did so partially because he wanted so desperately to involve her in his new life, saving his marriage.

When school was out and John Fell no longer provided a convenient excuse for Ellen's continued absence from Springfield, the gossip, of course, increased. By this time several of Stevenson's intimates were aware that Ellen was determined to sue for a divorce. The reasons were as obscure to them as they were, perhaps, to Ellen herself, and to Adlai. She felt "smothered," she said; she suffered a kind of "claustrophobia" in her marriage; she had to live her own

---

[1] Some in the governor's office thought that Ellen's Modern Woman was her view of herself. Modern Woman's opening speech was:

They say I'm distracted and lost	*I emote with a speed supersonic.*
I think I'm impacted and bossed.	*My dissatisfaction is chronic.*
When I was a kid	*I envy the peace*
They ruined my id;	*Of the Ancients of Greece;*
So now I raise Cain when I'm crossed.	*O Plato, please make me platonic!*

life, not a life as alien to her tastes as Adlai's now was. She had to be "free" in order "to write." A few intimates, mutual friends of hers and Adlai's, tried in vain to dissuade her. Wouldn't she at least agree to a separation without a divorce? She would not. It had taken her a long time to make up her mind, but now that it was made up there was no changing it.

Adlai, too, tried to dissuade her, pleading not just for himself but also for her own future happiness (he told a close friend that he was so terribly afraid of "what will happen to Ellen"), and then not for just the two of them but, especially, for their three sons. Ellen countered by saying that the three sons were virtually "raised"; Borden and "Little Adlai" were away at school, and John Fell would enter Milton Academy in September (he would enter, as a matter of fact, a year earlier than had been originally planned). She agreed, however, that everything must be done to protect the boys. In public statements it would be emphasized that the parting was "amicable." The boys would divide their holiday time equally between their parents, neither of whom would make any effort to alienate them from the other, and the Libertyville farm.

On the last Friday in September 1949 Stevenson made the formal announcement: "I am deeply distressed that, due to the incompatibility of our lives, Mrs. Stevenson feels a separation is necessary. Though I do not believe in divorce, I will not contest it. We have separated with the highest mutual regard." The press handled the story with rare restraint and sympathy. Said the Chicago *Sun-Times:* "Because of her growing distaste for the limelight as the wife of a man in public life, Mrs. Ellen Stevenson will divorce Governor Stevenson." Said the Chicago *Daily News:* "Though news of the Adlai Stevensons' impending divorce was dropped on the general public like a bombshell last weekend, friends of the couple sensed a smouldering fuse months ago. . . . Mrs. Stevenson never made any secret of the fact that she considered a political campaign disrupting of home life and that she found political banquets boring."

On December 8 a Chicago *Herald-American* reporter managed to get in touch with Ellen in Las Vegas, Nevada, where she had lived for the five preceding weeks, establishing her residence. Early in the following week she would file petition for divorce. "What will the grounds be?" she was asked. She replied: "I really can't say, but aren't they usually mental cruelty out here?" She was very cheerful. She had been "doing a lot of things I never seemed to have time to do before." She'd rented a typewriter and written at least fifty letters. She had read at least twenty books she had been planning to read for years. She was living in a ranch house about three miles from town. "There is a piano in my room, and I entertain myself a lot by playing it. Then I take long walks, sometimes hiking the three miles into town. I chose this spot because it's quiet, restful, and the weather is so nice. Why, right now while I'm talking to you"—she was interviewed by phone—"I can see the roses blooming outside my window." She planned to spend Christmas with the three boys at Libertyville, and then would try to obtain an apartment on the near North Side in Chicago. . . .

In the years that followed she engaged in a number of literary activities. She worked, intermittently, on a book. She wrote light verse. She became president of the Modern Poetry Association which published *Poetry* magazine, founded by Harriet Monroe in 1912. In the 1950s she established in her childhood home, now owned jointly by her and her sister, a new club devoted to the arts, calling it the 1020 Arts Center (from the address at 1020 Lake Shore Drive). She worked hard to make this club a success, displaying again her talent for interior decoration, providing for excellent service and excellent food and drink, scheduling first-rate art shows and chamber-music recitals by such stellar organizations as the Fine Arts String Quartet, arranging for lectures by such literary lights as W. H. Auden and Dylan Thomas. By the mid-1950s, this club absorbed most of her time and energy.

But by that time, too, the acid bitterness had worked very deeply into her, poisoning, it seemed, most of her life. Formerly she had seemed to resent the success and public acclaim which had come to her husband: it was not the limelight she disliked, said some of their mutual friends, but the fact that the limelight was not focused on her. "Everyone pays so much attention to Adlai!" she cried out, once, after a meeting of the Modern Poetry Association directors in the Newberry Library. "Why doesn't someone pay attention to me!" She laughed as she said it—but it was not a happy laugh. And her resentment of her former husband seemed to grow in direct proportion to his fame, as though this fame were for her a public humiliation. Certainly, if she felt she had made a mistake, if she suffered a sense of vital loss, the knowledge of the mistake and of her loss was inescapable: everywhere she turned she would encounter her former husband's face and hear his voice—in the press, on TV, over the radio, in newsreels.

Most of the friends she and Adlai had shared remained friends of his, and for that reason were repudiated by her as time went on. She began to make public statements which seemed obviously designed to hurt him, and she made malicious remarks about him at private affairs—remarks which were, of course, widely circulated.

She did succeed in hurting him, again and again, striking at the very roots of his pride, though he gave no outward sign of his hurt and made no public reply. She struck at him until some who loved him were driven into an actual hatred of her, and newsmen ceased to print the news she strove to make. She was, such people thought, an utterly selfish woman, a spoiled little rich girl who had never grown up and couldn't bear the knowledge that, measured against the man she had married, she now measured small. He had kept growing, they said, whereas she remained fixed in the Fitzgerald era, and she continued to believe that the fashionable, insouciant, not-very-important young man whom she had first met at parties was the "real" Adlai Stevenson and that all the other larger selves which now enveloped this first-known Adlai were "phony." . . . Such people pointed gratefully to the fact that Mrs. John Alden Carpenter, Ellen's mother, and Lady Spears, Ellen's aunt, publicly demonstrated their loyalty to Stevenson. . . .

He developed, at last, a kind of protective callus over those portions of his spirit where she had repeatedly hurt him, but he never ceased to care for her as a human being, nor to worry, helplessly, about what was happening to her. Particularly did he care what happened to her as it affected the boys; he was scrupulously careful to say and do nothing which would destroy their love and respect for her. He insisted, too, that they respect her, that they not neglect her. And close observers of him and his sons became convinced that his strategy in this respect was successful. He was, such observers agreed in later years, a remarkably successful father of three remarkably fine, strong sons. . . .

But in the immediate aftermath of the divorce he was convinced of his own failure. He worked incredibly hard for incredibly long hours all during the divorce period. He worked compulsively, as if afraid to stop—as if work were a pain-killing drug which, if it wore off, would leave him in unbearable agony.

One midnight Buffie went down to his basement office in the mansion to plead with him to go to bed. He'd been working into the morning hours every night that week; he'd collapse if he kept it up.

He looked at her through eyes that were dark with weariness and pain. He shook his head stubbornly, and made, unwittingly, one of his rare revelations of his hurt and of his excessively conscientious response to it.

"I've failed as a husband," he said. "I've failed as a father. I will succeed as governor!"

CHAPTER TWENTY-ONE

Governor Stevenson:

Personnel Recruitment and Administration

That good government requires good people in government had been a cardinal point of Stevenson's campaign. He had promised to improve the quality of the state's personnel. And on no phase of his administration did he spend more painstaking care than on the selection of personnel.

The problems the new governor faced, in this respect, were typical of American government. For the most part they stemmed from the fact that the salaries paid key officials were pitifully small when measured against the responsibilities those officials must shoulder. Consider his own salary, for example. He was paid twelve thousand dollars a year. In addition he received a house, a car and driver, and an expense allowance so modest that he had constantly to augment it from his own private income. Yet he was responsible for an enterprise directly employing some thirty thousand people and with a proposed budget, for the biennium beginning July 1, 1949, of some $1,055 millions. Moreover, his performance of his assigned duties, his efforts toward a genuinely creative administration were hampered at every turn by an archaic constitution, hostile political pressures, and public apathy. Much the same thing, if in different degree, was true of the key appointive officers.

It is a general rule of personnel management that if you pay less than the going wage you'll get, on the average, less than you pay for, whereas if you pay more, and can choose your employees from among many competing applicants, you're very likely to get more than you pay for. Failure to apply this general rule to public administration is by no means due wholly to popular ignorance. It is due also, and perhaps equally, to the fact that certain elements have a vested interest in corrupt, inefficient government. There are men who shout loudly for "economy" in government, bitterly opposing every effort to pay truly adequate government salaries, precisely because they profit personally from a system which virtually ensures mediocrity and venality among public servants. In few if any other states, historically, has such a system operated more effectively than in Illinois.

To fill his top appointive offices with first-rate men, therefore, required of Stevenson a great persuasive talent and administrative ingenuity. In nearly every case the man he wanted could accept appointment only at a considerable financial sacrifice—and he felt himself to be deeply indebted, in a personal way, for the sacrifices these others made. He sought to discharge this responsibility by making cash gifts at Christmas time to those whose services and sacrifices were greatest. For this he used some thousands which remained in his personal campaign treasury after (as a result of post-election fund raising) all his campaign debts had been paid. But most importantly he used a fund of ten thousand or so which had been made up, on their own initiative, by Dutch Smith and others of his well-to-do Chicago friends. ("He's down there fighting to give us decent government, using some of his own money to do it," said Dutch to his friends. "We have an obligation to help him out.")

The core of Stevenson's immediate staff—those personally associated with him in his daily work—was formed at the outset by people who had worked closely with him during the campaign. Carol Evans became the governor's personal secretary (she took the job on a six-month "trial" basis; nine years later she'd still be his secretary). Margaret Munn became her co-worker. James Mulroy, the campaign manager, became the governor's executive secretary, the only man close to Stevenson whose role might be compared to—though it was also very different from—that of Jim Farley in the early Roosevelt years; Mulroy it was who dealt directly with lawmakers and lobbyists in behind-the-scenes negotiations essential to the political process. Lou Kohn, taking leave of absence from his law firm, served as administrative assistant handling appointments for the first few months, returning then to his law practice.

To serve as administrative assistant in charge of patronage, he chose Lawrence E. Irvin, then thirty-eight, of Bloomington, a former Red Cross fieldworker and business manager of the Illinois State

Normal University. A plump-faced, smiling man, he was tactful, adroit, and firm; patronage problems became immediately less thorny as he handled them. William I. Flanagan, who had served as press-relations man during the campaign, became the governor's press secretary, with the high-sounding title of Superintendent of the Division of Department Reports.

The legislative assistant, a man of crucial importance to the administration, particularly in its first months, was Walter V. Schaefer, on leave from the Northwestern University Law School, where he was a professor. Stevenson had known him many years at the Bar in Chicago. He was a quiet, scholarly, yet eminently practical man of forty-one, chiefly responsible for translating the candidate's campaign promises into definite legal proposals for presentation to the legislature. After the first term of the legislature had ended, he returned to his Northwestern law professorship until, a vacancy occurring in the Supreme Court of Illinois, he was appointed to fill it by the governor. Subsequently Stevenson assured Schaefer's nomination and campaigned for his election to a full nine-year court term despite acute pressures for the selection of a "party faithful."

Carl McGowan assumed Schaefer's role on the staff, becoming the most important member of the governor's "inner circle" during the remainder of the term. McGowan, who had returned to Northwestern's law-school faculty after the war, was one of the first men Stevenson asked to come into the administration, but he had not felt free to do so until the school term ended in June of 1949. He then moved into a room in the mansion, living there until June of 1950 when his wife and family moved down into a rented house.

J. Edward Day, Stevenson's friend and associate in the Sidley firm, joined the initial group on March 3, 1949 (he'd always remember the date precisely). As administrative assistant, he worked closely with Schaefer, and later McGowan, on the legislative program; he also helped to choose personnel and acted as general adviser. Not the least of his contributions was the exercise of his talent for light verse, which not only brightened the lives of his associates but also made excellent "copy" for newspapers, helping to fill out the public picture of the Stevenson operation as a remarkably lighthearted and nimble-witted reform administration. In June of 1950 Day resigned as administrative assistant in order to accept Stevenson's appointment of him as Director of the Department of Insurance, succeeding Harry Hershey, a highly respected lawyer of Taylorville who had been Horner's choice for governor in 1940 and would soon become a member of the Illinois Supreme Court.

It was Day's resignation which led Stevenson, one early June morning, to place a call to William McC. Blair, Jr., in Chicago.

After his summer of work for the aid-Allies committee in Chicago, in 1940, Blair had returned to the University of Virginia Law School. Immediately after Pearl Harbor he enlisted in the Army and served as an intelligence officer in the China-Burma-India theater, head-quartered for a time in Calcutta and for a time in China. Released from the Army with the rank of captain (he'd be a major in the Reserves in the 1950s) in December 1945, he returned to the Virginia Law School, completed his work there, and was admitted to the Illinois Bar in the fall of 1948, entering one of the best of Chicago's law firms.

The law, however, bored him—not so much the actual law work as the "commuting rut" into which the law might put him. He had a horror of an increasingly dull and repetitious social life, a smothering of individuality in the homogenized culture of a fashionable subur-bia, a slow atrophy for lack of exercise of his capacity for excitement and innovation.

By March of 1950, thoroughly "fed up" with the life he was lead-ing, he resigned from his firm and went on an extended trip through Latin America. While in Mexico, he received a wire asking him if he would head up the Chicago office of the Hoover Commission. The job sounded interesting, having political overtones; he accepted it. He had been in the commission's Loop office precisely one hour and a half when the call from the governor came.

"I'm in need of an administrative assistant," Stevenson said. "If you're interested in the job, I'd appreciate your coming down this evening so that we can talk it over."

Blair did so and took the job, though he felt more than a little guilty about leaving the Hoover Commission in the lurch. A few days later he moved into the mansion and began a close working associa-tion with Stevenson which would last at least seven hectic years. . . .

Another who became a member of the immediate entourage, after the administration had run half its course, was Richard J. Nelson, a heavy-set man who, though only in his mid-thirties, had wavy gray hair. A stellar student of Schaefer's at the Northwestern University Law School, where he'd taken his degree in 1949, his interest in politics was matched by political talent; in June of 1950 he was elected president of the Young Democratic Clubs of America. As administrative assistant, Nelson often accompanied the governor on speaking trips, particularly those outside the state.

Yet another administrative assistant—the only one "inherited" from the preceding regime (a tribute to his abilities)—was T. Don Hyndman, who had served in the executive office since 1944 and was in his late thirties when Stevenson took office. A former newspaper-man, Hyndman's job under Green had been to write "nonpolitical" statements and proclamations, verbal productions which must be graceful, if possible substantial, yet politically innocuous. He continued in this role under Stevenson and served also, loyally and effectively, as general adviser.

II

Stevenson chose his cabinet slowly, carefully, presenting for Senate confirmation only six of thirteen code-department directors when he took office; the other seven were Green holdovers to be removed when and if he found better men to replace them. One of these, Dr. Roland R. Cross, had been director of the Department of Public Health since October 1940—a holdover from the Horner regime, whom Green had retained and whom Stevenson would retain throughout his administration.

Occasionally the new governor could obtain a good man with little effort. On the day after his election, he received some 250 telegrams urging him to appoint one Leonard Schwartz of Edwardsville to be director of the Department of Conservation. This aroused suspicions of a political "deal," but when Stevenson investigated he found that the wires came from sportsmen's clubs and that Schwartz was a nationally known writer for "outdoor" magazines, an organizer and former president of the Illinois Federation of Sportsmen's Clubs, and had helped to raise hundreds of quail and pheasant each year for Illinois hunters. The appointment was made and Schwartz did an excellent job.

Generally, however, appointment making was an arduous process during which the governor drew heavily upon the advice and good will of his long-time friends.

He was, for example, particularly anxious to obtain an outstanding man to serve as chairman of the Commerce Commission, which regulates public utilities and common carriers. No state agency is subject to greater pressure from "the interests" than this one, and none had fallen, deservedly, to a lower popular esteem during the Green administration. The first two men, approached by Stevenson, turned him down. Finally, just a few days before his inauguration, he took his problem to Laird Bell. Without real hope, he asked if Walter T. Fisher, a partner in the law firm of Bell, Boyd and Marshall, might be persuaded to take the job. He was surprised when Bell replied that Fisher just might be; but, he added, Fisher had no experience with public-utility regulation.

"That doesn't worry me because I know his intelligence, his industry, and his philosophy," Stevenson said.

"Well, he's a Republican," Bell said, smiling.

That made no difference either, Stevenson replied. He wanted outstanding men, regardless of party affiliation; besides, he well knew that Fisher's Republicanism was so "liberal" as to slide all the way over into political independence during election years.

The interview took place in a Loop hotel where Stevenson "hid out" some of the time between election and inaugural days.

At fifty-seven, Fisher was a tall, thin-faced, gray-haired man wearing rimless glasses through which clear gray eyes looked out with acute perception upon the world. His financial resources were such that he could afford the "luxury" of public service if he chose so to "indulge" himself. He had also a highly principled, philosophic mind, and it was stimulated by this interview to reflect long upon the psychology, the character of the man with whom he dealt.

Stevenson made his proposal and the two "kicked it around" for a while (the language was typical of Stevenson men). At one point Fisher said, "Ought I to do this, Adlai? Do you really think I should?" Stevenson's response took Fisher aback. "Well," said the governor-elect, "trade with me about it." From one point of view—the view Fisher initially held—this response was a kind of rebuff. Stevenson was refusing to join with Fisher in the making up of a mutual mind. He would not share in a joint decision. He remained isolate and kept Fisher isolated from him. But from another point of view—the view Fisher ultimately held—this was not a rebuff at all. On the contrary, it was an expression of respect for Fisher as an individual person who must make up his own mind, being responsible for his own character and acts. This was what human freedom meant. . . .

Fisher took the job. He was one of three commissioners appointed at that time, the other two being Democrats. Two Green appointees were held over, giving the commission temporarily a Republican majority, a fact much commented on by the press. As chairman, Fisher's salary was eight thousand dollars. "What a sacrifice you are making!" people said to him, intending praise. Fisher shook his head in reply, insisting that no sacrifice was involved. Some of his friends maintained yachts on Lake Michigan; these were expensive; yet no one regarded such expenses as "sacrifices." He, Fisher, chose to re-create himself through service on the Commerce Commission, a service which gave him compensations far more important to him, in his circumstances, than money could possibly be.

Another position for which the new governor was particularly anxious to find an outstanding man was that of director of the Public Welfare Department, by far the largest of all departments in Illinois government. He turned for advice to Dutch Smith, who was vice-president of the Community Fund of Chicago and a member of the executive committee of the Chicago Community Trust.

"The best possible man you could get," said Smith, "is Fred Hoehler."

Stevenson immediately agreed. Hoehler, a short, gray-haired man of fifty-five, was executive director of the Community Fund and had long been recognized as one of the outstanding professionals in his field. He was spectacularly well qualified for the state job.

There were, however, serious obstacles to his taking it. In the first place, his salary from the Community Fund was eighteen thousand dollars, whereas his salary as Illinois welfare director would be only eight thousand dollars. In the second place, Hoehler's health at that time was not good. It was largely for this second reason that he at first declined the offer Stevenson made to him. Both Stevenson and Smith continued to press him, however, until finally, one Sunday afternoon, he yielded to Stevenson's telephoned request that he at least agree to take the job for three months.

"That'll give me time to find a permanent director," Stevenson said.

But of course the governor made no effort to find another "permanent" director. Hoehler, as Stevenson had obviously expected, became so strongly committed to the state job that he stayed for the full term, writing during that period some of the brightest pages in the Stevenson gubernatorial record.

The Welfare Department, with a biennial budget of some $125,-000,000 and a payroll of nearly twelve thousand people, had in its jurisdiction children's hospitals, mental hospitals, correctional institutions, sanitoriums, schools for the deaf and blind—twenty-four institutions in all. These cared for some fifty thousand persons and had theretofore been staffed in many professional positions by political appointees. Hoehler changed this. He insisted that Public Welfare should be a career service staffed by professionals who were chosen and promoted on the basis of professional competence. Stevenson agreed and gave Hoehler full backing, despite loud protests by certain Democratic politicians who felt themselves to be robbed thereby of the fruits of party victory. These outcries were not lessened when Hoehler fired payroll parasites, eliminated what had been "standard" graft in the department's purchasing system, and canceled construction contracts where the costs were revealed, by investigation, to be from 5 to 10 per cent too high. He brought in out-of-state professionals to reorganize purchasing, rewrite specifications, and supervise the awarding of contracts.

Illinois's mental-health program was one of the worst among the forty-eight states when Stevenson took office. Within three years it had become very close to the best, enthusiastically praised by such world-famous psychiatrists as Dr. Karl Menninger of the Menninger Clinic, Topeka, Kansas. Hospitals which had been overcrowded and understaffed, often with incompetents, were expanded and staffed with first-rate people, their morale kept at a high level not only by Hoehler's inspired leadership but also by Stevenson's intense and knowledgeable interest in what they were doing.

In connection with the Peoria State Hospital, the first center devoted entirely to psychotic children in any state hospital in the country was opened in 1951. Basic research into the causes and treatment of mental illness was begun; a large research hospital was established for the study of geriatrics; research into special therapies for Mongoloid children and epileptics was conducted; and there was special research into the use of an ultrasonic-ray method of destroying brain tumors. A program for using special therapies on so-called "incurables" and senile patients was also begun.

When a Chicago civic organization awarded Governor Stevenson a citation for outstanding public service, it did so primarily because of his attraction of outstanding men into top state positions. Walter T. Fisher and Fred K. Hoehler were specifically mentioned. The citation would not have been awarded, however, if these two had been wholly unique among the Stevenson appointments. They were, on the contrary, typical of the high-caliber personnel he sought and often succeeded in obtaining—men like Henry F. Tenney, a civic-minded and wealthy lawyer (he was a friend and neighbor of Walter Fisher in Winnetka), whom he appointed to the Illinois Public Aid Commission, and women like Maude Meyers, an outstandingly capable career public servant whom he appointed to the Civil Service Commission.

His first Director of Revenue was Richard J. Daley, a former member of the legislature who was destined to become mayor of Chicago (with Stevenson's influential support) in 1955. Daley served as revenue director for some eighteen months and aided the new governor greatly, particularly with the legislative program, having "learned the ropes" thoroughly during his service in earlier sessions of the General Assembly.

George W. Mitchell became Stevenson's first director of finance, responsible for budget, purchasing, printing, and accounting controls. Mitchell, an officer of the Chicago Federal Reserve Bank, was a former president of the National Tax Association and had edited an eight-volume work on the organization and financing of local government. He did an outstanding job and Stevenson fought hard, though vainly, to keep him in the state government after his leave of absence from the bank was terminated. Mitchell, however, helped Stevenson to persuade Joseph Pois to come in as his successor. Pois, who had done consulting work on budgetary and taxation problems for the states of Michigan and Kentucky, was treasurer and member of the board of the Signode Steel Strapping Company of Chicago.

Closely allied with Pois in the elimination of graft and the increase of efficient and economical state operation was the state purchasing agent. The latter's job was one on which "money" politicians focused eager attention and which they would have been glad to help Stevenson fill. Instead, the governor turned for advice to acquaintances in the business world whose firms employed top-flight purchasing men. Among these, strangely enough, was General Robert E. Wood, chairman of the board of Sears, Roebuck and Company, who as head of the America First Committee had been bitterly opposed to Stevenson in the early 1940s. Wood told the governor that Sears' own purchasing agent, Carl Kresl, was retiring and might be persuaded to take the state job. Stevenson persuaded him.

Another state agency subject to great pressures and frequently corrupted by them in the past was the Parole and Pardon Board. He was able to obtain as chairman perhaps the best-qualified man in the country: Joseph D. Lohman, world-famous sociologist specializing in criminology.

The three-man Illinois State Liquor Commission, as Stevenson learned somewhat to his surprise, was yet another agency in which a certain kind of politician, and numerous other unsavory characters, took an inordinate interest. He discovered that there were abundant opportunities for commissioners to graft off the issuance or revocation of liquor licenses and that these opportunities had been abundantly realized in the past. Accordingly, he was determined to find a man whom he knew absolutely he could trust, and the man he ultimately found, W. Willard Wirtz, was to play a major role in the Stevenson story during the years ahead.

Then thirty-eight, Wirtz was a native of De Kalb, Illinois; a graduate of Beloit College in Beloit, Wisconsin; and had taken his law degree at Harvard Law School in 1937. At Harvard he had known J. Edward Day. From Harvard he had gone to the University of Iowa as a law-school faculty member (the dean there was Wiley Blount Rutledge, later an associate justice on the U. S. Supreme Court, whom Wirtz profoundly admired) and from Iowa he had come to Northwestern. At Northwestern, before the war, he had formed a close friendship with his law-faculty colleague, Carl McGowan, who became a neighbor of his in Winnetka. On leave from Northwestern during the war, he had been General Counsel of the Board of Economic Warfare in Washington. He had then served as Public Member of the Appeals Commission of the War Labor Board until it was replaced, after the surrender of Japan, by the National Wage Stabilization Board. On the latter he was chairman during its liquidation period, which lasted until January 1947. He had then returned to Northwestern, where he taught taxation, constitutional law, and trade regulation.

At a party in Wirtz's home one evening a few months after Stevenson took office, McGowan mentioned the difficulty of finding good men for state jobs. "Maybe that's because you don't ask," Wirtz said, half joking, yet serious, too, for he had long been interested in politics and was perhaps a trifle envious of the exciting experience his friend was having in Springfield. A week later Wirtz received a call in his law-school office from McGowan, who told him that the governor would like to see him at 160 North La Salle, the State

Office Building in Chicago. Wirtz went down and met Stevenson for the first time—this was in February of 1950—in a Finance Department office which the governor used as his Chicago headquarters until the penthouse atop the building was remodeled for his use. With no ado, Stevenson asked if Wirtz would accept appointment to a six-year term on the Liquor Commission.

"But I don't know anything about liquor control," Wirtz said.

"What we need, and find hard to get, is somebody who'll just keep his hands out of other people's pockets," Stevenson said, with a rueful grin. "That's the chief qualification."

Wirtz grinned, too. "If that's so," he said, "I'm not likely to deny that I'm qualified."

He took the job, and had barely returned to his office when his phone rang. It was Stevenson. The Liquor Commission was, by law, a bipartisan one, he said, and he had neglected to ask a key question: "Are you a Democrat?"

"Is it necessary that your appointee be a Democrat?" Wirtz asked. "It is."

"Then I'm a Democrat," Wirtz said. "As of now."

Other code-department heads were Roy E. Yung, Agriculture; Joseph K. McLaughlin, Aeronautics; Walter Eadie, Mines and Minerals; Michael F. Seyfrit, Public Safety; Charles P. Casey, Public Works and Buildings; Noble Puffer and C. Hobert Engle, successively heads of Registration and Education; and Frank Annunzio, Labor.

Even the lower echelons of the Labor Department profited from Stevenson's talent for personnel recruitment, a talent which was of a piece with his social charm.

At a party given by the head of the *Time* magazine bureau in Chicago, a year or so after the war, Stevenson had met for the first time Mrs. Stanley (Betty) Pargellis, wife of the librarian of Chicago's Newberry Library. In the course of their conversation he learned that Mrs. Pargellis, an active member of the League of Women Voters, was deeply interested in the women's and children's aspects of Illinois government labor policy. Then, and at a later date, the two held animated discussion of the Women's and Children's Division of the State Labor Department. Political appointments of women inspectors were being made—such appointments were among the few patronage spots for women—and Betty Pargellis was emphatic in her statements about the evils of this practice.

When Stevenson was elected governor he wrote to Betty Pargellis, among others, asking for personnel recommendations for the Labor Department, particularly of women. She recommended Miss Martha Ziegler, who'd been in such work in the federal government, to head up the Women's and Children's Division; she recommended Miss Florence Klever as Ziegler's second-in-command. Others confirmed these recommendations, and the appointments were made. The Ziegler-Klever team was a fortunate one for Illinois, despite the fact that much of its work, like much that Fred Hoehler's department did, was swiftly wiped out by the Republican administration which succeeded Stevenson's.

III

It was a concomitant of the kind of man he chose for government that Stevenson himself, as man and as administrator, should become the object of close study and penetrating observation by his associates.

Walter Fisher, for example, found the governor a fascinating human being. The Stevenson mind, from Fisher's point of view, was a lawyer's mind—and Fisher contrasted it with the businessman's mind or the mind of a general of armies.

A general or a business executive, facing the need for decision, consults his staff, who present him with "factors" to be "considered" in "solving a problem." These are presented and dealt with as though they were definite, static entities; and in business or military operations they often are relatively static, relatively definite. But sometimes—and almost always in politics—the "factors" are fluid and essentially indefinable: they flow into one another as processes instead of remaining distinct and separate things. In such cases the "problem" cannot really be "solved" in engineering terms, and when the chief executive of the military or business type says, "We'll do *this*" (he is likely to say it with a great show of force), the "decision" is an act of will rather than of intellect. Quite generally he has proceeded on hunch or impulse, his basic motivations remaining obscure to him. Of such a man it cannot be truly said that he has a decisive *mind*—though of course it often is said of him. He is more likely to have a vague, confused mind which has never really been made up, which shifts with shifting external pressures, and which has terrifying capacities for self-deception since its possessor has not heeded Socrates's urgent admonition to "Know Thyself."

Stevenson's lawyer mind proceeded very differently from this, in Fisher's view. Faced with the need for decision, Stevenson shaped a tentative hypothesis and then tested it against opposing arguments. To superficial observers, this might appear to be hesitation and vacillation, indicating an incapacity to decide. Fisher was convinced it was the precise opposite. People tend to confuse action with decision, whereas it is quite possible to act *without* deciding. Stevenson's acts (so Fisher concluded) were truly decisive, the proof of this being that they were "very firm"; they "stood up" against the pressures which were inevitably brought against them. In the Stevenson administration there was no backing and filling once a decision was made.

To all this, Jane Dick (Mrs. Edison Dick) added an observation with which Fisher thoroughly agreed. Mrs. Dick did not retire wholly to private life once the gubernatorial campaign was ended. She was persuaded to accept appointment as one of the five-man State Board of Public Welfare Commissioners, from which vantage point she (in her own words) "kept an eagle eye on the Stevenson administration for the next four years." It was her observation that Stevenson, as a part of the process of decision, always examined his own motives with scrupulous care and utter candor.

"He keeps asking himself, 'Why am I doing this?'" she said. "'Am I doing it because it's the right thing to do, or because it's the expedient thing?' He often acts on grounds of expediency, of course. Every politician has to. But when he does, he *knows* that he's doing it. He doesn't pretend to himself or anybody else that he's expressing in action some noble principle."

But perhaps Stevenson's working relationships with his immediate staff provided the deepest insights into his character as executive and human being. Significantly, the men closest to him were sharply distinguished from one another as personalities.

McGowan and Blair, for example, were actual contrasts in several respects. Blair disliked the law as a career; McGowan loved the law, was fascinated by its intricacies and challenged intellectually by its problems. Blair had a relaxed easy charm, the manners of a polished hedonist of the aristocracy, and a smiling warmth in his human relations. This caused people to like him at once, but it also caused many to underrate him as a mind and character: it was not until one knew him well, having observed him in action, that one realized the breadth as well as the acuteness of his intelligence and the seriousness of his purpose. McGowan, on the other hand, gave to many people an initial impression of rigidity and coldness. He seemed a stern Scotch-Presbyterian type—craggy, humorless, and intolerant of human frailties. Yet as one knew him better, this initial impression was modified by one's experience of the real human warmth of his nature, the concern he had for the welfare of those around him, so that this very "sternness" became an element of the attraction he had for people.

From all this it can be seen how each man might appeal strongly to Stevenson—though the appeal would be to different aspects of his nature. One can see how each could become an extension of Stevenson in action—though the extension would be of different elements of his character. In Blair, Stevenson might see the insouciant man about town, witty and debonair, whom he himself had once been and in some ways still was. Blair's pleasant affectation, like his own, was to take nothing very seriously, least of all himself, yet Blair's integrity and courage would stand any test and his capacity for hard work, like Stevenson's own, was almost unlimited when the objectives of work seemed worth while. In McGowan, Stevenson might see the Calvinist conscience which was his own inheritance from "Little Gabriel" and the Presbyterian divines of his ancestry. Indeed, close observers spoke of McGowan, in Springfield, as "Stevenson's conscience"—and Stevenson himself often said that McGowan and he "thought alike" and that never before had he met a man whose moral judgment so perfectly agreed with his own. Thus, in crude summary, one might regard McGowan and Blair as mirroring respectively the Puritan and the Cavalier in Adlai Stevenson, enabling him to realize and express his total self in the governor's office as he could not otherwise have done.

Blair became appointments secretary, personal facilitating officer, and the governor's most constant companion. He had always loved travel, and he was so relaxed on long trips, so eminently useful, that the governor seldom traveled without him. He knew how and when to keep silence. "I don't talk to him much, unless he wants to talk," Blair once explained, describing his "technique" of travel with Stevenson. "I don't even sit with him on a plane or train—unless he has some work to get done, as he often does, and wants me there as a kind of buffer. He needs privacy and solitude, he gets so little of it, and when he wants companionship, it does him good, refreshes him, to see new people."

As the months passed, Blair also became Stevenson's chief personal political agent and adviser, concentrating on the things Stevenson personally should do in order to advance his political fortunes. Yet this role was never specifically assigned to him. The fact is typical of Stevenson's relations with his immediate staff, and significant of his general administrative "style." Blair was required to assume his role, creating it in the process of assuming it—and it was never openly acknowledged by Stevenson himself. On the contrary, in later years Blair had often to proceed *despite* Stevenson, or even against the latter's stubborn resistance, in order to accomplish what he knew, deep down, to be his mission—the mission that Stevenson himself wanted Blair to perform.

Legendary among Stevenson associates would become Blair's bravery and skill as he entered what seemed to some a lion's den, there to persuade, and cajole, and often laugh the governor into doing something he'd flatly refused, at the outset, to do. At such times Blair was suave, even-tempered, firm, endlessly patient, quick to see openings through which he might thrust home his sword of persuasion; he was also adept at using Stevenson's own wants and commitments against him in a kind of mental and moral jujitsu. Politicians learned that it was often better—and perhaps generally so—to deal with Blair than with Stevenson directly on matters involving the governor's personal activity.

Typical was an episode which occurred some years later. Blair, having consulted with Stevenson (he never made such decisions without consulting him), committed the governor to a speech in Detroit, being persuaded by the Michigan Democracy, and by his own sense of values, that this was of importance to the welfare of Stevenson Democrats. Sometime later, when Blair was out of town, the Michigan people telephoned the Stevenson office, asking for Blair. The call was referred to the governor by a new employee who had not been warned of the governor's penchant for seizing such opportunities to get out of commitments, claiming afterward (to Blair) that he had "forgotten" he had agreed to them. On this occasion Stevenson told the Michigan people that his schedule was overcrowded (as indeed it always was) and that he just couldn't make the speech. That evening, walking along Jackson Street to his commuter's train, he told a friend of his "horrid afternoon"; the Michigan state Democratic chairman and the Michigan national committeeman had been on the phone with him for forty minutes.

"Forty minutes!" Stevenson said. "I timed them." He felt a little guilty about "pulling the rug out from under Bill," he went on. He was sure Bill had made the commitment in good faith and for what seemed to Bill good reasons.

"You're not going to do it, then?"

"I am not!" he said, with emphasis. . . .

A few weeks later he flew to Detroit and made the speech. Why, then, the initial resistance? Why his frequent reluctance to do things that he knew would serve his interests and were, indeed, necessary to the advancement of his political fortunes?

Such questions never ceased to intrigue, when they did not actively annoy, Stevenson's close working associates. Part of the answer doubtless lay, part of the time, in the surface irritability produced by the constant, galling pressures upon him. The more acute among his close observers were convinced, however, that the ultimate answer lay deep in Stevenson's character. Some wondered if the answer might not be related to the terrible accident of 1912, the accident in which the boy Adlai had been the inadvertent agent of Ruth Merwin's death. He seemed to punish himself. He seemed to feel that it was somehow *wrong* for him to succeed easily.

"He has to do it the hard way," one close observer said, "the hardest possible way."

If this were true—and it was a very tentative hypothesis—Bill Blair's role might come close, at times, to that of whipping boy. It would be up to him to help Stevenson, despite himself, toward success, and in the process to absolve the governor of the "guilt" of success. Stevenson himself, in later years, was inclined to assign to Bill Blair, in conversation, the responsibility for many of his self-promoting activities. "Bill made me go there," he would say. Or, "Bill says I have to do this." Of a quip of which he grew fond (and he grew inordinately fond of some of them), he would say wistfully that "Bill won't let me use it any more."

But it must not be assumed from this that he ever really regarded himself as, in any sense, Blair's puppet or any other man's, to be manipulated toward ends which he himself did not perceive. Certainly Blair himself never made that mistake. He neither manipulated nor was manipulated. There were occasions when Blair wholly failed to overcome an initial resistance, and if these failures were relatively few, it was only because Blair generally knew when this resistance was a false front, or an outer bastion which would not be strongly held. The inner citadel was impregnable, and he never knowingly attacked it.

If one assumes the validity of this tentative hypothesis, Carl McGowan's role in the Stevenson operation was less likely to go "unrewarded" in terms of an outward expression of gratitude than Blair's. As Stevenson's objectified "conscience"—as an extension of the Puritan in Stevenson's nature—McGowan could be assured of Stevenson's avowed appreciation of his services. Blair's might sometimes seem to Stevenson the voice of the tempter; his role might almost seem that of the devil's advocate. McGowan's voice and role would never seem so. When McGowan said, "there are things more important than winning an election, even an election to the Presidency of the United States," he expressed not only his own nature but also that which Stevenson regarded as highest and best in himself. His honest expression therefore (there was no doubt that McGowan meant what he said) could not fail to enhance Stevenson's respect for his subordinate's moral judgment and essential attitudes.

Moreover, Blair dealt with what Stevenson might regard as merely "formal" matters (at Springfield he was deemed the "handyman"), whereas McGowan certainly dealt with substantive matters. McGowan's work had to do directly with administration policy: he handled a great deal of Stevenson's official correspondence, he often served as Stevenson's alter ego in policy meetings or in the handling of administrative problems, he helped in the preparation of major speeches. He helped to prepare formal messages to the legislature, including the veto messages through which Stevenson's philosophy of law and government was revealed almost as completely as Justice Holmes's was in the famed dissenting opinions on the Supreme Court.

But if the roles of Blair and McGowan could be thus contrasted, they were in yet another respect essentially similar. By the time Blair came into the administration, McGowan had long assumed his particular role vis-à-vis Stevenson—and had created it in the process of assuming it—just as Blair found he had to do.

When McGowan first came to Springfield he took his problems into Stevenson's office somewhat as one might do who was assistant to an orthodox executive. But he discovered that Stevenson's tendency was to take over the problem in such cases. If, for example, McGowan brought in a letter concerning which he had some question, Stevenson was likely to keep it, saying, "I'll handle it." It quickly occurred to McGowan that he could hardly be of much help to Stevenson if this became a standard pattern of operation. He began to handle more and more matters "on his own," including matters of considerable importance but concerning which he was certain of Stevenson's position. As he did so he demonstrated a rare sagacity, both in his understanding of his chief and in his grasp of state problems.

"I tried to determine what I'd want as an assistant if I were in the governor's spot," McGowan explained, some years later. "I'd had an opportunity to observe how Stevenson worked for Knox during the war and it seemed to me that he'd now want me to work for him in the same way. It also seemed to me that, if I were Stevenson, I'd probably never spell out in any detail what I wanted from an administrative assistant. I'd probably not even know, in advance of problems, precisely what I wanted. But I'd certainly be grateful to my man if he handled things as much as possible on his own, and lightened my burden—even if he took risks, sometimes, and made mistakes. Stevenson had a crushing burden down there, you know. He worked terrifically hard for from ten to fifteen hours a day *every* day!"

Stevenson, McGowan added, was definitely a small-staff man. ("I do dislike having a lot of people bustling around me all the time," the governor himself said. "A measure of solitude and tranquillity is surely necessary to any man who would reflect upon his problems and solve them through concentrated thought.") He liked to handle things himself, being very much his own man and tacitly insisting that others be similarly self-possessed and "inner-directed."

IV

Though Stevenson professed to be an admirer of Governor Thomas E. Dewey's streamlined efficiency in New York (when a former top member of Dewey's administration visited Springfield, Stevenson questioned him at length about the manner in which Dewey organized his personal staff and worked with it), his imitations of Dewey's administrative methods, in so far as he made them, were too slight to be recognizable. He might be intellectually convinced of the value of a standardized "order" and "method" in the handling of his office's enormous work load, and that an efficiency expert could help him achieve it. But this intellectual conviction could make small headway against his deep, seemingly instinctive aversion to organization charts and the organization-chart mentality.

It was as if he felt, deep down, that there is a vital loss, unjustified by an increase of external efficiency, in any system which rigidly confines a man to a particular staff function, hedging him about with precise terms of reference (a detailed "job-description") and placing him as a static item in a chain of command. One can gain predictability of operation by doing so, he might have said, but by that same token one loses creativity. Moreover there is grave danger, he might have added, that decisive responsibility will be shifted from the individual person to the "system" if the latter becomes too slickly "efficient," with consequences destructive of human freedom and productive, over the long run, of disastrous errors. Politics, in his view, was an art rather than a science, and of politics his immediate staff operation was a part. . . .

The great defect of blurred delegations of authority, of course, is that they foment personnel discords. Status anxieties and power conflicts are likely to spring up as weeds on a ground uncultivated by a sharply defined authority. And to some extent this happened in the governor's office. "Adlai's a little like Roosevelt as an administrator," said one veteran of the Springfield days, years later. "If a man isn't working out quite right, Adlai'll often put another man in approximately the same spot without getting rid of the first one. That causes a lot of trouble, sometimes. And because his assignments of authority were so vague, there was a lot of jockeying for position in Springfield —people trying to get close to the throne." Stevenson very seldom used the governor's executive suite in the State House. He established his personal office in the basement of the Executive Mansion, and one result of this was a considerable jealousy between that portion of the immediate staff which worked in the State House office and that portion which was in daily contact with the governor in the mansion. . . .

Opinions varied as to Stevenson's own awareness of the anxieties and subtle conflicts which often swirled around him. Some people believed that status envy was so foreign to his nature, so alien to his personal experience, that he didn't recognize it for what it was when he encountered it; this meant that a "self-promoter" type might advance himself beyond his deserts or abilities. Others believed that Stevenson was perfectly cognizant of what went on around him, personnelwise, and that his seeming unawareness was, in part at least, a useful pose. "He believes in giving a man plenty of rope," one former associate said, contradicting the Springfield veteran quoted above, "but he knows damned well when that man has hanged himself, and he doesn't keep the dead body around the office too long." Yet others believed that Stevenson's whole administrative strategy was like Franklin Roosevelt's in more ways than one, having in it certain elements of craft and even of ruthlessness whereby his aides were tested and stimulated to do their best.

For if the defects of a loose organization with vague grants of authority are evident, the advantages of it are no less so to acute observers, provided that a proper care is exercised by the chief executive in the selection of his personnel. Certain it was that the conditions and general atmosphere of the Stevenson operation were fatal to mediocrity and vastly stimulating to many talents. Initiative, independence of judgment, imaginative thinking—these were prerequisites of success in that office. Every man was put on his mettle. And men like McGowan and Blair and Day, having created their private domains of order out of the initial chaos with which they were presented, became thorough masters of these domains, perfectly secure psychologically in their exercise of the authority which was theirs largely by right of creation.

"I was always sure of my own powers as the governor's counsel," McGowan later said. "I never worried about whether or not I had the authority to do this or that. I knew I had, and the responsibility too."

Such men became convinced that there was actually less backbiting, less soul-destroying anxiety, and a higher general morale in the Stevenson operation than in organizations more "efficiently" administered. They agreed, however, that this would not have been so had Stevenson not been the kind of man he was. His was a highly personal administration—his personality generated the climate in which work was done—and it could succeed only to the extent that Stevenson himself was profoundly respected as a mind, and much beloved as a person.

That he was beloved of his staff no man could doubt who talked to his staff members about him. "There is such *sweetness* in him," said one of these. "Oh, he's irascible at times. Who wouldn't be with the pressures he's constantly under? He says hurtful, cutting things at times to those who work intimately with him. But underneath, as a constant thing, there's the real sweetness of the man." Arthur Schlesinger, Jr., the historian, later regarded Stevenson as "approximately the most beguiling, seductive individual I've ever known." Yet another, who worked with the governor in Springfield, was convinced that Stevenson was as John Mason Brown once described him, "That rare, almost forgotten creature, a Christian gentleman."

Gaiety and wit, a youthful zest permeated by idealistic purpose, characterized the weekly staff meetings over which the governor presided. "Skull practice," these sessions were called, and they were swift and searching reviews of all manner of current state problems and of underlying policies. They were held with a rigid regularity, largely because Carl McGowan insisted upon it. "I knew that if I didn't insist, the governor, buried in work, would cancel them every so often," McGowan later explained. "Soon we'd be holding none at all—or holding them too infrequently." Regularly present, from the summer of 1950 on, were McGowan, Blair, Irvin, Day, Nelson, Flanagan, Hyndman, and Mulroy until his work relationship with Stevenson ended, as we shall see, tragically.

Something of the flavor of these sessions is revealed in a verse Ed Day read to one of the earliest of them. State Senator Roland Libonati of Chicago had introduced a bill which required that every room in every public building in the state be equipped with at least one cuspidor. On the floor the bill was amended, after solemn debate, to except public-school houses, and was then passed by the Senate. This provoked hilarity in Stevenson and his staff. Wrote Day:

> *A bill has passed the Senate*
> *About which some are skeptical:*
> *It would give a legal mandate*
> *To a rather crude receptacle.*
> *For those among the public*
> *Who may not approve of this,*
> *We point out that good government*
> *Should not be hit or miss.*
> *We recommend approval*
> *For Libonati's legislation;*
> *We feel sure it will live up*
> *To our best expectorations!*

On another occasion Johnson Kanady, the Chicago *Tribune's* Springfield correspondent, wrote in a typically snarling dispatch that "Stevenson's policy toward press conferences has always been to have aides carefully question newspapermen on what questions will be asked," and that this "accounts for his quick wit and ready answers." Howls of derisive glee were provoked by this among other Springfield correspondents as well as among Stevenson's staff. Ed Day's comment upon it was widely published. Wrote he: "This conjures up a rather improbable picture of the ebullient Stevenson occupying himself, amid mounds of paper work and lines of callers, in company with a group of 'aides,' drafting and redrafting impromptu bon mots to fit all possible questions at an approaching press conference."

CHAPTER TWENTY-TWO

Governor Stevenson:
His Legislative Record

Governor Stevenson presented to the Sixty-sixth General Assembly of Illinois the most extensive and ambitious legislative program that any governor of that state had ever tried to enact in a single session. Jack Arvey was convinced the program was too ambitious, and said publicly that the new governor, had he been more experienced, would not have attempted it. Stevenson himself was inclined to agree with this judgment, after the arduous session had ended. "But," he added, "I think campaign talk should be more than sweet, deceitful words. It's easy to talk big and act small when the responsibility suddenly falls on you like a ton of coal." Moreover, he was encouraged to believe that his proposals would be more likely to pass a Democratic House and a Republican Senate which were still enthralled by his tremendous electoral triumph.

In an unusually candid Report to the People, broadcast over forty-eight Illinois radio stations after the term's end, Stevenson pointed out that approximately two thirds of the legislation he had particularly recommended had been enacted. This legislation took the state highway police out of politics; upped state aid to schools from the $66 million for 1947–49 to $112 million for 1949–51 (he was forced to cut this by 10 per cent after the Senate blocked new revenue bills); increased unemploymnt compensation from a $20 to a $25 a week maximum, and extended eligibility to pregnant women, while reducing employers' contribution tax rates; improved mine safety equipment and took mine inspectors out of politics; increased from $50 to $65 a month the ceiling on pensions for the aged and the blind, with an escalator provision by which the ceiling went up or down in accordance with cost of living indices issued by the federal government; created a county superintendent of assessments for every county excepting Cook and St. Clair; and increased the salaries of all elective state officials, to be effective in 1953, and of all heads of departments and commissions, to become effective immediately. Simultaneously, he cut padded payrolls, greatly increased the efficiency of executive agencies, and effected economies in purchasing and the use of materials which would save millions of tax dollars during his term.

These were substantial victories for any new governor to achieve in his first General Assembly. They measured relatively small, however—in the public mind and for a time in Stevenson's own—against the defeat of proposals on which the governor had placed major emphasis. The three principal ones of these were (1) a referendum on calling a convention to revise the state's 1870 constitution; (2) a series of bills issuing from the Chicago Crime Commission and designed to speed and improve criminal justice; and (3) a bill to establish a Fair Employment Practices Commission to reduce job discrimination based on race, color, or creed.

The FEPC law, modeled on New York's, was introduced to both houses in mid-February of 1949. It was the first such administration-sponsored bill in Illinois history, and was strongly supported by ministers, the Illinois CIO, the Chicago Mayor's Commission on Human Relations, racial and religious minority organizations, and a few individual employers. It was fervently opposed by the Illinois Chamber of Commerce, the Illinois Manufacturers Association, the Illinois Small Business Men's Association, the Chicago Retail Merchants Association, and other employer groups as well as by leading newspapers, including the Bloomington *Pantagraph*, which asserted that the bill would prevent the hiring of people on the basis of ability and would subject employers to "nuisance lawsuits" for "shakedown purposes." A storm of controversy was aroused. A bulletin widely circulated by the Small Business Men's Association asserted that the bill was "class-legislation . . ." whose "motivating force" was "Communism."

Stevenson replied that the bill was in line with the Republican party's 1948 platform on civil rights and that in other states, like New York, New Jersey, and Connecticut, "which have adopted more stringent FEPC laws under Republican Governors, these laws have not caused any important difficulties for employers. . . ." In a radio Report to the People, he cited the argument that the answer to racial and religious discrimination is to be found, not in legislation, but in education. "There is," said he, "no conflict between legislation and education in our quest for economic justice."

The measure came to a vote in the House in mid-May, and passed by a margin of four votes. Sixty-eight Democrats and thirteen Republicans voted for it; three Democrats and forty Republicans voted against it; twenty-eight representatives didn't vote. The Senate vote was originally scheduled for June 15, but was postponed when Stevenson, having summoned Democratic leaders to his office, learned that he apparently had one less vote for his measure than was necessary for passage. That night he and his aides worked hard to gain votes. Next morning, after a bitter three-hour debate in which Republican leaders termed FEPC the "worst bill" in the session, one which "would put us back economically 25 years," the final vote was taken. With twenty-six votes needed for passage, the measure received twenty-three, with twenty-five votes against it and two senators not voting. Sixteen Democrats and seven Republicans voted for it, twenty-four Republicans and one Democrat voted against it. Stevenson, deploring the fact that Republicans in the "State of Lincoln" had defeated the measure, and this despite the 1948 national Republican platform, promptly pledged that the bill would be reintroduced to the next General Assembly. It was, but died in committee.

The resolution calling for a constitutional convention, which was immediately dubbed "Con-Con," was introduced to the legislature on February 2, 1949, after a night meeting of Democratic chieftains called by the governor at the Executive Mansion. It provided that the people be permitted to vote in the regular election of November 1950 on whether to call a convention in 1951 or later. Joined to it was a so-called "party-circle" bill, designed to ease the adoption of a new constitution. This called for a revision of the ballot law so that political parties, at their conventions, could endorse the calling of a constitutional convention, the endorsement then to appear at the top of the election ballot under the party's circle. A straight ticket vote in the circle, for all party nominees, would also be a vote for the calling of the convention. Split-ticket voters would be able to vote "yes" or "no" specifically on the constitutional question.

This was the number one item on the new governor's legislative program and the lines of battle over it were drawn even before the measure was introduced. In the vanguard of the supporting forces was the Illinois League of Women Voters, who had made an extensive study of the 1870 constitution and were convinced that it was, as Stevenson said, an almost insurmountable "roadblock to good government." Much more strongly organized was the opposition, consisting of powerful labor, farm, and manufacturing pressure groups, plus a bloc of downstate lawmakers who feared that convention delegates would approve legislative reapportionment on an actual population basis, giving Cook County control of the legislature. There were fears by businessmen that a new constitution might pave the way for a state income tax (none was permitted under the 1870 constitution), fears by some labor leaders that a new charter might wipe out labor's recent legislative gains, fears genuine or synthetic but loudly proclaimed that the bill of rights might be jeopardized, and protests that the proposed convention would cost from five to ten million dollars and would probably fail to produce an acceptable charter.

All these arguments were answered in extended public speech by administration supporters and by Stevenson himself, who pointed out that the risk of constitutional reform was the calculated risk of democracy, since democracy rests upon a faith in the people's judgment and capacity for self-government. A free society which refuses to take that risk, when changed circumstances demand it, is assured thereby of stagnation and ultimate death.

The measure came to a vote in the House on April 14. Two thirds of the House, or 102 votes, were required for passage, and Revenue Director Daley, who served as the governor's contact man with the legislature on this item, believed that he had them, though he knew that the predicted victory margin was paper thin. After a stormy seven-hour debate, during which two Democrats who had been brought from sickbeds were excused after being allowed to record "aye" votes, the roll-call ballot was taken on a resolution to approve the measure. This failed of passage by what would have been a five-vote margin had Democratic Speaker Powell stepped down from the rostrum to cast his favorable ballot. Ninety-six votes (76 Democrats, 20 Republicans) were cast for the resolution, 48 votes (46 Republicans and two Democrats) were cast against it. Only adroit floor management by Stevenson forces prevented a vote, then and there, to kill the measure completely. Thus the measure was kept alive for another attempt at passage.

Stevenson promptly announced that the attempt would soon be made, and he and his supporters began to exert all the pressure at their command upon the "doubtful" ones, offering, as a concession, to drop the "party-circle" proposal in return for Con-Con votes. As they did so, they themselves were offered a "deal" which would almost certainly have assured passage of the measure.

The two House Democrats voting against the measure were members of what was known as Chicago's West Side Bloc, whose other members included four Republicans. All came from the city's "tough wards" and they voted in concert against whatever anti-gambling and anti-racketeering bills were proposed. They now made it known to the governor that they would support Con-Con the next time around if the governor would withdraw his active support from the Crime Commission bills. There were five of these latter, introduced to both houses almost simultaneously with Con-Con in early February, and they were of course adamantly opposed by Chicago's politically organized hoodlums.

Dutch and Ellen Smith would never forget the effect this proffered deal had on their old friend Adlai. He visited them in Lake Forest, in their great house beside Lake Michigan, one bright spring day while the second vote on Con-Con and the vote on the crime bills were pending. He sat on the lake shore with the Smiths, looking far out across slate-green water on which the wind traced strange designs, and his face was so troubled that Ellen asked what the matter was. He was profoundly discouraged, he said. His legislative program was in serious trouble. He had been presented with an opportunity to put through an act of fundamental importance to Illinois's progress; he could have done it by scuttling an item of somewhat smaller importance. But if he chose the "lesser of two evils"—as it might appear to be—he gave a decisive power, in this one instance at least, into the hands of the worst political elements in the state. He had flatly refused to do so.

And then another deal had been offered him, he went on. A bill to permit dog racing in Illinois was before the General Assembly, and he had been assured of West Side Bloc support for Con-Con if he would merely promise not to veto this bill if it passed. Since its chance of passage through both houses was slight, he might argue that he could make the desired promise without seriously jeopardizing the general welfare; he might justify doing so on the ground that it was necessary to achieve the "greatest good for the greatest number." He had rejected the argument, however. He had refused the promise. Once again he had acted on principle, out of a conviction that ends and means, or effect and cause, are no more discontinuous in politics than they are in physics.

"But maybe I'm wrong in this approach to politics," he said. "Maybe it's impossible to accomplish anything at all if I keep on refusing deals like that."

Ellen and Dutch Smith merely looked at him, smiling sympathetically. He knew he wasn't wrong in his approach; they knew that he knew.

"Now I'll probably lose both the crime bills *and* Con-Con," he said. . . .

And as it turned out, he did lose them both. Con-Con came to its second vote on May 4 and received, this time, only 89 of the 102 votes needed for passage, despite the fact that Stevenson had ordered tabled the "party-circle" item in his bid for "doubtful" supporters. Seventy-three Democrats and 16 Republicans voted for the measure; 52 Republicans and the two West Side Bloc Democrats opposed it. As for the Crime Commission bills, they passed the Senate but were lost by a narrow margin in the House when they came to a vote in June.

A major factor reducing Con-Con support was a proposal by Republicans for a so-called "Gateway Amendment" to the constitution, as a substitute for the Stevenson measure. This would render more easy the amending of the 1870 constitution. It provided that an amendment could be adopted by two thirds of all those specifically voting on the question instead of by a majority (virtually impossible to obtain) of all those voting in a general election as had theretofore been required. There were reasons for believing that this Senate Republican proposal was cynically made. "They are attempting to nail down the lid on Con-Con!" cried Democratic Representative Paul H. Ferguson of Decatur. "They know that the Gateway Amendment proposal lost five times, but they are trying it again. Most of them don't even want constitutional reform." With this Stevenson agreed.

It occurred to him, however, that the Republicans had placed themselves on a rather small rug spread upon a very slick floor. The rug might be pulled out from under them. Moreover, by doing so, he might salvage something from what then appeared to him the crumbling ruin of his legislative program. Accordingly, as it became increasingly apparent that he hadn't enough votes for Con-Con, he prepared an alternative move, and immediately after the final Con-Con vote he issued a statement supporting the Gateway plan because, as he said, "we cannot wait forever for the most urgent constitutional reforms. . . . I doubt the sincerity of the 'Gateway proposal,' " he said, with a tinge of bitterness. "It looks like an effort to dodge responsibility for blocking much-needed changes." He doubted that the constitution could be effectively revised piecemeal. "But in spite of my misgivings, I feel it is better to have something than nothing," he went on. ". . . I will urge the Democratic party to join the Republican party in an all-out nonpartisan effort to secure ratification of the Gateway Amendment by the voters in 1950."

The Republicans, taken by surprise, were helpless to prevent what ultimately impressed itself upon the public mind as a Stevenson administration victory. Gateway passed the Senate almost unanimously. It passed the House by a vote of 138 to 2. It was presented to the voters on a separate blue ballot in 1950 (Stevenson supported the "blue-ballot" bill in the legislature) and was adopted.

Stevenson also had budget trouble with the Sixty-sixth General Assembly.

On April 10 he delivered his budget message, calling for the expenditure for the biennium of $1,273,400,000, the largest two-year budget in the state's history. For additional revenue he proposed the removal of the "service" exemption from the state's 2-per-cent sales tax, thus extending this tax to the building and construction industries and raising an additional twenty-five million dollars annually. He proposed that this money be used to aid cities, schools, and tuberculosis hospitals, providing needed relief from mounting local property taxes. Lobbyists of the affected industries reacted immediately, violently, effectively. The proposal was clearly in line with the legislative intent of those who first put through the sales tax in Illinois, and had been recommended by a Green-appointed tax-study commission of which seven Republicans still in the legislature were members. It was a disillusioning but educative experience for Stevenson when five of these seven actually voted against the Stevenson proposal—against, in other words, their own recommendation! The bill was defeated.

Small wonder that, a few weeks after the General Assembly session had ended, Stevenson told a cheering crowd at a Democratic rally that he "didn't know whether I love you so much after all. . . . But I guess," he added, "I'm like the everlasting optimist who fell off the skyscraper. As he passed the twentieth floor the horrified spectators in windows heard him shout, 'So far, so good!'" By that time, however, he had had time to assess profit and loss from his dealings with the legislature, and found reason to believe that what in late June had seemed the total ruin of his legislative program contained, after all, a number of new and solid structures. More importantly, he seemed to have retained if not enhanced his prestige with the general public, a fact which should produce Democratic gains in the election of 1950 and smooth the path toward his goals in the second session, especially so since he had learned a great deal about what to do and what not to do in his handling of legislators and of legislation.

II

Paradoxically it was during the crucial month of June, when he himself was somewhat discouraged, that his hold on public respect and affection became strongest. Courage, in the famous Hemingway definition, is "grace under pressure," and it was this kind of courage which Stevenson seemed to personify, in the public view, during weeks when every possible provocation toward partisan bitterness and personal animosity was given him. He fought hard for his program, but always in terms of principle, never in terms of personalities. He blasted "fiscal irresponsibility," not the Republican Senate leader, Wallace Thompson, who seemed bent on practicing it in government. He did not wash his hands of all responsibility for his defeats, as Mayor Kennelly seemed inclined to do; he gave no hint that he regarded Illinois politics too hopelessly "dirty" for him to engage in; he refused every temptation to slam the door on possible future co-operation with the men who now baited and frustrated him. Instead, "I blame myself," he said, for naïvely believing that Republican senators would practice what they preached. "I thought they really believed in conservative financial management," he told the people in a radio report, and he was grateful that "some of the Republican senators would not follow their leaders" in attempts to discredit him at the expense of the state's welfare.

"I think you people want legislators who do not put some small party advantage, real or fancied, over courage, intellectual integrity, and public responsibility," he asserted. ". . . I don't think most people even care much about party labels any more. What they want is honest, sincere, courageous performance. And what's more, I think the sooner politicians realized that that's the best politics the better it will be for them and for the people."

A few days before the General Assembly's end, he issued a statement in which he condemned Republican senators for approving sixty-five million dollars' worth of expenditures for which no budget provision had been made. Of this total, fifteen million was for township roads and fifty million for a city-aid program that conflicted with the one the governor had backed.

"The people will not be misled by false generosity," he declared. "If the appropriations voted exceed the revenue provided, I will be obliged to make reductions, by amendment or veto, in the aid programs I have recommended for education, health, and local governments. If these programs go out, local tax rates must go up or adequate local services won't be provided."

The Republican Senate (the Republicans had a 32 to 18 edge there) chose to regard this as a direct challenge. Its response was perfectly in line with its earlier actions. Customarily the Illinois General Assembly ends its session on June 30—and since it passes most of its bills during the session's last days, the governor can exercise his veto without fear that his action will be overridden. But if the governor was determined to use his veto to balance the budget, the Republicans were determined to unbalance that budget again, if possible, by overthrowing his vetoes; at the very least, impassioned appeals for worthy programs would embarrass an executive who struck those programs from the list of enactments on the ground that no money was available for them. The Republicans could do this, however, only if the legislature remained in session. Accordingly, on the night of June 30, when the legislature ordinarily adjourned *sine die* (that is, without date), the Senate voted to adjourn until July 18. Simultaneously the Democratic House voted to adjourn as usual, *sine die*. The official clocks had been stopped at midnight to permit the General Assembly to work into the morning of July 1.

The governor spent that night in his office on the second floor of the State House. Microphones in the two legislative chambers on the third floor picked up the floor action which blared through special loudspeakers mounted on the governor's office walls. When it became evident that the two houses disagreed on when to adjourn, a faint memory was stirred in Stevenson's mind. Way back in 1863, Illinois's Civil War governor, Richard Yates, had had to deal with a legislature torn by bitter party wrangles. Then, as now, the two houses had disagreed about adjournment. Yates had finally prorogued the legislature—that is, he had ended the session by executive order. The term "prorogue" and the device it named was an ancient one, referring originally to the ending of a session of Parliament by order of the Crown.

"Doesn't a governor still have that power?" Stevenson asked Walter Schaefer, who kept the nightlong vigil beside him.

"I was thinking precisely the same thing," said Schaefer. "I'm sure you *do* have the power. But let's see."

In a copy of the 1870 constitution he found what he wanted. He read aloud Article 5, Section 9: it said in effect that when the two houses cannot agree on when to quit, the governor can adjourn the Assembly until "such time as he thinks proper."

"It's a complicated procedure, though," Schaefer said. "We'd have to time everything perfectly, and it'd never work if the Republicans got wind of it."

"Let's do it," Stevenson said.

Schaefer, Day, Mulroy, and other Stevenson aides hurried back and forth between the executive office and the legislative halls, explaining the strategy to floor leaders and directing tactical moves. At five o'clock in the morning Stevenson gave the signal. A few minutes later, when only ten minor bills were left on its calendar, the House was suddenly presented with a resolution saying there was disagreement between it and the Senate regarding adjournment. The resolution was promptly passed by voice vote. Then Walter Schaefer handed Speaker Paul Powell a proclamation from the governor. Powell ordered the clerk to read it. At 5:30 A.M. Powell brought his gavel down.

Lieutenant Governor Sherwood Dixon, presiding officer of the Senate, and Senator Wallace Thompson, Republican Senate majority leader, were both in the House chamber as the clerk began reading. The two raced one another to the Senate chamber, Dixon carrying the governor's proroguing proclamation in his hand. Just as Dixon mounted to the presiding officer's chair, to take over, Thompson managed to get the floor from which he moved, breathlessly, that the Senate adjourn until ten o'clock Friday morning. If passed, this motion would render ineffective the governor's order, since the Senate would not be in session to receive it—and it is of course a basic rule of parliamentary procedure, incorporated in the Illinois Senate rules of order, that a motion to adjourn is not debatable and may not be tabled. Nevertheless Dixon promptly recognized Democratic Senator Kent Lewis who moved to table the Thompson motion. Angrily Thompson shouted his protests. Lewis shouted back.

And while this shouting was going on Dixon read the governor's order, from which no appeal was possible, and brought his gavel down. At five thirty-two in the morning of July 1, 1949, the Sixty-sixth General Assembly was ended. Thompson, white-faced with anger, was still shouting. . . .

III

A special session of the General Assembly was called by Governor Stevenson in the summer of 1950, chiefly to pass a rent-control bill made necessary by the Korean War, but also to provide more state aid for Chicago, which was in grave financial difficulties. The latter was wrecked against Republican opposition.

That autumn it appeared that the governor had lost every chance to put his program through the second of his regular General Assembly sessions, for in the November elections, contrary to his expectations in the summer of '49, the Republicans won control of the House, 84 to 69, while retaining control of the Senate, 31 to 20. Two factors influenced this result, neither of them under Stevenson's control. One was the entrance of the Chinese Communists into the war between North and South Korea, requiring the drafting of American youths into the armed services. The other was a widely publicized investigation of crime in politics conducted by a Senate committee headed by Estes Kefauver, Democrat of Tennessee. Both increased the Republican vote.

However, Stevenson had a greater success with this Republican-controlled legislature than he had had with the divided one of 1949. No doubt one cause of this was that one-party control meant one-party responsibility, with the result that Republican lawmakers became somewhat more concerned with the general welfare and somewhat less susceptible to petty partisanship. This cause would not have been as effective as it was, however, if Stevenson had not made it so through his own operation. His handling of the Sixty-seventh General Assembly was masterful, with the result that, at the session's end, he signed into law several bills he had vainly struggled to push through in 1949.

How did he do it?

His general method can perhaps be best defined by contrasting it with the method President Truman employed during those years. Truman's relations with the Republican Eightieth Congress had been of war, with no quarter asked or given. In the campaign of 1948 he attacked this Congress as the "worst" in history and castigated individual members of it unmercifully. When he won his amazing victory that year, he was confirmed in his belief that his brand of "give 'em hell" campaigning was the best if not the only kind for a Democrat to conduct and that the language of coercion was the proper executive language for communications with a recalcitrant legislature. Stevenson, campaigning for a Democratic legislature in 1950, hurled no charge of "worst" against the Republican Senate of the Sixty-sixth General Assembly; never did he attack his opponents by name; so that when his bid failed (and he was convinced it failed despite rather than because of his campaign style) he was not required to pay a ruinous forfeit to the victors. He had been reasonable and conciliatory. Before the Bar of public opinion, therefore, he could plead convincingly for reasonableness and a conciliatory attitude on the part of his opponents.

His general method, in other words, was that of nonviolence—and frequent result, in power-political situations, was the overthrow of his opponent from within, through a kind of moral subversion. The opponent's conscience was likely to become a Fifth Column which fought on Stevenson's side. Not that he depended wholly on moral suasion. He learned to employ with skill the traditional devices of political reward and punishment: the smile which prospers another's career, the frown by which that career is blighted, the patronage which can strengthen or weaken a legislator's hold upon his constituency. But in general he conceived his executive function to be the encouragement and facilitation of that desire for goodness and honor which he believed to be embedded in all men. The path of honor might never be as delightful to the senses as the primrose path, but there was no moral reason, in Stevenson's view, why it should not be made as smooth and easy to follow as possible.

Doing so required of him a quantity and quality of hard work which amazed his closest observers. He seemed determined to master every detail of the state's business, a task analogous to Thor's effort to drink up the sea and one whose hopelessness aroused protests from his associates. Once an aide found Stevenson at his desk late at night, engaged in a close study of the specifications for pipe insulation in a state hospital.

"Why do that?" the aide asked. "You don't know anything about insulation."

"That's why," the governor replied.

Always his presentations to the legislature were thoughtful, knowledgeable, and clear. Being armed himself, he armed his legislative leaders with such a wealth of factual argument that the artful dodgers of special interest had difficulty overcoming them. Moreover, through his press conferences and regularly scheduled reports over the radio, and through public speech in which he communicated to all kinds of audiences his passionate concern for good government, he mobilized public opinion behind his proposals in such a way that many legislators who could not otherwise have gone along with him without risking their next election were enabled to do so. Finally, he displayed as he had done in London an unsurpassed talent for face-to-face negotiation. By exercise of that talent he not only persuaded others toward the goals he defined but also committed them to him personally.

"Stevenson has a knack for making you *want* to help him," one legislator said.

All this—his careful preparation, his mobilizing of public opinion, his negotiating genius—was effectively employed in his handling of highway legislation during the second of his regular legislative sessions. In the early 1920s, if at a cost excessive to taxpayers under the Republican regime of the execrable Governor Len Small, Illinois had built one of the first and best state-highway systems. During the 1940s this system had been required to bear unprecedented burdens with inadequate maintenance. The result was that by 1948, like the Wonderful One-Hoss Shay, the highways began to fall apart all at once. Stevenson therefore proposed a ten-year building program to be financed (as he had proposed in '49, and proposed again in '51) by increasing the gasoline tax from three to five cents a gallon and increasing the license fee for trucks. Trucks were to be taxed on a ton-mile basis, so that heavy vehicles paid their fair share of the highway cost instead of shifting much of their proper burden to passenger cars doing relatively little damage to roads.

Inevitably, well-heeled lobbyists descended in droves upon Springfield to prevent both the gas tax and truck-license fee increase. They found their activities greatly hampered by the campaign of popular education on the "highway crisis" which the governor had conducted. Important segments of every legislator's constituency vehemently supported the governor's program. Newspaper support was almost unanimous—which meant that the lobbyists must pursue their ends in an unaccustomed and decidedly inhibiting glare of publicity. Their only hope was to create disputes among legislators as to how the increased revenue was to be distributed, playing off Chicago (whose motor clubs wanted arterial highways) against downstate residents (who wanted township roads), and special interest against special interest, in such a way that a hopeless deadlock resulted.

This strategy came very close to success. It would certainly have succeeded if Stevenson had not called the leaders of the contending groups to the Executive Mansion for a well-publicized night meeting in late June and exercised there his talent for negotiation. He proposed compromise solutions. When the meeting broke up at three o'clock in the morning, solid agreements had been made. Next day the necessary amendments of the bills were introduced. The amended bills passed.

After the 1949 General Assembly, Stevenson had established a Commission to Study State Government with Walter Schaefer as chairman. In the 1951 Assembly session 166 bills were introduced to carry out proposals of this commission, and of these 78 were passed in addition to approximately a dozen other bills growing out of the commission's findings.

He suffered defeats, too, of course. His FEPC law, as has been said, was rejected. So were several bills designed to improve law enforcement. When the Congress passed a law forbidding the shipment of slot machines in interstate commerce, Stevenson proposed a law prohibiting their manufacture in Illinois where, as a matter of fact, practically all slot machines were made. The legislature said no. He also proposed to strengthen the powers of the Liquor Control Commission, to halt gambling wherever liquor was sold. Again the legislature said no.

But in general his legislative leadership scored successes, and while doing so the executive branch continued to make a remarkable record of economy. It was remarkable in that the economy was achieved, not by reducing needed services, but by increasing administrative efficiency and eliminating waste.

IV

For weeks following the end of each General Assembly, Stevenson with his legal aides (Schaefer and Day in 1949, McGowan, Blair, and others in 1950) worked late every night over the more than eight hundred bills which were deposited by departing legislators on the governor's desk. Approximately 10 per cent of them were vetoed, and perhaps 2 per cent more were permitted to become law without the governor's signature.

The veto messages were carefully prepared. They revealed not only Stevenson's principles of government but also salient features of his character, notably his humor, his profound respect for the English language, and his equally profound contempt for all efforts to intimidate him. Some of them became famous.

Widely reprinted, for example, was his veto of a bill promoted by Illinois bird lovers and passed by both houses in 1949:

I herewith return, without my approval, Senate Bill No. 93 entitled, "An Act to Provide Protection to Insectivorous Birds by Restraining Cats." This is the so-called "Cat Bill." I veto and withhold my approval from this bill for the following reasons:

. . . I cannot agree that it should be the declared public policy of Illinois that a cat visiting a neighbor's yard or crossing the highway is a public nuisance. It is in the nature of cats to do a certain amount of unescorted roaming. Many live with their owners in apartments or other restricted premises, and I doubt if we want to make their every brief foray an opportunity for a small game hunt by zealous citizens—with traps or otherwise. I am afraid this bill could only create discord, recrimination and enmity. Also consider the owner's dilemma: to escort a cat abroad on a leash is against the nature of the cat, and to permit it to venture forth for exercise unattended into a night of new dangers is against the nature of the owner. Moreover, cats perform useful service, particularly in rural areas, in combatting rodents—work they necessarily perform alone and without regard for property lines.

. . . The problem of cat versus bird is as old as time. If we attempt to resolve it by legislation, who knows but what we may be called upon to take sides as well in the age-old problems of dog versus cat, bird versus bird, even bird versus worm? In my opinion, the State

of Illinois and its local governing bodies already have enough to do without trying to control feline delinquency.

Stevenson's conception of "free enterprise" and his commitment to logical consistency were both exemplified in his veto of the so-called "Sunday Car Bill," sponsored by a great majority of Illinois's used-car dealers who wished to restrain a minority from staying open on Sundays and thereby forcing all to stay open. The bill would have made it a criminal offense for any person to sell a motor vehicle on Sunday. Having cited an opinion of the attorney general that the bill was unconstitutional, Stevenson's veto message went on to say:

> *I cannot forbear to add that this is one case in which the constitutional objection and sound public policy clearly coincide. . . . If such a restriction on Sunday trade is sound for automobiles, why should it not be extended to newspapers, groceries, ice cream cones and other harmless commercial transactions? Carried to its logical extreme, any business group with sufficient influence on the legislature can dictate the hours of business of its competitors. And if hours, why not prices?*
>
> *Under our free enterprise system government should not interfere by regulatory or prohibitory laws in the business field except (1) where the activity in question is directly related to the public health, safety, morals, or welfare of (2) to enforce competition. Traffic in automobiles does not qualify under the one, and, so far as the latter is concerned, its only purpose and effect are to restrain competition.*

Also vetoed, on the grounds that government should be as local in character as possible, was a bill for state regulation of trailer camps. The veto message recognized that trailer camps had created a genuine public-health problem requiring public regulation but condemned the bill as "another example of the constant migration of local responsibility to higher levels of government."

But by far the most important of his vetoes, and the one most widely and heatedly discussed, was his veto of the final Broyles Bill. The bill had a lengthy title:

> *An Act to protect against subversive activities by making it a crime to commit or advocate acts intended to effect the overthrow of the Government of the United States or the State of Illinois or of any political subdivision thereof by violence or other unlawful means,*

or to attempt or conspire so to do, by defining subversive organiza-
tions and making them illegal, by establishing procedures to insure
the loyalty of candidates for public office and of public officers and
employees, and providing for the enforcement of the provisions of
said Act, and providing penalties for the violation thereof.

It was, of course, fervently promoted by its author, Republican Senator Paul Broyles, by the Illinois Department of the American Legion,
and by such champions of reaction as the Chicago *Tribune* and
Herald-American. It was inadvertently promoted—or so one assumes
—by the tactics and testimony of one Claude Lightfoot, the top Illinois Communist, who opposed the bill with such violence that he
had to be removed from a committee room by the sergeant at arms.
It passed the Senate by a vote of 35 to 15 and the House by 87 to 15.

Said Stevenson, in his veto message:

That the Communist party—and all it stands for—is a danger to
our Republic, as real as it is sinister, is clear to all who have the
slightest understanding of our democracy. No one attached to the
principles of our society will debate this premise or quarrel with
the objectives of this bill.

Agreed upon ends, our concern is with means. It is in the choice
of methods to deal with recognized problems that we Americans, in
and out of public life, so often develop differences of opinion. Our
freedom to do so is a great source of strength and, if not impaired
by mistakes of our own, will contribute greatly to the ultimate con-
fusion of the enemies of freedom.

The issue with respect to means raised by this bill has two aspects.
One is the question of the need for it in relation to existing weapons
for the control of subversives. The other is whether this addition to
our arsenal may not be a two-edged sword, more dangerous to our-
selves than to our foes.

He then reviewed existing legislation, federal and state, dealing
with treason and subversion, in support of his contention that no new
legislation in the field was needed and would, indeed, do harm by
increasing the already great legal confusion.

"But it is in the enforcement provisions that I find this bill most
objectionable," he said. These provisions required the state attorney
general to appoint a special assistant attorney general "who must

assemble and deliver to the State's Attorney of each county all information relating to subversive acts within such county." The local state's attorney was then required to present this matter to the Grand Jury. The assistant attorney general in Springfield was to maintain complete records of such information which might, with the permission of the attorney general, be made public. "I know of no precedent for any such interference with the normal discretion accorded to a public prosecutor," said Stevenson, and ". . . I can see nothing but grave peril to the reputations of innocent people in this perpetuation of rumors and hearsay." He also objected to provisions "intended to assure the loyalty of the employees of the State government and its political subdivisions" by requiring special loyalty oaths and ordering all governmental agencies to "establish procedures to ascertain that there are no reasonable grounds to believe that any applicant for employment is committed, by act or teaching, to the overthrow of the government by force or is a member of an organization dedicated to that purpose." Thus both applicants for employment and those already employed would be required to prove their loyalty—a radical departure from the basic principle of Anglo-Saxon justice whereby the burden or proof rests on the accuser rather than on the accused.

By such provisions as these, irreparable injury to the reputation of innocent persons is more than a possibility, it is a likelihood. If this bill becomes law, it would be only human for employees to play safe and shirk duties which might bring upon them resentment or criticism. Public service requires independent and courageous action on matters which affect countless private interests. We cannot afford to make public employees vulnerable to malicious charges of disloyalty. . . .

Does anyone seriously think that a real traitor will hesitate to sign a loyalty oath? Of course not. Really dangerous subversives and saboteurs will be caught by careful, constant, professional investigation, not by pieces of paper.

. . . I know full well that this veto will be distorted and misunderstood, even as telling the truth of what I knew about the reputation of Alger Hiss was distorted and misunderstood. . . . But I must, in good conscience, protest against any unnecessary suppression of our ancient rights as free men. . . . [We] will win the contest of ideas . . . not by suppressing those rights, but by their triumph.

v

The deposition regarding Alger Hiss's reputation to which Stevenson referred had been taken in May of 1949. It would be repeatedly used, and had already been used, to convey the impression that Stevenson was "soft" on communism in government, that he had joined in an attempt to "whitewash" Alger Hiss, and that at the very least he was, as Republican Senator Richard Nixon of California would say over and over again, guilty of "poor judgment"—so guilty, indeed, as to cast serious doubt upon his capacity to exercise governing power.

It will be recalled that Stevenson first met Hiss in 1933 when both men were members of the AAA's legal division. Both had worked on marketing agreements, but since they dealt with different agricultural commodities their association was not close. From then on until 1945, when Stevenson became Archibald MacLeish's assistant in Washington, the two men did not meet at all. In the spring of the latter year they met occasionally at intradepartmental meetings in Washington. They met again a few weeks later in San Francisco, where Hiss was secretary-general of the United Nations Conference and Stevenson was attached to the United States delegation. The two had no working contacts there but met now and then at official social functions. In July 1945 in Washington, Stevenson had conferences with Hiss regarding preparations for the presentation of the United Nations Charter to the Senate for ratification. The two did not then meet again until January 1946 in London, during the First General Assembly of the United Nations. There they met frequently at staff conferences and delegation meetings. Again in 1947, during the United Nations General Assembly in New York, they met to discuss the budget of the United Nations.

By then Alger Hiss was president of the Board of Trustees of the Carnegie Endowment for International Peace. He had been elected in December 1946 by a board whose members included John Foster Dulles. A few days later Dulles had been warned by a Detroit lawyer that Hiss had a "provable" Communist record. Said Dulles, in a reply dated December 26: "I have heard the report which you refer to, but I have confidence that there is no reason to doubt Mr. Hiss's complete loyalty to our American institutions. I have been thrown into intimate contact with him at San Francisco, London and Washington. . . . Under these circumstances I feel a little skeptical about information which seems inconsistent with all I personally know and what is the judgment of reliable friends and associates in Washington."

In December of 1948 Whittaker Chambers, a senior editor of *Time* magazine, testified as an admitted former Soviet agent before the House Un-American Affairs Committee. He asserted that in the 1930s he had worked with Alger Hiss, who, he said, was also a Communist party member at the time and had passed to him forty-odd confidential State Department documents for transmittal to a Soviet secret agent. One day that month Chambers led agents of the investigating committee to a hollowed-out pumpkin on his Maryland farm, where some of the documents allegedly passed by Hiss were found. Two weeks later Hiss was indicted by the Federal Grand Jury in New York on two counts of perjury, he having denied Chambers' charges under oath.

On May 24, 1949, the U. S. District Court in New York—the court before which Hiss was to be tried in June—directed the U.S. commissioner in Springfield to put certain questions to Stevenson on behalf of the Hiss defense, and certain cross-questions on behalf of the prosecution. This order was issued upon motion of Hiss's attorneys, who had, of course, ascertained in advance that Stevenson would make replies which did not damage their client. Hiss's attorneys had asked the governor to come to New York but he had declined, pleading press of duties. On June 2, Stevenson's deposition was taken at the mansion. (On that same day, at the Hiss trial in New York, Chambers admitted that he had committed perjury when, though then a Communist, he had taken an oath to defend the Constitution of the United States while accepting a federal job in 1937.) In response to the questions, Stevenson reviewed his past relationships with Hiss. The key testimony follows:

Q. No. 7. Have you known other persons who have known Mr. Alger Hiss?

A. No. 7. Yes.

Q. No. 8. From the speech of those persons, can you state what the reputation of Alger Hiss is for integrity, loyalty and veracity?

A. No. 8. Yes.

> *Q. No. 9 (a) Specify whether his reputation for integrity is good or bad?*
> A. No. 9 (a) Good.
> *Q. No. 9 (b) Specify whether his reputation for loyalty is good or bad?*
> A. No. 9 (b) Good.
> *Q. No. 9 (c) Specify whether his reputation for veracity is good or bad?*
> A. No. 9 (c) Good.

In the cross interrogation in behalf of the United States of America, "complainant in said cause," the following testimony was taken:

> *Q. No. 1. Were you ever a guest in the home of defendant Alger Hiss at any time in 1935, to and including 1938?*
> A. No. 1. No, I have never been a guest in Mr. Hiss's home.
> *Q. No. 3. Did you, prior to 1948, hear that the defendant Alger Hiss during the years 1937 and 1938 removed confidential and secret documents from the State Department and made such documents available to persons not authorized to see or receive them?*
> A. No. 3. No.
> *Q. No. 4. Did you, prior to 1948, hear reports that the defendant Alger Hiss was a Communist?*
> A. No. 4. No.

In 1950, after Hiss had been convicted of perjury in his second trial (the first ended with a hung jury), Everett Dirksen, the Republican candidate for U.S. senator from Illinois, repeatedly attacked Stevenson for having given this deposition.

"What would Dirksen have said?" asked Stevenson. "Would he have told a lie?" The Chicago *Tribune* then editorialized that Stevenson could have avoided giving the testimony, that by giving it he had "arrayed himself willingly beside Alger Hiss." To this Stevenson made no reply at the time. But on March 30, 1952, he would be interviewed on a nationally broadcast radio and television show, "Meet the Press," and would be asked about his Hiss testimony. He would tell, factually, how he had come to give it, then add: "And I would say this—I am a lawyer, and I think it is the duty of all citizens and particularly of lawyers, it is the most fundamental responsibility of lawyers, to give testimony in a court of law, honestly and willingly. And I think it will be a very unhappy day for Anglo-

Saxon justice when a man in public life is too timid to state what he knows or has heard about a defendant in a criminal case for fear that defendant would be ultimately convicted. That is the ultimate timidity."

On October 23, 1952, in a campaign speech in Cleveland, Ohio, Stevenson would reply directly to Senator Nixon's charge that he had exercised bad judgment in making the deposition. " 'Thou shalt not bear false witness,' is one of the Ten Commandments, in case Senator Nixon has not read them lately," Stevenson would say. "And if *he* would not tell and honestly tell what he knew of a defendant's reputation, he would be a coward and unfit for any office." Stevenson would also point out that General Eisenhower was elected to the Board of Trustees of the Carnegie Endowment at the same meeting at which Hiss was re-elected president and Dulles chairman of the board.

"After he had been indicted by the Grand Jury, Hiss tendered his resignation as president and trustee of the Carnegie Endowment," Stevenson would continue. "The Board of Trustees, of which General Eisenhower was a member, declined to accept his resignation and granted him three months' leave of absence with full pay so that he might defend himself. The General was not present at the meeting, but I do not find that he ever voiced disapproval of this concrete expression of trust and confidence. In May of 1949, the month in which I gave my deposition, and again in December 1949, after the first trial of Alger Hiss, the Board of Trustees, of which General Eisenhower was still a member, again voted to reject Hiss's resignation. . . . I bring these facts to the American people not to suggest that either General Eisenhower or John Foster Dulles is soft toward Communists or even guilty of the bad judgment with which I am charged. I bring them out only to make the point that the mistrust, the innuendoes, the accusations which this 'crusade' is employing, threatens not merely themselves, but the integrity of our institutions and our respect for fair play."

CHAPTER TWENTY-THREE

The Seamy Side of Politics Contrasted with the Governor's Life in the Mansion

The successor to the Capone gang of the 1920s in Chicago was a genuinely subversive organization as mysterious to ordinary citizens as it was sinister, and as corrupting to Illinois's governing processes as it was profitable for its members. Known as "The Syndicate," it was a firm yet shadowy working alliance between crime and politics whose agents were everywhere: no governor was able wholly to overcome it. Crucial portions of Stevenson's legislative program had been destroyed by it, as we have seen. Human beings high in the Stevenson administration were also destroyed by it.

One of these was Jim Mulroy.

Mulroy, as has been indicated, was the Stevenson staff member who did most of the political "horse trading" on which so much of legislative success depended. In the late spring of 1949 he was asked by the House majority leader Paul Powell if he would care to "take a flier" in the stock of Chicago Downs, a harness-racing association which had been legalized by a unanimous vote of the legislature a few weeks before. Chicago Downs did its racing at Sportsman's Park, generally deemed a syndicate operation and located in Capone's old home town of Cicero at the west side of Chicago. Mulroy had been ill a great deal; he was frequently in the hospital after he'd gone to Springfield. He needed money. He bought a hundred dollars' worth of the stock—one thousand shares at ten cents a share. A few months later each of those shares yielded a dividend of $1.65, which meant that Mulroy made $1750 on his hundred-dollar investment.

In the late summer of 1951 a publicity spotlight was turned on Chicago Downs. It revealed that some of the stockholders were close associates of members of the old Capone gang, that several Illinois legislators had been employed by the association, and that a very select list of politicians and state employees had been offered the ten-cent stock. Inevitably the spotlight focused with a special intensity upon stockholder Mulroy. He had done nothing illegal; he argued that the stock offer had been made *after* the legalizing bill had passed, so that the offer could not have been an effort to buy his influence; but few knowledgeable people could doubt that the stock offer had, in fact, been an influence-buying operation, whether Mulroy realized it at the time or not.

Stevenson himself was convinced his aide had been guilty only of thoughtlessness and impetuosity. For weeks, while public criticism mounted and other staff members insisted that Mulroy be fired, the governor refused to act. But in October he sadly told a mutual friend of his and Mulroy's that "Jim will have to go." He had talked to Mulroy about it. The interview had been heart-rending. Stevenson felt that he owed Mulroy a great deal (others pointed out that Mulroy also owed Stevenson a great deal), and he told Mulroy so, but he had an obligation to the people of Illinois which must override any merely personal loyalties. . . .

Less than six months later Mulroy died suddenly of a heart attack. His widow and close friends were convinced that his public disgrace, which he brooded over in black depression, had killed him. . . .

Another situation that caused some embarrassment to Stevenson was the affair of Frank Annunzio, director of labor. In early 1951 he had been named Democratic ward committeeman in Chicago's First Ward (the Loop) and had been ordered by Stevenson either to resign that position or his position in the cabinet. He had resigned the former. At the same time he resigned as president of an insurance agency called Anco, Inc., and sold his stock interest in that firm. Anco had been formed by Annunzio, early in '51, in partnership with John D'Arco, a member of the West Side Bloc in the 1941 legislature who had helped to kill the crime bills and Con-Con. D'Arco was vice-president of the firm whose other officers included a man who had been convicted of vote fraud in 1928 and had been wounded in the gang wars of the Capone days. The enterprise, though legal, was a highly dubious one for any cabinet officer to engage in.

Annunzio's connection with Anco became widely publicized during the investigations following the assassination of one Charles

Gross, a Chicago ward committeeman, in February of 1952. The fact that Annunzio had sold his stock failed to convince the public, or Stevenson, that the cabinet position had not been compromised and with it the prestige of the whole administration. The governor promptly asked for and received Annunzio's resignation, though he always insisted afterward that Annunzio had done an excellent job.

Far more serious than either the Mulroy or Annunzio affair was a scandal involving Charles W. Wray, the superintendent of Foods and Dairies in Roy E. Yung's Department of Agriculture.

Soon after his election Stevenson was warned by the kind of political pressures brought upon him that the Foods and Dairies superintendency was an office in which certain unsavory social elements took an excessive interest. He had therefore rejected every name pressed upon him and had hand-picked Charles Wray, a Lake County farmer who had been active in local politics, whose reputation for ability and honesty was high, and whose selection was approved both by farmers and food industry men. Of this appointment Stevenson had been particularly proud. It was therefore inconceivable to him that Wray could be in any way involved in the scandal which began to develop in the summer of 1951 when Director Yung of the Agriculture Department first heard reports that horse meat was being used to adulterate hamburger in Illinois and that this was being done with the connivance of state meat inspectors. Wray, who had charge of the inspectors, was ordered to conduct an investigation. He found nothing wrong.

By December of 1951, however, investigators for the Federal Office of Price Stabilization reported to Stevenson that something definitely *was* wrong. They were certain that specified meat packers were selling horse meat as beef. They were certain that some state inspectors were being bribed to overlook it. They had a list of the inspectors they suspected. Stevenson in January of '52 turned the matter over to Carl McGowan, whose handling of it enhanced the governor's opinion of his judgment. All the meat inspectors were called to Springfield and questioned by two assistant attorney generals. Wray was called also. At the end of two days, Wray, faced with incriminating evidence, confessed to McGowan that he himself was involved, that he had taken thirty-five hundred dollars from one Joe Siciliano who operated a packing plant in Lake and Henry counties and who was indeed selling horse meat as beef for use in hamburgers. He was fired, his statement turned over to the Lake County state's attorney. He was later indicted in Lake County on charges of bribery and conspiracy, though the charges were finally dismissed on a technicality. Joe Siciliano, however, was tried and convicted. (When he was arrested, his bond was set at thirty thousand dollars. "Thirty thousand!" cried Siciliano. "They must think I ground up Man O' War.")

No event in Stevenson's administration struck harder at his confidence in human nature than this one. His immediate response was stern. He pressed for a thorough investigation of the inspectors who had served under Wray, with the result that a dozen of them were fired or suspended. He enlisted a senior FBI agent to be his special personal investigator. He called his department directors to his State House office and there lectured them on their responsibility for the wrongdoing of their subordinates in so far as they failed adequately to supervise those subordinates. He said flatly that the "calm confidence" he had theretofore had in the men under him was being replaced by "an eager persistent surveillance." Thereafter, as his close associates noted, his faith in the essential decency of human beings was qualified by a greater awareness of human weakness. . . .

There was yet another major scandal during the Stevenson administration, but Stevenson was convinced that it was not an *administration* scandal. Rather was it, in his view, an administration triumph.

In 1951 Stevenson was informed that some Chicago wholesalers were cutting cigarette prices to an extent which would have been impossible had they paid the state tax on them. His response was prompt and highly effective. He instituted his own secret investigation, securing the appointment of a Chicago lawyer as a special assistant attorney general and employing a firm of private detectives. It was found that the cut-rate cigarettes bore counterfeit state tax stamps printed on the packages by stolen tax-meter machines for which new plates had been made. There was no doubt that the whole lucrative "business" was a syndicate operation. When sufficient evidence had been gathered, Stevenson ordered state police into raids on ten wholesale firms in greater Chicago. Several wholesalers were indicted and one was sent to the penitentiary. Stevenson also ordered an investigation of Department of Revenue employees, with the result that the head of the Chicago office of the cigarette tax collecting division and two inspectors there were fired. A third inspector resigned. They had refused to sign waivers of immunity.

II

Two disastrous events having political repercussions occurred during the Stevenson regime. One was an ugly race riot which broke out in Cicero in the summer of 1951 when a Negro family attempted to move into an all-white community. The other was an explosion in a coal mine at West Frankfort which killed 119 men on December 21, 1951.

Local law enforcement broke down completely during the Cicero riots and the governor ordered in five National Guard companies to restore order. Some 109 rioters were arrested on charges of unlawful assembly, but the handling of their cases by Cook County State's Attorney John S. Boyle so disgusted the governor that he was instrumental in having Boyle removed from the Democratic slate for re-election in 1952.[1] During the '51 General Assembly Stevenson had put through a measure transforming the Illinois Interracial Commission into the Illinois Commission on Human Relations, broadening its responsibilities to include "the promotion and encouragement of interfaith and interracial harmony and good will." To the first meeting of this commission on October 11 of '51, Stevenson said: "Deep beneath the Cicero disorders . . . lie the fears, the alarms, the pressures, the tensions of the continuously critical housing shortage. . . . Large numbers of the low income groups, and among these large numbers of the so-called minority groups, are inadequately housed, rigidly segregated and confined to slums and deteriorated residential areas. The demoralising effects . . . are placing a severe strain upon the whole range of State and municipal welfare services. This is . . . the grim reality underlying the tension and violence that accompany the efforts of minority group members to break through the iron curtain which confines so many of our fellow citizens."

One of the successes of the governor in the 1949 legislature session had been the reorganization of the Department of Mines and Minerals. This, however, was but the first step of the journey Illinois must make toward the goal of maximum practical mine safety. The governor therefore had called upon Dr. Harold Walker, head of the

[1] He let it be known that he was reluctant to stand for re-election and that one cause of his reluctance was the presence of Boyle on the ticket. Immediately after Boyle was removed from the slate, Stevenson let it be known that he would run again. See John Bartlow Martin's *Adlai Stevenson*, p. 114.

Department of Mines at the University of Illinois, to revise the patch-work mining code, assisted by the state mining department, by the governor's own aides, and by the Legislative Reference Bureau. On January 10, 1951, the resultant draft bill was submitted to the Mine Investigation Commission for review and comment. Examined by members of the commission and by representatives of the mine operators and the unions, the bill was unanimously rejected. (It is one of the distressing facts of Illinois politics that the mine operators and the union leaders are as one in their opposition to needed mine reforms.) Stevenson then had a breakfast at the mansion, to which he invited all the senators from the mining areas. These recommended that the bill not be introduced until the mining industry had had further time to consider it.

"Hence I am unable to make good my promise to present such legislation at this session," said Stevenson in a public statement issued May 16, 1951. "I hope the industry will bring in such further safety legislation as it can agree upon at this session. . . ." In that same statement he remarked that "currently our safety record is very good" but that "that situation could be sharply altered at any moment." No legislative proposals were made by the industry.

A little over seven months later the West Frankfort mine blew up. The Republicans attempted to tag Stevenson with responsibility for this disaster as Green had been tagged with responsibility for Centralia, but in order to do so they had to ignore or falsify a great many facts. It will be recalled that John Bartlow Martin's long, authoritative article in *Harper's* magazine on the Centralia tragedy had played a part in the 1948 campaign. In 1952 Martin reported[2] that the Centralia and West Frankfort tragedies were very different. Wrote he: "The cause of the Centralia disaster was clear and avoidable; the cause of West Frankfort was not clear. Many warnings had been given that the Centralia mine was dangerous; the West Frankfort mine was considered a 'model' mine. Centralia miners had repeatedly asked the Department of Mines and Minerals to make the company comply with the law and once had appealed to Governor Green; no such steps had been taken at West Frankfort. Investigation after Centralia disclosed that mine inspectors had been soliciting political campaign funds from operators; no such evidence was adduced after West Frankfort."

[2] Op. cit., pp. 139–40.

Stevenson was deeply moved by the Frankfort disaster. He flew at once to the scene, where he conferred with mine managers and rescue directors and visited many of the bereaved. He organized an extensive solicitation of funds for the dependents of the deceased miners. He also went to Washington to meet with John L. Lewis, head of the miners' union, and Secretary Oscar Chapman of the Interior department, about federal mine-safety regulation. It is significant that Stevenson opposed the proposed legislation, despite the pressure for it which mounted after the Frankfort tragedy. He stood firmly by his belief that in this area no more than in others should the states abdicate their responsibilities, forcing the federal government to assume them. It seemed to him that the states should be able to work out together some sort of uniform and effective mine-safety system.

III

In striking contrast to the seamy side of politics, with which Stevenson the governor had now and then to deal, was the life in the Executive Mansion of Stevenson the man. . . .

From the earliest possible moment in the spring until late in the fall he dined in the garden beside the house. In good weather he had his breakfast and luncheon upon the porch, save on days when he was so pressed for time that he lunched from a tray at his desk or had so many guests that luncheon was served in the dining room. Almost always people were with him—guests, or family, or staff members.

But on perhaps a half dozen occasions during his Springfield years he sat alone on a summer evening in the garden. It was a quiet place surrounded on three sides by a painted brick wall, on the fourth side by the tall stately mansion itself, and on all sides by history. In the center of the garden was a circular pool; in the center of the pool was a small stone figure from which water played. A garland of petunias edged the pool and edged, too, the garden wall over which green vines climbed to hide this place from the eyes of the street and muffle, as it seemed, the traffic roar of the twentieth century. Roses bloomed. Birds sang. He sat there on a few evenings until the last light of day died from timeless skies into a dark night brooding over all.

He might look up, then, at a star which seemed to perch on the peak of a mansion gable. He might let the night wind brush from his mind the burdens which weighted it. Lightened, his mind might rise and drift as on a wind of history until he could look down in tranquil contemplation not only upon himself, in this time, in this place, but also upon men and women long dead who had walked this garden and slept their nights away, or lay fretful and worried upon their beds, within those towering walls.

The mansion had been built in 1856. That was the year John C. Frémont, running as the first Republican candidate, had been defeated by Buchanan—poor self-divided Old Buck, soon to be crushed in the ruins of a House divided. Jesse Fell had fervently supported Frémont that year. So had youthful W. O. Davis. Adlai Ewing Stevenson, the governor's grandfather, then a college student, had as fervently supported Buchanan. All three men must at some time have trod this ground where the fountain now played and flowers bloomed. Abraham Lincoln must have done so, and certainly Richard Yates had paced up and down, up and down the grassy yard as he planned his strategy for dealing with an embattled legislature in the bitter summer of Gettysburg. Grandfather Davis had stayed often in the mansion when his good friend "Private Joe" Fifer was the governor of Illinois, and Adlai's own father and mother, and the stripling Adlai himself, had been constant visitors in the war-shadowed days of Governor Dunne.

So many had come here who now were long gone! It was well to remember—it was strangely soothing to remember—how many had here intensely lived whose bodies now mingled with the earth of Illinois. They had been great in their time who now, most of them, were utterly forgotten!

Forgotten. . . . To a drifting mind might come a poet's lines, the famous epitaph for John Peter Altgeld who, while living in this mansion in the 1890s, had dared to pardon the Haymarket radicals in a time of "loyalty" hysteria not unlike Stevenson's own. Sang the poet:

Sleep softly, . . . eagle forgotten, . . . under the stone,
Time has its way with you there and the clay has its own.
Sleep on, O brave-hearted, O wise man, that kindled the flame—
To live in mankind is far more than to live in a name.

Here Altgeld had stood firm on the principle of freedom and justice as he was "snarled at . . . , barked at . . . , foamed at . . . ," by the hounds of privilege, only to be forgotten after he had left this place by "the mocked and the scorned and the wounded, the lame and the poor that should have remembered forever. . . ." If his name was famous now, it was only because the poet had not forgotten.

And Adlai Stevenson, turning toward the southeast corner of the garden, might gaze upon the shabby gray house where that poet had lived.

It was an old house, as old as this mansion. When it was new a Mr. and Mrs. C. M. Smith had lived there. Mrs. Smith was a sister of Mrs. Abraham Lincoln, who lived just four blocks away, and in the house's front parlor many a party had been given the Lincolns; there had been an especially grand one in 1861, just before the President-elect said farewell to Springfield. Vachel Lindsay had been born in that house. He had lived in it all his life. There, precisely there above the wall, were the blank dark windows where he had often sat or stood, musing, above the garden. Through years of poverty and neglect he had slept in a sagging bed behind those windows, beside a bookcase that stood crooked because the poet who made it was clumsy with tools, and at a plain table had wrought, in mingled ecstasy and agony, the songs of Springfield which haunted Adlai Stevenson's mind:

> In this, the City of my Discontent,
> Down from this sky, up from the smoking deep
> Wild legends new and old burn round my bed
> While trees and grass and men are wrapped in sleep.

As he arose to enter the mansion, there to work far into the night at his desk, he might think that Vachel Lindsay's house should certainly become a shrine to the poet's memory, as Buffie wanted it to be—and his drifting mind, not yet engaged by the work which awaited him, might turn to Buffie and Ernest Ives, with gratitude for all they had done and were now doing for him. . . .

Ernest had stayed with him in the mansion through most of the hard spring and summer of 1949, when, amid the intense and novel pressures of his office, he'd tried so hard to save his marriage. Ernest's was a soothing presence: in the most literal meaning of the word, he was a gentleman—courteous, kind, self-effacing, devoted. He had lightened a grievous burden; he continued to do so. Unobtrusively, anonymously, he served in a hundred ways, taking care of family matters, helping entertain visitors, performing all manner of needed if inglorious chores, and above all providing relaxing companionship. Ernest knew how and when to keep silence. And Ernest was a good companion. The warm affection which everyone had for him was a great asset to the mansion, helping often to smooth out personnel difficulties which inevitably arose, now and then, among those who lived and worked there.

Buffie came and stayed for long periods, to serve as the governor's official hostess while Ellen remained in Libertyville. She lived there most of the time after the divorce, when Adlai rented his Libertyville farm to Marshall Field, Jr. At the same time she ran her homes in Bloomington and in Southern Pines, all of which, as she said, "took some doing." She it was who managed the mansion's domestic arrangements, working with Mrs. Van Diver, the housekeeper whose husband, a state police captain, was the governor's chauffeur; and with Gertie Dent, the cook.

Buffie loved the stately house. There were twenty-eight rooms in it. The so-called "basement," where the governor and his secretaries and personal aides had their offices, was really a ground floor, being level with the top of the knoll on which the mansion stood. The first floor, with the tall ceilings typical of its architectural period, consisted largely of "official" rooms, used not only for formal entertaining by the governor but also by Springfield's women's clubs and auxiliaries for special teas and the like. The two front parlors had long windows, reaching to the parquetry floor across which spread shaggy white rugs; mirrors rose to the ceilings above the mantels. From the ceilings hung crystal chandeliers whose teardrop prisms sparkled in the light. Adjoining each parlor was a long room with a bay window; one was the living room, the other the music room. Behind the music room was the state dining room whose beautiful paneling had been painted white and whose wallpaper was of a dogwood pattern; here was a complete silver service for eighteen which came originally from the battleship U.S.S. *Illinois* and bore the seal of Illinois. Behind the living room was the family dining room, and adjoining this was a sunroom and library which had been originally a side porch.

It was in the sunroom on the west side of the house that Stevenson and the Ives gathered before dinner and where they spent most of their informal moments. Occasionally Stevenson stretched out for a few moments before dinner on a long sofa there. The sofa, the armchairs had been newly slip-covered by Buffie in colors that harmonized with the green tile floor. One side of the room was lined with bookshelves that were entirely empty when Stevenson moved in and which he filled with books loaned by the historical library. Gradually these shelves became filled with books he received as gifts, particularly after it became generally known that he wished to establish a permanent library for the mansion. Many of these books were autographed at his request, "To Governor Adlai E. Stevenson, for the Executive Mansion."

Above the impressive entrance hall, with its curving stairway painted ivory-white with mahogany handrail, was a skylight of multicolored glass through which sunlight fell in rainbow hues. Buffie enthusiastically seconded, and helped to implement, her brother's desire that oil portraits of past governors be hung upon the downstairs walls, as permanent reminders that this was a house of history and tradition.

Upstairs were the bedrooms, the larger of which had fireplaces in them. One of these was transformed by Buffie into a memorial room to the early occupants of the mansion, a project in which her brother took a special pride. It began when Mrs. John Pickering, granddaughter of the Civil War governor, Richard Yates, gave to the state her grandfather's bed, bureau, and armoire. These pieces were supplemented by other period pieces and by pictures, vases, figurines. The room became as beautiful as it was historically fascinating, and Buffie and Ernest, and Stevenson, were grieved when the next administration abandoned the project and sent the room's furnishings into storage.

The house was well kept, and as thriftily as circumstances permitted. Buffie naturally would have liked to buy a few handsome pieces, but she respected her brother's conviction that the house, filled with flowers and pictures, should do as it was.

Soon after Buffie's arrival for her first extended visit in the mansion she and Ernest persuaded the governor to take a walk one chilly evening with her and Ernest, and Artie, the Stevenson dog. (Artie's full name was King Arthur. He was a melancholy Dalmatian whose wanderings through Springfield's streets, in defiance of the law, became famous in Illinois. People were always calling up the mansion to report that the governor's dog was at such and such an address, and could someone come fetch him?) Returning from the walk, Stevenson was horrified to see the mansion ablaze with light; electricity burned in a dozen empty rooms. "I never want to see that again!"

he told Buffie, with emphasis. "I keep preaching economy in government—and it's up to us to set an example."

He quite agreed that something should be done about the soiled, food-stained Scalamandré silk which was on the chairs in the state dining room, but he could not bring himself to approve the expenditure of two thousand dollars (the upholsterer's estimate) for that purpose. So Buffie had the silk removed, cleaned, and dyed gold. She had then slip-covered the gold silk of the chairs in the family dining room.

She strove mightily to please him, and he found her "indispensable. . . . I couldn't get along without her," he said.

She reminded him of what he had been, of what they both had been, in their childhood and youth. Some intimate observers felt that she occupied in his life a place somewhat analogous to that his mother had occupied long ago. She was so utterly committed to him, so profoundly convinced that he had greatness in him and could do no wrong. He needed that, an unwavering faith in him, during those trying years. Largely through Buffie he renewed friendships with Springfield people he had known in his teens, including Jim Patton, Mrs. Logan Hay, and the former Mary Douglas ("Dougie") Hay, who had been his favorite girl when he was a student in Springfield High and who was now Mrs. Donald Funk, wife of the chairman of the board of the Sangamo Electric Company.

When he went to Centre College in Danville, Kentucky, to receive an honorary degree and give an address, Buffie helped make the trip memorable for him. Together they explored the old college of which their great-grandfather Lewis Warner Green had been president and where Adlai Stevenson I had been a student. Together they visited Waveland, the brick mansion built in 1797 on the Wilderness Road by their great-great-grandfather Willis Green, now the homestead of a large dairy farm. Such vivid contacts with his own family traditions renewed and strengthened him. And to Buffie it seemed that he must draw upon that serene strength on their return flight from Danville in the governor's two-engine Beechcraft, for they flew into a terrible storm during which Buffie fervently prayed, while her brother calmly read official documents and made notes on them. (As an air traveler, Stevenson was notoriously brave to the point of rashness, and had sometimes to be overruled by his pilot, Major Dan Smith, when he wanted to make landings which radio-control towers ruled unsafe. Smith had to land by radar control in Chicago, on the return from Danville, because the Springfield airport was closed off.)

But it was not only the family past which gave him strength and serenity; it was also the family future, manifest in his three sons and in his strikingly handsome nephew, Timothy Ives. "I have always tried to live on a contemporary basis with my sons," he said, a few years later. "We have an easygoing relationship. I've tried to set an example for them and trust that they defer to me out of respect rather than authority. I believe in being patient with them. In the future, I would want them to be satisfied that they are giving rather than getting. I'd like to see them in teaching or law or business. Givers are needed in the business world, so I would like to see one of my sons go into it."[3]

Of all the hurtful charges Ellen had hurled at him during the period of their marriage's dissolution the one which had most deeply hurt was that, by entering public life, he was betraying and even "ruining" his sons. In solitary anguish he had examined that charge, striving with the objectivity characteristic of him in such concerns to determine whether it was true or false. And as he looked now upon his sons, and upon his relationship with them, he concluded that the charge was not true.

Each boy was a distinct personality. Adlai III seemed most closely to resemble his father; he was reflective, affable, a great reader, and interested in politics. Borden, the second son, believed himself to "take after" the Borden side of the family, but his father could see in him traces of the boy he himself had been. Borden was perhaps more the type of the "Princeton man" than the type of Harvard, where he would become a student; he was often baited—overbaited in fact—for being so little a scholar, so much a "playboy," and he developed an inferiority complex wholly unjustified by his innate abilities. John Fell was yet too young to have formed any clearly defined career ambitions, but it seemed unlikely that he would ever be interested in a political career. He was very shy—and very lovable. He had also what some described as a "monkey's curiosity." (Buffie once said that he had the lively curiosity of Kipling's Elephant Boy, though, as she promptly added, this was "not the best simile for the son of a Democrat.")

Every Christmas season there was a reception in the mansion and

[3] Quoted in *Look* magazine, 1956.

at least two big evening parties, one for the staff and one, a formal dance, for the Stevenson boys and Timothy. To the latter were invited young people from Chicago, from Lake Forest, from all over the state. The governor, and Buffie too, moved into the servants' quarters to make room for the guests, many of whom stayed overnight in the mansion, with the overflow quartered in a hotel where Ernest chaperoned them. Among the festivities was a solemn ritual which the governor never failed to honor: he took his young guests up into the attic of the mansion to view the mansion "ghost." This was a mannequin which he had carefully placed in a corner with just enough light upon it to make it gleam palely through the gloom, with eerie effect. John Fell was fourteen when the first dance was given and he attended it, his own first dance, donning one of his father's dinner jackets whose shoulders were so much too wide for him that whenever a girl placed her hand upon his arm, the jacket shoulders slid down. John Fell was unperturbed; he was wearing, he explained, the new "off-the-shoulder fashion."

During the holidays, too, the governor and the boys always managed to crowd in some trapshooting. . . .

All the boys, like Stevenson, loved the out-of-doors, and particularly the western mountains. In the summer of 1951 the three Stevenson sons and Adlai had a vacation trip they would never forget, going to the Jackson Hole wilderness south of Yellowstone Park.

Among the warm friendships which Stevenson formed during his Springfield years was one with the Reverend Dr. Richard Paul Graebel, pastor of the First Presbyterian Church. This was the church which Abraham Lincoln, never a church member, occasionally attended during the 1840s and '50s. It was rich in historic tradition, and none could have made this tradition more effective of good in the mid-twentieth-century community than Dr. Graebel.

Of German ancestry, a fair Nordic type physically, Graebel was yet a young man who, wherever he went, generated an electric excitement. During the 1948 gubernatorial campaign he had earned the wrath of the Chicago *Tribune*—a wrath displayed in front-page headlines—by arraigning the Green regime in his sermons for graft and corruption. Simultaneously, of course, he had earned the respect and gratitude of Adlai Stevenson.

The two, however, did not become close personal friends until February of 1950. There was in Springfield an organization known as the Midday Luncheon Club, which every year held a banquet in honor of Lincoln's birth. The banquet commemorating the 151st anniversary was held on a Sunday evening in the Centennial Auditorium. A great crowd was there. The club president, George C. Hoffman, introduced Adlai Stevenson, who, in turn, introduced with grace and wit Dr. Graebel, the principal speaker of the evening. Graebel's address, "Lincoln and the American Dream," was a powerful and moving one. (During it he paid tribute to Lloyd Lewis and was distressed to see, as he did so, that a woman in the audience wept; later he learned that she was Kathryn Lewis.) It made a profound impression upon Stevenson.

Thereafter the two men were often together. They enjoyed one another immensely in a social way—there was always a great deal of hearty laughter when they were together—but they also were often very serious together, talking over questions of ultimate faith, ultimate meaning. Some of the tone and temper of their talk was revealed, a few years later, when Stevenson made a recording for Edward R. Murrow's "This I Believe" broadcast over the CBS network. Stevenson, while preparing his statement, talked it over with Graebel, and in it he fused his Unitarian convictions with a religious feeling absent from any earlier one of his public statements.

At eleven o'clock every Christmas Eve, a candlelight carol service was held in the First Presbyterian Church. It was a beautiful service, and Adlai Stevenson, with his sons and the Iveses, never failed to attend. They sat just behind the "Lincoln pew," listening with rapt attention as the minister, standing alone, sang in German, in his rich warm voice, "Silent Night . . ."

Out of such things as these—out of the secret agony of his broken marriage, out of solitudes under infinite skies from which stars winked at him across light-years of space, out of the myriad human contacts and felt experiences of his crowded days, out of a sense of the countless generations that came and made and passed away, out of a growing conviction that to live in mankind under God is indeed far more than to live in a name—Adlai Stevenson added new dimensions to himself during those Springfield years. Constantly he became a richer, more lyrical personality, his character reaching outward and downward toward new heights and greater depths—and in proportion to his growth he became, in essential ways, more lonely. Did he become a stranger even to himself? To a future biographer it might seem so. All that he met became a part of him, but he met so much so rapidly as he passed his fiftieth birthday that he seemed for a time to grow beyond his own ken.

"What a man knows at fifty that he did not know at twenty is, for the most part, incommunicable," he would say four years later to the senior class at Princeton. ". . . The knowledge he has acquired with age is not the knowledge of formulas, the forms of words, but of people, places, actions—a knowledge not gained by words but by touch, sight, sound, victories, failures, sleeplessness, devotion, love— the human experiences and emotions of this earth and of oneself and other men; and perhaps, too, a little faith, a little reverence for things you cannot see."

Book Six

THE CALL TO GREATNESS

CHAPTER TWENTY-FOUR

Stevenson, Eisenhower, and Truman
in Early 1952

If there was a failure of self-knowledge, it by no means accounted for all the doubts and hesitations Adlai Stevenson publicly displayed during the first six months of 1952. From the moment of his gubernatorial victory in 1948 he had been talked of for President, the talk increasing in urgency and volume while he made his record as governor and other Democratic candidates of commanding stature failed to arise. He was stimulated by this talk to examine closely not only into himself and his obligation to Illinois but also into the contemporary national political scene. Both examinations fed his reluctance to heed the call to national duty. . . .

In the field of foreign policy, the most crucial of all fields of government during the Truman regime, the administration had been, on the whole, courageous and creative. The United Nations had been firmly supported and its congeries of specialized agencies now pursued their quiet labors on behalf of international co-operation and understanding largely because the United States participated fully in them and gave them, at the outset, the bulk of their financial support. Under the leadership of Secretary of State Dean Acheson, the "containment" policy vis-à-vis the aggressive Communist nations had been pursued with boldness and considerable success, particularly in Greece, the Middle East, and western Europe. The Truman Doctrine, the Berlin Airlift, the Marshall Plan, Point Four, NATO—all these stood as monuments to tough executive decisions intelligently made and effectively implemented. Though firm, foreign policy had been flexible, swiftly adapting itself to changing circumstances.

There had been failures. China had been lost to the Communists, and this was a defeat for the West of as yet incalculable world-historical significance. Perhaps Stevenson himself, had he been in power over the whole period of World War II and its aftermath, would have pursued a different policy. Perhaps the Chinese revolution, properly understood, could have been directed away from Moscow and toward the Western concept of democracy, if we had not committed ourselves so strongly and, as many said, so blindly to Chiang Kai-shek. But given the situation in China in the late 1940s, what could have been done by us to halt the march of communism there, short of initiating World War III? To this question the critics of our China policy had no clear answer. Some of them, indeed, seemed willing to risk a world atomic war.

But if China was a major defeat, Korea, in Stevenson's view, was a victory, when viewed in the proper historical perspective. He said so in an article he wrote in November of 1951 and which was published in the April 1952 issue of *Foreign Affairs*. "When North Korean forces invaded the Republic of Korea on June 25, 1950, with the full support of Peking and Moscow, most of us knew what was at stake," he said. "One of the men who took part in the long anxious meeting at Blair House gave the simplest explanation of the decision: 'This attack on South Korea is like Hitler's reoccupation of the Rhineland.'" He quoted the speech Senator William Knowland, California Republican, made on the floor of the Senate in immediate support of the President's announcement and reminded his readers that only one member of the Congress had opposed the Korean action and he, Representative Vito Marcantonio of New York, had been defeated for re-election.

Since then, of course, there had been a rising criticism of the conduct of the war—particularly of the removal of General Douglas MacArthur from his Korean command after he had repeatedly tried to take steps, in defiance of his commander-in-chief, which might have expanded the local war into a global atomic conflict. The immediate objective we had sought, namely to drive the North Koreans beyond the 38th parallel, had been achieved; the physical and psychological defenses of the West, and Western prestige among the uncommitted peoples of the Far and Middle East, had been immensely strengthened; there was every evidence that this tough demonstration of collective security had deterred the Soviet Union from other plotted conquests. Yet the war dragged on (it was limited mostly to air action in 1952) and was now dubbed, by certain Republicans, "Mr. Truman's War." The sobriquet seemed to Stevenson as palpably unfair as the repeated assertions that Truman and Acheson were "soft" on communism, and it was significant that both charges, despite their somewhat contradictory nature, were quite generally made by the same people. "There is, of course, no tidy solution to the Korean problem," Stevenson wrote, "precisely because it is only a part of the whole Soviet imperialist drive. . . . For that reason, the full settlement of the Korean problem is likely to take a long time and to wait upon the settlement of many other issues."

He had reason to know, that spring, the human anxieties, the angry impatience, which the military stalemate bred in a million families. His nephew, Timothy Ives, was training as a jet pilot in the U. S. Air Force at Byram Air Base and would soon go to Korea, there to fly scores of combat missions. His son, Adlai, Jr., would enter the Marines in June to train at Quantico and ultimately become a Marine lieutenant. It was a hard thing to say that the sacrifice of such young men was necessary to the prevention of a greater sacrifice. Yet Stevenson did say it. "[The] meaning of our experience in Korea as I see it is that we have made historic progress toward the establishment of a viable system of collective security," he asserted. "To deprecate our large and decisive share in that undertaking as 'useless' is both mischievous and regressive."

But if he could approve, on the whole, our foreign policy, he had reservations as he viewed the domestic scene. The latter was not, in all respects, an edifying one—and some of the most unedifying portions of it might strike an honest mind, looking at it in historical perspective, as due in part to twenty years of one-party control of the federal executive. During so long a tenure of power a political party's organization is likely to become fused almost to the point of identity with the institutions of government. These may then become as barrels of apples from which the few bad apples are unculled: corruption spreads through a process of secret deals and agreements until the public office which should be a public trust provides instead a currency for the payment of private debts and the satisfaction of strictly private desires.

Particularly is this likely to happen in the absence of an intelligently critical, morally responsible party opposition. History must record that little such opposition had been provided by the Republican party since 1932. During two decades of unparalleled national peril, when the country was threatened from within by economic collapse and from without by a rising tide of totalitarian imperialism, Republicans in the Congress, with few exceptions, had fought every measure of social and economic reform, every measure to strengthen Britain when she stood alone against the Nazi terror, almost every measure (at the outset) to develop an adequate military establishment. Small wonder that the Republicans had lost persuasive influence with a majority of Americans. Small wonder that their cries of "wolf" were largely ignored, since the "wolves" they had named in the past had so often proved to be the friendliest, most useful of hounds. The fact might embolden real wolves until a formidable pack of them roamed the forests of bureaucracy.

Had this happened? Adlai Stevenson would never believe that the wolf pack was anywhere near as large or as ravenous as Republican politicans proclaimed it to be, but he saw evidence that it was large enough. Quite large enough. So did millions of others.

Senator Kefauver's committee investigations, pursued before TV cameras, had stimulated popular disgust with the sordid alliance of crime and politics in many a big-city political machine. Though none dared allege that President Truman had ever been personally involved in such corruption, the Republican press and Republican politicians had not failed to reiterate the fact that he had begun his political career as a protégé of Tom Prendergast, whose Kansas City machine had been one of the most notoriously corrupt in the country during the 1920s and '30s. The doubts thus raised were repeatedly encouraged by disclosures of wrongdoing by men close to Truman, men whom he clung to with a machine politician's loyalty, as it seemed, when he should have repudiated them out of a statesman's loyalty to the national welfare.

There was a wave of such disclosures in late '51 and '52. The President himself, to his credit, admitted in practice that things had gone very wrong in the Internal Revenue Bureau, for he ordered a sweeping reorganization of that agency in early January, one which the Congress approved in March. A federal grand jury indicted E. Merl Young, former RFC examiner, charging him with giving false testimony to the grand jury. A House Appropriations subcommittee revealed that some eight millions of tax dollars had been lost through Commodity Credit Corporation operations whereby government buildings were rented and then leased back for up to twenty times the amounts paid the government by private contractors, the buildings being used for grain storage. And all this followed revelations that "influence peddling," or so the public was led to believe, had become a major Washington enterprise, corrupting minor governmental figures with "gifts" of mink coats and deep freezes.

True, a highly partisan Democrat might argue that all the thievery of twenty years of his party's power was but a tiny fraction of that which took place during a few months of the Harding regime following World War I, and that the Democratic party showed far more determination and capacity to clean its own house than the Republican party had demonstrated in the 1920s. He could point out that practically all these damaging disclosures had been made by congressional committees of which Democrats made up a majority and of which Democrats were chairmen. The Internal Revenue scandals were most glaringly revealed, not by the overwhelmingly Republican press, but by a normally Democratic newspaper, the St. Louis *Post-Dispatch*. And Senator Kefauver, announcing his candidacy on January 23 for the Democratic presidential nomination, frankly criticized the Truman administration (while upholding its foreign and domestic policies) for not doing all it could to clean up governmental corruption.

Nevertheless, an honest mind, remaining committed to Democratic principles, might wonder, as he surveyed the domestic scene, if a continuance of Democratic control of the executive was really in the best interests of party or country. Perhaps a respite from power would give the party opportunity to find new leadership, cleansing itself, whereas an assumption of power by the Republicans would force them to become realistic and responsible to a degree they had not been (they had, it seemed, developed a species of paranoia) during two powerless decades. There is no clear evidence that Stevenson had such explicit thoughts during those months, but there is a good deal of evidence that such "wondering" was part of the current of feeling which permeated his political thought.

It is true that an old broom sweeps poorly, whereas a clean sweep is easy with a broom that is new. The question, as always in politics, was one of alternatives. If the alternative to the old Democratic broom was the old Republican one, then the historical evidence was that the former would do a much better sweeping job. Like the Bourbons, the Republican Old Guard seemed to have learned and forgotten nothing during a world depression and a world war. Its leader was Senator Robert A. Taft of Ohio, who, judging from his voting record and public speech, would return the country to isolationism and big-business domination to precisely the extent that he was given the power to do so. In his now-desperate ambition to become President, he seemed even to have lost his former firm commitments to essential civil liberties for he now lent his support to the late Senator Joseph R. McCarthy of Wisconsin. One shuddered to contemplate what would happen to individual liberty in America, and to the painfully wrought system of collective security against Communist aggression abroad, if Taft occupied the White House, McCarthy had a free rein in the Senate, and the devotees of special privilege had again in hand the guardianship of the public weal.

But was this the only alternative?

As Stevenson often said, the GOP elephant was a two-headed beast. One head was the Old Guard, the other was the so-called "liberal" wing which seemed willing to hold most of the social gains made under the New and Fair Deals and to prevent a retreat into isolationism in foreign affairs. The latter group, since the days of Alf Landon, had been uniformly successful in its efforts to dictate the Republican presidential nominee: Willkie in '41, Dewey in '44, Dewey again in '48. It now appeared that the "liberals" had found a champion who could not only capture the nomination but might even reform the party, lopping off the head of reaction and enabling the party as a whole to take a new, more hopeful direction.

The champion's name was Dwight David Eisenhower. . . .

Stevenson in early 1952 may not have shared to the full the popular enthusiasm for the general as a potential political leader, but his admiration for Eisenhower as man and soldier was certainly great. This may have been one of the roots of his own reluctance to become a candidate that year.

Who, after all, could fail to admire the Eisenhower who had made of SHAEF a unique instrument of international co-operation, imbuing it with his own warm human qualities, his own strength and tolerance and sunny good will? Who could fail to admire the Eisenhower who seemed quite consciously to have made himself a symbol of Western unity, using his prestige to solidify American public opinion behind a foreign policy which might otherwise have split the people between an irreconcilable isolationism and internationalism? Like nearly all Americans, Stevenson believed he saw in the general a quality of moral goodness, an earnest desire to do good in the world, an innate human decency in which was rooted an apparently instinctive ability to make the proper public gesture on important occasions. The governor in late '51 and the first months of '52 might contemplate without serious qualms the possibility of the general as President.

Not until later would he wryly regard, as all too typical of the postwar Eisenhower, the manner in which the general had at last entered the presidential campaign.

Senator Henry Cabot Lodge, Jr., Massachusetts Republican, having just returned from a visit in Paris with Eisenhower, then commanding NATO armies, had told a press conference on January 6, 1952, that the general was a Republican, that the general would accept the Republican nomination if it were offered, and that this statement would not be denied by the general. On the following day Eisenhower, besieged by reporters, made his reply. In it he did not flatly state that he was a Republican; he said that Senator Lodge's announcement "gives an accurate account of the general tenor of my political convictions and of my Republican voting record." He did not clearly approve the political movement on his behalf; he said that "of course there is no question of the right of American citizens to organize in pursuit of their common convictions." He did not even clearly say that he would accept the nomination; he said that Senator Lodge and associates had a right to "attempt to place before me next July a duty that would transcend my present responsibilities" but that "in the absence . . . of a clear-cut call to political duty, I shall continue to devote my full attention and energies to the performance of the vital tasks to which I am assigned."

The only thing wholly unequivocal in the entire Eisenhower statement was his assertion that "under no circumstances will I ask for relief from this assignment in order to seek nomination to political office and I shall not participate in the pre-convention activities of others who may have such an intention with respect to me." Whereupon, in the late spring, he did just that; he sought relief from his assignment, returned to America, and engaged in an intense pre-convention campaign against Senator Taft.

On July 13, 1952, this campaign was crowned with success. At the Republican National Convention in the International Amphitheater in Chicago, following a bitter contest over delegates during which Taft supporters were charged with deliberate dishonesty in their attempt to claim the Texas delegation, Eisenhower won 585 votes on the first ballot, compared to 500 for Taft, whereupon the nomination, by floor motion, was declared unanimous.

II

Simultaneous with this was the campaign to secure the Democratic presidential nomination for Adlai Stevenson. Far different was its history. Not only did Stevenson refuse to "participate in the pre-convention activities of others," on his behalf, he opposed those activities so consistently and effectively that by the late spring of '52 they had collapsed into seeming utter futility. If some of his motives for doing so were never explicitly stated, his dominant motive was proclaimed to the world again and again: he wanted another four years as governor of Illinois.

On Sunday, January 20, Stevenson with Bill Blair flew to New York, where, on the following evening, in the grand ballroom of the Waldorf-Astoria, he delivered an address to the annual banquet of the National Urban League, an address which had been scheduled in November. It dealt with the harmful effect of racial discrimination in the United States upon our relations with other countries, particularly with Asian lands, and Stevenson had prepared it in the knowledge that it would be used as a "news peg" on which *Time* magazine, then edited by his old Princeton friend T. S. Matthews, would "hand" a cover story dealing with his record in Illinois. The speech was enthusiastically received by its immediate audience and next morning at breakfast Stevenson and Blair were gratified to see that it was well covered in the New York press. The *Herald Tribune* had an editorial lauding it.

Less gratifying was the information that all planes were grounded that morning by lowering, drizzling skies, for Stevenson and Blair were scheduled to fly down to Washington where the governor was to confer with Secretary of the Interior Oscar Chapman and John L. Lewis of the United Mine Workers concerning a proposal to place mine inspection under federal rather than state control. The weather failed to improve, so Blair and Stevenson took the noon train to Washington. They had planned to stay at the Metropolitan Club, but when they arrived there shortly after four o'clock they discovered that all rooms were taken. Reservations had been made for them at the Roger-Smith Hotel, the Metropolitan clerk told Blair, handing him some telephone messages. One of these, the two men noted with surprise, was from Blair House, where the President of the United States was living while the White House was being renovated. When Stevenson answered this call from his Roger-Smith room, he learned that the President wished to see him that evening.

Truman, in his *Memoirs*,[1] has given his version of the meeting with Stevenson: "I told him that I would not run for President again and that it was my opinion he was best-fitted for the place. He comes of a political family . . . had served the country in the State Department and the United Nations . . . had made an excellent Governor of Illinois. When I talked with him, I told him what I thought the Presidency is, how it has grown into the most powerful and greatest office in the history of the world. I asked him to take it and told him that if he would agree he could be nominated. I told him that a President in the White House always controlled the National Convention. Called his attention to Jackson and Van Buren and Polk. Talked about Taft in 1912, Wilson in 1920, Coolidge and Mellon in 1928, Roosevelt in 1936, 1940, 1944. But he said: No! He apparently was flabbergasted. . . ."

And Stevenson might well have seemed so to such eyes as Truman's. Certainly he was flattered, and even astonished, by the President's request. He was convinced that Harry Truman—despite his predilection for unfortunate off-the-cuff remarks and his sometimes dubious personal loyalties—would go down in history as one of America's strong chief executives. Few if any Presidents had displayed a greater personal and political courage than he in his great foreign-policy decisions and his campaign of '48, one of whose consequences had been an unprecedently swift advance of American Negroes toward their full rights as citizens of the United States. This gave to Truman's request a weight of honor to which Stevenson responded with gratitude.

Stevenson pointed out, however, that as an announced candidate for re-election as governor, he had an obligation to the people of Illinois, and particularly to the good people who had invested their talents, energy, and money in his campaign and administration on the assumption that he would see the job through to the end. He mentioned, also, his obligation to his three sons. Borden and John Fell were yet very young: a pitiless light of publicity would focus upon them if he ran for national office; they would be exposed to

[1] *Years of Trial and Hope*, Vol. II (New York: Doubleday & Co., 1956), pp. 491–92.

pressures and temptations which could warp their lives. Four years from now, he said frankly, the story would be different as far as his personal availability was concerned. By then he would have completed his job in Illinois in so far as it was possible for him to do so, and his youngest son would by then be a college student. He also, by then, would be better equipped for the presidency; as of the present moment he had doubts about his capacity to fill the job. . . . No, he was deeply moved, greatly honored, profoundly grateful, but he just couldn't do it.

Thus the words between these two men.

But beneath and beyond the words was a deeper, wider communication, flawed by misunderstanding. Because of it, this meeting took on (in subtle ways) some of the aspects of an encounter whose reverberations, echoing and augmented by subsequent events, would be heard throughout the land four years later.

These were two very different men—different in temperament, experience, attitudes, mind—and the difference was such that it was easier for Stevenson to appreciate Truman at the latter's full value than it was for Truman to appreciate Stevenson. That Truman misunderstood and underrated the man on whom he sought to bestow the nomination seems evident from the notes quoted above, written by the President soon after the meeting occurred. Stevenson—for all his outward deprecation, his seeming eagerness to defer to others—was not a man who could be "told" in this fashion; neither could he accept, easily, a "gift" of the nomination. His instinct for freedom, coupled with his obscure but powerful need to do everything the "hard" way, required that he earn whatever glory came to him and remain, always, his own man. . . .

His arrival at Blair House and his departure a little less than two hours later went unnoticed by White House news correspondents. But shortly after he breakfasted with Senator Paul Douglas next morning, the presidential visit was front-page news in the national press, having been released by the President himself. By nightfall Stevenson had been the focus of a dozen news cameras, the target of a score of pointed news questions, the subject of many a nationally syndicated columnist. And on the following day, Thursday, *Time* magazine with its cover story about him appeared. *Time* had shifted its news peg from the Urban League speech to the Blair House visit, saying: "Whatever the truth behind the rumors, this much was evident: in a cold season for the Democrats, Adlai Stevenson is politically hot, and Harry Truman feels the need of a little warmth."

Stevenson himself, having conferred on Wednesday with Chapman and Lewis concerning the mining law, continued to devote himself to Illinois business. On Thursday morning he breakfasted at the Metropolitan Club with a stocky, dark-haired, brown-eyed young man (he was then twenty-six) named Newton Minow, a graduate of the Northwestern University Law School, who was now the law clerk of Chief Justice Vinson of the U. S. Supreme Court. Minow had told McGowan he was interested in coming to Springfield as a Stevenson aide, and the breakfast conversation (a most congenial conversation, for the two liked one another immensely) dealt exclusively with that proposal and with state problems. An hour or so later Stevenson and Blair boarded a plane for Chicago.

Thereafter, the movement on behalf of Stevenson for President grew swiftly to boom proportions. In early February an Illinois Stevenson for President committee was organized in Chicago by a group of directors and former directors of the Independent Voters of Illinois, an Americans for Democratic Action affiliate. Of this draft Stevenson committee, Walter Johnson, professor of history at the University of Chicago, and George Overton, lawyer, were co-chairmen. Neither Stevenson nor anyone close to him had anything to do with organizing this committee nor with its work once it was organized—work which included mailing out literature and buttons (the latter said merely "Stevenson" so that they might be used in the gubernatorial campaign if the presidential movement collapsed), buying advertisements in newspapers, and in general focusing and keeping alive through doubtful times the draft movement. By spring the Illinois committee had become a national committee.

By that time, too, Stevenson was so far ahead of the other candidates for nomination that his selection on the first or second ballot seemed a certainty, if only he gave a word of encouragement to the movement on his behalf. He gave no such word. On the contrary, he refused to permit his name to be entered in any primaries (when it was entered without his permission in Oregon and could not legally be withdrawn, he urged Democrats to vote for Kefauver, the only other Democrat entered). Over and over again, to reporters, to visitors, and in answer to thousands of letters, he reiterated that he was a candidate for governor of Illinois and for that office only. "One does not treat the highest office within the gift of the people of Illinois as a consolation prize," he said in 1953, summarizing what he had told people in the preceding spring. "Moreover . . . I had little time to go around the country campaigning for an unwanted nomination to an unwanted office—an office, moreover, of such appalling difficulty and responsibility in the year of grace, 1952, that I felt no sense of adequacy." He urged Jack Arvey, national committeeman from Illinois, to do nothing on his behalf, and he urged this so persistently and consistently that Arvey did, in fact, nothing.

Meanwhile the campaign launched by Kefauver on the day following Stevenson's Blair House visit plodded through primary after primary, beginning with New Hampshire, where he inflicted a humiliating defeat upon the President, and ultimately winning the delegates of eight other states, plus half of Ohio's and part of Florida's. He also won the Pennsylvania presidential preference primary.

It was not such a campaign as Stevenson himself would have conducted. Launched with a criticism of Truman's alleged laxness in cleaning up governmental corruption, continued through the use of coonskin caps and an implacable handshaking folksiness, it seemed designed to advance the candidate at the expense of the party organization. One could not but admire Kefauver's courage and his indefatigable energy. Stevenson did so. But he was convinced that in the American political system good government depends very largely upon strong, effective party organizations, and he deplored the debilitating effects which the Kefauver campaign seemed to be having upon one of these. There seemed to him no necessity to conduct the battle against dishonesty in government in such a way as to weaken the party at its every level, from precinct and ward to the state and national committees. On the contrary, one should battle for governmental integrity in such a way as to *strengthen* the over-all party organization, thus exercising a necessary political art, as he was trying to do in co-operation with Jack Arvey and others in Illinois.

A future historian might find that Stevenson himself was giving a remarkable demonstration of the essential political art as he dealt, that spring, with the presidential movement on his behalf. The "pressure changed" somewhat, he wrote in early '53, as this movement proceeded. The question asked him was no longer, "Will you be a candidate for nomination?" but, "Will you accept the nomination?" "This was more difficult," he went on. "If I said, 'No,' how would it reconcile with all my preaching about public service and politics? How could I foretell then, long before the convention, what manner of deadlock and bitterness might develop to the lasting damage of my party? And, finally, could anyone in good health and already in public life refuse the greatest honor and greatest responsibility in our political system? So I concluded to keep still and say nothing more to anyone, contenting myself with confidence that no one could in fact be drafted by a modern convention against his often-expressed wish."

But his "confidence" that he could not be drafted was by no means a certainty that he would not be—and observe how his strategy served not only the ends he stated but also ends which were left unstated! By doing as he did, he neither burned the bridge behind him nor slammed the door in front of him. What he did do was ensure that if he at last entered the door, he would enter upright and free, without debts or obligations, and would have in his hands full control of party machinery. To assume that this was a conscious strategy on Stevenson's part, however, is to go against the external evidence and against Stevenson's own remembrance of his thoughts that spring. His strategy was more a function of circumstance than of choice, and the choice, in so far as it aimed to gain power, was a function of intuition rather than of conscious logic.

In early March Stevenson and Truman again met in Washington to discuss the presidential nomination. According to Truman's *Memoirs*,[2] this meeting was requested by Stevenson. According to Stevenson and his closest aides, he went because he had promised the President at the first meeting that he would come and talk to him again. The governor was at great pains to make the trip in secrecy, since a public knowledge of it could only feed the presidential boom which he wished, or believed he wished, to discourage. He was driven in a car with unofficial license plates to the St. Louis airport, where he boarded a commercial air-lines plane with a ticket issued to him in the name of William McC. Blair, Jr.

The plane stopped at Louisville, Kentucky, where Stevenson visited briefly with Barry Bingham of the Louisville *Courier-Journal*, an old friend who had been asked to meet him there. He wanted advice, and Bingham was full of it. "I argued, with as much force as the brief period allowed, my conviction that he should not fight against a fate which seemed to have settled upon him," Bingham told Walter Johnson in the spring of '54,[3] "I did not urge him . . . to

[2] Op. cit., p. 492.
[3] Walter Johnson, *How We Drafted Adlai Stevenson* (New York: Alfred A. Knopf, 1955).

make himself a candidate, or to promote his availability in any way at all. I only pleaded that he should leave himself uncommitted, so that a genuine draft could have an opportunity to develop. . . . As to his personal qualifications, I urged that the Democratic delegates and the people of the country in general should be allowed to judge for themselves on the basis of the public record. . . . He was modest, friendly, deprecating, seeking advice and yet protesting that he could not bring himself to take it. As we parted, he laughed and said: 'Well, you certainly haven't been much help to me!' "

In Washington he repeated to Truman what he had said in January. Re-election to the governorship of Illinois was the full measure of his ambition; he could not be a candidate for any other office. He then went to Florida for a few days of John Fell's spring vacation, and, while there, wrote a longhand letter to Charles Murphy, one of Truman's aides, expressing the hope that the President understood his position, and the gratitude he felt.

On the evening of Saturday, March 29, Stevenson was again in Washington, in the National Guard Armory, as one of fifty-three hundred Democrats gathered for the annual Jefferson-Jackson Day dinner. The President was the speaker of the evening, and near the close of one of his typical "give 'em hell" addresses he announced, as if casually, that he would not be a candidate for re-election nor would he accept a renomination. The chorus of protesting "noes" had scarcely died before newsmen were jammed around Adlai Stevenson, asking him the same old questions with more urgency than before, and with that "shift of pressure" he later recorded. Next day he was interviewed before TV cameras on the "Meet the Press" program, acquitting himself so well in answers to deliberately needling questions[4] that his stock received another boost in the political market. To the key question about his political future, he made his by then standard reply: "I must run for governor. I want to run for governor. I seek no other office. I have no other ambition." Said Lawrence Spivak: "Governor, doesn't this large studio audience give you any indication of how some people of the country feel about that?" Stevenson surveyed the audience with a smile. "It's very flattering indeed," he said, "and I suppose flattery hurts no one—that is, if he doesn't inhale."

In the days immediately following, however, he was convinced

---

[4] One of these concerned his Alger Hiss deposition. See pp.358–61.

that the "flattery" he was receiving was hurting him—if, indeed, it was flattery. The key question was asked him in a hundred forms, and he kept repeating his answer to it, with growing weariness and rare flashes of exasperation.

At last, on April 16, eight days after he received his formal nomination as Democratic candidate for governor of Illinois, he felt compelled to issue a statement which would, he thought, end any chance of his nomination. On April 17, a great Democratic fund-raising dinner was to be held at the Waldorf in New York, with W. Averell Harriman, then Mutual Security Director, as guest of honor. All the leading contenders for the presidential nomination were to be present, and for that reason Stevenson at first declined to attend: he was not a contender, and by appearing at the banquet and speaking there, as he was asked to do, he would be automatically classified as one. His initial refusal, however, raised an outcry among party leaders, who pointed out that, whether he liked it or not, he was the crowd getter, the publicity getter, and the party needed all the money and all the publicity it could raise. In response to this pressure Stevenson agreed to appear, but as he entered the plane for New York he issued the following statement, in order that his appearance would not be misconstrued:

I have been urged to announce my candidacy for the Democratic nomination for President. . . . Others have asked me merely to say that I would accept a nomination which I did not seek. To state my position now on a prospect so remote in time and probability seems to me a little presumptuous. But I would rather presume than embarrass or mislead. . . .

I have repeatedly said that I was a candidate for Governor of Illinois and had no other ambition. To this I must now add that in view of my prior commitment to run for Governor and my desire and the desire of many who have given their help and confidence in the unfinished work in Illinois, I could not accept the nomination for any other office this summer.

And that, it appeared, was that. Stevenson "seems effectively to have closed the door to his nomination," said the New York *Times*, adding that "many people will regret Mr. Stevenson's decision, for he is the type of man that either party should be proud to have for its leader." Political commentators accepted the "fact" that Stevenson was now definitely out of the race, ensuring that the Democratic convention would be "wide open" for the first time in twenty years. Yet the very papers which carried such comments also carried news stories about the "hit" Stevenson had made with his speech at the Harriman banquet, stories which kept alive (if feebly through the next weeks) the hope that, somehow, he would become the nominee after all.

III

Six days later Harriman formally announced his candidacy, and in the following weeks several others, overtly or covertly, took steps to advance their candidacies, among them Senator Richard Russell of Georgia, Senator Robert Kerr of Oklahoma, and Vice-President Alben Barkley.

The Walter Johnson committee, though discouraged, continued its operations. Its members drew what comfort they could from the fact that Stevenson had not said he "would not" accept the nomination but only that he "could not," thus suggesting that the decision was a function of circumstances rather than an expression of private will. Circumstances might change. . . .

In late April and in May, Stevenson spoke in Texas, Oregon, and California, filling engagements he had made in early January after he'd announced for governor and before the presidential boom had begun. Everywhere he was enthusiastically received. Everywhere he was hounded by reporters, and by partisans who insisted that he must run. Pressed in Portland, Oregon, to say whether or not he would accept a draft, he replied: "I cannot speculate about hypothetical situations. But I don't believe there ever has been a genuine draft of an unwilling man for the presidential nomination by either party.[5] I doubt if such a thing is possible." But suppose it happened? reporters kept asking him. Was he "afraid" to run against General Eisenhower? No, he replied in California, adding with a smile: "I don't think Ike is afraid of me." A few weeks later, when he visited the Illinois National Guard encampment in Wisconsin, a fervent supporter followed him around all day, pursuing him even to the airport, and as the governor climbed the steps to the plane's door, the man called out: "Well, what'll you do if we nominate you anyway?" Stevenson turned in weary exasperation. "Guess I'd have to shoot my-

[5] James A. Garfield was drafted against his will in the Republican convention of 1880, as Stevenson was soon reminded.

self," he said, and entered the plane. (Later, Republicans spread the story that Stevenson had threatened to commit suicide if he were nominated, clearly revealing that he was mentally unstable.)

On June 30, at the annual Conference of State Governors, he again told reporters that "without such participation on my part I do not believe [a] . . . draft can or will develop," but this time he added: "In the unlikely event that it does, I will decide what to do . . . in the light of conditions then existing." The latter remark kept alive the flame of hope in such men as Walter Johnson.

Others—professional politicians—fully shared the view of Jack Arvey and Stevenson that such a draft would "take a miracle." They were no strong believers in miracles. Some of them remembered only too vividly what had happened to them when, in 1948, they had participated in the movement to draft Eisenhower on the Democratic ticket.

Frank McKinney, chairman of the Democratic National Committee, repeatedly urged Stevenson to at least make his availability known covertly and became convinced that, in the light of the governor's attitude, the cause was hopeless. He and Harry Truman therefore turned their attention to other candidates, eliminating one after another of these as unsuitable for one reason or another. Dick Russell was impossible because of the race issue; Kerr was impossible because he had represented oil and gas interests in the Senate, introducing a bill on behalf of these which Truman had vetoed;[6] Harriman, who had served well in supremely important federal posts, had never run for elective office; Barkley was an old man, and there was doubt that labor would support him.

Nevertheless it was on Barkley that Truman and McKinney finally settled, two weeks before the convention opened. At a meeting in the White House, Truman told the Vice-President "that up to that time Stevenson had refused to run and if he [Barkley] was serious about wanting the nomination we would support him."[7]

---

[6] Wrote Truman on p. 494 of Vol. II of his *Memoirs:* "I have always felt that any man who goes either to the Senate or the House to represent a special interest in his own state and who sponsors legislation to help that special interest forfeits any claim to national leadership in the Democratic party. Historically, the Democratic party is not a special-interest party."

[7] Ibid., p. 495.

CHAPTER TWENTY-FIVE

"The Stark Reality of Responsibility"

There were three national news foci in Chicago during the week which began Friday, July 18. One was the International Amphitheater, vacated by the National Republican Convention a week before and now redecorated and refitted for the Democratic convention which opened on Monday, the twenty-first. A second was the Conrad Hilton Hotel, where the aspirants to the Democratic presidential nomination had their headquarters and where many of the convention delegates stayed and held their caucuses. The third was a large and handsome three-story brick house at 1416 North Astor Street, the home of Bill Blair's father, William McCormick Blair, Sr. Into this house, that Friday, moved Adlai Stevenson, with Carl McGowan and Bill Blair, an event which abruptly transformed this normally quiet neighborhood of the wealthy into a scene of hectic, crowded activity. Five phone booths were set up along the sidewalk to accommodate hordes of reporters who trampled into mud the walled garden between Chicago's suddenly famous "Blair House" and the house to the north where Bill's grandmother, Mrs. Joseph T. Bowen, lived. The crowds soon grew so large that the police were forced to close off the block.

On the fifteenth floor of the Conrad Hilton, on Wednesday the sixteenth, the National Stevenson for President Committee, with Leo Lerner now serving as a co-chairman with Johnson, had established a unique campaign headquarters. Like the headquarters of other candidates, it distributed buttons, literature, and free soda pop. Like the others, it was a scene of incessant noise and excitement as delegates came and went and crucial tactical conferences were held morning, noon, and night. But, unlike any other, this headquarters, manned by volunteers, had no contact, direct or indirect, with the candidate it sought to nominate. Johnson and his colleagues went to great lengths to *avoid* such contacts: when Bill Flanagan, the governor's press secretary, appeared there, he was asked by Johnson to leave; when John Fell and Borden came on Saturday afternoon, curious "to see the people who were trying to make . . . father do what he said he did not wish to do,"[1] the headquarters was thrown into consternation, and the boys were asked not to come back. It would have been fatal to the committee's strategy if the impression had got abroad that the reluctant candidate was merely another coy one. The draft which Johnson and the others sought to arrange must not only *be* genuine, it must also *seem* so.

On that oppressively hot Saturday the committee's primary concern was to make sure that Stevenson's name was put in nomination, and under conditions most favorable to his candidacy. In this it was greatly aided by a meeting called by Kenneth Anderson, National Committeeman from Kansas, in his headquarters at the Palmer House. Anderson and John Young, the Democratic state chairman from Kansas, were the first bona fide delegates to come out strongly and definitely for a draft of Stevenson, and though the Palmer House meeting broke up without clear-cut decisions having been made concerning nomination strategy, it initiated a process by which the Stevenson movement grew like a snowball rolling downhill—a simile peculiarly attractive to sweating delegates on that fervid day. Thereafter, Anderson, Young, and Anderson's youthful assistant, Milo Sutton, were ceaselessly active, getting in touch with other delegations, stimulating caucuses, and obtaining committed votes.

On that same Saturday an important meeting was held with members of the Pennsylvania delegation at the Morrison Hotel, a meeting at which Johnson and the leaders of the Pennsylvania group agreed to work together. One of the Pennsylvania delegation was an old Princeton friend of Stevenson's, Lewis M. Stevens, now a member of the Philadelphia City Council. Another, a man who would be of crucial importance to Stevenson's political future, was James A. Finnegan, president of Philadelphia City Council, who up to that time had never met the governor and would not meet him for some time thereafter. A key question, maddening under the circumstances, was: "Will Stevenson accept a draft?" (They could not know that

[1] Walter Johnson, op. cit., pp. 57–59.

Stevenson had decided he must do so: he had told McGowan and Blair that he would, though he continued to believe that a draft was a remote possibility and he continued to do all he could to discourage it.) By the time the meeting broke up, the Johnson group was fairly certain that the Pennsylvania caucus next day would produce a substantial number of Stevenson votes and that delegates emerging from that caucus wearing Stevenson buttons would produce a significant impact on the convention as a whole.

Meanwhile, on the second floor of Blair House, Stevenson worked with McGowan on the welcoming speech he would make to the delegates on Monday. On Sunday morning he attended services at the Fourth Presbyterian Church (the church in which he had been married), where his friend, the Reverend Harrison Ray Anderson, preached a sermon quite obviously aimed at him entitled, "How Men Know God's Will." When he left the church reporters asked him what he thought of the sermon. It was "superb," he said; the minister had "helped" him.

Later that day he attended the caucus of the Illinois delegation of which he was a member. The meeting was closed to reporters, but those enterprising gentlemen lay down on the floor with their ears to the crack beneath a sliding partition. They heard Stevenson insist again, with now-desperate sincerity, that he did not want the nomination. Of the presidency he said: "I do not dream myself fit for the job—temperamentally, mentally, or physically. And I ask therefore that you all abide by my wishes not to nominate me, nor to vote for me if I should be nominated." Emerging from this meeting, he was asked by reporters if he would yield to a draft if the convention became deadlocked. "Show me the deadlock first," Stevenson replied. The reporters already knew that he had done all he could to discourage the placing of his name in nomination. When he arrived in Chicago he had been told that either Governor Henry F. Schricker of Indiana or Archibald Alexander, a young friend of Stevenson's who was a candidate for senator in New Jersey, might make the nominating speech on his behalf. "I shall do all I can to prevent that," he promptly replied. And he did so. "I called them both by phone and asked them not to," he later said.[2] "Alexander agreed, but my esteemed friend, Governor Schricker, rebelled. . . ."

[2] *Major Campaign Speeches of Adlai E. Stevenson, 1952* (New York: Random House, 1953), pp. xxii and xxiii of Introduction.

Next morning, Monday, July 21, two determining events occurred. One was a breakfast given by Vice-President Barkley for sixteen labor-union leaders, in which he bid for their support and was refused it.[3] The other was Stevenson's speech of welcome. A spontaneous six-minute demonstration followed the governor's appearance on the rostrum, and only his departure from the rostrum ended the wild applause at the speech's close. For fifteen minutes the delegates and the nation listened to a politician like none they had heard before.

He said, in part:

Here, my friends, on the prairies of Illinois and of the Middle West we can see a long way in all directions. . . . Here there are no barriers . . . to ideas and to aspirations. We want none; we want no shackles on the mind or the spirit, no rigid patterns of thought, and no iron conformity. We want only the faith and the conviction that triumph in free and fair contest.

As a Democrat perhaps you will permit me to remind you that until four years ago the people of Illinois had chosen but three Democratic Governors in a hundred years. One was John Peter Altgeld, whom the great Illinois poet, Vachel Lindsay, called the Eagle Forgotten. He was an immigrant. One was Edward F. Dunne, whose parents came from the old sod of Ireland, and last was Henry Horner, but one generation removed from Germany. John Peter Altgeld, my friends, was a Protestant, Governor Dunne was a Catholic, Henry Horner was a Jew.

And that, my friends, is the American story, written by the Democratic party here on the prairies of Illinois.

He reviewed the Democratic era which had been ushered in, there in Chicago, with the nomination of Franklin Roosevelt. Then his wit sparkled and crackled, sending his audience into gales of laughter:

But our Republican friends have said that it was all a miserable

[3] Said Harry Truman, op. cit., p. 495: "[In] one essential respect Barkley failed to follow our suggestions to him. In meeting with the leaders of labor to enlist their support, we told him to be sure to see the leaders one at a time. . . . We knew that they would never commit themselves in a crowd, and all that came of this meeting . . . was a unanimous turndown. I am of the opinion that if Barkley had been advised by a manager skilled in dealing with labor this rejection would never have occurred and Barkley would have been the Democratic nominee."

failure. For almost a week pompous phrases marched over this landscape in search of an idea, and the only idea they found was that the two great decades of progress in peace, and of victory in war, and of bold leadership in this anxious hour, were the misbegotten spawn of bungling, of corruption, of socialism, of mismanagement, of waste and of worse. They captured, they tied and they dragged that ragged idea here into this hall and they furiously beat it to death for a solid week.

After listening to this everlasting procession of epithets about our misdeeds I was even surprised the next morning when the mail was delivered on time. . . . But we Democrats were by no means the only victims here. First, they slaughtered each other and then they went after us. And the same vocabulary was good for both exercises, which was a great convenience. Perhaps the proximity of the stockyards accounts for the carnage.

But he spoke also soberly, calling for a "sober understanding of the breadth and depth of the revolutionary currents in the world," and closed with a solemn exhortation:

And let us remember that we are not meeting here alone. All the world is watching and listening to what we say, what we do and how we behave. So let us give them a demonstration of democracy in action at its best—our manners good, our proceedings orderly and dignified—and, above all, let us make our decisions openly, fairly, not by the processes of synthetic excitement or mass hysteria. Let us make them as these solemn times demand, by earnest thought and prayerful deliberation.

And thus can the people's party reassure the people and vindicate and strengthen the forces of democracy throughout the world.

Even before that fateful Monday, the political columnist, Doris Fleeson, had written (on Sunday evening, the twentieth): "It now looks as though Gov. Adlai Stevenson will be dragged protesting to the presidential altar by the Democratic party. His shrieks are growing fainter, his suitor more importunate." On Monday evening Barkley issued a bitter statement in which he charged "certain self-annointed labor leaders" with forcing him to "withdraw my name from the consideration of the convention." On Tuesday, Anne O'Hare McCormick said in the New York *Times:* ". . . In one day . . . all the confused and unchanneled currents seemed to converge upon the shrinking figure of Governor Adlai Stevenson as the one and only, the almost automatic choice of the convention. Nothing but action by the President could alter the picture, and the general feeling here is that even that would now be too late. . . ." By that time, too, a firm coalition of the Draft Committee with the delegates of Pennsylvania, Kansas, Indiana, and New Jersey had been formed; Governor Schricker was at work on his speech nominating Stevenson; and former Senator Francis J. Myers of Pennsylvania was operating, despite Stevenson's public request that he not do so, as floor leader of the pro-Stevenson forces.

On Thursday afternoon the nomination speeches began. By late afternoon the names of Russell, Kefauver, Kerr, Senator J. W. Fulbright of Arkansas, and Averell Harriman had been presented to the convention with the usual demonstrations. Then Governor Schricker arose (Delaware having yielded to Indiana for the purpose) to speak for twelve and one half minutes, concluding: "Ninety-two years ago, the nation called from the prairies of Illinois the greatest of Illinois citizens, Abraham Lincoln. Lincoln, too, was reluctant. But there are times when a man is not permitted to say no. I place before you the man we cannot permit to say no, Adlai E. Stevenson of Illinois." There followed a wild demonstration which left no doubt that Stevenson was the convention's majority choice. Other names were then placed in nomination: Governor G. Mennen Williams of Michigan; Senator Hubert Humphrey of Minnesota; Governor Paul Dever of Massachusetts; Barkley; and Federal Security Administrator Oscar Ewing. But these were clearly anticlimactic.

On Thursday evening there was a bitter floor fight in the convention over a "loyalty pledge" aimed at the southern Democrats who, as "Dixiecrats," had bolted their party in revolt against Truman's civil-rights program in 1948. A resolution adopted on Monday required all delegates to sign a pledge that they would support the convention's nominees. Virginia, Louisiana, and South Carolina refused to do so. The floor fight then developed over the seating of the Virginia delegation, a resolution by Maryland to do so being vehemently opposed by supporters of Kefauver and Harriman, who hoped thus to halt the Stevenson draft. The resolution was finally adopted by a vote of 650½ for to 518 against—and the nomination of Stevenson, in the view of most observers, was assured. Even if the resolution had been rejected, that nomination would have been virtually certain. . . .

One can imagine at least some of Truman's feelings as he read such comments as Mrs. McCormick of the *Times* had made Tuesday morning and as Roscoe Drummond published in the *Christian Science Monitor* Tuesday evening: ". . . This convention is jelling so speedily, the prospect is that President Truman will have no opportunity to determine the presidential nominee—even if he could. . . . They say that Mr. Truman, who can recognize a trend as well as the next politician, is ready to give his favor to Governor Stevenson. The view here is that if he does not do so shortly, he will be waving at a bandwagon which has passed by." The President, it appeared, had been neatly cut off from power, and it must have been as salt upon the resulting wound to have Stevenson call him, on Thursday, July 24, to ask if it "would embarrass" the President if he, Stevenson, "allowed his name to be placed in nomination."

Stevenson meant this to be a courtesy call, but Truman's response to it clearly revealed the President's sense (an unadmitted sense) that party control had slipped from his hands. Wrote Truman of this telephone conversation: "I replied with a show of exasperation and some rather vigorous words and concluded by saying to Stevenson, 'I have been trying since January to get you to say that. Why should it embarrass me?'"[4]

II

During those historic days Stevenson emerged only twice from Blair House: to make his welcoming speech Monday morning and, on Friday morning, to breakfast in attempted secrecy with Averell Harriman at Ed McDougal's apartment on Lake Shore Drive, where Buffie and Ernest Ives stayed during the convention. He watched the proceedings intermittently on TV. When it became evident that his name would be placed in nomination in such circumstances as to make his selection likely, he began to write an acceptance speech, working in a second-floor bedroom on the north side of the house, with windows overlooking the walled garden. He wrote, as always, on a ruled yellow tablet, in longhand, slowly, painfully, conferring often with Carl McGowan, passing the written sheets to Carol Evans, who worked on a typewriter set upon a card table in the next room.

[4] Harry Truman, op. cit., p. 496. He added: "Actually, if Barkley had not withdrawn when he did . . . I would not . . . have been able to tell Stevenson that I would support him, and Barkley would have been the Democratic nominee."

After Governor Schricker's nominating speech Stevenson issued a brief statement: "I had hoped they would not nominate me, but I am deeply affected by this expression of confidence and goodwill."

On Friday afternoon he received a phone call from Frank Mc-Kinney, asking him to dine that evening with President Truman, who had just flown in from Washington. With thanks and regrets, Stevenson declined. He explained that by dining with the President he might appear to be promoting his chances for the nomination, in contradiction of all he had done and said before with regard to it. He did not say what was of course true, namely that by dining with Truman he would have given the public impression that he was Truman's man, restoring to the President some of the party power and prestige which had been lost through the course of recent events. To the precise extent that Truman's power was increased, under those circumstances, Stevenson's would be reduced, though it is quite possible that this idea did not explicitly occur to the governor.

Other ideas certainly must have, as the convention moved toward the balloting session. It must have occurred to him that, in point of fact, he did not have a clear choice between the governorship of Illinois—which he certainly did want—and the nomination for President. If he rejected the latter he might be defeated in his pursuit of the former. Obviously he was the strongest presidential candidate the Democrats could run against Eisenhower—the only candidate, people kept telling him, who had a chance to win against the popular military hero. And if Eisenhower won a landslide victory he might well carry into office the Illinois Republican gubernatorial candidate, William G. Stratton, a personable young man who bore a name well known in Illinois politics—and this despite Stevenson's record. . . . Stevenson may also have been reminded that the situation now facing him on the national level was similar to that which had faced him on the state level in late 1947, when he had been reluctant to run for governor. Dutch Smith had told him then that if he failed to run when the party needed him he would probably not be permitted to run when other conditions were more to his liking. . . .

The balloting took place on Friday afternoon. Of the 615½ votes needed for nomination, Kefauver received 340 on the first ballot. Stevenson was second with 273, Russell third with 268, and Harriman fourth with 123½. The other votes were scattered among ten candidates, led by Kerr, who received 65. On the second ballot Kefauver still led, having increased his vote to 362½. Stevenson's vote had increased to 324½, an increase which did not seem significantly large to many observers but which clearly indicated to convention "insiders" that the governor would be nominated on the third ballot with votes which had been committed for two ballots to other candidates. The convention then recessed for dinner (the time was six-fifteen).

At Blair House that night Adlai Stevenson dined with Buffie and Ernest Ives, and his two sons, Borden and John Fell. (They all regretted the fact that Adlai, Jr., then in Marine training at Quantico, could not be present.) Stevenson was completely relaxed. He joked with Buffie about her appearance on TV that day; a TV camera had crept up on her from behind, and Stevenson hugely enjoyed the resultant picture on the Blair House screen. "You'll have to learn to protect your rear," he laughed. After dinner he went back up to his second-floor bedroom, there to continue work on his speech.

When the convention reassembled, the crucial third ballot was taken; it required a long time, for there were many switches. The final official tally gave Stevenson 613 votes, two and a half less than needed for nomination. Utah then switched its twelve votes to Stevenson, Kefauver and Russell yielded to him, and thus, early in the morning of Saturday, July 26, he became the Democratic presidential nominee for 1952.

He had not yet said publicly that he would accept the nomination. . . . But after the balloting ended he crossed to the steps of Mrs. Bowen's house and made a short speech for TV and to the crowd in which he indicated he would accept. Then he left for the convention, where he joined President Truman in the Stockyard Inn for the short walk to the hall.

Meanwhile, at the International Amphitheater, Buffie Ives was taken to Mrs. Truman's box, where she sat beside the First Lady, with Perle Mesta, Secretary of the Treasury John Snyder, and other distinguished people. "I felt in a haze as hot white lights flashed on us," she later said, "and above my head floated one small balloon lettered 'KEFAUVER.'" Mrs. Truman explained that her husband would present the nominee to the convention. In the box assigned to Adlai Stevenson his aunt Letitia, the Edison Dicks, Dutch and Ellen Smith, Mrs. Harriet Welling, Borden and John Fell had "lived" nearly all that week. That night, though, the Dicks and some of the others were at Blair House, watching on TV. . . .

Time passed. Weary, restless, the great throng waited. The organ played, again and again, "Don't Let Them Take It Away," the campaign song.

There was a stir at last, then a hoarse roar as the President of the United States strode briskly to the rostrum, with Adlai Stevenson beside him.

The roar died.

The President—that familiar jaunty figure with the flat midwestern twang in his voice echoing, it seemed, almost nostalgically, out of an age already past and swiftly receding—spoke a fighting speech, as he had done in '48. Then he presented Adlai Stevenson. He lifted Stevenson's hand high as the convention rose to its feet, wildly cheering, its placards swinging as the organ boomed out again the campaign song.

And then, at what might have been a long moment of deflating anticlimax, came from Stevenson what to millions at that time seemed the voice of the future, a voice which sang with a lyric sense of the past and at the same time was clipped, precise. It was as though the great tradition of eloquence met here a prosaic present and a fearsome future, and advanced upon these with a firm intellectual discipline.

"I accept your nomination—and your program," he said.

"I should have preferred to hear those words uttered by a stronger, a wiser, a better man than myself," he said.

"None of you, my friends, can wholly appreciate what is in my heart," he said. "I can only hope that you may understand my words. They will be few."

And millions, listening that dark early-morning hour with a kind of awed astonishment, believed they understood. Many of them listened again next morning, in company with additional millions, as the "few words" were rebroadcast.

He said:

I have not sought the honor you have done me. I could not seek it because I aspired to another office. . . . I would not seek your nomination for the Presidency because the burdens of that office stagger the imagination. Its potential for good and evil now and in the years of our lives smothers exultation and converts vanity into prayer.

I have asked the Merciful Father—the Father of us all—to let this cup pass from me. But from such dread responsibility one does not shrink in fear. . . . So, "If this cup may not pass from me, except I drink it, Thy will be done."

. . . And now, my friends, that you have made your decision, I will fight to win that office with all my heart and soul. And, with your help, I have no doubt that we will win. . . .

He praised the conduct of the convention. He praised the platform which had been adopted. He strove to allay the fear that a continuation of Democratic control of the government would mean the death of the two-party system. It had seemed to him that the Republican party "looked brutally alive a couple of weeks ago, and I mean both Republican parties!" Nor was he afraid that the Democratic party was "old and fat and indolent"; it could never become so "as long as it looks forward and not back, as long as it commands the allegiance of the young and the hopeful who dream the dreams and see the visions of a better America and a better world." He said:

. . . When the tumult and the shouting die, when the bands are gone and the lights are dimmed, there is the stark reality of responsibility in an hour of history haunted with those gaunt, grim specters of strife, dissension and materialism at home, and ruthless, inscrutable and hostile power abroad.

The ordeal of the twentieth century—the bloodiest, most turbulent era of the Christian age—is far from over. Sacrifice, patience, understanding and implacable purpose may be our lot for years to come. Let's face it! Let's talk sense to the American people! Let's tell them the truth, that there are no gains without pains, that we are now on the eve of great decisions, not easy decisions, like resistance when you're attacked, but a long, patient, costly struggle which alone can assure triumph over the great enemies of man—war, poverty and tyranny—and the assaults upon human dignity which are the most grievous consequences of each.

. . . Better we lose the election than mislead the people; and better we lose than misgovern the people. Help me to do the job in this autumn of conflict and of campaign; help me to do the job in these years of darkness, doubt and of crisis which stretch beyond the horizon of tonight's happy vision, and we will justify our glorious past and the loyalty of silent millions who look to us for compassion, for understanding and for honest purpose. Thus we will serve our great tradition greatly.

Saturday morning. . . .

Though he has had little or no sleep for twenty-four hours, the Democratic candidate for President seems as fresh and cheery as always. We may glimpse him through the eyes of Newton Minow, who had arrived at the governor's Loop office on the preceding Monday wearing a big "Stevenson for President" button, earning thus a frown of disapproval from Carl McGowan. (Minow was an "innocent" in this; someone had pinned the badge upon him as he entered the building.) Now he enters Blair House to confer with Bill Blair, and as the two talk, he sees Stevenson with Averell Harriman in the next room. Then Stevenson comes out. "Why, hello, Newt!" he says, shaking hands. "I heard you were in town. I'm sorry I haven't had an opportunity to discuss things with you." Minow avers that the governor may have been a mite busy the last few days. Stevenson nods. "I'll see you in Springfield," the governor says. "Glad you're going to be with us."

Buffie Ives, that morning, is awakened from two hours of sleep by phone calls. Three highly important calls from highly important people come to her, for transmittal to her brother who seems to them barricaded behind an interminable busy signal. She dresses and hurries over to Blair House, delivering her messages to Bill Blair. Then she rides in the back seat of a car, between Stevenson and Harriman, to the convention hall. Harriman and Stevenson discuss the chairmanship of the Democratic National Committee as they ride; Truman is exerting tremendous pressure to ensure the continuance of Frank McKinney in that office and Stevenson is, as yet, noncommittal. (Desperately he strives to think of someone with whom to counter Truman's pressure, but it will not be until ten days later that he, lying awake one night, suddenly thinks of Stephen Mitchell, the lawyer who, with Lou Kohn and Dutch Smith, had launched the Stevenson political career in 1947.) There is no talk about the vice-presidency, for this matter was settled the night before. Truman, Stevenson, McKinney, and Sam Rayburn of Texas had met in a private room behind the stage and there agreed upon Senator John Sparkman of Alabama.

At the convention hall, soon after the Stevenson party's arrival, Senator Sparkman is nominated. He and Stevenson stand together on the rostrum, smiling and waving to cheering thousands. They turn this way and that to face a hundred cameras.

Sunday. . . .

Stevenson rides south from Chicago by train. A cheering throng awaits him at the Bloomington station, where the train pauses. He sees the faces of scores of boyhood friends. Alverta Duff presents him with a floral horseshoe as the crowd laughs and applauds. "If you can't get a good cup of coffee at the White House," says she, "just send for me." Twenty-five thousand people await him at Springfield. The ovation he receives there deeply moves him, more so than any other of these last hectic days. He speaks to the vast crowd with tears in his eyes—a rare thing with him: seldom does he reveal his deepest feelings. He speaks in the shadow of the courthouse, on the square Abraham Lincoln had known so well.

Monday night. . . . The hour approaches midnight as Bill Blair enters the governor's basement office in the mansion.

"The caretaker has been alerted," Blair says.

"Thanks, Bill," Stevenson says, arising. "Don't let a hint of this get out, will you not?"

"Not a hint," Blair says.

Stevenson slips furtively out a side door of the mansion and down a dark side street to the corner of Eighth and Market. He pauses for a second or two, looking up at Lincoln's home. Then he hurries up the short walk to the door, where the caretaker admits him. For an hour he sits alone in Lincoln's rocking chair. What does he think, feel, as he sits there? He will never say to anyone; perhaps he could not if he would. But a great calm is upon his spirit when he leaves that house and walks again the darkened side street. He has come to some sort of terms with the stupendous, the incredible thing that has happened to him. . . .

III

He had promised to "talk sense" to the American people. He proceeded, in early August, to map out a campaign which would do so, a campaign which would stimulate a "reasoned and precise debate" on the great issues emerging from the "ordeal of the Twentieth Century." He interpreted General Eisenhower's hard-won victory in the Republican convention as a "victory of the constructive and progressive men in the Republican Party over its bitter and reactionary elements." The entire campaign might therefore mean the elevating of the "national political dialogue" to a higher plane than any it had occupied, perhaps, in the whole of our national history. He realized that his views and he, personally, were little known in the country. He therefore planned in his early speeches to set forth his position as clearly, as unequivocally as possible upon such matters as agricultural policy, foreign policy, labor, natural-resource conservation, inflation, governmental corruption, and so on. These initial statements would, according to his plan, occupy the first half of the campaign. October, or the second half of the campaign, would be reserved for "amplification and rebuttal" and for dealing with "the exigencies and opportunities that were bound to develop as the campaign progressed."[5]

His chief consultant and partner in this planning was Carl McGowan, and McGowan was largely responsible for the hasty recruitment of a research and writing staff whereby the substantive aims of the campaign would be implemented. As a principal writing aide, Stevenson himself called in Arthur M. Schlesinger, Jr., Harvard historian and author of a Pulitzer prize-winning book, *The Age of Jackson*. Also called in were McGowan's old friend, W. Willard Wirtz; David Bell, who had served as a Truman assistant in the White House and who returned to Springfield with Stevenson after a conference with Truman in Washington on August 12; Robert Tufts, who had been a member of the State Department's Policy Planning Division; John Bartlow Martin; William Reddig, editor of an Olathe, Kansas, newspaper and formerly literary editor of the Kansas City *Star;* and Sidney Hyman, who had been closely associated with Harry Hopkins and Robert Sherwood in wartime Washington. With this core group was associated a group of in-and-outers—men who contributed as much of their time and energy as their other obligations would permit them to do. Among them were Kenneth Galbraith, Harvard economist; Jack Fischer of *Harper's* magazine; David Cohn, then closely associated with Senator Fulbright of Arkansas; Eric Hodgins of the Luce publications, author of the best-selling *Mr. Blandings Builds His Dream House;* and Bernard De Voto, historian of the American West and a conservation authority.

This group was dubbed the "Elks Club" because it headquartered in a large and noisy room on the third floor of Springfield's Elks Club. At the back were four bedrooms where some of the writers slept. They proved to be a congenial group, fortunately so in that they must engage in concentrated mental effort under frantic circum-

[5] The quotations are from the Introduction to *Major Campaign Speeches of Adlai E. Stevenson, 1952*, p. xxvi.

stances with six hours or less of sleep a night for many weeks. Contact with the governor was maintained through McGowan. The organization was as loose, as informal as it could possibly be, but Schlesinger functioned as its head, with David Bell as a kind of second-in-command, performing most of the duties of office manager. Writing assignments were made virtually automatically in terms of the special subject-matter competencies of the man, one or two of whom—different ones at different times—traveled with the governor and served as "pipe lines" back to the "Club."

All of them became convinced, if they were not at the outset, that Stevenson was a far better writer of Stevenson speeches than any of them could ever be. Most of them were initially perturbed by the fact that the final drafts of speeches generally bore little resemblance to the drafts they had painfully prepared, but whatever resentment they may occasionally have felt was submerged in the pride they took in a political candidate who was so fine a master of their own profession. With pride and truth they could proclaim that the speeches as Stevenson finally gave them—speeches which would be gathered into a best-selling book months after the campaigning had ended—were very much Stevenson's own.

Nevertheless, none in the campaign organization, save the governor himself, bore more of the health-breaking brunt of that campaign than did the "Elks Club" members (including, of course, McGowan), most of whom collapsed into a hospital bed at some point during the ordeal. None contributed more, save the governor, to that which would make the campaign memorable and perhaps unique in American political history. They were indispensable instruments of that extraordinary clarity and eloquence with which Stevenson discussed issues between mid-August and election eve.

There was one issue, however, on which neither they nor the governor prepared even an initial statement, one on which the governor's personal stand was not wholly unambiguous. That issue was President Truman and the portion of the administrative record which had been dubbed, in the Republican press, "Trumanism."

Stevenson stood firmly by the major domestic and foreign policies of the Democratic administration; he defended vigorously the overall record which President Truman had made; but at the same time, in Truman's own words, he seemed to give "the impression that he was seeking to dissociate himself from the administration in Wash-

ington, and perhaps from me."[6] He did so by replacing Frank Mc-
Kinney with Stephen A. Mitchell as chairman of the Democratic
National Committee (according to Truman he "fired" McKinney)
and by establishing his campaign headquarters, not in Washington
where the National Committee headquartered, but in Springfield.
The two acts were of a piece: had he not had his own man as national chairman, the problem of co-operating with the national
Democratic organization would have been insoluble. As it was, it was
so far from perfectly solved that some, even in Stevenson's organization, wondered if the GOP's "two-headed elephant" wasn't being
matched against a "two-headed donkey" in several respects.

There were other grave disadvantages to headquartering in
Springfield. Travel in and out of the town was much more difficult
than travel in and out of Washington would have been, and Springfield was deficient in mass-communications facilities. The latter com-
plication was enhanced by the apparent fact that Bill Flanagan,
whom Stevenson retained as his personal press secretary, seemed
not to enjoy the candidate's full confidence. When newsmen asked
Flanagan questions to which, they felt, he should have immediate
answers, Flanagan was likely to reply that he didn't know, he'd try
to find out. For this, and various "foul-ups" in news facilitation, the
unfortunate Flanagan was soon very much in the "doghouse" with
reporters. The situation was considerably improved when the White
House loaned to Stevenson one of the President's principal assistants, Clayton Fritchey, who had had a brilliant newspaper career
(he'd been editor of the New Orleans *Item,* managing editor of the
Baltimore *Post,* and won a Pulitzer prize for reporting while on the
Cleveland *Press*) before coming to Washington in '40 as assistant to
General Marshall, then Secretary of Defense.

Fritchey and Bell, however, were the only men closely associated
with Truman and the national organization who became closely associated with Stevenson during the campaign. A large red brick
house a half block from the Executive Mansion was rented, and
some thought it significant of the whole campaign effort that the
sign on the front porch identifying this house as "Stevenson Campaign Headquarters" was so small ("I want it small," Stevenson had
insisted. "Nothing gaudy!") that many who sought the house failed
to notice it. Soon this headquarters was vastly overcrowded with

[6] Harry S. Truman, op. cit., p. 498.

what many old-time Democrats regarded, disgustedly, as "amateurs" —so much so that considerable space was rented in Springfield hotels.

The chief "amateur" was Wilson Wyatt, whom Stevenson asked to become his personal campaign manager. Actually Wyatt, however "green" some might think him to be as regards national "politicking," was certainly no stranger to public life. A successful lawyer, he had been mayor of Louisville, Kentucky, in the early '40s; had served with the Board of Economic Warfare in North Africa for a time in '43; and had been National Administrator of Housing in Washington immediately after the war. He was a good friend of Barry Bingham and Mark Ethridge of the Louisville *Courier-Journal*, and of Carl McGowan, whom he had known in Washington during the war. Wyatt's chief assistant as campaign manager was Stevenson's old and close lawyer friend, George Ball. Dutch Smith and Jane (Mrs. Edison) Dick served as co-chairmen of the national Volunteers for Stevenson.

Bill Blair continued as Stevenson's personal facilitating officer and appointments secretary, proving under intense fire his good judgment and evenness of temper, his efficiency, his remarkable talent for human relations. Richard Nelson, the governor's aide who was president of the national Young Democrats that year, was another close assistant. Carol Evans and Margaret Munn continued their secretarial duties on the tours. Nearly all the others personally associated with him during those strenuous days were long-time associates and personal friends. As always, he seemed to need people immediately around him with whom he could relax and through whom he could keep in touch continuously with his own past, his own personal tradition. Thus Ernest and Buffie Ives traveled on the campaign trains and planes with him and so, part of the time, did John Fell, Borden, and Aunt Letitia Stevenson. Adlai, Jr., on leave, joined the party in Boston briefly.

Inevitably Truman took a sour view of much of this operation. The President was unpersuaded by Stevenson's "explanations" that the presidential candidate customarily chose his own man as National Committee head and that the campaign headquarters *must* be in Springfield since Stevenson continued to be governor of Illinois. In actual fact, of course, Stevenson was very seldom in Springfield during the whole of the campaign and the executive power was transferred to the lieutenant governor, Sherwood Dixon. He, however, had taken Stevenson's place as candidate for governor in Illinois, and was busy with his campaign.

The only occasion on which Stevenson felt obliged to make an emergency visit to Illinois between August and November was when an ugly prison riot broke out at Menard in late October. Stevenson was campaigning in Pennsylvania at the time. Back in Springfield, Michael Seyfrit, Director of Public Safety, and the lieutenant governor struggled to handle things in such a way as to make the governor's return unnecessary, especially since the governor's intervention might look like a "grandstand play." But the rioting convicts, some 339 of them, held seven guards as hostages in the east cell block and, after two days had passed, Sherwood Dixon felt compelled to put through a call to Carl McGowan on the campaign train.

"I immediately made the arrangements for the trip back," McGowan later recalled. "I knew that Stevenson had the same close feeling for the state police I did—a force he had taken out of politics and built up—and I knew he would want to be with them. When I told him of the plans he approved, without a flicker of hesitation. We also thought that, when the rioters knew the final authority was there on the spot, they would feel there was no more room for delay and bargaining, and that it might well help to prevent bloodshed."

Stevenson spoke on Thursday evening, October 30, before a great crowd in Hunt Armory in Pittsburgh, then slipped away to hasten with McGowan, Blair, and several news correspondents (the latter, covering his every move, could not be left behind), to Chester, Illinois, where the prison was located. He arrived at four o'clock in the morning, conferred with Dixon and others until dawn, then issued an ultimatum calling for immediate release of the hostages, "or the police will enter and use any force necessary to restore order." Shortly before noon the hostages were released unharmed and Stevenson personally entered the east cell block, with police, in what observers regarded as a demonstration of physical as well as moral courage. One or two shots were fired, one rioter was killed by a ricochet bullet, and it was all over. Stevenson returned to his plane and flew to New York.

There were, Truman complained, "two campaigns being waged by the Democrats" that year, for Truman was vigorously campaigning in defense of his record, giving the Republicans "hell" in the style of '48. There was between the two campaigns "overlapping and confusion," to use Truman's words. There was also a measure of bad feeling.

The latter focused particularly upon Stevenson's answer to a letter written him by a Portland, Oregon, newspaper editor who was considering endorsing the Stevenson candidacy. In this letter the editor asked, among other things, how the candidate proposed to deal with "the mess in Washington." In his reply Stevenson referred to this phrase as a means of identifying a specific point he meant to answer, without conceding either the accuracy or the propriety of the phrase itself but the stenographer neglected to put the phrase in quotation marks and Truman got the impression that Stevenson had promised to "clean up" the "mess." He was naturally outraged and personally hurt.

"How Stevenson hoped he could persuade the American voters to maintain the Democratic party in power while seeming to disown powerful elements of it, I do not know," Truman would write in his *Memoirs*. But of course the President sensed that it was precisely *by* seeming to do this that Stevenson hoped to persuade independent voters into his camp. Whether Stevenson was practically, or morally, right in this strategy is an unanswerable question. Truman himself was convinced that Stevenson would have received at least three million more votes than he did if he "had accepted in good faith the proposition I made to him on January 30, 1952, and enabled us to make the proper build-up. . . ."[7]

A few months later, Stevenson recorded some of his personal impressions of the "exacting ordeal" of a presidential campaign. "You must emerge, bright and bubbling with wisdom and well-being, every morning at 8 o'clock," he wrote,[8] "just in time for a charming and profound breakfast talk, shake hands with hundreds, often literally thousands of people, make several inspiring, 'newsworthy' speeches during the day, confer with political leaders along the way and with your staff all the time, write at every chance, think if possible, read mail and newspapers, talk on the telephone, talk to everybody, dictate, receive delegations, eat, with decorum—and discretion!— and ride through city after city on the back of an open car, smiling until your mouth is dehydrated by the wind, waving until the blood runs out of your arm, and then bounce gaily, confidently, masterfully into great howling halls, shaved and all made up for television with the right color shirt and tie—I always forgot—and a manuscript so

[7] Harry S. Truman, op. cit., p. 500.
[8] Introduction to *Major Campaign Speeches of Adlai E. Stevenson, 1952*, p. xii.

defaced with chicken tracks and last-minute jottings that you couldn't follow it, even if the spotlights weren't blinding and even if the still photographers didn't shoot you in the eye every time you looked at them. . . .

"But the real work has just commenced," he went on, "—two or three, sometimes four hours of frenzied writing and editing of the next day's immortal mouthings so you can get something to the stenographers, so they can get something in the mimeograph machines, so they can get something to the reporters, so they can get something to their newspapers by deadline time. . . . Finally sleep, sweet sleep, steals you away, unless you worry—which I do."

Actually, as his associates noted with awe, he had a remarkable capacity to relax and nap at odd moments, and his powers of recuperation, his resilience, were amazing. As the campaign ground toward its close, and others were breaking down around him, he seemed to grow stronger, as though he thrived on the incredible strain. As he himself recorded, he "gained weight on it" and that extra weight around his middle was "as tenacious as a campaign deficit."

He did so despite the disillusionment he increasingly suffered as he studied and sought to counter the tactics of his Republican opponents. He, who had "believed that an educational and elevating national discussion would result" from Eisenhower's Chicago victory, recorded with rare bitterness in late October[9] that this was "not a campaign by debate" but "a systematic program of innuendo and accusations aimed at sowing the seeds of doubt and mistrust." Nixon had set the pace. "Next Monday, I'm informed, the junior Senator from Wisconsin (Senator Joseph R. McCarthy) is going to make a highly advertised speech—the man who said last week that, if he were put aboard my campaign train with a club, he might be able to make a good American out of me." During that same week, nettled by charges that the Old Guard had captured him, General Eisenhower said emphatically that the decisions in the Republican campaign "have been and will be mine alone," and had added: "This crusade which I have taken to the American people represents what I, myself, believe."

"Crusade indeed!" cried Stevenson. . . .

But what, then, did it signify, this hard-fought campaign?

[9] In his speech at Cleveland, Ohio, dealing with the Hiss case, on October 23, 1952.

CHAPTER TWENTY-SIX

Stevenson Vs. Eisenhower:
The Issues of the '52 Campaign

Seldom in the history of American presidential campaigns have the two candidates been more different in character and personality, in background and education, in style and taste, in approach to historic issues, than were Stevenson and Eisenhower.

Raised as one of six sons of a humble family on the "wrong side of the tracks" in Abilene, Kansas—a town whose most famous citizen, until Eisenhower became famous, was Wild Bill Hickok—the boy Eisenhower was soaked through and through with Abilene's "Wild West" tradition, so much so that even after he became world famous his favorite reading for relaxation was western pulp magazines. He was passionately interested in athletics, particularly in football and baseball, and his courage as a fist fighter was notable even in a town where "kid" fights were brutal affairs. In school his grade record was no more distinguished than Stevenson's. His teachers remarked in him, however, a quick retentive mind, one concerned with "facts" rather than "theories." His natural bent was pragmatical, in the manner of the old western frontier, though qualified to some undetermined extent by the religious idealism of his parents, both of whom came of Mennonite stock (the Eisenhowers were River Brethren from Pennsylvania).

His education as a whole was highly specialized. At West Point he received a thoroughly technical training without being exposed to the humanities in any such way as to make them attractive to him in the absence of a natural interest in them. He was popular with fellow cadets and teachers; he demonstrated, indeed, what amounted to a genius for popularity, in that he achieved it without

apparently aiming to do so. And this genius served him well throughout his Army career, coupled as it was with an iron self-control and
fortitude, the kind of swift calculating logic employed by an expert
bridge player, and the ability to use this logic in situations whose
very vastness breeds in most men a species of superstition.

As a professional soldier he had been outwardly a-political through
most of his life; he had seemed to his intimates to have no strong
political convictions. And as a candidate for President he remained
curiously a-political, a universal hero rather than a partisan candidate. He maintained this role by being (or so his opponents believed) essentially passive, and this despite the hectic physical
activity which campaigning required. He appeared a static symbol,
presented at one place after another to speak words others had written, make over-all gestures others had prescribed, and take issue
stands others had advised.

Moreover, ambiguity seemed (to his opponents) to gather around
him in a thickening cloud. For instance he was billed as a modest
man who accepted adulation, and would accept high office, solely
from a sense of duty; and his opponents admitted that there was a
certain humility in what seemed to be his operation. There was even
an abject humility, they said, in that he seemed to set up no egoistic
resistance whatever to the ideas and wishes of others. But if he was
humble in this sense, might he not also be profoundly vain? As he
yielded to others, might not his primary concern be (as some said
it was) to avoid enmities at all costs, to "look good" and be personally "liked" by everyone?

Certainly his yielding qualities seemed notable when, at the very
outset of the campaign, he issued with Taft a joint statement prepared by Taft in which he conceded, it appeared, every point of
difference between his "liberal" Republican supporters and Taft's
"Old Guard." (Said Stevenson, "Taft lost the nomination but won
the nominee.") Campaigning in Indiana, he embraced Senator William E. Jenner of that state both figuratively and physically—the
same Jenner who, on the floor of the Senate, had called Eisenhower's
old friend and greatest benefactor, General Marshall, a "living lie."
When an emissary of Senator McCarthy of Wisconsin secretly visited Eisenhower in a Peoria hotel to insist that sentences praising
Marshall be removed from a speech to be given in Milwaukee, Eisenhower protested but did as McCarthy wished. He then gave rather
more than tacit support to McCarthy's campaign for re-election—a

campaign whose outcome was then uncertain—by saying that he and McCarthy were agreed as to "ends," only differing as to "methods." He also condoned what seemed to all Democrats and many independents a particularly nasty campaign of sly innuendo and partisan slander conducted by his running mate, Senator Nixon—a campaign all the more vicious, in the eyes of its opponents, for being so slick and well dressed.

As a matter of fact, it appeared to Stevenson and his staff that Eisenhower was being consciously presented to the people as a father image while his running mate was presented as a son image. When the son got into trouble over a large sum of money given directly to him by ten or so California businessmen, father forgave him. With the aid of TV-production experts and hours of rehearsal, Nixon allegedly bared his soul as well as his financial history to the public gaze. "Dick, you're my boy!" said Eisenhower, clasping Nixon to his bosom—this son who was so youthful and ardent and sincere—and the whole episode became classic-American, of a piece with George Washington's telling *his* forgiving father that he'd done it with his little hatchet. And indeed, claimed Democrats bitterly, the son was very busy with his little hatchet during that campaign, creating the impression in an indeterminate number of minds that the Democratic party was infiltrated with Communists and that Adlai Stevenson (whose reply we have presented[1]) had testified in defense of Alger Hiss.

He did not directly charge that Stevenson, too, had a "secret fund" for the advancement of his political ambitions, but he acquiesced in the strategy which created that impression. This was the one Dutch Smith and a few other public-spirited Chicagoans had presented to Stevenson[2] and which Stevenson used to supplement the salaries of men whom he had persuaded into Illinois government at financial loss to themselves. It was in no way analogous to the fund which had been given directly to Nixon for Nixon's personal use. So said Allan Nevins, the Columbia University historian, and several of his colleagues, in a public statement issued at the time. The donors of the Stevenson fund remained anonymous; they had no means of influencing, directly or indirectly, the official acts of those to whom Stevenson made his Christmas "gifts"; so that while the procedure might be deemed unwise in terms of effective personal management

[1] See pp. 358–61.
[2] See p. 319.

(it could easily lower rather than raise employee morale), it could not be deemed unethical. The episode ended when first Stevenson and Sparkman, then Eisenhower, made public their income-tax returns for the last several years,[3] by which time it seemed that the whole affair might have hurt Stevenson more than it had Eisenhower.

II

Small wonder that Stevenson, who had begun his campaign with such high hopes for an honest probing "national dialogue," was soon distressed and disillusioned. Only three specific issues developed during the whole campaign on which the general's position could be defined against Stevenson's with much sharpness or clarity, and even on these the general seemed, in his opponent's view, to waver a good deal.

One issue had to do with foreign policy. Stevenson defined as an aim of foreign policy the creation of a balance-of-power system whereby Soviet Russia and the West could maintain a peaceful if competitive coexistence until such time as a firmer world cooperation could be achieved through the United Nations. He said that Formosa must not be permitted to fall to the Chinese Communists after the Korean War was ended.

He had decided, as his closest aides knew, to go immediately to the Far East if he were elected, visiting not only the fighting front in Korea where his visit would raise the morale of our troops, but also Japan and India. Upon the teeming revolutionary masses of those far lands rested, he was convinced, the fulcrum of any workable balance-of-power system. Here, with the "uncommitted third" of the peoples of the earth, lay the center of gravity of a world caught up in a torrent of history. And Stevenson not only wanted firsthand information about these peoples but also wanted them to know that America purposed to be their friend. But he was adamantly opposed to any public disclosure of this plan of his. To publish

[3] Senator Sparkman's returns showed an income of $89,497 for the last eight years. He had never had a personal campaign fund, he said, but had employed his wife as office receptionist. Stevenson's personal income for 1942–51 had totaled $500,046, of which $211,980 went for taxes. These disclosures were made on September 15. Eisenhower published his returns on October 14, revealing that his personal income since 1942 had totaled $888,303, including $635,000 for rights to his book, *Crusade in Europe*. He paid $217,082 in income and capital-gains taxes during this period.

it in the midst of an election campaign would, in his view, amount to an attempt to buy votes in the coin of others' sacrifices, and at the expense of the general welfare. It could dangerously complicate negotiations then proceeding on the Korean question, it could conceivably prolong the war, and it would certainly raise hopes of an early peace which might prove false, thus weakening the popular will to do what, in Stevenson's view, must be done to secure the peace.

Eisenhower, addressing the national convention of the American Legion on August 25, urged that the United States help the people of Communist-controlled countries to "liberate" themselves from "Soviet tyranny," a proposal which, Stevenson later asserted, cruelly raised false hopes among oppressed peoples and was "far more frightening to our friends than our foes." The immediate and vociferous response of America's allies was one of alarm and protest. Did Eisenhower propose, if elected, to promote violent revolutions in the Communist countries and give them active American aid? If so, World War III would come inevitably and soon, in the view of London and Paris. Two days later, John Foster Dulles, the Republican foreign-policy adviser, was forced to explain that the general did *not* mean what he had seemed to mean; the general did *not* advocate a violent revolution in the satellite countries but, instead, "peaceful methods" (what they would be remained unsaid) which would lead to the "internal collapse" of communism.

Thereafter Eisenhower made no major statement on foreign policy until October 24 when, in Detroit, barely a week before the election, he pledged that if elected he would "go to Korea" to seek "an early and honorable" end to the war there. (On June 5, in Abilene, Kansas, he had said that he had no plan for ending the Korean War and that the United States should stand firm and try for a "decent armistice.") Stevenson, within hours, made public reply, saying that the general's proposal for a "slick, quick" way out of Korea risked a "Munich in the Far East" and increased the possibility of World War III. The root of the Korean problem, he indicated, lay not in Korea but in Moscow.

A second issue was that of state versus federal ownership of submerged oil lands off the shores of California, Texas, and Louisiana. The Supreme Court had ruled that, under existing laws, the federal government had the paramount interest in these submerged lands, that they were as much a part of the national public domain as the national forests, the national grazing lands, and the other public lands which belonged to all the people. When the Congress had adopted a joint resolution transferring ownership to the states, President Truman vetoed it. During the controversy Senator Lister Hill of Alabama had suggested legislation which would have earmarked the federal money received for these oil rights to be used for aid to education, alleviating the shortage of classrooms and teachers that became increasingly desperate as the population swiftly grew. Eisenhower came out for legislation giving the states title to the offshore lands. Stevenson complained that Eisenhower's precise position on the matter was difficult to define and that he took "at least three separate positions on the . . . question." ("I lack the versatility of my opponent," he added.) But the general's over-all position was clear enough, he favored the legislation Truman had vetoed. The issue, said he, was one of "States' rights." And this was as music in the ears of the managers of giant oil corporations whose headquarters' offices were in New York, whose interests extended to South America and the Middle East, and whose effective influence on state governors and legislatures was immensely greater than it could normally be upon the President and Congress of the United States.

Stevenson came out unequivocally for retaining federal ownership of the offshore lands. He did so against intense political pressure to take an ambiguous stand upon this issue, or none at all. In late August, Governor Allan Shivers of Texas called upon him in Springfield, personally to urge this course of action. Shivers never explicitly promised his support if Stevenson did as Shivers wished, nor did he threaten to support Eisenhower if Stevenson refused, but both threat and promise were implicit in the visit itself. Stevenson replied that, in his view, the Supreme Court's majority opinion was a valid statement of the public interest. He would say so forcefully during the campaign, "regardless of the possible effect upon electoral votes." And he chose to do so, not before an audience in New York, say, which would have been sympathetic to his stand, but to an audience in New Orleans, which was hostile to it.

The third issue was of a different order from those described above. It had to do with humor in the campaign. The general was against it.

In this, Eisenhower stood by a well-established tradition in American presidential politics—a tradition which said that candidates for President must, in their speeches, be "solemn as an owl." If they were not, if they indulged an ironical wit or even a storytelling humor, the electorate would write them off as "smart alecks" and "lightweights." In contrast, Stevenson's gift for laughter was remarkable and he dared to exercise it freely before an electorate whose intelligence he respected. It is an open question whether this actually cost Stevenson votes, but it is certain that his immediate audiences were so much more responsive and enthusiastic than the general's that the general's camp grew worried and the general himself was irked. There was nothing funny in the Korean War, high taxes, inflation, and governmental corruption, Eisenhower said—as if these were matters which Stevenson treated lightly.

Stevenson's reply was to laugh all the more. He noted that "in the midst of the terrible years of the Civil War, Abraham Lincoln—and the Republican Party still claims him—at least at election time—said of humor: 'If it were not for this occasional vent, I should die.'"

He averred that GOP must now stand for "Grouchy Old Pessimists" and that the general had chosen Cromwell as the "model" for the "crusade," chiefly because Cromwell could never be "accused" of having "cracked a joke." However, he added, "to be surrounded by the Republican Old Guard night and day would be a melancholy fate . . . and I can understand why it is no laughing matter for the general."

Nor was his humor confined to written speeches. It was sparked instantaneously by the unexpected. When a freight train roared by while he was speaking from his campaign train in Canandaigua, New York, he said, when he could resume, that "it must have been a Republican train—but don't worry—all the guys on it are for us." When he spoke in a town square and heard his voice tossed back at him in a disconcerting echo, he said, "I think what I am saying is worth listening to, but it's certainly not worth listening to twice." At Springfield, Massachusetts, he spoke from a railroad embankment high above the crowd. "I have often been accused of talking over the heads of the people," he said. "Thank goodness, at last you have given me an opportunity to do it."

Consistent with this style of humor, and indicative of the Stevenson frugality, was the most famous photograph taken of the candidate during his campaign. It showed him on the platform at Flint, Michigan, his legs crossed, a large hole in the sole of one shoe, and it was awarded a Pulitzer prize next spring. (Stevenson would learn of the award while in the Far East and would send a post card to

the photographer: "Congratulations. I'll bet this is the first time anyone ever won a Pulitzer prize for a hole in one.")

But he was forced to admit in retrospect that in the '52 campaign—
as in many presidential campaigns in the past—the discussion of issues was largely irrelevant to the campaign's outcome. The mood of
the country was in several respects similar to that which had prevailed in the America of 1920. Weary of war and politics, weary of
the burdens of self-government in an era of seemingly endless crisis,
disgusted with the "mess" of communism and corruption which they
were persuaded prevailed in Washington, Americans seemed eager
to believe in a hero who would take these burdens from them, leaving them free to pursue their private interests without guilt feelings
and without being called upon for great decisions. In terms of this
mood, the "Great Crusade," as Eisenhower labeled his campaign,
was shrewdly designed to win votes.

Republican strategists transformed the contest largely into one of
synthetic personalities: Eisenhower as hero, Truman as villain,
Stevenson as "eggheaded" clown. To do so they employed new
"public-relations techniques" on an unprecedented scale. The Republican treasury, as always, was far larger than the Democratic one,
which meant that Republicans could make much greater use of radio
and, especially, of the new and expensive medium, TV. In the closing days of the campaign, they employed "saturation" TV in some
crowded areas, presenting through Eisenhower's image, in that endless reiteration with which commercial products are sold, the twin
appeals to a revulsion against the high cost of living and to a revulsion
against the sending of "our sons" to Korea. Obviously aimed at
women voters, the appeals would seem, in the event, to have been
influential.

To the greater space and time which the Eisenhower forces could
buy from America's mass-communications agencies was added the
immense advantage derived from the ownership of those agencies by
Republican businessmen. Every influential mass-circulation magazine supported Eisenhower. A total of 993 daily newspapers with
40.1 million readers supported Eisenhower. Only 201 dailies supported Stevenson, and they were on the average papers of smaller
circulation, having altogether only 4.4 million readers. Eisenhower
received support from major papers in every state of the Union
whereas in at least nine states—Delaware, Maine, New Hampshire,

South Dakota, North Dakota, Rhode Island, Utah, Vermont, and Kansas—not a single daily supported Stevenson. Moreover, as Stevenson remarked in a speech on "The One-Party Press" in Portland, Oregon, nearly all these papers "rushed to commit themselves" to Eisenhower in the spring of '52, "long before they knew what [he] . . . stood for, or what his party platform would be, or who his opponent was, or what would be the issues of the campaign."

Truman had faced much the same situation in '48 (Roosevelt never faced a press so solidly committed to an opponent), but Truman at that time was President and his opponent was a man personally unpopular even among important segments of his supporters.[4] Under the circumstances Stevenson faced, press coverage became a major decisive factor—and it was but slender comfort for him to know that a majority of the journalists working for Republican publications were personally for him.

III

On Saturday, November 1, 1952, the Stevenson campaign train rolled through Ohio and Indiana toward Chicago. During the day the governor gave eight rear-platform talks, the last one at Gary, Indiana, shortly after five o'clock in the afternoon. That evening he spoke at a giant rally in the Chicago Stadium. He exuded confidence. "My friends of Chicago," he said, "it has not only been a great campaign for me—it's also a winner. There has been an electric feeling of victory in the air all the way home." He then flew to Springfield where he slept again in the mansion. Next morning, Sunday, he, with Buffie and Ernest Ives and a friend, Art Moore, drove from Springfield to Bloomington where they attended services in the Unitarian church. He lunched at the Ives's home, his own boyhood home, and napped afterward in the room which had been his as a boy (Alverta Duff tiptoed in to pull down the blinds and place a blanket over him). He was awakened, refreshed, an hour later to ride in a motorcade through a hailstorm to a reception at the Bloomington armory. He spoke there and returned to Springfield.

On the following day he went again to Chicago where he made,

---

[4] It was often alleged that the Roosevelt-Truman victories proved the press ineffective in a political campaign, but who could tell what the margin of victory would have been had Truman and Roosevelt been given a fifty-fifty break in the press?

that night, his election-eve address. "Anyone who runs for office wants to win," he said. "I want to win, of course; but win or lose, if I have kept faith with myself during the campaign, then I can await tomorrow—and the day after—and all the days after that—in good temper and sober contentment. . . . Tomorrow you will make your choice. . . . If your decision is General Eisenhower and the Republican Party, I shall ask everyone who voted for me to accept the verdict with traditional American sportsmanship. If you select me, I shall ask the same of the Republicans—and I shall ask Our Lord to make me an instrument of His peace."

He voted, next morning, at Half Day, near his Libertyville home. He talked informally before the school building, which was the polling place, to children assembled there. "I would like to ask all of you children to indicate, by holding up your hands, how many of you would like to be Governor of Illinois, the way I am," he said. Nearly all the children raised their hands. "Well, that is almost unanimous. Now I would like to ask all the Governors if they would like to be one of you kids." Whereupon Stevenson cheered.

He spoke, then, soberly to the children:

"I don't know whether you understand what is going on here this morning very well. I am not sure I do myself! But what you see here is something that does not happen everywhere in the world. Here are a lot of your parents and your neighbors going over to the schoolhouse there to cast their vote. That means they are deciding for themselves who is going to lead them—who is going to be their leader. . . . It is not everybody in the world who can do that. These are the things you read about in the history books, that your ancestors have been struggling for for generations—not only to get the right to govern themselves but to keep it. . . ."

He flew back to Springfield and was in the mansion by noon.

That day, Stevenson, Blair, and a few others on the governor's personal staff formed a pool to bet on the outcome of the election. Each contributed five dollars; each wrote his guess as to the distribution of the electoral votes on a slip of paper which was then initialed, folded, and sealed in an envelope. No man bet that Stevenson would lose, though Blair had a strong suspicion that he would. Blair, as a matter of fact, had renewed his passport on October 27, in the expectation of a trip abroad after the election—a clear indication of his dubious state of mind—and both Blair and McGowan shrewdly appraised the potency of Eisenhower's popularity com-

bined with the people's longing for a period of peaceful quiet. Nevertheless, Blair estimated an electoral vote of 270; only one guess in the
pool was lower, a guess of 267, the narrowest possible margin of
victory. Stevenson's own initialed slip, which Blair would keep as an
item of some historic interest, recorded his belief that he would
receive 381 electoral votes—a landslide victory!

The election-night party was held in the ballroom of the Leland
Hotel, where a giant scoreboard was erected on which votes were
recorded as the totals came in. There was a great crowd, including
many celebrities, in the room. An even greater crowd was outside
wanting to get in; and the "ins" had red stars stamped on their hands
so that they could move in and out at will. Carl McGowan cautioned
staff members, who had worked so hard, "Now, don't get your hopes
up too high. The news may be bad, you know." And from the first,
the news, recorded on the giant scoreboard, was bad. People began
to drink too much and to break down into tears.

Adlai Stevenson sat that night in his basement office at the mansion, working on items of state business as he listened to the returns
through a small portable radio. What did he think, feel, as he sat
there, listening alone, much of the time, to the news that what he
had offered the American people had been overwhelmingly rejected? "But I don't *have* to be President!" he had said often during
the campaign when someone had urged a course of action which
might gain votes but with which he disagreed. He had said it, then,
stubbornly. Could he now say it to himself serenely, adding that,
after all, with this defeat, "living doesn't end"?

Bill Blair came into the office sometime around nine o'clock.

"Well, Bill," said Stevenson cheerfully, being perfectly aware of
the answer, "which is it to be—'A' or 'B'?" He referred to statements
he had written out, one an acknowledgment of victory, the other a
concession of defeat.

Blair answered, "I'm afraid it's 'B,' Governor."

"Okay," Stevenson said. His tone was casual. His face was calm.

Nevertheless he delayed his announcement for several hours because Steve Mitchell, calling from Washington, pointed out that it
could have adverse effect on local candidates by causing Democratic poll watchers to cease watching the counting.

Buffie came in while he revised, as he always did up to the last
moment, the statement he was to give. Borden came in.

"I'm conceding," the governor said cheerfully. He read the telegram he was sending to General Eisenhower in the Commodore Hotel in New York: "The people have made their choice and I congratulate you. That you may be the servant and guardian of peace and make the vale of trouble a door of hope is my earnest prayer. Best wishes. Adlai E. Stevenson."

"I'll be broke for a year after I pay my election bets," said Borden gloomily.

They all drove over to the Leland Hotel. Stevenson passed through a crowd whose members, many of them, wept as they cheered his appearance. He spoke to those immediately before him whose lives, especially during these last weeks, had been bound by the strongest ties of affection and interest to himself and who had spent so much of themselves in behalf of the cause he represented. He spoke, through microphones, to the American millions:

General Eisenhower has been a great leader in war. He has been a vigorous and valiant opponent in the campaign. These qualities will now be dedicated to leading us all through the next four years. . . .

I urge you all to give to General Eisenhower the support he will need to carry out the great tasks that lie before him.

I pledge him mine.

We vote as many, but we pray as one. With a united people, with faith in democracy, with common concern for others less fortunate around the globe, we shall move forward with God's guidance toward the time when His children shall grow in freedom and dignity in a world at peace. . . .

He read to the silent, teary-faced crowd the telegram of concession he had sent. Then, looking out upon his friends and fellow workers, he added: "Someone asked me, as I came down the street, how I felt, and I was reminded of a story that a fellow townsman of ours used to tell—Abraham Lincoln. They asked him how he felt once after an unsuccessful election. He said he felt like a little boy who had stubbed his toe in the dark. He said that he was too old to cry, but it hurt too much to laugh."

Few in that room that night were too old to cry. Many sobbed aloud. . . .

Through the dark streets of midnight along which Abraham Lincoln had so often walked, Adlai Stevenson drove back to the mansion. Close friends were gathered there. His laughter spread over them, dissolving gloom. He called for champagne with which to toast "our defeat."

When at last his friends had gone and he was alone in his room Buffie came in to wish him good night.

"How are you?" she asked, trying to sound matter-of-fact.

He smiled a trifle wearily. Oh, he was "all right," he said. He hadn't asked for "any of this," he said. He had done the best he could. . . .

He who had believed he would win by an electoral vote of 381 to 150 had been defeated by a vote of 442 to 89. He had carried only nine states, none outside the South, and of the Solid South he had lost Virginia, Florida, and Texas, as well as the normally Democratic border states of Oklahoma and Tennessee. His opponent had received 6,621,260 votes more than he, out of an unprecedented total of 61,251,244. He might draw some comfort from the fact that he had polled the third largest vote of any presidential candidate in history, a total of 27,314,992. Aside from Eisenhower, only Franklin Roosevelt in 1936 had surpassed, and by less than 162,000, the popular vote Stevenson received in 1952. Moreover, on a proportionate basis Eisenhower's had not approached the majorities received by Franklin Roosevelt in 1932 and '36, by Harding in 1920 or Hoover in 1928. Stevenson might conclude that, in the circumstances, his defeat was by no means disgraceful.

All the same it was overwhelming, and during the two months following election day, as he busied himself with the completion of his term as governor and with a mountainous correspondence which climbed beyond the possibility of his scaling it, he told his friends he would cheerfully accept the usual fate of a defeated candidate, making way for another choice at the next Democratic convention.

He revealed a good deal of his state of mind in a hilariously funny speech he gave in early December before the Gridiron Club in Washington. This club, composed of newspaper writers and publishers, held annually a banquet at which members produced musical skits ridiculing the public figures of the day. At each banquet held after a national presidential campaign it was customary for the winner and the loser to make brief humorous talks at the close of the evening's entertainment—talks strictly "off the record." Stevenson's speech, however, was reprinted in pamphlet form following the dinner, in violation of the Gridiron rule, by one who heard it and felt it should be shared with a larger public. None who heard or read it could fail to be convinced that Stevenson in his own mind was "through" as a political figure. "A funny thing happened to me on the way to the White House!" he began. "Let me tell you something about it all." The general had run "so far ahead we never saw him. . . . I was happy to hear that I had even placed second." Stevenson wondered if he were not "entitled to some kind of record. . . . Did anyone starting from scratch ever enter our public life with such widespread approval, and then leave, with such widespread approval—all in the space of four years?" he asked. "Frankly, I think the chroniclers of our times have overlooked the meteoric beauty and brevity of my political career."

He laughed, he made others laugh with him, but it was a laughter not far removed from tears. This fact became clear when, a month later, on January 8, 1953, he made his farewell report as governor to the people of Illinois. The lieutenant governor, Sherwood Dixon, who had taken Stevenson's place on the Illinois ticket, had been defeated by the Republican William G. Stratton. Much of Stevenson's farewell address dealt with the "unfinished business" of his administration which he hoped the Stratton administration would complete: with the highway program, public schools, welfare services, the renovation of the constitution, the improvement of mine safety and labor laws, and so on. But at its close he expressed, in phrases reminiscent of Lincoln's farewell to Springfield, some of his own feelings as he left office, and as he did so he nearly broke down before his audience. He had wanted, so terribly much, to "finish the job."

"Illinois, where my family have lived and prospered for a century and a quarter, means a great deal to me," he said, "and I am humbly thankful for the opportunity that has been mine to serve it. I leave my high office content in one respect—that I have given it the best that was in me. It has been a richly rewarding experience, and the satisfactions have far outweighed the disappointments. To the people of Illinois who have honored me so generously, and to the associates in this great undertaking whose friendship and loyalty have meant so much to me, I shall be eternally grateful."

His gaze swept the audience before him. In a choked voice he spoke his final words: "And now, with a full heart, I bid you all goodbye."

Book Seven

CONCLUSIONS

CHAPTER TWENTY-SEVEN

An Increasing Purpose

On February 7, 1953, Adlai Stevenson basked in warm sunlight upon the green shores of Barbados in the British West Indies, enjoying another afternoon of his first extended vacation in many years. It had not been a time wholly free of work; another, in fact, might have found it a time of arduous labor, whose fruits, as he lolled back in a canvas lounge chair, lay in forty or fifty ruled yellow sheets of paper upon his knees. His fingers ruffled those pages, filled with his neat small script—an introduction to the book of fifty of his campaign speeches which a New York publisher would issue in the spring— as he rested his eyes upon the immense blue vistas of the Caribbean seas.

But he had written those pages far more easily than he usually wrote, as he told of why he was a Democrat, how he had happened to become a politician, what the campaign had meant to him.

"Did I talk over people's heads?" he had asked. And his reply had been, "No—and that's about the only aspect of the campaign I am sure of!" He conceded that radio, television, and press create the means of mass manipulation and the "sale" of political ideas and personalities. He conceded that "many of us may be taken in now and then by professionalized emotionalism, showmanship and huckstering." But, he had added, expressing perhaps more confidence than he really felt, "I am not much troubled by that danger."

His confidence was sustained by his review of the thousands of letters that had recently come to him. Letter after letter, he recalled, had expressed an almost pathetic gratitude for his effort to talk sense to the people—to speak, in other words, not as a front man for a collection of interests, not as a corporate personality whose brain was a board of directors, but as an individual human being who represented his party best by being true to his own values and his own sense of realities. Implicit in letter after letter had been the recognition that if the individual man is to be free he must, first of all, *be* an individual, with enough space around his essential self to define him as a unique person. He must have integrity. . . .

And as these ideas came to Stevenson's half-dreaming mind—there beside the calm blue waters—they might well have brought with them a homely phrase whose truth he had experienced in the campaign's immediate aftermath. He had felt, for a time, "all at loose ends," almost "undone." For to have integrity a man must not only be organized around a central core of conviction, he must also have a clear purpose in life. If he cannot be an individual who too much "gives himself away" in the common meaning of that phrase, neither can he be one who lives unto himself alone. "To save your life, you must lose it"—and the "losing" in this case was a process of commitment to an ideal goal. It was precisely this goal, this clear purpose, which he had for a time seemed to lack.

But now, upon this Caribbean isle, as he conversed relaxedly with friends, and slept, and soaked up the golden sunlight, he had felt himself to be knitting together again. In tranquillity he had recollected the campaign and re-collected his scattered thoughts about it; in tranquillity he began to cast long thoughts toward the future, defining new goals and purposes around which to organize his life. Vaguely at first, but with increasing clarity, he sensed the vital strategy by which he might maintain in his personal life a healthy balance between a private and a public self, making of the latter an addition to, rather than a reduction of, the former.

One chief determinant of all this in his mind was the fact that he remained—and would remain for nearly four more years—the titular head of the Democratic party. "In our country this role is a very ambiguous one," he would write in a later year.[1] "The titular head has no clear and defined authority within his party. He has no party office, no staff, no funds, nor is there any system of consultation whereby he may be advised of party policy and through which he may help to shape that policy. There are no devices such as the

[1] Adlai E. Stevenson, *What I Think* (New York: Harper & Brothers, 1956), pp. ix and x.

British have developed through which he can communicate directly and responsibly with the leaders of the party in power. Yet he is generally deemed the leading spokesman of his party. And he has— or so it seemed to me—an obligation to help wipe out the inevitable deficit accumulated by his party during a losing campaign, and also to do what he can to revive, reorganize, and rebuild the party." The Democratic party's deficit, at that time, amounted to some eight hundred thousand dollars.

Taking account of these things, he resolved, there in the golden sunlight, to play out the role assigned to him with more planned consistency than most if any of his predecessors in that role had done.

He must, of course, earn money, and for this purpose he would eventually return to the practice of law in Chicago—but he also re-solved to develop, informally but effectively, a staff of advisers (they must nearly all be unpaid volunteers) who could keep him informed on public questions and help him become a responsible critic of the Eisenhower administration's policies and actions. He resolved to emulate Wendell Willkie by journeying around the globe, at a more leisurely pace than Willkie had been able to do, to see for himself the people and the concrete problems of the world in which his country had so much power and therefore so much leadership responsibility. He resolved that, upon his return, he would revisit his own country to see it from coast to coast in the perspective of a world traveler and, in the process, help raise funds, through fund-raising dinners, which would not only wipe out the campaign deficit but also put into the party treasury funds with which to help finance the next campaigns. He further resolved that in the congressional campaign of '54 he would devote his full energy to his party's cause, as he himself would define it, for as many weeks as he could spare from his law practice.

Thus his plans for the future.

II

And, in the event, he carried out those plans. With a contract for articles from *Look* magazine, he set out on March 1 of '53 for the Far East, accompanied by Bill Blair, Walter Johnson, William At-wood of *Look* magazine, and Barry Bingham of the Louisville *Courier-Journal*. He had honestly believed that he could tour the world as a private citizen, albeit as one with special advantages for seeing and learning, but was abruptly disabused of this notion when a huge crowd greeted him at the airport in Tokyo. Thereafter, his world tour was almost as hectic as his '52 campaign had been, so much so that by the time he reached England on his way home he felt "numb." But during those nearly six months of incessant sightseeing and absorbed discussion he learned an immense amount about the psychology, the problems, the history of other lands, developing a yardstick for the critical measurement of the American performance in the field of foreign policy.

In January of '53 he had opened an office at 11 South La Salle Street in Chicago, consisting of a reception room and four small offices. It was not then nor for nearly two years afterward a law office but a personal office, staffed with Carol Evans, Phyllis Gustafson, Florence Meadow, and Juanda Higgins, all of whom had remained with him after the governorship ended. Bill Blair remained, too, as Stevenson's assistant. Here, after his return from the round-the-world tour, Stevenson wrote the immense number of speeches he must give; wrote articles for magazines; struggled to write another book, finally abandoning the project for lack of time; prepared the Godkin Lectures he gave at Harvard in 1954, lectures on world affairs published in book form under the title *Call to Greatness;* and dealt with a veritable flood of correspondence. That office, and Stevenson's Libertyville farm, became major centers of political intelligence in the country.

Headed by Thomas K. Finletter, former Secretary of the Air Force, an informal advisory group met at irregular intervals, sometimes in New York, sometimes for a weekend in Chicago or at the Stevenson farm, to discuss issues and present suggested "position papers." Its membership was fluid, but its core was composed of Finletter; Arthur Schlesinger, Jr.; Seymour Harris, Harvard economist who concentrated on fiscal policy; Kenneth Galbraith, Harvard economist who concentrated on agricultural policy; Chester Bowles, former governor of Connecticut and former ambassador to India, who concentrated on foreign policy; and W. Willard Wirtz. Governor Harriman of New York often met with the group, as did George Kennan, former ambassador to Russia, and Randolph Paul, tax expert, among others.

An increasing purpose began to dominate Stevenson's life during this period.

Through the first year and a half of the Eisenhower administration, when Republicans controlled both houses of the Congress, Stevenson watched with growing disapproval what seemed to him a failure of the President to function effectively either as chief executive or as party leader. Eisenhower's primary concern, it sometimes appeared, was to maintain intact his personal popularity by remaining "above the battle," at whatever cost to the general welfare, though Stevenson would concede that this concern might be motivated in part by a belief (mistaken in Stevenson's view) that the Republican party could in this way be unified and made, ultimately, an effective instrument of "conservatively liberal" or "liberally conservative" government. Occasionally the President proposed legislation which moderately extended the programs of the New and Fair deals, but he seemed content to let the Congress dispose of it without active intervention on his part. As a result, his key measures were often defeated, and in most cases received more support from Democrats than from Republicans in the Congress. Meanwhile there was formed, behind the smiling façade of Eisenhower popularity, what Stevenson regarded as a "hard coalescence" of big business, the executive bureaucracy, and the press, whereby the public domain was increasingly opened to private exploitation, creative intelligence in government was increasingly replaced by a stagnant mediocrity, and freedom of conscience and speech were increasingly threatened.

Emboldened by the apparent willingness of the White House to have "McCarthyism" used as a partisan political weapon, Wisconsin's junior senator embarked upon a program designed to brand Democrats as a party of pro-Communist traitors, asserting (on Lincoln's Birthday in 1954) that the regimes of Roosevelt and Truman had been "Twenty Years of Treason." Nor was McCarthy alone in his efforts to sow the seeds of suspicion, fear, and hatred in psychological ground prepared by the "Cold War." The Attorney General of the United States, Herbert Brownell, joined in the enterprise by publicly charging President Truman with having harbored in government a "known traitor" in the person of Harry Dexter White. The White House itself joined in by releasing figures on the number of security "risks" removed from government jobs (2,427 of them, the President finally announced), doing so in such a way as to indicate that the great bulk of these were "subversives," "spies and traitors," "Communists," as Governor Dewey, the Postmaster General, and Herbert Brownell openly said they were. This "numbers game," as Stevenson called it, was continued even after an administration spokesman was forced to admit that, out of more than two million federal employees, only one alleged active Communist had been found. Ultimately it was discovered that the over-all figure included not only people removed for a great variety of causes having nothing to do with "loyalty" but also some who had resigned their posts in blissful unawareness that they have ever been regarded (if, indeed, they ever had) as "risks."

It was this rending assault on individual liberty, combined with what seemed to him a potentially disastrous foreign policy of "bluff and backdown," which most outraged Adlai Stevenson. If the processes were permitted to continue, he asserted, the "end result" would be "a malign and fatal totalitarianism." He made this assertion in a fighting speech at Miami Beach, Florida, on March 7, 1954—a speech in which he pleaded for a restoration of honesty and human decency to a party which had become "half-McCarthy, half-Eisenhower. . . ." "Perhaps you will say that I am making not a Democratic but a Republican speech; that I am counseling unity and courage in the Republican party and administration," he went on. "You bet I am!— for as Democrats we don't believe in political extermination of Republicans, nor do we believe in political fratricide; in the extermination of one another. We believe in the republic which exists to serve, and we believe in the two-party system which serves it—that can only serve it, at home and abroad, by the best and noblest of democracy's processes. . . ."

In that same speech he criticized the doctrine of "massive retaliation" to Communist aggression which had just been announced by Secretary of State John Foster Dulles. "We are told, and I am quoting the words of Secretary Dulles, that we have rejected the 'traditional' policy of 'meeting aggression by direct and local opposition,'" he said. "We have taken the decision, he says, 'to depend primarily upon a great capacity to retaliate instantly, by means and at places of our choosing.' . . . Is this a 'new look' or is it a return to the pre-1950 atomic-deterrent strategy which made some sense as long as we had a monopoly of atomic weapons together with a strategic air force? Yet even then it didn't deter attack, and brought us to the brink of disaster in Korea where atom bombs were useless. . . . But, you say, we did not use the bomb against Russian and Chinese targets for fear of enlarging the war. Exactly: and if we should now use them in retaliation that way it would certainly mean World War III and atomic counter-retaliation. For the Russians [also] have massive power of retaliation. . . ."

Thus were stated the twin themes—the assault on civil liberties at home, the inflexible "either/or" policy abroad, implemented by tactics of vacillation—which wove through the campaign Stevenson waged on behalf of his party during the congressional elections of '54.

Shortly after he gave this speech, however, it appeared that he might play no role in the approaching campaign, nor any role in public life again. After "nineteen years plus" during which he had "never missed a day's work because of sickness," he suffered a serious illness. One day that spring he was abruptly doubled over with an agonizing pain in his abdomen. He was taken to the Passavant Memorial Hospital in Chicago. There, on April 12, he underwent surgery for the removal of a kidney stone lodged in his ureter. But in ten days he was out of the hospital, the only permanent consequences of his misfortune being his adherence thereafter to a low-calcium diet (he who had formerly drunk milk even at breakfast now drank no milk at all) and his giving up of smoking (he had formerly smoked a pack of cigarettes a day).

By the time the '54 campaign began he was as strong, as remarkably energetic as ever, his zest for the contest increased by the fact that his principal opponent was Vice-President Nixon, a "plausible young man" of "flexible convictions," for whom his contempt was profound. Demonstrating to the full his skill for scoring debater's points through innuendo and insinuation, Nixon sought to convey the impression that President Truman had been guilty of "treason" (his actual words were that the President had been a "traitor" to the "high principles" of his party, but the context was such that disloyalty to the nation was clearly implied) and that the Democratic party itself was "soft" on communism. In the autumn, aided in no small degree by Stevenson's efforts (he made eighty speeches from coast to coast and from North to South during the campaign), Democrats won a number of new governorships as well as control of both houses of the Congress—an unprecedented accomplishment for an opposition party during a popular President's first term.

It was a victory, Stevenson came to realize, which did little to prosper his personal political fortunes. With the removal of McCarthy and other right-wing Republicans from key committee chairmanships, with the restoration of power of Democrats who would support measures opposed by a majority of Republicans during the first two years of the administration, and through Eisenhower's continued exercise of his genius for popularity, the President again "looked good" in the eyes of those who had begun to doubt him. To a remarkable degree he was absolved of blame for his own party's deeds, even those of Vice-President Nixon, whose '54 campaign had outraged liberal minds while earning the public thanks of the President himself and who became, increasingly, the President's apparent first choice as successor. Senate Majority Leader Lyndon Johnson of Texas, House Speaker Sam Rayburn of Texas, Senator Walter George, who became chairman of the Senate Foreign Relations Committee—these and other conservative southern Democrats who led the Congress declined to attack Eisenhower effectively on issues, while the press surrounded him with what Stevenson called a "reverential hush." Never before, complained the titular head of the opposition, had a President been so protected against legitimate criticism.

"And I have become convinced through rather sad experience," Stevenson added in a later year, "that real issues cannot be developed, nor even effectively presented, during a political campaign. They must be sharpened and clarified largely through the legislative process *between* elections. In the campaign itself, about all a candidate can effectively do is present alternative courses of action."

III

But though an increasing purpose dominated Stevenson's life during this period—though his personal opposition to Eisenhower's leadership grew steadily harder and deeper—he had by no means decided that he himself would become a candidate for the presidency in 1956. This decision, he believed, should be the party's rather than his own. He was "available." Through words and deeds he let it be known that he was. But he would become an active candidate only if he had firm assurance that the party wanted him.

On December 4, 1954, in New Orleans, a Democratic National Committee conference was held. There Paul Butler was chosen to succeed Stephen Mitchell as national chairman. In the evening a dinner was held at which Stevenson was the principal speaker, addressing his audience on "The Challenge of Political Maturity." He deplored the "cruel, unjust, and foolish things" which had been said during the campaign, the fact that "patriots were slandered, evil motives imputed, parties traduced and defamed." The campaign had imperiled the "essential harmony" which, "especially in the conduct of our foreign policy," was a "necessity for our survival." "There is a relation between legitimacy of power and responsibility," he said. "The insecurity of knowing that power must be gained by tricks and deception breeds dynamic words coupled with irresponsible action. But power which comes legitimately . . . can be responsibly exercised with reason, patience, prudence, and wisdom. It is only from that sense of security that wisdom can be joined with innovation and that new paths can be explored. . . ."

In his pocket as he spoke was a handwritten statement which he had shown to no one save his immediate staff, because he wished to avoid the arguments which would be raised, he knew, against his presenting it. When his prepared address was completed he fished the statement from his pocket.

"Now that we are off the air," he said, "let me add a final, personal word. . . . As in the past I have no political ambitions. . . . For more than two years I have sought as best I could to discharge my obligations to the Democratic party which had honored me, and to the millions of my fellow Americans who have given me their confidence. . . . But now I must devote more time to my own concerns. So if henceforth I cannot participate in public and party affairs as vigorously as in the past, I hope you will understand and forgive me, and I assure you that it reflects no lesser interest in our party's welfare and no ingratitude for the inspiration and encouragement you have given me in such abundance."

In later years he would express surprise that this statement received virtually no attention in the press. He would speak of it as though it were an announcement of his intention to withdraw from political life. Actually, of course, it was no such thing. What it did do was give party leaders an opportunity to withdraw their support from him, should they choose to do so, while encouraging his supporters to express their wishes.

More than four months passed before he again made public speech.

By the beginning of 1955 he had come close to paying off single-handed the deficit his '52 campaign had accumulated—a feat, said John Mason Brown, "as revealing of his drawing power as of his probity,"[2] since he achieved it by speaking at dinners ranging from fifty to a hundred dollars a plate. By that time, too, he had formed his law partnership with Bill Blair, W. Willard Wirtz, and Newton Minow. It was a firm which practiced a good deal more law than the general public believed it did, though Stevenson's anxiety to keep the firm small and his obligations at a minimum caused them to reject far more clients than they accepted. Moreover, both Minow and Wirtz were impressed by Stevenson's professional competence as a lawyer. He personally handled few cases, but the matters he did handle were handled unusually well. "He sees things differently than most lawyers," Minow would explain. "He's quick and thorough, and sees implications and connections that most men don't see." And Wirtz would say that Stevenson went into "every facet" of a problem, was "ingenious in the development of strategy and argument," and obviously enjoyed the "challenge of a problem." The firm, soon after it was formed, moved to Suite 887 at 321 South La Salle Street—the Continental Illinois Bank Building—just across the hall from the law firm of Stevenson's '48 political opponent, Dwight Green.

During the Chicago mayoralty campaign in the spring of 1955 Stevenson gave active and probably decisive support to his former state director of revenue, Richard J. Daley, who defeated young Robert Merriam, a former Democratic alderman become a Republican. And while that campaign was being waged he lunched, one blizzardy March day, with Bill Blair and an out-of-town friend to whom he spoke of his personal career indecision. He still had not made up his mind, he said, whether or not to become an active candidate in '56. He spoke of the "subtlety" of issues in this mid-twentieth century. "They are no longer black and white, or not to anything like the extent they were in the 1930s," he said. "The contest is no longer so clearly one of the haves versus the have-nots. The issues are there. They are very real. But they are difficult to define now—and I must say the present administration does everything it can to blur and obscure them." They seemed to him to be more "philosophical" than they had formerly been, having to do now with "spiritual" values at least as much as they had to do with economic ones. He referred also to the operation he had had the year before.

"I'm not going to run again just for the exercise," he said emphatically. "I've had all that kind of exercise I need. Another race like the last one and I will *really* have had it."

[2] John Mason Brown, *Through These Men* (New York: Harper & Brothers, 1956).

Bill Blair smiled. "He always talks that way, as though he were about to collapse into his grave," Blair explained later. "Don't believe a word of it. The last physical examination showed him to be in perfect condition."

A few weeks later a crisis developed in the Far East which contained grave threats of global conflict. Telephone calls, letters, and telegrams poured in upon Stevenson urging him to address the nation on this crucial matter, and on April 11 he did so, speaking over a national radio hookup. The President had just asked for and received from the Congress a "blank check" on which to write his will, should Communist China attack, as she threatened to do, the tiny islands of Quemoy and Matsu which, as Stevenson said, "lie almost as close to the coast of China as Staten Island does to New York," which had "always belonged to China," and to which neither the U.S. nor the Nationalist China government on Formosa had any legal claim. That the President at this juncture should require the Congress to underwrite in advance any decision he might make seemed to Stevenson to set a dangerous precedent. Under the Constitution the President, as commander in chief of the armed forces, already had the right and responsibility to defend national interests against foreign aggression; by "passing the buck" to the Congress, Eisenhower diminished the power of the President's office. Said Stevenson:

"Having loudly hinted at American intervention in Indo-China just a year ago, and then backed away; having forced General Chiang Kai-shek to evacuate the Tachen islands when the Communists made menacing gestures just a couple of months ago, we now face the bitter consequences of our government's Far Eastern policy once again: either another damaging and humiliating retreat, or else the hazard of war, modern war, unleashed not by necessity, not by strategic judgement, not by the honor of allies or for the defense of frontiers, but by a policy based more on political difficulties here at home than the realities of our situation in Asia.

"Given these unhappy choices it appears that President Eisenhower will decide what to do if and when the attack comes, depending on whether in his judgement it is just an attack on these islands or a prelude to an assault on Formosa. While our President has great military experience, perhaps it is not improper to ask whether any man can read the mind of an enemy within a few hours of such an attack and determine whether, at some later date, the enemy plans to go further and invade Formosa. Is it wise to allow the dread question of modern war to hinge upon such a guess?"

Moreover, he reiterated, we stood at this juncture alone, our policy strongly opposed by our allies. Our Formosa policy was firm; it had been established five years ago when Truman sent the Seventh Fleet to defend that island from attack; but Quemoy and Matsu were in no sense essential to the defense of Formosa. Clearly the administration had placed the world in grave peril through Eisenhower's appeasement of the extremists in his own party, his refusal (it was of the essence of his genius for personal popularity) to take a firm and definite stand against those "inflammatory" elements who forward a "defensive war" against Communist China. "If the best hope for today's world is a kind of atomic balance, the decisive battle in the struggle against aggression may be fought not on the battlefields but in the minds of men, and the area of decision may well be out there among the uncommitted peoples of Asia and Africa who look and listen and who must, in the main, judge us by what we say and do."

As it turned out, the Chinese did not, that spring of '55, attack Quemoy and Matsu. The administration and its apologists were quick to say that this was due to the administration's "deterrent strategy." While not denying that the threat of war may indeed have deterred the Chinese at that moment, others remained convinced that the risk we had run had been a needless one and that the returns were by no means all in on the policy we had pursued. Quemoy and Matsu, fortified by the Chinese Nationalists with American approval and assistance, remained as irritating pinpricks in the flank of a huge and awakening dragon—and who could say but what that dragon merely waited, while Chiang's already overage army grew steadily older and weaker, until the time seemed ripe for a swift surprise seizure of the islands? What would we do if and when that time came?

IV

The weeks which immediately followed were unusually crowded for Stevenson, even by his own unique standards. He made a trip to Africa, partially for business reasons but also to visit a part of the world he had not seen before: Kenya, Rhodesia, the Belgian Congo, the Union of South Africa, the Gold Coast, Swaziland. At the latter place he had a wonderful time, particularly during his visit with the king. He returned from Africa in May, having prepared an article on Africa for *Look* magazine, and then made several long-scheduled speeches: before the General Federation of Women's Clubs in Philadelphia, where he protested against the rising tide of anti-intellectualism in America; at Oberlin College in Oberlin, Ohio, where his old Princeton friend, Bill Stevenson, was president; at the dedication of the New York-Bellevue Medical Center in New York, where he outlined a national health program; at the Smith College commencement in Northampton, Massachusetts, where he stressed the value of nonconformity of mind in a free society; before the annual meeting of the National Education Association in Chicago, where he presented a national educational policy outline.

The latter address was on July 6. He would never forget the date. In the morning he was terribly ill with fever, his voice so hoarse he could barely speak, and his doctor told him he must go at once to bed. "I have to speak," said Stevenson stubbornly. "Prop me up so I can do it." The doctor, with pills and hypodermics, managed to do so—though barely—and after an agonizing hour before the huge throng in the Chicago Stadium ("I never felt more miserable") Stevenson virtually collapsed and was taken to the Lake Forest Hospital, with what, in an earlier year, might have been a fatal case of virus pneumonia. But in a few days he was fit again.

On August 12 the Governors' Conference was held in Chicago, and while it was going on the Democratic governors removed whatever doubts may have remained in Stevenson's mind concerning the party's wishes for his candidacy. Some twenty governors called upon him at his Libertyville farm, including Governor Harriman of New York, and most of them thereafter issued statements paralleling Harriman's "I'm for Stevenson all the way." Stevenson's own mind was then just about made up: he began to lay plans for a campaign. While in Desbarats, Canada, with the Hermon Dunlap Smiths during the following August days he hired at least one major staff member and made decisions concerning others.

A few weeks later he went to Haiti and Jamaica on behalf of a law client, taking with him his son Adlai III and his daughter-in-law, the former Nancy Anderson of Louisville, Kentucky, a very attractive girl of twenty whom young Adlai had married in June. He asked his eldest son for opinions on whether or not he should run again. Adlai III, examining the matter as "problem" in the methodical way characteristic of him, favored his doing so. Then Stevenson talked to Borden by phone, Borden being then stationed in Hawaii as an Army lieutenant. Borden was not sure that running again was best for his father, but whatever his father thought best he wanted his father to do. John Fell, when his father talked to him, was, as Stevenson described it, "passively acquiescent."

Thereafter the only question about Stevenson's entrance into the campaign was one of timing. When should he announce formally? In July Truman had urged him to announce by Labor Day at the latest. Stevenson had not by then made up his mind. Now that he was sure of the party and of himself, he tentatively decided to make the announcement on November 19, following a huge Democratic National Committee dinner which was to be held in the International Amphitheater in Chicago and at which Stevenson was scheduled to make the principal address.

CHAPTER TWENTY-EIGHT

Preparations for 1956

The campaign of 1956, as Stevenson and his staff conceived it in the early autumn of 1955, was to be different in several important respects from that which he had waged in '52. Then he had been a reluctant candidate, doubtful of his personal qualifications for the presidency. Now he was a determined one, convinced that no available person was better qualified than he for the highest office. Then his role had been that of defender and apologist. Now his role would be that of critic and prosecutor. Then he had had to do everything at once, for he had started unprepared and little known; necessarily he had engaged in improvisation which was often frantic. Now he was a figure of world renown and was perhaps better prepared than any earlier presidential candidate had been for the campaign he foresaw.

The campaign he foresaw would be a long one, but it could be carefully planned and wholly focused on the opposing party, since he then appeared to be the inevitable and virtually unchallenged choice of the Democratic party. Already, with the aid of the Finletter advisory group and through a massive correspondence, he had accumulated much of the factual data and interpretative material he would need for attacks upon the administration and for the development of his own positions. Already he had gathered around him several of the key people of his campaign staff. These included, as a core group, his three law associates. Bill Blair, whose constant prodding had had no small part in keeping Stevenson's political aspirations alive, was the candidate's executive assistant. Newton Minow handled much of the law work in the firm while his colleagues became absorbed in politics, but he also served the candidate as a valued special assistant. W. Willard Wirtz began to function as head of the growing research and writing staff. Characteristically, this role, played in '52 by Carl McGowan, was not specifically assigned to Wirtz by Stevenson at the outset. The younger man assumed it and was even forced sometimes to defend it in subtle power struggles against newly recruited men who, being themselves without clear and definite status, sought to make places for themselves close to the throne.

The campaign plan called for the development, in the months immediately ahead, of a "reservoir of words," a reservoir which could be drawn upon at will and need during the late summer and the fall of the following year. It would contain not only full speech texts on all the basic issues, but also "appropriate language" for all manner of special occasions. Thus would be avoided the nerve-racking travail through which speeches had been born in the nick of time all through the campaign of 1952. Thus would be promoted the Stevenson concept of campaigns as "democratic dialogues," processes whereby the public was educated in the public's business and the final choices were made, not between competing personalities ("A presidential campaign ought not to be a popularity contest," said Stevenson repeatedly), but between the principles and proposals which the candidates expressed.

The major targets of Stevenson fire had already been selected. They radiated like spokes from a wheel whose hub was the alleged domination of government by big business. It was the business community that determined the nation's fiscal policy, which in turn affected our national defense, which in turn influenced our "bluff-and-backdown" diplomacy. It was the business community's hostility to public power, its primary commitment to personal monetary profit, which determined the administration's view of the TVA as "creeping socialism," incited the "give-away" (as Democrats called it) of natural resources in the public domain, and caused the government to make haste very slowly indeed in the development of atomic energy for productive uses. It was the business community's faith in the automatic beneficence of a "free market"—provided this market was not defined in such a way as to reduce protective tariffs drastically nor to produce effective "trust busting"—which determined the administration's apparent indifference to the plight of the family-sized farm. It was the business community's awareness that its concepts of government would prove vastly unpopular, if frankly stated, which determined the "duplicity" of the administration's public relations—its substitution of vague slogans for clear ideas, its constant effort to manipulate rather than inform public opinion—and it was the business community's domination of the means of mass communications which made this "duplicity" effective. In general it was the business community's self-centered conservatism—its unwillingness to recognize new problems of government or to explore new paths into the future—which must cause the Eisenhower years to be regarded in history as an era of missed chances for greatness, of lost opportunities to make giant strides toward a world of material abundance and permanent creative peace.

The process was encouraged by the fact that there were still two Republican parties, the Old Guard and the so-called "liberal wing." Eisenhower was the symbol of the latter, but in actual practice he continuously appeased the former, with the result that virtually every proposal, particularly in foreign affairs, was flawed by inner contradictions which made it ineffective if not actually dangerous to the general welfare.

So it was that the Stevenson men defined their political targets, and these were the terms by which their political ammunition was shaped. But it must be reiterated, as Stevenson himself reiterated, that the central theme of the proposed campaign was in no sense a hostility to the business community per se. Far less than some of his advisers was Stevenson inclined to attack big business as in itself a force inimical to our free institutions. What he did deplore, with increasing insistence, was the tendency to fuse big business and big government in such a way that business interests became the principal if not the sole determinant of major federal policies. He deplored the basic assumptions from which this tendency proceeded. In an article entitled "My Faith in Democratic Capitalism," published in *Fortune*, October 1955, he said that a great respect for "the concept of 'rugged individualism' (usually incorporated) is no warrant for the illusion that modern America was *created* by businessmen." Rather was it created "in a complex collaboration whereby the Federal government offered to individuals the best soil and nurture for enlightened capitalism ever devised." A vast program of internal improvements, paid for by taxpayers, had opened the frontier and moved it westward; tariffs had protected infant industries and now subsidized established ones, if generally to the detriment of world economic health; cheap public power had stimulated private enterprise in the Tennessee Valley and the Northwest; federal irrigation projects had transformed deserts into privately owned farms; and "much of the newspaper and magazine industry is carried by the taxpayer through the government's massive subsidy of second-class mail." Clearly there had always been an "interaction" and there must in our technological age be an ever closer "interdependence" of business and government, but for that very reason we must, said Stevenson, be careful not to confuse the functions of business with those of government. He suggested that we "think in terms of a doctrine of 'separation of powers' in this area of business and government relations—a separation resembling the constitutional differentiation between the executive, the legislative, and the judicial in the government itself. . . . Although commercial interests and national interests can and usually do walk a certain distance hand in hand, no full identity between them can ever be forced, and any attempt to force it would be apt to end in misery, or disaster, or both—and for both."

Addressing a University of Texas audience in late September of '55, he spoke of twentieth-century America as a "unique partnership between governmental and private enterprise, a mixed economy which is the despair of doctrinaire reactionaries as it is of doctrinaire radicals. . . . Slowly, sometimes painfully," he went on, "most of us have come to realize that mass production implies mass consumption, and that mass consumption in a free economy requires mass purchasing power. . . . To achieve a market whose demand keeps pace with an ever-expanding supply, we have used the power of representative government in several creative ways. Through graduated income taxes, through public works, through encouragement of labor unions and collective bargaining, through slum clearance and public housing, through the protection of the public domain, through the policy of equal treatment for the farmer—through these and other public measures we have helped to make our way to our present power and abundance. . . ."

But as party politician Stevenson was not loath to point out that little of the creative partnership he praised had been achieved under Republican administrations. The great gains had been made under Democratic administrations—those of Wilson, Roosevelt, Truman; during the 1920s, when key figures in the Republican administration openly proclaimed that government's primary purpose was to aid business, federal policies had contributed largely and directly to the most dangerous economic collapse in our history. "The Republican party has stood traditionally for an isolationist foreign policy, high tariffs, and other business subsidies," he asserted in an address to the Democratic State Convention in Green Bay, Wisconsin, October 7, 1955. "It has opposed most efforts of government to regulate business abuses, to conserve natural resources, to assure the growth of co-operatives, the development of cheap power, and the growth of organized labor." The reason for this was that the Republican party, which in Lincoln's day had been "the party of a single, compelling moral idea" had become "essentially the party of a single economic interest. . . . The Democratic party, on the other hand, has grown from many different groups and interests" and of it "there has been no dominance by any single interest." The nature of the democracy required that "the shaping of party policy" be "a process of reconciling discordant and often contradictory interests," with the result that the party had "an extraordinary record of accomplishment of doing things for the first time, of serving . . . the general welfare."

This Green Bay speech was illustrative of the manner, the attitudes with which Stevenson then faced the approaching campaign. Its central theme was farm policy, and during its preparation Stevenson was under severe pressure to endorse a return by the federal government to rigid high-price supports for basic crops, thus repudiating the flexible supports favored by the administration.

The administration argument was that high supports added to the mounting farm surplus and for that reason must reduce rather than increase farm income over the long run—but behind this argument lurked the belief that, due to the impact of technology on agriculture, there were now "too many farmers" and that a reduction in the farm subsidy, a greater reliance on the allegedly "free" market, would have the beneficial effect of reducing the number of farm units while increasing their average size. Both the stated argument and the unspoken belief were challenged by some of Stevenson's advisers. There was no clear evidence, they argued, that high supports were in any way responsible for the farm surplus, but there was considerable evidence that a reduction in support payments meant a further reduction in farm incomes at a time when those incomes, amid a booming industrial economy, were already dangerously low. No doubt this would further reduce the number of farmers, and perhaps this reduction might be justified if one's sole criterion of value was economic (though of this last there was no firm assurance). But was cold economics the sole valid criterion? Were not aesthetic and moral values concerned in the preservation of the family farm? Might not a considerable farm subsidy be justified on the ground that the family farm—farming as a "way of life"—was a strand of diversity we needed to retain in an increasingly uniform cultural pattern?

Thus the arguments and counterarguments, thus the opposing value judgments, which played upon Stevenson's mind. Concerning them, his mind was by no means made up. He was very sure that high rigid supports provided no real solution to the farm problem. He was unsure of their effect on surpluses, prices, and incomes. He had as yet no creative agricultural proposals of his own to make. He therefore resisted the pressures toward even a tentative and temporary endorsement of rigid supports. Instead, at Green Bay, he criticized the method "by which prices have been supported in the past, and which the Republicans adopted. . . ." He said that "we must explore new techniques" and mentioned "such devices as production payments" and the "temporary or permanent withdrawal" of some land from grain production, not only to reduce overproduction but also to conserve soil. Many of Stevenson's political advisers fumed. Why, in these circumstances, ignore the one clear vote-getting issue the Democrats then possessed? The odds against Stevenson's victory over Eisenhower seemed great enough without adding to them through a misguided perfectionism.

In reply, Stevenson counseled patience. The election was more than a year away. There was time enough to prepare a full-length exposition of the farm problem, with reasoned conclusions concerning it—an exposition giving full weight to those moral and aesthetic values which his materialistic-minded opponents seemed wholly to ignore.

II

Indeed, the definition of these latter values, not only in the farm problem but in every other political issue of our time, might well prove to be the central, unifying theme of the campaign Stevenson then foresaw. Perhaps he could develop the basic "philosophic" issue which he had vaguely mentioned to an out-of-town friend the preceding March.

Certainly a nagging sense of this issue, a felt need to clarify it, permeated all his thinking about specific, practical matters that autumn. "Technology, while adding daily to our physical ease, throws daily another loop of wire around our souls," he wrote in his *Fortune* article of October. "It contributes hugely to our mobility, which we must not confuse with freedom. The extensions of our senses, which we find so fascinating, are not adding to the discriminations of our minds, since we need increasingly to take the reading of a needle on a dial to discover whether we think something is good or bad, right or wrong." He had no doubt that America's material standard of living would continue to rise. "But spiritually, morally, and politically, I don't think we are doing too well." We need "a renewed understanding that the essence of our material power is a moral commitment whose maintenance against hostile outside pressures, and against our own inward corruption by the very power we wield, is our greatest mission as a people," said he at the University of Texas in late September.

But as he thought along these lines, he might come to recognize, as others who closely watched him recognized, a profound irony of American history—an irony in which his own career was involved and by which his ultimate political fate might be determined.

Here was a country that had been born of revolution and dedicated to the proposition that all men are created free and equal. It was a country committed to the belief that the individual human life is sacred and is the center and measure of all value. Its central political documents asserted over and over again, in various forms, that individual human beings are (in Kant's phrase) to be considered always as ends, never as means; and its political vocabulary centered on such words as "liberty," "freedom," "private enterprise," "self-reliance," "individualism." Yet as one surveyed the history of this country, one seemed to discern its dominant economic genius as a flat contradiction of individualism. It was a genius for planning and administering vast organization in which the individual played a sharply defined and limited role—a "genius," one might say, for mass production and mass consumption—and as such its natural tendency was to regard the individual as *always* a means, *never* an end.

In his Texas speech Stevenson referred to the inventive career of Eli Whitney as a kind of portrait-in-little of the process by which American enterprise, believing itself to be rooted in "rugged individualism," generated an economic environment in which such individualism became impossible. Having contracted to supply ten thousand muskets to the United States Government within the unheard-of period of two years, Whitney proposed (as he said) "to substitute correct and effective operations of machinery for that skill of the artist which is acquired by long experience." He proceeded to do so in the armory he established near New Haven. "And so," said Stevenson, "the system of manufacturing standardized interchangeable parts through a division of labor and the use of machines came into existence, to be followed by the assembly-line techniques of mass production which men like Henry Ford later applied with such huge success to industry in general. . . . Since the success of Whitney's armory, individual human skills, whether manual or mental, have become steadily less important to the actual work of producing goods. Machines took over. Organization took over. Routine took over. And they continue to take over with a frightening speed as we move into the age of automation—an age in which accounting and even the administration or direction of work is increasingly usurped by electronic brains." The America which Whitney foreshadowed and helped to create, Stevenson went on, was one in which "the shoemaker, the ironmonger, the gunsmith, the miller, the butcher, the merchant, was with increasing frequency not an individual but a corporation whose 'personality' was a legal fiction."

And surely a dangerous ambiguity was compounded by this application of the concepts and vocabulary of individual liberty to giant institutions and organizations! Surely only a species of totalitarian tyranny could result, ultimately, from the notion that the Declaration of Independence applied to U. S. Steel and General Motors, guaranteeing to these the fundamental human rights of "life, liberty and the pursuit of happiness"! Such a tyranny might come silently, imperceptibly, through the gradual growth of a single-minded control over industry, merchandising, and the agencies of mass communication. The communications control might then be used to transform human persons into bundles of conditioned reflexes, drowning their unique integrities in a dead sea of statistical averages. Consistent with this would be the rise of a new kind of ideal human— the "well-adjusted personality" perfectly balanced on dead center, whose "mind" was a barometer of social pressures, whose "decisions" were yieldings to such pressures, and whose appetite for economic goods was insatiable.

Neither Stevenson nor any responsible contemporary historian would argue that America had as yet come all the way to this sorry pass, but they might agree that there was a strong tendency in this direction. Stevenson had protested against it in his address at the Smith College commencement in early June. He deplored the theory of education which had as a "paramount aim" the production of citizens "who can fit painlessly into the social pattern. . . . While I am not in favor of maladjustment," he went on, "I view this cultivation of neutrality, this breeding of mental neuters, this hostility to eccentricity and controversy, with grave misgiving. . . . [We] need not just 'well-adjusted,' 'well-balanced' personalities, not just better groupers and conformers (to casually coin a couple of fine words) but more idiosyncratic, unpredictable characters (that rugged frontier word 'ornery' occurs to me). . . ." In this as in other addresses he reiterated his belief that human freedom was, ironically, threatened by the very "progress" which had resulted from a resurgence of human freedom during the Renaissance. By promoting an ever narrower economic specialization and an ever closer interdependence of specialities, an advancing technology drove hard "toward that extreme of machine state in which individual freedom is wholly submerged." The drive could be halted only by a renewed emphasis upon, and perhaps a new definition of, the ends—the human, personal, spiritual ends—which all economic devices should serve.

Nor could Stevenson be unaware that he was far from alone in regarding the essential political issue between himself and Eisenhower to be precisely this of human freedom. To many thoughtful observers the very contrast between the two men as personalities seemed to define this issue. Stevenson, the heir of a family tradition intertwined with American history, was essentially a historical person; Eisenhower was the product wholly of his time and immediate experience, essentially a-historical. Stevenson's formal education had been classical and general, with a major emphasis on the humanities; Eisenhower's had been highly specialized, a technical training through which he had no effective exposure to the humanities. Stevenson was, in philosophic bent, an idealist who tested the truth of an idea by its consistency with other true ideas; Eisenhower was a pragmatist whose test of truth was whether or not an idea "worked" toward some practical end in the immediate situation which called it forth. Stevenson's natural tendency was to view each moment as part of a continuous flow of time from past into future, and to deal with it in terms of a planned pattern of action and principle; Eisenhower in his farewell to the students of Columbia University, in

January of 1953, had advised his hearers not to "plan anything too carefully" because "in this life, you don't know what's around the corner." (More important than a plan, said he, was an attitude of "confidence—confidence that you can meet the problem of the day as it comes up.")

The issue thus defined in mid-twentieth-century America was consistent with that which had divided Jefferson and Hamilton at the very beginning of our national experience, but it differed from this not only in the concrete terms in which it was expressed but also, and primarily, in its psychological mood. In one real sense, the basic issue of 1952, and of the upcoming campaign as then discerned, seemed actually to *be* psychological in that it was an opposition of that which was active to that which was passive in the American spirit. It seemed to present a choice—an as yet far from clear choice —between a major emphasis on the values derived from physical sensation and a major emphasis on values derived from inwardness. One party seemed to insist that Americans must be "other-directed,"[1] the other party seemed to insist that Americans be "inner-directed," and John Mason Brown, in an unusually perceptive essay on the '52 campaign,[2] remarked how this difference was expressed in the very phrases which the two presidential candidates used "automatically" in their speeches, and even in the hand gesture which the two made toward their audiences. Stevenson, noted Brown, was constantly saying in his speeches, "This reminds me," or "I am reminded by," while Eisenhower "when making a serious point, was apt to say 'I am told' or 'Someone told me.'" When Eisenhower waved to crowds he made sweeping gestures, his arms held straight out; Stevenson "tended to keep his elbows at his sides and to make tentative, half-finished gestures." Brown further noted that the center of the famous Eisenhower smile was his mouth whereas the center of Stevenson's smile was his eyes.

But though the issue of human freedom seemed to Stevenson real and basic, though he longed to clarify and present it concretely, he was well aware of the difficulty of translating it into effective vote-getting terms.

Once an adviser submitted to him a memorandum arguing that a

[1] The phrases "other-" and "inner-directed" were made famous by *The Lonely Crowd*, David Reisman, Nathan Glazer, Reuel Denney (Yale University Press, 1950).

[2] John Mason Brown, *Through These Men* (New York: Harper & Brothers, 1956).

major full-length speech should be addressed to the "new suburbia," whose citizens were notoriously civic-minded without being in any sense politically minded, who depended wholly upon the standard agencies of mass communication for their national and international information, and who (mistakenly, as the memorandist said) identified their political interests with those controlling the Republican party. A rather smug materialistic complacency seemed to mark the people of suburbia, but beneath this, the memorandum argued, lay a deepening discontent—vague but powerful. These people had more and more leisure time and more and more gadgets with which to kill it, yet their lives, as they themselves felt in their moments of reality, were strangely empty of purpose and meaning. They were "spiritually unemployed. . . ."

The phrase interested Stevenson. Economic unemployment had been the great problem of the 1930s. Was spiritual unemployment the great problem of the '50s? "By all means write that speech," he said, "and we'll see what can be done with it." It might fit well into the "New America" theme which had been shaping itself in his mind and through which he hoped to stir the imaginations and arouse the highest aspirations of his countrymen. . . .

III

Then, with that total unexpectedness which (in Eisenhower's view) militated against planning anything "too carefully," there occurred an event which drastically transformed the nature of the coming campaign, setting at nought all of Stevenson's pre-convention plans.

On Friday, September 23, 1955, the President of the United States, on vacation in Denver, Colorado, played twenty-seven holes of golf at a Denver country club. That night, or early in the morning of Saturday the twenty-fourth, he suffered a heart attack and was taken from the house of his mother-in-law, Mrs. John S. Doud, to Fitzsimmons General Hospital. Major General Howard McC. Snyder, the White House physician, diagnosed the attack as a coronary thrombosis or blood-clot injury to the heart tissues.

The immediate and virtually unanimous conclusion of politicians and the general public was that Eisenhower, though he might complete his first term, would certainly not seek a second one. A concomitant of this was the probability that a Democrat would be the next President of the United States and that his party would score decisive victories in the '56 congressional and gubernatorial races. Certainly the financial community was convinced, in the immediate aftermath of Eisenhower's illness, that the President's political career had come to an end and that without him their party could not retain control of the executive branch. On Monday, September 26, the stock market broke with a computed loss of more than $12 billions—a loss second only to that of October 28, 1929.

It might be thought that this turn of events—apart from the natural human sympathy for a dangerously ill man—would cause secret jubilation in the Stevenson office. On the contrary, it caused a considerable measure of consternation and not a little dismay, particularly among those who were concerned with campaign research and writing. Every strategic calculation was thrown awry; every tactical concept must be revised. There was even a feeling, expressed by Wirtz among others, that the President's illness, if he made satisfactory recovery from it, might prove to be of a piece with the famous "Eisenhower luck," since it would remove him, for months at least, from the area of effective critical fire. For the time being, no direct attacks could be made upon him. "And just when we were getting him within our sights!" said Wirtz. Stevenson himself had looked forward to a sharply defined battle with "the champ" and deplored the fact that this new event must aid Republican strategists in that obscuring of real issues, that divorcement of the President from responsibility for the unpopular elements of his administration, which had characterized the last three years and for which Eisenhower himself had displayed a major talent. As for the possibility of any deep "philosophic" exploration of the historic issue, this too, it soon appeared, was drastically reduced if not actually destroyed.

For it was soon clear that Stevenson's relationship to his own party had been changed. Theretofore he had been assured by mutual friends of his and Kefauver's that the Tennessee senator would probably not seriously challenge his candidacy, while Harriman had placed himself solidly, unequivocally in the Stevenson camp. But soon Harriman was saying, with that slyness which caused some to dub him "Honest Ave the Hairsplitter," that while he was still "for" Stevenson, he was not necessarily "for him for President." ("What does he think I'm running for, county coroner?" asked Stevenson, who, though he laughed, was wounded by this defection of a man whom he had regarded as among the firmest of his political friends.)

Soon Harry Truman was letting it be known that he favored an "open" convention. Whereupon it appeared that Kefauver would again become an active candidate, laying plans for a formal announcement and a campaign for pledged convention delegates through the state primaries, such as he had waged in 1952.

It is possible that Stevenson, had he anticipated the intraparty struggle which now loomed, would have made a decision concerning his own candidacy different from that he had made a few months before. He indicated as much to Newton Minow when the two flew back from Texas following the university speech there on September 28. "Lyndon Johnson has been telling me I'll have to enter some primaries," Stevenson said. "What do you think?" Minow gave as his opinion that "of course" Stevenson would have to do so, now that the Democratic nomination was so obviously a prize any politician might covet. Stevenson shook his head and looked out the plane window upon the vast land he aspired to govern, and said, half sighing, that he certainly hadn't counted on this. . . .

As we have seen, he had been at great pains to make sure that he was the dominant choice of his party before he definitely committed himself to the battle. The kind of campaigning required of candidates in presidential primaries seemed to him demeaning of the candidates and unworthy of the high office toward which the campaigns aimed. The lack of uniform primary laws among the states (only nineteen states chose convention delegates in primaries), plus the effective presence of local factors unrelated to the national situation, seemed to him to make the primary results virtually unintelligible as guides to convention action. Moreover, in the present situation, Stevenson had everything to lose and nothing to gain by what would certainly prove to be a long, hard struggle, as expensive of his physical and mental stamina as of his campaign treasury. The governor of New York, Harriman, could justly say that he was unable to engage in a primary struggle; having made known his "availability," he might stand on the side lines and pick up the prize, painlessly, effortlessly, if Kefauver succeeded in fighting Stevenson to a standstill.

But at this juncture Stevenson was no longer a free agent in the political arena. Hundreds of people had already invested money, time, and effort in his cause, numerous staff commitments had been made, and he could not in honor forsake them even if he would. Nor would he have done so had the possibility of doing so been wholly honorable. Though a peaceable man, he had never shrunk in fear from a fight and his fighting spirit was roused by allegations that he wanted "glory" handed to him on a silver platter. He was convinced that of all available party leaders, he represented the area of widest possible agreement and the best chance of focusing all the party's resources on the opposition—and though he would never say so, he must have been convinced that he had earned the nomination, if anyone in the party had done so, through the effort he had made in '52 and the victories he had helped to gain in '54. Accordingly, albeit reluctantly, he revised his strategy and changed his posture to face the new situation. A first instance of this occurred in mid-October when, to counteract the effect of a forthcoming speech of Harriman's in Des Moines, he issued a statement favoring price supports of basic farm crops at 90 per cent of parity. He did so only after it became clear that the rights and interests of many other people, to whom he felt obligated, would be harmed by his failure to do so; and he flinched a bit, displaying an irritable resentment toward some of his staff, when the opposition promptly hurled at him the charge of "cheap political expediency."

Far more in character for him was the long-scheduled address he delivered a few weeks later, on November 11, during a Woodrow Wilson Centennial celebration at the University of Virginia. It would be the last, for many months, of the kind of foreign-policy review, on historical principles, he liked best to make. Subsequent events would bestow upon it a historical interest.

He referred to the violence which for five years had been "mounting . . . along the armistice lines" between Israel and her hostile Arab neighbors. "Unless these clashes cease there is danger of all-out war developing while we debate which side was aggressor," he said, insisting that a "major effort of statesmanship is required if we are to avert . . . disaster in this troubled area." Vital interests of the United States, the structure of the Western alliance against communism, the very existence of the United Nations were threatened by the "recent arms deal between Egypt and Russia," together with our failure to assure Israel of "an equitable balance of armed strength"—for the "Middle East has long been an area of Russian ambitions." While "we do not want to see an arms race in this area," neither side should feel "that it lives by the grace of its none-too-kindly neighbor. . . . We must help, if need be, to counteract any Soviet attempt to upset . . . [a] balance, and we must make it emphatically clear that the status quo shall not be changed by force."

But this was only the negative side of his proposal. It seemed to him that "we have shown little initiative within or outside the United Nations in devising measures to prevent these clashes," and this despite the fact that one device for doing so was clearly indicated. "After years of experience it would seem evident that the only way to avoid bloodshed and violence along the border is to keep the troops of these antagonists apart," he said. "And I wonder if United Nations guards could not undertake patrol duties in the areas of tension and collision. Certainly both sides would respect United Nations patrols where they do not trust each other."

Writing these sentences, Stevenson had had high hopes that his suggestion, striking fire from American imaginations, would spark the administration into a realistic, clearly defined Middle Eastern policy. It did cause some excitement among those who were convinced that a minimal world government was indispensable to genuine world peace. A long step might be taken in that direction, these people felt, if UN troops could be recruited, not as national units, but as individual volunteers owing allegiance only to the UN flag, and in numbers sufficient to enforce UN laws in areas where those laws were violated. But in general, as Stevenson ruefully admitted a few weeks later, his idea dropped quietly into the pool of national complacency, disappearing with scarcely a ripple. Far from facing the realities of the Middle Eastern crisis, the administration continued to address the Egyptian dictator, Colonel Nasser, in a language of threat-and-bribe which was self-defeating, while Israel, Britain, and France—acutely aware of the meaning of Soviet Middle Eastern penetration—grew daily more desperate.

As for Stevenson, he was by then in no position to lead a "loyal opposition" to policies which, as he told his friends again and again, were creating a dangerous power vacuum in the Middle East. By then he was engaged in an intraparty fight for his political life. . . .

IV

To reassure himself as to his fitness for the coming ordeal, Stevenson early in November had entered Passavant Hospital in Chicago for a comprehensive physical examination, supervised by Dr. Leander W. Riba. As if to counteract the politico-medical reports then issuing in a steady stream from Eisenhower's physicians, Dr. Riba told a reporter that Stevenson, upon examination, proved to be "in perfect health" with "far better than normal endurance for a man at his age." Heart, blood pressure, lungs, urinary tract, nervous system —all these were in excellent condition. His weight was "entirely satisfactory at 180 pounds." Stevenson had, said his doctor, a tremendous chest expansion—"nearly five inches between inspiration and expiration"—and had "legs on him like an ox." His arms were "well-muscled, too. . . . His health is better than at any time during the three years I have known him," the doctor concluded. "I was very agreeably surprised at how far within normal limits his tests fell."

The candidacy was formally announced on November 15. "In partnership with our friends and allies, with confidence born of strength and influence born of magnanimity, we must work to uproot the causes of conflict and tensions and to outlaw the very means of war in this atomic age," said Stevenson's announcement statement. "The task of the Democratic party is to make 'peace and prosperity' not just a political slogan but an active search for a better America and a better world. I am ready to do what I can to that end either as a worker in the ranks or at the top of my ticket if my party sees fit so to honor me." Next day, at a press conference in Chicago, he announced several major appointments to his staff.

The campaign manager was to be James A. Finnegan, whose role in the initial "draft-Stevenson" movement will be remembered. A short, gray-haired Irishman born in Philadelphia in 1906, Finnegan had been administrative assistant to former Senator William J. Myers and had been chairman of the Democratic County Executive Committee of Philadelphia from 1948 to 1952, during which time Philadelphia elected its first Democratic mayor in sixty-seven years. He was president of the Philadelphia City Council and secretary of the Commonwealth of Pennsylvania. Stevenson found him hard-working and efficient, "politically adroit and sophisticated, unusually effective in his handling of local politicians but with sound, informed judgment, too, on over-all issues." A man of gentle manner and even temper, he was greatly liked by the staff.

Finnegan's second-in-command was the executive director of the campaign committee, Hyman B. Raskin, a law partner of Stephen Mitchell's and a former deputy chairman of the Democratic National Committee. Born in 1909, Raskin was a big man with prematurely white hair, who worked well and effectively with Finnegan. Harry Ashmore, editor of the Arkansas *Gazette,* was a special assistant who played an important role during the primary campaign, particularly during its early weeks, returning to his newspaper in June of '56, after the last primary had been held. Mrs. Edison Dick and Barry Bingham served as co-chairmen of the National Stevenson for President Committee, with Archibald S. Alexander as that organization's executive director; their task was to recruit, organize, and direct the activities of Volunteers for Stevenson. Roger Tubby, former press officer of the Department of State and assistant press secretary in the White House for President Truman, became Stevenson's press secretary, a fact which initially caused widespread newspaper comment, since Tubby resigned from Harriman's staff in Albany, New York,[3] to accept the Stevenson assignment. Tubby's assistant was C. K. McClatchy, a young man who proved unusually efficient as facilitating officer to newspapermen who followed the primary campaign.

Stevenson, at this first press conference, also said he would call upon Stephen Mitchell and Wilson Wyatt for "continuous advice and counsel." He then made headline news by announcing his entrance into the Minnesota primary, to be held March 20. This, he said, was the only "firm decision" he had made with respect to primaries. "The others we will consider as we come to them."

During the question period he was asked if he expected Eisenhower to be his opponent. "I hadn't thought so," he replied, "but I read in the papers that his recovery is rapid and encouraging, and that there are those who believe that he may be fit to be a candidate again. That I just don't know. I can't speculate." He was asked whether, in his view, he was a "middle-of-the-road Democrat." In his reply he laughed at some of Eisenhower's favorite political slogans. "I am not one of those who believes that you can characterize a philosophy on public issues by slogans," he said. "I have never been sure what progressive conservatism means, or was it conservative progressivism? I have forgotten. And I am not sure what dynamic moderation or moderate dynamism means. I am not even sure what it means when one says he is a conservative in fiscal affairs and a liberal in human affairs. I assume what it means is that you will strongly recommend the building of a great many schools to accommodate the needs of our children, but not provide the money."

His hostility to "sloganeering" of course did not prevent the use

[3] Tubby's Albany assignment was in public relations for the New York Commerce Commission, but he had close working contacts with the governor's office.

of it against himself and his campaign. During his address to the Democratic National Committee dinner, a hundred-dollar-a-plate affair on November 19, he arraigned the administration for single-interest government, stressing the farm, public power, and foreign-policy issues. Truman promptly termed it the "best fighting New Deal speech" he had ever heard Stevenson give. But in the midst of it Stevenson said: "I agree that it is a time for catching our breath; I agree that moderation is the spirit of the times. But we best take care lest we confuse moderation with mediocrity, or settle for half-answers to hard problems." Next day Governor G. Mennen Williams of Michigan assailed Stevenson's "policy" of "moderation." Governor Harriman promptly announced that there "is no such word as 'moderation' or 'middle-of-the-road' in the Democratic vocabulary." Whereupon Truman discovered that he, too, was a champion of "immoderation," or at least was opposed to "moderation," and had lost his initial enthusiasm for Stevenson's speech.

Thus it was made evident that Stevenson would not only have to fight for his nomination but also that, as front-runner, he faced serious problems. He who had repeatedly attacked the GOP elephant as a two-headed beast now found himself the titular head of a party whose division might become as great, and as hampering to decisive government, as that separating the Republican Old Guard from the so-called "Eisenhower wing." He must establish and hold firm positions from which he could withstand fire from the left of his party, directed by northern liberals, and fire from the right, directed by southern conservatives, and he must do so in ways which would recommend him to the great mass of "independent" voters upon whose decision depended the outcome in November. The only alternative to this was a decision to write off the South, as Truman had done in 1948, and run as a candidate of the northern Democracy. The latter alternative was that chosen, in effect, by Harriman-Kefauver supporters, and it was here that the real issue lay between them and Stevenson in the struggle for control of the convention.

The split between the two regions had been greatly deepened by a unanimous decision of the U. S. Supreme Court, on May 17, 1954, declaring racial segregation in public schools to be unconstitutional. It had not been lessened by a decision on May 31, 1955, which assigned local authorities the task of integrating the schools and instructed federal courts to enforce "a prompt and reasonable start" toward integration, with the proviso that "additional time" be allowed where required by local conditions. "Good faith" was to be a major test of compliance with the law. In six southern states this ruling was openly defied by officials who denied that the Supreme Court had the authority to make it, and the violent disagreement on this point exacerbated every other difference between southern conservatives and those liberals who were convinced that southern congressional leadership since 1954 had played directly into Eisenhower's hands, immensely strengthening the administration as it approached the new election.

On December 16 Estes Kefauver announced his candidacy, promising a "vigorous campaign" through the primaries—and as the Christmas season came on, Stevenson knew that he could not avoid a head-on collision with the Tennessee senator in at least one primary and probably in several. His decisive defeat in any of these could, and probably would, cost him the nomination.

To his political concerns that Christmas was added a tragic personal concern.

On the morning of December 21 a car driven by nineteen-year-old John Fell Stevenson, on his way home from Harvard for the holidays, was struck head on by a truck on a railroad overpass near Goshen, Indiana. With him were three Harvard friends, two of them Chicago boys who had been intimates of his since childhood. These two, William S. North III and William C. Boyden, Jr., were instantly killed, while the third youth, riding in the back seat, suffered minor injuries. John Fell himself suffered a shattered kneecap which was subsequently removed, lost a number of teeth, and was badly cut and bruised. Adlai Stevenson learned of this when he arrived in his office that morning, his greatest relief from the pain of that dark hour being the firm assurance that his son was in no sense to blame for the accident: the truck had been passing another and its driver was soon indicted for reckless driving and involuntary homicide. Stevenson promptly flew to Goshen in a chartered plane, returning in an ambulance to Passavant Hospital in Chicago with his son a day or so later.

One of the first of the sympathy messages which poured in upon him was from the President of the United States, and to this Stevenson replied in longhand: "I am deeply grateful for your most thoughtful and kind message about John Fell; and he was at first incredulous and then profoundly impressed and grateful too!" John Fell joined in the "thanks," said Stevenson, "with all the emphasis a cracked jaw permits!" He spoke of the grave concern they all felt for the parents of the dead boys, and it was to this that he referred most emphatically in the form reply he was at last forced to prepare as the inpouring messages became a flood. Wrote he: "Your message of sympathy for John Fell was very kind and very helpful. While his body is recovering rapidly, the spirit will be slower to mend. But faith and love are healing powers, and there is a great reservoir of both in the world. . . . Our greater anxiety is that the families of his beloved friends will be given the strength to live through and beyond this tragedy."

Inevitably Stevenson was reminded of the great tragedy of his own childhood, the death of Ruth Merwin. In early January he drove with a friend from his farm to the Deerpath station. The friend asked how John Fell was getting along.

"Oh, fine," Stevenson replied. "He's been released from the hospital."

"Will he have a permanent limp?"

"No, he won't be crippled at all. It looked at first as though he would be, but the doctors say he'll make a complete recovery." Then Stevenson glanced away and went on, in a different tone, "That is, a complete physical recovery. Of course—a thing like this, it leaves scars on the spirit. They'll always be there."

And his friend, glancing at him, suddenly realized that Stevenson now spoke not only of John Fell but also of himself. . . .

CHAPTER TWENTY-NINE

An Ending: The Campaign of 1956

If a man's character is his fate, it becomes so in terms of the environment through which it must express itself, and in the politics of the Eisenhower years the dominant environmental condition seemed to be a fog of ambiguity whereby men and issues became badly blurred. They were blurred not only in the popular view but also in themselves, as though the fog dissolved all essential definitions.

Such, it might seem, was one lesson demonstrated by Stevenson's struggle in 1956 for the presidency of the United States. Four years before, as a drafted candidate of the party in power, he had projected a public image of himself which was true to his essential character. He had gone down in defeat. In 1956, as a challenged candidate of a party out of power, he seemed required by the "spirit of the times" to present to the public a "New Stevenson," one which blurred the image he had projected theretofore. Having suffered a nearly disastrous reverse as the "Old" Stevenson, he scored a series of tactical victories in his "New" form, but in the end he went down to a defeat worse than that of 1952 and one for which the blurring of his image seemed in some part responsible.

Some among his immediate staff would assert that this "New" Stevenson was wholly a public-relations myth invented by correspondents. Stevenson in '56 did nothing that he had not done in '52, they would claim; newsmen simply shifted their emphasis as they reported his activities, stressing in '56 elements they had largely ignored in '52. But no close objective observer would be likely to agree with this. Stevenson himself seemed to "shift emphasis" sufficiently to create a "New" public self as an overlay of the "Old."

He did not do so easily. Only with great reluctance, and only a step at a time, did he abandon his dream of a '56 campaign which would be in every way an improvement, as a contribution to the "democratic dialogue," over that he had conducted four years before. Particularly was he reluctant to abandon those attacks upon the administration's conduct of foreign affairs which he had conceived to be a principal element of his struggle for power; he was convinced that foreign policy was by far the most crucial of the real issues facing the American people, one fraught with the gravest dangers to the republic and to the world. As late as November 17, James Reston of the New York *Times* was reporting "talk" of Stevenson's "going abroad early in 1956 so that he can study some of the problems first hand and keep his campaign stocked with fresh themes."

At that time the Minnesota primary, as we have seen, was the only one Stevenson had definitely decided to enter, and it seemed unlikely that Kefauver would challenge him there, since Senator Hubert Humphrey, Governor Orville Freeman, and a Democratic farmer-labor organization which was reputedly one of the most effective state organizations in the nation was solidly supporting the Stevenson candidacy. Subsequently it became clear that Kefauver could hurt Stevenson's chances merely by making a good showing in Minnesota (no one, Kefauver included, thought he had a chance actually to defeat Stevenson there), whereupon Kefauver filed. Thus was scheduled the first of three major battles between the senator and Stevenson, the other two being the Florida primary on May 8 and the California one on June 5.

Even then Stevenson made no serious effort to match Kefauver's expenditure of time and energy in Minnesota. He had a personal distaste for the kind of folksy, handshaking, "coonskin-cap" campaigning which Estes Kefauver so assiduously practiced. This was not because he had a contempt for "common" folk and disliked to associate with them. On the contrary, it was precisely because he had so high a respect for people as individuals, so high an opinion of the intelligence of the electorate at large, that he hated to deal with them as mere elements in an emotion-ridden mass of flesh. He wanted to communicate with people *as* individuals, each with a mind of his own. Assembly-line handshaking seemed to him a travesty of this process: surely one who aspired to the highest office in the world should be primarily concerned to "touch minds" rather than "flesh." Hence, in those early weeks, he confined himself for the most part to large meetings before which he could present prepared addresses.

In one of these addresses, given in February, he reasserted those principles which had animated his '52 campaign and whose half-defiant, rather self-righteous expression seemed to some of his advisers unfortunate in his present circumstances. "I shall try in these coming months to fool no one, including myself," he said, "—not with slogans or false promises or easy answers to hard problems. . . . I must add frankly to what I've said about myself that it is quite possible that I would not be the best candidate for you, if winning is the first objective of any political race, because I have an allergy for false promises. . . . I am told that promises . . . are indispensable to victory and that keeping them is far less important than making them. Well, I don't agree." When he prepared these remarks he was about to campaign more arduously in Minnesota than he had originally planned to do, but far less arduously than Finnegan wanted him to do—and a campaign manager might be forgiven for believing that, no matter what the candidate said, the first objective of the race *was* victory and that victory was by no means as certain as the candidate seemed to believe.

Not until the New Hampshire primary of mid-March did Stevenson have a premonition of disaster. Though he was not entered in that primary and had not campaigned there, whereas Kefauver was formally entered and had shaken most of the Democratic hands in the state, Stevenson was encouraged by his supporters to expect a large write-in vote for himself. When this vote was not forthcoming, Stevenson confessed to his staff that he now "worried" a little about Minnesota.

On the evening of March 20 he had as his dinner guest at Libertyville his long-time friend, George W. Ball, who had been associated with him in the Sidley law firm, was now a partner in a New York and Washington law firm, and would serve after the convention as Stevenson's director of public relations. After dinner the two men sat before the fireplace in the living room, listening to the Minnesota returns. A few hours later they were joined by the Willard Wirtzes, the Edison Dicks, Archibald Alexander, and others. These latecomers found a Stevenson who was "fighting mad," though his anger was of a nature peculiarly his own in that it contained remarkably little personal bitterness. He was being licked in Minnesota. Indeed, his defeat there was of crushing, humiliating proportions.

Of Minnesota's thirty delegates Kefauver captured all but four while piling up a lead of some sixty thousand votes over Stevenson out of a total vote of a little over three hundred thousand. It seemed at once evident, and subsequent analysis proved it to be true, that Kefauver's margin of victory was largely made up of Republican votes, for Republicans were permitted by Minnesota law to vote in the Democratic primary and were encouraged to do so by Republican strategists, Eisenhower being virtually uncontested in the Republican primary and Stevenson being (as the Republican strategists believed) by far the strongest candidate the Democrats could run in November. Nevertheless Stevenson was abruptly removed from his front-running position. He must, it seemed, drastically revise his campaign strategy and tactics.

He cheerfully admitted as much next day at a large press conference, while denying emphatically that he was "through" or had any intention of withdrawing from the race. "When something like this happens, I don't feel bitter, or that an injustice has been done," said he. "I feel simply that I have failed to communicate, and that I must try harder." Asked if he now planned to shake more hands, he replied with a grin that apparently "a certain identity *is* established between shaker and shakee" when a hand is shaken.

Thereafter he ran, as he said, "like a singed cat." Gone from his prepared talks were the witticisms which had sparkled from his speeches of '52; gone was the evident reluctance to campaign for the presidency as though it were a popularity prize. The "New" Stevenson was bussed by pretty girls in California, donned cowboy boots in Arizona, carried a stuffed alligator and thumped a base fiddle in Florida, and everywhere shook hands by the hundreds, the thousands. He traveled continuously from coast to coast, and into the South, giving hundreds of talks to small groups and numerous prepared addresses before large audiences.

At first he betrayed a certain self-consciousness in this unwonted role, but as time went on he gave every outward appearance of thoroughly enjoying himself. He even managed, by the manner of his playing it, to make the role at least consistent with, if not truly expressive of, his essential self. His handling of the stuffed-alligator episode was typical. The alligator was thrust unexpectedly into his hands by one of the crowd around him on a Florida street. He laughed, but his laughter was a bit forced and his aides could see that he was annoyed. "What am I to do with this thing?" he muttered in an irritable aside. But as he went on down the street, he began to make extravagant gestures with the alligator, fumbling with it to indicate how it embarrassed him, laughing at the absurdity of his predicament, until, soon, the crowd was laughing uproariously in sympathy with him.

And his tactics, it seemed, "paid off." Forced to play Kefauver's game, he played it with a vengeance, to the delighted astonishment of his own staff, scoring a series of minor but significant victories in Alaska, the District of Columbia, New Jersey, Illinois, and Oregon on his way to Florida, where Kefauver was reputed to have the advantage. Stevenson won Florida, too, if narrowly. And in the crucial California primary on June 5 he scored an overwhelming victory, gaining some 1,100,000 votes to 627,000 for Kefauver. In early August the Tennessee senator withdrew from the race and, resisting the blandishments of Harriman forces, threw his support to Stevenson. He also made a handsome public apology for certain unfortunate remarks he had made about his opponent in the heat of the campaign, an apology which Stevenson, who had himself said some harsh things, gratefully accepted.

Thus was Stevenson restored, on the eve of the convention, to his position as front-runner for the nomination. And thus was it decided once and for all, or so it seemed, that the Democrats would enter the presidential race as a united party of North and South rather than of the North alone.

During this primary struggle, only two issues of national import were developed in such a way as to impress strongly the public mind. In February, before a Negro group in California, Stevenson opposed (a) the use of federal troops to force compliance with the Supreme Court's school desegregation decision and (b) an amendment to the pending school-aid bill denying federal aid to any segregated school. In so doing he used the term "gradually" to characterize what seemed to him the proper approach to a problem with deep historical roots and one imbued with passionate prejudice. This "gradualism," in his view, should be characterized by "all reasonable speed," but the term was one particularly hated by Negro leaders, who had learned from bitter experience that it generally meant the maintenance of the status quo. Stevenson was soon impelled to issue a prepared statement in which he reasserted his strong personal agreement with the Supreme Court decision while pointing out that the

Court itself had "recognized that we cannot by a stroke of the pen reverse customs and traditions that are older than the Republic. . . . Instead of establishing a fixed time limit for compliance with its decrees it has established the test of good faith as the measurement of progress in cases pending before the district courts. . . . We will not . . . reduce race prejudice by denying to areas afflicted with it the means of improving educational standards of all their people. Certainly we will not improve the present condition or future prospects of any Negro citizen by coercive federal action that will arm the extremists and disarm the men of goodwill in the South who, with courage and patience, have already accomplished so much."

Subsequently he called repeatedly for "positive leadership" by the White House to alleviate the dangerous situation in the South, where white citizens' councils were organized to defy the Court order and where state governments embraced a doctrine of "interposition" indistinguishable from Calhoun's Union-destroying "nullification." He suggested that the President call a conference of white and Negro leaders to work out means of implementing, in fair and orderly fashion, the "law of the land." The suggestion fell on deaf ears. The President even declined to say explicitly that he personally favored the Court's decision. It didn't matter what he personally thought, said Eisenhower; the Constitution was as the Court said it was, and he was under oath to uphold the Constitution. . . .

In April, before the American Society of Newspaper Editors, Stevenson suggested that the best way to frustrate Russia's competition and political penetration in the undeveloped areas was by channeling more of our economic aid through the United Nations' regional multilateral agencies and challenging the Soviet to do likewise.

A more significant proposal in the same speech was that the United States ban the further testing of hydrogen bombs, and announce the fact to the world. Such tests, he pointed out, were poisoning the earth's atmosphere with deadly Strontium 90, and while there was some disagreement among scientists as to the immediacy of the danger (there were scientists who claimed that the "tolerance point" was being rapidly approached), there was none at all that the ultimate effect, if the tests continued, would be race suicide. Moreover, this was a disarmament move which the United States might make unilaterally, without serious risk to our national security: scientists had means of knowing immediately when and approximately where a massive atomic explosion occurred, so that if Soviet Russia tested a bomb we could promptly resume the tests ourselves if we wished to do so. In any case, the risk of the proposal was small compared to the gains the United States might make from it in the esteem of all the peoples of the earth and as a contribution to peace and sanity. But this suggestion, too, fell on deaf ears in the administration, and was initially opposed by Kefauver, though a majority of the nation's physical and biological scientists seemed to favor it strongly. Indeed, key administration spokesmen treated the proposal with contempt, indicating that it was presumptuous of Stevenson to make it to the greatest military leader of the age.

II

Meanwhile it had become apparent that the President's heart attack, far from being a hazard to his re-election, was probably a political asset. Having passed through the valley of the shadow of death, he was now a greater hero, more beloved of the populace, than before. In large part this was due to his personal qualities—to the perfection with which he expressed the dominant mood of the country and to the warm affection he personally inspired. But it was also due to a triumph of public-relations engineering unprecedented in American political history, as several writers on political affairs pointed out at the time.

While the President yet lay part time in an oxygen tent, Dr. Paul Dudley White, an eminent specialist from Boston, had joined White House Press Secretary James Hagerty in a massive "Operation Candor" to publicize every phase of the sick man's recovery. Within days Dr. White announced that he saw "no medical reason" why Eisenhower should not run for re-election. When the sick man, on September 30, initialed a couple of documents, the fact received banner headlines in the nation's press. This gesture was followed by others in ever closer succession, all of them immensely publicized to indicate that the President, though he still had "a long way to go" for full recovery, remained in effective control of all his essential duties. On November 11, seven weeks after his attack, he was flown to Washington. November 11 happened to be Veterans Day; parades and crowds were on Washington's streets in memory of martial events in which General Eisenhower had played so conspicuous a part. Grinning broadly and waving to the crowds, providing visible evidence of his returning health, the President announced that, according to his doctors, he would have to "ease" rather than "bulldoze" his way into a full exercise of his responsibilities, but that he felt fine. He then proceeded to his Gettysburg farm where he convalesced for several weeks, working part time in a headquarters established in the town's post office.

Long before he had returned to the White House, nearly all the nation's press and all Republican politicians were praying in chorus that he run again. And by early spring, when he announced that he would indeed run, though he might have to transfer some of his nonessential functions to his "associates" during a second term, his physical fitness for the office seemed no longer an issue of even the "silent" kind in the minds of most voters; public-opinion polls continued to show him the overwhelming choice of the electorate.

Whatever slight doubts may have remained concerning his health were presumably removed by a comprehensive physical examination in Walter Reed Hospital May 10 to 12. "His general condition continues good," said the vastly publicized medical report. "He is physically active and mentally alert." Among the "special" examinations was one of his digestive tract. "The X-ray examinations of the gastro-intestinal tract with barium studies showed a normally functioning digestive tract," the report concluded.

It was through his digestive tract, however, as the culmination of what one doctor said was an ailment of long standing, that the sixty-five-year-old President was struck down on June 8 by his second dangerous illness within nine months. Rushed to Walter Reed Hospital, he underwent emergency surgery at two fifty-nine on the morning of June 9 to relieve obstruction of the ileum, or lower part of the small intestine.

Here, surely, was an ultimate test of Republican public-relations skills. But within hours, or so it appeared to knowledgeable observers, a successful strategy had been decided upon. This strategy was to minimize the seriousness of the President's affliction and to refuse to admit that it could have any effect upon his candidacy. Eleven hours after the operation began, Major General Leonard D. Heaton, who had performed the surgery, told a jam-packed news conference that he saw no medical reason why the President should not run again. A "rapid and complete recovery" was anticipated. The President should be able to resume the "full duties" of his office in four to six weeks and to play golf again by mid-August. OKAY

FOR IKE TO RUN SAY DOCTORS was the standard banner head-line in the nation's press that afternoon.

Thereafter, in marked contrast to the tactics following the heart attack, no press conferences at which reporters could question the doctors were held. Embarrassing questions concerning the recur-rence rate of ileitis were brushed off by Press Secretary Hagerty. One Republican leader after another indicated that "of course" the President's decision to run remained unchanged. And while he was yet in acute misery, with a tube running through his nose, Eisen-hower was reported to have "personally decided" (Hagerty stressed it as a *personal* decision) that American military leaders should not visit the Soviet Union as the Soviet government had invited them to do. Thereafter, his physical recovery was almost as rapid as Heaton had predicted while his popularity with voters, according to the polls, remained undiminished. A Gallup poll in early August showed Eisenhower to be favored by 61 per cent of the voters as against 37 for Stevenson.

Awesome to all, gratifying to most, dismaying to the few who be-lieved that a complacent and ill-informed America drifted in a dangerous world, was this renewed evidence of Eisenhower's tre-mendous appeal—or the appeal of his public image—to the average citizen. His popularity seemed to tower like a rock above the political seas. Every adverse argument, every citation of adverse evidence, seemed to break futilely against it. Stevenson and his supporters must realize that he, if nominated, must run not only against a man but also against a myth. The man was formidable enough to make his defeat difficult. The myth was sustained by so powerful a "will to believe," so firm and skilled a control of mass media, as to make its defeat nearly impossible.

III

Nevertheless, the Democrats who began to gather in Chicago during the week of August 5 in preparation for their national con-vention, which would open August 13 in the International Amphi-theater, were by no means downhearted. All that the presidential polls indicated, in Democratic opinion, was that the American peo-ple had not yet begun to take the election seriously. The people were being asked to re-elect a President whose principal recommen-dation, in the Democratic view, was an amiable personality, who in good health had been the opposite of vigorous in the discharge of his responsibilities, and who was now both overage and in failing health. Surely they would take a good hard look at actuarial figures, if at nothing else, and would decide that a vote for Eisenhower would be, in all probability, a vote for Vice-President Nixon as President. Few Democrats doubted that this decision, if widely made, would be fatal to the Republican ticket. It was a cardinal article of their faith that the average American disliked Nixon as much as they did, and in this faith they were not wholly alone. At that very moment, Harold Stassen, one of the President's principal advisers, was leading a "dump-Nixon" movement which, though it would doubtless fail in the Republican convention, dramatized the views of many an "independent," many an "Eisenhower Republican."

There was no denying, of course, that the Republican slogan, "Peace, Progress, Prosperity," was a potent one in the prevailing circumstances. It would remain so, however, only to the extent that it obscured what, to Democrats, seemed the plain facts. In fact, there had been no progress in government but instead a retreat in several areas. In fact, the "peace" was a precarious armed truce during which Russia profited hugely from the administration's incredible bungling. In fact, the much-vaunted prosperity, in so far as it was affected by governmental action, was determined by inherited Democratic policies, had been damaged by every departure the administration had made from these, and now contained several soft spots, notably in agriculture and closely related industries. And did not Democratic victories in every recent election show these facts to be realized by an increasing number of Americans? Did not the very polls which predicted an Eisenhower landslide predict that Democrats would increase their number of governorships and their majorities in the Congress? In view of all this, what reason was there to assume that even the Ike myth was invulnerable? After all, in four years of politics Eisenhower had faced less hostile fire than Truman and Roosevelt had faced in an average month, and who could say that he would not swiftly wither in the heat blasts of a fighting campaign?

But it must be a fighting campaign, led by a fighting presidential candidate committed to New and Fair Deal "principles." So said Averell Harriman, who, at last formally announcing his candidacy on the weekend of the President's ileitis attack, proclaimed himself precisely the fighter which the situation demanded. So, too, said

Harry Truman who, having thus far declined to say whom he favored for the nomination, dominated the pre-convention scene from the moment of his arrival in Chicago. The ex-President would, he told a press conference, "let the people know for whom I stand before the convention meets," and then dropped broad hints (he was "no bandwagon fellow," he had no faith in political polls, he had no use for presidential primaries) that his choice would be Harriman.

The probability, combined with an earlier event of that hectic week, struck more dismay into the heart of the Stevenson camp than any other development since the Minnesota primary. This earlier event was a curbstone TV interview in which Stevenson had said that, in his opinion, the party platform "should express unequivocal approval of the [Supreme] Court's decision" on school desegregation. Southern delegates, who theretofore had seemed firm Stevenson supporters, had reacted promptly and wrathfully against him. There now loomed the distinct possibility that Harriman, aided by concerted southern "favored son" votes, could prevent Stevenson's nomination on an early ballot, deadlock the convention, and ensure the victory of a dark horse compromise candidate. To the eyes of many an outside observer this possibility came close to becoming a probability when, on Saturday, August 11, Truman announced that his choice was indeed Harriman. The New York governor, said Truman, had "the ability to act as President immediately upon assuming that office, without risking a period of costly and dangerous trial and error." The ex-President then made it clear that he personally would fight with every ounce of his strength to stop Stevenson.

But by that time Stevenson and his staff had carefully assessed the probable effect of Truman's move and, though they remained acutely concerned, were no longer dismayed. The move, they believed, had been made too late. Truman, they were convinced, mistook his personal popularity with the delegates for persuasive power over them, whereas in fact his popularity had waxed to almost the precise extent that his power had waned. They conceded that it might now be impossible for Stevenson to win on the first ballot, but they were confident, if far from overconfident, that he would win on the second or third.

Thus did Stevenson pay a final installment on the pre-convention and campaign strategy he had followed, partly from conscious choice and partly from character-determined necessity, in 1952. He was aided greatly to do so by the fervent support of Mrs. Franklin D.

Roosevelt, who should know, if anyone did, whom her husband would have been most likely to favor—or so most delegates might assume. All that weekend Stevenson's staff members and leading supporters went from caucus room to caucus room in Loop hotels, working for new pledges and for the reaffirmation of old ones. Nor did the pace slacken after the gavel came down opening the convention on Monday. On that day and the next, Stevenson himself visited several state caucuses and was everywhere greeted with great enthusiasm. While the convention struggled toward adoption of a civil-rights platform plank which rejected "all proposals for the use of force to interfere with the orderly determination" of desegregation matters in the courts and which asserted the Supreme Court decisions to be "the law of the land" (other planks called for repeal of the Taft-Hartley Law, international control of the Suez canal, arms for Israel, and high rigid supports of farm prices), the battle for delegates went on. By Wednesday it became clear that Stevenson had won it despite Truman's increasingly harsh strictures upon him. (On Tuesday night a stubbornly defiant Truman, seemingly bent on ruining what he could not rule, asserted that Stevenson was a "conservative" who follows the "counsel of hesitation" and "lacks the kind of fighting spirit we need to win.") At two-thirty that morning, most of Michigan's forty-four delegates, led by Governor Williams, voted to support Stevenson. A few hours later, New Jersey's thirty-six votes were pledged to Stevenson when Governor Robert Meyner, a Stevenson man from the outset, absolutely refused to stand as a favorite son. It was more than enough to ensure a first-ballot nomination. . . .

On Wednesday evening Stevenson, his name having been placed in nomination a few hours before by youthful Senator John F. Kennedy of Massachusetts, sat in his office at 231 South La Salle. During the preceding weeks he had come to a decision which he planned, later that night, to announce to the convention, and he revised his statement of it as he sat there. He paid scant attention to the telecast of the convention's balloting session where the Stevenson vote grew steadily toward the 686½ votes needed for nomination. He was watching, though, at approximately ten o'clock when TV cameras focused on a jubilant governor of Pennsylvania rising to cry his delegation's vote into the microphone. "Pennsylvania casts seven votes for Harriman . . ." shouted Governor Leader, pausing dramatically before adding, "and for Stevenson, enough to put him over the top

—sixty-seven!" Stevenson watched pandemonium break loose on the convention floor, then walked from his office into a glare of TV lights and an explosion of photographers' bulbs, smiling a trifle wanly. "I feel fine," he said, ". . . relieved and happy."

He went down to the Clark Street entrance of the bank building and into the limousine waiting for him there. He drove the miles southward to the Amphitheater in precisely twelve minutes, escorted by police cars and motorcycles whose sirens screamed through the warm summer night, arriving at the Stockyards Inn, adjacent to the convention hall, at about the time the conclusion of the roll call showed Stevenson's total vote to be 905½.

While the convention, by thunderous voice vote, was making his nomination unanimous, Stevenson himself was engaged in heated argument. The move he planned to make was strongly opposed by Sam Rayburn, Lyndon Johnson, and Paul Butler, none of whom had had prior inkling of it. It would, they claimed, "deadlock the convention." The move was supported, however, by Jack Arvey, Dick Daley, David Lawrence of Pittsburgh, and Governor Abraham A. Ribicoff of Connecticut, none of whom had had any inkling of it either. For fifteen minutes they exchanged views vigorously, until at last Sam Rayburn, the convention chairman, said that, under duress, he would do as Stevenson wished.

"Are you absolutely sure this is what you want to do?" asked Rayburn.

"It's what I want to do, Sam," replied Stevenson, his face somewhat flushed but his voice calm.

Then, facing the roaring hall, the TV cameras again, and the news-reels and the flashing bulbs, he announced in a brief statement his unprecedented decision, one shrewdly designed to serve not only the political interests of the immediate present but also, he was convinced, those of the future. The choice of his running mate, he said, would be the convention's alone; he himself would have no part in it. "The American people have the solemn obligation to consider with the utmost care who will be their President if the elected President is prevented by a Higher Will from serving his full term," he explained. "It is a sober reminder that seven out of thirty-four Presidents have served as the result of such an indirect selection. The responsibility of the Presidency has grown so great that the nation's attention has become focussed as never before on the office of the Vice-Presidency. The choice for that office has become almost as important as the choice for the Presidency." For this reason he wished to depart from the custom of having the presidential candidate choose his running mate for reasons of geography, political expediency, or personal liking. "Until tomorrow night," he concluded, "my heartfelt thanks, and may God be with you."

The convention's stunned surprise had not passed before Senators Humphrey, Kefauver, and Kennedy had become active vice-presidential candidates—and all that night the Loop hotels were scenes of frenzied activity as the intense campaigns for delegates went on. Stevenson himself, having downed a glass or two of champagne at a party in his suite at the Sheraton-Blackstone, and appeared briefly at a party for the Volunteers for Stevenson in the Conrad Hilton, slept peacefully. Next day he received a phone call from Harry Truman offering to come down from his suite two floors above Stevenson's in order to congratulate the nominee. "Don't do that," said Stevenson. "I'll come to see you." And he did, staying for approximately three minutes with the man who had so bitterly fought him, who had said things which would plague Stevenson throughout the campaign, and who now offered to do whatever the candidate wished him to do in the struggle for election. Just what was said between them was not disclosed. Stevenson then went to 231 South La Salle, where he worked on his formal acceptance speech and also watched, on TV, the convention's most exciting afternoon. Humphrey's candidacy, damaged by the Minnesota primary results, swiftly waned. The vice-presidential race was between Kefauver and Kennedy, with the South—out of dislike for Kefauver rather more than love for Kennedy, whose Catholic religion was a handicap among southern agrarians—fervently supporting the latter.

Stevenson himself remained scrupulously neutral, outwardly at least, impressing upon staff members that they must not, by word or sign, indicate a preference. While the roll-call vote on the convention floor seesawed between Kefauver and Kennedy, he worked calmly in his office on the speech he was to give that night. Occasionally Bill Blair, in whose office the TV set was located, came in to tell Stevenson the latest development; once or twice Stevenson came into Blair's office to watch the screen for a few moments. And whatever his secret preference may have been, Stevenson was certainly not dismayed when, on the second ballot, Kefauver emerged the victor by the narrowest of margins. He respected the Tennesseean's senatorial record, and whatever dislike he may have had for the man had been overcome by the events which followed June 5. Certainly no one could doubt that Kefauver would be an indefatigable campaigner on the national ticket. Moreover he would have one important advantage over Kennedy as candidate: the Massachusetts senator had voted against the Democratic farm program a few months before and would, it appeared, have been unable to make a strong bid for the farm vote, whereas Kefauver's popularity with farmers was notable.

In the nature of things, Stevenson's acceptance speech that night could not be as dramatic, as full of surprise, as that he had made four years before, and there were some among his supporters who regretted that it was not more clearly organized, more sharply focused on a few central issues. It was eloquent, however, stimulating no less than fifty-three bursts of enthusiastic applause as he proceeded.

History, he proclaimed, had brought us to the threshold of a "new America." "I mean an America where poverty is abolished and our abundance is used to enrich the lives of every family. I mean a new America where freedom is made real for all without regard to race or belief or economic condition. I mean a new America which everlastingly attacks the ancient idea that men can solve their differences by killing each other." On his way to these shining generalities, he arraigned the Eisenhower administration in terms highly pleasing to his supporters. The men around the President, said he, had dealt "the ultimate indignity to the democratic process" by attempting to "merchandise candidates like breakfast cereal." They "cynically coveted" Eisenhower as candidate but "ignored" him "as leader." And indeed Eisenhower had shown little desire or capacity for leadership. His major talent, Stevenson indicated, was for *mis*-leading the people. For instance, the President had proclaimed that our prestige abroad "has never been higher," when the blunt truth was that "it has probably never been lower." We were, said Stevenson, "losing the cold war."

The following week, in San Francisco, the Republican National Convention renominated Dwight Eisenhower and Richard Nixon in a session enlivened only by the expulsion from the hall of an irreverent Nebraska delegate who—apparently in an excess of boredom with the prevailing "Ike" adulation—sought to place in nomination a mythical "Joe Smith."

Thus, for the first time in fifty-six years, the two major-party presidential candidates were the same men who had faced each other four years before. The last time this had happened was in 1900, when McKinley ran for re-election against Bryan, and on that occasion the Democratic vice-presidential candidate had been Adlai Ewing Stevenson I.

The fact could not but stir in the present Adlai Stevenson a renewed sense of that family tradition, of history as family process, which had been a central theme of his growth. Both family past and family future seemed to meet among the events which had crowded around him during the last two weeks. Buffie, with Ernest Ives, had been close beside him. His sons, John Fell and Adlai III, had been there too, and young Adlai had worked hard and effectively for his father among the delegates during Truman's effort to block the Stevenson candidacy. Borden was still with the Army in Hawaii (a typical photograph showed him sitting at ease, clad in gaudy sport shorts, listening to convention reports on the radio), but soon he would be discharged and would join his father in the later phases of the campaign. It was with pretty, young Nancy Anderson Stevenson, however, Adlai, Jr.'s wife, that the family future lay. She had been one of the most photographed and televised personalities at the convention, being a wonderfully alive girl whose wholehearted reactions to the convention's abundant stimuli were delightful to behold, and all the world now knew that she carried the unborn first grandchild of the Democratic nominee. Moreover, this grandchild would be born, the doctors said, on or very near election day. . . .

IV

In retrospect it would appear that Stevenson, making his acceptance speech on August 17, stood at the apex of his political career. He had fought his way over one harsh obstacle after another on his way to party dominance, displaying in the process a rare courage, gaiety, intelligence, and integrity. His example had persuaded into active party work thousands of idealistic and energetic young people who would not otherwise have thought of entering practical politics, and his labors had contributed directly to the financial health of the party and to the victories it had scored at the polls since '52. No man could have earned in harder ways the public glory which was wrapped about him, in roaring acclaim, as he stood that night in the spotlight, behind the lectern and the microphones. He, of course, faced great odds as he again entered the lists against Eisenhower. Those who cheered him that night knew it. But they knew, too, that he had faced great odds before and had overcome them through the exercise of theretofore unsuspected strengths and talents. They were convinced he had a fighting chance, and this might be all that was needed by so shrewd, valiant, and experienced a warrior, armed as he now was with a battle-tested staff whose headquarters this time were in Washington, D.C., and whose organization was much more efficient than it had been before.

The campaign strategy, as worked out by the astute Finnegan, with Paul Butler and others, had two major tactical phases. One was a "pinpoint" tactic whereby Stevenson would focus on those states, and even on those counties and wards, where a relatively slight shift of votes would transform an Eisenhower victory into a Stevenson one. The other tactic, one which was indeed required by "pinpointing" on so vast a scale, was a public display of energy and stamina which Eisenhower could not match, indicating, as mere words could never do, the contrast between a relatively young man in the full tide of vigorous health and an aging man whose health was waning. Great reliance was placed on the apparent fact that the Democrats were the majority party; Stevenson, by being thoroughly identified with his party, might therefore gain as much as Eisenhower would lose if somehow the President could be identified, in the popular mind, with *his* party. In this strategy Stevenson had concurred. He was dismayed, however, when he saw what it actually entailed. The travel and speaking schedule which had been worked out for him was, he vehemently protested, worse than grueling; coming as it did atop the primary and convention struggles, it was a "man-killer." He wouldn't have a minute's relaxation from mid-August through election day; he'd have no solitude in which to ponder his problems and shape for them creative solutions.

And indeed, or so it would appear in retrospect, the advantages gained by this incessant activity were outweighed by the effects it had upon the candidate himself. Every other error of the campaign was rooted in this initial one, Stevenson later believed, though he could not and would not blame anyone but himself for this. When the strategy was planned he had not realized how near to nervous exhaustion (though his physical condition remained excellent) the long struggle for the nomination had brought him. Nor did he realize, other observers would assert, how badly this struggle had blurred his popular image, how greatly it had contributed to a disillusioned view of him as "just another politician" who would do anything to gain votes—and this during a period when Ike adulation was mounting, or being carried, to unprecedented heights. If the Democratic party had united solidly behind Stevenson in the fall of '55, devoting its every resource to a carefully planned build-up of him, it probably could not have matched, in the present state of mass communications, the Eisenhower build-up through those months. As it was, major portions of party strength had been devoted to tearing down Stevenson, and Republican campaign orators had been provided thereby with an ammunition they would now use gleefully against him.

But the chief blame, if blame there was, attached to a failure by Stevenson's staff and by Stevenson himself to take sufficient account of his essential character and temperament. The staff had assumed, and he himself had at least tacitly assumed, that the "New Stevenson" could do what the "Old" one had never been able to do, namely delegate to trusted lieutenants more of the "brainwork"—the actual writing of speeches and policy statements—leaving himself free to concentrate on public appearances and personal "politicking." His inability to do this, he had long realized, was a serious handicap. In private conversation, not many months before, he had spoken of it. He had two roles to play, he had said; one was "executive," the other "creative." And he had deplored the fact that, though he felt he could play either role adequately, he could not play them simultaneously nor shift easily, instantaneously from one to the other.

"What I ought to do is what everybody tells me to do—delegate the 'creative' thing (which is what I *like* to do, it's the fun of my life) and concentrate on the 'executive,'" he went on, "because so much of the latter is stuff that just can't be delegated. There are so many people who have to be dealt with on the top level, you know. They have to see *me*, or talk to *me*, and nobody else. And there are decisions to make, operating decisions, which nobody else can make."

The man to whom he spoke had replied that he understood all that, but added that millions of people over the country were hoping and praying that he would not become "just another candidate," that he would be able to retain the "high-level" approach he had made in '52.

"I know," Stevenson had said. "I just hope they realize what I'm up against. There's a limit to what any one man can do."

This limit was reached and passed in the two and a half months following the convention. In effect, Stevenson attempted to conduct simultaneously *two* campaigns, either of which was sufficiently arduous to absorb all his energies. One was the campaign Finnegan had devised with Stevenson's concurrence. The other was the campaign Stevenson himself had envisaged in the weeks preceding Eisenhower's heart attack. Actually he made somewhat fewer public appearances, and fewer set speeches, than he had made in '52. Bill Blair could prove this by comparing the schedule followed in the earlier campaign with that being followed in this one, and he did so when Stevenson complained bitterly that the present ordeal was the "worst" he had ever endured. But the candidate was now much more tired than he had been before, and certainly the demands made upon him were severe enough. He traveled incessantly. He made as many as five talks in a single day. He was constantly meeting and mingling with local Democratic groups and appearing with local candidates. (In the event, it would appear to many that this helped local Democrats far more than it helped him; certainly he gathered for these larger crowds and more publicity than they could have gathered for themselves, while enabling his opposition to picture him as hanging ignominiously upon the coattails of these same candidates.) He also gave dozens of full-length addresses, supplementing these with five policy statements averaging ten thousand words each, in which he spelled out his "New America" program for "Older Citizens," "Education," "The Nation's Health," "True Economics," and "Natural Resources."

Thus the total "brainwork" required in '56 was probably in excess of that required in '52. The staff he had to perform it, however, was smaller than it had been four years before. Headed by Wirtz, the writers included Arthur Schlesinger, Jr.; John Bartlow Martin, who had joined the staff during the primary campaign; and Robert Tufts. Incidental help was given by Kenneth Galbraith, John Hersey, and William Lee Miller, among others. As in '52, most of the writers suffered breakdowns from overwork before the campaign ended (Wirtz himself was ill for three weeks after election day), and as in '52, or even "worse" than in '52, in the opinion of Bill Blair, Stevenson wrote and rewrote constantly in moments when he might otherwise have had some relaxation from the extreme tensions of his days. Nor was he as much at ease with the products of these labors as he had been with the speeches of '52. Though their intellectual content was at least as high as that of his earlier speeches, though many of them were wholly successful, they were in general less direct expressions of himself than former speeches had been and gave evidence, at times, of the haste, amid crowding distractions, in which they had been composed. He lacked the time in which to absorb them completely into his consciousness before he gave them; he had often not so much as five quiet and solitary minutes in which to "get hold" of himself before he went again before the multitude, under the floodlights and the staring camera eyes.

In consequence of all this, the image of him projected on TV screens was, very often, precisely the opposite of that intended when the campaign was planned. He often appeared tired, driven, harassed, his delivery stumbling and awkward as it had never been before. Moreover there were, now and then, incredible production failures, notably at Harrisburg where he made his "kickoff" speech over a nationwide hookup costing a quarter of a million dollars and where the teleprompter, on which he had been urged to rely, failed to work properly. Such mistakes were not likely to plague Eisenhower, whose campaign was much less arduous and whose natural genius for public relations was sustained by the most talented of Madison Avenue technicians. Indeed, Eisenhower on TV, carefully made up and staged by such production experts as the actor Robert Montgomery, often appeared actually younger, at once more vigorous and more relaxed, than his opponent—an irony far from amusing to Stevenson's supporters. . . .

But though these things were apparent at the time, they did not assume the relative importance given them here until after the event. Even then they would not appear to have been, of themselves alone, decisive of the outcome. Every losing campaign appears in retrospect to have been a succession of errors, just as every winning one appears to have been a triumph of intelligent planning. Republican strategists would later claim that the outcome had been determined by their decision, in early March, to conduct the "briefest" campaign in history—a five-week TV campaign in which they would capitalize on Eisenhower's personality and on the mistakes Stevenson must "inevitably" make. The fact that Eisenhower began to add trips and speeches to his itinerary in September and October was due, they would explain, merely to the fact that "Ike loves crowds." They would not admit what to the Stevenson camp seemed true, namely that there had been three distinct phases of the struggle during which there were major shifts in voter sentiment, and in all save the last of these the shifts had been away from Eisenhower and toward Stevenson.

The first phase, in the Stevenson view, began with the dramatic last day of the Democratic convention, whose color and excitement stood out in marked contrast to the performance of the Republicans in the following week. Stevenson took off on a flying three-week regional tour during which he presented his farm program to a responsive audience in Iowa and made, there and elsewhere, a series of hard-hitting attacks on the administration's domestic policies. The polls immediately showed a gain in Stevenson's strength, particularly in farm states whose normally Republican ground Kefauver assiduously cultivated. And the gains continued for some time, so narrowing the gap between Stevenson and Eisenhower that political dopesters who theretofore had spoken of an "Ike landslide" as a "sure thing" began to forecast a "close race." It was at this point that Eisenhower began to add speeches and appearances to his itinerary.

There followed, in the Stevenson view, a leveling-off period of some weeks during which the Democratic candidate, having seemingly provoked his opponent into a more active defense, failed to make gains and may even have lost ground. He was a little worried about this personally. He spoke of it to Jane Dick, who was immediately reassured by Senator Lehman of New York. This happened in every campaign, Lehman said, and it was well to have it happen in the middle of the struggle. "He'll come up again," predicted Lehman confidently.

And he appeared to do so. There were signs that his candidacy had been given a boost among Negro voters and among northern independents when, before a pro-segregationist crowd in Little Rock, Arkansas, he said that he personally regarded the Supreme Court's desegregation decision to be morally "right." Some of his staff had sought, rather desperately, to dissuade him from this and were immensely relieved when the audience, in apparent admiration of his courage and honesty, actually applauded the statement. (Eisenhower, during a brief swing into the South, failed to mention the desegregation problem.) There were further signs of gain when Stevenson, having earlier said little about foreign policy because his staff was convinced, and the polls showed, that there was little public interest in it, began a series of slashing attacks upon Republican efforts to label itself the "peace" party and the Democrats the "war" party.

Peace, said Stevenson, could not be defined as merely the absence of overt hostilities; it involved the "building of a community"; and the Republican administration, far from trying to build a world community, was weakening the foundations for such a structure through its vacillation between threats and appeasement vis-à-vis the Communists and through its reckless disregard of the opinions and feelings of our allies. (Replied Eisenhower: "But why this anguished cry of some politicians that we have no peace? Do they think they can make America's parents and wives believe that their sons and husbands are being shot at?") Again and again Stevenson scored the Republicans for "misleading the people" concerning our foreign affairs, for proclaiming "peace" when there was no peace, for asserting (as Eisenhower did in mid-October) that there was "good news" from Suez, where world crisis then centered, when in fact the news was all "bad."

It was at the opening of this phase of the campaign that Stevenson made what his Republican opponents regarded as major errors. Stevenson's own supporters thought it a serious tactical error when their candidate, in the midst of a speech on the West Coast to an American Legion convention, said that the time had come to take a "new look" at our defense establishment and to consider the possibility of "ending the draft" as a means of assuring adequate military manpower. He did so in part because he was advised that Eisenhower planned to call for an end of the draft at the last moment of his campaign, in a move similar in its intent to the "I will go to Korea" statement of 1952. It was well known that influential voices in the Pentagon said the draft was wasteful, inefficient, wholly unsuited to the manpower needs of the armed services in this age of technological warfare. The defense services should be "career services," and the draft was no way of obtaining these. It would be far cheaper and more effective to employ higher pay and other attractions to recruit volunteers who would make careers of the military. So said Stevenson some days later, when he spelled out in detail his "end-draft" proposal. But by that time the damage had been done by his one-sentence statement so far as vote getting was concerned. The initial pronouncement had made the headlines and reaped a harvest of hostile Republican editorial comment; the exposition of it seemed defensive and was relatively unpersuasive.

The second "error" was a renewal, with some elaboration, of his H-bomb proposal. The "professionals" warned him that this was not a vote-getting issue and might well be a vote-losing one, Eisenhower being the number one military hero of the country. Stevenson agreed. But he was convinced that what he had to say desperately needed saying, that it might open the way toward ending the disarmament deadlock and the threat of nuclear warfare, and that he had therefore a moral obligation to advance the proposal, regardless of its effect upon his personal political fortunes. Eisenhower's initial response to both the end-draft and end-H-bomb-tests proposals was to dismiss them contemptuously. Both the draft and the tests must be continued in order that the United States could "negotiate" from a "position of strength rather than weakness," he said, and in a press conference in the second week of October he responded with a show of irritation to questions about the proposals. He had "said my last words on these subjects," he announced. Stevenson had not done so, however, and neither, it soon appeared, had Eisenhower.

On October 15, in a nationwide TV address from Chicago, Stevenson said that, if elected President, he would make an effort to achieve world agreement on the ending of H-bomb tests "the first order of business." He reminded his listeners that he had proposed last April that the United States take the initiative on this matter. Since then, both the Soviet Union and Great Britain had declared their willingness "to join us in trying to establish the kind of policy I have suggested." He reiterated that "little danger to national security" was involved, "because if another power conducts further tests we would know it and, as I have said, would have no choice but to resume such tests ourselves." Pending the agreement, the United States should proceed, he now said, with the production of hydrogen weapons and with further research in this field. That night and next day, a flood of telegraph and telephone messages poured in upon the Stevenson office, in support of his proposal. One was from Dr. Henry DeWolf Smyth of the Institute for Advanced Studies in Princeton, N.J., who endorsed Stevenson's stand as "transcending the partisanship of the current campaign." Five nuclear scientists from the Argonne National Laboratories in Lemont, Illinois, telegraphed Stevenson that "nuclear physicists firmly believe your plan, far from being 'catastrophic nonsense,' is workable, wise, and in the best interests of the United States." ("Catastrophic nonsense" was the epithet Nixon had applied to the Stevenson proposal.)

In Portland, Oregon, three days later, Eisenhower found that he had, after all, quite a few more "words" to say on this subject. Stevenson's call for an end to H-bomb tests, said he, was a compound of "pie-in-the-sky promises and wishful thinking," presenting to the nation a choice between this and "hard sense and experience. . . . We reject any thought that we will say: We are going to disarm and we hope that you will too one day," he went on, as if this were what Stevenson had actually proposed. ("Along with other Democrats, I have been doing all I can to keep the Eisenhower Administration from slashing our defense establishment during the last four years," replied Stevenson some days later. "It ill becomes the President to talk about dropping our guard when his Administration has consistently put dollars ahead of defense. I want to see our defenses strengthened, not weakened, and there is nothing in my H-bomb proposal inconsistent with this object.") Subsequently the President ordered the preparation and release of a "history" of the H-bomb and a statement of why the tests should be continued. This document Stevenson branded a "campaign pamphlet" which "even as a political paper is remarkable for misstatements and distortions." He answered it, on October 29, with a point-by-point analysis of the President's argument. By then the scientific public was convinced (as, indeed, it had been from the outset) that Stevenson had by far the better of the scientific argument, but the politicians, including those in Stevenson's camp, were convinced that he had had by far the worse of the question's political argument.

The latter was in part due to a letter Premier Nikolai A. Bulganin of the Soviet Union had seen fit to address on October 21 to President Eisenhower and to publish in Moscow before it had been translated and delivered to the White House. In it Bulganin had taken cognizance of the fact "that an election campaign is being conducted in the United States, in the course of which the discussions of various questions of international significance . . . acquires the form of polemic." However, "we fully share the opinion recently expressed by certain prominent public figures in the United States concerning the necessity and the possibility of concluding an agreement on the matter of prohibiting atomic weapon tests and concerning the positive influence this would have on the entire international situation." He accused Secretary of State Dulles of "obvious distortion of the policy of the Soviet Union concerning the above-mentioned questions. . . . As far as the Soviet Government is concerned," he asserted, "it is prepared to conclude an agreement with the United States of America immediately for discontinuing atomic tests. We proceed, of course, on the basis of the assumption that other states having atomic weapons at their disposal will likewise adhere to such an agreement." The President's prompt response was a stern reprimand of the Premier for unwarranted interference in the United States' domestic affairs. The statement concerning Dulles, he said, "is personally offensive to me." The Soviet Union had consistently opposed every system of international inspection and control of armaments, including Eisenhower's "open-skies" proposal. "However, though disappointed, we are not discouraged," Eisenhower went on. ". . . We will close no doors which might open a secure way to serve humanity."

"I share fully President Eisenhower's resentment at the manner and timing of Premier Bulganin's interference in the political affairs of the United States," said Stevenson in a statement released October 22, adding that Bulganin earlier had said he hoped that Eisenhower would run for re-election. ". . . But the real issue is not Mr. Bulganin's manners or Russian views about American politics. The real issue is what we are going to do to save the world from hydrogen disaster. Viewed from the standpoint, not of politics, but of peace, I think the President's reply is unfortunate.

"There are two possibilities. One is that the Bulganin offer [to stop tests through agreement] . . . is made for propaganda purposes only. . . . If that is true, it should be exposed for all the world to see. The other possibility is that the Russian offer, ill-timed as it is, reflects an opportunity to move ahead now toward a stop to the further explosion of hydrogen bombs. In either event, there seems to me only one course to follow. That is to pursue this opening immediately and all the way."

But no reasoned argument could now undo the damage the Bulganin statement had done to Stevenson. As a residue from the era of McCarthy and the Nixon campaign of '54, there was a widespread belief that the Democrats were not only a "war" party (witness Korea) but also a party of Communist appeasers (witness Yalta), and the fact that the two views were flatly contradictory did not prevent their effective exploitation in '56 by Dewey and Nixon. The latter was now a "high-level" candidate, but his talent for sly innuendo and plausible distortions of truth remained, in the Democratic view, his principal campaign weapon. In tones of sorrow rather than anger, Nixon the Statesman rebuked Stevenson the Politician for having walked into a "Communist mousetrap," risking the national security in order to gain votes. He was enabled to do so the more effectively by the fact that the Bulganin letter had appeared amid the most dangerous international crisis since World War II. . . .

v

The whole campaign had been conducted in the deepening shadow of this crisis, whose explosion into bloody violence on October 29 determined the final, decisive phase of the American political campaign. And it was the ultimate irony of the campaign that this explosion, which seemed to prove in blood and terror the truth of Stevenson's strictures upon the Eisenhower foreign policy, actually increased hugely Eisenhower's strength at the polls.

Thus there was a sense in which the outcome on November 6 was partially determined by a Middle Eastern policy decision taken by the Eisenhower administration more than three years before. In 1953, when Major General Mohammed Naguib was the newly installed Premier of Egypt, the Eisenhower administration, perhaps more strongly motivated by American oil interest in Arab countries than the preceding administration had been, began to court Arab friendship while de-emphasizing the friendship for Israel and the determination to help the latter country defend herself against armed aggression. This represented a major shift in American policy, and it was dramatized when Secretary Dulles presented to Naguib, as a personal gift from the President, an automatic pistol. Israeli leaders at once protested vehemently, warning that the real power in the new Egyptian regime was Colonel Gamal Abdel Nasser and that the colonel, far from being a "moderate," was a fanatic Arab nationalist whose ambition was to lead an Arab bloc in a war of extermination against Israel. Britain and France, too, were dubious; the new regime seemed to them intransigent in its anti-Westernism.

Nevertheless, the Eisenhower administration persisted in its pro-Nasser policy even after the colonel, having taken over the premiership in 1954, made in 1955 his deal with Moscow to obtain heavy arms from the Soviet bloc in return for commitments to Russia whose scale and scope would remain secret a year later but whose nature was revealed in the anti-Western propaganda which the Egyptian leader immediately increased in volume and violence. The U.S. arms which Israel requested, with British and French support, were refused—a decision which, as we have seen, was roundly criticized by Stevenson at the time. A reluctant Britain was persuaded to join the United States in the offer to Nasser of a massive economic-aid program, including (in December of '55) help in building the $1.3 billion Aswan dam on the Nile, the prime object of Nasser's domestic program. Significantly the colonel did not accept the offer. Instead he "considered" it while, throughout the early months of '56, he organized a "neutralist" bloc of Arab states, worked to undermine the British position in Jordan, challenged Britain's control of vital oil fields on the Arabian coast, and gave active aid to nationalist Arabs fighting against the French in North Africa. He also financed, trained, and equipped anti-Israeli commandos who stepped up their raids across the Israeli border while he built up his regular forces for war. Israel warned Washington, with increasing desperation, that the stockpile of Communist arms was mounting to terrifying heights. So did Britain and France, again urging the United States to send arms to Israel in order to restrain Nasser. The Eisenhower administration refused to do so.

But in July of '56, in a typically abrupt reversal of policy, the administration withdrew its offer of help with the Aswan dam, doing so in a way calculated to be most humiliating to Nasser personally and most damaging to his prestige in the Arab world. Nasser's predictable response was a prompt seizure of the Suez Canal, whereupon Britain and France demanded that the canal be internationalized—by force, if necessary. They were restrained by Dulles, who proposed, as an alternative, a "users association" to operate the canal. When Britain and France agreed to this, Dulles, faced by angry Nasser threats, "weakened" the proposal "out of all recognition," as the normally pro-American London *Times* bitterly complained.

By October, Britain and France were convinced that Nasser planned to bar their use of the canal (vital to them), take over their Middle Eastern bases, and cut off their oil supplies. Israel was convinced that, soon, he would attack her. All three were convinced that no reliance could be placed upon the United States for help in what, to them, seemed a crisis of survival.[1] On Monday, October

[1] It was on October 12 that Eisenhower, in a carefully staged television campaign show, said that he had "the best announcement that I think I could possibly

29, Israeli armor and paratroops thrust deep into Egypt's Sinai Peninsula. Within two days after that, British bombs had fallen on Egyptian airfields, Israeli troops had sealed off the Gaza Strip, and Anglo-French landing forces were moving toward Suez. . . .

Stevenson would point out with some bitterness, in private conversation, that the Eisenhower administration had not seen fit theretofore to work through the United Nations in the development and implementation of its Middle Eastern policy. The economic-aid program, for example, might conceivably have been offered through the UN in such a way as genuinely to serve the people of the Middle East, making peace between Israel and her neighbors and solving the Arab refugee problem. Instead, the Aswan-dam offer had been handled in crude power-political terms, and with no intelligent consideration of Nasser's problems, psychology, and power-political resources. It was only now, on the brink of World War III, that Eisenhower suddenly discovered that the UN was responsible for making and keeping the peace.

And on Friday, in the UN, the United States found herself strangely allied with the Soviet Union against her own long-time friends and allies, demanding a cease-fire which, on the following day, was rejected by Britain, France and Israel. The United States then increased her pressure for a withdrawal, though Eisenhower had promised—with a flatness which seemed to Stevenson unfortunate for peace, if effective as a vote getter—that no U.S. troops would be sent into the Middle East. Period. Ultimately the withdrawals were made after the Russians, encouraged no doubt by Eisenhower's "no-troop-involvement" pledge, had threatened to use "volunteer" troops on the side of Nasser and had "warned" Paris and London that their countries were vulnerable to Soviet atomic attack.

(Concurrent with these developments had come, that summer, the first really serious break in the Iron Curtain across central Europe. A rebellious Poland had been granted important concessions from Moscow in return for continued acceptance of a Polish Communist government. Soon thereafter, actual and initially successful revolution had flared in Hungary. For these events, Republican orators at first took credit, claiming that they stemmed from the Eisenhower administration's "liberation" policies. They claimed no responsibility

---

make to America tonight"; namely that progress in settling the canal dispute had been "most gratifying" and that it looked as though "a very great crisis is behind us." The statement was given streamer headlines in the nation's press.

for the disaster, however, when Russia, taking advantage of the break in the Western alliance, moved in with tanks and troops to drown in blood the Hungarian bid for freedom. . . .)

For a few days after the Israeli attack, it appeared to Stevenson that the event must greatly reduce his opponent's vote and aid his own chances. Surely the American people must now see the truth of his criticisms, though he regretted that he had not launched these more specifically at the Suez crisis earlier in the campaign. (He had refrained from doing so, as he had publicly announced, because he wished to do nothing which might weaken Eisenhower's hand in the dangerous situation.) Surely they would see that Nasser, with our open aid, had been built up into a most formidable foe of American interests and a most dangerous threat to world peace; that Russia, with our inadvertent aid, was now established as a major power in the Middle East, an object she had pursued for centuries in vain; and that the Western alliance, largely through our fault, was seriously if not fatally wounded. Surely they would conclude that to continue in office an administration capable of such blunders would be to invite even worse disaster. He was swiftly disillusioned. By midweek he had begun to realize that the great majority of Americans were seeing what they had been long conditioned to see. "Ike is a great military hero and a Man of Peace; he loves you; he knows best. Have faith in Ike." This had been the burden of Republican propaganda, echoed and amplified by an unprecedentedly adulatory press, for four long years. And in this time of trouble, it was to Ike that millions turned who might otherwise have voted for Stevenson.

The irony was bitter to the Democratic candidate, moving from the East toward Chicago through that final crucial week. Had he, after all, overrated the critical intelligence of the electorate? His draft and H-bomb proposals, deliberately distorted by his opponent into proposals for unilateral disarmament; the Bulganin episode; the long image-distorting battle for the nomination; even the wit and gaiety which had formerly made him so appealing to civilized minds —all these now combined with the father image of Ike to work disastrously against him. In one of the most effective speeches of the campaign, he soberly analyzed the crisis, tracing the steps through which it had developed. The speech was well received, but it could not command any such attention, in the circumstances, as Eisenhower's moves to "save" the world from the catastrophe for which (in Stevenson's view) he was so largely responsible. Thereafter, Stevenson began to raise his voice in an effort to be heard above the tumult of foreign war. His denunciations of the administration became more harsh than any he had made before.

In Minneapolis, on the morning of Monday, November 5, he reminded his listeners that Nixon, who "has put away his switch-blade and now assumes the aspect of an Eagle Scout," had said not long ago in that very city, "There will be no war in the Middle East." He also reminded them of "President Eisenhower's role in the making of our Middle Eastern policy. . . .

"In February of this year, the Eisenhower administration started to send a shipload of tanks to Saudi Arabia," he went on. "This was at the time that we were declining to send arms to Israel. When protests mounted, the administration first embargoed the shipment. And while it was trying to decide what to do, where was the President of the United States? On February 17, he played golf. On February 18, he shot quail. On February 22, when the ban was finally removed, the President shot eighteen holes of golf. . . . Toward the end of March, as the situation grew worse, Prime Minister Eden sent the President an urgent message about the Middle East. But some days later the President, when asked about it in a press conference, said, 'I can't recall how long it has been since I have had a letter from the Prime Minister.' On April 9 the White House announced: 'The President and the Secretary of State regard the situation (in the Middle East) with the utmost seriousness.' On the same day the President began a golfing vacation in Georgia.

"When Egypt took over the Suez Canal in July, the President was at Gettysburg. On August 4, when the New York *Times* called the Suez impasse the 'gravest challenge to the West since Berlin and Korea,' the President played golf. On August 11, when Britain rejected Communist proposals for a Suez conference, the President played golf. As the crisis mounted toward the end of August the press reported that the President, now at Pebble Beach, California, golfed happily at one of America's toughest and most beautiful courses. . . . And even when we have been forewarned, we have still failed to act. Our government knew about the impending arms deal between Egypt and the Communists a full month before President Eisenhower met with the Russian leaders at Geneva. Yet our President made no protest of this action. . . . If there had been less hearts and flowers and more firm talk at Geneva, the Communists would never have dared to arm Egypt. . . .

"The last four years have presented America and the free world great opportunities to exploit the weaknesses in the Communist ranks and advance the cause of peace. But this administration has failed to take advantage of them. The death of Stalin caught us off-guard. The uprisings in East Berlin caught us off-guard. The uprisings in Poznan caught us off-guard. The most recent revolts in Poland and Hungary obviously caught us off-guard. . . . And America reached the summit of foolishness when Mr. Nixon hailed the collapse of our alliance [with Britain and France] as 'a declaration of independence that has had an electrifying effect through the world.'"

That night, in Boston, he reiterated in substance these foreign-policy criticisms before proceeding to deal, in unprecedentedly frank terms, with the issue of the President's health. "[Distasteful] as the matter is, I must say bluntly that every piece of scientific evidence we have, every lesson of history and experience, indicates that a Republican victory tomorrow would mean that Richard M. Nixon would probably be President of this country within the next four years." The statement of course called down upon Stevenson's head wrathful charges of "dirty tactics" and "bad taste," and there were many among Stevenson's supporters who regretted that it had been made. However true as a statement of probability, it seemed a poor note on which to end what had been, take it all in all, an extraordinarily gallant and high-minded campaign against overwhelming odds.

VI

He was originally scheduled to make his election-eve speech in Chicago. But on Sunday afternoon he had received a jubilant message from Adlai III, who had returned to the Harvard Law School in September: Nancy Anderson Stevenson, in Boston's Lying-in Hospital, had given birth to a baby boy whose name was Adlai Ewing Stevenson. Immediately the candidate had revised his schedule. From Minneapolis next day he flew, with John Fell and Borden beside him, to Boston.

Sirens screaming, police cars and motorcycles escorted him from the airfield to the hospital on whose third floor, in the late afternoon, he gazed down happily upon his plump, brown-haired, one-day-old grandchild. Flash bulbs popped. "He doesn't seem to mind at all," laughed Stevenson as the baby slept on undisturbed. "He must be a born pol." He then said he would "punch in the nose" anyone who said the baby looked like him. The baby, reporters laughingly agreed, was much better-looking. And this family happiness sustained him as, numb with weariness, he returned from his Boston speech to Chicago.

On Tuesday he voted at Half Day. That evening, in the President's Suite of the Sheraton-Blackstone in the Loop, he shared a buffet dinner with his family and close friends, some twenty people in all. Buffie and Ernest Ives were there, and John Fell and Borden. The Edison Dicks were there, and Bill Blair. The atmosphere reflected the candidate's outward mood: he was tired but smiling, a bit rueful yet gay, expecting the worst but by no means conceding it. Nor did this atmosphere noticeably change as, after dinner, they all watched the election returns on TV. Stevenson lounged back in an easy chair, sometimes shaking his head a little as, one by one, his enfeebled hopes were crushed to death, but not for a moment did he lose, outwardly, his good cheer.

At nine o'clock, by which time it was already clear that he was losing, he left his party to confer in another room with Jim Finnegan and Bill Wirtz concerning the timing of and general arrangements for his concession. He then went into his bedroom to write out the statement whose general form he had already well in mind. He would use in it a quotation from Fra Giovanni's Christmas Letter of 1513, and another, from Proverbs, which he had memorized from his mother's lips when he was a child. By the time he emerged, the proportions of his defeat were revealed as overwhelming. There would be no surprises for him on the morrow when he learned that he had won only 74 electoral votes compared to Eisenhower's 457, and 26,028,887 popular votes compared to Eisenhower's 35,582,236. He had carried Missouri and six southern states. He had lost Oklahoma, Texas, Louisiana, Florida, Virginia, Kentucky, and Tennessee, of the states deemed solidly Democratic. Clearly he had come to the end of the road he had entered upon just eight and a half years ago (how much longer ago it seemed than that!); he could not but feel, deep within him, the gnawing pain of disappointment and failure. There seemed to be, in so crushing a defeat, a large measure of personal humiliation. Yet he smiled at Buffie, at Ernest.

"It's a pathetic night," Buffie said. . . .

He shook his head at her, still smiling. Someone had asked him once what he considered to be his greatest personal asset as a candidate. "Well, I should say, serenity of spirit," he had replied. "I can contemplate in tranquillity the distinct possibility that I will never be President of the United States. I can see many reasons for not wanting to be President during the next four years, for everything is likely to start unraveling within the next year or two. Of course," he had added, "I shall do my best to win." Well, he was, now, quite serene—and certainly he had done his best.

At twelve-twenty on the morning of Wednesday, November 7, he emerged from the Sheraton-Blackstone, with John Fell at his left arm and Borden at his right, with Buffie and Ernest behind him. He crossed the street to the Conrad Hilton where, in the Grand Ballroom, a tearful crowd of some twenty-five hundred supporters awaited him. And there, for those who saw him in the room and for millions who watched him over TV, he came again sharply into focus as the Stevenson of old, the gallant, urbane, witty man, sensitive and gay, whom they had long loved. He smiled and waved to the crowd upon whose faces, for the first time that evening, broad smiles appeared.

He said that he had sent a telegram to President Eisenhower. He read it:

" 'You have won not only the election but also an expression of the great confidence of the American people. I send you my warm congratulations.

" 'Tonight we are not Republicans and Democrats, but Americans. We appreciate the grave difficulties your administration faces, and, as Americans, join in wishing you all success in the years that lie ahead.' "

Stevenson paused, looked out over the crowd.

"And now," he went on, "let me say a word to you, my supporters and friends, all over the country.

"First, I want to express my respect and thanks to a gallant partner in this great adventure—Estes Kefauver. I wish there was some way I could properly thank you, one by one. I wish there was some way I could make you feel my gratitude for the support, the encouragement, the confidence that has sustained me through these weeks and months and years that I have been privileged to be your leader. Thanks to many of you, I have twice had the proud experience of being selected by the Democratic Party as its nominee for the most exalted office on earth. Once again I have tried hard to express my views and make clear my party's hopes for our beloved country.

"To you who are disappointed tonight, let me confess that I am, too! But we must not be downhearted, for 'there is radiance and glory in the darkness, could we but see, and to see, we have only to look.'

"For here, in America, the people have made their choice in a vigorous partisan contest that has affirmed again the vitality of the democratic process. And I say God bless partisanship, for this is democracy's life blood. But beyond the seas, in much of the world, in Russia, in China, in Hungary, in all the trembling satellites, partisan controversy is forbidden and dissent suppressed. So, I say to you, my dear and loyal friends, take heart—there are things more precious than political victory; there is the right to political contest. And who knows better how vigorous and alive it is than you who bear the fresh, painful wounds of battle?

"Let me add another thought for you who have traveled with me on this great journey: I have tried to chart the road to a new and better America. I want to say to all of you who have followed me that I am supremely confident that our cause will ultimately prevail, for America can only go forward. It cannot go backward or stand still.

"But even more urgent is the hope that our leaders will recognize that America wants to face up squarely to the facts of today's world. We don't want to draw back from them. We can't. We are ready for the test that we know history has set for us.

"And, finally, the will of our society is announced by the majority. And if other nations have thought in the past few weeks that we were looking the other way and too divided to act, they will learn otherwise. What unites us is deeper than what divides us—love of freedom, love of justice, love of peace.

"May America continue, under God, to be the shield and spear of democracy. And let us give the administration all responsible support in the troubled times ahead.

"Now I bid you goodnight, with a full heart and fervent prayer that we will meet often again in the liberals' everlasting battle against ignorance, poverty, misery and war.

"Be of good cheer. And remember, my dear friends, what a wise man said: 'A merry heart doeth good like a medicine, but a broken spirit dryeth the bones.'"

His smile broadened as, to his prepared statement, he appended a typical "Adlaiism":

"Let there be no tears for me. If I have lost an election, I have won a grandchild."

The crowd laughed, and cried, and cheered him while, for a last time, the floodlights poured down and the flash bulbs popped and the camera eyes focused upon him. The photographers, as always, called upon him to turn first this way, then that. Amidst the frenzy, Borden grasped his father's right hand and lifted it high in the traditional gesture of victory.

Index